A BUDDHA LAND IN THIS WORLD

Before you start to read this book, take this moment to think about making a donation to punctum books, an independent non-profit press,

@ https://punctumbooks.com/support/

If you're reading the e-book, you can click on the image below to go directly to our donations site. Any amount, no matter the size, is appreciated and will help us to keep our ship of fools afloat. Contributions from dedicated readers will also help us to keep our commons open and to cultivate new work that can't find a welcoming port elsewhere. Our adventure is not possible without your support.

Vive la Open Access.

Fig. 1. Detail from Hieronymus Bosch, *Ship of Fools* (1490–1500)

A BUDDHA LAND IN THIS WORLD: PHILOSOPHY, UTOPIA, AND RADICAL BUDDHISM. Copyright © 2022 by Lajos Brons. This work carries a Creative Commons BY-NC-SA 4.0 International license, which means that you are free to copy and redistribute the material in any medium or format, and you may also remix, transform and build upon the material, as long as you clearly attribute the work to the authors (but not in a way that suggests the authors or punctum books endorses you and your work), you do not use this work for commercial gain in any form whatsoever, and that for any remixing and transformation, you distribute your rebuild under the same license. http://creativecommons.org/licenses/by-nc-sa/4.0/

First published in 2022 by punctum books, Earth, Milky Way.
https://punctumbooks.com

ISBN-13: 978-1-68571-034-7 (print)
ISBN-13: 978-1-68571-035-4 (ePDF)

DOI: 10.53288/0373.1.00

LCCN: 2022936379
Library of Congress Cataloging Data is available from the Library of Congress

Book design: Vincent W.J. van Gerven Oei

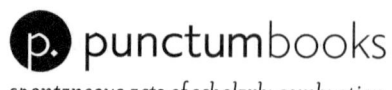

spontaneous acts of scholarly combustion

HIC SVNT MONSTRA

Lajos Brons

A BUDDHA LAND IN THIS WORLD

PHILOSOPHY, UTOPIA, AND RADICAL BUDDHISM

p.

Contents

Preface   13
Abbreviations, Transliterations, and Other Technicalities   15

PART I — Groundwork

1. Radical Buddhism   21
   Secularity • Secularity as Naturalism • The Sociopolitical Dimension: Secularity as Privatization • Locating Radical Buddhism • Naturalism • A Plethora of *-isms* • A Guide to This Book • What This Book Is Not About •

2. Protectors, Monks, and Jeweled Trees   39
   Early Buddhism • Aśoka • Mahāyāna • From Nāgārjuna to Zhiyi • From Saichō to Nichiren • A Buddha Land in This World

3. Reality and Utopia   61
   Secular Buddhism • Sri Lanka — Dharmapāla and Ariyaratne • Realism and Reform in Japan — Inoue Enryō • Uchiyama Gudō and Early Buddhist Socialism • Seno'o Girō and the Youth Leagu • China/Taiwan — A Pure Land in the Human World • Activist Alternatives and Lin Qiuwu • Korea — Han Yongun's Buddhist Socialism • Vietnam — Thích Nhất Hạnh's Engaged Buddhism • Thailand — Buddhadāsa's Dhammic Socialism • Burma — Buddhist Marxism and U Nu • Tibet — Gendun Chopel and the 14th Dalai Lama • Ambedkar and the "New Vehicle" in India

4. Materialism, Ideology, and the Specter of Marxism   113
   The Problem(s) with Materialism(s) • Physicalism • Moralistic versus Systemic Critique • Economic Materialism • Ideology • Materialism, Superstition, and Other Themes

5. What Makes Something Buddhist? 137
   The Idea of an "Original Buddhism" • The Four Noble Truths • Suffering • Karma, Rebirth, (No-)self, and Nirvāṇa • The Middle Way • Metaphysics, Rationality, and Free Inquiry • Meditation, Pacifism, and Dependent Origination • Defining "Buddhism" and "Buddhist" • What Is a Buddhist? • Postscript

6. Radicalizing Radical Buddhism 171
   Sources and Schools • A Very Sketchy Overview of Parts II and III • Between Science and Religion

PART II — सत् Sat

Introduction 187

7. Conceptual Matters 193
   Realism (1) — Universals and (Anti-)Essentialism • Realism (2) — External Reality • Idealism • The "Noumenal" • Apophasis, Kataphasis, Skepticism, and Mysticism • Relativism, Pluralism, and Perspectivism • An Analogy

8. Realism and Reality in Yogācāra and Tiantai 211
   A Bit of Historical Context • Yogācāra Realism • Tiantai/Tendai Non-dualism • Relativism and Perspectivism in Yogācāra and Tiantai • *Apoha* and Its Implications • Triangulation, *Kalpanā*, and Kataphasis

9. Epistemic Justification, Science, and Austere Realism 247
   Avisaṃvāda • Objections to the Coherence Principle • Perspectives and Science • Essences, Freedom, Paradise, and Other Incoherences • Posits and Phenomenal Reality • Summary of Chapters 8 and 9

10. Perspectives on Perspectival Realism 279
    The Baseline — Post-Yogācāra Realism • New Pragmatism — Davidson, Putnam, and Quine • Classical Perspectives — Zhuangzi, Heraclitus, and Epicurus • Religious Perspectives — Ibn Rushd, Dooyeweerd, and *Anekāntavāda* • Perspectives in Modern Western Thought • Some Concluding Remarks

PART III — 道 Dao

Introduction — 309

11. Intersubjectivity and Moral Epistemology — 313
Three Arguments for Convergence • Moral Theory — A Primer • Meta-ethical Convergence

12. Expected Consequences — 327
The Metaphysics of (Expected) Consequences • Consequences in Consequentialism • Problems for Subjective Consequentialism • Foreseeable and Intended Consequences • Consequences and Consequentialism in Mahāyāna • Expectivism and Free Will

13. The Badness of Death and Suffering — 351
Instrumental and Intrinsic Goods • Universal Intrinsic Evil • Suffering, Death, and Bodhisattva Ethics • Some Objections • Suffering, Shock, and Intoxication

14. The Metaphysics of Acts and Rules — 371
Maps *for* and *of* Behavior • Public Maps and Rules • A Dao of Compassion

15. The Case against Capitalism — 387
The Ideology of Supply and Demand • Free Trade Ideology • Playing with FIRE • Misery for the Many • A Cautious Conclusion

16. The Other Side of Utopia — 425
Ideal Theory, Utopia, and Ideology • *Mappō* • A Buddha Land in This World

PART IV — Conclusion

17. Radical Buddhism for the 21st Century — 443
Lokamātra • Labels, Hesitations, and Rafts • Radical Buddhism in This World

References — 455

Preface

Winter tends to be cloudy and rainy or snowy on Sado Island (Japan), but today the sun was shining, so I decided to go on a small excursion. A twenty-minute walk over country roads bordered by stubby rice fields led me to Konponji 根本時, the temple built at the location where Nichiren initially lived when he was banished to Sado in 1271. Although Nichiren wasn't a radical Buddhist by the standards of this book,[1] for a number of reasons,[2] a visit to Konponji seemed to be an appropriate "ceremony" to mark the end of the process of writing it.

Nichiren was by far the most radical of the Kamakura-era reformers of Japanese Buddhism. Buddhism had always served the state, but in Nichiren's view this was the world upside down. The state itself should follow (Nichiren's interpretation of) Buddhism to assure peace and harmony in the realm, and its failure to do so was what caused poverty, famines, attempted foreign invasions, and other disasters.[3] That the Kamakura rulers were less pleased with such radical ideas (and decided to banish him) is hardly surprising. Furthermore, Nichiren was also a major influence on Seno'o Girō, the most radical of the early-twentieth-century radical Buddhists, and possibly the main inspiration for this book.[4]

Nevertheless, this isn't a book I was planning to write. Although I have been interested in Buddhism since the middle of the 1980s, I never thought I'd write a book about a topic related to Buddhism. Instead, I've been pondering for years to write a book about perspectival realism (i.e., metaphysics and epistemology), or perhaps about moral theory, but I never managed to draft an outline that satisfied me. But then, a couple of years ago, I read some papers by James Mark Shields about "radical Buddhism," and while contemplating that rather intriguing phenomenon, somehow various bits and pieces of the things I had been working on the past decade started to fit together. That, eventually, resulted in this book. The book about perspectival realism that I never wrote somehow evolved into part II of this book, and the book about moral theory became the core of part III.

Like my previous book, *The Hegemony of Psychopathy*,[5] I didn't write this book just for an audience of academic philosophers (or Buddhologists), but for anyone who is interested in the topics addressed: Buddhist philosophy, ethics and social

---

1 See chapter 4.
2 I can't deny that the fact that it was merely a twenty-minute walk anyway is among those reasons.
3 See the section "From Saichō to Nichiren" in chapter 2.
4 See the section "Seno'o Girō and the Youth League" in chapter 3.
5 Lajos Brons, *The Hegemony of Psychopathy* (Earth: punctum books, 2017).

philosophy, radical thought and anti-capitalism, metaphysics and epistemology (i.e., the branches of philosophy dealing with questions about existence and knowledge), the relation between naturalism and religion, and so forth. For this reason, I tried to make the book as accessible as I could to different audiences by refraining as much as possible from jargon and by adding explanations (sometimes in footnotes) of things that might need no explanation to experts. (To what extent I succeeded in doing this is another matter.)

Most but not all of the content of this book is new. Parts of chapters 8 and 9 are based on earlier publications but have been completely rewritten. Earlier versions of most of the sections of chapter 16, of smaller parts of other chapters in part III, and of the sections on secular Buddhism and on Seno'o Girō in chapter 3, as well as much of the introduction to part II have been published before on my blog, *F=ma*,[6] which typically deals with topics that are quite similar to those addressed in this book. And parts of chapter 14 have been presented at a conference before but have not yet been published.

Aside from this preface, the parts mentioned in the previous paragraph, and chapter 17, this book was written in the first half of 2020, while the Covid-19 pandemic gradually started to envelop the planet. Except for this paragraph, Covid-19 is not mentioned in this book. I briefly considered discussing it in chapter 15, "The Case against Capitalism," but while it is certainly true that countries with more draconian neoliberal capitalist regimes have been hit by the pandemic much harder, it is our abusive relation with nature more than capitalism per se that is to blame for the spread of zoonotic diseases.[7]

It is customary to end the preface of a book like this by acknowledging colleagues and others who helped shape the ideas presented in it, and I'll follow that custom. The person who more than anyone helped sharpen my arguments and clarify my ideas in the last decade is Iida Takashi. For that — but also for making it possible for me to carve out a path on the academic fringe — I owe him gratitude.[8] Aside from Iida, the anonymous referees of various journals that published my papers related to topics addressed here, as well as my students, have also been instrumental in improving and clarifying my ideas. Most of all, however, I owe gratitude to Tomoko and Nagi, for being there and for keeping me sane in an insane world.

Sado, Japan
December 9, 2020

---

[6] *F=ma*, http://www.lajosbrons.net/blog/.

[7] David Quammen, *Spillover: Animal Infections and the Next Human Pandemic* (London: Bodley Head, 2012).

[8] Much earlier, Piet Pellenbarg played a similar role, and I remain as grateful to him for that as I am to Iida.

Abbreviations, Transliterations, and Other Technicalities

Throughout this book, abbreviations are used to refer to Buddhist canonical sources and to collections of writings by a few Western philosophers that are relatively frequently referred to. Occasionally other abbreviations are used in a single chapter or section — those are introduced there.

The abbreviations used for canonical sources are the following:

AN   *Anguttara Nikāya* (*The Numerical Discourses*).
     Followed by text number, page/section.[1]
DN   *Dīgha Nikāya* (*The Long Discourses*).[2]
MN   *Majjhima Nikāya* (*The Middle-Length Discourses*).[3]
SN   *Samyutta Nikāya* (*The Connected Discourses*).[4]
Sn   *Sutta Nipāta.*[5]
T   *Taishō Tripiṭaka* 大正新脩大藏經.
     Followed by volume number, text number, page.[6]

See footnotes for editions and translations used. All page references and other references are to those editions. Translations, as well as the original Pāli, are also available at *Sutta Central.*[7] The source of all non-Buddhist (classical) Chinese texts referred to is *The Chinese Text Project.*[8] Many Sanskrit philosophical texts are available at the

---

1 *The Numerical Discourses of the Buddha: A Translation of the Anguttara Nikāya*, trans. Bhikkhu Boddhi (Somerville: Wisdom, 2012).
2 *The Long Discourses of the Buddha: A Translation of the Dīgha Nikāya*, trans. Maurice Walshe (Somerville: Wisdom, 1995).
3 *The Middle Length Discourses of the Buddha: A New Translation of the Majjhima Nikāya*, trans. Bhikkhu Ñāṇamoli, rev. Bhikkhu Bodhi (Somerville: Wisdom, 1995).
4 *The Connected Discourses of the Buddha: A New Translation of the Samyutta Nikāya*, trans. Bhikkhu Boddhi (Somerville: Wisdom, 2000).
5 *The Suttanipāta: An Ancient Collection of the Buddha's Discourses together with Its Commentaries*, trans. Bhikkhu Boddhi (Somerville: Wisdom, 2017).
6 Source for volumes 1–55: CBETA, http://tripitaka.cbeta.org/. For other volumes: *The SAT Daizōkyō Text Database*, http://21dzk.l.u-tokyo.ac.jp/SAT/index_en.html.
7 *Sutta Central*, https://suttacentral.net/.
8 *The Chinese Text Project*, https://ctext.org/.

Digital Sanskrit Buddhist Canon.⁹ For translations, see the list of references at the end of this volume.

The following abbreviations are used in references to collections of papers and other writings by Western philosophers:

EAE   Donald Davidson, *Essays on Actions and Events*.¹⁰
FLPV   W.V.O. Quine, *From a Logical Point of View*.¹¹
ITI   Davidson, *Inquiries into Truth and Interpretation*.¹²
MEW   Karl Marx & Friedrich Engels, *Werke* (i.e., their collected works in German).¹³ The number following the abbreviation and preceding the colon refers to the volume number.
OROE   Quine, *Ontological Relativity & Other Essays*.¹⁴
PoR   Davidson, *Problems of Rationality*.¹⁵
SIO   Davidson, *Subjective, Intersubjective, Objective*.¹⁶
TLH   Davidson, *Truth, Language, and History*.¹⁷
WPOE   Quine, *The Ways of Paradox and Other Essays*.¹⁸

Transliterations and Translations

The transliteration used for Pāli and Sanskrit is the International Alphabet of Sanskrit Translation (IAST). In most cases, Sanskrit terms are preferred to their Pāli equivalents, unless the Pāli term is better known (e.g., Pāli *dukkha* rather than Sanskrit *duḥkha*). Consequently, titles of *sūtras* in the Pāli canon are given in Pāli — hence, as ... *Sutta* — but these texts are referred to as *sūtras*.

The romanization used for Chinese is pinyin without tone marks, except in case someone or something is better known under another romanization (as in case of the Taiwanese monk Chengyen 證嚴 and the organization Tzu Chi 慈濟 she founded — pinyin: *Zhengyan, Ci Ji*). Revised Hepburn transliteration is used for Japanese. Names in other languages are transliterated according to what appears to be the most common transliteration system for those languages.

Foreign (i.e., non-English) words are italicized, with two kinds of exceptions. The first concerns foreign words that have no English equivalents, that are relatively well known, and that occur frequently throughout the text. Examples included "*sūtra*," "*dukkha*," "*karma*," "*nirvāṇa*," "*bodhisattva*," "*dao*" (道; the only Chinese term on this list), and "the Dharma" (with a capital "D," referring to Buddhist teachings; *dharmas*

---

9 *Digital Sanskrit Buddhist Canon*, http://www.dsbcproject.org/.
10 Donald Davidson, *Essays on Actions and Events*, 1st edn. (Oxford: Clarendon, 1980); 2nd edn. (Oxford: Oxford University Press, 2001). The second edition has some additions at the end but does not otherwise differ from the first.
11 W.V.O. Quine, *From a Logical Point of View* (Cambridge: Harvard University Press, 1964).
12 Donald Davidson, *Inquiries into Truth and Interpretation*, 1st edn. (Oxford: Clarendon, 1984); 2nd edn. (Oxford: Oxford University Press, 2001). The second edition has some additions at the end but does not otherwise differ from the first.
13 Karl Marx and Friedrich Engels, *Werke* (Berlin: Dietz, 1962–68).
14 W.V.O. Quine, *Ontological Relativity and Other Essays* (New York: Columbia University Press, 1969).
15 Donald Davidson, *Problems of Rationality* (Oxford: Oxford University Press, 2004).
16 Donald Davidson, *Subjective, Intersubjective, Objective* (Oxford: Oxford University Press, 2001).
17 Donald Davidson, *Truth, Language, and History* (Oxford: Oxford University Press, 2005).
18 W.V.O. Quine, *The Ways of Paradox and Other Essays*, 1st edn. (Cambridge: Harvard University Press, 1966); rev. and enl. edn. (Cambridge: Harvard University Press, 1976).

in italics and without a capital refers to the partless elements that ultimate reality consists of; to avoid confusion between the two terms *dharmas* is always italicized). Secondly, if a foreign word is used a lot in a relatively short passage (such as a section) it is only italicized when it is first introduced. If a foreign word is mentioned rather than used, it is always italicized and no additional quote marks are used.

If the only reference given for a quote is in another language than English and thus, no translator is mentioned, then the translation is my own. In most cases I will give the same quote in the original language in a footnote. (While this is standard practice in case of non-European languages, it is uncommon for European languages. Since I could not come up with a good non-Eurocentric argument to support that distinction, I decided to give the original in case of European language quotes as well.)

All Western names are given in the order given name · family name; all East-Asian names in the order family name · given name, except in case someone's name is better known in a different order. (The latter is often the case for Japanese or Chinese authors working in Western countries.)

PART I

GROUNDWORK

1

Radical Buddhism

About fifty meters south of Ōhiradai station in the mountainous, rural area of Hakone (Japan) there is a small and inconspicuous temple named *Rinsenji* 林泉寺. The temple belongs to the Sōtō sect of Zen Buddhism and was established in 1559. It is not a particularly interesting or noteworthy temple except for one brief episode in its history. In May 1909 the police arrested Rinsenji's chief priest, Uchiyama Gudō 内山愚童, and searched the temple. They found an illegal printing press under the main altar, and they also claimed to have found dynamite and fuses.

The printing press was used by Uchiyama to print socialist and anarchist pamphlets as well as some of his own radical writings in which he argued for land reform, for anarcho-communist revolution, against fatalistic belief in karma (i.e., the belief that one's current misery is due to bad karma resulting from bad deeds in previous lives), and against the emperor.[1] The latter was used as "evidence" for an accusation of his involvement in a plot to kill the emperor, the so-called *High Treason Incident* 幸徳事件. After a show trial that was "mostly based on circumstantial evidence and orchestrated by the Japanese government to get rid of the radical left,"[2] he and several others were sentenced to death. He was executed on January 24, 1911.

Uchiyama is one of the best known so-called "radical Buddhists," although he never used that term himself. The notion of radical Buddhism is a fairly recent academic invention for the purpose of categorizing and characterizing a rather loose collection of trends and movements in mostly early twentieth century Buddhism.[3] James Mark Shields and Patrice Ladwig, probably the foremost academic experts on the subject, define the notion of "radical" in "radical Buddhism" as a "position that is (1) politically engaged; and (2) in opposition to the hegemonic socio-political and/or economic ideology (or ideologies) of a given period," and a "radical Buddhist" as "anyone engaged in the explicit or implicit use of Buddhist doctrines or principles to foment resistance to the state and/or the socio-political and/or economic status

---

1   See the section "Uchiyama Gudō and Early Buddhist Socialism" in chapter 3 for a brief discussion of Uchiyama's thought.
2   Fabio Rambelli, *Zen Anarchism: The Egalitarian Dharma of Uchiyama Gudō* (Berkeley: Institute of Buddhist Studies and BDK America, 2013), 5.
3   The phrase "radical Buddhism" was occasionally used before, but the here relevant term was coined by James Mark Shields in a conference paper that was published in 2012. James Mark Shields, "Radical Buddhism, Then and Now: Prospects of a Paradox," *Silva Iaponicarum* 日林 23/24/25/26 (2012): 15–34.

quo."⁴ Most radical Buddhists were not just radical in this sociopolitical sense, however, but also in their strive to reform or modernize Buddhism. For example, two decades after Uchiyama's death, the Youth League for New Buddhism 新興仏教青年同盟 accepted a mission statement that pledged both "to reform [the capitalist economic system] and realize the society of the future" and "to promote a Buddhism appropriate to the new age."⁵

Furthermore, this two-fold aim of reforming both society and Buddhism is by no means unique to radical Buddhism. Since the 1880s there have been a great number of Buddhist monks and laymen in various countries arguing for some kind of Buddhism that is rationalized or modernized on the one hand, and activist or socially engaged on the other. Several labels have been introduced to group together thinkers and movements expressing varieties hereof: Buddhist modernism (or modernist Buddhism),⁶ engaged Buddhism,⁷ secular Buddhism,⁸ Protestant Buddhism,⁹ and so forth. There are, of course, significant differences between the Buddhisms these labels cover — especially in the extents of their engagement or activism — but they are all rooted in a desire "to promote a Buddhism appropriate to the new age." They all strive (or strove) to somehow make Buddhism more relevant for and in modern society, or in other words, to *modernize* Buddhism or key aspects thereof.

Modernization is often associated with secularization, and proposed modernizations of Buddhism generally involve aspects of secularization. This is most obvious in case of secular Buddhism, which flat-out rejects any supernatural or mythical element in Buddhism, but most Buddhist modernists, engaged Buddhists, radical Buddhists, and so forth, also rejected or rethought supernatural elements in traditional Buddhism and argued for more naturalist interpretations. The aforementioned rejection of fatalistic belief in karma by Uchiyama may be seen as an example hereof.

Secularity

Until a few decades ago, the ruling paradigm in the sociology of religion was the *secularization thesis*, the idea that modern societies are becoming increasingly secular. Reality is a bit more complex, however, and there is a mountain of historical evidence against this thesis, or at least against some varieties thereof.¹⁰ The idea of

---

4   Patrice Ladwig and James Mark Shields, "Introduction," *Politics, Religion & Ideology* 15, no. 2 (2014): 187–204, at 16.
5   Kashiwahara Yūsen 柏原祐泉, 『日本仏教史　現代』(Tokyo: Yoshikawa Kōbunkan 古川弘文館, 1990), 214. See the section "Seno'o Girō and the Youth League" in chapter 3 for the full three-point mission statement.
6   Usually Heinz Bechert is credited with coining the term "Buddhist modernism" and starting the academic study thereof. See Heinz Bechert, *Buddhismus, Staat und Gesellschaft in den Ländern des Theravāda-Buddhismus: Grundlagen. Ceylon* (Berlin: Metzer, 1966).
7   Thích Nhất Hạnh is usually credited with coining the term "engaged Buddhism." See the section "Vietnam — Thích Nhất Hạnh's Engaged Buddhism" in chapter 3.
8   I am not sure who used the (English) term "secular Buddhism" first, but by far the best known advocate of the notion is Stephen Batchelor. See the section "Secular Buddhism" in chapter 3.
9   The term "Protestant Buddhism" was coined in Gananath Obeyesekere, "Religious Symbolism and Political Change in Ceylon," *Modern Ceylon Studies* 1 (1970): 43–63. See also Richard Gombrich and Gananath Obeyesekere, *Buddhism Transformed: Religious Change in Sri Lanka* (Princeton: Princeton University Press, 1988).
10 For a review of the historical evidence against the secularization thesis, see J.C.D. Clark, "Secularization and Modernization: The Failure of a 'Grand Narrative'," *The Historical Journal* 55, no. 1 (2012): 161–94.

a process of secularization presupposes that societies or ideas can be more or less secular, or, in other words, that there are *gradations* in secularity, and regardless of whether there are discernible historical trends with regards to secularity, the notion of gradations of secularity is helpful to get a better grip on radical Buddhism and adjacent phenomena.

On such a scale of secularity, there is a more radical secular end, a more traditional non-secular end, and much in between. There is no such single scale, however. In *Public Religions in the Modern World*, José Casanova argues that

> what usually passes for a single theory of secularization is actually made up of three very different, uneven and unintegrated propositions: secularization as differentiation of the secular spheres from religious institutions and norms, secularization as decline of religious beliefs and practices, and secularization as marginalization of religion to a privatized sphere.[11]

Casanova's three kinds of secularization presuppose three kinds of secularity: (1) secularity as the extent of separation between religious and non-religious institutions; (2) secularity as a measure of the pervasiveness and influence of religious beliefs and practices; and (3) secularity as the extent to which religion has been forced out of the public sphere and into the private sphere. But even these might not be singular dimensions. Most importantly, the second seems to cover several different — albeit probably related — aspects of secularity including (2a) the extent to which people adhere to traditional religious beliefs and practices; (2b) the importance of religious beliefs and practices (either traditional or new) to people; and (2c) the extent to which religious beliefs and practices are reinterpreted or reformed to conform to secular, non-religious beliefs and practices.

Radical, modernist, and secular Buddhism move away from the traditional non-secular end of the spectrum in this last sense (i.e., 2c), but that is not the only dimension of secularity that matters here. Jessica Main and Rongdao Lai have pointed out that one of the central features of engaged Buddhism is "the rejection of the historical and ideological aspects of *secularization*."[12] In other words, engaged Buddhism is *anti*-secular in the third sense distinguished above (i.e., 3): it does *not* accept marginalization to the private sphere, but sees an explicit public, social, or political role for Buddhism. And radical Buddhists who argue for revolution, like Uchiyama, are even more radically anti-secular in this sense. Hence, radical Buddhism is radically secular in one sense of secularity, and radically anti-secular in another.

Modernist, radical, secular, and related Buddhisms can be positioned in a two-dimensional space defined by two of the aspects of secularity distinguished above: the extent to which religious beliefs and practices are reinterpreted or reformed to conform to secular, science-based beliefs and practices, and the extent to which religion is forced into the private sphere and denied a public, social, or political role. The first of these aspects or dimensions identifies secularity with naturalism; the second identifies it with *privatization*.

On both dimensions, the two extremes of radical secularity and radical anti-secularity are idealizations. Few if any thinkers or currents exemplify these end points

---

11 José Casanova, *Public Religions in the Modern World* (Chicago: University of Chicago Press, 1994), 211.
12 Jessica Main and Rongdao Lai, "Introduction: Reformulating 'Socially Engaged Buddhism' as an Analytical Category," *The Eastern Buddhist* 44, no. 2 (2013): 1–34, at 4. Italics in original.

on the two scales, although some may have gotten quite close. In between there is a whole spectrum of intermediate positions. The opposite of "radical" as an adjective is "moderate," but in case of a spectrum only positions roughly in the middle can be considered moderate. Furthermore, the moderate category on either dimension does not just include relatively well-developed positions that are equally distant from both radical extremes, but also a kind of neutrality resulting either from a quietist unwillingness to develop a more definite position (because the issue is not considered important, for example) or from incapability to develop a clear position due to a lack of access to necessary information. Uchiyama should probably be classified as a moderate on the secularity-as-naturalism dimension in this sense because he lacked the necessary background in science and philosophy, including Buddhist philosophy, to develop a more rigorous position in this respect.

I suppose that some people might be inclined to choose moderation over the radical extremes on the basis of an assumption that the middle ground is always better. This is a form of fallacious reasoning called the "argument to moderation" or "middle ground fallacy" that might be especially attractive to some Buddhists, given that Buddhism preaches "the Middle Way."[13] However, the Buddha's Middle Way is one between two very specific extremes,[14] and that the middle way is the right way in *some* specific case(s) does not imply that one should always opt for the middle way. Sometimes one of the extremes is right.

Secularity as Naturalism

Radical secularity-as-naturalism implies an acceptance of science as supreme authority and a rejection of supernatural explanations. The anti-secular end on this dimension, on the other hand, accepts religious tradition or scripture as supreme authority and accepts supernatural explanations. In case of Buddhism, the secular end's rigorous naturalism leads to a rejection of belief in karma and reincarnation. This implies the necessity of reinterpretation of at least some texts and doctrines or the bracketing of problematic doctrines, and consequently, the secular end is radically reformist. The anti-secular end, in contrast, is staunchly traditionalist.

Radical secularity-as-naturalism conflicts with the identification of Buddhism as a religion, or at least appears to do so, but not with its identification as philosophy, provided that philosophy is assumed to be part of science. The latter is itself not an uncontroversial claim, however. The question how philosophy relates to the sciences is closely related to the question of how to define philosophy and its subject matter, which is one of the core questions of the branch of philosophy called "metaphilosophy."[15] Many philosophers saw and see their discipline as something inherently different from the sciences, but not always for the same reasons. The most important but not only exception is W.V.O. Quine. For Quine, philosophy and science are continuous, and neither deals in absolute certainties. Rather, *any* scientific idea, and thus any philosophical idea, is open for revision.

---

13 Ichikawa Hakugen has suggested that this is one of the reasons why radical philosophies such as socialism and anarchism are relatively rare among Buddhists. Ichikawa Hakugen 市川白弦,『仏教者の戦争責任』(Tokyo: Shunshūsha 春秋社, 1970).

14 Namely, asceticism and hedonism. *Dhammacakkappavattana Sutta* (SN 56.11). See the section "The Middle Way" in chapter 5.

15 See, for example, Søren Overgaard, Paul Gilbert, and Stephen Burwood, *An Introduction to Metaphilosophy* (Cambridge: Cambridge University Press, 2013), chapter 2.

Quine's naturalism is rooted in pragmatism, a philosophical movement that sprung up in nineteenth-century America and that advocated giving up the traditional quest for absolute certainty and to settle for the more modest goal of finding what works. On the basis of the contrast underlying this suggestion, we can sketch a picture showing how science, religion, and philosophy relate to each other. Traditionally, philosophy has been a quest for certainty,[16] while religion claimed to have already found certainty. Science, on the other hand, does not aim for certainty, but for prediction and explanation (i.e., for what works), and any scientific explanation is only provisional (i.e., open for revision if contrary evidence is found).

Radical secularity-as-naturalism, then, aiming to make Buddhism "scientific" or naturalist, first collapses religion into philosophy by giving up on the pretense that certainty has already been found,[17] and then collapses philosophy into science by giving up the quest for certainty altogether. In this sense, radical secularity-as-naturalism is, or should be, pragmatist or Quinean naturalist, or something very similar.

Moderate positions on this dimension often seem to be motivated by a conscious or unconscious desire to give some key beliefs protected status (or conversely, to only reform or discard some unwelcome beliefs). In such cases, naturalism is only accepted halfheartedly or partially; that is, as long as scientific findings do not threaten core beliefs they are accepted, and some peripheral beliefs may even be revised in light of contrary scientific evidence, but core beliefs are effectively immune from revision. That effective immunity may be the result of a lack of awareness or understanding of that contrary evidence, of ignoring that evidence, of trying to explain it away, of a pseudo-skeptical appeal to uncertainty, or of some combination of these. None of these options are available to an austere naturalist, but the appeal-to-uncertainty strategy is especially dubious. An example thereof would be to hold on to a belief in an immortal soul because science has not with absolute certainty proven that there are no souls. The latter is true for the obvious reason that science never proves anything with *absolute* certainty — that just is not how science works. But that is no reason to accept the opposite. Rather, science — and thus naturalism — always provisionally accepts the most well-supported and most coherent theory or explanation. There is no empirical evidence for souls,[18] the notion of a soul conflicts with basic laws of physics,[19] and the only motivation for a belief in souls appears to be a human craving for immortality.[20] That is more than sufficient ground to reject the notion. It is true that science can be wrong (and it is always science itself that shows when

---

16   The quest for certainty does not just characterize Western philosophy, but Chinese and Indian philosophy as well. For example, classical Chinese philosophy aimed to find the constant or unchanging dao 常道, and much of Indian philosophy has been concerned with the nature of ultimate truth. In all three traditions the quest for certainty at some point developed into its counterpart, the critical realization of the certain failure of that quest (in skepticism, Daoism, and Mādhyamaka), therein finding some kind of certainty after all.
17   This is only applicable to religious explanation, of course, but religion also serves other functions, and radical secularity-as-naturalism may not necessarily have to give up those. See the section "Between Science and Religion" in chapter 6.
18   Contrary to popular belief, near-death experiences are not evidence of an afterlife or an immortal soul but are better explained as hallucinations of an oxygen-deprived brain. Dean Mobbs and Caroline Watt, "There Is Nothing Paranormal about Near-Death Experiences: How Neuroscience Can Explain Seeing Bright Lights, Meeting the Dead, or Being Convinced You Are One of Them," *Trends in Cognitive Sciences* 15, no. 10 (2011): 447–49. See also the first part of chapter 2 in Mark Johnston, *Surviving Death* (Princeton: Princeton University Press, 2010).
19   See the section "Physicalism" in chapter 4.
20   Idem, but see also section "Between Science and Religion" in chapter 6.

it is wrong!), but the scientific approach is to provisionally accept the best scientific theory until it is proven wrong, not to reject some scientific theory that does not fit with one's worldview because it might eventually be proven wrong. That's not naturalism — that's cherry-picking.

Such cherry-picking, when it occurs, rarely seems to be intentional, however. Humans have a psychological need to protect the beliefs that are most central to their worldview,[21] and that need trumps almost everything else. For this reason, a consistent and austere secularity-as-naturalism may not really be humanly possible. We are all biased, and we all protect the beliefs we hold dearest. Probably the most prominent example of this kind of unintentional cherry-picking is the fourteenth Dalai Lama, who has shown great interest in the dialogue between Buddhism and science and who has written that "if science proves some belief of Buddhism wrong, then Buddhism will have to change,"[22] but who has also shown to be unwilling or unable to give up beliefs in mind–body dualism and reincarnation.[23] The latter is quite understandable given the centrality of those beliefs in his belief system, but it implies that he does not genuinely embrace science, or naturalism, and thus that he should be classified as moderate on the secularity-as-naturalism dimension.[24]

The Sociopolitical Dimension: Secularity as Privatization

The secularity-as-privatization dimension concerns the public, social, or political roles of Buddhism (or religion in general). Radical secularity in this sense is the position that religion belongs in the private sphere exclusively. Buddhists who take up a position close to this extreme argue that suffering or *dukkha* in Buddhism is just psychological and thus private and that other kinds of suffering (such as poverty) have nothing to do with dukkha and are, therefore, no concern for Buddhism. They may still be a concern for Buddhists, but that concern is not motivated by Buddhism itself.[25]

Moving away from radical secularity in this sense we find a range of positions that, to an increasing extent, stress the importance of addressing other kinds of suffering, often called "material suffering" or "worldly suffering," and that, to a decreasing extent, accept the sociopolitical and economic status quo. The anti-secular extreme roundly rejects the status quo and aims for a complete overhaul of society. In other words, radical anti-secularity in this sense is revolutionary. Moderate positions closer to the secular end largely accept the status quo and focus their attention on charity; moderate positions closer to the anti-secular end are less accepting of the status quo and aim for more or less radical reform.

Some moderate positions may seem more radical than they really are, although this is probably more obvious in the case of Christianity than that of Buddhism. The Christian right, for example, may seem radically anti-secular in their aims to

---

21 See the section "Between Science and Religion" in chapter 6.
22 Tenzin Gyatso, the 14th Dalai Lama, "Our Faith in Science," *The New York Times,* November 12, 2005, https://www.nytimes.com/2005/11/12/opinion/our-faith-in-science.html. See also Tenzin Gyatso, *The Universe in a Single Atom* (New York: Morgan Road, 2005), 3.
23 Tenzin Gyatso, *The Universe in a Single Atom.* Tenzin Gyatso, "Reincarnation," *His Holiness the 14th Dalai Lama of Tibet,* 2011, http://www.dalailama.com/biography/reincarnation.
24 For a more extensive discussion of the Dalai Lama's views on science and society, see the section "Tibet — Gendun Chopel and the 14th Dalai Lama" in chapter 3.
25 About *dukkha* and the concept of suffering in Buddhism, see the section "Suffering" in chapter 5.

ban abortion and euthanasia and to implement various other religiously motivated policies. However, they accept the sociopolitical and economic status quo and do not aim to create a society based on the values expressed in, for example, the *Sermon on the Mount* (Matthew 5–7). Hence, they effectively accept that the ethics of the New Testament has no place in politics and are a private matter. All they aim for is a few minor, or even cosmetic, adjustments to the status quo, which makes them moderates, and closer to the secular than to the anti-secular end.

It is important to notice that when religion is allowed in the public and political sphere, it is nearly always in this moderate form. Religious involvement in politics is accepted as long as it just concerns relatively superficial matters like abortion and euthanasia, but it has to stay outside more important areas such as economic policy, national security, and so forth. In the last half century, not just religion has been marginalized in this sense, however, but most political ideologies as well. Politics now presents itself as technocracy — preferred policies are no longer motivated by openly ideological arguments but by apparently neutral "science." Hence, political ideology has been privatized as much as religion, or so it seems.

This is not exactly the case, however. Rather than that all religion and political ideology has been forced out of politics, one specific religion or ideology has become hegemonic. That religion or ideology is neoliberal capitalism. It tolerates no competition in the political sphere, but it depends on masking itself as ideologically neutral to maintain that monopoly. Creating this image of ideological neutrality, or non-ideologicality, is the main task of mainstream, neoclassical economics. The latter pretends to be a science, but it is about as scientific as numerology or astrology and has more in common with religion or political ideology than with science.[26] This is a topic that we will return to in chapter 15, but for now it needs to be noted that the degree of secularity-as-privatization (of some position) coincides with the degree of acceptance of the hegemony of neoliberal capitalism or the *hegemony of cultural psychopathy*, as I called it elsewhere.[27] Acceptance of the status quo is acceptance of *that* hegemony.

Locating Radical Buddhism

Modernist Buddhism, which originated in the 1880s in Ceylon (Sri Lanka), Japan, and Western academies is, or was, moderate to secular on both dimensions. Secular Buddhism is a recent, Western radicalization of Buddhist modernism,[28] which effectively means that it moved closer toward the secular extremes on both dimensions. Engaged Buddhism and radical Buddhism also grew in modernist soil (although they have deeper roots; see next chapter), but are much more anti-secular on the privatization dimension. Engaged Buddhists occupy themselves with charity

---

26 Robert Nelson, *Economics as Religion: From Samuelson to Chicago and Beyond,* rev. edn. (University Park: Penn State University Press, 2014); John Rapley, *Twilight of the Money Gods: Economics as Religion and How It All Went Wrong* (London: Simon & Schuster, 2017); David Orrell, *Economyths: Ten Ways Economics Gets It Wrong* (Ontario: John Wiley, 2010); John Weeks, *Economics of the 1%: How Mainstream Economics Serves the Rich, Obscures Reality and Distorts Policy* (London: Anthem, 2014); and Norbert Häring and Niall Douglas, *Economists and the Powerful: Convenient Theories, Distorted Facts, Ample Rewards* (London: Anthem, 2012). See also chapter 15, as well as the section "Problems for Subjective Consequentialism" in chapter 12.
27 Lajos Brons, *The Hegemony of Psychopathy* (Earth: punctum books, 2017).
28 Although it had a forerunner in late-nineteenth-century Japan. See the section "Realism and Reform in Japan — Inoue Enryō" in chapter 3.

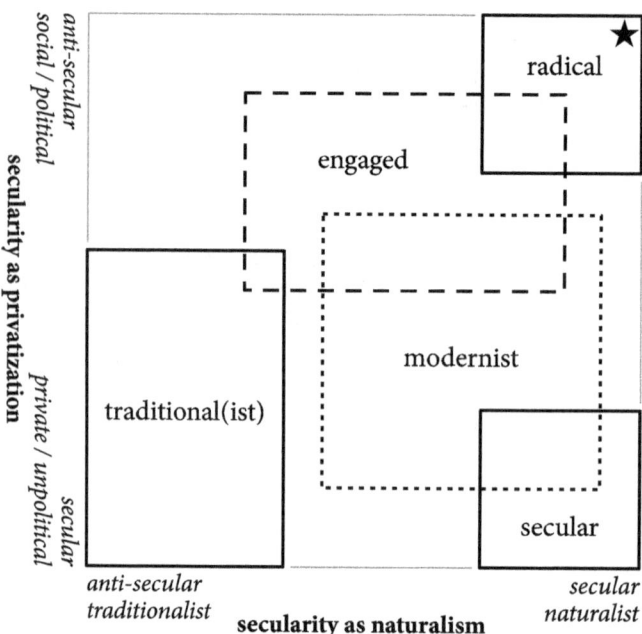

Fig. 1.1. Five Buddhisms in a two-dimensional space.

and often argue for political reform, while radical Buddhists demanded much more radical social change or even revolution, although generally a peaceful revolution. Figure 1.1 roughly locates these four modern "Buddhisms" as well as traditional(ist), mainstream Buddhism in a two-dimensional space defined by the two dimensions of secularity described above.

This map of five Buddhisms is merely intended to give a clearer view of the terrain and not to give some kind of definitive classification of modern currents in Buddhist thought and practice. Nevertheless, it must be noted that my understanding of "radical Buddhism" is based on this map and, consequently, that it deviates slightly from the definition by Shields and Ladwig cited a few pages back. While their definition focuses on the political aspect, I define radical Buddhism as being radical in two respects. That is, *radical Buddhists adopt a broadly naturalist stance with respect to Buddhist doctrine* (and are thus secular in that sense), and *they adopt a radically anti-hegemonic, revolutionary stance in political and economic affairs* (and thus reject the secular marginalization of religion to the private sphere).

This book is about radical Buddhism in this sense. More specifically, it is concerned with the question whether a position in the top right corner of figure 1.1 (marked with "★") is possible. Since there have been people who have defended positions very close to that — Seno'o Girō 妹尾義郎 probably came closest[29] — the answer to that question may seem to be that it is obviously possible, but that answer would be too hasty. What I am asking here is whether it is possible to develop a position that simultaneously satisfies all of the following criteria: (1) it is radically naturalist, (in a roughly Quinean or pragmatist sense); (2) it is politically radical in the sense that it rejects the status quo (meaning that it rejects neoliberal capitalism and the hegemony of psychopathy); (3) it is recognizably and defensibly Buddhist;

---

29 See the section "Seno'o Girō and the Youth League" in chapter 3.

and (4) it is radical in the sense of being uncompromising, rigorous, and consistent. It is by no means obvious that any combination of just two of the first three criteria is possible, let alone all three of them, and the fourth criterion obviously adds a further complication. Nevertheless, I think the answer to my question is "yes," but it will require more than a few pages to explain that answer. Just to be clear, the purpose of this book is not to reconstruct *the* philosophy of radical Buddhism, because that does not exist, but rather to take radical Buddhism to its logical conclusion, and thus to radicalize it.

Naturalism

A radicalized radical Buddhism is radically naturalist. This is the first criterion mentioned above. But it is not entirely clear what "naturalism" means, so before we proceed, some clarification is needed. One helpful way to classify the various naturalisms is the distinction between metaphysical naturalism, scientific naturalism, and methodological naturalism.[30]

Metaphysical naturalism makes a claim about the nature of reality and about what exists — roughly, the only things that exist are things that are part of the natural world. Hence, metaphysical naturalism entails the rejection of *super*natural entities like gods, ghosts, spirits, and souls, but the boundary between the supernatural and the natural is not always clear. Mark Johnston has attempted to naturalize the notion of God, for example,[31] and the ancient Greek philosopher Democritus naturalized the soul by claiming that it consists of especially small atoms. However, metaphysical naturalism does not just reject supernatural entities, but all non-natural entities, including abstract objects such as numbers, unless they can somehow be reduced to natural things. Many philosophers believe that numbers exist and that science depends on the assumption that numbers exist, but Hartry Field has famously argued against these beliefs.[32]

According to *scientific naturalism*, the natural sciences are the only source of reliable knowledge about reality. There is much to say for this view considering the success of the sciences, especially when compared to other models of inquiry like religion and tradition, but it is not immediately clear why the social sciences and humanities must be excluded. This exclusion seems to be based on the idea that there is something special about the scientific method of the natural sciences that is lacking in the other, lesser (?) sciences. But it is also supported by the widely shared belief that there can be one and only one correct description of reality and that the natural sciences are best positioned to give that one description. W.V.O. Quine, Hilary Putnam, Richard Rorty, and others have argued against these and related ideas and have thereby undermined at least some versions of scientific naturalism. Quine explicitly rejected the idea that there is just one correct description of reality. Rather, multiple descriptions are possible, and in a given context we should choose the one that best fits our interests and purposes.[33] Rorty has attacked the same idea but has

---

30 See, for example, Kelly James Clark, "Naturalism and Its Discontents," in *The Blackwell Companion to Naturalism*, ed. Kelly James Clark (Chichester: Wiley Blackwell, 2016), 1–15.
31 Mark Johnston, *Saving God: Religion after Idolatry* (Princeton: Princeton University Press, 2009).
32 Hartry Field, *Science without Numbers: A Defense of Nominalism*, 2nd edn. (Oxford: Oxford University Press, 2016).
33 W.V.O. Quine, "On What There Is" (1948), FLPV: 1–19; *Word and Object* (Cambridge: MIT Press, 1960); and "Ontological Relativity" (1969), OROE: 26–68.

also argued that there is no such thing as *the* scientific method, and that there is no good reason to put the natural sciences on a pedestal.[34] And Putnam has pointed out that scientific naturalists tend to overlook the methodological similarities between the natural and other sciences; if there is a scientific method, it is not unique to the natural sciences.[35]

While metaphysical naturalism makes a claim about what kind of things exist and scientific naturalism aims to restrict our way of knowing things, including what exists, *methodological materialism* has more modest aims — it tells us how we should conduct our inquiries. What exactly it prescribes or forbids differs a bit between interpretations, but typically, methodological materialism forbids the appeal to supernatural entities and explanations and recommends modeling our approach to inquiry and explanation on the methods and approaches that are common in the natural sciences. These two "rules" are not entirely independent from each other. Thales is often considered the father of Western science and philosophy and of the scientific method because he was the first, as far as we know, to reject supernatural explanations. He suggested, for example, that the periodic floods of the Nile were caused by wind, while the traditional explanation appealed to the gods or other supernatural entities or events.[36] Hence, the first rule is an essential part or aspect of the second.

The most outspoken advocates of modeling philosophical inquiry and philosophical ideas on scientific practice were the nineteenth-century American pragmatists, Charles Sanders Peirce, William James, and John Dewey, and some of their twentieth-century heirs including Quine, Rorty, and Putnam, who were mentioned above. James argued that we should think of truth "instrumentally," that is:

> Any idea upon which we can ride, so to speak; any idea that will carry us prosperously from any one part of our experience to any other part, linking things satisfactorily, working securely, simplifying, saving labor; is true for just so much, true in so far forth, true *instrumentally*.[37]

According to James, in advocating this "instrumental view of truth" he and his allies "have only followed the example of geologists, biologists and philologists."[38] (Notice that he does not just mention natural sciences.) His point is that science treats truth instrumentally: scientists accept as true that what works, "any idea upon which we can ride."

Half a century and some scientific revolutions later, it has become clear to even the most casual observer of science that there can be big changes in the ideas upon which we ride, although this should not be exaggerated. Relativistic physics has not completely replaced Newtonian physics, for example; in the physical circumstances of the world of our ordinary circumstances Newtonian physics works fine, and

---

34 Richard Rorty, *Philosophy and the Mirror of Nature* (Princeton: Princeton University Press, 1979), and *Consequences of Pragmatism* (Minneapolis: University of Minnesota Press, 1982).
35 Hilary Putnam, *Realism and Reason* (Cambridge: Cambridge University Press, 1983); *The Many Faces of Realism* (La Salle: Open Court, 1987); and *Realism with a Human Face* (Cambridge: Harvard University Press, 1990).
36 His explanation is false, of course, but that does not matter. What matters is that it is a naturalistic explanation, while supernatural explanation was the norm.
37 William James, "Pragmatism: A New Name for Some Old Ways of Thinking" (1907), in *Pragmatism and the Meaning of Truth* (Cambridge: Harvard University Press, 1978), 1–166, at 34. Italics in original.
38 Ibid.

relativistic physics adds little. Nevertheless, these scientific revolutions lead to an increasing awareness that the instrumental truth of science is not final truth: scientists accept ideas and theories as true, but only *provisionally*. (Peirce thought that if inquiry continues long enough we will eventually reach the truth, rather than some provisional, instrumental truth, but it is hard to see how we would know that we have arrived.) Influenced by pragmatism and responding to what he considered "dogmas of empiricism," Quine argued in the 1950s and '60s that *all* scientific and philosophical ideas are provisional and thus open to revision.[39] Nevertheless, any revision of scientific ideas starts at the edges of our web of belief and central beliefs are only revised as a last resort. Thus, while the belief that $1 + 1 = 2$ is open to revision in principle, there are very many more peripheral scientific and other ideas that are candidates for revision before considering to revise "$1 + 1 = 2$."

Partially on this ground, but also motivated by a version of scientific naturalism, Quine also rejected the common idea of a fundamental difference between science and philosophy:

> There have been philosophers who thought of philosophy as somehow separate from science, and as providing a firm basis on which to build science, but this I consider an empty dream. Much of science is firmer than philosophy is, or can ever perhaps aspire to be. I think of philosophy as continuous with science, even as a part of science. [...] Philosophy lies at the abstract and theoretical end of science. Science, in the broadest sense, is a continuum that stretches from history and engineering at one extreme to philosophy and pure mathematics at the other.[40]

There is, then, no fundamental difference between science and philosophy in how we should choose between competing theories and ideas, and all are open to revision. Nothing is excepted: there are and can be no immutable truths. Rather, we select the theory that best explains the facts that need explaining, without appeals to dogma, without appeals to supernatural entities or processes, and we accept that our selection is no final truth.

Although I present Quinean, pragmatist naturalism here as a kind of methodological naturalism, it can also be seen as a variety of scientific naturalism, albeit a rather modest variety that does not idealize science and that does not discard the social sciences and humanities. This does not mean that all nominally "scientific" views are equally valuable in all circumstances, however. Quine's insight that alternative descriptions of reality — physical descriptions, psychological descriptions, and so forth — are possible does not mean that all descriptions are equally valuable or justified.[41] Some nominally "scientific" descriptions might be useless given our purposes. Others may be insufficiently supported by evidence or even be incoherent.

---

39 W.V.O. Quine, "Two Dogmas of Empiricism" (1953), FLPV: 20–46; *Word and Object*; and "Epistemology Naturalized" (1969), OROE: 69–90. On Quine's pragmatist naturalism, see also Paul Gregory, *Quine's Naturalism: Language, Theory, and the Knowing Subject* (London: Continuum, 2008), and Jeffrey Roland, "On Naturalism in the Quinean Tradition," in *Philosophical Methodology: The Armchair or the Laboratory*, ed. Matthew Haug (London: Routledge, 2014), 43–61.

40 Bryan Magee, *Talking Philosophy: Dialogues with Fifteen Leading Philosophers* (Oxford: Oxford University Press, 1982), 143.

41 In addition to previous references to Quine's writings, see also W.V.O. Quine, "Posits and Reality" (1955), WPOE: 246–54.

Yet others may violate principles of naturalistic explanation. Supernatural explanations most obviously violate such principles, and thus it may seem that metaphysical naturalism is implied by methodological naturalism, but even the acceptance of metaphysical naturalism (i.e., the rejection of gods, souls, spirits, etc.) is provisional. It is in principle possible that new evidence forces a change of mind, but given all we know now, that is almost as unlikely as that we would have to revise our belief that $1 + 1 = 2$.

The quest for certainty is a religious quest, not a scientific one; and philosophy should side with science, not with religion. Of all naturalisms, Quine's is the most radical exactly because it incorporates the pragmatic rejection of the dogma of absolute and final certainty. Furthermore, the fourth criterion mentioned at the end of the previous section interprets "radical" as "uncompromising, rigorous, and consistent," and the consistency of metaphysical and standard scientific naturalism is quite debatable. The first depends on a vague or even obscure boundary between the natural and the non-natural and an a priori denial of everything that lies on the wrong side of that boundary. The second is based on a heavily idealized view of the natural sciences. Such a priori rejections and idealization are very much against the spirit of naturalism, but what is even more problematic is that these naturalisms are themselves outside the scope of science. They are presented and defended as non-empirical, evidence-independent, and unchanging (i.e., unrevisable), hence, as the very opposite of naturalism.

There are, moreover, other reasons to accept some version of Quinean naturalism here. Aside from implying variants of metaphysical and scientific naturalism and helping to make sense of the modernist reidentification of Buddhism as philosophy or science (see above), the philosophy of Quine and his student Donald Davidson will also help fill in some details where Buddhist philosophy alone does not provide sufficiently clear answers. There are important similarities between Davidson's and Quine's philosophy of language and the ideas of the Yogācāra philosophers Dignāga and Dharmakīrti, for example,[42] and especially Davidson's ideas will help to merge elements of Yogācāra and Tiantai 天台 into a coherent whole that can serve as the metaphysical and epistemological foundation of a radical Buddhism as well as to connect that foundation to a theory of normative ethics that builds on ideas found in the writings of Asaṅga and Śāntideva.[43]

Aside from four Buddhist philosophers mentioned in the previous paragraph, this section has only mentioned Western philosophers, which might give the impression that naturalism is a Western affair. But nothing could be further from the truth. Variants of naturalism have become influential in parts of Western philosophy — analytic philosophy mainly — but this is really quite a recent development and if one looks further back in history there are probably more examples of naturalism (or ideas close to naturalism) to be found in India and China than in Europe. The most obvious example in the Indian philosophical tradition is Cārvāka, but Dale Riepe suggested that the possibly mythical philosopher Uddālaka, mentioned in the

---

42 Lajos Brons, "Dharmakīrti, Davidson, and Knowing Reality," *Comparative Philosophy* 3, no. 1 (2012): 30–57, and "Meaning and Reality: A Cross-Traditional Encounter," in *Constructive Engagement of Analytic and Continental Approaches in Philosophy,* eds. Bo Mou and R. Tieszen (Leiden: Brill, 2013), 199–220. See also the last two sections of chapter 8.

43 Buddhism has no clear meta-ethics, for example, and Davidson's philosophy provides what is needed to construct a meta-ethics that creates a coherent bridge between metaphysics and epistemology on the one hand and normative ethics on the other.

Upanishads, and early Vaiśeṣika were naturalistic as well, and he found elements of naturalism in Jainism and Buddhism.⁴⁴ To what extent Uddālaka and early Vaiśeṣika were naturalistic is debatable, but the latter "Hindu" school is an interesting case because, like Democritus, it naturalized the soul by assuming that it consists of a special kind of atoms.

By far the most interesting naturalist in the Chinese philosophical tradition is the first-century philosopher Wang Chong 王充, an autodidact with an encyclopedic knowledge who was driven by a strong aversion to fashionable nonsense and the "flowery and artificial writing" 華偽之文 that he perceived to be customary in his day. In contrast to the latter, his book Lunheng 論衡, was intended to promote truth and to dispel falsehoods by means of a two-faced philosophical method of questioning 問 what is unclear and challenging 難, what is false or invalid.⁴⁵ The latter he generally did by means of clear, unadorned, and direct arguments.⁴⁶ For example, the chapter on spirits or ghosts 鬼 opens with the following passage:

> People say that the dead become spirits, have consciousness, and can harm people. [If we] test this [idea] by examining different kinds of creatures [we can] verify that the dead do not become spirits, don't have consciousness, and cannot harm people. How can we verify this? We can verify it from [other] creatures. Man is a creature, and [other] creatures are also creatures. If [another] creature dies it doesn't become a spirit, so for what reason would only humans become spirits when they die? [...] If we cannot separate [humans from other creatures], we have no reason to assume that [humans] can become spirits.⁴⁷

This introduction is then followed by a battery of short arguments intended to prove that there is no soul or spirit and that nothing is left after death after the body has rotted away.⁴⁸

As mentioned, Wang Chong particularly disliked "flowery writing." He argued that the "common people" are all too easily bewitched by exciting ideas in an attractive package:

> It is the nature of common people to enjoy strange sayings and uphold false and absurd writings. Why is this? [Because] the truth cannot be grasped quickly [or] easily, while flowery falsehoods astound the hearers and move their minds.⁴⁹

---

44   Dale Riepe, *The Naturalistic Tradition in Indian Thought* (Delhi: Motilal Banarsidass, 1961).
45   About Wang Chong's philosophical method, see Alexus McLeod, "A Reappraisal of Wang Chong's Critical Method through the 'Wenkong Chapter'," *Journal of Chinese Philosophy* 34, no. 4 (2007): 581–96. On Wang Chong in general, see Alexus McLeod, *The Philosophical Thought of Wang Chong* (Cham: Palgrave MacMillan, 2018).
46   Many of Wang's arguments are in *modus tollens* (if *p* then *q*; not *q*; therefore, not *p*), which is not remarkable in itself — rather, according to Christoph Harbsmeier, *Science and Civilization in China*, Vol. 7: *The Social Background*, Part 1: *Language and Logic in Traditional China* (Cambridge: Cambridge University Press, 1998), *modus tollens* was a very common argument form in ancient China — but his application stands out for its transparency and explicitness.
47   世謂死人為鬼，有知，能害人。試以物類驗之，死人不為鬼，無知，不能害人。何以驗之？驗之以物。人，物也，物，亦物也。物死不為鬼，人死何故獨能為鬼？世能別人物不能為鬼，則為鬼不為鬼尚難分明。如不能別，則亦無以知其能為鬼也。人之所以生者，精氣也，死而精氣滅⋯ 如不能別，則亦無以知其能為鬼也。 — Wang Chong 王充,《論衡》,〈論死〉(ca. 80), §§1–2.
48   Most of these arguments are in *modus tollens*. See two notes before this one.
49   世俗之性，好奇怪之語，說虛妄之文。何則？實事不能快意，而華虛驚耳動心也。— Wang Chong,《論衡》,〈對作〉, §2.

And consequently, "in the writings of the people all truth is lost, and false and absurd doctrines subvert what is real and virtuous [or] beautiful."[50] There is an obvious anti-populist or even elitist sentiment in these claims, but Wang has a point that "flowery and artificial writing" has an advantage in the marketplace of ideas. The relative obscurity of Wang may even confirm this point. He responded to the proliferation of "empty falsehoods" 虛 with relatively dry and unexciting arguments, which probably did not contribute much to his popularity. Nevertheless, it is an example worth following. Excitement is not a proxy for truth. More often the opposite is true. The more exotic and exciting an idea, the more likely it is false.

Methodological naturalism is, as the term implies, primarily concerned with *how* to conduct inquiries. It can be said with a very high degree of confidence that naturalistic inquiry leads to metaphysically naturalistic conclusions, but it is the way that determines the inquiry's nature, and not its end or findings. The consistency criterion, the fourth criterion mentioned at the end of the previous section, requires that if some form of methodological naturalism is adopted here, it must be adopted as a guiding principle in how this inquiry is conducted as well. This has at least two important implications. Firstly, methodological naturalism restricts the grounds for acceptance of some theory or idea. That is, it should (provisionally!) be accepted if and only if it is supported by the best available evidence. Tradition or authority do not count as evidence and are thus not appropriate grounds for acceptance, and neither is scripture, unless there are independent reasons to accept the content of some text as probably true. And secondly, methodological naturalism requires clarity, and thus takes exception to ambiguity, obscurity, and "flowery writing."

The reliance on the best available evidence commanded by naturalism has an important corollary. If a view, theory, or idea is based on the best available evidence, then that evidence justifies the provisional acceptance of that view, theory, or idea as true. And consequently, if a view simultaneously satisfies the criteria of naturalism and is "recognizably and defensibly Buddhist" (criterion 3 in the previous section), then this implies that the right view is a Buddhist view, or in other words, that I should (again, provisionally) accept a variant of Buddhism as true. I do indeed accept that conclusion, but despite that, I do not consider myself a "Buddhist" for reasons explained in chapter 5.[51]

A Plethora of *-isms*

One implication of the clarity requirement (i.e., the second methodological implication of naturalism mentioned above) is that much attention will be given in this book to problems of language. "Philosophical problems arise when language goes on holiday," said Wittgenstein famously,[52] and some of the worst philosophical problems arise due to equivocations — confusions of different meanings of the same word. While there are terms in the Buddhist tradition that are ambiguous or polysemous,[53] it is Western philosophy that is probably the worst offender in this respect. And worst of all are the various *-isms*. Many philosophical terms ending

---

50 起眾書並失實, 虛妄之言勝真美也。— Ibid.
51 See the section "What Is a Buddhist?" in chapter 5.
52 Ludwig Wittgenstein, *Philosophische Untersuchungen* (1953; Frankfurt a.M.: Suhrkamp, 1975), §38.
53 Chapter 5 will discuss several, including the notion of a "middle way" and the concept(s) of *dukkha* (suffering).

in -ism — such as "realism," "idealism," "materialism" — have at least two entirely different meanings within philosophy and another unrelated meaning in ordinary language. Other, more technical -isms are ill-defined and differently interpreted. If a word ends in -ism that is almost a guarantee that there is widespread disagreement and misunderstanding about the meanings (in the plural!) of that word. Indeed, even the term "Buddhism" is ambiguous.

Unfortunately, -isms are unavoidable in this book, and consequently, many pages are devoted to distinguishing and describing variants of various -isms in an attempt to improve clarity and avoid confusion and equivocation. The previous section, discussing "naturalism," is a case in point. "Materialism" and the related concept of "physicalism" are discussed in chapter 4. "Buddhism," obviously a key concept here given the aim of this book, is the topic of chapter 5. The polysemy of "realism" is addressed in chapter 7 and also touched upon in chapter 2. "Idealism" is discussed briefly in chapters 2 and 4 and more extensively in chapter 7. Other -isms examined in this book include "essentialism," "relativism," "perspectivism" (all in chapter 7), "coherentism" (in chapter 9), "consequentialism" (in chapter 12), "capitalism" (in chapter 15), and "Utopianism" (in chapter 16).

A Guide to This Book

This book consists of four parts. The aim of the book as a whole is to radicalize radical Buddhism, and the purpose of part I is to clarify what that means. Toward that end, it sketches the history and prehistory of radical Buddhism and adjacent modern Buddhisms, discusses some important patterns and trends therein, investigates what it means to call something or someone "Buddhist," and considers what all of this implies for the project of this book. That project — radicalizing radical Buddhism — is the topic of parts II and III, which focus on metaphysics and epistemology (in part II) and on ethics and social philosophy (in part III), respectively. The final, and very short part IV returns to the four criteria of this book's goal and presents some closing thoughts and conclusions.

Part I consists of six chapters including this one. Chapters 2 and 3 sketch parts of the prehistory and history of radical Buddhism and related modern Buddhisms such as Buddhist modernism, engaged Buddhism, secular Buddhism, and so forth. Chapter 2 discusses the philosophical roots of radical Buddhism and related modern Buddhisms in the history of Buddhist thought. The aim of the chapter is not to give a complete account of the history of Buddhist philosophy, but to selectively sketch some of the precursors and foundations of the social engagement, this-worldly focus, and rationalism that characterize radical Buddhism.

Chapter 3, the longest chapter of this book, introduces relevant ideas of a number of radical Buddhists, engaged Buddhists, and others. Like chapter 2 it does not give a complete overview. That would make this book at least two times thicker than it already is.[54] Rather, it focuses on the more radical among the many modern Buddhists.[55] This, of course, raises the question what it means to be more or less radical.

---

54 Nevertheless, chapter 3 aims for geographical completeness by covering as much of the Buddhist world as possible.
55 Explicitly excluded from the scope of chapter 3 are radicals and activists who do not primarily identify themselves as Buddhist but merely take some inspiration or ideas from Buddhism. This should not be taken to imply that those have nothing to offer, however, but chapter 3 is already long enough. One example of such "radicalism with Buddhist elements," as opposed to "radical Bud-

Roughly, a Buddhism or Buddhist is more radical on the *sociopolitical dimension* if they demand more sweeping reform, more explicitly (or more prominently) reject capitalism, or demand (or allow, at least) a greater political role for Buddhism. Many radical Buddhists associate themselves with some kind of socialism or anarchism and there are levels of radicality in that respect as well; that is, Marxism and communism are more radical than social democracy or utopian socialism,[56] and anarchism based on the ideas of Kropotkin is more radical than that based on Tolstoy or other primitivist anarchisms. A Buddhism or Buddhist is more radical on the *naturalistic dimension* to the extent that it or they unconditionally accept science, reject supernatural entities and explanations, and focus on this world and this life, rather than on some kind of afterlife or otherworldly paradise.

Based on these and other criteria, Chapter 4 opens with a provisional map of the landscape of radical Buddhism and its neighbors. The chapter is mainly concerned, however, with some patterns and trends among radical and engaged Buddhists, particularly the reluctance to accept materialism. To a large extent this reluctance is rooted in misunderstandings which are partially caused by the polysemy of "materialism." As mentioned in the previous section, within philosophy, "materialism" means a number of very different things, and it has a further unrelated meaning in ordinary language. Chapter 4 also discusses the common lack of "systemic" perspectives in Buddhism and the consequent tendency to seek the causes of worldly suffering in moral defects, thereby often missing their real causes, and looks into the role of ideology.

The goal of this book — developing a naturalist and sociopolitically radical philosophy that is recognizably and defensibly Buddhist — only makes sense if there is a clear way or criterion to tell whether something is indeed "recognizably and defensibly Buddhist," but deciding whether some doctrine, theory, or idea is "Buddhist" is not as easy and straightforward as it may seem, as will be shown in chapter 5. Attempts to define Buddhism by appealing to some kind of essence end up excluding much of what has been called "Buddhist" and stumble upon other problems as well. For that reason, the approach adopted in this book is more or less genetic or historical: a theory, doctrine, practice, or idea is Buddhist if most of what it is based on is Buddhist and if it could not just as well be based on non-Buddhist sources.

The final chapter of the first part of the book wraps up the "groundwork" by summarizing some of the key findings of part I and zooming in on the most important schools and sources for parts II and III. Additionally, chapter 6 also discusses the common Buddhist modernist idea that Buddhism is a philosophy rather than a religion.

Based on the groundwork of part I, parts II and III of this book focus on reality and what we can know about it, and on social and ethical questions respectively. Part II proposes a "perspectival realism" that is based mostly on Yogācāra and Tiantai

---

dhism," can be found in the writings of the Dutch Marxist philosopher Jasper Schaaf, *Boeddhisme en betrokkenheid: Kan de Boeddha-Darma bijdragen aan een marxistisch georiënteerde inzet van maatschappelijke betrokkenheid?* (Groningen: Dialectiek, 2000). Schaaf argued for a Buddhist-inspired "middle path" between excessive social engagement and involvement (Dutch: *betrokkenheid*) leading to burnout or disillusionment on the one hand and excessive detachment on the other. A "reasonable distance" is needed to allow long-term, genuine social engagement, and Buddhism offers the tools toward that end.

56 The term "utopian socialism" does not refer to non-Marxist socialism here but to any kind of socialism that is centered on a picture of an ideal society.

Buddhism and, to a lesser extent, on the philosophy of W.V.O. Quine and Donald Davidson. Building on these metaphysical and epistemological foundations but also appealing to the thought of important moral thinkers from the Buddhist traditions such as Asaṅga and Śāntideva, part III defends a moral theory that could be called "negative expectivism," and discusses this theory's implications. Of particular concern in part III is an assessment of the anti-capitalism shared by most radical Buddhists. More detailed chapter overviews of parts II and III can be found at the end of the introductions to those two parts.

What This Book Is Not About

A corollary of the sociopolitical dimension of secularity is a focus on society rather than the individual. And a corollary of the secularity-as-naturalism dimension is indifference to traditional, supernatural-oriented ritual. This has important implications for a radicalized radical Buddhism, the hypothetical position located at the "★" in figure 1.1.

Western Buddhists and many other Buddhist modernists appear to identify Buddhism primarily with meditation, and the aim of traditional monastic Buddhism is personal liberation (i.e., awakening, enlightenment, nirvāṇa). But these practices and aims are focused almost exclusively on the individual[57] and are consequently outside the scope of radical Buddhism. Many Asian Buddhists are more likely to identify Buddhism with rituals or with stories that help make sense of the world and give meaning to their lives, but these too are outside the scope of radical Buddhism.

Because of its social and naturalistic orientation, radical Buddhism is not really concerned with mindfulness meditation, personal liberation, ritual, and other individual or traditional aspects of Buddhism. It is relatively indifferent to the aspects of Buddhism that seem to be most paradigmatically "Buddhist" to most Buddhists. This does not mean that it is incompatible with those, or that it rejects them. On the contrary, most radical Buddhists also emphasized the importance of these aspects of Buddhism at times. What it does mean is that they are not part of *radical* Buddhism. And this has two important implications. Firstly, it could be argued that radical Buddhism as a variety of Buddhism is incomplete and needs to be supplemented with "non-radical" practices and other elements.[58] Secondly, because this book is about radical Buddhism, most of these "non-radical" practices and elements are outside the scope of this book. Hence, mindfulness meditation, personal liberation, and ritual will receive very little attention here.[59]

---

[57] This is not entirely true in the case of Mahāyāna Buddhism. Therein, the primary purpose of personal liberation is to acquire the capability to help others achieve liberation as well. See next chapter.

[58] The question whether and to what extent it is possible to combine radical Buddhism with certain elements of traditional Buddhism to remedy this incompleteness is addressed in the section "Posits and Phenomenal Reality" in chapter 9.

[59] Some other kinds of meditation are discussed briefly in the section "Suffering, Shock, and Intoxication" in chapter 13.

2

Protectors, Monks, and Jeweled Trees

Many different Buddhas are worshiped in different schools and sects of Buddhism. There are eternal Buddhas, Buddhas of the past, and Buddhas of the future. The Buddha that is revered most in modernist, secular, and radical Buddhism was born on November 10, 1844 in Paris, France. On that day Eugène Burnouf published his *Introduction à l'histoire du buddhisme indien*,[1] in which he depicted the historical Buddha as an undogmatic, rational, and very human thinker. His Buddha was not the supernatural Buddha worshiped in parts of South and East Asia, but Burnouf never visited that part of the world and did not meet many Buddhists either. Rather, he believed that Buddhism and the Buddha were to be found in ancient texts exclusively. It was Burnouf's demythologized Buddha, rather than the Buddhas worshiped by countless Buddhists in Asia, that would come to dominate academic research and the popular imagination in the West. And within a few decades it would be exported back to Asia.[2]

Burnouf's approach to the study of Buddhism was as influential as his image of the Buddha: real Buddhism could only be understood by scrutinizing ancient texts, and actual Buddhist practice was nothing but a corruption, which had the convenient implication that Western scholars of Buddhism never had to suffer the inconvenience of traveling to more "primitive" parts of the world. Instead, from their comfortable armchairs, they would tell the distant natives what their religion really is about. The history of the Western reception of Buddhism is Orientalism at its "finest."[3]

More recently, the accusation of Orientalism has been leveled against scholars researching the history of *engaged* Buddhism. Two camps have emerged in that field, one arguing that sociopolitical engagement is the result of relatively recent Western (modernist) influence, the other pointing at ancient precedents.[4] What must be noted, however, is that this controversy concerns the origins of Buddhist engage-

---

[1] Eugène Burnouf, *Introduction à l'histoire du buddhisme indien*, Vol. 1 (Paris: Imprimerie Royale, 1844).
[2] On this aspect of the history of modern Buddhism, see, for example, Donald Lopez, Jr., *Buddhism and Science: A Guide for the Perplexed* (Chicago: University of Chicago Press, 2008), chapters 1 and 4.
[3] Orientalism is a view of Asia or the East as more or less irrational, childish, erotic, feminine, weak, conservative or backward, and so forth, and simultaneously of the West as the Enlightened opposite of all that. See Edward Said, *Orientalism* (New York: Pantheon, 1978), and Richard King, *Orientalism and Religion: Postcolonial Theory, India, and "The Mythic East"* (London: Routledge, 1999).
[4] The most important paper on Orientalism in this context is Thomas Freeman Yarnall, "Engaged Buddhism: New and Improved? Made in the USA of Asian Materials," in *Action Dharma: New Studies in Engaged Buddhism*, eds. Christopher Queen, Charles Prebish, and Damien Keown (London: RoutledgeCurzon, 2003), 286–344.

ment and not the origins of the demythologized Buddha. As far as I know, there is widespread agreement that the latter was born in Europe in the nineteenth century.

Nevertheless, the controversy about the origins of Buddhist engagement does raise a problem for any attempt to give some kind of historical overview. Should I start in the nineteenth century with the arrival of Henry Steel Olcott in Ceylon (Sri Lanka)? Or should I start with king Aśoka in the third century BCE, for example? Fortunately, I can bypass this conundrum as my aim in this and the next chapter is not to sketch the history of engaged Buddhism, but to present some key ideas of a number of important radical, engaged, and modernist Buddhists and to provide some historical context to those ideas, most importantly, the focus on this-worldly suffering. Given the latter aim and the fact that not all readers of this book will be equally familiar with basic Buddhist doctrine, I should start early, but that only raises another problem: we do not know much about early Buddhism and some of what we do seem to know conflicts with traditional accounts, and consequently, the history of early Buddhism is controversial as well. Here I have no easy way to avoid controversy as the commitment to naturalism in this book requires me to avoid supernatural explanations, to limit myself to evidence-based accounts and, thus, to take a side. But given that the goal and topic of this book are probably rather controversial, it would be foolish to insist on avoiding controversy anyway.

Early Buddhism

Buddhism, as well as Jainism and Ājīvikism, arose in a part of north-east India that Johannes Bronkhorst has called "Greater Maghada."[5] Greater Maghada consisted of a number of states, mostly kingdoms, of which Maghada was the most important. The culture of this area was significantly different from the Vedic culture to its south and west, but later the two would mix into Brahmanic culture. Based on historical and archaeological research, there are a few things that we know about Greater-Maghadan culture: they worshiped *stūpas*, and they believed in karma and rebirth or reincarnation. The former would not be adopted in Brahmanic culture, but the latter would. Evidence suggests a few other differences between Greater-Maghadan and Vedic culture, but about these we can be less certain. Bryan Levman, among others, suggests that the people of the region may have worshiped snakes and trees, for example.[6] And Greater-Maghadan medicine appeared to have been more empirical and rational, while according to Kenneth Zysk, "Vedic medicine may be characterized as a magico-religious system."[7]

Zysk and Bronkhorst agree that the Greater-Maghadan physicians were a subset of the *śramaṇas* or wandering mendicants that founded or followed the aforementioned new religions (or related religions that we do not know about). We do not know much about the historical Buddha — there is a lot of myth, but very little

---

5 Johannes Bronkhorst, *Greater Maghada: Studies in the Culture of Early India* (Leiden: Brill, 2007). My account of Greater-Maghadan culture in this section is largely, but not exclusively, based on this book. Jainism is still practiced in India. Ājīvikism has died out.
6 Bryan Levman, "Cultural Remnants of the Indigenous Peoples in the Buddhist Scriptures," *Buddhist Studies Review* 30, no. 2 (2013): 145–80.
7 Kenneth Zysk, *Religious Medicine: The History and Evolution of Indian Medicine* (1985; rpt. London: Routledge, 2017), 7.

evidence, and some scholars even doubt his existence[8] — but he almost certainly was a śramaṇa who lived in Greater Maghada some time between the sixth and fourth centuries BCE. What exactly he taught is almost as hard to unravel, but what we do know strongly suggests that he taught a kind of meditation.[9] We do know a lot more about how his followers understood his teachings, and most of the basic elements are present in the *Dhammacakkappavattana Sutta*,[10] which is traditionally regarded to be the Buddha's first sermon after reaching awakening or enlightenment.[11]

Before his awakening, the Buddha had tried and given up asceticism, which may have been Jainism or Ājīvikism, the main ascetic movements of his time. The sūtra opens with the claim that the path toward knowledge, peace, awakening, and nirvāṇa is a middle way between asceticism and hedonism (i.e., the pursuit of sensual pleasure). This middle way is then defined as the Noble Eightfold Path of right view, right intention, right speech, right action, right livelihood, right effort, right mindfulness, and right concentration (the last two of which refer to meditation). Following this, there are four claims that together have become known as the Four Noble Truths. (1) The noble truth of suffering: "birth is suffering, aging is suffering, illness is suffering; union with what is displeasing is suffering; separation from what is pleasing is suffering; not to get what one wants is suffering."[12] (2) The noble truth of the origin of suffering, namely "craving for sensual pleasures, craving for existence, craving for extermination."[13] (3) The noble truth of the cessation of suffering, which is achieved by the fading away of craving. (4) The noble truth of the path towards the cessation of suffering, which is the aforementioned Noble Eightfold Path. The Four Noble Truths would become one of the most central doctrines of Buddhism, and indeed, engaged and radical Buddhisms are often motivated by versions or adaptations thereof to worldly suffering.

The word "suffering" in this summary of the Four Noble Truths translates Pāli *dukkha* (Sanskrit *duḥka*), which is notoriously difficult to translate into English. *Dukkha* refers to anything that is uncomfortable, unpleasant, painful, or causing sadness, sorrow, or distress. (The opposite of dukkha is *sukha*, which means something like happiness or comfort, suggesting "unhappiness" or "discomfort" as possible translations of *dukkha*.) The explanation of the first Noble Truth seems to cover the whole breadth of the notion of dukkha ranging from physical pain to displeasure and from mental anguish to sorrow, but in the subsequent Noble Truths and in much of the Buddhist tradition, the notion appears to refer to a kind of spiritual distress mainly.[14]

Both Vedic and Greater-Maghadan religions were primarily concerned with *mokṣa* or liberation from suffering (duḥka/dukkha), but they differed in their identification of causes and remedies. In Vedic and later Brahmanic religions, knowledge lead to liberation, but Buddhism, Jainism, and Ājīvikism suggested different paths related to the Greater-Maghadan belief in karma and rebirth. They shared the idea that life inherently involves suffering and thus that rebirth was a cause of suffering.

---

8   David Drewes, "The Idea of the Historical Buddha," *Journal of the International Association of Buddhist Studies* 40 (2017): 1–25. See the section "The Idea of an 'Original Buddhism'" in chapter 5.
9   On what the Buddha may or may not have taught, see chapter 5.
10 SN 56.11.
11 The Sanskrit/Pāli term that is often translated as "enlightenment" is *bodhi*, which derives from the root *budd* meaning both "to wake up" and "to understand."
12 SN 56.11, 1844.
13 Ibid.
14 The Four Noble Truths and the concept of *dukkha* will be discussed in detail in chapter 5.

The standard view of karma, adopted by both Jainism and Ājīvikism, was that action causes rebirth, and consequently that mokṣa requires non-action, that is, asceticism and, ideally, starving yourself to death. Buddhism, however, rejected the traditional view of karma and claimed that intentions or volitions (*cetanā*) rather than actions cause rebirth (and moreover, that good intentions lead to a good rebirth and bad intentions to a bad rebirth).[15] Intentions are rooted in desires (i.e., craving), and consequently, without desire there are no intentions and no rebirth.[16] This is what is expressed in the second Noble Truth: craving (i.e., desire) is the cause of suffering. And importantly, the explanation mentions craving for life and extermination (*vibhava*, literally "non-existence," here probably referring to mokṣa), stressing the focus on the existential anguish related to rebirth and re-death.

Elsewhere, the cause of suffering is elaborated by means of the doctrine of the Twelvefold Chain of Dependent Origination. This doctrine is based on the idea that everything has a cause and declares that there is a chain of twelve kinds of causes ending in suffering and originating in ignorance.[17] Ignorance of what exactly differs a bit from source to source and theory to theory, but the *Dhammapada* suggests that it is ignorance of the Three Marks of Existence: impermanence, suffering, and no-self. This is rather cryptic, but what it appears to mean is the following: (1) All conditioned things (i.e., all things that depend on causes) are impermanent; (2) All conditioned things are unsatisfactory (dukkha); (3) No conditioned things have essences (i.e., selves).[18]

Early Buddhism was primarily concerned with preserving the Dharma, that is, the teachings or doctrine of the Buddha. There was no written language yet in Greater Maghada at the time of the Buddha and for many centuries the doctrines were preserved by memorizing and reciting them. Parallel to memorization and recitation there was a process of scholastic systematization resulting in the *Abhidharma*. The scholastics had a preference for numbered lists, and consequently, there is reason to be suspicious about the authenticity of such lists as original teachings of the Buddha. There also may have been considerable Vedic and later Brahmanic influence in this period. For example, the identification of a liberating knowledge — dispelling ignorance as the ultimate cause of suffering according to the Twelvefold Chain of Dependent Origination — was probably an import from Vedic/Brahmanic religions, which, contrary to the Buddha, held that mokṣa, or liberation, depends on knowledge.[19]

Abhidharma scholasticism also involved a turn towards metaphysics, the branch of philosophy concerned with the nature of existence, which started with listing things that exist and culminated in the *dharma theory*. Important lists in this respect include the five *skandhas*, material and mental aggregates that play a role in the arising of craving or desire; the eighteen *dhatūs* or elements of existence; the four *paramatthas* or ultimate realities; and so fourth. The first of these lists was the most important and included *rūpa* (form or matter, i.e., the physical, non-mental aspect of an object), *vedanā* (sensation or pre-conceptual sensory experience of that object), *saṃjñā* (perception or cognition and conceptual classification of the object),

---

15 In *Chakkanipāta* (AN 63.5/III.415), the Buddha is recorded as saying, "[i]t is volition, bhikkhus, that I call kamma" (963).
16 There are other explanations of the relation between karma, rebirth, and intention.
17 *Nidānasaṃyutta*, SN 12.
18 *Dhammapada* §§277–79.
19 Johannes Bronkhorst, *Buddhist Teaching in India* (Boston: Wisdom Publications, 2009), 25–44 and 57.

saṃskāra (mental imprints and conditioned thoughts triggered by the object), and *vijñāna* (the conscious awareness of the object and its various parts and aspects).

The concept of *dharma* originally meant something like "teaching" or "doctrine," but also "law," "order," and a lot more, but it was also used by the scholastics to refer to something like mental contents or mental properties, and these dominated the aforementioned metaphysical lists. Of the five skandhas, for example, four refer to mental things. Consequently, these lists came to be conceived as lists of *dharmas*, and the word *dharma*, especially in the plural, became an ontological category. The scholastics further argued that composites do not exist and that only partless parts are real. The resulting *dharma* theory held that

> the list of dharmas is not only a list of all the building blocks of the world as it is known to us but also a list of everything that exists. The dharmas therefore became *elements of existence*, and from then on Buddhist doctrine included an exhaustive ontology, a complete enumeration of all that exists. From the point of view of the Abhidharma Buddhists then, only the dharmas really exist. The other objects that we know from everyday life do not really exist.[20]

Under the influence of this theory, Buddhism developed a tendency to look for ultimate truth beyond the phenomenal world — the world as we experience it around us — which in some schools of thought even lead to a denial of the existence of phenomenal reality altogether. This devaluation of the phenomenal was unique to Buddhism but may have developed in response to Brahmanism. As mentioned, according to Vedic/Brahmanic religions, liberation (mokṣa) depends on knowledge or insight, and under their influence, early Buddhists tried to identify a liberating knowledge within their tradition as well. No such knowledge is clearly identified in the sūtras, however, which could be taken to imply that it is a kind of knowledge that cannot be expressed in words. If this idea is combined with the emphasis on meditation as the path towards liberation, then an obvious conclusion would be that there must be some kind of ultimate reality hidden behind the world of ordinary experience, which is only accessible through meditation.[21]

Not all schools of Abhidharma recognized the latter part of this idea. According to the influential Sarvāstivāda school, liberating knowledge was knowledge of the dharmas and meditation played no major role in acquiring that knowledge. The resulting emphasis on gaining metaphysical knowledge as well as the increase of debate with representatives of competing systems of thoughts (including Greeks in north-west India, many of whom converted to Buddhism) reinforced the rational and philosophical elements in Buddhist thought.

Aśoka

Aśoka was the third emperor of the Mauryan empire, which originated in Greater Maghada, and ruled over most of India from approximately 268 BCE until his death in 232 BCE. His first major act as emperor was to wage a bloody war of conquest against Kaliṅga, which included one of the largest and deadliest battles in Indian his-

---

20 Ibid., 77. Italics in original. On Abidharma philosophy, see also Jan Westerhoff, *The Golden Age of Indian Buddhist Philosophy* (Oxford: Oxford University Press, 2018), chapter 1.
21 Bronkhorst, *Buddhist Teaching in India*, 80.

tory with more than 100,000 casualties according to Aśoka himself. At some point in his life Aśoka "converted" to Buddhism, and he is revered by many Buddhists as *the* exemplary ruler. He is mostly remembered for his edicts, a number of inscriptions he left on pillars and rocks throughout his empire. These edicts are chiefly religious, moral, or political in nature, and they document some of his works and concerns, such as the availability of medicine to the people, safe travel, and spreading Buddhism.[22]

Buddhist legends about Aśoka tend to sketch him as a much more benevolent and pious ruler than available evidence warrants, and tend to ignore or downplay the Kaliṅga massacre, and because of this he is sometimes mentioned as a predecessor of engaged Buddhism.[23] One may wonder, however, how Buddhist Aśoka really was. Romila Thapar rightly raises the question what his "conversion" to Buddhism really could have entailed and points out that religious tolerance and acceptance or even protection of *all* sects was a key pillar of his rule (but that he also wanted forest-dwelling *atavikas* exterminated for no apparent reason).[24] Major rock edict number 12 says that "promotion of the essentials (is possible) in many ways" and, thus, that "all sects should be both full of learning and pure in doctrine."[25] Christopher Beckwith argues that the content of Aśoka's edicts suggest that his Buddhism was "an early, pietistic, 'popular' form perhaps akin to pre-Mahayana" and that the aspects of Dharma, or doctrine, mentioned "might be called 'generic' piety and morality" and are common to most (Indian) religions.[26]

Mahāyāna

The sūtras are not very clear about what it means to be awakened or liberated — to be an *arhat* — but there was no similar ambiguity about the status of the Buddha, and probably because of that, some monks strove to become Buddhas instead of arhats. This is the origin of Mahāyāna, which originally was no separate sect or school. Mahāyāna monks were found in the same monasteries as their mainstream colleagues and did not originally have separate doctrines either. Probably, Mahāyāna monks meditated more — and it may be the case that the outrageously grandiose scenes in many Mahāyāna sūtras describe meditative experiences[27] — but several centuries would pass before Mahāyāna and the "mainstream" started to drift apart.[28]

---

22 Robert Thurman, "The Edicts of Asoka," in *The Path of Compassion: Writings on Socially Engaged Buddhism*, ed. Fred Eppsteiner (Berkeley: Parallax, 1985), 111–19.
23 Illustrated, for example, by the inclusion of a reprint of a text by Robert Thurman on Aśoka's edicts in a collection of writings on engaged Buddhism. See previous footnote.
24 Romila Thapar, "Ashoka — A Retrospective," *Economic & Political Weekly* 44, no. 45, November 7, 2009, 31–37. The term *atavikas* (probably) refers to the descendants of the people who inhabited India before the immigration of Dravidians and Indo-Aryans. Hence, it appears that Aśoka was a racist advocating genocide.
25 E. Hultzsch, *Inscriptions of Asoka*, new edn. (Oxford: Clarendon Press, 1925).
26 Christopher Beckwith, *Greek Buddha: Pyrrho's Encounter with Early Buddhism in Central Asia* (Princeton: Princeton University Press, 2015).
27 Paul Harrison, "Buddhānusmṛti in the Pratyutpanna-Buddha-Saṃmukhāvasthita-Samādhi-Sūtra," *Journal of Indian Philosophy* 6, no. 1 (1978): 35–57, at 54, and Bronkhorst, *Buddhist Teaching in India*, 118.
28 The term "mainstream Buddhism" here denotes what is sometimes called *Hīnayāna*. In the early history of Buddhism that was the mainstream, although later Mahāyāna became much bigger. Currently, there are about half a billion nominal Buddhists in the world. More than two-thirds of those belong to Mahāyāna sects. The only remaining "mainstream" sect is Theravāda.

Someone who is on the path to become a Buddha is called a *bodhisattva*. Hence, the Buddha himself was a bodhisattva before becoming a Buddha. Arhats and the Buddha were supposed to have all kinds of supernatural powers, and the same applies to advanced bodhisattvas, but these were to play a more important role in Mahāyāna than in mainstream Buddhism. A prominent theme in the *Perfection of Wisdom Sūtras* is the realization of the unreality of the phenomenal world. These sūtras present the world as we experience it as an illusion. Advanced bodhisattvas, who are themselves free from illusion, can manipulate that illusion, and thus, phenomenal reality. The most important characteristic of a bodhisattva, however, is his compassion or even altruism, which is beautifully expressed in Śāntideva's *Bodhicaryāvatāra*:

> Those who have developed the continuum of their mind in this way, to whom the suffering of others is as important as the things they themselves hold dear, plunge down in the Avīci hell as geese into a cluster of lotus blossoms.[29]

Legendary bodhisattvas typically vowed to save all sentient beings — to help them reach awakening — and in later Mahāyāna, this became a defining feature of the bodhisattva, as attested, for example, by Atiśa's eleventh century *Bodhipathapradīpa*, a synthesis of various schools and doctrines of Buddhist philosophy.[30] The combination of supernatural power and the intention to save all sentient beings was taken to its logical conclusion in the *Sukhāvatīvyūha Sūtras*, which tell the story of the bodhisattva Dharmakāra's vow to create a Pure land in which anyone who called upon him would be reborn and would be instructed by him in the Dharma until they become bodhisattvas and, ultimately, Buddhas themselves. Dharmakāra became the Amitābha Buddha, and as such he is worshiped in Pure Land Buddhism, which is widely practiced in East Asia.

Dharmakāra/Amitābha's Pure land is not the only Buddha land (or Buddha field, *Buddhakṣetra*; the term "Pure land" 淨土 is East-Asian), however. Other Buddhas have their own Buddha lands. Mañjuśrī, for example, supposedly has one of the greatest Pure lands, located somewhere in the east,[31] while Amitābha's Pure land lays to the west. In East-Asian Buddhism, Pure lands or Buddha lands are conceived as paradise-like places, "lands of bliss," where one goes after death, but the notion was also sometimes understood in a more this-worldly, utopian sense, especially in twentieth-century radical and engaged Buddhism. Several radical Buddhists, but also some more cautious reformers, argued for the realization of a Buddha land, or Pure land, in this world.[32]

A bodhisattva's compassion does not only concern the final liberation of all sentient beings, but also the alleviation of their suffering in this world, that is, suffering caused by hunger, poverty, fear, sickness, oppression, and so forth. For example, the *Avataṃsaka Sūtra* states that a bodhisattva aims, among other aims, to "cultivate total giving to put an end to poverty for all sentient beings, practice transcendent giving for endless eons and satisfy all sentient beings with gifts of food and drink,

---

29 Śāntideva, *The Bodhicaryāvatāra* (8th c.), trans. Kate Crosby and Andrew Skilton (Oxford: Oxford University Press, 1995), §8:107.
30 Paul Williams, *Mahāyāna Buddhism: The Doctrinal Foundations*, 2nd edn. (London: Routledge, 2009), 194–95. The section starting on 194 gives a good overview of the bodhisattva ideal, and how it was understood and developed in Tibet.
31 According to the *Avataṃsaka Sūtra*, also known in English as the *Flower Garland Sūtra*.
32 And this is, of course, what gave this book its title.

and satisfy all beggars by giving away all goods" and to protect "beings by providing what they require."[33] According to Stephen Jenkins, statements of a similar nature can be found in very many sūtras (and he lists several), and therefore, the widely shared belief that Mahāyāna sūtras are only concerned with spiritual suffering and "not with identifying material sources of suffering simply will not hold." Rather, "the ideal practitioner should materially support others."[34]

Importantly, this requirement does not just apply to advanced bodhisattvas. According to the *Lotus Sūtra* we are all destined to become Buddhas and are thus, in a sense, bodhisattvas already. It is perhaps for this reason that the Buddha says that "The Buddha-tathagatas only teach and transform bodhisattvas. Their one purpose is to demonstrate the Buddhas' insight to all beings and have them apprehend it."[35] This passage makes sense only if "only bodhisattvas" in the first sentence and "all beings" in the second co-refer.[36] But even in Mahāyāna currents in which the *Lotus Sūtra* plays no major role, the idea of the bodhisattva is not some kind of abstract ideal one might hope to realize after many rebirths, but an exemplar of moral action right now and right here. It is for this reason that it is common for Mahāyānins to take a bodhisattva vow. The form and content thereof differs between schools and regions, although there are many shared elements. The vows typically taken in East Asia were first formulated in the sixth century by Zhiyi 智顗 in his *Exposition on the Dharma Gateway to the Perfection of Meditation* 釋禪波羅蜜次第法門:

> These are the four Bodhisattva vows. […] Even though sentient beings are unlimited [in number], I vow to liberate [or] save [them all]. […] Even though the *kleśas*[37] are innumerable, I vow to stop [them all]. […] Even though the Buddhist teachings are inexhaustible, I vow to know [them all]. […] Even though Buddhahood is unsurpassable, I vow to attain [it].[38]

It should be fairly obvious that realizing these vows would require much more than what is humanly possible, but making a vow does not commit one to succeeding, merely to trying, and it's the intention (i.e., the trying) that matters. In the *Bodhicaryāvatāra*, Śāntideva wrote:

> If the perfection of generosity consists in making the universe free from poverty how can previous Protectors [i.e., Buddhas and Bodhisattvas] have acquired it, when the world is still poor, even today? The perfection of generosity is said to result from the mental attitude to relinquishing all that one has to all people, to-

---

33 Thomas Cleary, *The Flower Ornament Scripture: A Translation of the Avatamsaka Sutra* (Boston: Shambala, 1984), 1414–15, and 805.
34 Stephen Jenkins, "Do Bodhisattvas Relieve Poverty?" in *Action Dharma: New Studies in Engaged Buddhism*, eds. Christopher Queen, Charles Prebish, and Damien Keown (London: RoutledgeCurzon, 2003), 38–49, at 44.
35 Translation from Gene Reeves, *The Lotus Sutra* (Boston: Wisdom, 2008), 83.
36 On this interpretation of chapter 2 of the *Lotus Sūtra*, see also Brook Ziporyn, *Emptiness and Omnipresence: An Essential Introduction to Tiantai Buddhism* (Bloomington: Indiana University Press, 2016), 71.
37 *Kleśas* are afflictions or negative emotions such as ignorance, attachment (or craving, desire, and so forth), and aversion, or hatred.
38 四弘誓願者。… 亦云眾生無邊誓願度。… 亦云煩惱無數誓願斷。… 亦云法門無盡誓願知。… 亦云無上佛道誓願成。— Zhiyi 智顗,《釋禪波羅蜜次第法門》(6th c.), T46n1916, 476b.

gether with the fruit of that act. Therefore, the perfection is the mental attitude itself.[39]

If one has a *genuine* intention to save everyone, then one will try to get closer to that goal, even if it is just a little bit. And if one has a *genuine* intention to learn everything that matters (here limited to Buddhist teachings, but we'll encounter different views later in this book), then there is a fairly good chance that there will be at least some success. But still, what ultimately matters is not just the success, but the genuine commitment to save all sentient beings.[40]

Nevertheless, considerable effort has been made by Buddhists in China and Japan to put the bodhisattva's commitment to alleviating suffering into practice.[41] "Buddhist activities included road and bridge building, public work projects, social revolution, military defense, orphanages, travel hostels, medical education, hospital building, free medical care, the stockpiling of medicines, conflict intervention, moderation of penal codes, programs to assist the elderly and poor [...], famine and epidemic relief, and bathing houses."[42]

From Nāgārjuna to Zhiyi

It was mentioned at the start of the previous section that Mahāyāna only started to deviate from the mainstream after a few centuries. The schism resulted from a growing body of Mahāyāna sūtras and their study, leading to new insights and new ideas, although they had to be defended as old ideas to avoid accusations of heresy. The philosopher monk who is more than anyone else responsible for the birth of Mahāyāna philosophy is Nāgārjuna (second century). In fact, aside from the Buddha himself, there probably is no known Buddhist thinker who is more influential than Nāgārjuna.

In his most important work, the *Mūlamadhyamakakārikā* (*Fundamental Verses on the Middle Way*), Nāgārjuna tried to prove the "emptiness" of the phenomenal world. Phenomena, things as we experience them, are dependent on words — they are conceptual constructions. But together with some further assumptions, this insight leads to all kinds of contradictions, which implies that those phenomena are "empty." "Empty" (*śūnya*) here means lacking an essence or intrinsic nature (*svabhāva*). That phenomenal or conventional reality is empty does not imply that it does not exist, however, because that would in turn imply that suffering and the cessation of suffering — that is, the Four Noble Truths — are also unreal.[43] Rather, everything is empty. The key passage is the following:

> Whatever is dependently co-arisen | That is explained to be emptiness. | That, being a dependent designation, | Is itself the middle way. | Something that is not

---

39 Śāntideva, *Bodhicaryāvatāra*, 5:9–10.
40 See also the section "Consequences and Consequentialism in Mahāyāna" in chapter 12.
41 Unfortunately, we do not know to what extent this was the case in India, aside from the aforementioned case of Aśoka. However, according to Chinese sources, the standard curriculum at Nālandā, the biggest monastic university in the history of Buddhism that functioned from the fifth to twelfth century, included medicine, which suggests at least some concern with health care.
42 Jenkins, "Do Bodhisattvas Relieve Poverty?" 39.
43 Nāgārjuna, *Mūlamadhyamakakārikā* (2nd–3rd c.), 24:1–6.

dependently arisen, | Such a thing does not exist. | Therefore a nonempty thing | Does not exist.[44]

This passage, often referred to as "the emptiness of emptiness," requires some unpacking. Whatever is dependently co-arisen is phenomenal or conventional (or conventionally real). Hence, the first sentence merely states that conventional or phenomenal reality is empty (i.e., phenomena do not have essences). However, "emptiness" is itself a "dependent designation," meaning a mere conceptual construct, and is thus itself empty. Or in other words, emptiness is not some kind of ultimately real substance, but is itself also only conventionally real. Furthermore, there is no thing that does not depend on causes and there is no thing that is not empty. Thus, everything is empty, and as emptiness marks conventional or phenomenal reality, even ultimate reality is ultimately only conventionally real.

In addition to the *Mūlamadhyamakakārikā*, Nāgārjuna also wrote several other texts, and many more are attributed to him. Among those, the most interesting here is the *Ratnāvalī* (*Precious Garland*), which was addressed to a king. The relevant portions of the text appear to be another version of the Buddhist trope of the compassionate king: Nāgārjuna advises the king, "through compassion you should always generate an attitude of help."[45] However, the chapter on royal policy also makes several specific policy recommendations, such as to "create centers of doctrine" and sustain already existing centers of doctrine, to appoint suitable and capable people to official positions, to avoid harsh punishments,[46] to

[c]ause the blind, the sick, the lowly, | The protectorless, the wretched | And the crippled equally to attain | Food and drink without interruption. | [And to] Provide all types of support | For practitioners who do not seek it | And even for those living | In the realms of other kings.[47]

The archetype of the Buddhist trope of the compassionate king who takes the wellbeing of his citizens to heart — with Aśoka as the most famous supposed historical example — is probably the doctrine of the "Ten Duties of the King" found in the Jātaka tales, a collection of stories about the previous lives of the Buddha. The king's ten duties are (1) generosity/charity; (2) moral character; (3) altruism ("sacrificing everything for the good of the people"); (4) honesty and integrity; (5) kindness; (6) austerity; (7) freedom from hatred; (8) non-violence; (9) patience and forbearance; and (10) non-opposition to the will of the people.[48] Nāgārjuna's recommendations are considerably more concrete than this list of royal virtues, however. Robert Thurman suggests that what Nāgārjuna is describing is "the welfare state, astoundingly millennia ahead of its time, a rule of compassionate socialism based on a psychology

---

44 Ibid., 24:18–19, trans. Jay Garfield, *The Fundamental Wisdom of the Middle Way: Nāgārjuna's Mūlamadhyamakakārikā* (Oxford: Oxford University Press, 1995), 69.
45 Nāgārjuna and Kaysang Gyatso, the 7th Dalai Lama, *The Precious Garland and The Song of the Four Mindfulnesses,* trans. Jeffrey Hopkins and Lati Rimpoche with Anne Klein (New York: Harper & Row, 1975), §311.
46 Ibid., §310, §318, §§322–25, and §§332–37, respectively.
47 Ibid., §§320–21.
48 Walpola Rahula, "The Social Teachings of the Buddha," in *The Path of Compassion: Writings on Socially Engaged Buddhism,* ed. Fred Eppsteiner (Berkeley: Parallax, 1985), 103–10.

of abundance achieved by generosity,"⁴⁹ but that ignores the fact that this supposed "welfare state" depends entirely on the good will of the king, a benevolent dictator, and history teachers that dictators never remain benevolent for long.

Nāgārjuna laid the foundations of the Mādhyamaka school of Indian Mahāyāna. Its main competitor was Yogācāra, which developed a few centuries later, and which initially bridged the Mahāyāna-mainstream schism. There are several early Yogācāra texts that belong to the mainstream, for example, and the Dārṣṭāntika and Sautrāntika schools that both belonged to the mainstream appear to have been very closely affiliated with early Yogācāra.⁵⁰

One of the central doctrines of Yogācāra is that any awareness of something is awareness of an object that exists in the mind itself rather than outside of it. Hence, we are never aware of objects outside the mind. Because of this doctrine Yogācāra philosophy is often called "idealism," but that classification is somewhat deceptive as the term "idealism" is ambiguous. In philosophy the term "idealism" is used mainly in reference to two kinds of theories that are not always sufficiently clearly distinguished. The first kind, most famously represented by Berkeley,⁵¹ claims that there is no external world and that *everything* is in the mind. According to the second kind, the properties of things *as we experience them* are created by the mind. Hence, the second kind of idealism does not necessarily reject external reality, but merely claims that it is, more or less, unknowable. Kant, who explicitly affirmed the existence of a largely (but not completely!) unknowable, external, noumenal world, is the most influential idealist in this second sense. What makes the term "idealism" even more prone to causing confusing is that it is often opposed to "realism," which is at least as ambiguous. Strictly speaking, realism — in the here relevant sense — merely claims that there is an external, mind-independent reality, and by implication, Kant and many other idealists, in the second sense of "idealism," were realists.⁵²

If Yogācāra is idealist, then it is idealist in the second sense. It holds that what we are aware of exists in the mind only, but this does not imply that there is no mind-external world, and consequently, Yogācāra "idealism" does not necessarily conflict with realism.⁵³ Indeed, it has been interpreted as a form of realism by several monks and philosophers later.⁵⁴

Yogācāra gave birth to the "logico-epistemological" school of Dignāga (sixth century) and Dharmakīrti (sixth or seventh century), who wrote extensively about logic, rhetoric, philosophy of perception, and epistemology (the branch of philosophy concerned with the nature and sources of knowledge), and who should be credited

---

49 Robert Thurman, "Nagarjuna's Guidelines for Buddhist Social Activism," in *The Path of Compassion*, ed. Eppsteiner, 120–44, at 128.
50 Robert Kritzer, *Rebirth and Causation in the Yogācāra Abhidharma* (Vienna: Arbeitskreis für Tibetische und Buddhistische Studien, 1999), 297–81. See also Bronkhorst, *Buddhist Teaching in India*, 157–58.
51 At least, this is more or less the standard interpretation of Berkeley, but as is usually the case in philosophy, there are other interpretations.
52 About the notions and varieties of realism and idealism, see chapter 7.
53 Bronkhorst, *Buddhist Teaching in India*, 161; Sallie King, *Buddha Nature* (New York: SUNY Press, 1991); Ian Charles Harris, *The Continuity of Madhyamaka and Yogācāra in Indian Mahāyāna Buddhism* (Leiden: Brill, 1991); and Dan Lusthaus, *Buddhist Phenomenology: A Philosophical Investigation of Yogācāra Buddhism and the Ch'eng Wei-shih lun* (London: RoutledgeCurzon, 2002). Lusthaus denies that Yogācāra is idealist in the second, epistemological sense as well because it assumes the possibility of gaining some kind of nonconceptual knowledge of ultimate reality. We'll return to the question whether Yogācāra is idealist or realist in chapter 8.
54 See, for example, Zhiyi, and much of Chinese Buddhism in general, in this chapter; and Inoue Enryō and Inoue Tetsujirō in the section "Realism and Reform in Japan — Inoue Enryō" in chapter 3.

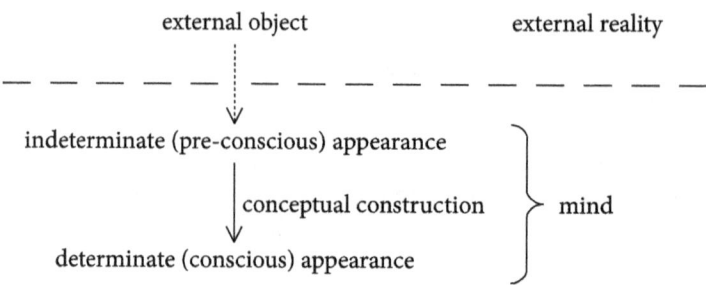

Fig. 2.1. A metaphysical picture.

for strengthening the rational element in Buddhist philosophy. Much of their writings are from a Sautrāntika perspective rather than a Yogācāra perspective, which may seem odd considering that Sautrāntika belonged to mainstream Buddhism (although possibly no longer mainstream in a literal sense at that time) and Yogācāra to Mahāyāna, and even more peculiar if Yogācāra is assumed to be idealist while Sautrāntika is realist.[55] It is less strange if Sautrāntika is something like a mainstream version of Yogācāra, however, and even less strange if it is taken into account that Yogācāra does not *necessarily* deny the existence of an external world. And importantly, Dignāga, who founded the logico-epistemological school, did not deny external reality.[56]

The picture that emerges from Yogācāra, Sautrāntika, and their combination in Dignāga and Dharmakīrti's writings — a picture that would be immensely influential on the further development of Buddhist thought in China and Tibet — is something like the diagram in figure 2.1.[57] There is some variation in the terms used for various parts of this diagram, but *pratibhāsa* and *pratibhasa-pratīti* appear to be the most common terms to refer to the indeterminate (preconscious) and determinate (conscious) appearance, respectively, and the external object is usually referred to as *artha* or *svārtha*. Nevertheless, other terms occur and there are other ambiguities in addition to the lack of terminological consistency. Does the external object and external reality exist or not? If the external object exists, how is it related to the indeterminate, preconscious appearance in the mind? If the external object exists, how does one talk about it, given that it is inherently beyond or before language? Perhaps, the greatest source of ambiguity, however, concerns the question how this apparent threefold division maps to the twofold division of conventional or phenomenal and ultimate reality. It makes most sense to me to identify determinate appearance with conventional or phenomenal reality and external reality with ultimate reality, but that is certainly not the only option.[58]

---

55 On the realism of Sautrāntika see, for example, Jadunath Sinha, *Indian Realism* (Delhi: Motilal Banarsidass, 1999).
56 Shōryū Katsura, "Dignāga and Dharmakīrti on 'Apoha'," in *Studies in the Buddhist Epistemological Tradition*, ed. Ernst Steinkellner (Vienna: ÖAW, 1991), 129–46, at 138.
57 According to Dan Lusthaus, Yogācāra rejected metaphysical theorizing, which would probably imply that the school would reject this picture as well. That they might not accept this picture as a picture of their thought does not necessarily mean it is an inaccurate picture, however. Lusthaus, *Buddhist Phenomenology*.
58 Questions like those asked in this paragraph and related issues of interpretation of Yogācāra philosophy are addressed in chapter 8.

One effect of all this ambiguity is that it sometimes seems that the interpretation of a later Buddhist philosopher is determined more by the philosophical background of the interpreter than by the position of the interpreted. A good example of this is Zhiyi 智顗, who was already mentioned in the previous section as the author of the most common version of the bodhisattva vow. Western philosophy split up into two major schools in the twentieth century: analytic philosophy, which rejects idealism and in which realism about the external world is the default; and continental philosophy, which tends to be anti-realist but refrains from calling itself idealist.[59] JeeLoo Liu is an analytic philosopher who also writes about Chinese philosophy, and who interprets Zhiyi as a realist.[60] Brook Ziporyn writes mostly about Tiantai 天台 Buddhism (the school founded by Zhiyi) and Daoism, but has a background in continental philosophy and interprets Zhiyi as an anti-realist.[61]

I'm not sure whether there is a definite answer to the question what the correct interpretation of Zhiyi is, but any attempt to get a better understanding of his philosophy needs to place him in his broader philosophical context. A key feature of that context is the Chinese preference for *kataphatic* over *apophatic* discourse. In Christian theology this distinction concerns the question whether and to what extent we can describe or talk about God, but in the context of Buddhism it refers to the attitude we take towards ultimate reality.

As explained earlier in this chapter, Buddhism rejects essences, but an anti-essentialist can take two very different attitudes towards conventional or phenomenal reality and the conceptual constructions it is based on or consists of. She can take a more negative attitude and stress the fact that conceptual constructions do not match ultimately "real" things, and therefore, that conceptual constructions are effectively mistaken and that any apparent (i.e., phenomenal) reality based on or consisting of them is illusory. Or she can take a more positive attitude and stress that conceptual construction is at least partially caused or guided by external reality (and thus, that conceptual constructions are not *completely* arbitrary), and therefore, that they show a partial view or perspective, which implies that they are incomplete rather than mistaken. This is roughly what the difference between kataphatic and apophatic discourse about ultimate reality is about: the positive attitude is the kataphatic attitude; the negative attitude is the apophatic attitude.

Most of Indian Mahāyāna philosophy, and especially that of Nāgārjuna and the Mādhyamaka school, was apophatic. For Nāgārjuna, ultimate reality was empty, and emptiness was itself empty — beyond conceptual description — and thus apophatic. Later Indian thinkers often took a somewhat less negative (i.e., less apophatic) attitude, but Nāgārjuna's shadow was long. Dignāga and Dharmakīrti argued a few centuries later that conceptual categories are social conventions with roots in ultimate reality, but even this was couched in apophatic terms. Conceptual construction was supposed to take place through a process called *apoha* that avoids positive or

---

59 Continental "anti-realisms" tend to reject a collection of theses most of which are not really "realist" in a strict sense at all. See the section "Realism (2) — External Reality" in chapter 7.
60 JeeLoo Liu, *An Introduction to Chinese Philosophy: From Ancient Philosophy to Chinese Buddhism* (Malden: Blackwell, 2006).
61 Ziporyn's anti-realism and rejection of analytic philosophy, which he considers "reactionary" is, perhaps, most explicit in *Being and Ambiguity: Philosophical Experiments with Tiantai Buddhism* (Chicago: Open Court, 2004), 108. The most complete version of his interpretation of Zhiyi can be found in his *Emptiness and Omnipresence*.

affirmative (i.e., kataphatic) statements. That is, we learn a concept of "cow" not by classifying things as cows but as not non-cows.

Apophasis played no significant role in Chinese pre-Buddhist philosophy and may not have fit well in the ancient Chinese worldview, but in India apophasis was not universally accepted either. Rather, as Robert Gimello argues, philosophical challenges to Mādhyamika — and thus the further development of Mahāyāna philosophy — developed out of "profound dissatisfaction with the seemingly relentless apophasis of Nāgārjuna." Especially in China, the challengers stressed "the spiritual utility of positive and affirmative language" — "they chose [...] eloquence over silence."[62] The kataphatic attitude and the idea that ultimate reality is inherently beyond or before language pull in different directions, however, leading to a kind of tension, and sometimes obscurity, in East-Asian Buddhist writings. Some of Zhiyi's writings exemplify this tension. Paul Swanson writes that

> affirmation of the use of language tempered by the awareness of its limitations is exactly the position taken by [Zhiyi], who is constantly re-affirming the inadequacy of language to describe reality, yet immediately affirms the necessity to use language in the attempt to describe the indescribable and conceptualize that which is beyond conceptualization.[63]

The latter point is important to keep in mind when reading Buddhist writings from China and Japan: language is necessary but inadequate to describe ultimate reality, and consequently, Buddhist monks and philosophers often had to resort to dense metaphors. A reader who fails to look beyond those metaphors would completely miss the point.

While Nāgārjuna's theory of the emptiness of emptiness entails that even ultimate reality is only conventionally real, kataphatic Chinese Buddhist philosophy turned this on its head: from Nāgārjuna's conventionality of the ultimately real, it developed into the ultimate reality of the conventional, that is, a kataphatic affirmation of conventional reality.[64] In Fung Yulan's *Short History of Chinese Philosophy*, the result of this transformation is summarized as follows:

> The reality of the Buddha-nature [ultimate reality] is itself the phenomenal world, [...]. There is no other reality outside the phenomenal world, [...]. Some people in their Ignorance, see only the phenomenal world, but not the reality of the Buddha-nature. Other people, in their Enlightenment, see the Buddha-nature, but this Buddha-nature is still the phenomenal world. What these two kinds of people see is the same, but what one person sees in his Enlightenment has a significance quite different from what the other person sees in his Ignorance.[65]

---

62 Robert Gimello, "Apophatic and Kataphatic Discourse in Mahāyāna: A Chinese View," *Philosophy East and West* 26, no. 2 (1976): 117–36, at 119.
63 Paul Swanson, *Foundations of T'ien-T'ai Philosophy: The Flowering of the Two Truths Theory in Chinese Buddhism* (Berkeley: Asian Humanities Press, 1989), 23.
64 Lajos Brons, "Meaning and Reality: A Cross-Traditional Encounter," in *Constructive Engagement of Analytic and Continental Approaches in Philosophy*, eds. Bo Mou and R. Tieszen (Leiden: Brill, 2013), 199–220.
65 Fung Yu-Lan, *A Short History of Chinese Philosophy*, ed. and trans. Derk Bodde (New York: MacMillan, 1948), 252–53.

This kataphatic, world-affirming attitude is unavailable to anyone who denies the existence of external reality, and by implication, most of Chinese Buddhist philosophy cannot possibly have been anti-realist.[66] But there is at least one other reason to doubt the accuracy of an anti-realist interpretation of Zhiyi: the *Lotus Sūtra*.

Chinese Buddhism imported Buddhist philosophy from India as a whole, without much awareness of its historical development and sectarian divisions. This lead to a problem because there are obvious contradictions between the doctrinal positions of different schools, and even between and within the sūtras themselves. Fortunately, Mahāyāna had a tool to deal with this problem: the doctrine of skillful means (*upāya-kauśalya*). According to this doctrine, the Buddha taught different things to different people, depending on their abilities and understanding. Consequently, there are provisional teachings that are not ultimately true but that were just the most efficient way for the Buddha-as-teacher to help people progress on the path towards awakening. If two or more of the Buddha's teachings are in conflict with each other, this conflict can always be resolved by appealing to skillful means. The problem, however, is figuring out which teachings are the provisional teachings and which teaching is the final truth. Different schools had rather different ideas about this, and Zhiyi placed the *Lotus Sūtra* at the pinnacle of his pyramid of teachings. Coincidentally, the most famous parables about skillful means can also be found in this sūtra.

The *Lotus Sūtra* (*Saddharma Puṇḍarīka Sūtra*) is a very strange text. It is supposed to be the Buddha's final teaching, but it appears to be mostly about itself and it is filled with exaggerated exotic imagery of flying jeweled stūpas, gigantic audiences, and supernatural feats. The *Lotus Sūtra* represents pretty much everything many Western "secular" Buddhists dislike about Buddhism as a living religion in East Asia, which is probably most neatly illustrated by an anecdote in Donald Lopez's book about the sūtra.[67] In his university course, "Introduction to Buddhism," he starts with a series of lectures on more or less philosophical topics addressed by Buddhism — the kind of topics Western Buddhist and Westerners with an interest in Buddhism are typically interested in, ranging from metaphysical questions to meditation and the Four Noble Truths. Much of the second half of the course is dedicated to the *Lotus Sūtra*, which tends to provoke disappointment and even outrage in students. The Lotus Sūtra is too fantastic, too supernatural, too inauthentic (its earliest parts date to the first century BCE), too religious and not enough philosophical, and so forth for secular Western preferences. He quotes a student as asking, "How can people accept the words of one monk who decided to write a text to completely change Buddhism?" To some extent, the outrage and rejection is understandable. It is indeed extremely unlikely that the *Lotus Sūtra* was taught by the Buddha, and the text is indeed overly self-referential and overly ornate, but it is not true that it represents a radical deviation from other, earlier teachings and there is more lurking below the ornate surface than a casual glance might suggest. Like many religious texts, the *Lotus Sūtra* requires patience and study.[68]

---

66 See also Klein, *Buddha Nature,* and Robert Sharf, *Coming to Terms with Chinese Buddhism: A Reading of the Treasure Store Treatise* (Honolulu: Kuroda Institute/University of Hawai'i Press, 2002).
67 Donald Lopez, Jr., *The Lotus Sūtra: A Biography* (Princeton: Princeton University Press, 2016).
68 For an excellent introduction to and explanation of the *Lotus Sūtra*, see Donald Lopez, Jr. and Jacqueline Stone, *Two Buddhas Seated Side by Side: A Guide to the Lotus Sūtra* (Princeton: Princeton University Press, 2019).

Aside from its many parables, the two most important teachings in the *Lotus Sūtra*, although opinions might differ about this, can be found in chapters 2 and 16. The former was already briefly discussed: we are all destined to become Buddhas and are thus in some sense bodhisattvas already. In chapter 16, the Buddha speaks in verse about this world, the world where he is preaching the *Lotus Sūtra*, Vulture Peak. He says that this world is in fact his Buddha land (*Buddhakṣetra*), that he is always residing here, in this world, and that his apparent death was merely another example of skillful means.

> [This world] is in fact my tranquil land [i.e., a Buddha land], | [...] | All the gardens and palaces | Are adorned with various gems. | The jeweled trees abound with flowers and fruits, | And the sentient beings are joyful among them. | [...] | Although my Pure Land never decays, | The sentient beings see it as ravaged by fire | And torn with anxiety and distress; | [...] | To the deluded and unenlightened I say that | I have entered nirvana, | Although, in fact, I am really here.[69]

But if this is a Buddha land, it cannot possibly be a mere phenomenal deception. Rather, this world, this Buddha land, is the only world there is. There is no separate, ultimate reality. The world described in the sūtra, with its flying stūpas, shaking earth, and various other supernatural fables, is reality seen through the eyes of awakened beings: ultimate reality. But that fantastic, ultimate reality is not a different world: it is the world we live in and are familiar with; it is merely seen with or through different eyes. As Gene Reeves has pointed out, the *Lotus Sūtra*, despite its fantastic imagery, is "radically world-affirming."[70] Conventional or phenomenal reality and ultimate reality are not different worlds. Rather, there is just one world, which can be perceived or thought about in different ways. Recall the quote by Fung Yu-lan a few pages back: what different "kinds of people see is the same, but what one person sees in his Enlightenment has a significance quite different from what the other person sees in his Ignorance." This is a central idea in much of Chinese Buddhism, and it is based directly on the *Lotus Sūtra*.

Anti-realism is the rejection of external reality and the claim that phenomenal reality is all there is, but that would imply that this world, this Buddha land, is merely phenomenal and not ultimately real. Zhiyi cannot possibly have believed that. Most likely he would have considered this idea heretical. And if that is right, then Zhiyi cannot have been an anti-realist. It is not difficult to find passages in his writings that confirm this, moreover. For example, in his *Profound Meaning of the Lotus Sūtra* 妙法蓮華經玄義, Zhiyi argued that the Lotus Sūtra teaches the non-duality of reality:

> The (ultimately) real is identical with the conventional, and the conventional is identical with the (ultimately) real. True nature is like a pearl: the pearl is analogous to the (ultimately) real and its function is analogous to the conventional [or conventionally real]. The pearl is identical with the function and the function is identical with the jewel; they are non-dual, but two; it is merely a [conceptual]

---

69 Tsugunari Kubo and Akira Yuyama, *The Lotus Sūtra, Translated from the Chinese of Kumārajiva* (Berkeley: Numata Center for Buddhist Translation and Research, 2007), 229–30.

70 Gene Reeves, "The Lotus Sutra as Radically World-Affirming," in *A Buddhist Kaleidoscope: Essays on the Lotus Sutra*, ed. Gene Reeves (Tokyo: Kosei, 2002), 177–99.

division between [what we call] the (ultimately) "real" and [what we call] the "conventional."[71]

Hence, for Zhiyi, and pretty much all of the thinkers, sects, and schools that were influenced by him, which includes most of East-Asian Buddhism, reality is non-dual. Ultimate reality and conventional reality are not two different realities, but two different perspectives on one and the same reality. This non-dualism is a widely shared doctrine in East Asian Buddhism but is often expressed in more soteriological terms. For example, the apocryphal Chinese *Treasure Store Treatise* 寶藏論 states that upon reaching enlightenment and learning to see ultimate reality "there is nothing to be realized, nothing to be attained, and yet if there is no realization or attainment, the mind will forever be confused."[72]

From Saichō to Nichiren

Zhiyi's Tiantai philosophy was brought to Japan by Saichō 最澄 in the beginning of the ninth century. There are, however, significant differences between Zhiyi's Tiantai and Saichō's Tendai (both written 天台, but pronounced differently in Chinese and Japanese). Saichō's influences and focus were simultaneously broader and more restricted than Zhiyi's. Saichō's teacher Gyōhyō 行表 had introduced him to the teachings of the competing Huayan 華嚴 and Chan 禅 (Japanese: Zen) schools, and he expressed a strong interest in esoteric Buddhism (*mikkyō* 密教) throughout his career. On the other hand, while Zhiyi studied and quoted other sūtras besides the *Lotus Sūtra*, Saichō unequivocally prioritized the *Lotus Sūtra*.[73]

Like Zhiyi, Saichō argued for the non-duality of the phenomenal and the ultimate, but curiously, he did so on the basis of his interpretation of the teachings of Fazang 法藏, the most prominent philosopher of the Huayan school. Paul Groner writes that "On the basis of [Huayan] doctrines, Saichō argued that the absolute was not separate and isolated from the phenomenal world. Rather, the phenomenal arose from the absolute. The absolute and phenomenal merged and interpenetrated."[74] Saichō's interpretation of Fazang was somewhat unorthodox, however, as Jacqueline Stone has pointed out, but the result was a "profound valorization of empirical reality,"[75] strengthening the kataphatic, this-worldly turn discussed in the previous section.

After Saichō, Tendai thought developed further and incorporated more elements of esoteric Buddhism such as the chanting of *mantras*. The school also got increasingly involved in politics and war in the eleventh and twelfth century, leading to growing dissatisfaction and a number of split offs and new sects in the end of the twelfth and beginning of the thirteenth centuries. All of the major current sects of Japanese buddhism were founded by disenchanted Tendai monks in this period. The

---

71 真即是俗；俗即是真。如如意珠，珠以譬真，用以譬俗。如如意珠，珠以譬真，用以譬俗。即珠是用，即用是珠，不二而二，分真俗耳。— Zhiyi 智顗,《妙法蓮華經玄義》(6th c.), T33n1716, 703b.
72 Translation from Sharf, *Coming to Terms with Chinese Buddhism*, 159.
73 Victor Forte, "Saichō: Founding Patriarch of Japanese Buddhism," in *The Dao Companion to Japanese Buddhist Philosophy*, ed. Gereon Kopf (Dordrecht: Springer, 2019), 307–35.
74 Paul Groner, *Saichō: The Establishment of the Japanese Tendai School* (Honolulu: University of Hawai'i Press, 2000), 104.
75 Jacqueline Stone, *Original Enlightenment and the Transformation of Medieval Japanese Buddhism* (Honolulu: University of Hawai'i Press, 1999), 14.

Pure Land 浄土 sect by Hōnen 法然, the True Pure Land 浄土真宗 sect by his pupil Shinran 親鸞, the Sōtō 曹洞 and Rinzai 臨済 sects of Zen Buddhism by Dōgen 道元 and Eisai 栄西, and the Nichiren sect by Nichiren 日蓮.

Aside from Dōgen, all of these reformers were heavily influenced by *mappō* 末法 thought. The term *mappō* (literally, "end of the Dharma") refers to a period in which the Buddha's teachings are in decline. The notion appears to be a Chinese innovation. Jan Nattier has shown that the concept has no clear Sanskrit equivalent but is a Chinese "apocryphal word" and "is as rare in the canonical *sūtra* literature as it is ubiquitous in the East-Asian commentaries."[76] The idea of a period of decline of the Dharma became extremely influential in Chinese and Japanese Buddhism, and by the twelfth century many Japanese Buddhist monks believed that *mappō* had already started. Supposedly, in that period traditional methods of reaching liberation or awakening are no longer available, so Hōnen and Shinran recommended to put one's faith in Amitābha Buddha to achieve rebirth in his Pure land, and Nichiren required his followers to chant the title of the *Lotus Sūtra*.[77]

The this-worldly focus that was already present in Tendai is also clearly visible in some of these reformers, most notably in Dōgen and Nichiren, albeit in very different ways. Dōgen suggested that dualism (i.e., the view that ultimate reality and phenomenal reality are different worlds) is a kind of "foolishness." He wrote that "opening flowers and falling leaves [i.e., the phenomenal world] is nature (such) as it is. However, fools think that there are no opening flowers and falling leaves in the world of Dharma-nature [i.e., ultimate reality]."[78] Nevertheless, Dōgen also emphasized that the realization that the phenomenal is not ultimately unreal should not lead to the opposite kind of foolishness: "[a]lthough people now have a deep understanding of the contents (heart) of seas and rivers, we still do not know how dragons and fish understand and use water. Do not foolishly assume that all kinds of beings use as water that what we understand as water."[79] So, while the conventional is not ultimately unreal, it does not represent the whole of ultimate reality either but merely one particular perspective.[80]

Nichiren considered himself the only true follower of Saichō. In his view Tendai had become corrupted with esoteric influences and had deviated from the one and only true teaching of the *Lotus Sūtra*. Like Saichō, Nichiren rejected metaphysical dualism. Lucia Dolce writes, "[f]or Nichiren [...] there is only one [...] world. Vulture Peak, the place where the Lotus Sutra is taught represents both this world of ours and the most perfect world, the only possible 'paradise'. There is no other reality,

---

76 Jan Nattier, *Once Upon a Future Time: Studies in a Buddhist Prophecy of Decline* (Berkeley: Asian Humanities Press, 1991), 103 and 98. Interestingly, it seems that the first one to use the term in its later standard sense was Zhiyi's teacher Nanyue Huisi 南嶽慧思 (ibid., 110).
77 About the notion of *mappō*, see also the section with that title in chapter 16.
78 シカアレハ開華葉落。コレ如是性ナリ。シカアルニ愚人オモハクハ。法性界ニハ。開華葉落アルヘカラスト。— Dōgen 道元, 『正法眼藏』(1231–53), 「法性」, T82n2582, 202b.
79 イマ人間ニハ。海ノココロ江ノココロヲフカク水ト知見セリトイヘトモ。龍魚等ハ。イカナルモノヲモテ。水ト知見シ。水ト使用ストイマタシラス。オロカニワカ水ト知見スルヲ。イツレノタクヒモ。水ニモチキルラント認スルコトナカシ。— Dōgen, 『正法眼藏』, 「山水經」, T82n2582, 65c.
80 Hee-Jin Kim, *Dōgen on Meditation and Thinking: A Reflection on His View of Zen* (Albany: SUNY Press, 2007); Bret Davis, "The Philosophy of Zen Master Dōgen: Egoless Perspectivism," in *The Oxford Handbook of World Philosophy*, eds. Jay L. Garfield and William Edelglass (Oxford: Oxford University Press, 2011), 348–60; Brons, "Meaning and Reality." See also chapter 8.

neither for humanity, nor for the Buddha."[81] However, this one world is in a state of disarray. In Nichiren's most famous writing, *Establishing the Peace of the Country* 立正安國論,[82] his imaginary interlocutor observes the sad state of the world and asks Nichiren what is wrong.

> Famine and disease rage more fiercely than ever, beggars are everywhere in sight, and scenes of death fill our eyes. Cadavers pile up in mounds like observation platforms, dead bodies lie side by side likes planks on a bridge. [...] [W]hy is it that the world had already fallen in decline [...]? What is wrong? What error has been committed?[83]

Nichiren answers that he has "pondered the matter carefully" and "searched rather widely in the scriptures for an answer."[84] The cause of all the suffering and disasters, he argues, is that people have turned their backs on what is right, namely the *Lotus Sūtra*. If only the people would

> embrace the one true vehicle, the single good doctrine of the Lotus Sutra [...] then the threefold world[85] will all become the Buddha land, and how could a Buddha land ever decline? The regions in the ten directions will all become treasure realms, and how could a treasure realm ever suffer harm?[86]

Nichiren's diagnosis and proposed cure of worldly suffering was explicitly sociopolitical. To some extent Buddhism has always been political — throughout history, Buddhism has been used by rulers to legitimize their rule, and for a long time the main function of Buddhism in Japan was to carry out rituals to protect the state — but Nichiren inverted that hierarchy and argued that the state should serve Buddhism (or Buddhist goals) rather than the other way around. Moreover, he did not give advice, hoping for the good will of the king (like Nāgārjuna), but he made demands; he and his followers routinely admonished the state for not following the right path (i.e., that of Nichiren's interpretation of the *Lotus Sūtra*).

There is, however, a very different reading of Nichiren that directly contradicts the foregoing. Early-twentieth-century readings of *Establishing the Peace of the Country*, especially by proponents of so-called "Nichirenism," were strongly nationalist or even fascist. The cornerstone of this far-right reading, which unfortunately continues to be influential, is just one short sentence that occurs roughly halfway in the text: "[f]irst we should pray for the nation, and after that we should establish the Buddhist law."[87] The nationalist interpretation of this sentence is that for Nichiren

---

81 Lucia Dolce, "Between Duration and Eternity: Hermeneutics of the 'Ancient Buddha' of the Lotus Sutra in Chih-i and Nichiren," in *A Buddhist Kaleidoscope*, ed. Reeves, 223–39.
82 T84n2688.
83 Nichiren 日蓮,『立正安國論』[*Establishing the Peace of the Country*] (1260), trans. Philip Yampolsky, ed., *Selected Writings of Nichiren*, trans. Burton Watson and Others (New York: Columbia University Press, 1990), 14.
84 Ibid.
85 The "threefold world" 三界 is this world, that is, the world of unawakened beings, which does not just include humans, but also animals, hungry ghosts (*pretas*), *asuras*, gods, and so forth. It is called "threefold" due to a traditional classification of the realms of these various beings into three kinds.
86 Nichiren,『立正安國論』, trans. Yampolsky, *Selected Writings of Nichiren*, 40–41.
87 For a more literal translation and reference, see the block quote below.

the state or nation has priority over the Buddhist law (rather than the other way around). But this interpretation is absurd for a number of reasons.[88]

First, the word "state" 國家 occurs only twice in the text. In all other cases Nichiren used the word *kuni* 國, which means something like land, country, district, or area including its inhabitants, but which does not mean "state," and which has no nationalistic connotation.[89] This should be kind of obvious, as the notion of the nation was only invented in Europe much later and imported in Japan in the nineteenth century. In the two cases were Nichiren used 國家 he was clearly referring to the state or government, rather than the country. *Kuni* 國, on the other hand, was a neutral term — the topic of the text was creating peace and harmony in some area, and not the creation of some harmonious state.

Second, the idea that Nichiren prioritized the state is obviously incorrect if the quote is not lifted out of its context.

> The country is prosperous because it relies on the Dharma. The Dharma is valuable because of the people. If the country would be destroyed and the people exterminated, who can [still] revere the Buddha? How can one [still] have faith in the Dharma? [Therefore] One must pray for the state first, and then establish the Dharma.[90]

Hence, what Nichiren is saying here is that to establish a Buddha land, we must first ensure peace, harmony, and prosperity. In other words, a functioning (and benevolent!) state is a prerequisite for establishing the Dharma, but that does not make the state a priority. That would be confusing means and ends.

Third, Nichiren repeatedly stated throughout his writings that he "vowed to summon up a powerful and unconquerable desire for the salvation of *all beings*, and never falter in [his] efforts."[91] He did not just aim for the elevation of Japan or the Japanese people, but he considered himself a bodhisattva aiming for the liberation of all of mankind. (Nevertheless, he did believe that Japan had a special role to play in saving and spreading Buddhism, and in saving or liberating people elsewhere.[92])

A Buddha Land in This World

In the chapter "The Dharma-Door of Nonduality" of the *Vimalakīrti Sūtra* it is written that "Matter itself is void [i.e., empty]. Voidness does not result from the destruc-

---

88 See also Satō Hiroo, "Nichiren's View of Nation and Religion," *Japanese Journal of Religious Studies* 26, nos. 3–4 (1999): 307–23.

89 On Nichiren's use of the word *kuni* 國 and the lack of nationalistic or ethnic connotations in that use, see also Jacqueline Stone, "Placing Nichiren in the 'Big Picture': Some Ongoing Issues in Scholarship," *Japanese Journal of Religious Studies* 26, nos. 3–4 (1999): 382–421, at 412.

90 夫國依法而昌。法因人而貴。國亡人滅。佛誰可崇。法誰可信哉。先祈國家須立佛法。— Nichiren,『立正安國論』, T84n2688, 206b.

91 Nichiren 日蓮,『開目抄』 [*The Opening of the Eyes*] (1272), trans. Yampolsky, *Selected Writings of Nichiren*, 79. Emphasis added.

92 Nichiren observed that Buddhism has spread from India to China and from China to Japan but had since disappeared in India and was on the decline in China. This geographical direction had to be turned around. Only Japan could bring Buddhism back to China, India, and then the rest of the world. For "Nichirenists" this was an attractive way to legitimize Japanese conquests and hegemony in East Asia in the early twentieth century. See also Stone, "Placing Nichiren in the 'Big Picture'."

tion of matter, but the nature of matter is itself voidness."[93] Robert Thurman, the translator of the sūtra, explains this passage as follows:

> [T]he fact that matter is voidness is absolutely affirmative of matter, not negative of matter. [... T]he first implication of the statement [...] that matter is voidness [... is that] our immediate reality *is* ultimate, cannot be escaped or negated, and must be accepted as it is — at least to start with, before we try to do something about it in a relative way — with no false hope of ever making it ultimate, since it already is so. We are left with the seemingly contradictory tasks of becoming conscious of its ultimacy on the one hand and, on the other hand, of devoting our energies to the improvement of the unavoidable relative situation as best we can. For the successful accomplishment of this dual task we need, respectively, wisdom (*prajñā*) and great compassion (*mahākaruṇā*), and these two functions are the essence of the Great Vehicle (*Mahāyāna*), and of the Middle Way.[94]

Here we encounter two of the themes I attempted to highlight in the brief and selective historical sketch presented in the preceding sections: (1) non-duality, or the claim that ultimate reality and phenomenal or conventional reality are not two different worlds; and (2) compassion and the importance of worldly suffering. (The third and less important theme was the rationalist element in Buddhism.) These two themes are not unrelated — if there is no other world, no ultimate or alternative reality we can hope to escape to, then we must address the suffering in this world.

Supposedly, only awakened beings can perceive ultimate reality, but ultimate and conventional reality have also been associated with different worlds as places. Conventional reality, then, is not just the world as we experience it but is the world *we live in*, the world of endless suffering, while ultimate reality is the world of the Buddhas and their Buddha lands; and the goal of Buddhist practice is not just to achieve awakening and *see* ultimate reality, but to actually *go* there. If one gives up on dualism, if there is just one world, then this radically changes. Then there is no other world, there is just this one world. But this raises a question: how does one go to the Buddha land if one, in some sense, is already there?

Two very different answers can be given to this question. According to the first answer, the Buddha land is literally here already — this world is the Buddha's Pure land — and thus, all we need to do is learn to see it. "Is it because the sun and moon are impure that those blind from birth do not see them?" asks the Buddha rhetorically in the *Vimalakīrti Sūtra*. Of course, it is not, and "in the same way," he continues, "the fact that some living beings do not behold the splendid display of virtues of the Buddha-field of the Tathāgata is due to their own ignorance."[95] Hence, all one needs to do is to dispel one's ignorance by study and meditation, purify one's mind, and reach awakening.

This interpretation carries dualism back in through the back door. It implies that ultimate reality and conventional reality are radically different, incompatible perspectives on the same world. Thus, instead of a dualism of worlds, we get a dualism of perspectives. But the kataphatic, non-dualistic turn lead to a rejection of that

---

93 Translation from Robert Thurman, *The Holy Teaching of Vimalakīrti: A Mahāyāna Scripture* (University Park: Pennsylvania State University Press, 1976), 73.
94 Robert Thurman, "Introduction," in *The Holy Teaching of Vimalakīrti*, 1–9, at 3.
95 Translation from Thurman, *The Holy Teaching of Vimalakīrti*, 18.

dualism as well. Moreover, it *must* be rejected, because the Buddha's teachings were taught in the world-as-conventionally-real (i.e., the world as we ordinarily experience it). If the conventional and ultimate are radically different, then this would imply that the Buddha's teachings would *only* be conventionally real. "If all of this is empty, [...] it follows that the Four Noble Truths do not exist," wrote Nāgārjuna in response to the idea that conventional reality does not really exist.[96] And analogously, if all of this is illusion because our conventional experience of this world is radically different from the ultimate, then it follows that the Four Noble Truths are illusion. That cannot be an acceptable conclusion, to a Buddhist at least. Hence, the ultimate and the conventional are *not* radically different, the conventional is not mere illusion, and, to speak with Dōgen, only fools think that there are no opening flowers and falling leaves in ultimate reality. And this implies in turn that the Buddha land cannot be something that is literally here *already*. Rather, in the same way that we can realize our potential of seeing through awakening, we can realize the world's potential of becoming the Buddha land.

Non-dualism implies that there is only this world, and therefore, that a Buddha land (or paradise, or utopia) can *only* be realized in this world. Moreover, it must be realized in this world. Ultimate reality is not something one sees already but something one needs to learn to see, and analogously, if there is just one world and ultimate reality is a perspective or aspect of that one world, then that perspective or aspect is not really there (i.e., seen) already, but waiting to be realized. Or in other words, aiming for awakening (i.e., "learning to see") is aiming for the realization of a Buddha land, or something like it, in this world. This is the second answer.[97]

Hence, contrary to the first answer that discourages any form of activism or social engagement, this second, more consistently non-dualist answer is also an activist answer. In embryonic form, much of this activist interpretation was already present in the thought of some of the thinkers mentioned above, most explicitly in Nichiren, but versions of this idea would play a much more central role in the thought of several twentieth century Buddhist thinkers.

---

96 *Mūlamadhyamakakārikā* 24, no. 1, trans. Garfield, *The Fundamental Wisdom of the Middle Way*, 67.
97 See also the last section of chapter 16, which suggests a less utopian and more pragmatic or pragmatist attitude toward the idea of a Buddha land in this world.

3

Reality and Utopia

The appeal of Eugène Burnouf's demythologized Buddha[1] derived mostly from the rational and undogmatic picture of Buddhism that came with it. *That* Buddhism was very much the opposite of how Christianity was increasingly viewed in the late-nineteenth century. And contrary to Christianity, *that* Buddhism did not conflict with science. So, Buddhism was simultaneously very old and very modern. Of course, romantic exoticism also played and continues to play a major role in the Western attraction to Buddhism, but the apparent rationality and naturalism have always been the main selling points of the Buddhism of Burnouf's Buddha. Furthermore, this has not only been the case in the West, but also in the East. There, this modern Buddha was exactly what anti-colonial and nationalist movements needed to respond to the Western, Orientalist charge of Eastern backwardness. If the Buddha was already modern in some sense, while Christianity was pre-modern, then the East was already better adapted to modernity, and it was the Christian West that was backward instead.

Different stories can be told about how the various modern Buddhisms mentioned in the first chapter of this book grew out of these trends. There is a Western-centric or Orientalist story that starts with the arrival of Henry Steel Olcott (1832–1907) in Ceylon (present day Sri Lanka) in 1880, and that credits him — often together with Paul Carus (1852–1919) whose book *The Gospel of Buddha* (1894) played a key role in the introduction of Buddhism to a wider audience in the West — for kick-starting the modernization of Buddhism.[2] There is a more Asia-centric story that minimizes Western influences and maintains that the modernization of Buddhism was largely an indigenous response to colonialism and Western dominance. And there are more nuanced stories that aim for some kind of middle path between the Western-centric and Asia-centric extremes.[3]

The question which of these stories is the most accurate is outside the scope of this book, but I have the impression that it is probably much closer to the second than to the first story. Except in case of Ceylon/Sri Lanka, I have seen little evidence for *direct* Western influence on twentieth-century developments in Asian Buddhist thought.[4] It is sometimes suggested that Western scholarship played an important

---

1 See the introduction of the previous chapter.
2 Paul Carus, *The Gospel of Buddha* (Chicago: Open Court, 1894).
3 For such a nuanced and very well-researched account, see David McMahan, *The Making of Buddhist Modernism* (Oxford: Oxford University Press, 2008).
4 And even in case of Sri Lanka that influence appears to be very minor.

role, but that is probably an exaggeration as well. The writings by Japanese academic Buddhologists[5] and scholar-monks like Yinshun 印順 (China/Taiwan) were much more widely read and certainly much more influential than those by any Western author.

This does not mean that trends in Western Buddhism (and/or the Western understanding of Buddhism) are irrelevant here, however. On the contrary, while engaged Buddhism may be a predominantly Asian phenomenon, at least originally, the current wave of secular Buddhism is almost exclusively Western, although it had a precursor in late-nineteenth-century Japan, and secular Buddhism is relevant here because it is the clearest attempt to take the naturalist dimension of secularity to its extreme.

Secular Buddhism

While there are substantial differences between Western Buddhism and Asian Buddhist modernism, the two also have much in common. When Heinz Bechert introduced the notion,[6] he argued that Buddhist modernism emphasizes the rational elements in Buddhist thought, increases attention to this-worldly affairs, and increases the role of the laity. This also applies to Western Buddhism, but these three aspects of Buddhist modernism work out a bit differently in the East and West. Lacking a Buddhist monastic tradition, the emphasis on the laity is obviously even greater in the West; this-worldliness generally translates to usefulness rather than engagement; and rationalization is taken further than what is common among Asian Buddhist modernists as well. Secular Buddhism takes all of this to its extreme.

Gananath Obeyesekere has pointed out another common feature of Buddhist modernism: a strong orientation towards a kind of text-based, "authentic" Buddhism.[7] Because this is also a characteristic of Protestantism, Obeyesekere has coined the term "Protestant Buddhism." The term is appropriate, as Protestantism may very well be the source of the fixation on texts and on authenticity. According to Gregory Schopen, early Buddhology was heavily influenced by Protestantism from which the field inherited a number of methodological assumptions. He wrote that: "The methodological position frequently taken by modern Buddhist scholars, archaeologists, and historians of religion looks, in fact, uncannily like the position taken by a variety of early Protestant reformers who were attempting to define and establish the locus of 'true religion'."[8] Through Olcott and Dharmapāla, this "Protestantism" seeped through into Sinhalese Buddhism (see below), but it seems to have played a much less important role in the rest of Asia. Western Buddhism, however, tends to be extremely "Protestant."

The demythologized and rationalized picture of Buddhism and the Buddha sketched by Burnouf and popularized by Carus and others in the nineteenth and

---

5   Academic research into Buddhism started to develop in Japan at the end of the nineteenth century, only a few decades later than it did in Europe.
6   Heinz Bechert, *Buddhismus, Staat und Gesellschaft in den Ländern des Theravāda-Buddhismus: Grundlagen. Ceylon* (Berlin: Metzer, 1966).
7   Gananath Obeyesekere, "Religious Symbolism and Political Change in Ceylon," *Modern Ceylon Studies* 1 (1970): 43–63. See also Richard Gombrich and Gananath Obeyesekere, *Buddhism Transformed: Religious Change in Sri Lanka* (Princeton: Princeton University Press, 1988).
8   Gregory Schopen, *Bones, Stones, and Buddhist Monks: Collected Papers on the Archaeology, Epigraphy, and Texts of Monastic Buddhism in India* (Honolulu: University of Hawai'i Press, 1997), 13.

early twentieth century remained dominant throughout the twentieth and twenty-first century,[9] although more traditional (or "exotic," from a Western point of view) interpretations started to gain some ground in the last quarter or so of the twentieth century. From quite early in its history, this rationalist picture tended to involve the idea that Buddhism was somehow scientific, or supported by science. For example, in his *Buddhist Catechism*, Olcott claimed that a version of the doctrine of karma and rebirth is supported by the theory of evolution:

> The broad rule [of the doctrine of karma and rebirth] is that if we have an excess of merit, we will be well and happily born the next time; if an excess of demerit, our next birth will be wretched and full of suffering. [...] True science entirely supports this doctrine of cause and effect. Science teaches that man is the result of a law of development, from an imperfect and lower, to a higher and perfect, condition.[10]

For secular Buddhists who reject all supernatural and mythical elements in Buddhism, this does not go nearly far enough, however. So, while Olcott largely accepts the mythical biography of the historical Buddha and a version of the doctrine of rebirth or reincarnation, Stephen Batchelor, for example, rejects both.

As far as I know, the English term "secular Buddhism" was coined around the year 2000, but I do not know who used it first.[11] The term gained prominence when Batchelor published a paper titled "A Secular Buddhism" in 2012.[12] (He also used the term "Buddhism 2.0" in that paper to refer to his version of secular Buddhism.) The topic of that paper was not entirely new, however: Batchelor has proposed, developed, and defended something he has called "secular Buddhism" and "Buddhism 2.0" among others in a series of books and articles starting in the 1990s.[13]

Batchelor's Buddhism 2.0 inherits most of the tenets of the Western current of Buddhist modernism and then radicalizes them. It strives to be rational or scientific, "authentic," and useful in this world and age, and it is inherently private, which is another aspect of Protestantism, either Christian or Buddhist. Because secular Buddhism radicalizes these trends, it exposes some of the weaknesses thereof.

Secular Buddhism uncritically accepts the modern, Western normative ideal of authenticity. While this ideal is rooted in Protestantism and nineteenth-century romantic thought, it has more recently become incorporated by capitalism in a number of ways. One fashion of authenticity is the misguided, and rather un-Buddhist,

---

9   See, for example, McMahan, *The Making of Buddhist Modernism*, 5.
10 Henry Steel Olcott, *A Buddhist Catechism: According to the Canon of the Southern Church* (Colombo: The Theosophical Society, 1881), 11.
11 The Japanese equivalent, 世間仏教, predates the English "secular Buddhism" by more than a century. It was used first in Inoue Enryō 井上圓了, 『仏教活論序論』 (1887), in 『井上円了選集』 (Tokyo: Tōyō University 東洋大学, 2003), vol. 3: 327–93, at 388.
12 Stephen Batchelor, "A Secular Buddhism," *Journal of Global Buddhism* 13 (2012): 87–107.
13 Books: Stephen Batchelor, *Buddhism without Beliefs: A Contemporary Guide to Awakening* (New York: Riverhead, 1997); *Confessions of a Buddhist Atheist* (New York: Spiegel & Grau, 2011); and esp. *After Buddhism: Rethinking the Dharma for a Secular Age* (New Haven: Yale University Press, 2015). Relevant papers are collected in *Secular Buddhism: Imagining the Dharma in an Uncertain World* (New Haven: Yale University Press, 2018). The aforementioned paper "A Secular Buddhism" is included in this collection, but I will refer to the original version in the following.

ideal of being authentic,[14] but more important here is the fashion of authentic consumption — the attempt by consumers to acquire or experience authentic "things" (in the broadest possible interpretation of "thing").[15] Thus, a Western tourist under the influence of this cult of authentic consumption will only want to see and experience authentic buildings, including authentic ruins, authentic landscapes, authentic cultures, authentic foods, and so forth, and will reject hybrids and modern or Western influences on, or "corruptions" of the "pure," traditional, original, authentic ideal. And similarly, a Western Buddhist under the same influence will want to find or reconstruct the most "authentic" Buddhism possible and will reject what she sees as corruptions, deviations, and non-purely-Buddhist (i.e., "inauthentic") influences.

While the ideal of authenticity is not exclusively Western, as Protestant Buddhism is also found in Asia, it is certainly modern. There is nothing quite like the Protestant attempt to reconstruct some kind of "authentic" Buddhism in the pre-twentieth-century Buddhist tradition. In fact, the whole idea of reconstructing the historical Buddha and his "real" historical message is quite alien to traditional Buddhism and even clashes with widely held Buddhist beliefs about historical factuality.[16] Perhaps, this could be taken to imply that the reconstructionist project is an "un-Buddhist" project or not an *authentically* Buddhist project.

Regardless of whether authenticity as a normative ideal is properly "Buddhist" or authentic, it is deeply problematic for a number of reasons. Batchelor appears to be aware of at least one of these problems:

> The more I am seduced by the force of my own arguments, the more I am tempted to imagine that my secular version of Buddhism is what the Buddha originally taught, which the traditional schools have either lost sight of or distorted. This would be a mistake; for it is impossible to read the historical Buddha's mind in order to know what he "really" meant or intended.[17]

It seems, however, that the seductive force of the ideal of authenticity is strong, given that much of Batchelor's work is an attempt to reconstruct the life and original (i.e., authentic) teachings of the Buddha anyway.[18] To what extent such reconstruction is possible is a topic we'll address later (see chapter 5), but it should be noted here that any such reconstruction will be offensive to some sectarian sensibilities and, therefore, quite controversial. There are more fundamental problems for the ideal of authenticity, however. Firstly, it is unclear why authenticity should be an ideal at all. And secondly, idealizing authenticity may conflict with some of the other modernist tenets.

Authentic ruins may be more interesting to visit than fake ruins, but Buddhism is not like a ruined building; it is a collection of beliefs, values, and ideas that serve

---

14 For an excellent critique of this notion of authenticity, and an explanation of why one should not usually strive to be authentic in this sense, see Simon Feldman, *Against Authenticity: Why You Shouldn't Be Yourself* (London: Lexington, 2015).
15 For a useful review of the sociology of such authentic consumption, see Amanda Koontz, "Constructing Authenticity: A Review of Trends and Influences in the Process of Authentication in Consumption," *Sociology Compass* 4, no. 11 (2009): 977–88.
16 See Jan Westerhoff, *The Golden Age of Indian Buddhist Philosophy* (Oxford: Oxford University Press, 2018), 24–34.
17 Batchelor, "A Secular Buddhism," 90.
18 Or in his own words, he seeks "to return to the roots of the tradition and rethink and rearticulate the dharma anew." Batchelor, *After Buddhism*, 19.

certain purposes and there is no a priori reason to assume that more "authentic" versions of those beliefs, values, and ideas serve those purposes any better than less authentic versions. Actually, the contrary is considerably more plausible, although, as Jay Garfield has pointed out, this may itself be a modernist or Western point of view.[19] Thales is arguably the father of Western science and philosophy. If authentic beliefs would be more valuable than later "corruptions," then we should reject Newton, Einstein, and everything modern science and philosophy has taught and return to Thales's original teachings. We'd have to reject plate tectonics and explain earthquakes by claiming that land floats on water, for example.

As mentioned, Batchelor attempts to reconstruct the life and teachings of the historical Buddha, but the more human the Buddha thereby becomes, the more he becomes like Thales. That is, he becomes the father of a certain tradition, but nothing more than that. Being simply human, the Buddha then no longer has any special authority, and there is, therefore, no special reason to believe his teachings. In other words, the more "authentic" the reconstruction of the Buddha's teachings and their origins, the less reason there is to accept them. Destroying the last bit of authority the Buddha has after humanizing him, Batchelor remarks that the Buddha "did not stand out among his peers because his knowledge of reality was somehow more accurate or superior to theirs."[20] Oddly, he does not seem to realize how devastating this remark is. If there was nothing special about the Buddha, then there is no reason to accept his teachings, *unless* they would satisfy some standard of knowledge, but the only standard of knowledge available to a genuinely *secular* Buddhist would be the standard of science. The Buddha's teachings cannot possibly satisfy criteria for good scientific theory, however, as they are not rooted in, and might not even be coherent with, a scientific worldview, and whether there is scientific evidence for the Buddha's teachings is a rather controversial question as well, not in the least due to lack of agreement about what exactly those teachings are.[21]

And this brings us to the second problem: the normative ideal of authenticity itself clashes with the naturalist aspect of secularity. An attempt to go back to the authentic teachings of the Buddha makes sense only if one accepts that the Buddha had some special, supernatural access to truth and wisdom, much like Mohamed's direct line of communication with Allah.[22] But while a traditional Buddhist typically believes that the Buddha was omniscient,[23] a *secular* Buddhist cannot possibly accept that.

If authenticity is not problematic enough, one can try to go one step further and reconstruct the Buddha's original teachings by purifying them from later "corruptions" *and then* purify the original teachings from non-Buddhist influences as well. The aim, then, is for something that is explicitly unauthentic, for something

---

19 Jay L. Garfield, "Buddhism and Modernity," in *The Buddhist World,* ed. John Powers (London: Routledge, 2016), 294–304, at 303, writes: "From a Buddhist point of view, history is often conceived as degeneration from an omniscient teacher through more and more fallible human beings, with the Dharma gradually attenuating on the way to disappearance. That vision is central to Buddhism's self-conception. In a Western context, however, we think the other way around about history. We conceive of history as progress from a primitive to a more enlightened view."
20 Batchelor, *After Buddhism,* 129.
21 Donald Lopez, Jr., *Buddhism & Science: A Guide for the Perplexed* (Chicago: University of Chicago Press, 2008); *The Scientific Buddha: His Short and Happy Life* (New Haven: Yale University Press, 2012); and Evan Thompson, *Why I Am Not a Buddhist* (New Haven: Yale University Press, 2020).
22 It was only a direct line of communication if Gabriel was a mere messenger, of course.
23 See, for example, the quote by Garfield in note 19.

more "pure" than historical reality. Batchelor adopts a variant of this attitude. He writes that "my starting point in dealing with dogmatic statements is to bracket off anything attributed to Gotama that could just as well have been said by another wanderer, Jain monk, or brahmin priest of the same period."[24] Mark Siderits has suggested something like this as a possibility as well but more as a theoretical exercise than as a normative ideal.[25] A charitable reading of Batchelor suggests that his approach should be understood much in the same way. His point in "bracketing off" is not so much hyper-purification but rather the arrival at a more interesting theory.

There is a long list of candidate ideas that could be bracketed off on these grounds (i.e., on the grounds that they were part of the shared cultural background rather than particular to the Buddha's thought). An obvious example is reincarnation or rebirth, suggested by Siderits. Mind–body dualism and other varieties of substance dualism are other examples, as well as the belief in gods and spirits, the theory of karma, which is closely related to the idea of rebirth, and so forth. One may wonder, however, how many of such background ideas can be discarded without changing Buddhism into something else entirely.[26] In any case, much of Buddhist doctrine would have to be radically rethought. Batchelor, of course, realizes this very well and much of his project is aimed at doing exactly that.

In the first chapter of this book I distinguished two dimensions of secularity: secularity as naturalism and secularity as privatization. While radical Buddhism and related engaged Buddhisms are anti-secular in the second sense, secular Buddhism is secular in both respects. In other words, secular Buddhism accepts the banishment of religion to the private sphere and denies it any significant social or political role.

Secular Buddhists share with other modern Buddhists the idea that Buddhism must be relevant in this world and this age, but in case of secular Buddhism, this relevance generally means "usefulness" and the world and age themselves are more or less taken as given. There is a certain blindness in secular Buddhism for important features of the surrounding culture, and consequently, those are unconsciously and uncritically, or unthinkingly, accepted. One such feature of modern culture is that it is extremely individualistic or even narcissistic[27] and idealizes "autonomy," although there is considerable geographical variation in this respect.

Another, equally important feature is that "usefulness" itself is a rather fashionable idea — in modern, capitalist consumer society what is useless is worthless. Since the nineteenth century, "useful" has become inseparable from the originally utilitarian concept of "utility," which itself — under the influence of the hegemony of liberalism and mainstream economics — has effectively turned into a synonym of "profitability." Hence, something is useful to the extent that it is profitable, but there are many ways in which something can be profitable. It might help you make more money directly. Or it might help you cope with the conditions of life more effec-

---

24 Batchelor, *After Buddhism*, 26.
25 Mark Siderits, "Buddhism and Techno-Physicalism: Is the Eightfold Path a Program?" *Philosophy East & West* 51, no. 3 (2001): 307–14; *Buddhism as Philosophy: An Introduction* (Aldershot: Ashgate, 2007).
26 Lopez, *The Scientific Buddha*. This obviously is a problem for the project of this book as well. See also chapter 5.
27 Jean Twenge and Keith Campbell, *The Narcissism Epidemic: Living in the Age of Entitlement* (New York: Atria, 2009).

tively. Or it may help in creating acceptance of the status quo (i.e., hegemony[28]) and thereby make your employees less likely to dissent or revolt. And so forth.

Stephen Batchelor states explicitly that he does "not envision a Buddhism that seeks to discard all trace of religiosity, that seeks to arrive at a dharma that is little more than a set of self-help techniques that enable us to operate more calmly and effectively as agents or clients, or both, of capitalist consumerism."[29] However, one may wonder how successful he is. His reinterpretation of the Dharma is thoroughly individualist. For example, item seven of his *Ten Theses of Secular Dharma* is that "the community of practitioners is formed of autonomous persons who mutually support each other in the cultivation of their paths."[30] The same individualism permeates his rethinking of the doctrine of "no-self,"[31] emphasis on self-reliance,[32] and response to social ills.[33] The "secular dharma" may be "grounded in a deeply felt concern and compassion for the suffering of all those with whom we share this earth,"[34] but it remains focused on the practice of autonomous individuals. As in liberalism and mainstream economics, the "autonomous" individual takes center stage and is the only actor worth considering. This, of course, is very fashionable, but it also denies the "secular dharma" a social or political role, which makes it rather useful for those who profit from the status quo as well. Individualistic concern with suffering without social, communal, and political action to alleviate that suffering is impotent and harmless to those who profit from the continuation of suffering.[35]

In the end, what secularized Buddhisms typically aim to achieve is a kind of acceptance of suffering rather than a desire to end it. Almost as an afterthought, Batchelor's eighth thesis of secular dharma preaches "empathy, compassion, and love for all creatures who have evolved on this earth,"[36] but this appears to be an empty plea. Without actual commitment to alleviate suffering, this so-called "empathy" or "compassion" is nothing but a pornographic indulging in pity.

Although secular Buddhism may be rather interesting from a sociological point of view, it turns out to be of limited relevance here. It is diametrically opposed to radical Buddhism on one dimension of secularity, namely, secularity-as-privatization (see chapter 1). And while it purports to be located at the same end on the other dimension, namely that of secularity-as-naturalism, its Protestant craving for authenticity undermines this. Secular Buddhism, thus, is not a good model for a coherent secularity-as-naturalism. An alternative will be formulated in part II of this book (based on groundwork laid in part I), but here we'll return to the East, and to the nineteenth century.

---

28 Hegemony (or cultural hegemony) is the more or less spontaneous, "unthinking" assent to or acceptance of the sociopolitical and economic status quo. See also the section "Uchiyama Gudō and Early Buddhist Socialism" in this chapter.
29 Batchelor, *After Buddhism*, 17.
30 Ibid., 321.
31 Ibid., 201–3.
32 E.g., ibid., 275.
33 E.g., ibid., 305.
34 Ibid., 16.
35 The failure of secular Buddhism to be much more than self-help is also illustrated by its most common defense by adherents when facing criticism: "it works for me." That's apparently all that matters: that it "works" for me in better coping with the stresses caused by this world.
36 Batchelor, *After Buddhism*, 321.

Sri Lanka — Dharmapāla and Ariyaratne

In 1880, in a public ceremony in Ceylon (Sri Lanka) Henry Steel Olcott and Madame Blavatsky officially converted to Buddhism. A few years earlier Blavatsky and Olcott had founded the Theosophical Society that aimed to investigate occultism and to reveal the shared universal truths behind the world's religions.[37] In Ceylon, Olcott became more heavily invested in Buddhism. He became acquainted with prominent Buddhists and wrote the aforementioned *Buddhist Catechism*. He did not arrive in a vacuum, however. Buddhists had been engaged in debates with Christian missionaries for some years, and Olcott was a rather useful asset in the anti-colonial and nationalist struggle for a modern Buddhist self-identity in opposition to the Christian, colonial oppressor. The Buddhist revival movement, which was closely associated with this struggle, presented Buddhism as a rational, democratic, and modern religion, much more suitable to this modern age than backward Christianity. The fact that an educated Westerner converted and joined their ranks helped greatly in spreading that message.

The most prominent figure in the anti-colonial, Buddhist revival movement was Anagarika Dharmapāla (1864–1933), who was closely affiliated with Olcott for a while.[38] Dharmapāla was an activist and missionary more than a theoretician but is, more or less, the paradigmatic Protestant Buddhist. He claimed that "Buddhism is a scientific religion, in as much as it earnestly enjoins that nothing whatever be accepted on faith,"[39] and that "the Message of the Buddha [...] is free from theology, priestcraft, rituals, ceremonies, dogmas, heavens, hells and other theological shibboleths."[40] His Buddhism was rational and optimistic, and was therefore the religion that is most suitable for the modern age; it was individualist and lay-centered, and he stayed a layman himself for most of his life. Furthermore, he presented Buddhism primarily as an ethical teaching and emphasized meditation. And he fully embraced the idea of a return to an uncorrupted, text-based (rather than practice-based) "authentic" Buddhism. As David McMahan points out, "Dharmapala's representation of Buddhism, though it could be fiercely critical of Christianity and the West, was deeply informed by Protestantism, Enlightenment rationalism, and Victorian cultural forms."[41]

Dharmapāla's Buddhism also involved elements of social engagement and a kind of reactionary or primitivist utopianism common among Buddhist reformers around that time. He wrote that "the basic doctrine of Buddhism is to relieve human suffering,"[42] and his notion of suffering explicitly included poverty and related this-worldly suffering. Furthermore, he was at times very critical of capitalism. For example, he wrote that "The British consciousness so long has been led by the immoral

---

37 This kind of perennialism remains popular among Western Buddhists (as far as I can see), but has been rejected by most Buddhist Modernists etc. in Asia.
38 On Dharmapāla, see, for example, George Bond, *The Buddhist Revival in Sri Lanka: Religious Tradition, Reinterpretation and Response* (Columbia: University of South Carolina Press, 1988), 53–61; Gombrich and Obeyesekere, *Buddhism Transformed*; and McMahan, *The Making of Buddhist Modernism*, 91–97.
39 Anagarika Dharmapāla, "The World's Debt to Buddha" (1893), in *Return To Righteousness: A Collection of Speeches, Essays and Letters of the Anagarika Dharmapala*, ed. Ananda Guruge (Colombo: Ministry of Education and Cultural Affairs, 1965), 3–22, at 18.
40 Anagarika Dharmapāla, "Message of the Buddha" (1925), in *Return to Righteousness*, 23–34, at 27.
41 McMahan, *The Making of Buddhist Modernism*, 95.
42 Dharmapāla, "The World's Debt to Buddha," 20.

class of Capitalists who loves gold more than human life,"⁴³ and that "Everywhere in Europe capitalism is introducing class hatred. The poor have no place in society. Plutocracy has destroyed love."⁴⁴ However his analysis of such this-worldly evils and suffering was almost entirely moral, and all he had to offer as an alternative was the myth of Aśoka and similar utopian dreams of the restoration of some idyllic past.

As mentioned, this last aspect of Dharmapāla's thought is by no means unique. In the contrary, a common, but not universal, feature of Buddhist modernism that has not yet been mentioned is an often primitivist and always utopian rejection of modernity and longing for some more or less idyllic past, often embodied in the Aśoka myth. Another good example of this anti-modern aspect of Buddhist modernism is A.T. Ariyaratne (1931–), the founder of the Sarvodaya Shramadana Movement, which is sometimes heralded as an example of engaged Buddhism in action.⁴⁵ Like Dharmapāla, Ariyaratne sketches a very idyllic picture of precolonial Sri Lanka.⁴⁶ Supposedly, it was a very equal society without caste or class in which wealth was shared and "everyone's worth and dignity was well recognised." In a scathing review of the first volume of Ariyaratne's collected writings, Susantha Goonatilake points out that Ariyaratne's idyll is "completely imaginary" and that much of it is "patently false." Precolonial Sri Lanka was very unequal and had a caste system, and people of lower caste or class were addressed like animals.⁴⁷

Something else Ariyaratne's thought shares with many other engaged and radical Buddhisms is a rethinking of the Four Noble Truths, but to Ariyaratne, this rethinking is unusually radical. Often it just involves broadening the scope of "suffering,"⁴⁸ but Ariyaratne reinterprets the first Noble Truth, "There is suffering," as "There is a decadent village," and the second locates the causes of this decadence in "factors such as egoism, competition, greed, and hatred."⁴⁹ The general approach of the Four Noble Truths — identify the problem, identify the cause, and so forth — also had a rather practical implementation: Sarvodaya Shramadana volunteers went into the villages to research what was needed, resulting in a list of basic needs including a clean environment, water, food, health care, energy, and education.

While Ariyaratne and his Sarvodaya Shramadana Movement can certainly be seen as an example of engaged Buddhism, they are about as far away from the radical end of the spectrum as possible. They aim for an awakening of individuals and society and are officially critical of capitalism, but in practice they do not even work for reform and aim for charity within the narrow confines offered by neoliberalism.

In a book documenting several decades of research on the role of private Non-Governmental Organizations (NGOs) like Sarvodaya Shramadana in Sinhalese soci-

---

43 Anagarika Dharmapāla, "The Repenting God of Horeb" (1922), in *Return to Righteousness*, 401–25, at 408.
44 Anagarika Dharmapāla, "The Constructive Optimism of Buddhism" (1915), in *Return to Righteousness*, 391–400, at 394.
45 Bond, *The Buddhist Revival in Sri Lanka*, chapter 7; George Bond, "A.T. Ariyaratne and the Sarvodaya Shramadana Movement in Sri Lanka," in *Engaged Buddhism: Buddhist Liberation Movements in Asia*, eds. Christopher Queen and Sallie King (Albany: SUNY Press, 1996), 121–46.
46 Susantha Goonatilake, "Review of Collected works of A.T. Ariyaratne," *Journal of Contemporary Asia* 13, no. 2 (1983): 236–42. See also Bond, "A.T. Ariyaratne and the Sarvodaya Shramadana Movement in Sri Lanka," 131.
47 Goonatilake, "Review of Collected Works of A.T. Ariyaratne," 238–39.
48 This is assuming that the original scope of "suffering" (*dukkha*) was narrow, which is quite debatable. See the section "Suffering" in chapter 5.
49 Bond, "A.T. Ariyaratne and the Sarvodaya Shramadana Movement in Sri Lanka," 129–30.

ety, Goonatilake remarks that "the aim of NGOs was to shrink the role of government in developing countries."⁵⁰ Since the emergence of the Washington Consensus in the 1980s, developing countries have been forced to reduce government activities by means of austerity and privatization and to refrain from supporting domestic industry to get access to International Monetary Fund or World Bank loans. Intentional or not, the privatization of poverty alleviation is part of this package. Increased poverty due to the enforced shut-down of support programs for the poor and other domestic economic policy was to be addressed by private NGOs rather than by the state. The background of the Washington Consensus is an ideologically driven program to cut down governments and promote "free" markets. One of its effect is what Goonatilake aptly calls "recolonisation": an increased usurpation of former government activities by foreign-funded, private organizations like Sarvodaya Shramadana, and thereby, a gradual loss of domestic control to foreign financial control.⁵¹

Ariyaratne embraced the role of Sarvodaya Shramadana in this privatization and recolonization scheme, which does not just make him an accomplice in the neoliberal destruction of the state but raises doubts about the genuineness of his "philosophy" and stated aims. His criticism of capitalism rings hollow if at the same time Sarvodaya Shramadana "takes the form of a normal capitalist enterprise working on commercial criteria."⁵² And so does his idyllic picture of traditional village life when Sarvodaya Shramadana's vision of economic development appears to be focused on retraining villagers to provide cheap materials and labor for Western multinationals, and souvenirs and services for Western tourists.⁵³ The latter can, perhaps, be excused as some kind of "economic realism." The point here, however, is not so much to criticize Ariyaratne and Sarvodaya Shramadana but to illustrate how conformist and *anti*-radical engaged Buddhism can be.

Realism and Reform in Japan — Inoue Enryō

Olcott visited Japan for the first time in 1889, together with Dharmapāla. He stayed for little more than three months, during which he claims to have "visited 33 towns and delivered 76 public and semi-public addresses, reaching […] 187,500 hearers."⁵⁴ Like when he arrived in Ceylon before, Olcott did not arrive in a vacuum; Japanese Buddhism had been experiencing turbulent times that were in some ways similar but in other ways very different from the situation in Ceylon.

---

50 Susantha Goonatilake, *Recolonisation: Foreign Funded NGOs in Sri Lanka* (New Delhi: Sage, 2006), 285.
51 Ibid. See also Goonatilake, "Review of Collected Works of A.T. Ariyaratne," 241. Another effect of the Washington Consensus is that it actually prevents "developing countries" from developing, and this makes Goonatilake's term "recolonisation" particularly appropriate. One of the pillars of colonial policy was to make sure that the colonies were unable to build up industries that could compete with those in the colonizing state, and thus to prevent them from economically developing. Rather, colonies were to be providers of cheap resources, including labor. As economists Ha-Joon Chang and Erik Reinert have pointed out, the effect of the policies enforced by the Washington institutions is exactly the same. See also the section "Free Trade Ideology" in chapter 15 and Ha-Joon Chang, *Kicking Away the Ladder* (London: Anthem, 2002); *Bad Samaritans: Rich Nations, Poor Policies, and the Threat to the Developing World* (London: Random House Business, 2007); and Erik Reinert, *How Rich Countries Got Rich… and Why Poor Countries Stay Poor* (London: Constable, 2007).
52 Goonatilake, "Review of Collected Works of A.T. Ariyaratne," 240. See also Goonatilake, *Recolonisation*, 59.
53 Ibid.
54 Henry Steel Olcott, *Old Diary Leaves: The Only Authentic History of the Theosophical Society, Fourth Series: 1887–92* (Madras: Theosophical Publishing Society, 1910), 164.

Unlike Ceylon, Japan was never colonized, but it shut itself off from the rest of the world for centuries. After it finally opened up in the 1860s it decided to catch up with the West and to become modern. Buddhism did not fit in the modernist self-image of the new or future Japan. It was repressed from 1867 to 1871 and continued to be seen as backwards for some time after that. In the middle of the 1880s this started to change under the influence of the philosopher, educator, and former Buddhist priest Inoue Enryō 井上圓了 (1858–1919) who adopted Western, modernist discourse and used Western philosophy and science in an attempt to show the backwardness and irrationality of Christianity and the scientific nature of Buddhism. His books and articles, which were read widely, played a key role in the birth of Buddhist modernism in Japan.[55]

It is in this historical context that Olcott and Dharmapāla arrived, and the success of his first tour, which he described as a "successful crusade," is closely related to the reason why he was such a valuable asset to the nationalist Buddhist revival movement in Ceylon: he was the modern, Western convert underlining the modernity of Buddhism. However, Japan's infatuation with Olcott did not last long. His *Buddhist Catechism* had been translated into Japanese in 1886 and was reprinted in 1889 for the occasion of his visit but was never reprinted again and quickly faded into obscurity. And when he visited Japan again in 1891 he had a hard time connecting with Japanese Buddhists. Part of the reason for this was that Inoue, Olcott, and others had been somewhat successful in presenting Buddhism as modern. Hence, Olcott was not necessary anymore as a tool to spread that message. Japan had moved on. Furthermore, Olcott's association with Theosophy and Theravāda Buddhism, the only remaining school of formerly "mainstream," non-Mahāyāna Buddhism, were also increasingly seen as problematic in Mahāyāna Japan.

Inoue Enryō would soon be joined by a number of other philosophers combining Buddhism or Chinese philosophy with Western philosophy, such as Inoue Tetsujirō 井上哲次郎 (1855–1944), Kiyozawa Manshi 清沢満之 (1863–1903), Nishida Kitarō 西田幾多郎 (1870–1945), and Suzuki Teitarō 鈴木貞太郎 (also known as Suzuki Daisetz 鈴木大拙; 1870–1966). The 1880s and 1890s would also see the establishment of academic research into the history of Buddhism and Buddhist philosophy in Japan. More than a century earlier, Tominaga Nakamoto 富永仲基 (1715–1746) was the first to take a historical approach to the rather large and varied collection of Buddhist sūtras in existence, but he was ahead of his time and — although his writings had some influence on the Nativist 国学 thinker Motoori Norinaga 本居宣長 (1730–1801) who rejected Buddhism — his writings proved too controversial, and he was all but forgotten only a few decades later.[56] Nakamoto's historical approach, or something very much like it, would be revived in the late nineteenth century. In 1894, exactly one and a half century after Tominaga published his book about Buddhism, Furukawa Isamu 古河勇 (also known as Rōsen 老川; 1871–1899) published a paper in which he wrote that academic Buddhology had shown that the Mahāyāna sūtras cannot be attributed to the Buddha and were products of a later time, something Nakamoto had also claimed before.[57]

---

55 Yoshinaga Shin'ichi, "Theosophy and Buddhist Reformers in the Middle of the Meiji Period: An Introduction," *Japanese Religions* 34, no. 2 (2009): 119–31. Rainer Schulzer, *Inoue Enryō: A Philosophical Portrait* (New York: SUNY Press, 2019).

56 Katō Shūichi, "Tominaga Nakamoto, 1715–46: A Tokugawa Iconoclast," *Monumenta Nipponica* 22, nos. 1–2 (1967): 177–93.

57 Yoshinaga, "Theosophy and Buddhist Reformers in the Middle of the Meiji Period."

The strongest Western influence on Japanese society and emerging academia at that time was Germany, and the dominant philosophy in Germany was idealism. According to German idealist philosophers, the properties of things as we experience them are created by the mind and we cannot know the thing-in-itself, as Kant called it, or the thing outside the mind.[58] The Japanese philosophical response to this reminds of the shift from apophasis to kataphasis when the Chinese imported Indian Buddhist philosophy.[59] That is, there was a shift from the negative, apophatic attitude Japanese philosophers found in German idealism,[60] to a more positive and reality-confirming, kataphatic attitude in the works of Inoue Enryō, Inoue Tetsujirō, and Kiyozawa Manshi, among others. Nevertheless, there is an important difference with the Chinese apophasis-kataphasis shift many centuries earlier. The Chinese Buddhist philosophers intended to work *within* a single tradition, namely Buddhism, and reinterpreted the materials within that tradition. The equivalent would have been if these Japanese philosophers would have reinterpreted German idealism from within, but that's not really what they did. Rather, they constructed their metaphysics largely out of Buddhist and Chinese materials, even if they presented them in a Western style and in Western terms.[61]

Inoue Tetsujirō advocated a kind of realism which he called "the theory of identity of phenomena and reality" 現象即実在論 and which he explicitly opposed to idealism.[62] The character 即 *soku* is used in Buddhist philosophy to express some kind of identity or co-occurrence of two things (and not in the same sense outside Buddhist philosophy), but the term as a whole is his translation of German *Identitätsrealismus* (identity realism) or *Identitätstheorie* (identity theory).[63] These terms did not occur in German philosophy at that time, however, at least, as far as I know.[64] But the term *Identitätsphilosophie* was used by Hegel in reference to Schelling, and this indeed appears what Inoue Tetsujirō was referring to.

While Inoue Enryō did not use the same label (i.e., 現象即実在論) for his metaphysics, his ideas were very similar in this respect to Inoue Tetsujirō's.[65] He defended a kind of neutral monism that seems somewhat similar to Schelling's, who had argued that nature and spirit are essentially identical.[66] Inoue Enryō's neutral mon-

---

58 See also the second to fourth section of chapter 7.
59 See the section "From Nāgārjuna to Zhiyi" in chapter 2.
60 For example, Inoue Enryō found Kant's philosophy ultimately unsatisfactory because it "drives the noumenal substance of all things outside [the scope of] knowledge" 万の物の本体を、知識の外に放ち去り. Inoue Enryō 井上圓了, 『奮闘哲学』(1917), in『井上円了選集』, Vol. 2 (Tokyo: Tōyō University 東洋大学, 2003), 207–444, at 245.
61 Kosaka Kunitsugu, "Metaphysics in the Meiji Period," 国際哲学研究 [*Journal of International Philosophy*] 3 (2014): 291–307, and John Maraldo, "The Japanese Encounter with and Appropriation of Western Philosophy," in *The Oxford Handbook of Japanese Philosophy*, ed. Bret Davis (Oxford: Oxford University Press, 2014), 333–63.
62 Inoue Tetsujirō 井上哲次郎,「現象即実在論の要領」(1897), in (『井上哲次郎集』, Vol. 9 (Tokyo: Kress クレス出版, 2003), 153–99.
63 Or the other way around: *Identitätsrealismus* is Inoue Tetsujirō's German translation of his term 現象即実在論. See also the next footnote.
64 I have found no occurrence of the term *Identitätsrealismus* outside the context of Inoue Tetsujirō's philosophy, and Rainer Schulzer, *Inoue Enryō*, also suggested that the term was coined by Tetsujirō himself. The term *Identitätstheorie* is the German translation of "mind/brain identity theory" (in the philosophy of mind) and was coined in the middle of the twentieth century.
65 According to Schulzer, *Inoue Enryō*, 227, Enryō's version of 現象即実在論 (again, not Enryō's label) even predated Tetsujirō's.
66 Monism in the philosophy of mind or metaphysics comes in three kinds: idealist monism holds that only the mind exists and thus that everything is in the mind; materialist monism or physicalism

ism is most clearly expressed in his *Philosophy of Struggle* 奮闘哲学 where he wrote, "Either to claim that materialism is the truth or that idealism is the truth is one-sided; viewed from the outside one understands that these two are nothing but two extremes of the same thing, two faces of the same object."[67] However, in Schelling's *Identitätsphilosophie*, ultimate reality, or "the absolute," is absolutely unknowable (i.e., apophatic), and for that reason Inoue Enryō preferred Hegel's refutation of Schelling's philosophy[68]; in Hegel, he saw the Western equivalent of the non-dualism of Tendai/Tiantai 天台 and the logico-epistemological school:[69]

> The [theory of] dependent origination of suchness of Tendai is similar to the idealist school in Western philosophy as well as the logico-epistemological school [in Buddhist philosophy]. The position of that sect [i.e., Tendai] that "all dharmas are suchness and suchness is all dharmas" is the same as Hegel's argument that "the phenomena are the non-phenomena [i.e., things-in-themselves[70]] and the non-phenomena are the phenomena."[71]

This claim is significant, as the metaphysics of Inoue Enryō and Inoue Tetsujirō is indeed similar to a realist interpretation of Yogācāra and the logico-epistemological school and to Zhiyi 智顗, the founder of Tiantai. Like Zhiyi, Inoue Tetsujirō and Inoue Enryō explicitly rejected the dualism that separates the phenomenal or conventional from an unknowable noumenal or ultimate reality. This is not very surprising, as something like this had been the dominant view in Japanese Buddhism since Saichō 最澄,[72] but by developing new arguments for Buddhist realism and connecting it with Western science and philosophy, they changed it into something new: a philosophy.

The quote by Inoue is also interesting because it and its surrounding text suggests a comparison with Hegel's remark (in the chapter on Heraclitus in his *Lectures on the*

---

holds that only the physical world exist and thus that the mind is physical as well; and according to neutral monism both matter and mind are forms or expressions of something else. See also the first sections of chapter 4 in this volume.

    Schelling argued for a version of neutral monism around 1800. See, for example, F.W.J. Schelling, "Darstellung des Systems meiner Philosophie" (1800), in *Sämtliche Werke*, Vol. 4 (Stuttgart: Cotta, 1859), 105–212; as well as the texts collected in *Sämtliche Werke*, Vol. 3 (Stuttgart: Cotta, 1858).

67 あるいは唯心論が真理であるなどというのは、いずれも偏見にして、局外より観察すれば、この二者全く一物の両端、一体の両面に過ぎぬことが分かる。— Inoue Enryō,「奮闘哲学」, 237. See also Inoue Enryō,『哲学要領』(1886), in『井上円了選集』, Vol. 1: 87–215, at 154.
68 Inoue had rejected Kant for very much the same reason. See note 60.
69 See the section "From Nāgārjuna to Zhiyi" in chapter 2.
70 The term "non-phenomena" 無象 is rather obscure, but can be gleaned from the contexts in which it occurs throughout the text. Most often the two characters are part of the compound 無象界 which is contrasted with 現象界. The latter means "phenomenal world," and thus the former can only mean "noumenal world," or "ultimate reality" in Buddhist terms. By implication, "non-phenomenon" 無象 refers to the noumenon or thing-in-itself.

    The argument in quotes (in my translation) that Inoue attributes to Hegel presumably refers to G.W.F. Hegel's argument in the section "Die Erscheinung" in his *Wissenschaft der Logik* (1813), Vol. 2, in *Werke*, Vol. 6 (Frankfurt a.M.: Suhrkamp, 1969–71), 124–25, that "the phenomenon is that what the thing-in-itself is, or its truth" ("Die Erscheinung ist das, was das Ding and sich ist, oder seine Wahrheit").

71 天台の真如縁起は、西洋哲学中の論理学派すなわち理想学派に似たり。その宗立つるところの万法は真如、真如是万法というはヘーゲル氏の現象是無象、無象是現象と論ずるところに同じ。— Inoue Enryō,『哲学要領』, 104.
72 See the section "From Saichō to Nichiren" in chapter 2.

History of Philosophy) that "here we see land; there is no sentence by Heraclitus that I haven't included in my Logic."[73] Hegel read the history of philosophy from his own philosophical perspective and found a kindred spirit in Heraclitus, and similarly, the context of the quote by Inoue Enryō above is a short overview of Western philosophy culminating in Hegel where Inoue finally "saw land," that is, he found a metaphysics that appeared similar to his own. In other words, Inoue was not a Hegelian who found a parallel in Buddhist thought, but a Buddhist thinker who thought to have found similar ideas in Hegel.[74]

While Inoue Tetsujirō was an academic philosopher focusing on German philosophy and Buddhism, Inoue Enryō was an educator, and initially a Buddhist priest, who wrote about many aspects of Buddhism and who aimed to reform Buddhism. Like many Buddhist reformers after him, he advocated a new Buddhism that transcended the traditional sects. He also argued for some kind of socially engaged Buddhism and was the first to call for a "secular Buddhism" 世間仏教, more than a century before the rise of secular Buddhism in the West. However, Inoue's secular Buddhism was very different from Stephen Batchelor's Buddhism 2.0.[75] One key difference is that the cult of authenticity had no pull on him. Under the influence of the then-new idea of evolution, Inoue Enryō developed an organic view of Buddhism as a living thing 活物 in his *Living Discourse on Revealing the Truth* 顕正活論. As an evolving, living thing, Buddhism had always adapted to its environment, and consequently, throughout its history Buddhism reformed many times and will continue to reform in response to changes in its social and intellectual environment. And while it is true that the seeds of this continuously reforming, living thing were found in ancient India, Mahāyāna is like its flowers and fruit.[76]

Authenticity was irrelevant for Inoue because he adopted a more genuinely secular view than the "secular" Buddhists who are stuck on the absolute authority of the Buddha. In the preface of the *Prolegomena* to the series that *Living Discourse* was part of, he wrote:

> Although there is much talk among Christians that the original texts of Buddhism are Indian, that Mahāyāna is not the Buddha's teaching, that Śākyamuni [i.e., the Buddha] really did no exist, and so forth, this doesn't even concern me a little bit. That person's biography may not be detailed/accurate and the origin of those teachings may be unclear, but I would never be so blind and ignorant to believe those teachings based on biography or origin. I will only believe it if it agrees with today's philosophical reasoning, and I will reject it if does not.[77]

---

73 G.W.F. Hegel, *Vorlesungen über die Geschichte der Philosophie*, Vol. 1 (1837), in *Werke*, Vol. 18, 320.
74 To what extent Inoue Enryō's and Inoue Tetsujirō's metaphysics really is similar to Hegel's is quite debatable, however, but unfortunately I must admit that I find Hegel far too obscure to contribute much to that debate. It should also be noted that although Enryō can be classified as a "Buddhist thinker" in this stage of his intellectual development, gradually other elements, particularly Confucianism and nationalism, became more prominent.
75 See the section on "Secular Buddhism" above.
76 Inoue Enryō,『仏教活論本論、第二編: 顕正活論』(1890), in『井上円了選集』, Vol. 4 (2003): 189–371, 218–21. See also Rainer Schulzer, "Inoue Enryō's Philosophy of Buddhism," in *The Dao Companion to Japanese Buddhist Philosophy*, ed. Gereon Kopf (Dordrecht: Springer, 2019), 565–73.
77 故にヤソ教者中、インドに仏教の原書なし、大乗は仏説にあらず、釈迦は真に存するものにあらず等と喋々するものあるも、余がすこしも関せざるところなり。その人の伝記つまびらかならず、その教の由来明らかならざるも、余は決して伝記由来をもって、その教を信ずるがごとき無見無識のものにあらず。ただ余がこれを信ずるは、その今日に存するもの哲学の道理に合す

This may be a surprising statement for a onetime Buddhist priest, and it may be doubted whether he would really have rejected his Buddhist beliefs if he would be faced with contrary evidence, but this is the strongest expression of a naturalist attitude within Buddhism that we have encountered thus far.

Uchiyama Gudō and Early Buddhist Socialism

In its modern history, the dominant ideology in Japan has been on the far right of the political spectrum. This does not mean that the majority of Japanese are rightwing extremists, but that political culture, public discourse, and public policy have been predominantly nationalist (and sometimes even racist), authoritarian, antifeminist or sexist, obsessed by loyalty, discipline, and conformity, and enchanted by a glorious but mythical past. Indeed, Inoue Enryō and Inoue Tetsujirō were fervent nationalists, worshiped the emperor, and enthusiastically supported Japan's war efforts, and consequently, were enemies of radical Buddhism more than allies. Nevertheless, there also always have been liberal and socialist undercurrents in modern Japan, and while Buddhism has mostly been allied to the reactionary mainstream,[78] there have been a number of notable exceptions as well.

In 1894 Furukawa Isamu (Rōsen) founded the Warp and Woof Society 経緯会, which was heavily influenced by Inoue Enryō's ideas. It was aiming for a new Buddhism that was free of superstitions,[79] this-worldly in focus, and trans-sectarian.[80] The society was disbanded in 1899 after Furukawa died, but some of its members, including several former students of Inoue, founded a new organization with very similar goals in that same year: the New Buddhist Fellowship 新仏教同志会.[81]

In the first issue of its journal *Shin Bukkyō* 新仏教 (*New Buddhism*), the Fellowship specified its six founding principles. Like its predecessor, it aimed to exterminate all superstitions, but also — and this was new — to "work for the radical reform of society."[82] And Buddhism itself was also in need of radical reform. In the same issue it was written that

るにより、これを排するは哲理に合せざるによるのみ。— Inoue Enryō,『仏教活論序論』(1887), in『井上円了選集』, Vol. 3 (2003): 327–93, at 327–28.

78 The complicity of mainstream, sectarian Buddhism in militarism, fascism, and war in the first half of the twentieth century has been well documented. See Ichikawa Hakugen 市川白弦,『仏教者の戦争責任』(Tokyo: Shunshūsha 春秋社, 1970); Robert Sharf, "The Zen of Japanese Nationalism," *History of Religions* 33, no. 1 (1993): 1–43; and Brian Victoria, *Zen at War*, 2nd edn. (Lanham: Rowamn & Littlefield, 2006), as well as several other writings in Japanese by Ichikawa Hakugen. About Ichikawa's work, see Christopher Ives, *Imperial-way Zen: Ichikawa Hakugen's Critique and Lingering Questions for Buddhist Ethics* (Honolulu: University of Hawai'i Press, 2009).

79 On Inoue's rejection of superstitions, see Jason Ānanda Josephson, "When Buddhism Became a 'Religion': Religion and Superstition in the Writings of Inoue Enryō," *Japanese Journal of Religious Studies* 33, no. 1 (2006): 143–68.

80 James Mark Shields, "Awakening between Science, Art and Ethics: Variations of Japanese Buddhist Modernism, 1890–1945," in *Rethinking Japanese Modernism*, ed. Roy Starrs (Leiden: Brill, 2011), 105–24, and *Against Harmony: Progressive and Radical Buddhism in Modern Japan* (Oxford: Oxford University Press, 2017).

81 James Mark Shields, "Immanent Frames: Meiji New Buddhism, Pantheism, and the 'Religious Secular'," *Japan Review* 30 (2017): 79–95, at 87, and Shields, *Against Harmony*, 97–104.

82 社会の根本的改善を力む — Quoted in Hoshino Seiji 星野靖二, "'Rational Religion' and the Shin Bukkyo [New Buddhism] Movement in Late Meiji Japan," in『近代日本における知識人宗教運動の言説空間—「新佛教」の思想史・文化史的研究』, Report of Grants-in-Aid for Scientific Research no. 20320016, ed. Yoshinaga Shin'ichi, 2012, 205–18.

over time, religions have no choice but to gradually develop and evolve. Therefore it is clear that there will be differences between the faith that was necessary for the establishment of Buddhism as a religion during the ancient period of Śākyamuni [i.e., the Buddha], that of the period of Shinran and Nichiren, and that of our own (Meiji) times. [...] As such, when we see people trying to bring back the old faith of Śākyamuni, Shinran, or Nichiren today in the Meiji period, all we can do is laugh at such a stupid and worthless idea.[83]

Like the Warp and Woof Society, the Fellowship also aimed for a this-worldly Buddhism. Founding member Tanaka Jiroku 田中治六 (1869–?) grounded this this-worldly orientation in Inoue Enryō's realist metaphysics, calling it *genseshugi* 現世主義, "this-world-ism."[84] *Genseshugi* was not so much a metaphysical or philosophical theory, however, as it was a shift from the traditional focus on death in Japanese Buddhism to a focus on life in this world, and thus on this-worldly suffering and its alleviation. Hence, like Inoue, Tanaka and many other members of the Fellowship called for a socially engaged Buddhism.

Another founding member who argued for a socially engaged, this-worldly Buddhism was Watanabe Kaikyoku 渡辺海旭 (1872–1933). Watanabe was a priest as well as an academic and studied Buddhism, Sanskrit, and Pāli in Germany for ten years. Soon after his return to Japan in 1910 he published an article in *Shin Bukkyō* in which he developed a this-worldly orientation into an analysis of this-worldly suffering. He argued that industrial society leaves many people behind, treating them as disposable (屑, literally "scrap" or "debris"). The cause of this problem and related social problems such as poverty is industrial capitalism. If left untreated, these problems would eventually lead to socialist revolution. The remedy he suggested to avoid that was very much like social-democratic welfare.[85]

Despite the call for "radical reform of society," the members of the Fellowship had very moderate political views.[86] Most radical was probably Inoue Shūten 井上秀天 (1880–1945) who traveled extensively through south and east Asia, met Dharmapāla in Ceylon, and was acquainted with Taixu and Uchiyama Gudō, both of whom we'll meet below, as well as a number of other radicals. His travels throughout south Asia lead to an interest in Theravāda Buddhism and the principle of nonviolence (*ahimsā*). Inoue became a pacifist and, for that reason, strongly opposed Japanese imperial aggression and war in general. He was interested in socialism because socialists shared his antiwar stance and was a member of a socialist organization, but about his political views other than his pacifism, little is known.[87]

The first Buddhist priests to openly embrace "socialism" were Takagi Kenmyō 高木顕明 (also known as Enshō 遠松, 1864–1914) and Uchiyama Gudō 内山愚童 (1874–1911). Takagi was a True Pure Land 浄土真宗 priest with a large number of

---

83 Translation from Shields, "Immanent Frames," 87.
84 Hoshino, "'Rational Religion' and the Shin Bukkyo [New Buddhism] Movement in Late Meiji Japan," 210–12.
85 James Mark Shields, "The Scope and Limits of Secular Buddhism: Watanabe Kaikyoku and the Japanese New Buddhist 'Discovery of Society'," in *Buddhist Modernities: Re-Inventing Tradition in the Globalizing Modern World*, eds. Hanna Havnevik et al. (New York: Routledge, 2017), 15–32, and Shields, *Against Harmony*, 116–19.
86 Which is nicely illustrated by Watanabe's aim to avoid revolution mentioned in the previous paragraph.
87 Shields, *Against Harmony*, 124–28.

burakumin 部落民, Japan's outcasts, in his parish. The *burakumin* have long been discriminated and were generally poor, and Takagi became a social activist on their behalf. It was this activism that got him in contact with several more radical socialists, and because of those associations, he was arrested in the *High Treason Incident* 幸徳事件 along with Uchiyama and twenty-four others. Takagi was sentenced to death in 1911, but this was commuted to life imprisonment a day later. He died in prison, apparently by suicide, a few years later.

Socialism was still a very new idea at the time in East Asia and was not always well understood. Anarchism and socialism were rarely distinguished from each other and Marx was still relatively unknown, especially in China. For this reason, it may be more appropriate to call the political ideologies of early-twentieth-century radicals in Japan and China "anarcho-socialism." Within this anarcho-socialism there were two main currents: a primitivist, Romantic current based mostly on the writings of Tolstoy, and a progressive, rationalist current based mostly on Kropotkin. While Tolstoy was critical of industrialization and wanted to return to a preindustrial, rural, idyllic past (that probably never existed),[88] Kropotkin strove to reorganize rather than abolish industrial production,[89] and explicitly connected his anarchism with modern science.[90] And while early twentieth century anarcho-socialism in China was mostly of the Kropotkinian variety,[91] "radicals" in Japan were more often Tolstoyans.

In his "My Socialism" 余が社会主義 (written in 1904 but not published until 1959),[92] Takagi explicitly rejected Tolstoy and Marx, but like Tolstoy's anarchism, his "socialism" was primarily individual (rather than social) and primarily moral (rather than political and economic). He did not aim for political revolution but for a "revolution of thought." Furthermore, Takagi was deeply religious, and his interpretation of socialism is inseparable from his Pure Land beliefs. He wrote, for example, that he considered "the Land of Bliss (Amitābha's Pure land) to be the place in which socialism is truly practiced."[93]

Uchiyama Gudō was a Sōtō 曹洞 Zen priest and abbot of a small temple in a poor and mountainous area near the tourist resort Hakone, where many upper class Tokyoites owned a vacation home. Like Takagi, he was surrounded by poverty and suffering, and like Takagi, he turned to socialism in response, but his turn was considerably more radical. Uchiyama discovered anarcho-socialism in the pages of *Heimin Shinbun* 平民新聞, a short-lived socialist newspaper, in 1904. In that same paper he explained his attraction to socialism in a short letter:

> As a propagator of Buddhism I teach that "all sentient beings have the Buddha nature" and that "within the Dharma there is equality, with neither superior nor inferior." Furthermore, I teach that "all sentient beings are my children." Having taken these golden words as the basis of my faith, I discovered that they are in

---

88 See, for example, Leo Tolstoy, "The End of the Age" (1905), in *Government Is Violence* (London: Phoenix, 1990), 21–52, at 41.
89 Peter Kropotkin, *Fields, Factories, and Workshops* (London: Swan Sonnenschein, 1909).
90 Peter Kropotkin, *Modern Science and Anarchism* (New York: Mother Earth, 1908).
91 See, for example, Alif Dirlik, *Anarchism in the Chinese Revolution* (Berkeley: University of California Press, 1991).
92 Takagi Kenmyō 高木顕明, "My Socialism," trans. Robert Rhodes, *The Eastern Buddhist* 33, no. 2 (2001): 54–61.
93 Ibid., 57.

complete agreement with the principles of socialism. It was thus that I became a believer in socialism.[94]

The three quotes come from the *Great Nirvana Sūtra*, *Diamond Sūtra*, and *Lotus Sūtra* respectively, but the first also expresses a central theme of the *Lotus Sūtra*.[95] About these quotations of scripture, Fabio Rambelli writes that "it seems that Gudō chose these passages out of context and re-signified them in a socialist fashion by translating Buddhist soteriology (salvation) as social liberation."[96] Unfortunately, this is all Uchiyama seems to have written, or all that remains, at least, on the relation between socialism and Buddhism. He was no theoretician but an activist, and as Brian Victoria remarks, he did not claim or possess "special expertise in either Buddhist doctrine or social, political, or economic theory."[97] Nevertheless, he did write a few pamphlets and many letters, and some key aspects of his socialist Buddhism (or Buddhist socialism) can be gleaned from those.[98]

Uchiyama's most important text is his pamphlet *Anarchist Communist Revolution* 無政府共産革命, which he printed himself in 1908 on the illegal press he hid below the altar in his temple. The tone of the pamphlet is angry and incendiary, and it does not seem a particularly philosophical piece, but it includes a rather interesting critique of ideology (in the Marxian sense of that term) or hegemony, which makes it even more radical than it may seem at first glance.

The pamphlet argues against a number of "superstitions," "wrong ideas that people hold precious like sacred things" and "that have penetrated deeply" in everyone's minds.[99] The first superstition that Uchiyama rejects is a common interpretation of karma and rebirth, namely, the fatalistic belief that birth as a poor tenant farmer is retribution for bad deeds in previous lives. He writes that "if today, in our world of the twentieth century, you are still deceived by this kind of superstition, you will really end up like cows and horses."[100] The other superstitions he discusses are economic and political rather than religious, however; these are the beliefs that tenant farmers owe rent to the landowner and tax to the state, and that a country needs an army. While these beliefs are of a different nature than the belief in karma, they serve the same purpose: protecting the status quo, and especially, protecting the interests of landowners and the rich. "If you give up these superstitions the emperor and the rich will no longer be able to afford their own lives of ease and luxury."[101]

---

94 Translation from Victoria, *Zen at War*, 41.
95 See Fabio Rambelli's *Zen Anarchism: The Egalitarian Dharma of Uchiyama Gudō* (Berkeley: Institute of Buddhist Studies & BDK America, 2013), 12 and 86n, for exact locations of the three quotes in the sūtras. Rambelli remarks that "Gudō's citations of the scriptures are incorrect, perhaps due to his lack of familiarity with kanbun (the form of Chinese language in which they are written)" (86n4).
96 Ibid., 13.
97 Victoria, *Zen at War*, 39.
98 Translations of Uchiyama's most important writings as well as several quotes from his letters can be found in Rambelli, *Zen Anarchism*. The original Japanese texts can be found in Kashiwagi Ryūhō 柏木隆法,『大逆事件と内山愚童』(Tokyo: JCA, 1979).
99 Rambelli, *Zen Anarchism*, 48.
100 Translation from ibid., 45.
101 Ibid., 47.

While the term "superstition" recalls Inoue Enryō,[102] Uchiyama's use of the term is much closer to Marx's "ideology" or Gramsci's "hegemony." Marx and Engels wrote in *The German Ideology*:

> The ideas of the ruling class are in every epoch the ruling ideas — that is, the class that is the ruling *material* force of society, is simultaneously its ruling intellectual force. The class that has the means of material production at its disposal thereby commands the means of intellectual production at the same time, [...] The ruling ideas are nothing more than the ideal expression of the dominant material relationships; [...][103]

Uchiyama's "superstitions" play exactly this role: they are the ideas of the ruling class that through that class's dominance become the ruling ideas, and they express the dominant economic (i.e., "material") relations in society, thereby reinforcing and safeguarding them. In other words, "ideology" refers to the values and beliefs that support the interests of the ruling class. Part of that ideology — or of those ideological "superstitions" — in Uchiyama's time was the Buddhist doctrine of karma. He was neither the first nor the last to point out the abuse of this doctrine to justify social injustice,[104] but he was almost certainly the first to embed this in a broader critique of ideology.

Nevertheless, there is an important difference between Uchiyama's "superstitions" and the notions of ideology or hegemony. Ideological or hegemonic ideas are assumed to permeate society more or less automatically. This is especially clear in case of Gramsci, who defines "hegemony" as

> the "spontaneous" consent given by the great masses of the population to the general direction imposed on social life by the dominant fundamental group; this consent is "historically" caused by the prestige (and consequent confidence) which the dominant group enjoys because of its position and function in the world of production.[105]

Uchiyama did not believe that the consent of the masses can be entirely spontaneous, or that the elite's sociopolitical and economic dominance (and consequent prestige) is sufficient to guarantee the spread of the ideological superstitions they depend on. Rather, it requires some form of concerted action to spread and continuously reinforce these ideas. And thus, "[t]he government, using everyone from university professors down to elementary schoolteachers, is doing everything in its

---

102 Inoue was a distant relative of Uchiyama's mother, and Uchiyama may have known him personally, but there is no historical evidence that they ever met. It is unlikely that he was not aware of some of Inoue's works. On Inoue's rejection of superstitions, see Josephson, "When Buddhism Became a 'Religion'."
103 Die Gedanken der herrschenden Klasse sind in jeder Epoche die herrschenden Gedanken, d.h. die Klasse, welche die herrschende materielle Macht der Gesellschaft ist, ist zugleich ihre herrschende geistige Macht. Die Klasse, die die Mittel zur materiellen Produktion zu ihrer Verfügung hat, disponiert damit zugleich über die Mittel zur geistigen Produktion, [...] Die herrschenden Gedanken sind weiter Nichts als der ideelle Ausdruck der herrschenden materiellen Verhältnisse, die als Gedanken gefaßten herrschenden materiellen Verhältnisse; [...] — Karl Marx and Friedrich Engels, *Die deutsche Ideologie* (1846/1932), MEW 3: 9–530, at 46.
104 See, for example, the section "Ambedkar and the 'New Vehicle' in India" below.
105 Antonio Gramsci, *Selections from the Prison Notebooks* (New York: International Publishers, 1971), 12.

power to prevent you from giving up these superstitions."¹⁰⁶ Uchiyama did not mention the responsibility of Buddhists priests or institutional Buddhism in spreading the ideology of karma here, but this may be due to the fact that his focus in this part of the text has shifted to economic and political ideology.

Furthermore, while Uchiyama called the theory of karma and rebirth (without explicitly using those terms) a "superstition" and suggested that it is outdated, this does not imply that he fully accepted a scientific or naturalist worldview. He rejected the theory of karma and rebirth because it was ideological — that is what "superstition" means in *Anarchist Communist Revolution* — and not because it conflicts with science. He did not say anything about the latter.¹⁰⁷

Uchiyama's socialism, like that of his contemporaries, was utopian and romantic; that is, he saw a model of the ideal society in the communal lifestyle of Buddhist monasteries in the past. The Buddhist *saṃgha* (monastic community) with its lack of private property was his ideal. But he was also quite realistic at the same time and sought the causes of this-worldly suffering and poverty in this-worldly economic and political conditions. For this reason, he advocated land reform to alleviate rural poverty. Furthermore, he did not share the insistence on non-violent means typical of utopian socialists and socialist Buddhists. In the contrary, in a letter to Itō Shōshin 伊藤証信 (1876–1963), he wrote that "if priests today are really serious about creating a paradise, they must first overthrow the government. The hand that holds the rosary (juzu) should also always hold a bomb."¹⁰⁸

Uchiyama Gudō was arrested on May 24, 1909 on his way back from religious training at his sect's main temple. The police searched his temple and found the illegal press. They also claimed to have found dynamite, but the truth of this claim is disputed, and even if it is true, it may have been used for railway constructed and only stored at the temple temporarily. He was convicted to twelve years in prison, later reduced to seven, and stripped of his status as a priest by the Sōtō Zen sect. While in prison several other socialists and associates including three more Buddhist priests were arrested in relation with a plot to kill the emperor. It is unlikely that Uchiyama had anything to do with this plot, and the same is true for the vast majority of other suspects, but his pamphlet *Anarchist Communist Revolution* explicitly rejected imperial rule and was considered to be key evidence for his involvement. Uchiyama and twenty-three others were sentenced to death. For twelve convicts, including Takagi, this was commuted to life imprisonment a day later, but Uchiyama was executed on January 24, 1911.

The plot to kill the emperor was itself the result of the suppression of socialism — lacking any other way to give expression to their ideas, the plotters believed that assassinating the nominal head of the government that suppressed them was the only way forward — but the "High Treason Incident" 幸徳事件, as the plot is called, also gave the government the perfect pretext to raise that suppression a few levels.

---

106 Translation from Rambelli, *Zen Anarchism*, 47.
107 In Uchiyama's other main text, *Common Consciousness* 平凡の自覚, he suggested that there is an immortal "mysterious holy spirit" 不可思議の聖霊 within mankind that lead us away from primitive existence and "that makes us progress without pause until we reach the ultimate" (Rambelli, *Zen Anarchism*, 54). This could, of course, be interpreted as a distinctly unscientific, or non-naturalist, view, but the way he used the term "spirit" suggests that it refers to a shared characteristic of human psychology, a longing for freedom and progress we all share, and not to some kind of supernatural entity.
108 Translation from Rambelli, *Zen Anarchism*, 24.

They rounded up the most prominent radicals of the time, executed half of them and locked away the rest, and with the help of the Buddhist sects and leading intellectuals including Inoue Enryō and Inoue Tetsujirō, they orchestrated a propaganda campaign against the left and in favor of nationalism, militarism, and emperor worship. The most important result of the High Treason Incident and its aftermath was that "through the end of the Pacific War no major Buddhist or Christian leader ever again publicly spoke out in any organized way against government policies."[109] Brian Victoria observes that

> this blind and total obedience to the government on the part of Japan's religious leaders, Buddhist and non-Buddhist alike, was destined to become the most enduring religious legacy of not just the High Treason Incident but of the entire Meiji period.[110]

This does not mean that anarchist or socialist undercurrents within and outside Buddhism completely disappeared, but after the High Treason Incident they tended to avoid any open associations with radical ideologies. Itō Shōshin, for example, never used the term "socialism," but instead used the term *muga-ai* 無我愛, "selfless love," as a name and catchphrase for his mixture of Buddhism, pacifism, and a sprinkling of socialism.[111] Other Buddhist thinkers of the following decades with socialist leanings similarly tended to avoid to associate them with the revolutionary left. Instead, they preached a kind of Tolstoyan utopianism that idealized traditional agrarian life. The most famous among them was Miyazawa Kenji 宮澤賢治 (1896–1933), a devout follower of Nichiren who is now best known for his stories and poems.[112]

Seno'o Girō and the Youth League

Several decades earlier in the 1880s, Tanaka Chigaku 田中智學 (1861–1939) had founded Nichirenism, a blend of Nichiren 日蓮 Buddhism and nationalism that gradually moved further and further to the right.[113] Miyazawa was associated with *Nichirenism* for some time, and so was Seno'o Girō 妹尾義郎 (1890–1961), probably the most radical among Japanese radical Buddhists.

Seno'o discovered the *Lotus Sūtra* when he was in high school and started spending time at a local Nichiren temple when he became ill, his sister died of lung disease, and the family business began to fail. He became close with the priest who suggested him to read Nichiren. Several years later, in 1915, he started a pilgrimage. His health had not improved and neither had his family's fortune, so he was forced to give up at the first temple that did not send him away. He stayed at that temple for a few years, studying under the guidance of its head priest, and entered the Nichiren priesthood. In 1918 he joined and started working for the Nichirenist movement. He organized

---

109 Victoria, *Zen at War*, 54.
110 Ibid.
111 Shields, *Against Harmony*, 172–77.
112 Steve Odin, "The Lotus Sutra in the Writings of Miyazawa Kenji," in Gene Reeves, *A Buddhist Kaleidoscope: Essays on the Lotus Sutra* (Tokyo: Kosei, 2002), 283–96, and Shields, *Against Harmony*, 188–97. Part of Miyazawa's most famous poem is quoted in the section "Suffering, Death, and Bodhisattva Ethics" in chapter 13.
113 See also the section "From Saichō to Nichiren" in chapter 2.

meetings, edited and wrote in Nichirenist journals, and traveled around Japan to lecture on Nichirenism and related topics.

Some time in the 1920s, Seno'o started to have doubts about capitalism and its compatibility with his Buddhist beliefs. He started reading Japanese and European left-wing writings, including works by Marx and Engels, Kautksy, Lenin, and Bukharin. Slowly, he moved away from Nichirenism and turned towards the left. In 1931 he published a book titled *Turning towards a New Buddhism* 新興佛教への転身 in which he explained his turn away from Nichirenism and toward a "New Buddhism" 新興佛教.[114] In the same year, he founded the Youth League for New Buddhism 新興仏教青年同盟. The Youth League gained several hundreds of members over the following years and forged links with various other groups on the left, arousing concern by the government, which was increasing its suppression of left-wing and liberal thought from the middle of the 1930s. In 1936 Seno'o was arrested and imprisoned for treason. After five months of interrogation. he confessed his "crimes" and pledged his loyalty to the emperor, for which he apparently never forgave himself. In 1942 he was released from prison, but he stayed in the shadows after that.[115]

In his *History of Japanese Buddhism: The Modern Era*, Kashiwahara Yūsen reports that the Youth League adopted a three-point mission statement in its founding ceremony:

1) Looking up with great respect to the Śākyamuni Buddha, the greatest person that mankind has been endowed with, we vow to realize the establishment of a Buddha land in accordance with the principle of brotherly love.
2) Recognizing and denouncing the wrecked existence of all the established sects that have desecrated the spirit of Buddhism, we vow to promote a Buddhism appropriate to the new age.
3) Recognizing that the capitalist economic system goes against the spirit of Buddhism and obstructs the livelihood and welfare of the general public, we vow to reform this and realize the society of the future.[116]

---

114 Seno'o Girō 妹尾義郎,『新興佛教への転身』(1931), in『妹尾義郎宗教論集』, ed. Inagaki Masami 稲垣真美 (Tokyo: Daizō 大蔵出版, 1975), 260–301.
    I have translated *Shinkō Bukkyō* 新興仏教 here as "New Buddhism." *Shinkō* 新興 means something like "emerging," "developing," or *sometimes* "new." Neither "emerging" nor "developing" is appropriate here, which leaves only "new" as a translation. Shields translates 新興 as "revitalized" or "revitalizing" in his many writings about Seno'o (see next footnote), but I think that this deviates a bit too much from both its literal and intended meaning. Alternatively, one might want to split up the compound and translate 新興 as "newly flourishing," but that sounds rather contrived.
115 Whalen Lai, "Seno'o Girō and the Dilemma of Modern Buddhism: Leftist Prophet of the Lotus Sūtra," *Japanese Journal of Religious Studies* 11, no. 1 (1984): 7–42; Stephen Large, "Buddhism, Socialism, and Protest in Prewar Japan: The Career of Seno'o Girō," *Modern Asian Studies* 21, no. 1 (1987): 153–71; James Mark Shields, "A Blueprint for Buddhist Revolution: The Radical Buddhism of Seno'o Girō (1889–1961) and the Youth League for Revitalizing Buddhism," *Japanese Journal of Religious Studies* 39, no. 2 (2012): 333–51; James Mark Shields, "Seno'o Giro: The Life and Thought of a Radical Buddhist," in *Buddhists: Understanding Buddhism through the Lives of Practitioners*, ed. Todd Lewis (Chichester: Wiley Blackwell, 2014), 280–88; and *Against Harmony*, chapter 6.
116 結成式で可決された三綱領は、一、我等は人類の有する最高人格・釈迦牟尼仏を鑽仰し、同胞真愛の教綱に則って仏国土建設の実現を期す。二、我等は全既成宗団は仏教精神を冒瀆したら残骸的存在なりと認め、之を排撃して仏教の新時代的宣揚を期す。三、我等は現資本主義経済組織は仏教精神に背反して大衆生活の福利を阻害するものと認め、之を改革して当来社会の実現を期す。— Kashiwahara Yūsen 柏原祐泉,『日本仏教史　現代』(Tokyo: 古川弘文館, 1990), 214.

In short, the mission of the Youth League was (1) to realize a Buddha Land (i.e., a more or less utopian society) in this world; (2) to reform Buddhism and reject sectarian Buddhism; and (3) to reject capitalism and reform society. The last point, and to some extent the first two as well, is also evident in a proclamation read in the same meeting: "Recognizing that the suffering in present society is mainly caused by the capitalist economic system, and cooperating [with others] to fundamentally correct that, New Buddhism pledges to [focus on] the welfare of the general public."[117]

The first stated goal in the Youth League's mission statement — realizing a Buddha Land in this world — is more or less the same as Nichiren's,[118] but there is an obvious difference between the Youth League and Nichiren in their ideas about how this goal is to be realized (i.e., reforming society versus worshiping the *Lotus Sūtra*). The second stated goal reminds of Nichiren's critique of the established Buddhist sects at his time, about six centuries earlier. Nichiren also believed that he was formulating a Buddhism appropriate to his age and also repeatedly claimed that the established sects had desecrated Buddhism. Hence, two out three goals in the Youth League's mission statement align closely with Nichiren's ideas. Translations of those two into Late Middle Japanese might have been written or spoken by Nichiren.

Seno'o's book *Turning towards a New Buddhism*, which was published in the same year, is in dialogue form and opens with an answer to a question about his aims in writing it:

> Firstly, rejecting the corrupted established religious organizations, I want to show the true value of Buddhism to the current era. Secondly, I want to unify divided Buddhism and suppress the ugly rivalry between the sects. Thirdly, I want to realize an ideal society of love and equality by participating in a movement to reform the capitalist economic system, which conflicts with the spirit of the Buddha.[119]

These aims are very similar to those of the Youth League, and that is no coincidence, of course. The first and second of Seno'o's aims are combined into the second goal in the Youth League's mission statement, while Seno'o's third aim is split up into the first and third goals in the mission statement. Two years later, Seno'o published another book, titled *New Buddhism on the Way to Social Transformation* 社会変革途上の新興佛教, in which he listed six "demands of modern/contemporary society" 現代社会の要求:

> First, contemporary science advocates atheism, denying the reality of superhuman gods or Buddhas.

---

117 新興仏教は、現社会の苦悩は、主として資本主義経済組織に基因するを認めて、これが根本的革正に協力して大衆の福利を保障せんとする。— 新興仏教青年同盟 (New Buddhist Youth League),『宣言』[Proclamation], 1931, reprinted in Inagaki Masami 稲垣真美,『仏陀を背負いて街頭へ—妹尾義郎と新興仏教青年同盟』(Tokyo: Iwanami 岩波新書, 1974), 3–6, at 4.

118 Near the end of his *Establishing the Peace of the Country* 立正安國論, Nichiren wrote that if people would embrace the *Lotus Sūtra* then this world will become a Buddha land. See the section "From Saichō to Nichiren" in chapter 2.

119 第一は堕落した既成教団を排撃して佛教の真価を現代に発揮したいのだ。第二は分裂した佛教を統一して醜い宗派争ひを絶ちたいのだ。第三は佛陀の精神に反する資本主義経済組織の改造運動に参加して、愛と平等の理想社会を実現したいのだ。— Seno'o Girō,『新興佛教への転身』, 260.

Second, contemporary science advocates "aspiritualism,"[120] denying the doctrine of nirvāṇa that recognizes a life after death.

Third, people nowadays are not satisfied with fairytale-like happiness, but desire the enjoyment of complete happiness in actual daily life.

Fourth, desiring stability in economic life, the general public nowadays demands a reform of capitalism.

Fifth, awakened mankind sublates[121] nationalism and is elated by internationalism.

Sixth, adherents of progressive Buddhism break with sectarian Buddhism and desire its unification.[122]

These "demands" make very clear how Seno'o and the Youth League approached Buddhism. Their "New Buddhism" 新興仏教 was an atheist Buddhism without gods, spirits, or souls, and without an afterlife or nirvāṇa. It was a more or less naturalistic Buddhism with as deep a respect for modern science as for the teachings of the Buddha. Furthermore, the third to fifth demands reveal that New Buddhism was also a humanistic and ethical Buddhism focusing on worldly happiness and worldly suffering, on well-being and misery. This New Buddhist focus on worldly suffering also reminds of how Nichiren described the main problems of his time: "Famine and disease rage more fiercely than ever, beggars are everywhere in sight, and scenes of death fill our eyes."[123]

Seno'o built on Nichiren (he had rejected Nichirenism, but not Nichiren), radicalized his thought, and to some extent transcended it. Even Seno'o's naturalism and this-worldly focus are much more in Nichiren's spirit than they may appear. In a letter to a follower, Nichiren wrote:

> The true path lies in the realities of the world. The [...] [Sūtra of the golden light] states, "If one profoundly discerns secular dharmas, that is precisely the Buddha-Dharma." And the *Nirvāṇa Sūtra* states, "All secular and external scriptures and writings are in each case the Buddha's teaching. They are not heterodox teachings." When the Great Teacher Miao-lo [...] cited the passage from [...] the *Lotus Sūtra*, "All worldly affairs of livelihood and property in no case differ from the true aspect," comparing it with the other [passages cited here] and elucidating its meaning, [he explained that,] although the first two sūtras have a profound intent, [in comparison] they are still shallow and cannot approach the *Lotus Sūtra*.

---

120 Seno'o coins a neologism here that mirrors the Japanese term for "atheism," which occurs in the first "demand." "Atheism" is *mu-shin-ron* 無神論, "no-God-theory." "Aspiritualism," my translation of Seno'o's neologism, is *mu-reikon-ron* 無霊魂論, "no-spirit/soul-theory."

121 "Sublates" translates the Japanese term for Hegel's notion of *Aufheben,* which shows a clear Marxist influence on Seno'o's thought.

122 一　現代科学は超人間的な神佛の実在を否定して無神論を説く。　二　現代科学は死後の生活を認める彼岸主義を否認して無霊魂論を説く。　三　現代人は幻想的幸福に満足しないで実際生活の中に全幸福の享受を欲する。　四　現代大衆は経済生活の安定を欲して資本主義の改造を要求する。　五　目覚めた人類は国家主義を止揚して国際主義を高調する。　六　進歩的佛教信者は宗派的佛教を清算してその統一を熱望する。— Seno'o Girō,『社会変革途上の新興佛教』(1933), in『妹尾義郎宗教論集』, ed. Inagaki Masami 稲垣真美 (Tokyo: Daizō 大蔵出版, 1975), 325–88, at 330.

123 Nichiren 日蓮,『立正安國論』[*Establishing the Peace of the Country*] (1260), trans. Philip Yampolsky, ed., *Selected Writings of Nichiren,* trans. Burton Watson and others (New York: Columbia University Press, 1990), 14. See also the section "From Saichō to Nichiren" in chapter 2.

Where they explain secular dharmas in terms of the Buddha-Dharma, this is not so of the *Lotus Sūtra*. It interprets secular dharmas as immediately comprising the whole of the Buddha-Dharma.[124]

Background of this passage is Nichiren's non-dualism: there is just one world. But if there is just one world, there is also just one epistemology and just one science. Then, there is no fundamental difference between Buddhist insights and scientific insights — insight is just insight, and truth is just truth. Thus, secular dharmas (i.e., theories, teachings, doctrines) are Buddhist teachings. Or in other words, Buddhism ought to incorporate and adjust to scientific knowledge.[125]

Furthermore, there being just one world, this one, a Buddha land can only be realized in this world. Nichiren observed that the world he lived in was very far removed from the ideal. The world he lived in was one of poverty and disaster. To the best of his knowledge, the cause of all this misery was a corruption of Buddhism, insufficient reverence of the *Lotus Sūtra* by the people and state, and therefore, that was what needed to be rectified. But science and philosophy have progressed considerably since Nichiren's time, and to the best of our or Seno'o's knowledge the causes of misery are very different, and consequently, the remedy must be different as well.

The proclamation of the Youth League stated that "the suffering in present society is mainly caused by the capitalist economic system," and Seno'o repeatedly made similar claims. As an explanation of the cause of misery, this seems considerably more plausible than Nichiren's — given all we know, it's rather hard to believe that a lack of reverence of the *Lotus Sūtra* is the cause of poverty in the "developing" world or of the destruction of our planet's climate system, which is already causing massive suffering in most parts of the world and might even threaten mankind's survival. That neoliberal capitalism is to blame for these is considerably more plausible. Erik Reinert, Ha-Joon Chang, and others have documented how capitalist ideology has ruined the "developing" world, preventing it from really developing.[126] Mike Davis, John Rapley, and Naomi Klein have written about the misery and suffering resulting from capitalism's quest to enrich the few.[127] Klein, Bill McKibben, and many others have shown that climate change is driven by capitalism and that the same ideology is to blame for the lack of willingness to prevent climate change from becoming catastrophic.[128] And so forth. And so on.[129] So, contrary to Nichiren's diagnosis, Seno'o's

---

124 Nichiren, "Offerings in Principle and Actuality" (also known as "The Gift of Rice"), trans. Jacqueline Stone, *Some Disputed Writings in the Nichiren Corpus: Textual, Hermeneutical and Historical Problems*, PhD thesis, University of California at Berkeley, 1990, 485–86.
125 There are precedents for this idea in earlier Buddhist texts, including in the Pāli canon itself, where it is stated (in AN8.8) that "[w]hatever is well spoken is all the word of the Blessed One [i.e., the Buddha]." See also Paul Williams, *Mahāyāna Buddhism: The Doctrinal Foundations*, 2nd edn. (London: Routledge, 2009), 42.
126 Reinert, *How Rich Countries Got Rich… and Why Poor Countries Stay Poor*; Chang, *Kicking Away the Ladder*; and Chang, *Bad Samaritans*.
127 Mike Davis, *Late Victorian Holocausts: El Niño Famines and the Making of the Third World* (London: Verso, 2001); John Rapley, *Twilight of the Money Gods: Economics as Religion and How It All Went Wrong* (London: Simon & Schuster, 2017); and Naomi Klein, *The Shock Doctrine: The Rise of Disaster Capitalism* (New York: Henry Holt, 2007).
128 Naomi Klein, *This Changes Everything: Capitalism vs. the Climate* (New York: Simon & Schuster, 2014), and Bill McKibben, *Falter: Has the Human Game Begun to Play Itself Out?* (New York: Henry Holt, 2019).
129 See also chapter 15.

does not seem particularly far-fetched. And assuming that he is right, to realize a Buddha land in this world, capitalism needs to be reformed or replaced.

Seno'o's anti-capitalist conclusion follows from premises that he mostly shared with Nichiren and from a line of reasoning that is also very similar to Nichiren's. Hence, in a sense, he radicalized Nichiren and the *Lotus Sūtra*; that is, he took those to their logical conclusion. But in doing so, Seno'o also transcended Nichiren and the *Lotus Sūtra*. While for Nichiren the Lotus Sūtra was both the starting and end point of his argument (it provided the anti-dualist premise and the solution or conclusion), in case of Seno'o, the *Lotus Sūtra* and associated ideas were more like a ladder that, to borrow Wittgenstein's metaphor, once used to climb up, can be discarded.[130] That is, the *Lotus Sūtra* and the philosophy based on it lead to the non-dualist premise that there is just one world and just one epistemology but plays no further role beyond that. In other words, Seno'o has left the *Lotus Sūtra* behind, or transcended it.

Furthermore, contrary to Nichiren who believed that the *Lotus Sūtra* was the Buddha's final and ultimate teaching, Seno'o was well aware of the key findings of academic research on Buddhism of his time and argued that the *Lotus Sūtra* and other Mahāyāna Sūtras did not literally record the Buddha's sermons at all. In his *Turning towards a New Buddhism*, Seno'o wrote:

> When the times change and social conditions and culture advance, Buddhism develops as well, and the Mahāyāna Sūtras are the many new Sūtras that were produced by later followers of the Buddha in order to adapt to the age [they lived in]; therefore, because the Mahāyāna Sūtras are no direct recordings of the sermons of the Buddha, I say that "Mahāyāna is not the view/doctrine of the Buddha."[131]

Consequently, Seno'o's "transcendence" of the *Lotus Sūtra* is not just an accident of the line of reasoning he radicalized but also a necessity. The *Lotus Sūtra* did not represent the words of the Buddha but was a later production that was appropriate to that later time. It was still appropriate to Nichiren's time according to Seno'o,[132] but has mostly lost its relevance since. Hence, the need for a "New Buddhism," a Buddhism based equally on modern science, on the conditions of this world, and on an interpretation of the teachings of the Buddha.[133]

One of the most common definitions of what it means to be a Buddhist is "one who has taken refuge in the three jewels of Buddha, Dharma, and *saṃgha*." Perhaps unsurprisingly, Seno'o reinterpreted the three jewels as well, thereby implicitly giving an account of what it means to be a "New Buddhist" 新興仏教徒. The term *saṃgha* usually refers to the Buddhist, monastic community (i.e., monks and nuns primarily but sometimes also including lay followers), and "Dharma" refers to the Buddha's teachings, or to Buddhist teachings more broadly. Seno'o reinterpreted

---

130 Or like a raft, which is discarded after crossing a river. Ludwig Wittgenstein, *Logisch-philosophische Abhandlung, Tractatus logico-philosophicus* (1921), Kritische Edition (Frankfurt a.M.: Suhrkamp, 1998), §6.54. The raft metaphor is found in *Alagaddūpama Sutta*, MN 22.13–14. See also chapter 17.

131 佛教も、時代が進移し世態文化が進歩するにつれて発展して、時代に適応すべく幾多の新しき経典が後来の佛弟子によって創作されたのが大乗経典で、従って、大乗経典は直接佛陀の説法記録でないから「大乗非佛説」といふのだ。— Seno'o Girō, 『新興佛教への転身』, 265–66.

132 Ibid., 266–68.

133 Somewhat similar ideas where expressed by Inoue Enryō and in the inaugural issue of the journal of the New Buddhist Fellowship before. See the section "Realism and Reform in Japan — Inoue Enryō" in this chapter.

both terms in a way consistent with his philosophy, but also changed the order of the three jewels, albeit mostly for an expository purpose.

The third jewel, the vow to take refuge in the saṃgha, "is the creed [or] principle of the realization of a cooperative society without exploitation."[134] Seno'o defended his interpretation of saṃgha by arguing that the original community of the Buddha's followers was, more or less, this kind of society. Hence, he interpreted the term not so much as referring to the religious or monastic aspect of the original saṃgha but as referring to its social aspect. (Uchiyama Gudō's ideal society was similarly based on his vision of the monastic community, and variants of the same idea can be found in the thought and writings of many other radical and engaged Buddhists.)

The second jewel, the refuge in the Dharma, "is the fundamental philosophy of the realization of a cooperative society." Seno'o added that "'Dharma' does not so much refer to meditation on emptiness[135] or [the doctrine of] dependent origination as to the denial of private property and the practical '*muga*-ism' (selflessness) of mutual dependence."[136] This reinterpretation of Dharma as incorporating *all* relevant knowledge or doctrine is in line with the rejection of a dualism of worlds and epistemologies already explained above: the secular dharma is part of the Buddhist Dharma (and the other way around). A new term here is "muga-ism," although this is by no means the first occurrence of the term or variant terms in Seno'o's writings and it is also related to Itō Shōshin's *muga-ai* 無我愛.[137] *Muga* 無我 means something like "selflessness" but is also the Japanese translation of the Buddhist term *anātman* or "no-self," referring to the Buddhist teaching that the self is an illusion or that there is no essential, stable, unchanging self. Seno'o used the term "muga-ism" mainly as an apparent antonym to selfishness or egoism.

The first jewel, the refuge in the Buddha, "is the reverence of Śākyamuni Buddha as the ideal experiencer and guide of the second and third [refuges]," recognizing that "there is no need for abstract, ideal Buddhas like Amida [i.e., Amitābha] Buddha, Dainichi Buddha, or the eternal Buddha as idealizations of Śākyamuni Buddha."[138]

---

134 第三の「自帰依僧」は搾取なき共同社会実現の信条である。— Seno'o Girō,『社会変革途上の新興佛教』, 387.

135 The phrase "meditation on emptiness" translates 空観, which is a technical term from Tendai/Tiantai philosophy. 空観 is one of a set of three meditations 三観, including meditation on ultimate/noumenal truth/reality or truth or emptiness 空観, the meditation on phenomenal/conventional truth/reality 假観, and meditation on the mean 中観. The three meditations 三観 are themselves a reflection of Zhiyi's theory of threefold truth: ultimate truth 空, conventional truth 假, and the truth of non-duality 中, which is the truth that ultimate reality and phenomenal reality are not different worlds. (See the section "From Nāgārjuna to Zhiyi" in chapter 2 and the section "Tiantai/Tendai Non-dualism" in chapter 8.)

Seno'o's use of "meditation on emptiness" 空観 as an example of traditional, sectarian Buddhism is interesting. He was, of course, a Nichiren Buddhist and Nichiren considered himself a Tendai Buddhist, which may explain the choice, but 空観 can also be understood as contemplation or meditation on some kind of reality beyond the world of daily experience. The latter is not just an appropriate designation for the kind of Buddhism Seno'o rejects, but by using this term, he grounds that rejection in Tendai/Tiantai philosophy itself. The conventional and ultimate are non-dual, and 空観 is part of a set of meditations aimed at realizing that, and thus at realizing that there is no other world beyond this one: there is only this world.

136 第二の「自帰依法」は、共同社会実現の基礎哲学である。法とはいうまでもなく空観・縁起のそれで、私有否定、相依相関の実践的無我イズムだ。— Seno'o Girō,『社会変革途上の新興佛教』, 387.

137 See the end of the previous section.

138 第一の「自帰依佛」は第二第三の理想的体験者・唱導者としての佛陀釈尊への渇仰である。…、佛陀釈尊の理想内容としての阿弥陀佛や大日如来さては久遠本佛等々の抽象てき理

While the other two refuges as well as the first five of the six "demands of modern [or] contemporary society" may suggest that Seno'o had transcended or left behind Buddhism altogether, his interpretation of the refuge in the Buddha shows that this is not the case. Seno'o's "New Buddhism" may have been unconventional in several ways — it was atheist, humanist, socialist, and more or less secular and naturalist — but he was still very much a Buddhist. The Buddha remained his first and final refuge.

Furthermore, while it can be argued that Seno'o attempted to secularize Buddhism, he simultaneously "Buddhified" secularity. The term "muga-ism" is a good example. Superficially, it may seem to be just a secular term denoting an antonym to selfishness or egoism, but it is very unlikely that it is a mere coincidence that *muga* also means no-self (*anātman*).[139] According to Mahāyāna texts about *bodhicitta* (becoming a Bodhisattva) such as Śāntideva's *Bodhicaryāvatāra*, the selfless compassion (or muga-ism?) that more or less defines a Bodhisattva is inseparable from a deep understanding of no-self (*muga, anātman*). One cannot have one without the other: the wisdom of no-self requires genuine compassion and lovingkindness and the other way around. And this strongly suggest that Seno'o's normative ideal (on the individual rather than the social level[140]) of muga-ism is a variant of the Bodhisattva ideal — a genuine muga-ist is a Bodhisattva.

China/Taiwan — A Pure Land in the Human World

As mentioned above,[141] early anarcho-socialism in China was more often inspired by Kropotkin than by Tolstoy. This difference may partially explain why radical Buddhism was less rare in Japan than in China. Tolstoy was a Christian and explicitly combined religion with his anarchist views, and Tolstoyan Buddhists could relatively easily follow that example. Kropotkin, on the other hand, had a much more secular but also much more radical world view, and was thus much harder to combine with Buddhism. Nevertheless, there also were some radical Buddhists in mainland China and Taiwan. The most important are Taixu 太虛 (1890–1947), who advocated anarchism for some years before becoming a more or less apolitical reformer of Buddhism, and Lin Qiuwu 林秋梧 (also known as Zhengfeng 證峰; 1903–34), a Taiwanese socialist who became a monk, who will be discussed in the next section.

In 1904, Taixu left home and became a monk. In the following years, he would study Buddhist scriptures with some eminent monks, but this left him unsatisfied. From 1908 onward, he became increasingly interested in modern science and politics. He started reading revolutionary literature and got more and more involved in movements for Buddhist reform and revolutionary politics. He gravitated towards anarchism (or anarcho-socialism), was active in the Socialist Party, and published a few articles in anarchist journals. Around 1913 the political climate changed drastically and left-wing movements were increasingly suppressed, and Taixu was also starting to lose faith in some of his anarchist beliefs himself. In October 1914 he had himself sealed in a cell in a monastery, where he mainly studied Yogācāra texts for

---

想佛を必要としない。— Seno'o Girō, 『社会変革途上の新興佛教』, 387.
139 And the reference to mutual dependence, which is another important Buddhist notion, albeit mainly a metaphysical one, in the same phrase is probably no coincidence either.
140 On the social level, the ideal is a Buddha land in this world.
141 In the section "Uchiyama Gudō and Early Buddhist Socialism."

almost three years. In 1917 he left his cell and returned to the world, but he did not return to his radical ideas. Rather, he revived an old Maitreya Pure land cult as an alternative to the Amitābha Pure land cult of Pure Land Buddhism and continued to work for Buddhist reform.[142]

Of the thinkers who influenced Taixu, two are worth briefly discussing here: Kang Youwei 康有為 (1858–1927) and Zhang Taiyan 章太炎 (1869–1936). Kang was a Confucian scholar with an interest in Western science, who argued for political reform. Among his ideas, the one with the greatest impact on early twentieth century Chinese thought in general and Taixu in particular was his progressive, evolutionary reinterpretation of a doctrine found in the Confucian classic, the *Book of Rites* 禮記. In the chapter *Li Yun* 禮運 of that text, three historical or mythical ages are distinguished: the utopian age of "Great Unity" *Datong* 大同 in the distant past, the age of "Lesser Tranquility" 小康, and the "State of Disorder" 亂國.

> When the Great Way was practiced, everyone acted fairly. They elected virtuous and able men, spoke the truth, and cultivated peacefulness. Thus people did not just love their own parents as parents, and did not just [treat] their own children as children. They arranged provisions for the old, employment for the able, and means of growth for the young. They showed sympathy for widows, orphans, the lonely, and the sick, arranging support for all [of them]. Men had work and women had homes. [...] Theft, disorder, and treason did not arise, and thus doors to the outside were not closed. This was what is called the "Great Unity" (*Datong*).
>
> Now the Great Way has become obscured, everyone acts [in the interest of their own] family, [loving only their own] parents as parents, and [only their own] children as children, [only] using goods and power [or] influence for themselves. [...] Thus, [selfish] schemes are flourishing, and [even] the use of force is on the rise. [...] This is what is called the "Lesser Tranquility."[143]

The age of Lesser Tranquility followed the age of Great Unity or Datong, and the age of Lesser Tranquility will itself eventually give way to the State of Disorder,[144] mainly due its lack of a proper morality (i.e., the "Great Way" or "Great Dao" 大道).

In his *Book on the Great Unity* 大同書, Kang argued that the State of Disorder would be followed by another Datong, which he sketched in a mixture of Confucian (mainly Mencian) and liberal, Western terms. It would be a world "without any social distinctions based on property, class, race, or sex." And "the nation-state itself would be suspended by a global parliamentary government, and all people would accept common customs and be united in a common faith."[145] "Social customs would

---

142 Justin Ritzinger, *Anarchy in the Pure Land: Reinventing the Cult of Maitreya in Modern Chinese Buddhism* (Oxford: Oxford University Press, 2017), and Eric Goodell, "Taixu's Youth and Years of Romantic Idealism, 1890–1914," *Chung-Hwa Buddhist Journal* 21 (2008): 77–121.
143 大道之行也，天下為公。選賢與能，講信修睦，故人不獨親其親，不獨子其子，使老有所終，壯有所用，幼有所長，矜寡孤獨廢疾者，皆有所養。男有分，女有歸。... 盜竊亂賊而不作，故外戶而不閉，是謂大同。今大道既隱，天下為家，各親其親，各子其子，貨力為己，... 故謀用是作，而兵由此起。... 是謂小康。—《禮記》[*Liji*],〈禮運〉, §§1–2.
144 Ibid., §10.
145 Charlotte Furth, "Intellectual Change: From the Reform Movement to the May Fourth Movement, 1895–1920," in *The Cambridge History of China, Volume 12: Republican China 1912–1949, Part I*, ed. John Fairbank (Cambridge: Cambridge University Press, 1983), 322–405, at 329.

have cast off all [...] 'selfishness', and would perfectly reflect a spirit of undifferentiated universal love," 仁.[146]

The main significance of Kang's rethinking of the Datong myth is his relocation of utopia from the (mythical) past to the (real) future. He turned Datong from a reactionary into a progressive ideal. Furthermore, Kang presented a very optimistic view of the future. He saw history as an evolutionary process leading more or less automatically towards Datong — utopia would not be brought about by Confucian sages but by history itself (but it would take a few centuries).

From Kang, Taixu inherited Datong utopianism, which would be a lasting element of his thought. From Zhang Taiyan, he learned that anarchism and Buddhism are compatible, and that anarchism can even be grounded in Buddhist thought.[147] This would not be a lasting influence, but it is quite possible that Taixu's interest in Yogācāra in his later thought partially originates in Zhang's influence as well.

Zhang was involved in the nationalist, revolutionary struggle and spent some time in Japan and some time in prison. In Japan, but also in China itself, he studied Yogācāra philosophy, which was an important topic in Japanese academic Buddhology. He was also interested in Daoism (Zhuangzi 莊子 especially) and in Western science, but his attitude towards the latter was very different than that of Kang and many of his contemporaries.[148]

A key term used by Chinese intellectuals around that time was "public/universal principle" *gongli* 公理. A gongli was a single, abstract principle explaining the whole of social or physical reality and thereby justifying certain sociopolitical developments and arrangements. The theory of evolution as it was understood in China at the time was a gongli, and so were materialism and naturalism or the modern, Western scientific worldview in general, as well as the political theories and ideologies based thereon. Zhang was extremely critical of gongli, however, calling them "fundamental intellectual delusions."[149] His criticism was based on the distinction between ultimate and conventional truth he found in Yogācāra. Gongli are fixed, permanent principles, but ultimately everything is impermanent. Permanence is merely apparent — it is a hallmark of conventional reality and illusion. And therefore, gongli are not ultimately true. But if gongli are unreal, then so are the social aggregates — such as the state, society, or the nation — based on them.

Furthermore, based on Yogācāra thought, Zhang also argued for the ontological primacy of the individual. He wrote that "all entities are composed of myriad constituents and thus do not possess their own being. The individuated entities that form the composite, however, can be said to have true being. In contrast, the composite has false being."[150] Hence, states, nations, and other collectives are not ultimately real — both because they are composites and because they are based on gongli — and because they are not ultimately real, they can have no claim on indi-

---

146 Ibid., 330.
147 Ritzinger, *Anarchy in the Pure Land*, 36–37.
148 John Jorgensen, "Indra's Network: Zhang Taiyan's Sino-Japanese Personal Networks and the Rise of Yogācāra in Modern China," in *Transforming Consciousness: Yogācāra Thought in Modern China*, ed. John Makeham (Oxford: Oxford University Press, 2014), 64–99, and Viren Murthy, "Equality as Reification: Zhang Taiyan's Yogācāra Reading of Zhuangzi in the Context of Global Modernity," in ibid., 123–45.
149 Quoted in Wang Hui, "Zhang Taiyan's Concept of the Individual and Modern Chinese Identity," in *Becoming Chinese: Passages to Modernity and Beyond*, ed. Wen-hsin Yeh (Berkeley: University of California Press, 2000), 231–59, at 235.
150 Ibid., 238.

viduals who are "nearer to reality than the composite."[151] The individual comes first, ontologically speaking, and therefore, the individual should also come first sociopolitically speaking. This motivated Zhang's Yogācāra anarchism. The individual "does not come into being because of the world, the society, the nation, or other people. Thus the individual fundamentally has no responsibility toward the world, the society, the nation, and toward people."[152]

While Zhang's Yogācāra anarchism was important for the younger Taixu, Kang's Confucian Datong utopianism was probably more influential in the long run. Taixu came out of his three-year seclusion a moderate reformist and Maitreya cultist. Justin Ritzinger suggests that his vision of the ideal society was still informed by his earlier anarchist ideals,[153] but it seems to me that very little anarchism or socialism is left and that the utopian vision of Taixu after seclusion is just the traditional Confucian ideal of Datong, albeit in Kang's progressive interpretation.

Furthermore, although Taixu rejected gods, ghosts, and other superstitions, he believed in rebirth and otherworldly Pure lands, and he never wholeheartedly embraced science or naturalism. In the contrary, whenever he perceived a conflict between science and his Buddhist beliefs, he always claimed that science was wrong. The best science could hope for was to confirm some of the eternal truths that Buddhism had already found, but ultimately, Buddhism, Yogācāra particularly, gave a more expansive and more accurate view of the nature of reality than science ever could.[154] Hence, the later Taixu was certainly not a radical Buddhist, and even the early, anarchist Taixu was only radical with respect to the sociopolitical dimension.

Nevertheless, there can be no doubt that Taixu advocated a socially engaged Buddhism. The Buddhism he envisioned was a "Buddhism for human life" 人生佛教 or "Buddhism for the human world" 人間佛教, focusing on this life rather than the afterlife, and striving to create a "Pure land in the human world" 人間淨土.

> In the future, Buddhism should pay more attention to problems in this life and should not focus on problems after death. In the past, Buddhism was used by emperors as a tool to fool people with ghosts and gods, but in the future it should be used to study the universal truths of life to guide the development and progress of the people of the world.[155]

The "Pure Land in the human world" is Datong, the utopian future, but in some of Taixu's early writings, it was an explicitly anarchist utopia. For example, the journal article "Three Evils of the World," published in 1913 ends as follows:

> Only by arousing the sense of universal love that is present in everyone can anarchism be implemented. Only by the implementation of anarchism can people break free from the evil of seeking names [i.e., seeking conceptual determina-

---

151 Ibid.
152 Ibid., 234.
153 Ritzinger, *Anarchy in the Pure Land.*
154 Scott Pacey, "Taixu, Yogācāra, and the Buddhist Approach to Modernity," in *Transforming Consciousness,* ed. Makeham, 150–69.
155 今後佛教應多注意現生的問題, 不應專向死後的問題上探討。過去佛教曾被帝王以鬼神禍福作愚民的工具, 今後則應該用為研究宇宙人生真相以指導世界人類向上發達而進步。— Taixu 太虛,〈我的佛教改進運動略史〉(1940), in《太虛大師全書》, Vol. 19/29, ed. Yinshun 印順 (Taipei: Yinshun Culture and Education Foundation 印順文教基金會, 1998), 77.

tions]. To arouse the sense of universal love is the virtue of (human) nature; to implement anarchism is the virtue of wisdom; to break free from the evil of names is the virtue of cutting off [negative mental states; *kleśas*]. When [these] three virtues are perfected, bliss [i.e., the Pure Land] appears. Then all people equally achieve the supreme awakening of the five states of enlightenment.[156]

For the early Taixu, Datong, the Pure Land of bliss (in which everyone works towards their awakening), and anarchist utopia were all one and the same. Anarchism is a requirement for universal awakening, and consequently, the path towards anarchism is the path towards Buddhahood (and vice versa).[157] But the possibility of anarchism — and thus of the Pure Land or Datong — depends on universal love or fraternity 博愛, and although "universal love [or] fraternity is inherent in human conscience,"[158] it does not actually arise because of "false morality" 偽道德. The main obstacles posed by false morality are self-interest and the preferential treatment of close relatives, which are, not coincidentally, exactly the main causes of the degeneration of Datong mentioned in the long quote from the *Book of Rites* in the beginning of this section, and thus also the problems that need to be countered to re-establish Datong. Hence, Taixu argues that "we cannot overthrow the [current] evil system unless we eradicate false morality,"[159] and for that reason, moral education is key to achieving a Pure land in the human world.

While Taixu's analysis of the causes of this-worldly suffering and the path towards its cessation in the Pure Land in "Three Evils of the World" is primarily moral and cultural, in another journal article published a year earlier, he argues for a very different view. According to that article, "A Cursory Discussion of the Equalization of Wealth" 均貧富淺言,[160] "the world's problems are rooted in economic inequality."[161] This, of course, implies a much more radical solution than moral education: to solve the world's problems we must abolish private property and equalize wealth.[162]

It appears that this radical phase in Taixu's thought did not last long; one year later he already saw "false morality" rather than economic inequality and capitalism as the main problem. And the radical elements that were left in his thought further eroded in that of his main intellectual descendants. His most important student, Yinshun 印順 (1906–2005), was a scholar rather than an activist and rejected political activity as a means towards the establishment of a Pure land in the human world. And Yinshun's most important student, Chengyen 證嚴 (1937–), who founded the charity organization Tzu Chi 慈濟, explicitly forbids her millions of followers to

---

156 唯喚起人人本有之博愛心, 乃能實行無政府主義, 唯實行無政府主義, 人類乃能脫離幹名之罪惡。喚起博愛心, 性德也, 實行無政府主義, 智德也; 脫離名之罪惡, 斷德也。三德圓, 極樂出。幹是乎一切眾性皆成就無上正等五覺。— Taixu,〈世界之三大罪惡〉(1913), in《无政府主义思想资料选》, eds. Ge Yichun 葛懋春, Jiang Jun 蔣俊, and Li Xingzhi 李兴芝 (Beijing: Peking University Press 北京大学出版社, 1983), 266–68, at 268. The "five states of enlightenment" 五覺 is a reference to the *Awakening of Faith*.
157 Ritzinger, *Anarchy in the Pure Land*, 87.
158 博愛心既為人類良心本有 — Taixu,〈世界之三大罪惡〉, 266.
159 不鏟除偽道德, 不能傾覆惡制度 — Ibid., 267.
160 Full title:〈均貧富淺言: 以平等教育為手續, 以共產主義〉. Taixu's anarchist writings are not included in his collected writings 太虛大師全書 (probably because its editor, Yinshun, did not have access to them), and are only available at a small number of libraries in mainland China. Unfortunately, I have been unable to obtain a copy of this article, so I'm relying on Ritzinger's discussion here.
161 Ritzinger, *Anarchy in the Pure Land*, 75.
162 Ibid., 77.

engage in politics. (Moreover, Chengyen teaches a very conservative Confucian morality.[163])

There are several reasons that can explain this further de-radicalization of Taixu's "Buddhism for the human world" (or for human life). One is a general tendency of social movements to become less radical over time. Another explanation is the changing political context. In 1949, after the Chinese revolution, Yinshun fled to Taiwan which became a one-party state ruled by the Kuomintang. The latter heavily repressed left-wing ideas and any other kind of socio-political engagement or opposition. Probably the most important explanation, however, is Yinshun's philosophical rather than practical orientation. His primary interest was always Buddhist philosophy, Indian Mādhyamaka in particular, and he rejected many of the popular superstitions and "corruptions" that characterized actual Buddhist practice. He argued in his *New Treatise on the Pure Land* 淨土新論 that there are as many Pure Lands as there are Buddhas and that the way to a Pure land is not to chant some Buddha's name (as Taixu did, hoping to achieve rebirth in Maitreya's Pure Land), but to become a bodhisattva and, ultimately, a Buddha and create a Pure land oneself.[164] Hence, creating a "Pure land in the human world" means bodhisattva practice, or in more practical terms, charity, and thereby creating one's own spiritual Pure land, rather than realizing some kind of ideal society. And consequently, Chengyen's Tzu Chi runs hospitals and is active in disaster relief in many countries but has no socio-political agenda and plays no political role.

Activist Alternatives and Lin Qiuwu

After the end of martial law in Taiwan in 1987, more activist variants of engaged Buddhism emerged. For those, Tzu Chi's charity work was insufficient, and creating a Pure land in the human world also required protecting and cleaning up the environment, socioeconomic reform, and cultural change.[165] The mouthpiece of this movement was the journal *Buddhist Culture* 佛教文化, edited by Li Zhenglong 李政隆.[166]

In his editorials in the first two issues of *Buddhist Culture*, Li targeted the idea that Buddhism is a matter of personal practice and suggested that "Buddhists should examine themselves and should no longer just pursue inner peace or life in the land of bliss";[167] rather they should engage in social welfare work to improve the economic and social environment. Li wonders, "wouldn't 'building a Pure land in the human

---

163 Scott Pacey, "A Buddhism for the Human World: Interpretations of Renjian Fojiao in Contemporary Taiwan," *Asian Studies Review* 29 (2005): 61–77, at 70.
164 Charles Jones, *Buddhism in Taiwan: Religion and the State, 1660–1990* (Honolulu: University of Hawai'i Press, 1999), 126–31; Marcus Bingenheimer, *Der Mönchsgelehrte Yinshun (1906) und seine Bedeutung für den Chinesisch-Taiwanischen Buddhismus im 20. Jahrhundert* (Heidelberg: Forum, 2004); and Ritzinger, *Anarchy in the Pure Land*, 223–34.
165 Charles Jones, "Transitions in the Practice and Defense of Chinese Pure Land Buddhism," in *Buddhism in the Modern World: Adaptations of an Ancient Tradition*, eds. Steven Heine and Charles Prebish (Oxford: Oxford University Press, 2003), 125–42.
166 In his first editorial in that journal, Li wrote positively about the socially engaged spirit of Christianity, which he considered to be lacking in Buddhism, and a few years later he converted to Christianity.
167 佛教徒應自我檢省, 不應再一味消極地只追求內心的平靜, 或追求往生極樂世界 — Li Zhenglong 李政隆,〈什麼是人間淨土?〉,《佛教文化》1 (1990): 2.

world' be more in line with the essence of Buddhist thought?"[168] Like Yinshun, he considers this work the "way of the Bodhisattva," which is not surprising considering Yinshun's immense influence on Taiwanese Buddhism. Li argues that the goal should be "to create a better environment for the propagation of Buddhism and for benefiting life, aiming for a world in which bodhisattvas would want to be reborn."[169]

In a symposium organized by Li and reported in *Buddhist Culture*, Yang Huinan 楊惠南, a professor in the philosophy department of Taiwan National University, argued that Mahāyāna strives for "universal liberation" 普渡 and that there are two ideas about how to achieve this. The first aims to develop a pure conscience in every living being individually. He called this method "mechanical" 機械論式 and suggested that it is influenced by Confucianism. The second method, which he called "organic" 有機論式, "pays attention to the relationships between sentient beings and sentient beings."[170] In other words, the organic approach takes into account that we are social beings rather than isolated individuals, and infers from this that it is more "efficient" to help many interrelated people reach awakening together. According to Yang, the approach of Tzu Chi and similar organizations is mechanical and merely aimed at one's own awakening. Instead, Buddhists should aim for universal awakening, and the state should play a central role in making that possible. If, as often assumed, it is the task of bodhisattvas to bring about a or the Pure land, then this implies that the state should be like a bodhisattva.

An interesting, but almost forgotten thinker who was revived in the pages of *Buddhist Culture*, and also in academic writings by Yang,[171] is Lin Qiuwu (who was already mentioned in the previous section). As an educated youth, Lin was able to help people who found themselves in trouble with the Japanese authorities, which made him a local hero to the Taiwanese but a troublemaker to the Japanese occupying forces. He studied philosophy in Taipei until he was expelled for his anti-Japanese activism only eleven days before his planned graduation. This did not end his activism, but after some further trouble he went to mainland China where he came into contact with Marxist thought and started visiting Buddhist temples. He returned to Taiwan in 1925 and toured around the country lecturing until in 1927 he suddenly became a monk. As a monk, he studied at Komazawa University 駒沢大学, a Sōtō Zen university in Japan. He returned to Taiwan again in 1930, where he became active as Buddhist reformer trying to eradicate "superstitions" and a political activist until his untimely death of tuberculosis in 1934.[172]

Most of Lin's Buddhist writings were published in *South Sea Buddhism* 南瀛佛教. In 1928, not long after he had become a monk, he wrote, "How can we emphasize [rebirth in] the Pure land in the afterlife, while ignoring the reality in Taiwan?!"[173] His answer was that we should not ignore reality but instead create a Pure land in

---

168 建「人間淨土」的宏願, 豈不更契合佛教思想本質？— Li Zhenglong 李政隆,〈共建人間淨土的社會福利工作〉,《佛教文化》o (1990): 2.
169 使成就一個未來更美好的弘法利生環境, 便成爲現世乘願再來的菩薩們所應努力的方向。— Li,〈什麼是人間淨土?〉.
170 注重衆生興衆生的關係 — Yang Jiaqing 楊家青 et al.,〈建設人間淨土：座談會〉,《佛教文化》1 (1990): 10–16, at 15.
171 Especially in the chapter on Lin Qiuwu in his *Outlook of Contemporary Buddhist Thought*. Yang Huinan 楊惠南,《當代佛教思想展望》(Taipei: 三民, 1991).
172 Charles Jones, "Buddhism and Marxism in Taiwan: Lin Qiuwu's Religious Socialism and Its Legacy in Modern Times," *Journal of Global Buddhism* 1 (2000): 82–111.
173 怎樣能偏重來世的淨土、而忽略現實的臺灣！— Lin Qiuwu 林秋梧,〈為臺灣佛教熱叫!!〉,《南瀛佛教》6, no. 6 (1928): 50–53, at 52.

this world 現世的淨土. Lin developed his notion of a "Pure land in this world" independently from Taixu's "Pure land in the human world" 人間淨土 around the same time, and despite the apparent similarity, there are substantial differences between the two notions. As explained above, Taixu's "Pure land in the human world" was strongly influenced by Kang's progressive reinterpretation of traditional Confucian Datong utopianism. Lin's "Pure land in this world" was an expression of his mixture of Buddhism and Marxism. He used the term for the first time, as far as I know, in an article from 1929 titled "Class Struggle and Buddhism" 階級鬥爭與佛教. In that article, he first explained the Marxist idea of class struggle, and then gave a Buddhist perspective on how to overcome class struggle and create an ideal society. That ideal society, the Pure land in the human world, is described as follows:

> From each according to his ability, to each according to his needs;[174] without a trace of selfishness, all of the people will spare no effort to produce collectively. In this society, there will be enough for everyone, and naturally, there will be no theft. In Buddhism, such a world is called the Pure land of bliss.[175]

Lin argued that according to Buddhist teachings of cause and effect, class struggle, capitalism, and all the suffering they produce are ultimately rooted in "the greed of a small part of mankind."[176] And only Buddhism can lead the world away from this suffering and away from the greed that is causing it.

> If mankind can have faith in the one Buddha, follow the Dharma, and act as one, then the shadows of war, possessions, and laws will naturally be completely annihilated in this swirling world. At that time, the Pure land in this world will naturally come true.[177]

This would not happen by itself, however, and a few years later, he suggested that it is the task of bodhisattvas to take the initiative in realizing the Pure land in this world:

> The bodhisattva is the vanguard of social reform. Their fundamental goal is to build a heaven on earth, the [Pure] Land in the west, to make all of mankind (and eventually all living beings) experience no suffering but enjoy various kinds of happiness.[178]

Lin's Buddhism was focused on this world rather than on some hypothetical afterlife. He advocated a modernist view of Buddhism as a rational philosophy rather than a religion. The modernist elements in this view are probably the results of his educa-

---

174 The slogan "from each according to his ability, to each according to his needs" comes from Karl Marx's *Kritik des Gothaer Programms* (*Critique of the Gotha Program*, 1875), MEW 19: 11–32, at 21 and is also quoted by Vladimir Lenin in his *The State and Revolution* (London: G. Allen & Unwin, 1917).
175 各盡所能、各取所需、沒有絲毫的私意、人民個々盡力於公共的生業。在這個社會裡面、家給人足、自然沒有盜竊的事。這樣的世界、佛教則叫做極樂淨土。— Lin Qiuwu,〈階級鬥爭與佛教〉,《南瀛佛教》7, no. 2 (1929): 52–58, at 56.
176 一小部分的人類之貪欲 — Ibid., 55.
177 人類能信一佛、奉一法、行一行、那末兵革、財產、法律等々的形影、自然會由這個娑婆世界完全消滅了。又到這個時候、現世淨土自然就會實現了。— Ibid., 58.
178 菩薩行的便是社會改革的前衛分子。他們的根本目標在於建設地上的天堂此土的西方。使一切人類(再而及於一切生物)無有眾苦但受諸樂。— Lin Qiuwu,〈婦人講座 佛說堅固女經講話(二)〉,《南瀛佛教》11, no. 12 (1933): 18–25, at 22.

tion in Japan where such views were very common at the time, but there is a strong Marxist influence on Lin's thought predating that. Reinforcing his view of Buddhism as a social philosophy rather than a religion was his acceptance of the Marxist idea that religion is a product of historical economic conditions and has always been a tool used by the rich and powerful to make the masses accept their lot.[179] Nevertheless, while Lin accepted many elements of Marxism, the foundations of his thought remained firmly Buddhist.

Near the end of his life Lin started writing about his holistic metaphysics (recalling the Huayan 華嚴 school of Chinese Buddhism) and its relation to his social thought, but tuberculosis unfortunately cut that project short. About a passage in the fairly obscure *Fu Shuo Jiangu Nü Sūtra* 佛說堅固女經[180] he wrote:

> It explains the truth that everything is (the) Buddha. A single person is an individual life from the point of view of the whole, but self and others are inseparable. When individuals gather together, society emerges. In society, we use our strength to help others, and the strength of all others but oneself returns to oneself to support oneself. The universe is even greater than society. The universe is one vast organized system. Just like all the individuals in a society who mutually depend on each other for support and [thereby] form the entire society, all the connected phenomena in the universe — people, animals, mountains and trees, rocks, iron, gold and silver, cloth, and [the four elements] earth, water, fire, and wind — are all maintained in a precise order. Such a universe is the one/whole body of the Buddha![181]

Korea — Han Yongun's Buddhist Socialism

Like Taiwan, Korea was occupied by Japan for most of the first half of the twentieth century, and like Lin Qiuwu, Han Yongun 韓龍雲 (also known as Manhae 萬海 or 卍海; 1879–1944) started his career by getting into trouble with the occupying force. Having become a monk in 1905, Han immediately turned his attention to reformist ideas. Although he was very much interested in Japanese Buddhist modernism, the most important influence on Han's early reformist thought was the Chinese Confucian modernist Liang Qichao 梁啓超 (1873–1929), a student of Kang Youwei.[182] From Liang, he learned about social Darwinism and Western science and philosophy. He largely adopted social Darwinism, but struggled to reconcile the idea of the survival of the fittest with Mahāyāna altruism. Furthermore, while he believed at the time that capitalism and economic inequality were natural and inevitable consequences

---

179 Jones, "Buddhism and Marxism in Taiwan," 97. See also the section "Uchiyama Gudō and Early Buddhist Socialism" in this chapter.
180 T14n0574. Supposedly translated by Narendrayaśa in the late sixth century but probably only preserved in its Chinese translation.
181 說明著一切皆佛的真理。個體即一個一個的生命由全體的來看、自己與他人是不可分開的。個人集合起來便是社會。在社會中用自己之力去扶助別人，而自己以外一切別人之力卻歸於自己保持我們自己。比社會更大的就是宇宙。宇宙是一個大組織體。和社會的各個個人互相相依靠扶助而形成整個社會一樣，宇宙中的森羅萬象一人啦、畜生啦、山川樹木啦、石啦、鐵啦、金銀啦、布匹啦、地水火風啦、一切皆以整然的秩序維持而成的。這樣的宇宙、就是一大佛身。— Lin Qiuwu, 〈婦人講座　佛說堅固女經講話(吾)〉,《南瀛佛教》12, no. 3 (1934): 12–18, at 12.
182 About Kang Youwei, see the section "China/Taiwan: A Pure Land in the Human World" in this chapter.

of the evolutionary struggle for survival, he also became increasingly aware of the inhumanity of capitalism.

Han played a leading role in the nationalist independence movement and was arrested in 1919 and imprisoned for three years for his involvement with the anti-colonial (i.e., anti-Japanese) resistance. Around that time socialism was quickly gaining popularity, especially among younger people. The communists especially were fiercely anti-religious. Because socialists and communists were playing an important role in the anti-colonial movement, Han needed to build bridges, but he also needed to reach an audience that thought that Buddhism was outdated and that socialism was new and progressive. For this reason, he started to write and speak about "Buddhist socialism."[183]

The short article "The Buddhism I Believe in," published in 1924, was such an attempt at bridge-building, but seems to sketch what Han really believed as well. He wrote that "the main article of faith in Buddhism is equality" because all humans and things are endowed with the Buddha-nature (i.e., the ability to reach awakening).[184] By this time Han had shed his earlier belief in social Darwinism, and Kropotkin's notion of mutual aid as an evolutionary principle had replaced selfish competition and the survival of the fittest. "What then is the practical activity of Buddhism?" he asked, answering, "It is universal love and mutual aid."[185]

A somewhat puzzling passage in "The Buddhism I Believe in" is Han's apparent attempt to address the Marxist materialist objection to Buddhism on the ground that it involves an idealist metaphysics:

> The biggest contradiction among modern scholarly theories or principles is that between idealism and materialism. But the impression that Buddhism is built upon an idealist theory is only a superficial one — in reality, mind and matter are not independent from one other in Buddhism. Mind is becoming matter ("emptiness is form"), and matter is becoming mind ("form is emptiness"). So, mind in Buddhism is the mind that includes matter. If we pay heed to the Buddhist sayings, "only the mind exists in the three worlds" and "there is no matter outside of the mind," it becomes even clearer that the mind in Buddhism is inclusive of matter.[186]

First he denies that Buddhism is based on idealism (that is "only superficial") because the two are interdependent or even interchangeable, suggesting some kind of neutral monism.[187] But then he says that "mind includes matter," which is exactly what idealism in the here relevant sense claims, and indeed, near the end of the article he writes that Buddhism "is based upon idealism, which is inclusive — nay, transcendent — of both mind and matter."[188] Does that mean that "the impression that Buddhism is built upon an idealist theory" is *not* "superficial" after all?

---

183 Vladimir Tikhonov and Owen Miller, "Introduction," in Han Yongun, *Selected Writings of Han Yongun: From Social Darwinism to "Socialism with a Buddhist Face,"* trans. Vladimir Tikhonov and Owen Miller (Folkestone: Global Oriental, 2008), 1–36.
184 Han Yongun, "The Buddhism I Believe In" (1924), in *Selected Writings*, 153–54, at 153.
185 Ibid., 154.
186 Ibid.
187 Like Inoue Enryō had suggested before. See the section "Realism and Reform in Japan — Inoue Enryō" in this chapter.
188 Han Yongun, "The Buddhism I Believe In," 154.

Unfortunately, he did not write much else about the topic. In "Meditation and Human Life," the only other explicit discussion of materialism and idealism I'm aware of, Han appears to reject materialism because it denies the role of the mind in human action — "The famous *Communist Manifesto* came not out of Marx and Engels's hands, but out of their minds"[189] — but that is a straw man argument. Materialism does not deny the mind but reduces it to matter. That is, according to materialism mental processes are material or physical processes, usually brain processes.[190]

Han did not write much about his vision of Buddhist socialism. In an interview published in 1931, the interviewer asked him: "If we were to express Buddha's economic ideas in modern language?" Han's response is that "it would be Buddhist socialism."[191] He did not mention "mutual aid" again, and all he said about the Buddha's economic ideas is that he rejected caste, class and social inequality and that

> Sakyamuni was negative about the accumulation of property. He criticized economic inequality. He himself always made his clothes from grasses and wore them while he travelled around preaching. His ideal was to live without the desire to own anything. Aren't the distinctions between "good" and "bad" people really a chronic disease caused by the lust for ownership?[192]

Han's Buddhist socialism was more or less forgotten after his death. The war in Korea lead to the establishment of dictatorial regimes, allowing no opposition, on both sides of the border. Only after democratization toward the end of the 1980s did something like engaged or radical Buddhism reemerge in South Korea. The most important example thereof is the JungTo Society, founded by Pomnyun 法輪 (1953–) in 1988. The JungTo Society is a community of Buddhist activists taking the bodhisattva path seriously. They are involved in charity work, famine relief, environmental activism, and peace activism, among others. The name "JungTo" means "Pure land," and their ultimate aim is to build a Pure land on earth. Members of the society have to take a number of vows. Part of those is the following, summarizing the organization's goals:

> To build a Pure Land (*JungTo*) I vow to let go of self, possessions, and attachment to my own views, and strive to become a bodhisattva who is compassionate towards all sentient beings. [...], we vow to build a peaceful and happy world, a Pure Land, by cultivating a happy life (a pure mind), a peaceful society (good friends), and a beautiful environment (clean land).[193]

---

189 Han Yongun, "Meditation and Human Life" (1932), in *Selected Writings*: 165–80, 165–66.
190 See the sections "The Problem(s) with Materialism(s)" and "Physicalism" in chapter 4.
191 Han Yongun, "Sakyamuni's Spirit: Dialogue with a Journalist" (1931), in *Selected Writings*: 158–64, at 160.
192 Ibid.
193 Quoted in Frank Tedesco, "Social Engagement in South Korean Buddhism," in *Action Dharma: New Studies in Engaged Buddhism*, eds. Christopher Queen, Charles Prebish, and Damien Keown (London: RoutledgeCurzon, 1991), 154–82, at 169.

Vietnam — Thích Nhất Hạnh's Engaged Buddhism

Thích Nhất Hạnh (1926–2022) is credited for coining the term "engaged Buddhism."[194] He became a monk in 1947 and almost immediately started pushing for a modernization of monastic education, eventually leading to the establishment of a new Buddhist university in 1964. During the 1960s and '70s he was involved with the peace movement in Vietnam and with efforts to help the many Vietnamese boat refugees.[195] Because of his anti-war efforts, he was forced to live in exile from 1966 until his return to Vietnam in 2018.

One of the most important influences on Nhất Hạnh's thought was Yinshun. He read all of Yinshun's works, translated at least two of them into Vietnamese, and once called Yinshun "the Buddhist teacher who I revere most."[196] Furthermore, the term "engaged Buddhism" is the English translation of *Nhân gian Phật giáo*, which is the Vietnamese translation of Yinshun's, and originally Taixu's, "Buddhism in the human world" 人間佛教. Like Yinshun, Nhất Hạnh stressed individual bodhisattva practice and rejected political activity. Sally King suggests that Nhất Hạnh's position implied "that an engaged Buddhist can only engage in political protest and opposition and that there is no constructive role that a Buddhist can play in politics, no contribution to the creation of a more just and humane political system" and that "such constructive work should be left to others."[197]

Nhất Hạnh's aversion of participation in politics is probably not just due to Yinshun's influence, however, but also influenced by his own experiences. In his commentary on the *Sutra on the Eight Realizations of the Great Beings* 佛說八大人覺經,[198] he wrote:

> Practicing generosity means to act in a way that will help equalize the difference between the wealthy and the impoverished. Whatever we do to ease human suffering and create social justice can be considered practicing generosity. This is not to say that we engage in any political system. To engage in partisan political action that leads to a power struggle among opposing parties and caused death and destruction is not what we mean by practicing generosity.[199]

Here Nhất Hạnh rejects participation in politics because it involves violent power struggles, and his experiences in Vietnam — and outside Vietnam, but still related to Vietnam — may indeed have suggested that this is the case. However, if this passage is read as a rejection of all participation in politics, then the argument for that rejection fails, because it certainly is not true that party politics always, or even generally, causes "death and destruction."

---

194 Nhất Hạnh used the term "engaged Buddhism" first in Thich Nhat Hanh, *Vietnam: The Lotus in the Sea of Fire* (New York: Hill & Wang, 1967).
195 Sallie King, "Thich Nhat Hanh and the Unified Buddhist Church of Vietnam: Nondualism in Action," in *Engaged Buddhism*, eds. Queen and King, 321–63.
196 Bingenheimer, *Der Mönchsgelehrte Yinshun*, 79. On Yinshun, see the section "China/Taiwan: A Pure Land in the Human World" in this chapter.
197 King, "Thich Nhat Hanh and the Unified Buddhist Church of Vietnam," 354.
198 T17n799.
199 Thich Nhat Hanh, "Commentary," in *The Sutra on the Eight Realizations of the Great Beings*, trans. Diem Thanh Truong and Carole Melkonian (Loubès-Bernac: Dharma Books, 1987), 10–25, at 19.

Understandably, peace and compassion are key themes in Nhất Hạnh's writings. Most of his books focus on mindfulness meditation, and many of them can be described as self-help guides (for a Western audience!) from a Vietnamese Zen Buddhist perspective. For Nhất Hạnh, concrete and practical issues in people's daily lives and more lofty goals like peace are not really different topics — both fall under the same header of "engaged Buddhism." In *Being Peace* he wrote that "engaged Buddhism does not only mean to use Buddhism to solve social and political problems, protesting against the bombs, and protesting against social injustice," but that "first of all we have to bring Buddhism into our daily lives."[200] And one brings Buddhism into one's daily live by practicing mindfulness in whatever one does. This is the real meaning of "engagement" for Nhất Hạnh. "Buddhism must be engaged. What is the use of practicing meditation if it does not have anything to do with our daily lives?"[201]

There is not just one Buddhism, argued Nhất Hạnh. Rather, "the teaching of Buddhism is many" and "when Buddhism enters one country, that country always acquires a new form of Buddhism."[202] Due to his peace activism and exile, Nhất Hạnh's audience became a Western audience, and thus he took it upon himself to help the West to acquire "a new form of Buddhism." Nhất Hạnh was a teacher more than an innovator, however, which is clearest in his more philosophical writings, such as his sūtra commentaries. For example, in his commentary on the *Diamond Sūtra*, he espouses a fairly conventional Zen Buddhist view.[203] What is new or different to some extent is the way of teaching, not the teaching itself. Hence, it could be said that Nhất Hạnh was practicing "skillful means,"[204] and considering his success as a teacher, those means were quite skillful indeed.

Thailand — Buddhadāsa's Dhammic Socialism

Among the monks and activists discussed in this chapter, there probably is no other who has written as much as Buddhadāsa (1906–93; also known under too many other names and titles to list here), whose collected lectures take up almost seventy volumes. Buddhadāsa was in many respects a typical Buddhist modernist: he strove to return to the Buddha's "original" teachings, rejected superstitions and magical beliefs and practices, believed that Buddhism is scientific, and insisted that Buddhism must be relevant in this world and this life.[205] Nevertheless, his attitude toward modernity was mixed, but that too is something he shared with many of the other Buddhist modernists that we have already met in this chapter. While he accepted much of the modern, scientific worldview, he simultaneously idealized a pre-modern, preindustrial past. The latter evolved into his theory of "Dhammic socialism," but also played a role in his personal life choices: rather than settling in Bangkok, he moved into an abandoned temple in the countryside in 1932.

Buddhadāsa went back to the Pāli canon with the intention of identifying therein what the Buddha originally taught and thereby the "fundamental principles of

---

200 Thich Nhat Hanh, *Being Peace* (Berkeley: Parallax, 1987), 58.
201 Ibid., 116.
202 Ibid., 85.
203 Thich Nhat Hanh, *The Diamond That Cuts through Illusion*, rev. edn. (Berkeley: Parallax, 2006).
204 On "skillful means" (*upāya-kauśalya*), see the section "From Nāgārjuna to Zhiyi" in chapter 2.
205 Donald Swearer, "Bhikkhu Buddhadāsa's Interpretation of the Buddha," *Journal of the American Academy of Religion* 64, no. 2 (1996): 313–36.

Buddhism."²⁰⁶ For an idea to qualify as such a fundamental principle it must satisfy two criteria. It must aim at quenching dukkha (which Buddhadāsa or his translators define loosely as "pain, misery, suffering"), and it must have "a logic that one can see for oneself without having to believe others."²⁰⁷ The first criterion captures what was arguably the Buddha's core concern; the second is based on a famous passage in the *Kesamutti Sutta* (also known as *Kālāma Sutta*) in which the Buddha tells people not to rely on tradition, scripture, or reason but only on what they know for themselves.²⁰⁸ What does not pass these two criteria is not part of the fundamental core of Buddhism and must, therefore, be rejected. One of the most important implications hereof is Buddhadāsa's rejection of karma and rebirth.²⁰⁹

> Take the question of whether or not there is rebirth after death. What is reborn? How is it reborn? What is its "karmic inheritance"? These questions don't aim at the extinction of dukkha. That being so, they are not the Buddha's teaching nor are they connected with it. They don't lie within the range of Buddhism.²¹⁰

Furthermore, Buddhadāsa argues that karma and rebirth are inconsistent with what he takes to be a fundamental principle: no-self. If one would develop understanding "to the extent of being able to extinguish *dukkha*" then

> one sees without doubt that there is no self or anything belonging to a self. There is just the feeling of "I" and "mine" arising due to our being deluded by the beguiling nature of sense experience. With ultimate understanding, one knows that, because there is no one born, there is no one who dies and is reborn. Therefore, the whole question of rebirth is quite foolish and has nothing to do with Buddhism at all.²¹¹

Because extinguishing dukkha requires overcoming the illusion of the self, Buddhadāsa's argument depends on the plausibility of the claim that the self is indeed an illusion. There are, of course, very many arguments for this claim in Buddhist scriptures and commentaries, but instead of quoting those, Buddhadāsa opted for a modern, naturalistic approach:

> The Buddhist teachings aim to inform us that there is no person who is a self or belongs to a self. The sense of self is only the false understanding of the ignorant mind. There exist merely the natural processes of body and mind, which function as mechanisms for processing, interpreting, mind, which function as mechanisms for processing, interpreting, and transforming sense data. If these natural processes function in the wrong way, they give rise to foolishness and delusion, so

---

206 Santikaro Bhikkhu, "Buddhadasa Bhikkhu: Life and Society through the Natural Eyes of Voidness," in *Engaged Buddhism*, eds. Queen and King, 147–93.
207 Buddhadāsa Bhikkhu, *Heartwood of the Bodhi Tree* (Somerville: Wisdom, 2014), 3.
208 AN 3:65. For a discussion of the relevant passage in this sūtra, see the section "Metaphysics, Rationality, and Free Inquiry" in chapter 5.
209 Strictly speaking, Buddhadāsa Bhikkhu did not so much reject rebirth as radically reinterpret it. In *Another Kind of Birth* (Bangkok: Sivaphorn, 1969), he defined birth as "the arising of the idea 'I am'" (p. 4). Consequently, whenever the illusion of the self arises in the mind, one is "reborn."
210 Ibid., 4.
211 Ibid.

that one feels that there is a self and things that belong to self. [...] This being so, it follows that in the sphere of the Buddhist teachings there is no question of rebirth or reincarnation.[212]

Ultimately, Buddhadāsa aimed to go even beyond the Buddha's teachings, to a universal truth behind those and behind all other religions. (He shared this aim with Olcott, which was one of the reasons for Dharmapāla's eventual break with Olcott.[213]) This deeper universal truth is the Law of Nature (*saccadhamma*), which Buddhadāsa identified with the Buddhist principle of dependent co-origination or inter-dependency (that is, everything depends on something else for its existence or nature, and ultimately everything depends on everything else). On the basis of this principle, he argued that collectives or wholes have priority over the inter-dependent parts that make up those collectives or wholes. "Dhammic socialism" is the application of this idea to society. Hence, for Buddhadāsa, "socialism" means prioritizing the interests and needs of society over the interests and needs of the individuals within that society.[214] And because socialism, understood as such, follows from the Natural Law, it is the natural state, while capitalism is an immoral deviation.

The aim of Buddhism is peace — both the inner peace resulting from quenching dukkha and worldly peace resulting from alleviating worldly suffering. The cause of dukkha is the illusion of the self and the cause of worldly suffering is selfishness and greed, which is rooted in that same illusion of the self. Dhammic socialism is modeled on the Buddhist *saṃgha*, the community of monks; instead of selfishly taking as much as one can, members of the community take no more than their fair share. In contrast to such Dhammic socialism, socialism *simpliciter* (i.e., "normal" socialism) in Buddhadāsa's view, does not aim for peace but for revenge. Marxist socialism is "just the revenge of the worker"[215] and must, for this reason, be rejected.

The somewhat abstract ideal of Dhammic socialism in which the needs of society or the community outweigh the needs of the individual and in which no one takes more than their fair share raises the question how to organize society to realize this ideal. Buddhadāsa's answer to that question is one we encountered before: a virtuous king, or actually a virtuous dictator. The Dhammic socialist state ultimately depends entirely on a dictator who strictly observes the "Ten Duties of the King" of the Jātaka tales[216] and who, thus, is perfectly virtuous and perfectly committed to the wellbeing of the society he serves. And of course, Buddhadāsa pointed at king Aśoka as the best example of such a benevolent and virtuous dictator.[217]

Buddhadāsa's most influential follower, the social and peace activist Sulak Sivaraksa (1933–), does not accept this latter aspect of Dhammic socialism. He considers it a "weak point" in Buddhadāsa's social thought "because dictators never possess dhamma."[218] For Sivaraksa, the ideal ruler, who still is modeled on king Aśoka and other mythical virtuous kings, is a democrat.

---

212 Ibid., 5.
213 See the section "Sri Lanka — Dharmapāla and Ariyaratne" in this chapter.
214 Buddhadāsa Bhikkhu, *Dhammic Socialism* (Bangkok: Thai Inter-religious Commission for Development, 1986); Tavivat Puntarigvivat, *Thai Buddhist Social Theory* (Bangkok: World Buddhist University, 2013); and Santikaro, "Buddhadasa Bhikkhu."
215 Quoted and translated in Santikaro, "Buddhadasa Bhikkhu," 167.
216 See the section "From Nāgārjuna to Zhiyi" in chapter 2.
217 Santikaro, "Buddhadasa Bhikkhu." On king Aśoka, see the section "Aśoka" in chapter 2.
218 Quoted and translated in Puntarigvivat, *Thai Buddhist Social Theory*, 144.

Sivaraksa advocated "Buddhism with a small 'b'," a kind of Buddhism that is not institutionalized and stripped of ritual, myths, and unessential accretions. The most fundamental teaching of that small-"b" Buddhism is the shared core of all the world religions: the rejection of selfishness.[219] All of this is rather similar to Buddhadāsa, of course, except for the new term "Buddhism with a small 'b'." Sivaraksa's own most important contribution to Buddhist social thought is probably his reinterpretation of the Four Noble Truths and the Five Precepts.[220] Donald Swearer summarizes Sivaraksa's views on suffering, its cause, and its cessation (i.e., the Four Noble Truths) in a this-worldly context as follows:

> Sulak interprets suffering [...] as dehumanizing social, economic, and political forces that sacrifice the long-term common human good for vested self-interest and short-term economic and political gain. The solution to this kind of suffering must come from broad-based, nonviolent, grass-roots movements that challenge narrow self-interest and dehumanizing power.[221]

The first and second of the Five Precepts are the rules that one should not take a life and should not steal, respectively. Sivaraksa interprets the first to not only mean literally killing someone, but also making weapons, depriving people of their livelihood, using chemical fertilizers and insecticides, destroying forests, polluting the environment, and living a wasteful life of excessive consumption. Similarly, the precept against theft becomes a principle of economic justice, and thus a rejection of the exploitation and institutional violence that is an inherent part and aspect of the current capitalist economic system. Hence, the precept against theft implies that one should live a simple life without exploiting others and without becoming complicit in "the unethical tendencies built into the status quo," but it also means that society must be radically reformed or, in other words, that we must "overturn the structures that compel others to live in poverty involuntarily."[222]

Burma — Buddhist Marxism and U Nu

When Buddhism was first introduced to China, Buddhist concepts and ideas were translated and understood in Daoist terms (and other indigenous vocabulary). Somewhat similarly, the introduction of Marxism to Burma in the 1930s by Thakin Soe (1906–89), Ba Swe (1915–87), and others made heavy use of Buddhist terminology. Marxist philosophy was the Marxist *Abhidhamma*, the goal of struggle was *Lokka Nibban* (the Earthly Nirvāṇa), and so forth.[223] According to Emanuel Sarkisyanz, "as the Buddhist aim is the overcoming of *universal* suffering and the Marxist aim is to overcome *economic* suffering, Marxism at one time came to be accepted in Buddhist

---

219 Sulak Sivaraksa, *Seeds of Peace: A Buddhist Vision for Renewing Society* (Berkeley: Parallax, 1992), and Donald Swearer, "Sulak Sivaraksa's Buddhist Vision for Renewing Society," in *Engaged Buddhism*, eds. Queen and King, 195–235.
220 See, for example, Sulak Sivaraksa, "Buddhism and Contemporary International Trends," in *Inner Peace, World Peace: Essays on Buddhism and Nonviolence*, ed. Kenneth Kraft (New York: SUNY Press, 1992), 127–37.
221 Swearer, "Sulak Sivaraksa's Buddhist Vision for Renewing Society," 217.
222 Sivaraksa, "Buddhism and Contemporary International Trends," 131.
223 Emanuel Sarkisyanz, *Buddhist Backgrounds of the Burmese Revolution* (Dordrecht: Springer, 1965).

Burma as a partial or lower truth."²²⁴ Consequently, Ba Swe and others saw Marxism as an economic method for Buddhism. Gradually, some Buddhist thinkers started to push back against this integration of socialist thought into a Buddhist framework. Marxism was seen by them as aiming merely for economic goals and thus as "materialist." Rather than adopting socialism, Buddhism should opt for a middle way between socialism and capitalism, avoiding the materialistic focus on material wellbeing shared by both.

Probably the most important thinker and politician emerging from these intermingling currents of thought was U Nu (1907–95), who rejected Marxism and argued for a kind of Buddhist socialism that was not materialist and that was ultimately aimed at religious rather than economic goals. According to U Nu, capitalism is immoral because it turned people away from religion (i.e., Buddhism). The concentration of wealth in the hands of the elite in capitalism results in a shrinking group of people that are able to perform acts of merit, and consequently, eliminating the inequality caused by capitalism would be a good deed for a Buddhist. However, eliminating poverty and inequality is not a goal in itself: it is merely the economic means towards a religious goal. That goal is to create a world in which everyone can achieve peace of mind by overcoming greed, hatred, and delusion, and in which everyone can work towards their own perfection and future Buddhahood.²²⁵

The means to achieve or approach that end advocated by U Nu can be characterized as a welfare state, but one in which education would be at least as important as providing material welfare. The main obstacle to achieve socialism — a world of plenty wherein people voluntarily share the fruits of their labor and in which there is no poverty, theft, or crime — is ethical. Only moral beings can establish such a socialist society, and consequently, moral and religious education is the key to establishing Buddhist socialism.

Tibet — Gendun Chopel and the 14th Dalai Lama

In the middle of the twentieth century Tibet was one of the most backward parts of the planet. It was so backward that Gendun Chopel (Dge 'dun chos 'phel, 1903–51) felt the need to publish an essay titled "The World Is Round or Spherical" under a pseudonym. The idea that the world is not a flat plane with mount Meru (or Sumeru) in its center was a very controversial idea in Tibet, and it remains controversial among ultra-conservative lamas until this day. According to Gendun Chopel the Buddha actually knew that the world is "round or spherical," but taught that is is flat anyway because he thought that would be most helpful to his audience(s), hence, as a kind of "skillful means."²²⁶

Gendun Chopel became a monk at an early age but continuously ran into trouble for being unusually critical. He enthusiastically embraced science, although there was much he did not understand, and he did not completely reject the supernatural and magical. From 1934 until 1946 he traveled in India and Sri Lanka. Half a year after his return to Tibet he was arrested and imprisoned for approximately three years

---

224 Ibid., 196–97. Ba Yin even claimed that Marx must have been influenced by the Buddha (ibid., 193).
225 This goal is virtually identical to that of a Pure land in this/the human world, but it is based on Theravāda Buddhism rather than Mahāyāna Pure Land Buddhism here.
226 Lopez, *Buddhism and Science*.

on unclear charges. He died in 1951, shortly after he was released from prison, due to liver disease caused by heavy drinking.[227]

While Gendun Chopel certainly was an eccentric, by Tibetan standards at least, and can perhaps be thought of as a Buddhist modernist, he was not a *radical* Buddhist in the sense adopted here. He did not fully accept a naturalistic worldview and aside from his criticism of British colonialism in India he never wrote anything political.[228] About the British, he wrote:

> They introduce the new aspects of modern times, such as railroads, schools, and factories. Their law is only good for the educated and for wealthy families. If one has money and education, anything is permitted. As for the lowly, their small livelihoods that provide the necessities for life are sucked like blood from all their orifices. Such a wondrous land as India appears to be filled with poor people who are like hungry ghosts.[229]

Unlike Gendun Chopel, Tenzin Gyatso, the fourteenth Dalai Lama (1935–), does not believe that the Buddha actually knew that the earth is not flat.[230] For many conservative Tibetans, this must have been a shocking point of view, as it implies the rejection of the age-old dogma of the Buddha's omniscience, a dogma that even many apparent Buddhist modernists have difficulty shaking off. As mentioned in chapter 1, the Dalai Lama explicitly embraces science. In *The Universe in a Single Atom*, he wrote that "if scientific analysis were conclusively to demonstrate certain claims in Buddhism to be false, then we must accept the findings of science and abandon those claims,"[231] and that

> if science shows something to exist or to be non-existent (which is not the same as not finding it), then we must acknowledge that as a fact. If a hypothesis is tested and found to be true, we must accept it. Likewise, Buddhism must accept the facts-whether found by science or found by contemplative insights. If, when we investigate something, we find there is reason and proof for it, we must acknowledge that as reality — even if it is in contradiction with a literal scriptural explanation that has held sway for many centuries or with a deeply held opinion or view.[232]

---

[227] Donald Lopez, Jr., *The Madman's Middle Way: Reflections of Reality of the Tibetan Monk Gendun Chopel* (Chicago: University of Chicago Press, 2006).

[228] But it appears that he was somehow associated with a pro-Chinese revolutionary party at some point. See ibid, 39–40.

[229] Translation: from Donald Lopez, Jr. and Thupten Jinpa, "Gendün Chöpel on British Imperialism," in *Sources of Tibetan Tradition*, eds. K. Schaeffer, M. Kapstein, and G. Tuttle (New York: Columbia University Press, 2013), 751–55, at 754.

[230] Tenzin Gyatso, the 14th Dalai Lama, *The Universe in a Single Atom* (New York: Morgan Road, 2005), 79–80.

[231] Ibid., 3. The Dalai Lama made a similar statement in an op-ed in *The New York Times*: "if science proves some belief of Buddhism wrong, then Buddhism will have to change." Tenzin Gyatso, "Our Faith in Science," *The New York Times,* November 12, 2005, https://www.nytimes.com/2005/11/12/opinion/our-faith-in-science.html.

[232] Tenzin Gyatso, *The Universe in a Single Atom*, 24–25.

A closer look shows that statements like these cannot be taken at face value, however.[233] Firstly, it appears that the Dalai Lama expects a very high degree of certainty from science, especially when science appears to contradict his beliefs. Science must "*conclusively* demonstrate" things. But science does not deal in certainty — that's religion. All that science can do is tell us what, given the evidence, we should provisionally accept as true. The lack of absolute certainty in science is, of course, a rather convenient tool to anyone who prefers not to accept some scientific finding, and this is one of the tools the Dalai Lama uses to maintain his belief in mind–body dualism and reincarnation. Science has not "*conclusively* demonstrated" that those beliefs are false, and thus there is no reason to give them up.[234]

Secondly, Buddhism only needs to give up something if science shows that thing "to be non-existent." Hence, Buddhism only needs to give up mind–body dualism — the thesis that minds are not existentially dependent on the body and are a separate kind of substances — if science shows that such separate, nonphysical minds do not exist. However, this requirement is absurd. Showing that something exists is easy — just hold it out in front of someone or if it's too big, point someone in the right direction — but it should be fairly obvious that it is impossible to *show* something that does not exist. It is fundamentally impossible to show nonexistence of something. The only way to prove that something does not exist is to explain why it cannot possibly exist. (And in case of mental substances in a physical universe, philosophers have done a pretty good job at that centuries ago.) Furthermore, it is impossible to show the nonexistence of something that is not even supposed to be part of the physical universe. Showing or detecting something is a physical act, and therefore, something outside the physical universe cannot possibly be shown, observed, or detected. It cannot possibly interact with the physical universe either, which is one of the main reasons why the notion of mental substances such as souls is nonsensical.[235]

Thirdly, the Dalai Lama does not really accept the authority of science as these quotes might suggest. *The Universe in a Single Atom* is a good example of a trope that is widely shared among Buddhist modernists: science is discovering what the Buddha already knew.[236] The role of science is not that of a teacher telling Buddhism what is true and what is false, but the other way around: science is the student discovering for itself what the teacher (i.e., Buddhism) has already been saying for ages, albeit often in somewhat cryptic terms. Furthermore, there are some areas of knowledge that, in this view, are outside the domain of science. "A real understanding of the true nature of the mind can only be gained through meditation,"[237] said the Dalai Lama elsewhere. Science is limited; Buddhism is not. And consequently, science can never be more than some kind of assistant, humbly confirming some of the more superficial teachings of the master, occasionally dis-confirming something trivial, like the flat earth, but lacking the ability to delve into anything more important or profound.[238]

---

233 On the Dalai Lamai's relation with science, see also Lopez, *Buddhism and Science*, 131–52 and 193–95.
234 This is a kind of fallacious reasoning, called "appeal to ignorance," which is rather common in encounters between science and religion.
235 See also the section "Physicalism" in chapter 4.
236 See, for example, Tenzin Gyatso, *The Universe in a Single Atom*, 50.
237 Quoted in Lopez, *Buddhism and Science*, 34.
238 A similar attitude towards the relation between science and Buddhism can be found in the thought of Taixu. See the section "China/Taiwan — A Pure Land in the Human World" above.

The Dalai Lama has built some impressive defense works around his most sacred beliefs. He requires "conclusive" counter-evidence that is fundamentally impossible for at least two reasons, and to top all of that off, he declares the matter to be beyond the reach of science anyway. None of this should be surprising. On the contrary, it would be foolish to expect otherwise. The Dalai Lama is the spiritual leader of the Gelug school of Tibetan Buddhism. His primary responsibility is to that school, and his primary intellectual commitment is to the teachings of that school. His admission that the Buddha was not omniscient was already shocking enough — to expect that he would throw out mind–body dualism and reincarnation, which he considers core teachings, would be absurd.

The Dalai Lama is not a naturalist. He is often described as an "engaged Buddhist," but he is considerably more radical than most others who share that label. He may be a moderate with respect to matters of science, naturalism, and so forth, but his sociopolitical views are certainly not moderate. He has called himself a "Marxist" or "communist" in several interviews, for example. As far as I know, the earliest interview in which he said something like that dates to 1993 and was published a few years later. In that interview, the Dalai Lama said:

> Of all the modern economic theories, the economic system of Marxism is founded on moral principles, while capitalism is concerned only with gain and profitability. Marxism is concerned with the distribution of wealth on an equal basis and the equitable utilization of the means of production. It is also concerned with the fate of the working classes — that is, the majority — as well as with the fate of those who are underprivileged and in need, and Marxism cares about the victims of minority-imposed exploitation. For those reasons the system appeals to me, and it seems fair.[239]

This does not mean that he identified with nominally Marxist regimes like the former Soviet Union or China, however. On the contrary, he considered those failures and not "true" Marxist regimes. Buddhadāsa rejected Marxist socialism because he saw it as a revenge of the working class against the elite, and the Dalai Lama adopts a similar view.

> I think the major flaw of the Marxist regimes is that they have placed too much emphasis on the need to destroy the ruling class, on class struggle, and this causes them to encourage hatred and to neglect compassion. Although their initial aim might have been to serve the cause of the majority, when they try to implement it all their energy is deflected into destructive activities. [...] The failure of the regime in the former Soviet Union was, for me, not the failure of Marxism but the failure of totalitarianism. For this reason I still think of myself as half-Marxist, half-Buddhist.[240]

In a more recent interview he identified power as a source of corruption:

---

[239] Tenzin Gyatso, the 14th Dalai Lama and Marianne Dresser, *Beyond Dogma: Dialogues and Discourses* (Berkeley: North Atlantic, 1996), 109.
[240] Ibid., 109–10.

> So now in all communist countries, they don't think much, you see, about equal distribution or exploitation. Their main concern is power. [...] I feel I am more Marxist than those Marxist parties [laughs]. Their main concern is power and money. They don't care about equal distribution, about exploitation. I do. I do still.[241]

In a similar spirit, he said in another interview that he is "not only a socialist but also a bit leftist, a communist. In terms of social economy theory, I am a Marxist. I think I am farther to the left than the Chinese leaders."[242] Statements like these raise the question what exactly the Dalai Lama means when he calls himself a "Marxist" or "communist," especially considering that by his own admission, he is not an expert on Marxist philosophy or economics.[243]

According to the Dalai Lama, "original Marxist ideology is very much related to [or] with a sense of altruism, a sense of concern for the well-being of the majority,"[244] and Marxism developed from "the sensibility and concern for the well-being of the majority, of the needy, of the poor, of the suffering people."[245] Contrary to capitalism, which only cares about "gain and profitability," "Marxism is concerned with the distribution of wealth on an equal basis and the equitable utilization of the means of production."[246] Somewhat similar to the onetime Burmese understanding of Marxism as Buddhism in the economic sphere, the Dalai Lama appears to see Marxism as the Buddhist principle of compassion applied to this-worldly suffering.[247] To what extent it is appropriate to call that "Marxism" is debatable, but it should not be brushed aside too easily. When the Dalai Lama said that religious and community leaders "could be invoking karma to support ruling-class ideology,"[248] he consciously expressed a concern shared by many Buddhist modernists and engaged Buddhists in very Marxist terms. Furthermore, he has also said that he encourages Marxism as a tool "to generate courage in poor peasants and workers."[249] And regardless of whether the Dalai Lama's socialism can really be called "Marxism," it certainly is not some kind of halfhearted reformism or romantic utopianism. He demands drastic change, including the abolition of capitalism, and he is not afraid to call for political action to achieve that change:

> The show of wealth by the rich makes the poorer feel envious, jealous. Shouldn't the poorer sections of society embark on some movement, albeit in a nonviolent path, against this show of wealth and this inequality? With support from Marxist theory?[250]

---

241 Anup Dhar, Anjan Chakrabarti, and Serap Kayatekin, "Crossing Materialism and Religion: An Interview on Marxism and Spirituality with the Fourteenth Dalai Lama," *Rethinking Marxism* 28, nos. 3–4 (2016): 584–98, at 588.
242 Noriyuki Ueda and Tenzin Gyatso, the 14th Dalai Lama, *The Dalai Lama on What Matters Most: Conversations on Anger, Compassion, and Action* (Charlottesville: Hampton Roads, 2013), 66.
243 Dhar, Chakrabarti, and Kayatekin, "Crossing Materialism and Religion," 586–87.
244 Ibid., 587.
245 Ibid., 588.
246 Tenzin Gyatso and Dresser, *Beyond Dogma*, 109.
247 Ibid., 15.
248 Dhar, Chakrabarti, and Kayatekin, "Crossing Materialism and Religion," 588.
249 Ibid.
250 Ibid., 591.

Ambedkar and the "New Vehicle" in India

Finally, we return to India. Buddhism had virtually disappeared from India between the tenth and twelfth century due to a combination of factors including foreign invasions and the loss of patronage to Hinduism, but it returned in the twentieth century, mostly but not exclusively due to the mass conversion of *Dalits* (outcasts or "untouchables") following B.R. Ambedkar's (1891–1956) conversion in 1956. Ambedkar was a Dalit himself, but was given the opportunity to pursue higher education. He obtained degrees from American and English universities in law and economics, was the first minister of law and justice after India's independence, and a co-author of India's constitution. He was also an activist for Dalit rights.

In 1956, the year of his conversion and death, Ambedkar wrote an essay "Buddha or Karl Marx" in which he compared Buddhism with Marxism.[251] The comparison is not exactly fair, however. The picture he sketches of Buddhism is highly idealized and isolated from historical reality, while he subjects Marxism to severe but rather facile criticism. Nevertheless, the text is interesting because the very fact that he felt the need to discuss the choice between Buddhism and Marxism illustrates that he thought of the two as addressing similar concerns.

At the time he wrote "Buddha or Karl Marx," Ambedkar had already been researching Buddhism for years, and this research resulted in his magnum opus, *The Buddha and His Dhamma*, which was published posthumously.[252] In this book, Ambedkar presented an original interpretation of the Buddha's teachings that adheres neither to Theravāda nor to Mahāyāna orthodoxy, but borrows from both, and that is often called *Navayāna* or "New Vehicle."

According to Ambedkar, Buddhism is not a religion, but a *dhamma* (the Pāli equivalent of Sanskrit *dharma*). A dhamma is a social contract and moral theory and thus normative: "The purpose of Religion is to explain the origin of the world. The purpose of Dhamma is to reconstruct the world."[253] While there are many possible dhammas, only the Buddha's Dhamma concentrates on suffering and its cessation: "The world is full of suffering and [...] how to remove this suffering from the world is the only purpose of [the Buddha's] Dhamma."[254] Ambedkar's interpretation of suffering or dukkha is unorthodox. He points out that the term includes "sorrow and suffering from social and economic causes" and that "the Buddha was very much aware that poverty was a cause of sorrow," and concludes that "the Buddha's conception of Dukkha is material,"[255] which directly contradicts the common interpretation of dukkha as mainly a kind of spiritual or existential suffering. Obviously, this focus on worldly or material suffering has profound implications.

---

251 B.R. Ambedkar, "Buddha or Karl Marx" (1956), in *Writings and Speeches*, Vol. 3 (New Delhi: Dr. Ambedkar Foundation, 1987), 441–62.
252 There are two more or less "standard" editions of B.R. Ambedkar's *The Buddha and His Dhamma* (1957): the version in *The Buddha and His Dhamma*, in *Writings and Speeches*, Vol. 11 (New Delhi: Dr. Ambedkar Foundation, 1979), and a critical edition, *The Buddha and His Dhamma* (New Delhi: Oxford University Press, 2011). When quoting this book in the following, I'll give page references to both, prefixing page numbers respectively with W (for "Writings and Speeches") and C (for "critical edition").
253 Ambedkar, *The Buddha and His Dhamma*, W322/C172. On dhamma as social contract and moral theory, see ibid., W316–17/C168, W322/C172, W324/C172.
254 Ibid., W121/C68.
255 Ibid., W510–11/C264–65.

A recurring theme in the book is class and caste as a source of suffering. According to Ambedkar, the Buddha left his home to become a wanderer because of war. Contemplating war, the Buddha realized that "the conflict between nations is occasional. But the conflict between classes is constant and perpetual. It is this which is the root of all sorrow and suffering in the world."[256] For this reason, the Buddha rejected class, caste, and the Brahmanic social order locking those in place.

> It was clear to him that [the Brahmanic social order with its caste system] did not serve the interests of all, much less did it advance the welfare of all. Indeed, it was deliberately designed to make many serve the interests of the few. In it man was made to serve a class of self-styled supermen. It was calculated to suppress and exploit the weak and to keep them in a state of complete subjugation.[257]

Inequality causes misery and suffering, and inequality and class struggle are themselves caused by craving and greed. Thus, only righteousness can remove the root causes of inequality and its effects,[258] or in other words, the solution is moral — the Eightfold Path, or Ambedkar's interpretation thereof, will remove "all injustice and inhumanity that man does to man."[259] The Buddha did not teach people to aim for "some imaginary heaven" but rather that "the kingdom of righteousness lies on earth and is to be reached by man by righteous conduct."[260] This focus on moral improvement is not the only feature Ambedkar's vision shares with many of the other Buddhist utopianisms mentioned above. He also saw the *saṃgha* (i.e., the monastic community) as the exemplar of a moral society,[261] and he believed that the virtue of a righteous king would trickle down to his subjects, thus leading all of them to righteousness.[262]

As mentioned, Ambedkar's *Navayāna* (he never used that term himself, by the way) integrates elements of both Theravāda and Mahāyāna. From the latter he adopted the bodhisattva perfections,[263] and compassion is an important virtue in his view. Regarding compassion, he made the rather important point that compassion without wisdom is a potential source of evil.[264] As social and moral psychologists have argued and shown, having compassion with someone can lead to a one-sided focus on that person's interests and disastrous neglect of the interests of others.[265] This is one of the main reasons why some moral theorists reject empathy.[266] Compassion in Buddhism, however, is not supposed to be one-sided but to be extended to all living beings equally.[267]

---

256 Ibid., W57–58/C41.
257 Ibid., W91/C58. On the rejection of caste, class, and inequality, see also ibid., W301ff/C161ff.
258 Ibid., W283–84/C152, W239/C129.
259 Ibid., W129/C73.
260 Ibid., W283/C152.
261 Ibid., W434/C232.
262 Ibid., W406/C219.
263 Ibid., W232/C125.
264 Ibid., W130/C74.
265 C. Daniel Batson, *Altruism in Humans* (Oxford: Oxford University Press, 2011), chapter 8.
266 See, for example, Paul Bloom, *Against Empathy: The Case for Rational Compassion* (London: Bodley Head, 2016).
267 See the last sections of chapter 13.

Ambedkar's Buddha rejected the supernatural, "accepted that reality must rest on proof," and taught that "thinking must be based on rationalism."[268] His teaching did not depend on souls, gods, or an afterlife,[269] nor on his own infallibility,[270] but was entirely aimed at removing this-worldly suffering. He especially rejected the belief in God because that belief only leads to prayer and worship, which lead to the institution of the priesthood in turn, and priests only produce superstition.[271] Superstition, prayer, worship, and priests have no place in Buddhism, and neither do rituals or ceremonies.[272]

According to Ambedkar's Buddha, "It is hard for mankind to give up its belief in the immortality of the Soul and accept my doctrine that the Soul as an independent entity does not exist and does not survive after death."[273] This, however, created a problem for Ambedkar, as the Buddha supposedly claimed that he was not an "annihilationist."[274] He solved this problem through a creative reinterpretation of rebirth. Ambedkar argued that life is essentially energy, and that energy is always preserved.[275] Thus, if one dies, one's life energy just dissipates in the universe, but is not lost.

He also rethought the theory of karma and uncoupled it from rebirth. Karma, in Ambedkar's view, is just the general principle that actions have effects, that good actions tend to have good effects and that bad actions tend to have bad effects, which he considered the foundation of the moral order.[276] His relatively naturalistic approach to Buddhism was not the only reason for rejecting a more traditional interpretation of karma, however. He argued that the Buddha reinterpreted the Brahmanic theory of karma because it "was calculated to sap the spirit of revolt completely" by implying that "no one was responsible for the suffering of man except he himself" and that "revolt could not alter the state of suffering; for suffering was fixed by his past Karma as his lot in this life."[277]

---

268 Ambedkar, *The Buddha and His Dhamma*, W86/C55. See also ibid., W131/C75 and W249ff/C133.
269 Ibid., W121/C68.
270 He rejected superhuman explanations, and therefore, did not claim that he was infallible himself either. See ibid., W222/C121.
271 Ibid., W254–55/C136.
272 Ibid., W121/C68.
273 Ibid., W111/C64. On the rejection of the soul, see also ibid., W259ff/C138ff.
274 In Indian philosophy, the term "annihilationism" is used to refer to schools of thought that claimed that death is the absolute end and that there is no afterlife, soul, rebirth, or anything else that continues, thus that death completely annihilates a living being.
275 Ambedkar, *The Buddha and His Dhamma*, W329ff/C173ff and W348ff/C184–85.
276 Ibid., W243–45/C131–32 and W337ff/C178ff.
277 Ibid., W91/C58.

4

Materialism, Ideology, and the Specter of Marxism

Not all of the Buddhists introduced in the previous chapter are radical Buddhists, and those who might be considered radical are not all radical to the same extent. Given that the goal of this book is to radicalize radical Buddhism — to construct some kind of combination of radical naturalism and radical sociopolitical engagement that is evidently Buddhist — an obvious question is how close these thinkers and activists come to that goal. That question is not easy to answer, however, or at least not objectively.

The section "A Guide to This Book" in chapter 1 mentioned a number of complementary ways in which a position or person can be more or less radical. A position is more radical on the naturalistic dimension to the extent that it involves a more unconditional acceptance of science, a rejection of supernatural entities and explanations, and a focus on this world rather than on some kind of afterlife or otherworldly paradise. And it is more radical on the sociopolitical dimension if it demands more sweeping reform or even revolution, more explicitly or more prominently rejects capitalism, or demands (or allows, at least) a greater political role for Buddhism. Additionally, it was suggested that Marxism and communism are more radical than social democracy or utopian socialism and that an anarchism based on the ideas of Kropotkin is more radical than one based on Tolstoy or some kind of primitivist anarchism. Further criteria of radicality could be distinguished. For example, someone who does not categorically reject violence as a means is more radical on the sociopolitical dimension than someone who does, and a systemic analysis of the causes of worldly suffering is more radical on both dimensions than a more idealist approach suggesting that moral improvement of individuals is sufficient to bring forth a more utopian society.

All of these criteria can, in principle, be operationalized and measured, but this is considerably more difficult in practice than it is in theory. It is not equally clear in all cases where exactly to locate a thinker with regards to all of these and other criteria, and "measurement" is not really a matter of putting a ruler next to the text. There is a lot of subjectivity involved. Despite these problems — which are further aggravated by the fact that I have not studied all of the thinkers and activists introduced in the previous chapter sufficiently to be confident about how they "measure up" — an attempt is still worth the effort because it provides a clearer overview of the terrain. The resulting map is by no means perfect and might even be wrong about some details, but a sketchy map is often preferable to no map at all, as long one realizes that the map is sketchy indeed and does not treat it as if it were conclusive or definitive.

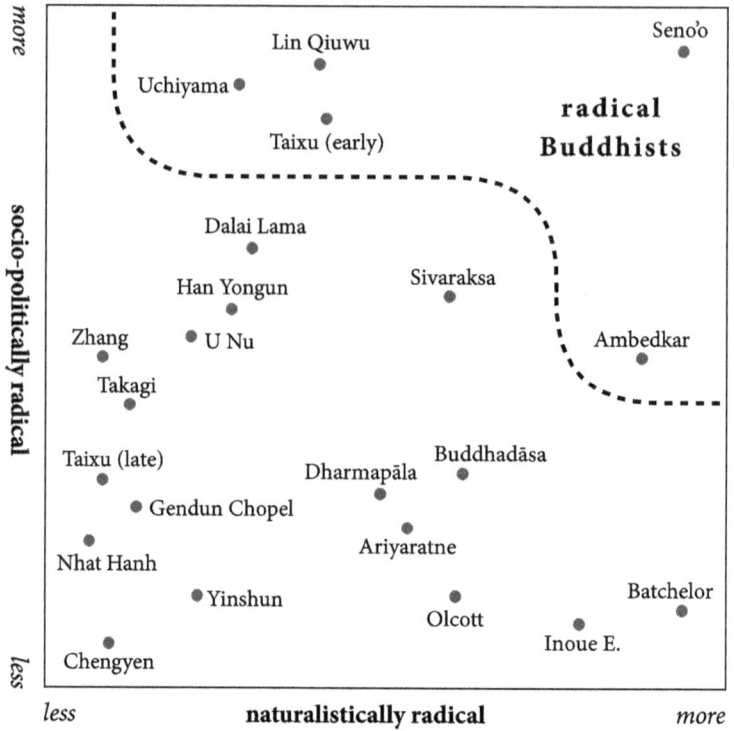

Fig. 4.1. A very provisional map of radical Buddhism and its neighbors.

Figure 4.1 presents such a map. In addition to *roughly* locating the most important Buddhists mentioned in the previous chapter in a two-dimensional space, it separates the "radical Buddhists" from the rest of the field, thereby helping to clarify that designation. Although the figure may appear similar to that in chapter 1, it must be emphasized that the two figures do not map the same area. Firstly, the axes in figure 1.1 are dimensions of *secularity*, while the axes in the figure presented here show degrees of *radicality* on very similar but not identical dimensions. And secondly, all of the thinkers and activists mapped in figure 4.1 can be considered engaged Buddhists or Buddhist modernists, while figure 1.1 also included non-engaged, traditional Buddhism, such as the funeral Buddhism that is common in Japan.

While figure 4.1 illustrates that there are significant differences between these modern Buddhists,[1] there are also important similarities. The main aim of the present chapter is to point out and discuss some of those similarities, and this map helps in separating the more important from the less important patterns. What radical Buddhists like Lin Qiuwu 林秋梧 and Seno'o Girō 妹尾義郎 have in common matters more here than what is shared by Gendun Chopel and Henry Steel Olcott.

---

1 The figure only includes modern Buddhists covered in chapter 3. The most "radical" Buddhist mentioned in chapter 2 is probably Nichiren 日蓮. By more or less the same procedure, adjusting measures somewhat to take the different sociopolitical and economic context into account, Nichiren would end up close to U Nu in figure 4.1, well outside the radical cluster. Hence, while Buddhist engagement may have ancient roots, *radical* Buddhism is very much a modern development.

The figure also illustrates that radicality is rare: half the people in the figure are in the leftmost third, and half of them are in the bottom third. This is not just an artifact of the way the two dimensions are measured, but it reflects the facts that few if any of these thinkers and activists fully accept a naturalist world view and that many allow only a limited sociopolitical role for Buddhism. The latter is related to a widely shared acceptance among non-radicals of the sociopolitical status quo as a given, constraining what is considered possible and thinkable, and limiting the scope of engagement.[2]

Almost all of the Buddhists discussed above share a this-worldly focus, but there are differences in both the foundations and expression thereof. Many emphasize that Buddhism should not only focus on death and better rebirth, but on this life. Tanaka Jiroku 田中治六 called this "this-world-ism" 現世主義,[3] but the most famous expression of this idea is probably Taixu's 太虛 term "Buddhism for human life" 人生佛教. For some of the more radical Buddhists, however, this this-worldly focus is rooted in an austerely realist metaphysics that recognizes only this world and only this life. If there are no other worlds — no other-worldly Buddha lands, Pure lands, heavens, or hells — and if there is no rebirth or afterlife, then this world and this life is all there is, which generates a sense of urgency about this-worldly suffering. If there is only this world and only this life, then nothing can make up for this-worldly suffering, and preventing or alleviating that suffering becomes a top priority. This sense of urgency is absent in less radical thinkers whose this-worldly focus is moral rather than metaphysical, and consequently, their motivation for social engagement is different: preventing or alleviating suffering is part of the bodhisattva path, which seems to imply that it is all about the progress of the believer on that path rather than about the suffering of others.[4]

Almost all of the Buddhists in figure 4.1 who strive for significant sociopolitical and economic reform, which includes more than half of them, model their ideal society on the *saṃgha* (or *saṅgha* in Pāli), the monastic community of monks and nuns.[5] Invariably this saṃgha-based utopianism depends on a heavily idealized picture of the monastic community, a picture that has little to do with historical reality. For example, according to the monastic rules (*vinaya*), monks are not supposed to own anything except for a very small number of personal belongings, but early Indian inscriptions reveal that the vast majority of financial donations made to temples were by wealthy monks.[6] Hence, reality was very different from the scriptural ideal. And the feudal, monastic order that ruled Tibet until 1959 was responsible for a system

---

2   As James Mark Shields observed, "most liberal or progressive writers on Buddhist economics [...] tend to assume that Buddhism is compatible with global capitalism," and "the current ideas of Buddhist economics are unable to imagine real alternatives to contemporary industrial capitalism." James Mark Shields, "Buddhist Economics: Problems and Possibilities," in *The Oxford Handbook of Buddhist Ethics*, eds. Daniel Cozort and James Mark Shields (Oxford: Oxford University Press, 2018), 407–31, at 427, 425. Italics in original.
3   See the section "Uchiyama Gudō and Early Buddhist Socialism" in chapter 3.
4   Yinshun and Chengyen are the best examples of this effectively self-centered version of engagement. See the section "China/Taiwan — a Pure Land in the Human World" in chapter 3.
5   Orders of nuns have died out in much of the Buddhist world. The only remaining lineage of nuns is part of east-Asian Mahāyāna, and consequently, there are no officially recognized nuns in south-Asian Theravāda or in Tibetan Buddhism. Outside Taiwan, where there is a significant number of nuns, the *saṃgha* is almost exclusively male.
6   Gregory Schopen, *Bones, Stones, and Buddhist Monks: Collected Papers on the Archaeology, Epigraphy, and Texts of Monastic Buddhism in India* (Honolulu: University of Hawai'i Press, 1997).

of serfdom, slavery, torture, rape of child monks by other monks, and other atrocities.[7] Indeed, many ordinary Tibetans welcomed the Chinese invaders as liberators (which does not necessarily imply that they still support the Chinese occupation). And a few decades earlier in Mongolia, the socialist revolution also gained support from anti-Buddhist sentiments caused by a similarly feudal and parasitical monastic order. The saṃgha has been quite capable of creating dystopian conditions for many but a tiny elite.

This neglect of historical reality and one-sided focus on a scriptural ideal is not just expressed in this saṃgha-based utopianism, moreover, but it is a common feature of Buddhist modernism or even of religious modernism in general. Protestantism was more or less a scripturalist response to Roman-Catholic ritualism, and Clifford Geertz has observed similar scripturalism in Islamic modernism, for example.[8] An interesting illustration of this scripturalism in Buddhist modernism is Ambedkar's "Buddha or Karl Marx," which compares a scriptural ideal of Buddhism with a rather simplified version of Marxism, and only considers to what extent the theses of Marxism have been "disproved by history" or "demolished by opponents."[9] Apparently, the theses of Buddhism cannot be similarly disproved or demolished — their scriptural authority makes them immune from historical reality.

Another common theme is a call to reform Buddhism or transcend sectarianism. Often, this reformist aim is closely related to scripturalism, as it was in protestantism, but is also linked to the aforementioned this-worldly focus. A common complaint about sectarian Buddhism is that it is just concerned with rites and rituals for the dead rather than with the needs of the living, and this is one of the main issues that reform should address. It seems to me that this charge is somewhat misguided, however. Funeral rites and other rituals for the dead are indeed nominally for the dead, but their real audience is the living, and much of the focus of traditional, sectarian Buddhism on death serves to help believers manage their fear of death, and thereby serves an important psychological need in this life.[10] Hence, this-worldliness and a focus on death are not necessarily as contradictory as they are sometimes or often made out to be. In any case, the topic of reform of Buddhism is outside the scope of this book.

The Problem(s) with Materialism(s)

One of the most widely shared characteristics of the thinkers and activists introduced in the previous chapter is a hesitation to accept materialism. Many of them even explicitly reject materialism, but it is not always clear what exactly they reject. "Materialism" means many different things in different contexts and much of the hesitation and lack of clarity appears to be rooted in ambiguity and confusion resulting from this jumble. At the very least, the following three notions of materialism need to be distinguished.[11]

---

7 Michael Parenti, "Friendly Feudalism: The Tibet Myth," *New Political Science* 25, no. 4 (2003): 579–90.
8 Clifford Geertz, *Islam Observed: Religious Development in Morocco and Indonesia* (Chicago: University of Chicago Press, 1968).
9 B.R. Ambedkar, "Buddha or Karl Marx" (1956), in *Writings and Speeches*, Vol. 3 (New Delhi: Dr. Ambedkar Foundation, 1987), 441–62, at 444.
10 See also the section "Between Science and Religion" in chapter 6.
11 James Mark Shields observed the same problem and made the same distinction between notions of materialism, but his terminology and framing of the distinction is strongly influenced by Marxism

1. *Metaphysical materialism* is the idea that only matter exists, and thus, that the mental can be reduced to material processes and events. Because this implies that energy does not exist either, this view has been superseded by *physicalism*, which holds that everything that exists is physical. In practice there is no essential difference between metaphysical materialism and physicalism — in the context of metaphysics "materialism" is just an outdated name for physicalism. Physicalism contrasts with idealism, which holds that only the mental exist, and thus that matter is just in the mind; substance dualism, according to which both the mental and the material or physical exist as two fundamentally different kinds of substances; and neutral monism, which holds that the mental and the material are two different forms of some neutral "stuff." Hence, physicalism is the denial of mental substances such as spirits and immaterial minds. The mind is somehow ontologically dependent or supervenient on, or emergent from the brain. There is, however, considerable variation in views on how exactly the mental depends or supervenes on, or emerges from the material or physical.

2. *Economic materialism* (or historical materialism) is the view, most famously associated with Karl Marx, that certain economic aspects of society determine or strongly influence certain other aspects of society. Marx suggested, for example, that the distribution of ownership and control of the means of production (e.g., factories, tools, fields, labor power, and so forth) determines key aspects of a society's political and cultural conventions and institutions. A materialist understanding or analysis of history or society focuses on how economic aspects determine or influence other aspects. Consequently, a materialist analysis of suffering seeks the causes of suffering in the economic arrangements, systems, conventions, and institutions that create poverty, inequality, and other forms of material suffering. As such, a materialist analysis is a variety of systemic analysis, which investigates the causal roles of social systems. Another, less common kind of systemic analysis focuses on the roles of power. Systemic analyses and approaches contrast with idealist ones, which assume that morality, culture, and ideas are the factors that determine social institutions, problems, and changes.

3. *Axiological materialism* (also called "vulgar materialism" or "commodity fetishism," among others things) is the more or less single-minded strive for wealth, possession, and material welfare. Materialism in this sense prioritizes "material" goals, such as wealth, capital, goods, and so forth, both for individuals and for society as a whole. Capitalism as a political ideology rather than economic system, for example, is materialist in this sense because its primary aim is economic growth. And some forms of socialism are also primarily focused on increasing material welfare for the masses. Like the other two materialisms distinguished here, axiological materialism contrasts with idealism, which prioritizes immaterial goals like justice and fairness, but it also contrasts with views that prioritize spiritual goals.

A fundamental difference between the first two materialisms and the third is that the first two are descriptive, while axiological materialism is normative. To accept physicalism is to accept the view that reality is physical, and to accept economic

and neo-Marxism, while I aim for a more neutral approach here. Shields, "Buddhist Economics," 421.

materialism is to accept the view that certain economic developments drive other social developments. But to accept axiological materialism is to accept the view that people and societies *should* aim for material goals, such as wealth or some distribution thereof.

Buddhism rejects axiological materialism,[12] but because these three kinds of materialism are not always carefully distinguished, many Buddhists end up rejecting the other two as well. The three are independent from each other — none of the three implies either of the remaining two. And consequently, a rejection of the third should not be a ground to reject either physicalism, as updated metaphysical materialism, or economic materialism.

Many of the Buddhists introduced in the previous chapter rejected Marxism or mainstream socialism because they associated it with axiological materialism.[13] While it is certainly true that there are varieties of socialism that are just concerned with decreasing economic inequality and increasing the material welfare of the masses, this is not the case for Marxism, or at least not for Marx himself. Marx was a metaphysical materialist and an economic materialist, but he surely was no axiological materialist. On the contrary, one of his main reasons for opposing capitalism was the *alienation* it causes. Alienation is the separation of individuals from their own labor power and what they use it for, which thereby denies them agency and changes them into things. Capitalism effectively denies workers their humanity. And consequently, a main goal of Marxian socialism is to reorganize society in such a way that alienation does not occur, which is very much an "immaterial" goal.

Perhaps, most of the modern Buddhists who rejected Marxism did not know or understand this aspect of his thought. In practice, socialists, including many Marxists, tend to focus on material goals such as economic and political equality indeed, and the main text in which Marx developed his views about alienation are his *Economic and Philosophic Manuscripts of 1844*, which were not published until 1932.[14] Nevertheless, that Marx rejected capitalism because it dehumanizes and enslaves people can also be gleaned from the *Communist Manifesto*, which was translated into all major languages of the Buddhist world and widely available from very early on. Describing the "revolutionary role" that the bourgeoisie has played by substituting capitalist exploitation and misery for feudal exploitation and misery, Marx and Engels wrote:

> The bourgeoisie, wherever it came to dominate, destroyed all feudal, patriarchal, idyllic relations. It has mercilessly torn the motley feudal bonds that tied people to their "natural" superiors, and left no other bond between man and man than naked (self-)interest, than callous "cash payment." It has drowned the holy showers of pious exaltation, chivalrous enthusiasm, and bourgeois melancholy in the freezing water of selfish calculation. It has dissolved personal worth into exchange value, and replaced the countless chartered and rightfully acquired freedoms with the single unprincipled [freedom of] free trade. It has, in one word, replaced ex-

---

12 With a possible exception for Ambedkar, whose suggestion that "the Buddha's conception of [suffering] is material" seems to indicate that his *Navayāna* accepts some form of axiological materialism. Ambedkar occasionally contradicted himself, however, so it is not always clear how to interpret him. See the section "Ambedkar and the 'New Vehicle' in India" in chapter 3.
13 The Fourteenth Dalai Lama is an important exception in this respect.
14 Karl Marx, *Ökonomisch-philosophische Manuskripte aus dem Jahre 1844*, MEW 40: 465–588.

ploitation hidden by religious and political illusions with open, shameless, direct, dry exploitation.¹⁵

Here and elsewhere, the main charge against capitalism is not that it produces inequality and material suffering, but that it systematically dehumanizes people by denying them their personal worth and turning them into commodities (i.e., labor power) that have no value other than exchange value. Hence, the goal of Marxism is not an axiological-materialist goal (i.e., wealth or the distribution thereof), but liberation from exploitation, dehumanizing commodification, and alienation. The Dalai Lama called this Marxist sense of concern for the wellbeing of others "spiritual,"¹⁶ and that seems indeed a more appropriate qualification than "materialist." Nevertheless, even if Marxism aims to overcome some kind of spiritual suffering, this is not the same kind of spiritual suffering as that addressed by Buddhism — alienation is not the same as dukkha, although it may be one form or aspect thereof.¹⁷

Physicalism

A naturalist should accept some version of physicalism because there is no plausible alternative, or at least, not from a naturalist perspective. This may sound like a bold claim, but it is one of the few claims that the majority of living philosophers agree about,¹⁸ and for good reasons. The alternatives, as mentioned in the previous section, are idealism, dualism, and neutral monism, and all three are deeply problematic, while the problems for physicalism tend to be vastly exaggerated or based on misunderstandings. An extensive defense of physicalism is outside the scope of this book, but given the importance of the topic, it seems appropriate to briefly rehearse some of the main arguments.

The most influential version of dualism in Western philosophy was proposed by Descartes in the seventeenth century. He argued that the mental and the material are two fundamentally different kinds of substances. Almost immediately, the objection was raised that if they are indeed fundamentally different substances, then the mental and the material cannot possibly interact; that is, a physical event (such as

---

15 Die Bourgeoisie, wo sie zur Herrschaft gekommen, hat alle feudalen, patriarchalischen, idyllischen Verhältnisse zerstört. Sie hat die buntscheckigen Feudalbande, die den Menschen an seinen natürlichen Vorgesetzten knüpften, unbarmherzig zerrissen und kein anderes Band zwischen Mensch und Mensch übriggelassen als das nackte Interesse, als die gefühllose „bare Zahlung." Sie hat die heiligen Schauer der frommen Schwärmerei, der ritterlichen Begeisterung, der spießbürgerlichen Wehmut in dem eiskalten Wasser egoistischer Berechnung ertränkt. Sie hat die persönliche Würde in den Tauschwert aufgelöst und an die Stelle der zahllosen verbrieften und wohlerworbenen Freiheiten die eine gewissenlose Handelsfreiheit gesetzt. Sie hat, mit einem Wort, an die Stelle der mit religiösen und politischen Illusionen verhüllten Ausbeutung die offene, unverschämte, direkte, dürre Ausbeutung gesetzt. — Karl Marx and Friedrich Engels, *Manifest der Kommunistischen Partei* (1848), MEW 4: 459–93, at 464–65.
16 Anup Dhar, Anjan Chakrabarti, and Serap Kayatekin, "Crossing Materialism and Religion: An Interview on Marxism and Spirituality with the Fourteenth Dalai Lama," *Rethinking Marxism* 28, nos. 3–4 (2016): 584–98, at 588.
17 What exactly dukkha is and what kinds of suffering it includes is somewhat controversial. If dukkha is understood broadly, it certainly includes alienation and even material or economic suffering. See the section "Suffering" in chapter 5.
18 Slightly more than half of academic philosophers accept (some form of) physicalism, but this increases to a comfortable majority among those who accept (some form of) naturalism as well. Naturalists tend to be physicalists and vice versa. See *The 2020 PhilPapers Survey*, https://survey2020.philpeople.org/.

stepping on a sharp stone) cannot cause a mental event (such as pain), and a mental event (such as my desire to relieve that pain) cannot cause a physical event (such as moving my foot off the sharp stone).[19] Furthermore, if fundamentally different mental and physical substances would interact, this would violate the law of conservation of energy, one of the most fundamental principles of physics,[20] because physical or mental interaction would either destroy or create energy. The physical universe is a closed system — nothing can go in or out of it. If there would be a separate mental universe, then that would be really separate, without any links or interactions between the two.

Some attempts to save substance dualism accepted this conclusion. For example, according to parallelism, the physical and the mental are like two clocks constructed by God to run in perfect parallel. So, when I_{body} step on a sharp stone in the physical universe, then I_{mind} feel pain in the mental universe. This does, of course, imply that the course of both universes is completely fixed — both are just running two programs decided and implemented by God. Alternatively, according to occasionalism, the material event of me stepping on a sharp stone is an occasion for God to cause the mental event of feeling pain, and my mental event of desiring that pain to end is an occasion for God to cause the material event of me moving my foot of the stone.

Unsurprisingly, parallelism and occasionalism gained few adherents, as did other equally desperate attempts to save substance dualism. Soon a broad consensus arose that the latter cannot be saved, and thus, some version of monism must be accepted. According to monism, there is only one kind of substance. Metaphysical idealists hold that that one substance is mental (and thus that matter is in the mind); according to materialists it is matter, and according to physicalists — that is, updated materialists — it is physical; and neutral monists suggest it is something else. The third of these options has never been popular because it raises more questions than answering them. If matter and mind are both different forms or expressions of some third kind of "neutral" stuff, then what is that stuff? We sort of understand the idea of mental and material substances, but the suggestion of some third kind of substance that is neither mental nor material, but somehow gives rise to both, makes little sense and explains even less.

Idealism in the here relevant sense grew out of empiricism.[21] The British empiricist argued that all our knowledge is based on experience, but the corollary thereof is that all we know is those experiences themselves through mental content and not the supposed external sources of those experiences. And if that is the case, Berkeley argued, then we really have no ground to assume the existence of that external reality and must conclude that everything is in the mind. In other words, contrary to physicalism or materialism, which holds that mental processes are material processes

---

19 One of the first to raise this objection was Elisabeth of Bohemia, who also doubted Descartes's strict separation of mind and body (i.e., matter). She may also have been one of the first to make the important point that the mind (or the "I") is not merely present in the body, but is closely connected to it. See Jacqueline Broad, *Woman Philosophers of the Seventeenth Century* (Cambridge: Cambridge University Press, 2003).
20 Technically, this law has been superseded by the law of conservation of energy and matter since Einstein showed that matter and energy can be converted into each other by his famous formula $E=mc^2$, but that does not help dualism.
21 The topic here is metaphysical idealism rather than epistemological idealism. The former holds that only the mental exists, and therefore, that the material is in the mind; the latter holds that all we can know is our mental representation of the external world and never that external world itself, or some view very much like this. See the section "Idealism" in chapter 7.

(i.e., brain processes), according to idealism what we take to be matter is just mental representation of matter, or matter in the mind.

There are at least two serious problems for idealism. Firstly, as Malebranche was quick to point out, idealism assumes that we actually know what is in our own minds, and we have no reason to believe that that assumption is true. It may actually be the case that we know more about the external world, the world around us, than about our own mental content. Recently, Peter Carruthers confirmed this. In *The Opacity of Mind* he reviews a mountain of empirical evidence that shows that the mind is not nearly as transparent as idealists and many others assumed; most of the time we have no clue about our own mental states and mental contents.[22] Secondly, idealism appears to imply solipsism: if everything is in our mind, then so are other people. Then, only my mind exists. This conclusion appears absurd (and it is), but idealism has considerable difficulty avoiding it.

One may wonder, if the alternatives to physicalism — dualism, idealism, and neutral monism — are so implausible, then why did so many philosophers defend these views, and why does dualism continue to be so common among non-philosophers? It seems to me that there are three main reasons for this: misunderstandings about physicalism, ignorance about cognitive science, and craving for an immortal soul. An example of the first was Han Yongun's rejection of materialism on the grounds that "the famous *Communist Manifesto* came not out of Marx and Engels's hands, but out of their minds."[23] Apparently, Han thought that materialism or physicalism denies the existence of minds and ideas, but that is nonsense. Materialism or physicalism merely denies their *independent* existence. Or in other words, according to physicalism, minds, ideas, and other mental contents are ultimately reducible to, or emergent from physical things and processes. About how that reduction or emergence works there is considerable disagreement, but that does not matter here.

The second reason to reject physicalism is the mistaken belief that cognitive science cannot explain important aspects of the mental, such as consciousness.[24] Cognitive science has made some huge leaps in the past decades, but even if it had not, there is another serious problem for this kind of argument against physicalism: it depends on the assumption that positing an immaterial or non-physical mental substance (as in idealism or dualism) better explains consciousness and other difficult aspects of the mind than physicalist, cognitive science, but that assumption is absurd. We do not know anything about such supposed mental substances or even how we could get to know anything about them, and consequently, those cannot explain anything. Rather than explaining consciousness, dualism or idealism changes it into an unexplainable mystery.

Both historically and sociologically, the third reason why dualism and idealism have been so attractive to many — and why such desperate attempts have been made to save it — is probably by far the most important. Contrary to physicalism, dualism and idealism appear to leave open the possibility of an immortal soul, which is a central dogma in many religions. If the mind is just a brain process, or otherwise ontologically dependent on the brain, then when our bodies die, we die. But if our

---

22 Peter Carruthers, *The Opacity of Mind: An Integrative Theory of Self-Knowledge* (Oxford: Oxford University Press, 2011).
23 See the section "Korea — Han Yongun's Buddhist Socialism" in chapter 3.
24 The Dalai Lama is a good example. See Tenzin Gyatso, the 14th Dalai Lama, *The Universe in a Single Atom* (New York: Morgan Road, 2005). See also the section "Tibet — Gendun Chopel and the 14th Dalai Lama" in chapter 3.

mind is something else, some kind of mental substance, then we might survive our bodily death. We are programmed to crave immortality,[25] which explains why substance dualism is so common, but it takes only a moment of reflection to realize that dualism or idealism cannot deliver the goods either. Again, we do not know anything about mental substances, if they exist, so we do not know whether they are immortal either. For all we know, our immaterial minds, if we would have those, die every time we fall asleep and a new mind is generated when we wake up.

From a naturalist point of view, physicalism is the only game in town,[26] but it is a game with many variants — behaviorism, functionalism, eliminativism, mind-brain identity theory, epiphenomenalism, anomalous monism, and so forth — and all of those have sub-variants that differ in subtle ways. Which of those variants is right is a difficult question, but fortunately, the answer is largely irrelevant here.[27] A question that does need an answer, on the other hand, is whether physicalism is compatible with Buddhism. Mark Siderits answers that question in the affirmative, for Indian Buddhism except Yogācāra, at least. He argues that

> there do not seem to be any insuperable obstacles to accommodating the basic Buddhist project within a physicalist framework. But there remains one major hurdle, namely the doctrine of karma and rebirth. [...] Why would this [doctrine] require an ontology containing nonmaterial elements? Is it because the rebirth process requires some entity that travels from an old to a new body bearing the karmic seeds, and nothing physical could play this role? But this picture of rebirth as transmigration is precisely what Buddhism rejects.[28]

Nevertheless, physicalism does conflict with most interpretations of this doctrine, and it is for that reason that Ambedkar proposed a radical reinterpretation of rebirth and karma, for example.[29] We'll return to the question of the compatibility of rebirth, karma, and related notions with a physicalist or naturalist worldview in chapter 9,[30] but one may wonder how essential the doctrine of karma and rebirth really is. Of course, the Dalai Lama and many others consider it a cornerstone of Buddhism,[31] but it is not immediately clear why that should be the case. Siderits suggests that

> while [the doctrine of karma and rebirth] has played an important role in many Buddhist cultures, it is not crucial to the central project of Buddhism. Indeed, if

---

25 This psychological need and its relation with religion will be discussed in section "Between Science and Religion" in chapter 6.
26 Apparent arguments against physicalism in more recent philosophical literature often depend on the mistaken idea that mental substances can explain anything, or on exotic thought experiments (which can be interpreted in multiple ways and tend to be rather unconvincing from a methodological naturalist perspective), or are merely arguments against specific varieties of physicalism (reductionism, particularly) rather than against physicalism in general.
27 For my answer, see Lajos Brons, "Patterns, Noise, and Beliefs," *Principia* 23, no. 1 (2019): 19–51.
28 Mark Siderits, "Buddhism and Techno-Physicalism: Is the Eightfold Path a Program?" *Philosophy East & West* 51, no. 3 (2001): 307–14, at 311.
29 See the section "Ambedkar and the 'New Vehicle' in India" in chapter 3.
30 See the sections "Essences, Freedom, Paradise, and Other Incoherences" and "Posits and Phenomenal Reality" in chapter 9.
31 But Buddhadāsa, for example, explicitly rejected karma and rebirth as a Buddhist doctrine. See the section "Thailand — Buddhadāsa's Dhammic Socialism" in chapter 3.

I take myself to live only one life instead of the indefinitely many lives promised by rebirth, then the fact of my own mortality takes on even greater significance, for I cannot then defer seeking a solution to the problem of suffering to some future life.³²

If anything, physicalism makes the problem of suffering, and thus the need for a solution, more urgent. And this it has in common with the this-worldly realism that rejects supernatural heavens and Pure lands.³³

Moralistic versus Systemic Critique

In the *Shōbōgenzō* chapter *Genjōkōan*, Dōgen 道元 wrote that "of all the many aspects of things, we can only see those that we have learned to see."³⁴ What we see in phenomenal reality around us depends on what kinds of things we have learned to recognize and categorize, and we mostly remain unaware of other perspectives.³⁵ Dōgen's point does not just apply to metaphysics, but to pretty much anything. We only see what we have learned to see.

The worldview of traditional Buddhism is pre-modern. Buddhist modernists attempted and attempt to modernize that worldview, but such attempts at modernization are almost inevitably incomplete. Dogmas (such as karma and rebirth) are effectively immune to modernization, but in addition to those, there are also aspects of Buddhism that many modernizers have not learned to see and thus remain unaware of. One important remnant of pre-modernity in the thought of many but not all of the modern Buddhists discussed in the previous chapter is a kind of *pre-modern individualism*.

One of the most important revolutions in European intellectual history took place in and around the period that Reinhart Koselleck has called the *Sattelzeit* (saddle-time; "saddle" in the sense of a pass in a mountain ridge).³⁶ Europeans living before and after the Sattelzeit — which lasted from approximately 1750 to 1850 in Germany but started a bit earlier in France, for example — were living in different worlds and not only because of the industrial revolution, which took place around the same time. People before the Sattelzeit were lacking many of the abstract social concepts that we are used to now — concepts like "state," "society," "culture," and so forth. Some of the *words* were already in use, but they did not mean exactly the same things.

The concept of the "state" was one of the first to develop, and this development actually started before the Sattelzeit. The closest pre-modern equivalent of the state was the household of the king. There was no notion of the state as some kind of social

---

32 Siderits, "Buddhism and Techno-Physicalism," 312.
33 See the this chapter's introduction, as well as chapter 9.
34 This is a paraphrase of the following passage: "Either in dust [i.e., as layman, seeing nothing but the ordinary phenomena] or outside the frame [i.e., as an accomplished monk, seeing beyond the ordinary], of all the numerous aspects [of things], we can see and understand only those that we have developed eyes of learning [i.e., capability] for." 塵中格外。オホク様子ヲ帯セリトイヘトモ。參學眼力ノオヨフハカリヲ見取會取スルナリ。— Dōgen 道元,『正法眼藏』,「現成公案」(1231–53), T82n2582, 24b.
35 See the section "Relativism and Perspectivism in Yogācāra and Tiantai" in chapter 8.
36 Reinhart Koselleck, "Einleitung," in *Geschichtliche Grundbegriffe: Historisches Lexikon zur politisch-sozialen Sprache in Deutschland*, Vol. 1: *A–D*, eds. Otto Brunner, Werner Conze, and Reinhart Koselleck (Stuttgart: Klett Cotta, 1972), xiii–xxvii, at xv.

abstraction or institution separate from the person of the king and his possessions and entitlements yet. An even more important step was the development of the concept of "society" as something separate from the state or the household of the king and the individuals within a society.[37] It is hard to overestimate the importance of the invention of "society" — without it, there would have been no social science, no social philosophy,[38] and no political ideologies.[39] And without it there can be no analysis of the *social* causes of social problems, and no critique of social problems in *social* terms.

This lack of a social perspective is further reinforced by another common aspect of ancient cultures: *ahistoricism*. In an overview of possible indicators separating "civilized" from "uncivilized" societies — in a descriptive rather than normative sense of the term "civilized" — Robert Bierstedt mentioned that uncivilized societies have "history but no historiography."[40] In other words, ancient and "primitive" cultures have histories but no awareness thereof. More specifically, they lack an awareness of historical change and development. Instead, it is assumed that almost everything has stayed the same and will always stay the same. Numerous Buddhist sūtras and Jātaka tales assuming time-spans of many millions of years without any kind of sociopolitical, technological, or other kind of change are a case in point.

Ahistoricism and the lack of a concept of "society," or the "social" as a sphere of life, together lead to *system blindness*, the inability to perceive social structures and systems and how they shape and are shaped by society and the people in it. If everything would be the same color, that would effectively be the same as there not being color at all. If all societies would be organized more or less the same and share the same sociopolitical and economic systems and structures, it would appear as if there would be no social structures and systems at all. Without a concept of the "social," one cannot really think about society, and without an understanding that one's society once was very different, one cannot really appreciate that different systems, structures, and institutions are possible.

Pre-modern individualism and system blindness are two sides of the same coin. Without an understanding of social systems and what roles they play, one can only think of social processes and problems in individual terms, without realizing they are *social* processes or problems. Without systems, only individuals exist and only the

---

37 Manfred Riedel, "Gesellschaft, bürgerliche," in *Geschichtliche Grundbegriffe: Historisches Lexikon zur politisch-sozialen Sprache in Deutschland*, Vol. 2: *E–G*, eds. Otto Brunner, Werner Conze, and Reinhart Koselleck (Stuttgart: Klett Cotta, 1975), 719–800; Manfred Riedel, "Gesellschaft, Gemeinschaft," in ibid., 801–62; Hans Boldt et al., "Staat und Souveränität," in *Geschichtliche Grundbegriffe: Historisches Lexikon zur politisch-sozialen Sprache in Deutschland*, Vol. 6: *St–Vert*, eds. Otto Brunner, Werner Conze, and Reinhart Koselleck (Stuttgart: Klett Cotta, 1990), 1–154; and Johan Heilbron, Lars Magnusson, and Björn Wittrock, eds., *The Rise of the Social Sciences and the Formation of Modernity: Conceptual Change in Context, 1750–1850* (Dordrecht: Kluwer, 1998).

38 There would be and was political philosophy (as the branch of philosophy that is concerned with the legitimacy and organization of the state), but there could be no philosophical inquiry into questions about the good society. Most of the core concerns of social philosophy — justice, equality, liberty, distribution of wealth and power, and so forth — depend on the concept of the "social" as a sphere of life.

39 Because political ideologies (to be distinguished from the Marxian notion of ideology) are collections of ideas about what society should be like and how to realize those ideas.

40 Robert Bierstedt, "Indices of Civilization," *The American Journal of Sociology* 71, no. 5 (1965): 483–90, at 490.

thoughts and actions of individuals can have causal efficiency.[41] And consequently, for pre-modern Buddhism, suffering is an individual problem with individual causes and an individual solution. Pre-modern individualism and related aspects of a pre-modern worldview are expressed in Buddhist thought in many other ways, however. One obvious example is that Buddhist political thought is nearly always based on the idea of a virtuous king (with king Aśoka as the preferred historical exemplar) and does not involve the concept of "society" or even a notion of the state as something different from the holdings of the king.

Another interesting example is anger. From a pre-modern individualist point of view, anger is always anger *with someone*. And because anger with someone involves a desire to harm the other that one is angry with, and thus an intention to cause suffering, it is always bad.[42] There are other kinds of anger, however. One can, for example, be angry at a social system that causes suffering, but system blindness makes *such* anger inconceivable, and consequently, it has rarely been recognized by Buddhist thinkers. Perhaps, the most noteworthy and not coincidentally very recent exception is the Dalai Lama, who in an interview in 2006 said:

> There are two types of anger. One type arises out of compassion; that kind of anger is useful. Anger that is motivated by compassion or a desire to correct social injustice, and does not seek to harm the other person, is a good anger that is worth having.[43]

Closely related to the individualist view of anger is the widespread misconception, expressed by Buddhadāsa, the Dalai Lama, and many others, that class struggle or Marxist socialism is, or is motivated by, a kind of revenge of the working class against the elite.[44]

A much more fundamental problem than these examples is that the only kind of analysis and critique of worldly suffering and its causes allowed by pre-modern individualism or system blindness is a moralistic perspective that puts the blame on individuals and their actions and desires. Consequently, subtle variations of the same theme can be found in the thought of Dharmapāla, Taixu, Ambedkar, Sivaraksa, and many others mentioned in the previous chapter: the worldly suffering caused by capitalism is rooted in greed or selfishness or some other closely related moral defect, which itself originates in delusions about an autonomous, essential self. As James Mark Shields pointed out, from Marx's perspective, this turns things on their heads: these delusions and moral defects are not causes of capitalism, but its consequence.[45] Or in other words, it is the capitalist *system* that is the root cause of worldly

---

41 In Buddhist metaphysics, having causal efficiency (i.e., the ability to cause things) is the most common mark of existence. What does not have causal efficiency does not exist. By this standard, social systems exist because they do have effects.
42 Anger can be useful if handled skillfully (i.e., by a Bodhisattva), but that does not make it less bad. See, for example, Stephen Harris, "The Skillful Handling of Poison: *Bodhicitta* and the *Kleśas* in Śāntideva's *Bodhicaryāvatāra*," *Journal of Indian Philosophy* 45 (2017): 331–48.
43 Noriyuki Ueda and Tenzin Gyatso, the 14th Dalai Lama, *The Dalai Lama on What Matters Most: Conversations on Anger, Compassion, and Action* (Charlottesville: Hampton Roads, 2013), 99.
44 Santikaro Bhikkhu, "Buddhadasa Bhikkhu: Life and Society through the Natural Eyes of Voidness," in *Engaged Buddhism: Buddhist Liberation Movements in Asia*, eds. Christopher Queen and Sallie King (New York: SUNY Press, 1996), 147–93. Tenzin Gyatso, the 14th Dalai Lama and Marianne Dresser, *Beyond Dogma: Dialogues and Discourses* (Berkeley: North Atlantic, 1996), 15–16.
45 Shields, "Buddhist Economics: Problems and Possibilities," 419.

and spiritual suffering rather than the actions and desires of individuals. Hence, while the typical Buddhist analysis and critique of capitalism and worldly suffering is individualist and moralistic, Marx's analysis and critique is social and systemic.

Economic Materialism

Marx and Engels's thought about the causal relations between aspects of a society's economy and aspects of its culture and prevailing ideology is usually called "historical materialism" and is a variety of a broader collection of theories and perspectives called "economic materialism." Economic materialism is not a single theory as there are nearly infinitely many ways in which economic aspects could be hypothesized to influence or determine other social aspects. Historical materialism, however, is generally treated as if it were a theory, but whether it deserves that status is debatable.

The first statements of historical materialism date to the second half of the 1840s and can be found in *The German Ideology* (written in 1846 but not published until 1932), *The Poverty of Philosophy* (1847), and the *Communist Manifesto* (1848). Two quotes from the second and third of these texts may illustrate the general idea (or ideas!):

> With the obtainment of new production forces people change their mode of production, and with the change of the mode of production, the way in which they earn their living, they change all their social relations. The hand mill yields a society with feudal lords; the steam mill one with industrial capitalists.[46]

> Does it require deep insight to understand that with people's living circumstances, that with their social relations and with their social being, their representations, views, and concepts — in one word, their consciousness — also change? What else does the history of ideas prove than that the intellectual production alters with the material production?[47]

In these two quotes, people's material living circumstances appear to be the decisive factor, but in the first the way "people earn their living" is equated with the technological mode of production, while in the second it is their social relations. And while in the first quote the dependent variable is the overall organization and class structure of society, in the second it is people's perception and understanding of the world around them.

The *locus classicus* of historical materialism is a passage in the preface to Marx's *Critique of Political Economy* from 1859:

---

46 Mit der Erwerbung neuer Produktivkräfte verändern die Menschen ihre Produktionsweise, und mit der Veränderung der Produktionsweise, der Art, ihren Lebensunterhalt zu gewinnen, verändern sie alle ihre gesellschaftlichen Verhältnisse. Die Handmühle ergibt eine Gesellschaft mit Feudalherren, die Dampfmühle eine Gesellschaft mit industriellen Kapitalisten. — Karl Marx, *Das Elend der Philosophie: Antwort auf Proudhons "Philosophie des Elends"* (1847), MEW 4: 63–182, at 130.
47 Bedarf es tiefer Einsicht, um zu begreifen, daß mit den Lebensverhältnissen der Menschen, mit ihren gesellschaftlichen Beziehungen, mit ihrem gesellschaftlichen Dasein, auch ihre Vorstellungen, Anschauungen und Begriffe, mit einem Worte auch ihr Bewußtsein sich ändert? Was beweist die Geschichte der Ideen anders, als daß die geistige Produktion sich mit der materiellen umgestaltet? — Marx and Engels, *Manifest der Kommunistischen Partei*, 480.

In the social production of their lives, people enter into certain necessary, involuntary relations, [namely] production relations, which correspond with a particular stage of development of the material production forces. The totality of these production relations constitutes the economic structure of society, the real base, on which a legal and political superstructure is erected that corresponds with certain forms of social consciousness. The mode of production of material life determines the social, political, and intellectual life in general. Is is not people's consciousness that determines their existence, but the other way around, their social existence that determines their consciousness. At a certain stage of their development, the material forces of production of a society come in contradiction with the existing production relations [or production conditions], or — what is just a legal expression [for the same thing] — with the circumstances of ownership within which they have operated until then. [...] Then begins an era of social revolution. With the change of the economic foundation, sooner or later the whole superstructure transforms.[48]

The key idea here appears to be that the relations and conditions of ownership (*Eigentumsverhältnissen*) — particularly the distribution of ownership of the means of production — largely determines the legal, political, and ideological "superstructure," that is, institutions, systems, and organization of a society. While this idea is considerably clearer than the vague hints in the previous two quotes, it is still very imprecise and virtually impossible to test mainly because it allows too many exceptions.[49] Presumably the same core idea was further elaborated in Engels's *The Origin of the Family, Private Property, and the State* (1884),[50] which was influenced as much by developments in evolutionary anthropology, Lewis Morgan's *Ancient Society*,[51] published a few years earlier, especially. Engels sketches history as a series of stages in which each transition from one stage to the next is determined by changes in a society's economic base (i.e., institutions, systems, and technologies related to ownership and production).

Regardless of whether Engels's stage theory is really an elaboration of the same idea expressed by Marx in the preface of his *Critique of Political Economy*, it should

---

48 In der gesellschaftlichen Produktion ihres Lebens gehen die Menschen bestimmte, notwendige, von ihrem Willen unabhängige Verhältnisse ein, Produktionsverhältnisse, die einer bestimmten Entwicklungsstufe ihrer materiellen Produktivkräfte entsprechen. Die Gesamtheit dieser Produktionsverhältnisse bildet die ökonomische Struktur der Gesellschaft, die reale Basis, worauf sich ein juristischer und politischer Überbau erhebt und welcher bestimmte gesellschaftliche Bewußtseinsformen entsprechen. Die Produktionsweise des materiellen Lebens bedingt den sozialen, politischen und geistigen Lebensprozeß überhaupt. Es ist nicht das Bewußtsein der Menschen, das ihr Sein, sondern umgekehrt ihr gesellschaftliches Sein, das ihr Bewußtsein bestimmt. Auf einer gewissen Stufe ihrer Entwicklung geraten die materiellen Produktivkräfte der Gesellschaft in Widerspruch mit den vorhandenen Produktionsverhältnissen oder, was nur ein juristischer Ausdruck dafür ist, mit den Eigentumsverhältnissen, innerhalb deren sie sich bisher bewegt hatten. ... Es tritt dann eine Epoche sozialer Revolution ein. Mit der Veränderung der ökonomischen Grundlage wälzt sich der ganze ungeheure Überbau langsamer oder rascher um. — Karl Marx, *Zur Kritik der Politischen Ökonomie* (1859), MEW 13: 1–160, at 8–9.
49 This is a problem because a theory that allows many exceptions can never be proven wrong, and if a theory cannot possibly be proven wrong, then it cannot be tested at all.
50 Friedrich Engels, *Der Ursprung der Familie, des Privateigentums und des Staats: im Anschluß an Lewis H. Morgans Forschungen* (1884), MEW 21: 25–173.
51 Lewis Morgan, *Ancient Society: or, Researches in the Line of Human Progress from Savagery through Barbarism to Civilization* (Chicago: Kerr, 1877).

be fairly clear that the term "historical materialism" does not denote a single theory linking a clearly defined cause to a clearly defined effect. Rather, the term refers to a vaguely bounded cluster of concepts, ideas, and interpretations found in or inspired by the writings of Marx and Engels. Attempts have been made to find (or create) some order in the profusion,[52] but the only shared idea uniting all the variants of historical materialism is that some aspects of the economic "base" of a society determine (or very strongly influence, at the very least) some aspects of the legal, political, ideological, and cultural "superstructure." Furthermore, varieties of historical materialism are typically either too imprecise to be tested, like the vague suggestions in the first two quotes above, or are based on outdated ideas that have proven to be false, such as aspects of Engels's stage theory.

Perhaps, then, we should not treat historical materialism as a theory but as a perspective that can spawn hypotheses and theories. This blurs the line that sets it apart from economic materialism in general, but there are some features of historical materialism that make it a recognizably distinct approach within that larger category: firstly, historical materialism is explicitly associated with Marxism; and secondly, it typically focuses on institutional and organizational aspects of production, such as the distribution of the ownership of the means of production. Within the broader category of economic materialism, other, non-Marxist theories of economic influence on cultural and ideological aspects of society have been proposed. For example, Georg Simmel suggested that a money-based economy promotes a selfish kind of individualism,[53] and many others have claimed that societies become more individualist as they become wealthier.[54] "Individualism" is itself a contested concept, however, and Ronald Inglehart has argued in a number of publications that increasing wealth leads to "post-materialism," a higher valuation of immaterial life goals, and thus a rejection of axiological materialism,[55] which is more or less opposite to the selfish and materialist notion of individualism found in many other theories, such as Simmel's.

Economic materialism belongs to a larger class of systemic perspectives on society that take social systems, structures, and institutions to be the main determinants of values, ideas, beliefs, and so forth. Alan Carter suggested a systemic perspective called "analytical anarchism" focusing on the distribution of power rather than economic factors,[56] but the vast majority of theories and ideas adopting a systemic perspective are economically materialist. In a direct confrontation between economic and political systemic perspectives, the first appears to fare better, which might partially explain the dominance of the economic perspective.

---

52 One of the more interesting attempts that I have seen is Jolanta Burbelka, "Historical Materialism: General Theory and Forms," in *Poznań Studies in the Philosophy of the Sciences and the Humanities*, Vol. 6: *Social Classes, Action & Historical Materialism*, eds. J. Brzeziński et al. (Amsterdam: Rodopi, 1982), 211–35.
53 Georg Simmel, *Philosophie des Geldes* (1900), in *Gesamtausgabe*, Vol. 6 (Frankfurt a.M.: Suhrkamp, 1989).
54 For an overview, see Lajos Brons, *Rethinking the Culture–Economy Dialectic*, PhD Thesis, University of Groningen, 2005, 232–38. Table 7.1 therein identifies thirteen different economic causes and sixteen different cultural effects that have been suggested in the literature surveyed.
55 See, for example, Ronald Inglehart, *The Silent Revolution* (Princeton: Princeton University Press, 1977), and *Culture Shift in Advanced Industrial Society* (Princeton: Princeton University Press, 1990).
56 Alan Carter, "Analytical Anarchism: Some Conceptual Foundations," *Political Theory* 28, no. 2 (2000): 230–53.

For example, one possible interpretation of a variant of historical materialism is that the distribution of ownership of the means of production determines the distribution of political power, or in other words, that the social class that has economic power will sooner or later end up with political power as well. If political power is the driving force, this would be the other way around. History suggests that political power of social classes (rather than individual) follows economic power, even though it may occasionally be the other way around for individuals. In the sixteenth to eighteenth centuries, economic power had shifted from the old feudal order to a new class of merchants and industrialists in much of Europe, and that class eventually grasped political power and disposed of feudalism everywhere. And in part of the nineteenth and twentieth century, with the spread of wealth and economic power to a growing middle class came a spread of political power in the form of democratization.[57] The last half century, however, has seen a concentration of wealth and economic power in the hands of a continuously shrinking elite, and that elite has also gained more and more political power.[58]

The opposite of economic materialism is economic idealism, the idea that certain "ideal" aspects of society — such as values, beliefs, and ideas — strongly influence or even determine certain economic (i.e., "material") aspects of society. For example, an economic idealist might hold that a rise in consumerism, which is itself a kind of axiological materialism, has caused the rise in capitalism, while an economic materialist might claim that capitalism causes consumerism. In the case of this example, they might both be wrong. Frank Trentman's majestic study of the history of consumerism from the fifteenth century until the present, *Empire of Things*, suggests that consumerism predates capitalism and thus cannot be caused by it, and predates it by so much that it cannot be the cause of capitalism either. He observes that "complaints about conspicuous consumption by the rich and by others who spend beyond their means in an attempt to imitate them are as old as human civilization. There is nothing particularly new or modern about it."[59] The form that consumption takes might be influenced by various circumstances, but the drive to consume — to spend one's available resources — appears to be as old as mankind. And consequently, "ideals of frugal self-reliance have been no match [to the 'undisputed cultural ideal' of consumption], or have been limited to short-lived and self-destructive experiments."[60]

The most influential theorist of economic idealism is Max Weber, who in *The Protestant Ethic and the Spirit of Capitalism* argued that Protestantism had lead to an increase of entrepreneurship which in turn lead to the rise of capitalism.[61] In response to Weber, R.H. Tawney argued that it was not Protestantism but individualism that had produced capitalism.[62] Historical research by Alan Macfarlane has suggested that Tawney *may* have been right in case of England; in that country, an earlier rise of individualism seems to have played a key role in the rise of both

---

57 This is a bit of an oversimplification, but it is not wide off the mark. For a useful review of some relatively recent books on the topic, see Daniel Ziblatt, "How Did Europe Democratize?" *World Politics* 58 (2006): 311–38.
58 William Robinson, *Global Capitalism and the Crisis of Humanity,* new edn. (Cambridge: Cambridge University Press, 2014), and Peter Phillips, *Giants: The Global Power Elite* (New York: Seven Stories, 2018). See also the next section, "Ideology."
59 Frank Trentman, *Empire of Things: How We Became a World of Consumers, from the Fifteenth Century to the Twenty-First* (New York: Harper, 2016), 677.
60 Ibid., 680.
61 Max Weber, *Die Protestantische Etik und der "Geist" des Kapitalismus* (Tübingen: J.C.B. Mohr, 1905).
62 R.H. Tawney, *Religion and the Rise of Capitalism: A Historical Study* (London: Murray, 1926).

Protestantism and capitalism.[63] However, entrepreneurship and capitalism have also blossomed under very different conditions, and individualism does not explain the bursts of entrepreneurship in some Italian cities during the Renaissance or among the Chinese diaspora all over Asia, for example.

In the 1990s and 2000s there was a major revival of Weberian economic idealism. The origin of this revival was a failure of mainstream, neoclassical economic theory to explain why its recipes for economic success did not work in less developed countries in the global south. Through the IMF and World Bank, mainstream economists had enforced free trade and austerity on these countries because, according to their theories, that would help them to develop economically.[64] They did not, but rather than considering that their theories might have been wrong, mainstream economists sought an alternative explanation: it must have been these countries' culture. They lacked "the entrepreneurial spirit," or something like that. Around that time, I did some research into the supposed relations between culture and the economy,[65] but much to my embarrassment, I never realized the origins of this "neo-Weberianism." And neither did I notice its Orientalist or even racist overtones: at bottom, the neo-Weberian claim that poor countries did not develop economically due to their lack of "entrepreneurial spirit" is just a rehash of the old racist trope of the lazy African, Asian, or other non-Westerner.

In addition to these dubious origins, there also is little empirical support for neo-Weberianism (which did not seem to affect its attraction much). The idea consists of two main parts: culture influences entrepreneurship, and entrepreneurship leads to economic growth. Variants of both parts have been researched extensively, but for both the evidence is inconclusive at best. Economists typically assume that entrepreneurship measured as start-ups leads to job creation, for example, but many studies failed to find such an effect.[66] The other part of the equation did not fare any better. Both culture and entrepreneurship can be operationalized and measured in a variety of ways, and while some measures of culture are positively related to some measures of entrepreneurship, others are negatively related. After reviewing most of the published research on this supposed relation and adding a few more empirical tests myself, all I found was that "the only cultural dimension (if it is one) that seems to have a consistent and significant positive effect on self-employment is dissatisfaction."[67]

As mentioned above, economic materialism and economic idealism are better understood as perspectives than as theories, and perspectives in the sense intended here cannot be judged on their truth or falsity but should be assessed for their usefulness instead. A perspective is better to the extent that it spawns more testable theories and ideas. A perspective is worse to the extent that it misleads.[68] By this standard,

---

63 Alan Macfarlane, *The Origins of English Individualism: The Family, Property and Social Transition* (Oxford: Blackwell, 1978).
64 See also chapter 15.
65 Resulting in *Rethinking the Culture–Economy Dialectic* as well as a few minor publications.
66 Ibid., 255.
67 Ibid., 278.
68 Perspectives play a more important role in part II of this book (chapter 9 especially), but the notion of perspectives employed there is not exactly the same as the notion used here. Perspectives as theory-spawning ways of looking at things are one kind of perspective in the sense of part II, but only one kind, and there are other kinds or notions of perspective that can be tested (although not "judged on their truth or falsity" strictly speaking, but that is for other reasons that are explained in the introduction to part II). Scientific theories, for example, can also be understood as perspectives in the sense of part II, and scientific theories are testable by definition. Consequently, what makes a

economic materialism is the better perspective. There is evidence that an increase of (distributed!) wealth leads to an increase in individualism, after a multi-decadal gap, and other cultural changes, for example.[69] And history suggests that the thesis that political power follows economic power may very well be right. There is no consistent evidence for idealist theories, like neo-Weberianism, on the other hand. Furthermore, the idealist perspective is misleading in as far as it tends to obscure the role of social systems, structures, and institutions in shaping values and beliefs.

The tendency among Buddhists to seek the causes of worldly suffering in moral defects rather than in systemic factors — and thus, to resort to moralistic critique and avoid systemic critique — is rooted in a pre-modern worldview akin to economic idealism because it assumes that values and beliefs are independent variables rather than themselves effects of socioeconomic systems and conditions. Like economic idealism, the pre-modern individualism and systemic blindness of traditional Buddhism are misleading because they make the systemic causes of suffering invisible and put the blame squarely on individuals and their ideas and desires. And thereby, rather than blaming capitalism for the suffering it causes,[70] traditional Buddhism blames its victims.

Ideology

The individualist, anti-systemic bias of Buddhism is not just rooted in a pre-modern worldview, but is also reinforced and simultaneously obscured by similar biases in modern society. The hegemony of neoliberal individualism makes pre-modern individualism almost invisible — it looks too much like the default view and, therefore, not as a view at all — and something similar is the case for system blindness. The economist Yanis Varoufakis has pointed out that certain methodological assumptions of neoclassical economics, which is as hegemonic as neoliberal individualism, preclude the conceptualization and modeling of any genuine alternative to capitalism because those assumptions imply that capitalism is the only possible system, and if there are no conceivable alternative systems, then effectively there are no systems at all.[71] Consequently, the individualist, anti-systemic bias of Buddhism is almost indistinguishable from the dominant ideology of the present age, and it is probably partially for this reason that the vast majority of Buddhist modernists accept the sociopolitical and economic status quo as given and, therefore, limit the scope of Buddhist engagement to charity or calls for minor reform.[72] As mentioned, radicality is rare.

Uchiyama Gudō 内山愚童 believed that the ruling elite spreads "superstitions" to support and maintain their status. As pointed out in the section "Uchiyama Gudō and Early Buddhist Socialism" in chapter 3, Marx and Gramsci made apparently similar claims, but there is an important difference. Uchiyama's "superstitions" are imposed or reinforced by concerted action from above, while in case of Marx's "ideology" or Gramsci's "hegemony," the values and beliefs that support the status and

---

"perspective" as a theory-spawning way of looking at things better or worse may not make all kinds of perspectives, in the sense intended in part II, better or worse.
69 Brons, *Rethinking the Culture–Economy Dialectic.*
70 See chapter 15.
71 Yanis Varoufakis, *Economic Indeterminacy: A Personal Encounter with the Economists' Peculiar Nemesis* (London: Routledge, 2014).
72 See above, as well as Shields, "Buddhist Economics."

position of the ruling class trickle down more or less automatically. "The ruling ideas of an era were always just the ideas of the ruling class," wrote Marx and Engels,[73] and not so much because of some kind of conspiracy, but because of their influence and social dominance. The acceptance of hegemonic values and beliefs is "spontaneous" according to Gramsci, and it is on this spontaneous acceptance that the authority and power of the ruling elite rests.

Ideology, in this sense, is a collection of values, beliefs, ideas, perspectives, and so forth that serve the interest of some social group. The dominant ideology in a society, according to Marx, is always the ideology of the ruling class, that is, the values and beliefs that serve the interests of the ruling class. Uchiyama's "superstitions," which include karma and the ideas that we owe taxes and land rents to the state and landowners, respectively, are ideological in this sense. And so are individualism and the anti-systemic bias — those obscure the role of capitalism as the source of human suffering because they make it seem that capitalism is "natural," or that, in Margaret Thatcher's words, "there is no alternative." The result is that for most people in modern society "it is easier to imagine the end of the world than to imagine the end of capitalism."[74] This is is the essence of hegemony: spontaneous acceptance of the status quo due to manufactured ignorance of alternatives.[75]

The key difference between Uchiyama on the one hand, and Marx and Gramsci on the other, is whether this manufactured ignorance is orchestrated by the elite (as suggested by Uchiyama) or is a by-product of their social dominance (as suggested by Marx and Gramsci). In any case, it is not disputed that the ruling elite spreads their ideology to the rest of society, but the question is whether they do this explicitly to *create* acceptance and consent or because they believe the "superstitions" they spread themselves. All evidence seems to point at the second.

Leslie Sklair, William Robinson, and others have shown in a number of books and articles that the past decades saw the rise of the *Transnational Capitalist Class* (TCC).[76] This class constitutes the global economic and political elite. Estimates of the size of the TCC differ from several thousands to tens of thousands. Recently, Peter Phillips has listed the 389 most powerful members of that elite and has shown how they control the global financial sector, politics, and the mainstream media.[77] Phillips also stresses repeatedly that these core members of the TCC genuinely believe in the ideology they spread. He writes, for example, that "[t]ransnational power elites hold a common ideological identity of being the engineers of global capitalism, with a firm belief that their way of life and continuing capital growth is best for all humankind."[78] The same ideological self-delusion is illustrated in Anand Giridharadas's *Winners Take All*, which describes, as the subtitle indicates, "the elite charade of changing the world."[79] The elite believes that they use charity for good, but all they

---

73 Die herrschenden Ideen einer Zeit waren stets nur die Ideen der herrschenden Klasse. — Marx and Engels, *Manifest der Kommunistischen Partei*, 480.
74 Fredric Jameson, "Future City," *New Left Review* 21 (2003): 65–79, at 76.
75 See also Lajos Brons, *The Hegemony of Psychopathy* (Earth: punctum books, 2017).
76 Leslie Sklair, *The Transnational Capitalist Class* (New York: Wiley, 2000), and Robinson, *Global Capitalism and the Crisis of Humanity*.
77 Phillips, *Giants*.
78 Ibid., 29.
79 Anand Giridharadas, *Winners Take All: The Elite Charade of Changing the World* (New York: Knopf, 2018).

really do is preventing real change and making sure that their own wealth and power remains unchallenged.

There is no elite conspiracy to control the world by *intentionally* manufacturing consent. Surely, the elite does manufacture consent,[80] and their power depends on that consent, but they do so by spreading values and beliefs they hold themselves. They are blind more than evil. Nevertheless, Uchiyama was not far off when he wrote that the government "is doing everything in its power to prevent you from giving up" the superstitions that keep them in power. It's just that most of the time they are not aware they are doing that — they have deluded themselves as much as they are deluding everyone else. Perhaps, the main defect in Uchiyama's analysis is another difference with Marx that I have glossed over thus far. He focuses his attention on the government and ignores the role of social class. Consequently, what he did not foresee — but probably also could not foresee — is that governments themselves became tools in the hands of the ruling elites. The TCC is indeed doing everything in its power to prevent you from giving up the superstitions on which their (immense!) power rests.

Buddhism, obviously, has not been immune from ideological superstitions, and among the modern Buddhists discussed in the previous chapter only a few were aware of something like ideology and its effects. Uchiyama has already been mentioned. One of the superstitions he mentioned explicitly was karma. The Dalai Lama has also said that karma could be invoked "to support ruling-class ideology,"[81] and somewhat similarly, Ambedkar argued that the notion of karma "was calculated to sap the spirit of revolt completely" by implying that "no one was responsible for the suffering of man except he himself."[82] But aside from these examples, Buddhists have mostly been blind for the effects of ideology, and consequently, most of them uncritically accepted the status quo, or even enthusiastically embraced it.

Materialism, Superstition, and Other Themes

One of the most widespread ideological superstitions among modern Buddhists is that materialism and Marxism are antithetical to Buddhism.[83] Perhaps, they are right *if* "Buddhism" is equated with some kind of traditional, sectarian Buddhism that is heavily invested in the status quo and that is mostly concerned with selling promises of an afterlife, in the Pure land or elsewhere. But neither materialism, nor Marxism should scare *radical* Buddhists.[84]

Many people seem to believe that there is no progress in philosophy, but that is a mistake. The misconception is understandable, however, because much of the progress in philosophy is negative. Many ideas and theories have been proposed and

---

80 Edward Herman and Noam Chomsky, *Manufacturing Consent: The Political Economy of the Mass Media* (London: Vintage, 1988).
81 Anup Dhar, Anjan Chakrabarti, and Serap Kayatekin, "Crossing Materialism and Religion: An Interview on Marxism and Spirituality with the Fourteenth Dalai Lama," *Rethinking Marxism* 28, nos. 3–4 (2016): 584–98, at 588.
82 B.R. Ambedkar, *The Buddha and His Dhamma* (1957), in *Writings and Speeches*, Vol. 11 (New Delhi: Dr. Ambedkar Foundation, 1979), 91, and (New Delhi: Oxford University Press, 2011), 58. See section "Ambedkar and the 'New Vehicle' in India" in chapter 3.
83 The handful of exceptions includes Seno'o Girō, Lin Qiuwu, the Dalai Lama, and a few Burmese Marxist Buddhists, but none of them went as far as accepting either materialism or Marxism.
84 On this topic, see also James Mark Shields, "Liberation as Revolutionary Praxis: Rethinking Buddhist Materialism," *Journal of Buddhist Ethics* 20 (2013): 461–99.

have been proven incoherent or deeply flawed for other reasons. We may not have widely accepted, definite answers to many philosophical questions, but we know many wrong answers and why they are wrong. Substance dualism, the idea that minds and bodies are fundamentally different kinds of things or substances, is one of those wrong answers. And many of the alternatives are similarly unattractive. From a more or less naturalistic point of view, and thus the point of view of radical Buddhism, there really is just one option: physicalism, an updated version of metaphysical materialism.

A radical Buddhist should provisionally accept economic materialism as well, but for very different reason. Contrary to metaphysical materialism or physicalism, economic materialism is not a theory about the nature of reality or some part thereof but a way of seeing and thinking about the world we inhabit, a perspective. And it is a useful perspective, especially for radical Buddhists, for at least two reasons. Firstly, it has produced more credible theories and ideas than competing perspectives. And secondly, it is indispensable to help free Buddhism from some of its traditional baggage and ideological blinkers, that is, from the system blindness and pre-modern individualism that Buddhism inherited from the pre-modern soil in which it grew, reinforced by the hegemony of neoliberal capitalism. Economic materialism puts the spotlight on the role of economic and sociopolitical systems, structures, and institutions in the (re)production of suffering and away from the traditional facile moralism that puts all the blame for suffering on individuals and their flawed beliefs and desires.

Nevertheless, economic materialism is merely a tool, an instrument to see some things more clearly, and tools or instruments have their uses and limits. Economic materialism is not a panacea and should not become a dogma. Naturalism accepts no dogmas and subjects everything to the same rigorous standards.[85] This is one point were radical Buddhism and Marxism diverge: for the latter historical materialism (i.e., the Marxist version of economic materialism) is a dogma. Other points of divergence have similar backgrounds. There are many interesting insights in the works of Marx, Engels, and later Marxists, but there is also much that is too imprecise to be testable, too obscure to be meaningful, self-contradictory, or refuted by empirical evidence. Hence, a naturalist — and thus, a radical Buddhist — should learn from but not embrace Marxism, and that, indeed, is what Seno'o Girō and Lin Qiuwu, for example, did.

They did not do so exactly for this reason but because they rejected axiological materialism — the strive for material goals such as individual or national wealth — which they associated with Marxism and the other two kinds of materialism. Axiological materialism may very well be incompatible with Buddhism indeed, but Marx was not an axiological materialist and, moreover, axiological materialism is independent from metaphysical and economic materialism. Accepting those does not imply or even suggest an acceptance of axiological materialism, or the other way around.

In addition to their somewhat ambivalent attitudes toward materialism and Marxism, the radical Buddhists and nearby neighbors in figure 4.1 have several other things in common. One of the most important shared ideas is an austere, this-worldly realism that affirms the reality of the world we live in and rejects supernatural heavens and other-worldly Pure lands. As mentioned above, this this-worldly real-

---

85 See the section "Naturalism" in chapter 1.

ism, which is affiliated with but not identical to naturalism and physicalism, evokes a sense of urgency about this-worldly suffering that is absent in other-worldly Buddhisms. If there is only this world and only this life, then nothing is as important as suffering in this world and this life. The radicalization of radical Buddhism in this book is based on this idea: part II discusses the Buddhist credentials of such an austere or this-worldly realism, and part III incorporates it in the foundations of a radical and Buddhist moral and social philosophy.

Some other common themes will be addressed in the next two chapters. Chapter 5, which aims to answer the question what it means to call something or someone "Buddhist," discusses the application of (something like) the Four Noble Truths to worldly suffering,[86] as well as the modernist emphasis on the supposed rationality of Buddhism.[87] The closely related and equally modernist idea that Buddhism is a philosophy rather than a religion, which very many Buddhist modernists emphasize, will be examined in chapter 6.[88] Another idea that almost all modern Buddhists mentioned in chapter 3 share is that Buddhism rejects all violence. The main exception is Uchiyama Gudō, who wrote that "the hand that holds the rosary should also always hold a bomb."[89] As is often the case, things get complicated when you look closer: there is no unequivocal rejection of all violence in Buddhism, and whether violence must be categorically rejected is a considerably more difficult question than it might seem to be.[90]

---

86 See the sections "The Four Noble Truths" and "Suffering" in chapter 5.
87 See the section "Metaphysics, Rationality, and Free Inquiry" in chapter 5.
88 See the section "Between Science and Religion" in chapter 6.
89 See the section "Uchiyama Gudō and Early Buddhist Socialism" in chapter 3.
90 For a very short discussion of Buddhist views on violence, see the last paragraph of the section "Meditation, Pacifism, and Dependent Origination" in chapter 5. See also the section "Ideal Theory, Utopia, and Ideology" in chapter 16.

5

What Makes Something Buddhist?

The goal of this book, as explained in chapter 1, is to develop a naturalistic and sociopolitically radical philosophy that is recognizably and defensibly Buddhist. That goal only makes sense if there is a clear way or criterion to tell whether something is indeed "recognizably and defensibly Buddhist," but deciding whether something or someone is Buddhist is not as easy as it may seem to be, especially if one wants to avoid the Orientalist penchant of telling the "natives" what their belief system really is about. If a definition of "Buddhism" or "Buddhist" excludes schools of thought, practices, ideas, sects, or people that are generally considered to be Buddhist *by Buddhists*, then that is not an acceptable definition.[1]

So then, how does one define what can be properly called "Buddhist"? The two most obvious approaches are both essentialist, albeit in different ways: one aims to identify the original teachings of the historical Buddha and defines Buddhism in terms of those original teachings; the other tries to identify a set of shared teachings uniting all the different Buddhist sects and schools. The first of these approaches is exclusivist, as it denies "Buddhist" status to anything that deviates too much from supposed "original Buddhism," but is problematic for other reasons as well. This *originalist* approach is typical for Buddhist modernism, and especially Protestant Buddhism, but as mentioned in chapter 3,[2] is rather uncharacteristic for more traditional Buddhism. Buddhist hermeneutics has never assumed that it is possible or even desirable to reconstruct a single "original Buddhism,"[3] but instead tried to make sense of the "bewildering profusion of doctrines" that were usually presented and accepted as authentic in some sense.[4] Perhaps, a more serious problem is that it is rather doubtful whether it is even possible to reconstruct the Buddha's original teachings.

The second essentialist approach may not really be feasible either. There is too much disagreement even about apparently basic doctrines between schools and sects to identify a substantial shared core, and some widely shared doctrines may not have been taught by the Buddha, or at least not in the same form. Most of this chapter is concerned with the assessment of the main candidates for inclusion in such a hypothetical shared core, but the ultimate failure to identify a substantial shared core

---

1   By this standard, most sectarian definitions are not acceptable either because they tend to exclude whatever deviates too much from that sect's vision.
2   See the section "Secular Buddhism" in chapter 3.
3   Jan Westerhoff, *The Golden Age of Indian Buddhist Philosophy* (Oxford: Oxford University Press, 2018), 24–34.
4   Robert Thurman, "Buddhist Hermeneutics," *Journal of the American Academy of Religion* 46, no. 1 (1978): 19–39, at 20.

necessitates a third, non-essentialist approach, which, considering that most Buddhisms are anti-essentialist, seems more appropriate anyway. First, we'll look into the problem of "original Buddhism."

The Idea of an "Original Buddhism"

There are two kinds of skepticism about the project of reconstructing the original teachings of the historical Buddha. According to the first kind this is practically impossible because we lack reliable evidence about what those teachings could have been. According to the second this is fundamentally impossible because there was no historical Buddha. The second, more extreme skepticism is rare and must be distinguished from the much more common view that most of the stories about the historical Buddha are myths. According to the latter view there is a real historical person hidden behind those layers of myth, which is exactly what this extreme skepticism denies: there are just layers of myth and no historical person hiding below them. The Buddha did not exist.

A recent example of this second kind of skepticism is David Drewes's "The Idea of the Historical Buddha." He claims that "no basis for treating the Buddha as a historical figure has yet been identified,"[5] which is true if the basis required is some kind of direct, hard evidence. Drewes points out that Western Buddhologists at some point accepted this lack of evidence, decided not to worry about it, and from then on just assumed that the Buddha existed. This, he argues, is premature, as there are inconsistencies in even the most basic supposed facts about the Buddha such as his name and ethnicity.[6]

Unsurprisingly, Drewes's paper invoked some vitriolic responses. Perhaps, the most interesting is Alexander Wynne's "Did the Buddha Exist?"[7] which denigrates Mahāyāna,[8] accuses some of the most outstanding scholars of Buddhism "of not really knowing anything about the primary sources,"[9] and at one point begs the question by assuming the authenticity of canonical texts reporting the Buddha's sayings in an attempt to prove that the Buddha existed.[10] Hence, he does a fine job presenting himself as a sectarian fanatic and undermining his scholarly credentials, but he also points out several historical and geographical details — such as the rarity of bricks and the absence of gold coins — that are unlikely to be invented by later editors or writers. Bryan Levman makes a similar point about flora and fauna that are indigenous to the area were the Buddha was supposed to live, but not to the area where the most important editing of the canonical texts took place.[11] Such details are significant because myths and other texts from ancient societies are almost always ahistoricist: they assume very little, if any, social, cultural, or technological progress, and are thus rarely aware that some things they take for granted were absent in earlier

---

5   David Drewes, "The Idea of the Historical Buddha," *Journal of the International Association of Buddhist Studies* 40 (2017): 1–25, at 1.
6   Ibid., 17.
7   Alexander Wynne, "Did the Buddha Exist?" *Journal of the Oxford Centre for Buddhist Studies* 16 (2019): 98–148.
8   Ibid., 140.
9   Ibid., 144.
10 Ibid., 110.
11 Bryan Levman, "The Historical Buddha: Response to Drewes," *Canadian Journal of Buddhist Studies* 14 (2019): 25–56.

times or other places.¹² Nevertheless, such geographical and historical details do not prove that the Buddha existed. What they establish is that much of the setting of the canonical stories about the Buddha and his teachings is almost certainly accurate, but not that what is reported to have taken place within that setting is accurate as well. And considering that it is much more likely that editors focused on what took place in those settings than on the settings themselves, this is only to be expected.

According to the first kind of skepticism mentioned above, we cannot really know what the Buddha taught because we lack reliable sources. None of the texts we have date back to the time the Buddha was supposed to live, and there is no other contemporary evidence either. The oldest rock inscriptions date to several centuries after the Buddha, for example. We have some snippets of texts that are very old, all in verse form, but our main source is the Pāli canon. Buddhist modernists tend to assume authenticity of the Pāli canon, but that assumption has been proven false.

Supposedly, until the sūtras in the Pāli canon were written down they were recited in periodic meetings of monks, but we have no consistent evidence about the nature, form, and frequency of these meetings, nor about how reliable this process was.¹³ They were written down in Ceylon (Sri Lanka) between 29 and 17 BCE, after which a long process of selection and redaction started.¹⁴ Texts were edited and organized into collections or "baskets" in a context of inter-sectarian rivalry. Different sects created different collections and redactions to legitimize their sectarian views and lineages. This process of classification, organization, and redaction continued until in the fifth century the redaction of the Mahāvihārin lineage became more or less fixed, resulting in what we now know as the "Pāli canon."¹⁵ With one exception, none of the competing and earlier redactions survived, and there are only a few text collections that we have multiple versions of.¹⁶ That one exception is the Chinese

---

12 See the section "Moralistic versus Systemic Critique" in chapter 4.
13 This paragraph is mostly based on the following two sources: Steven Collins, "On the Very Idea of the Pali Canon" (1990), in *Buddhism: Critical Concepts in Religious Studies, Volume I: Buddhist Origins and the Early History of Buddhism in South and Southeast Asia*, ed. Paul Williams (London: Routledge, 2005), 72–95, and Gregory Schopen, *Bones, Stones, and Buddhist Monks: Collected Papers on the Archaeology, Epigraphy, and Texts of Monastic Buddhism in India* (Honolulu: University of Hawai'i Press, 1997).
14 Sri Lanka was not the only place where the Buddha's teachings were written down around this time, and probably it was not the first either. Thomas McEvilley, *The Shape of Ancient Thought: Comparative Studies in Greek and Indian Philosophies* (New York: Allworth, 2002), 372, has suggested, for example, that the Gandhārī "canon," which was written down in an area that is now part of Pakistan and that had large Greek, Persian, and Central-Asian immigrant populations, predated the earliest steps towards a Pāli canon by at least several decades. How canonical these early "canons" were is quite debatable — hence, the scare quotes. Furthermore, it appears that at least some Mahāyāna sūtras were written down around the same time or even earlier as well. Allegedly, parts of the *Aṣṭasāhasrikā Prajñāpāramitā* (*Perfection of Wisdom*) *Sūtra* date to approximately 100 BCE, for example. See Richard Salomon, *The Buddhist Literature of Ancient Gandhāra: An Introduction with Selected Translations* (Boston: Wisdom, 2018).
15 Despite the content of the Pāli canon becoming more or less closed by this time, the version of the canon we have now did not become completely fixed until king Parakkamabāhu I of Sri Lanka intervened in sectarian debates in favor of one sect and one version of the canon in the twelfth century. Not coincidentally, the language most of the Pāli canon is written in also dates to that century. See Collins, "On the Very Idea of the Pali Canon," and Helmer Smith, *Saddanīti: La grammaire palie d'Aggavaṃsa*, Vol. 1 (Lund: Gleerup, 1928), vi.
16 There are, on the other hand, many individual texts of which we have multiple versions, and more keep being discovered, and typically there are significant differences between versions, especially between versions written by different sects or in different languages.

version of the *Numerical Discourses*, one of the aforementioned baskets, which is very different from the Pāli version and must have been composed separately.¹⁷

The Pāli canon, then, is not a neutral record of the Buddha's life and teachings. Its content has been organized and reorganized and edited and reedited again and again, and much of this organization and editing was colored by sectarian views and sectarian interests. Nevertheless, the aforementioned accuracy of geographical and historical setting implies that it is composed from ancient materials, and if that is the case, we may be able to distill more from the texts. If some passage conflicts with what we now know about the culture in which Buddhism arose and seems more in line with a later Brahmanic idea, for example, then that is a likely later redaction. Other criteria have been proposed and used by researchers trying to reconstruct the Buddha's original teaching, but the most common method is usually called "higher criticism" and is based on the assumption that if all versions of some passage agree in the Pāli canon, then that passage is probably authentic. But this is a very strange idea.

Imagine that you are a detective investigating two crimes. In the first crime you have a bunch of witnesses who all have subtly different accounts of what they claim to have seen, and it is quite credible that they actually did witness the crime. On the basis of the similarities of their accounts you can puzzle together a good picture of what happened, while you can explain the differences from the facts that they saw the crime from slightly different perspectives and that they will remember things differently.

In the second crime there is a bunch of people who all claim to have witnessed the crime and who all give you the exact same story in the exact same words — say, that the butler did it, with a knife, in the library. You would probably find this highly suspicious, unless you are very lazy or gullible. Most likely, the butler did not do it at all. Rather, someone wants you to believe that the butler did it and orchestrated a bunch of fake witness accounts.

Much of the Pāli canon is more like the second case than like the first. There is a lot of word-for-word repetition suggesting extensive redaction rather than authenticity. As the detective, you should ask yourself in the second case who would want you to believe that the butler did it and why. Similarly, the suspicious repetitions in the Pāli canon should raise questions about the authorship and purpose of those redactions, especially considering that we know that much redaction had a specific purpose: supporting some sect's point of view in inter-sectarian rivalry.

Gregory Schopen makes a very similar point: "If all known versions of a text or passage agree, that text or passage is probably late; that is, it probably represents the results of the conflation and gradual leveling and harmonization of earlier existing traditions."¹⁸ Furthermore, according to Schopen, this can actually be shown in a few cases where we have an older, perhaps unrevised, version of a text. He compares five versions of the same text, four of which are late, and a fifth, which was recently discovered and which is significantly older. The four newer versions largely agree with each other, but not with the earlier version. Schopen concludes that the later

---

17 Johannes Bronkhorst, *Buddhist Teaching in India* (Boston: Wisdom Publications, 2009), 63. Given that Buddhism passed to China through Gandhāra, it is possible, perhaps even probable, that the Chinese version of the *Numerical Discourses* was based on, or influenced by the Gandhārī canon mentioned in note 14.
18 Schopen, *Bones, Stones, and Buddhist Monks*, 27.

versions "agree not because they represent the old presectarian version, but because they almost certainly represent later, conflated, and fundamentally altered versions of an earlier tradition."[19]

All of this may seem to prove the first skeptic right — we cannot know anything about what the Buddha taught — but that conclusion only follows if we accept the skeptic's criterion for knowledge. Both kinds of skepticism assume that to know something, we must have incontrovertible evidence. Knowledge, more or less, requires certainty. But that is a view that a pragmatist or Quinean naturalist does not accept. The skeptic and the naturalist might agree that everything is open to counter-evidence and revision, and thus that there is no such thing as incontrovertible evidence or absolute certainty. But while the skeptic concludes that this implies that we cannot know anything, the naturalist retorts by pointing out that the skeptic confuses scientific knowledge with religious dogma. The latter claims absolute certainty; the former does not. Everything scientists "know" is only accepted provisionally. What we call "knowledge" is just what we have the best evidence for. And sometimes that "best evidence" is just our best explanation for the observed facts. This is how we know about planets around other stars, for example: we do not have direct evidence for their existence, but they are the best explanation for aspects of our observations of those stars.

Something similar applies here. We do not have rock-solid evidence for the Buddha's existence, but the assumption that he existed is by far the most parsimonious explanation of the many things that we know with greater confidence. If he would be invented, his inventors inserted him into texts that were themselves at least partially authentic because the geographical and historical setting of those texts is almost certainly not invented. Why they would have made that effort is hard to explain. Perhaps, even harder to explain are the various less flattering details about the Buddha and his surroundings. In the *Attadaṇḍa Sutta*,[20] for example, the Buddha appears to be motivated by cowardice and a fear of social conflict more than by lofty ideals, which makes him a lot more human and a lot less like an invented great founder and sage.[21]

However, while we can be fairly confident that the Buddha indeed did exist, there is a lot more uncertainty and a lot more disagreement about what *exactly* he taught. The traditional view is that the essence of Buddhism is to be found in the Buddha's first sermon at Deer Park after he reached awakening, which is recorded in the *Dhammacakkappavattana Sutta*[22] (the title can be translated as "setting the Dharma wheel in motion"). However, it is unlikely that this text indeed represents the first sermon. At the very least it was heavily edited, but it might even be a later construction entirely.[23] Instead of *recording* the first sermon, "the compilers of the Canon put in the first sermon what they knew to be the very essence of the Buddha's Enlightenment."[24] However, we do have other texts describing the events surrounding the first sermon,

---

19 Ibid., 29.
20 Sn 4.15.
21 See also Levman, "The Historical Buddha."
22 SN 56.11.
23 See, for example, Tilman Vetter, *The Ideas and Meditative Practices of Early Buddhism* (Leiden: Brill, 1988); Richard Gombrich, *Theravāda Buddhism: A Social History from Ancient Benares to Modern Colombo*, 2nd edn. (London: Routledge, 2006); and Bronkhorst, *Buddhist Teaching in India*.
24 Gombrich, *Theravāda Buddhism*, 62.

such as the *Ariyapariyesanā Sutta*[25] and *Mahāsaccaka Sutta*,[26] and these — together with text-critical, linguistic, and historical research — help in sketching a more credible version of what the Buddha may have taught.

The *Dhammacakkappavattana Sutta* presents five related doctrines in summary form:

1. The Buddha's path is a middle path between asceticism and the pursuit of sensual pleasure (i.e., hedonism). This Middle Way leads to vision, knowledge, peace, awakening, and nirvāṇa (*nibbāna* in Pāli).

2. The Middle Way is the Noble Eightfold Path consisting of right view, right intention, right speech, right light action, right livelihood, right effort, right mindfulness, and right concentration.

3. The Four Noble Truths of suffering (dukkha), the origin of suffering, the cessation of suffering, and the path towards the cessation of suffering. That path is the Noble Eightfold Path.

4. Further explanation of the Four Noble Truths. Suffering must be fully understood. The origin of suffering must be abandoned. The cessation of suffering must be experienced or realized by oneself. The path towards the cessation of suffering must be developed.

5. Knowledge of the Four Noble Truths lead to the Buddha's awakening.

For a number of reasons it is virtually certain that not all of these doctrines were part of the Buddha's original teaching, and certainly not in this form. According to Tilman Vetter, "very likely the first section reflects the oldest teaching and the following sections subsequent stages."[27] If this is right, then there really was no first sermon. The Buddha's initial teaching was just a "middle way" between the asceticism of Jainism and Ājīvikism and the pursuit of worldly pleasure, and this middle way was the kind of meditation that had lead to the Buddha's own awakening. One reason to believe that this is the case is that in the *Ariyapariyesanā Sutta* the Buddha explains that he was instructing two or three of his first five students while the others went to beg for alms. As Vetter points out, this makes no sense if what he was instructing was just some doctrine — even if it was all of the doctrines in the supposed first sermon — but it makes perfect sense if he was teaching them a kind of meditation.[28]

Furthermore, there are other reasons to doubt that most of the aforementioned five doctrines were part of the Buddha's initial teaching. According to Johannes Bronkhorst, an important difference between the Buddha's teaching and Vedic/Brahmanic religions is that only in the latter liberation or awakening depends on knowledge or insight.[29] Under Brahmanic influence, early followers of the Buddha tried to identify a liberating knowledge within the Buddha's teachings as well, and

---

25 MN 26.
26 MN 36.
27 Vetter, *The Ideas and Meditative Practices of Early Buddhism*, xxviii.
28 Ibid., xxix.
29 Bronkhorst, *Buddhist Teaching in India*, and Johannes Bronkhorst, *Greater Maghada: Studies in the Culture of Early India* (Leiden: Brill, 2007). See also the section "Early Buddhism" in chapter 2.

the fifth doctrine in the *Dhammacakkappavattana Sutta* is probably a result of that attempt. The idea of some kind of knowledge acquired in meditation is a Vedic/Brahmanic idea. Moreover, even if the Buddha believed in a liberating knowledge, the Four Noble Truths are an unlikely candidate because, as Bronkhorst points out, their aim is to point the way to liberation. They are like a sign at the beginning of the path rather than what is to be found at the end of that path. Doctrine 5, then, is almost certainly of much later date, and so is doctrine 4, which mainly acts as a bridge between the Four Noble Truths (doctrine 3) and the idea of the Four Noble Truths as liberating knowledge (doctrine 5).

K.R. Norman has decisively shown that the Four Noble Truths (doctrine 3) cannot have been part of the Buddha's original teaching *in this form* either.[30] His argument is mainly linguistic, but there are other reasons to think that that the Four Noble Truths may not have been part of the original teaching at all.[31] First, they are too formulaic. As pointed out in chapter 2,[32] the early Abidharma scholastics had a strong preference for formulas, lists, and especially numbered lists, which is reason to doubt the authenticity of any formulaic, numbered list in the corpus, such as the Four Noble Truths and the Noble Eightfold Path (doctrine 2). Nevertheless, while it is very likely that the form of these doctrines is of much later date, their content is probably authentic, although it is not completely clear what exactly that content is either. But this does not imply that the first sermon included some less formulaic expressions of the same or similar ideas. The second reason to doubt that the Four Noble Truths were part of the first teaching is that the *Ariyapariyesanā Sutta* makes no mention of the "cessation of suffering" or anything similar as the goal of the "Middle Way." Rather, the goal is the same as that in doctrine 1 listed above: nirvāṇa.

Given all we know, it seems very likely that what the Buddha taught, at least at first, was some kind of meditation more than a doctrine, but it is far less clear what kind of meditation that was exactly and what *exactly* it aimed to achieve. There is a bewildering variety of kinds and purposes of meditation in Buddhism, and various meditation-based sects will doubtlessly claim that their preferred kind of meditation was what the Buddha taught, but there is no evidence of any kind to back up such claims.

The goal of the Buddha's meditation technique may seem less ambiguous: it is awakening or enlightenment or nirvāṇa. But what exactly does that mean? The *Ariyapariyesanā Sutta* describes nirvāṇa (*nibbāna* in Pāli) as "the unageing, unailing, deathless, sorrowless, and undefiled supreme security from bondage."[33] The English term "deathless" translates the Pāli *amata* (*amṛta* in Sanskrit), which is otherwise usually translated as "immortal" or "immortality." *Amata* or *amṛta* is a pre-Buddhist term with obvious Vedic overtones and with connotations of the kind of immortality or very long lifespans of gods and other god-like beings and it is extremely unlikely that the Buddha and his followers were not aware of this. Hence, this strongly suggests that nirvāṇa is a state like immortality that is further characterized as being free from aging, ailments, sorrow and defilement. However, one sentence later, the same

---

30 K.R. Norman, "The Four Noble Truths: A Problem of Pali Syntax," in *Indological and Buddhist Studies: Volume in Honour of Professor J.W. de Jong on His Sixtieth Birthday*, ed. L.A. Hercus (Canberra: Australian National University Press, 1982), 377–91.
31 Carol Anderson, *Pain and Its Ending: The Four Noble Truths in the Theravāda Buddhist Canon* (London: Routledge, 2013), 20–21.
32 See the section "Early Buddhism."
33 MN 26, §30/265.

sūtra says "this is our last birth; there is no renewal of being," which suggests the very opposite of immortality, namely extinction — if there is no "renewal of being" then there is no more being and thus no existence, and non-being or nonexistence is not a state one can be in.[34] This tension in the interpretation of nirvāṇa would never be resolved, and consequently, if the goal of Buddhist practice is nirvāṇa, then its goal is fundamentally unclear.

Much of the foregoing is controversial outside academic Buddhology,[35] but I want to emphasize that I'm not claiming here that the foregoing is the one and only true interpretation of the Buddha's original teaching. My aim is more modest than that. It is to illustrate how hard it is to uncover that original teaching — if it can be done at all — and that "canonical" sources cannot be taken at face value. But there is another, even more important point: it is a virtual certainty that the vast majority, if not all, of present Buddhist practices and doctrines deviate to greater or lesser extent from "original Buddhism," whatever that was.[36] And consequently, an originalist approach to defining Buddhism is exclusivist. It would imply that very many people who consider themselves Buddhists would be mistaken. In my view, it is the person who proposes such a definition who is fundamentally mistaken, however. As mentioned in the introduction of this chapter, an acceptable definition of Buddhism, or of what it means to call something or someone "Buddhist," cannot exclude a substantial number of people, schools, ideas, practices, or texts that are considered "Buddhist" *by Buddhists*.

The Four Noble Truths

The most obvious alternative to the originalist approach to defining Buddhism is to seek the essence of Buddhism in a set of doctrines or practices rather than in its source. This approach aims to identify a number of core ideas, practices, doctrines or other kinds of characteristics that make something "Buddhist." Contrary to the originalist approach, this approach is not necessarily exclusivist: if there is a collection of doctrines or practices that is shared by all schools and sects, and perhaps even by lay varieties of Buddhism, and *not* by non-Buddhists, then that collection could be used to inclusively define Buddhism. This and the following sections discuss some candidates for inclusion in such a set of defining core features.

If Buddhism would have to be represented by a single doctrine, then the most obvious candidate for that defining doctrine would be the Four Noble Truths. It should already be clear from the foregoing, however, that this is not an unproblematic suggestion, but the problem may be even deeper. According to Carol Anderson,

> evidence demonstrates that the four noble truths were probably not part of the earliest strata of what came to be recognized as Buddhism, but that they emerged

---

[34] Another possible interpretation, however, is that "renewal of being" implies another, new being after the present one. "No renewal of being," then, could also mean an indefinite continuation of the present being (i.e., the present life), or in other words, immortality (*amata*).

[35] Traditional, sectarian Buddhists probably considering it "slandering the Dharma," one of the worst crimes one can possibly commit.

[36] More often than not, "original Buddhism" is a modernist reconstruction that accords with the views of the person or persons doing the reconstruction.

as a central teaching in a slightly later period that still preceded the final redactions of the various Buddhist canons.[37]

In other words, the Four Noble Truths (hereafter 4NT) may not have been taught by the Buddha *at all*. It might date to some time between the Buddha's passing and the fifth century canonization instead. If that is the case indeed, and 4NT would be a defining doctrine of Buddhism, then this would rather paradoxically imply that the Buddha's teaching was not Buddhism. However, that 4NT was not taught by the Buddha in the form known to us now and was not part of his first teachings does not necessarily imply that he did not teach something *like* 4NT, which raises the question: What reasons might we have to believe that he did or did not teach some kind of proto-4NT?

K.R. Norman has shown that the original form of 4NT is that "this is suffering, this is the origin of suffering, this is the cessation of suffering, this is the path leading to the cessation of suffering."[38] But this may still be a later version, only one that predates the even later addition of the "noble truth" labels. If the Buddha taught a proto-4NT, it must have been something even more basic.

Hendrik Kern was the first to suggest a link between 4NT and medical practice in his *History of Buddhism* in India published in 1882. He claimed that

> [t]he four truths are derived from the art of medicine: 1. the physician identifies the disease; 2. acknowledges its cause, [...]; 3. he realizes that this must be repressed, eliminated; 4. proceeds towards this end to means, either medical or surgical.[39]

This is an interesting suggestion. If he is right, then there may have been a proto-4NT as a summary of medical procedure: (1) identification of the disease; (2) identification of the cause; (3) identification of the cure; (4) treatment, or application of the cure.[40]

The Buddha was a *śramaṇa*, a wandering mendicant. The ancient Greek geographer Strabo reports that according to Megasthenes, whose book on India is lost, there were two kinds of śramaṇas: forest-dwellers (ὑλόβιοι) and physicians (ἰατρικοί or ἰατροί). The physicians were "humanitarian philosophers, men who are of frugal habits" who "go about begging alms from village to village and from city to city," and who cure diseases.[41] The Buddha seems to have belonged to this second kind, but that does not necessarily imply that he was a physician himself. It does make it very likely, however, that he was well-acquainted with other śramaṇas who were physicians and that he was to lesser or greater extent influenced by them. This is also suggested by the medical analogies in the Pāli canon and elsewhere. Their prevalence indicates

---

37 Anderson, *Pain and Its Ending*, 21.
38 Norman, "The Four Noble Truths," 388. I changed Norman's translation of *dukkha* from "pain" into "suffering."
39 De 4 waarheden zijn ontleend aan de geneeskunst: 1. de geneesheer constateert de ziekte; 2. erkent de oorzaak er van, [...]; 3. hij beseft dat deze moeten onderdrukt, uit den weg geruimd worden; 4. gaat over te dien einde tot de middelen, medische of chirurgische. — Hendrik Kern, *Geschiedenis van het Buddhisme in Indië*, Vol. 1 (Haarlem: Tjeenk Willink, 1882), 207n4.
40 See also Terry Clifford, *Tibetan Buddhist Medicine and Psychiatry: The Diamond Healing* (1984; Delhi: Motilal Banarsidass, 1994), 38–39.
41 Translation, as well as the original Greek, in Strabo, *The Geography of Strabo*, Vol. 7, trans. Horace Leonard Jones (London: Heinemann, 1930), 102–5.

medical influence, but their superficiality and somewhat marginal role — their use for explanation or clarification and their being no fundamental part of the doctrine — suggest that the Buddha was not a physician himself.[42]

Taking this into account, Kern's suggestion does not seem at all implausible. However, according to Sylvain Mazars, 4NT does not occur in pre-Buddhist Indian medical literature, and "moreover, one could find these 'four truths of medicine' in any other medical culture in the world, since the goal and the working method of the physician are reasonably the same everywhere."[43] He is probably right that 4NT was not a pre-Buddhist medical doctrine, but that does not preclude a medical source of the idea. The Buddha's proto-4NT — something like the diagnosis–cause–cure–treatment tetrad — may very well have been his interpretation of the approach of some of the physician–śramaṇas he knew. Moreover, it is not exactly true that the goal and working method of medicine are the same everywhere, as Mazars claims. Kenneth Zysk has pointed out that the medicine of Greater Maghada, the culture in which the Buddha lived, was very different from the Vedic medicine practiced in much of the rest of Northern India. While the latter was magical and religious,[44] Greater-Maghadan medicine was naturalistic and rational, and took an empirical attitude to studying the causes of diseases and how to cure them.[45] Hence, the diagnosis–cause–cure–treatment tetrad closely matches *their* working method, and closely matches modern medicine, but deviates significantly from more magical approaches to medicine, which are or were widespread among "primitive" cultures.

Furthermore, in the *Mahāsaccaka Sutta* and the *Sāmaññaphala Sutta* the basic formula of 4NT is applied to something other than suffering: "These are the taints; [...] This is the origin of the taints; [...] This is the cessation of the taints; [...] This is the way leading to the cessation of the taints."[46] The wording here is close (but not identical) to the original 4NT as reconstructed by Norman but applied to the taints (*āsavas*) rather than to suffering (*dukkha*).[47] Assuming that only the wording of this passage has been altered in later redaction, this passage indicates that proto-4NT, whatever its exact form may have been, was a general approach used by the Buddha to analyze some human problems and their solution.

Taking all of this into account, it seems to me that the most probable biography of 4NT is something like the following. From physician–śramaṇas he encountered or knew, the Buddha learned a certain naturalist and rational approach to diseases and their causes, cures, and treatments, which he adopted and transformed into a proto-4NT. This proto-4NT was his interpretation of that medical method and may have been very similar to the diagnosis–cause–cure–treatment tetrad. In the earliest stage

---

42 Sylvain Mazars, *Le bouddhisme et la médecine traditionnelle de l'Inde* (Paris: Springer, 2008), 59–63.
43 Aucune source ne démontre que la médecine indienne possédait une quelconque expression des quatre vérités avant le bouddhisme. [...] De plus, on pourrait trouver ces «quatre vérités de la médecine» dans n'importe quelle autre culture médicale du monde, puisque le but et la méthode de travail du médecin sont sensiblement les mêmes partout. — Ibid., 56.
44 Kenneth Zysk, *Religious Medicine: The History and Evolution of Indian Medicine* (1985; rpt. London: Routledge, 2017), 7.
45 Kenneth Zysk, *Asceticism and Healing in Ancient India: Medicine in the Buddhist Monastery,* corr. edn. (Delhi: Motilal Banarsidass, 1998), 29, and Bronkhorst, *Greater Maghada,* 59. See also the section "Early Buddhism" in chapter 2.
46 *Mahāsaccaka Sutta,* MN 36, §42/342. A similar passage can be found in the *Sāmaññaphala Sutta* (DN 2, §97/107), but notice that *āsavas* is there translated as "corruptions."
47 Taints (*āsavas*) are mental dispositions such as the craving for continued existence that keep one in samsara, the world of death and rebirth, and that prevent one from reaching awakening.

of his thought, this proto-4NT did not play a significant role yet, but in its further development he applied it to what he considered to be the most important problem, suffering (dukkha), and to closely related problems (such as the taints). Long after his death, the Buddha's application of the proto-4NT to the problem of suffering, through centuries of recitation and redaction, gradually developed into the Four Noble Truths as we know them today.

This story is, of course, somewhat speculative, but the point is this: given what we think we know about the Buddha, his thought, and his cultural environment, as sketched in the foregoing, it seems implausible that something very similar to 4NT was *not* part of his philosophy. The form of 4NT as we know it today may be of much later date and may have gone through several redactions, but the basic approach underlying that doctrine — what I called proto-4NT — and the application of that approach to the problem of suffering are unlikely to be later inventions. Those must have been part of the Buddha's thought, but possibly not in its earliest stages.

Nevertheless, this does not imply that a 4NT-like analysis of suffering (hereafter 4NT/S) is a sufficient condition for some body or school of thought to count as "Buddhist." Mazars was right when he pointed out that 4NT/S is too widespread. The resulting definition would be too broad and would include substantial parts of medicine and social philosophy, for example, although this depends on what "suffering" means exactly. Whether 4NT/S is a *necessary* condition can be debated as well. 4NT/S does not seem to play a significant role in lay Pure Land Buddhism (i.e., the most common form of Buddhism in East Asia), for example, but as the main purpose of defining "Buddhism" here is to assess whether certain philosophies, theories, or ideas can be called "Buddhist" this may not be a serious concern. For a school of thought to count as "Buddhist," some form of 4NT/S is probably a necessary, but not a sufficient, condition.

This does not help, however, if we want to know whether some more specific theory can be properly called "Buddhist." If 4NT/S is a necessary condition for a *theory* to count as "Buddhist," then any Buddhist theory of metaphysics or epistemology that is not directly concerned with suffering would *not* be Buddhist, and that would obviously be absurd. This problem cannot simply be evaded by decreeing that such specific theories are Buddhist if they are part of broader theory or philosophy that includes 4NT/S, because that would make anything Buddhist as long as it is an element in some eclectic combination of ideas that includes 4NT/S.

Suffering

The problem addressed by the Four Noble Truths is dukkha (*duḥkha* in Sanskrit), which is translated as "suffering," "pain," or "unsatisfactoriness," among others. While it is not entirely clear whether overcoming dukkha played an important role in the earliest stage of the Buddha's philosophy (the *Ariyapariyesanā Sutta* suggests it did not), it seems beyond dispute that it was the primary concern in his more developed thought, and in virtually all Buddhist thought of later ages.

Nevertheless, a shared concern with dukkha and its transcendence is a unifying thread only if it is a shared concern with the same thing, and it is not entirely clear whether it is. The concept is not defined in the canonical sources, leaving considerable room for interpretation. In narrower views, dukkha is simply a kind of unsatisfactoriness of life caused by an inevitably frustrated desire for permanence. In this view, dukkha is personal and psychological or mental. It is a kind of stress more than a kind of pain. In broader views, on the other hand, dukkha *includes* this unsatisfactoriness, but also physical pain and worldly suffering. Additionally, there are more heterodox views such as Ambedkar's, who suggested that dukkha is, in the first place, material suffering such as poverty.[48]

A definition of "Buddhism" according to the narrow view would exclude Ambedkar's Navayāna but might also imply that the engagement of engaged and radical Buddhism is "un-Buddhist." James Deitrick seems to argue for something like this. He accuses engaged Buddhists of forgetting "the most basic of Buddhism's insights, that *suffering has but one cause and one remedy*, that is, attachment and the cessation of attachment."[49] An example of a contrasting point of view can be found in the typical response Joanna Macy got from learned Buddhist monks in Sri Lanka to her questions about the application of the Four Noble Truths to worldly suffering by engaged Buddhists. She writes that she expected an answer corresponding to the narrower view, but

> instead, almost invariably, they seemed surprised that a Buddhist would ask such a question — and gave an answer that was like a slight rap on the knuckles: "But it is the same teaching, don't you see? Whether you put it on the psycho-spiritual plane or on the socio-economic plane, there is suffering and there is cessation of suffering."[50]

Rather than defining dukkha, the *Dhammacakkappavattana Sutta* illustrates the first Noble Truth by giving a number of examples:

> [B]irth is suffering, aging is suffering, illness is suffering, death is suffering; union with what is displeasing is suffering; separation from what is pleasing is suffering; not to get what one wants is suffering; in brief, the five aggregates subject to clinging are suffering.[51]

This suggests a broad interpretation of dukkha, which is also supported by the scholastic classification of dukkha into three kinds. The most basic kind of dukkha is physical and mental pain, which may even include dissatisfaction, annoyance, boredom, and fatigue. The second, more subtle kind of dukkha derives from change and the impermanence of things (in the broadest possible sense of "thing"). Any gain, any achievement, any satisfaction, any positive sensation or emotion, and so forth only lasts for a brief while, leading to unhappiness and craving for more after it has drained away. The third, even subtler kind of dukkha results from the fact that this change and impermanence is fundamentally outside of our control because everything is interdependent or conditioned. Nothing is permanent and nothing is independent of causes, conditions, and other things, including we, ourselves. Dukkha in this third sense, *sankhara-dukkha*, is related to existential dread and to a general

---

48 See the section "Ambedkar and the 'New Vehicle' in India" in chapter 3
49 James Deitrick, "Engaged Buddhist Ethics: Mistaking the Boat for the Shore," in *Action Dharma: New Studies in Engaged Buddhism*, eds. Christopher Queen, Charles Prebish, and Damien Keown (London: RoutledgeCurzon, 2003), 252–69, at 263. Italics in original.
50 Joanna Macy, "In Indra's Net: Sarvodaya & Our Mutual Efforts for Peace," in *The Path of Compassion: Writings on Socially Engaged Buddhism*, ed. Fred Eppsteiner (Berkeley: Parallax, 1985), 170–81, at 179.
51 SN 56.11, 1844.

dissatisfaction resulting from the fact that things never are or can be as we expect and as we want them to be.

The narrow view effectively redefines dukkha as simply this third kind on the grounds that the second to fourth of the Four Noble Truths appear to be concerned only with dukkha in this third sense. The argument appears roughly to be that because the Buddha was really only interested in sankhara-dukkha, Buddhism is, by definition, only concerned with dukkha in that sense. But this argument raises two questions. What did dukkha mean for the Buddha? And if his concept of dukkha was broad rather than narrow, then why did he focus on just one kind of dukkha?

Dukkha or duḥkha is typically contrasted with *sukha*, meaning something like happiness, pleasure, or bliss. The etymology of both terms is uncertain and disputed, and some suggestions appear rather far-fetched. Hermann Jacobi suggested well over a century ago that the etymological, literal meaning of the two words is "well standing" and "badly standing," and this remains the most plausible analysis I have seen.[52] But in this case, etymology does not really tell us anything relevant.

A major difficulty in uncovering what dukkha may have meant to the Buddha is that Greater-Maghadan culture had no writing at the time he lived. Jainism originated from the same culture, but its scriptures, the Jain Agamas, were written down in the fifth century and are for that reason as unreliable as the Pāli canon. The oldest Indian texts are the Vedas, but those belong to Vedic culture, which later developed into Brahmanic culture, and as explained in chapter 2,[53] there were significant differences between the Vedic/Brahmanic and Greater-Maghadan cultures. Hence, we cannot just assume that the Greater-Maghadan concept of dukkha was the same as the Vedic or Brahmanic concept. But at the same time, lacking other contemporary sources, there is not much else we can do.

Duḥkha does not occur in any of the four Vedas, and its opposite, *sukha* is rare as well and almost exclusively used in reference to chariots;[54] but both terms occur in the Brāhmaṇas and Āraṇyakas, the next layer of Vedic texts, which predate the Buddha by a few centuries. In those,

> the terms sukha and duḥkha are used with fair frequency, almost always together, and with a semi-technical psychological meaning. In these passages sukha and duḥkha are the experiences of the "body," as "actions" are of the "hands," and "sight" of the "eyes." Buddhist texts never reveal an acquaintance with this technical usage but it no doubt was in the background of their descriptions of sukha and duḥkha as the characteristic experiences of man.[55]

Significantly, duḥkha in the Vedic sources is nothing like sankhara-dukkha; it is a much broader notion that is closer to "pain," "suffering," or "distress." And the Pāli canon and Jain Agamas suggest that the Greater-Maghadan notion of dukkha was not a narrow notion either. In the contrary, the notion of dukkha encountered in those is usually suffering in the broad sense, including pain, sickness, sorrow, loss,

---

52 Hermann Yacobi, "Ueber Sukha und Duḥkha," *Zeitschrift für vergleichende Sprachforschung auf dem Gebiete der Indogermanischen Sprachen* 25, no. 4 (1881): 438–40.
53 See the section "Early Buddhism."
54 Paul Younger, "The Concept of Duḥkha and the Indian Religious Tradition," *Journal of the American Academy of Religion* 37, no. 2 (1969): 141–52.
55 Younger, "The Concept of Duḥkha and the Indian Religious Tradition," 144–45.

and so forth, but *also* including something like existential dread.⁵⁶ As mentioned, reliability is an issue because these texts were written down much later and are heavily redacted, but it would be hard to explain why redaction would have *broadened* the term's meaning. If Buddhism is essentially concerned with sankhara-dukkha, as supposedly expressed in the doctrine of the Four Noble Truths, then one would expect redaction to narrow the use of the term dukkha in accordance with that core concern, and not broaden it. That dukkha was not narrowed suggests that it is was not and should not be interpreted narrowly.

Furthermore, the traditional biography of the Buddha does not suggest a narrow interpretation either. According to the Jātaka tales, the kinds of suffering the Buddha witnessed and that motivated him to become a śramaṇa were aging, disease, and death. The story is probably apocryphal, but it suggests that in the early Buddhist tradition the concept of dukkha and the kind of suffering the Buddha was concerned with was broad.

Based on these considerations, it seems rather unlikely that the Buddha's concept of dukkha was narrow. But then why did he focus on sankhara-dukkha?

Perhaps, he did not. Perhaps, the idea that he did is a misunderstanding. The point of the examples of dukkha following the statement of the first Noble Truth in the *Dhammacakkappavattana Sutta* appears to be that life inevitably involves suffering, and if that is the case, then the remedy is obvious. If birth is suffering, as the sūtra explicitly claims, then the solution is no longer being born, and that is exactly the purpose of the Buddha's "Middle Way." Furthermore, rebirth is caused by karma, which according to the Buddha is accumulated by intentional or volitional action, and intention or volition depends on something like desire. Thus, the doctrine that became known as the Four Noble Truths may originally have been something like the following: (1) Life inherently involves suffering (in the broad sense); (2) New lives or rebirths are caused by intentional actions (karma) and thus by craving or desire; (3) There is a way to end suffering, namely, by eliminating karma and rebirth (i.e., new lives with new suffering); (4) That way is the "Middle Way." If this interpretation is correct, then the Buddha was never specifically concerned with existential dread, sankhara-dukkha, or dukkha in some other narrow sense, but always with suffering in a very broad sense.

But this is not the only possible answer to the question. Perhaps, the Buddha did indeed focus on curing sankhara-dukkha. If the problem diagnosed in the first Noble Truth is suffering in a broad sense, however, then there must be a reason why only a cure is offered for dukkha in a narrow sense (i.e., for sankhara-dukkha), but as far as I can see, no explicit reason or argument is offered. This could imply that the Buddha was not aware of the narrowing of the notion of dukkha, which seems implausible, or that he did not see a need to mention a reason or argument for narrowing of the notion. The latter may have been the case if that reason or argument was too obvious to be considered explicitly in the cultural context. If cultural circumstances such as pre-modern individualism and system blindness make many kinds of suffering seem like inevitable facts of life,⁵⁷ then there is no point in trying to diagnose and remedy

---

56 It may be the case that the explicit inclusion of existential dread (or dukkha in the narrow sense) in the concept of *dukkha/duḥkha* is a typical feature of Greater-Maghadan culture. But this is a topic that requires further research.

57 On pre-modern individualism and system blindness, see section "Moralistic versus Systemic Critique" in chapter 4.

those. And if life inevitably involves aging, sickness, death, and a variety of other forms and kinds of suffering, and there is, therefore, little if anything one can do about that, then it makes sense to focus one's attention on a kind of suffering that *can* be remedied.

Other answers are possible, and it is also possible that the Buddha's ideas about dukkha subtly changed during his long life. If we can trust his biography, the Buddha lived and taught for many decades after his awakening and it is rather unlikely that during this long period his views did not somehow further develop. Nevertheless, regardless of what exactly the Buddha taught, available evidence does not suggest that his concept of dukkha was narrow, even if he focused on remedying just sankhara-dukkha or some related specific variety of dukkha. Furthermore, the notion of dukkha in early Buddhism does not seem to be narrow either. Therefore, Buddhism is not essentially concerned with dukkha in some specific, narrow sense. It could be said that it is essentially concerned with dukkha, but given the variety in interpretations of that term — from broad to narrow and with all kinds of sub-species of the narrow interpretation — this is not a very meaningful statement.

A suggestion that Buddhism is essentially concerned with suffering would be similarly meaningless as a defining characteristic for the same reason and may even be false if there is a substantial difference in meaning between "suffering" and *dukkha*. Obviously, "suffering" is not a good translation of the very specific notion of sankhara-dukkha, but it is less clear whether it is equally inaccurate or even misleading as a translation of the more general or broader notion.

According to the linguist Anna Wierzbicka, "suffering" is not a linguistic universal, that is, it is not a concept shared by all languages and cultures; but it is a European concept with strong Christian overtones. And "suffering" is fundamentally different from *dukkha*. In her analysis, suffering involves a kind of helplessness or involuntariness that is missing in dukkha, and conversely dukkha is rooted in frustrated desire, which plays no essential role in "suffering."[58] She appears to be unaware of much of the literature on the concept of "suffering," however, and her interpretation of *dukkha* is based on a very small number of secondary sources.[59] Moreover, that interpretation of *dukkha* is heavily influenced by Buddhist thought and misrepresents the more general notion of dukkha found in non-Buddhist sources and probably even in much of the Pāli canon itself. Desire is not an essential component of that general notion but is what causes dukkha according to Buddhism.

Wierzbicka does have a point that suffering is involuntary. One would not normally say that someone who is getting a painful tattoo is suffering, for example, and it is the fact that the pain involved in getting a tattoo is voluntary which seems to make the difference. Dukkha appears to be broader than this, as it includes pain, but the more subtle forms of dukkha distinguished in the Buddhist tradition are certainly involuntary and outside one's control.

---

58 Anna Wierzbicka, "'Pain' and 'Suffering' in Cross-Linguistic Perspective," *International Journal of Language and Culture* 1, no. 2 (2014): 149–73.
59 This is, moreover, fairly typical in the research program called "Natural Semantic Metalanguage" that Wierzbicka founded. In Lajos Brons, "Recognizing 'Truth' in Chinese Philosophy," *Logos & Episteme* 7, no. 3 (2016): 273–86, I remarked that the claims about linguistic universals in this research program generally "seem to be based on extensive knowledge of language, but remain extremely opaque, and often evoke the suspicion of armchair speculation (or even of being driven by the theory they are supposed to support more than by available data)," and that surely seems to be the case here.

Perhaps, this is the main difference between "suffering" and *dukkha*: the former is contrasted to pain while the latter includes pain. By far the largest body of literature on pain and suffering outside Buddhism belongs (unsurprisingly) to medical and nursing science, and an important question in that literature is how to distinguish the two concepts. The most influential answer to this question is based on Eric Castell's definition of "suffering" "as the state of severe distress associated with events that threaten the intactness of a person,"[60] wherein the term "person" refers more or less to someone's self-concept or the things and capabilities that matter most to someone and which are, therefore, part of one's self-concept.[61] Among critical responses to Castell's definition two of the most important are those by Steven Edwards and Franco Carnevale.[62] The first stressed that suffering is something felt, must have a significant duration, and must have "a fairly central place in the mental life of the subject."[63] The second argued convincingly that suffering is an emotion, while pain is a localized sensation. Nevertheless, while Edwards and Carnevale succeeded in showing some oversights or weaknesses in Castell's definition, neither rejected it completely, and for that reason, I'm inclined to see their critique as proposals for amendment or supplements more than rejections. What stands is that suffering is subjective (i.e., can be judged by the sufferer only), and that suffering is associated with threats to the self or its self-defining attachments.

Again, the notion of dukkha is broader than suffering, but what is problematized most about suffering in the Buddhist tradition is not pain, but more subtle forms and aspects of suffering such as its involuntariness and its subversion of what matters to us most — what Castell called "the intactness of the person" — and those are exactly what separate suffering from mere pain. Consequently, while "suffering" and *dukkha* are not strictly identical indeed, the first is a pretty good translation of the second.

Karma, Rebirth, (No-)self, and Nirvāṇa

One of the main differences between modernist and traditional versions of Buddhism concerns the reality of karma and rebirth. Some modernists and academic Buddhologists have argued that neither doctrine is essential to Buddhism,[64] while others, such as Ambedkar and Buddhadāsa, have proposed changes to these doctrines that are so substantial that they imply a dismissal of the traditional doctrines as well.[65] On the other hand, if the original teaching of the Buddha was that life

---

60 Eric Castell, "The Nature of Suffering and the Goals of Medicine," *The New England Journal of Medicine* 306, no. 11 (1982): 639–45, at 640, and *The Nature of Suffering and the Goals of Medicine* (Oxford: Oxford University Press, 1991), 33.
61 In his analysis of the concept of "suffering," the philosopher Thomas Metzinger reaches a similar but not identical conclusion about the centrality of something like a self-concept in suffering. Suffering is "owned" by a person. Metzinger writes that "the essence of suffering lies in the fact that a conscious system is forced to identify with a state of negative valence and is unable to break this identification or to detach itself" ("Suffering," in *The Return of Consciousness: A New Science on Old Questions*, eds. Kurt Almqvist and Anders Haag [Stockholm: Axel and Margaret Ax:son Johnson Foundation, 2017], 237–62, at 246).
62 Steven Edwards, "Three Concepts of Suffering," *Medicine, Health Care and Philosophy* 6 (2003): 59–66, and Franco Carnevale, "A Conceptual and Moral Analysis of Suffering," *Nursing Ethics* 16, no. 2 (2009): 173–83.
63 Edwards, "Three Concepts of Suffering," 65.
64 See the section "Secular Buddhism" in chapter 3.
65 See the sections on Buddhadasa and Ambedkar in chapter 3.

inherently involves suffering and that the only way to prevent future suffering is not being reborn and passing into nirvāṇa, as suggested as a possible interpretation in the previous section, then *that* "original Buddhism" would make no sense without karma and rebirth. Furthermore, according to Johannes Bronkhorst, the Buddha revised the Greater-Maghadan theory of karma and rebirth, which suggested that he believed that his revised theory was important.[66] That revision concerns the role of intention or volition. As mentioned in chapter 2,[67] the Greater Maghadan view was that all actions lead to the accumulation of karma and thereby to rebirth, while the Buddha held that intentions or volitions (*cetanā*) lead to rebirth. This revision is a key premise in the interpretation of the Four Noble Truths suggested above. In that interpretation, the second Noble Truth *is* the Buddha's revised theory of karma and rebirth: new lives (i.e., rebirths) are caused by intentional or volitional actions, which are themselves rooted in craving or desire. What follows from this premise is that the only way to eliminate future suffering is the elimination of the cause of rebirth: karma, and thus craving or desire.

If one, on the other hand, interprets the Four Noble Truths as being concerned with the analysis and transcendence of some more specific kind of suffering similar to existential anguish, then neither karma nor rebirth plays any significant role. In the contrary, as Mark Siderits has suggested, "if I take myself to live only one life instead of the indefinitely many lives promised by rebirth, then the fact of my own mortality takes on even greater significance" and remedying my suffering only becomes more urgent.[68]

I do not know whether either of these two interpretations of the Four Noble Truths is right, and I expect that adherents of one will consider the other a heresy, but both are defensible and many other interpretations are possible and have been defended. Lacking sufficient reliable evidence, there is no objective and non-dogmatic criterion to decide between such competing interpretations aside from coherence. By implication, there are legitimate interpretations of Buddhist doctrine that do not presuppose karma and rebirth, and consequently, karma and rebirth cannot be necessary elements of a definition of Buddhism. Furthermore, even if it would be the case that all legitimate interpretations of Buddhist doctrine involve karma and rebirth, these could only be considered essential elements of Buddhism if karma and rebirth are themselves singular, unequivocal doctrines, and that is not the case.

First of all, it is not entirely clear how to understand the theories of karma.[69] Is it a metaphysical theory that holds that karma is some kind of thing, process, substance, or natural law? Or is it something else? Francisca Cho, for example, claims that karma is not a metaphysical notion but is used "performatively" by traditional Buddhists "in order to orient their personal experiences."[70] I'm not convinced by her argument, however. As far as I can see most Buddhists claim that karma exists in some form or other, and thus make a metaphysical claim. Often karma is claimed to be something like a law or process, but if karma is something that can accumulate,

---

66 Bronkhorst, *Greater Maghada*, 19–20.
67 See the section "Early Buddhism" in chapter 2.
68 Mark Siderits, "Buddhism and Techno-Physicalism: Is the Eightfold Path a Program?" *Philosophy East & West* 51, no. 3 (2001): 307–14, at 312. See also the section "Physicalism" in chapter 4.
69 On this problem, see, for example, Wendy O'Flaherty, "Introduction," in *Karma and Rebirth in Classical Indian Traditions*, ed. Wendy O'Flaherty (Berkeley: University of California Press, 1980), ix–xxv.
70 Francisca Cho, "Buddhism, Science, and the Truth about Karma," *Religion Compass* 8, no. 4 (2014): 117–27, at 117.

then it appears more like a substance, albeit a virtual one. As virtual substance, karma may be similar to money in a bank account. By doing good deeds or having right intentions, one's karmic bank balance grows; by doing bad deeds or having wrong intentions, one's karmic bank balance declines.[71] The better your karmic balance, the better your next lives, and if you accumulate a lot, you may not be reborn anymore at all and pass into nirvāṇa. That this is close to how many Buddhists think about karma is also illustrated by the ancient and widespread belief that one can make donations to other people's karmic bank accounts. Throughout the Buddhist world, people make offerings to improve their ancestors' merit, and as Gregory Schopen has shown, this practice is very old and has mainstream (i.e., non- or pre-Mahāyāna) roots.[72] This "transfer of merit," however, only makes sense if it is roughly analogous to a transfer or donation of funds, and thus if karma indeed works much like a bank account, but that view seems to conflict with another theory of karma — namely, that karma is and can only be the balance of one's own actions or intentions.

The notion of caste is closely related to that of karma, but never played an important role in Buddhist doctrine, and Ambedkar has suggested the rejection of caste as a key element of the Buddha's teachings.[73] Whether this is a justifiable claim is hard to say. Bryan Levman has suggested that caste was not part of the Buddha's cultural heritage,[74] but according to Donald Lopez "there is no evidence that the Buddha sought to 'reform' or destroy what has been called the caste system,"[75] and there are references to caste in the Pāli canon. It is possible, however, that those references and the Buddha's apparent adherence to caste are the result of later redactions under Brahmanic influence.

The notions of rebirth and nirvāṇa are as central to Buddhist doctrine as karma, if not more, and are at least as ambiguous. Much of this ambiguity is the product of the interplay of these notions with the doctrine of no-self. According to the latter doctrine, there are no self-defining essences — there is nothing, *no thing*, that is me. This doctrine, or collection of doctrines perhaps, is little understood, and plays virtually no role in *lay* Buddhism. Furthermore, it is not even certain whether the Buddha himself held this belief, as Bronkhorst has pointed out. According to Vedic and Brahmanic beliefs, knowledge of the self is a prerequisite for liberation, and it is this belief that the Buddha denied. There is no liberating knowledge of the self, but the metaphysical question whether there *is* a self is quite irrelevant.[76]

Regardless of whatever the Buddha himself exactly believed, all schools of Buddhism accept some doctrine of no-self. An obvious implication of this doctrine is that there is nothing that can transmigrate from this life to the next and nothing that can enter nirvāṇa after one's final life, but this is not what the majority of Bud-

---

71 While the "karma bank" might seem an inappropriately Western or modern metaphor, this impression would be mistaken. Both in India and China Buddhist monasteries gained some of their income from lending money on interest. Hence, monasteries functioned among others as banks. See, for example, Gregory Schopen, "Doing Business for the Lord: Lending on Interest and Written Loan Contracts in the *Mūlasarvāstivāda-vinaya*," in *Buddhist Monks and Business Matters: Still More Papers on Monastic Buddhism in India* (Honolulu: University of Hawai'i Press, 2004), 45–90.
72 Schopen, *Bones, Stones, and Buddhist Monks*.
73 See the section "Ambedkar and the 'New Vehicle' in India" in chapter 3.
74 Bryan Levman, "Cultural Remnants of the Indigenous Peoples in the Buddhist Scriptures," *Buddhist Studies Review* 30, no. 2 (2013): 145–80.
75 Donald Lopez, Jr., *Buddhism & Science: A Guide for the Perplexed* (Chicago: University of Chicago Press, 2008), 80.
76 Bronkhorst, *Buddhist Teaching in India*, 27.

dhists believe. Richard Gombrich has found that "belief in personal survival after death is a fundamental feature of Sinhalese Buddhism in practice,"[77] and if you ask any lay adherent of Japanese Pure Land Buddhism she will tell you that she hopes to be personally reborn in Amitābha's Pure land after death. Aside from a small minority of intellectuals and learned monks, Buddhists believe in personal survival after death, and thus in a surviving self. But traces of such beliefs can also be found in the canonical texts. Nirvāṇa is usually not described as complete extinction, as no-self would imply, but as peaceful, wonderful, marvelous, blissful, pure, and so forth,[78] and thus as a place where the self can go or as a state the self can enter. Furthermore, as already mentioned above, the *Ariyapariyesanā Sutta* associates nirvāṇa with immortality.[79]

Karma, rebirth, nirvāṇa, and related notions may play important roles in much Buddhist thought, but these terms do not refer to singular, unequivocal doctrines. Rather, understanding of what these terms refer to differs widely between sects, schools, and believers. There is no such thing as a single doctrine of karma and a single doctrine of rebirth and so forth, and consequently, these cannot be defining features of Buddhism.

The Middle Way

A very similar problem occurs in case of the notion of the or a Middle Way, which is so ingrained in Buddhist self-identity that "the Middle Way" has often been used to designate Buddhism as a whole. Ichikawa Hakugen 市川白弦 has pointed out that this self-identification of Buddhism as "the Middle Way" has lead to conformism and a compromising attitude in sociopolitical matters, and considers it to be one of the factors that lead to the complicity of the Buddhist sects in Japanese militarism and fascism in the first half of the twentieth century. Furthermore, the notion seems to imply that less compromising attitudes and radical alternatives are inherently "un-Buddhist," and consequently, the Middle Way doctrine has hampered the development of Buddhist socialism and anarchism and other radical Buddhisms, which makes the notion especially relevant in the present context.[80]

However, the notion of *the* Middle Way is also deeply flawed, which is most clearly illustrated by means of an analogy. Imagine three travelers arriving at a fork in the road as shown in figure 5.1 (they come from the left bottom corner). There's a road to the left and a road to the right, but they do not like either of those roads. "They're too extreme," says one of them to the others. "We should take the middle way," another replies. So the first one decides to go between the two forks in the direction of the arrow labeled "A" in the figure. The second turns around and decides to go back (arrow B). And the third gets a shovel from his backpack and starts digging straight down (arrow C). Clearly, it makes no sense to say that all three of these travelers are taking *the* middle way. The point of the analogy is that it makes no sense to call Buddhism "the Middle Way" for exactly the same reason.

---

77 Richard Gombrich, *Buddhist Precept and Practice: Traditional Buddhism in the Rural Highlands of Ceylon* (Oxford: Clarendon, 1971), 243.
78 Jan Westerhoff, "Buddhism without Reincarnation? Examining the Prospects of a 'Naturalized' Buddhism," in *A Mirror Is for Reflection: Understanding Buddhist Ethics*, ed. Jake David (Oxford: Oxford University Press, 2017), 146–65, at 154.
79 See the section "The Idea of an 'Original Buddhism'" in this chapter.
80 Ichikawa Hakugen 市川白弦, 『仏教者の戦争責任』 (Tokyo: Shunshūsha 春秋社, 1970).

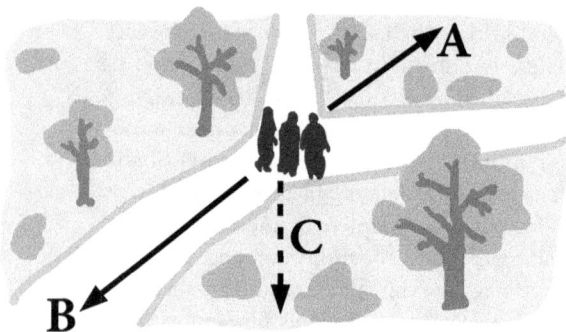

Fig. 5.1. Three travelers take the "middle way."

The most prominent occurrence of the term "Middle Way" in Buddhist texts is in the *Dhammacakkappavattana Sutta*, which opens with the Buddha's doctrine of a Middle Way between asceticism and the pursuit of sensual pleasure, a Middle Way that leads to vision, knowledge, peace, awakening, and nirvāṇa. This is arrow A in the figure: the Buddha carves a new path in between the two existing forks in the road, both of which he deems to extreme.

Importantly, this is the only use of the term "Middle Way" about which we can say with a fair degree of confidence that it goes back to the Buddha himself. A similar, but not identical phrase occurs in the *Nidānavagga* section of the *Connected Discourses*, where it says that the Buddha "teaches the Dhamma by the middle" between the extremes "all exists" and "all does not exist"[81] or between "eternalism" and "annihilationism."[82] This "middle" is not called "the Middle Way," however. And more importantly, it is not like arrow A in figure 5.1 either. Rather, *this* "middle" is more like the skeptical strategy of denying an assumption that underlies both of the options presented. It is a return to an earlier overlooked fork in the road where that assumption was made, and consequently, this "middle" is more like arrow B than like A. Eternalism is the view that there is a self, soul, or person, that survives death; annihilationism is the view that the self does not survive death, but is annihilated at death. The "middle" in this case is the rejection of the assumption underlying both of these views that there is a self in the first place.

So, while the Middle Way between asceticism and hedonism is like a compromise between two extremes, a middle path in a very literal sense, this second middle is no compromise at all, but a rejection of both options. It is a return (like B) to an earlier fork in the path, where both of the options presented took the same road by making the same assumption, and a continuation on the alternative, overlooked path from that fork by rejecting that shared assumption.

A third version of the "middle way" emerged in later Buddhist thought in response to the "middle" between the extremes "all exists" and "all does not exist" mentioned above. This middle way is associated mainly with Nāgārjuna and his Tibetan interpreters like Tsong Khapa. "All exists" is taken to be the position that everything we experience exists *as such* (i.e., as experienced) — let's call this "naive realism." The opposing view is called "nihilism." Jay Garfield explains that the strategy of the

---

81 SN 12.15/544.
82 SN 12.17/547.

middle here is another skeptical move but one that turns the order of explanation around.⁸³ The nihilist points at problems and inconsistencies the naive realist cannot explain. The strategy of the middle follows the nihilist up to this point but then argues that what is taken for granted in demonstrating those problems and inconsistencies is itself problematic. This may sound rather obscure, but what matters here is just that this strategy is neither the middle way as compromise (arrow A), nor the middle as rejection of an underlying assumption and return to a previous fork in the road (arrow B), but a third kind of "middle" (but whether it is analogous to arrow C, I do not know).

The fall-out of all of this is that it makes little sense to call Buddhism "the Middle Way." It may have been an effective rhetorical device, but it certainly cannot define Buddhism. A second important conclusion is that there is no reason to believe that the Buddha had a general preference for compromise or other kinds of middle paths. He argued for a middle between asceticism and hedonism — that much seems reasonably certain — but that is all. And consequently, Buddhist conformism and antiradicalism is based on a mistake.

That said, there is reason to believe that the Buddha tended to avoid radical positions in sociopolitical matters, but this has little to do with a purported doctrine of moderation. As mentioned above, the *Attadaṇḍa Sutta* suggests that it was partially motivated by a fear of social conflict,⁸⁴ but probably more important was a general reluctance on the Buddha's account to take a position in matters that he did not consider important for achieving liberation or awakening. The latter could be added to figure 5.1 as a fourth traveler who, upon reaching the fork in the road, refuses to take any of the available paths and just stays there. What this fourth traveler's choice is analogous of is not a further "middle way," however, but *quietism*.

Metaphysics, Rationality, and Free Inquiry

It is often claimed that the Buddha adopted quietism with regards to metaphysical questions. There are indeed many sūtras in which the Buddha refuses to answer metaphysical questions or to take a position in metaphysical debates on the ground that such metaphysical speculation is "unbeneficial," "does not belong to the fundamentals of the holy life," and "does not lead to disenchantment, to dispassion, to cessation, to peace, to direct knowledge, to Nibbāna."⁸⁵ However, it is not true that the Buddha rejected all metaphysics — his beliefs in karma and rebirth, for example, were metaphysical beliefs — and it is certainly not the case that the Buddhist tradition rejected metaphysical speculation. In the contrary, Abhidharma scholasticism in the centuries after the Buddha's death involved a grand theory about the nature of reality, and most later sects and schools implicitly or explicitly developed or adopted metaphysical positions as well.

Nevertheless, there also have been schools that rejected metaphysical speculation, or appeared to do so, on quietist or meta-metaphysical grounds.⁸⁶ Within Buddhist

---

83 Jay Garfield, "Epochē and Śūnyatā: Skepticism East and West" (1990), in *Empty Words: Buddhist Philosophy and Cross-Cultural Interpretation* (Oxford: Oxford University Press, 2002), 3–23.
84 Sn 4.15.
85 *Cūḷamālunkya Sutta*, MN 63, §8/536. See also *Aggivacchagotta Sutta*, MN 72, and *Brahmajāla Sutta*, DN 1.
86 Meta-metaphysics, or meta-ontology, is a twig of a branch of philosophy that is concerned with the nature, possibility, methods, and core concepts of metaphysics.

philosophy, both of the main branches of Mahāyāna developed meta-metaphysical views, but there is considerable disagreement about what exactly those views were. For example, Mark Siderits suggests that Yogācāra held a metaphysical position, namely a form of idealism, while Mādhyamaka took the meta-metaphysical stance that no coherent metaphysical position is possible, but according to Dan Lusthaus it is more or less the other way around, that is, Yogācārins did not take a metaphysical position because attachment to metaphysical views was part of the problem.[87]

There are many disagreements and controversies like this in the academic study of Buddhist thought, but what is beyond dispute is that the Buddhist tradition is also a philosophical tradition. Some Buddhists modernists even claim that Buddhism is a philosophy rather than a religion. This does not seem exactly right to me, but I'll address that topic in the next chapter. Closely related to the idea that Buddhism is a philosophy more than a religion is the perception of Buddhism as inherently rational and anti-dogmatic. There is much in the history of Buddhism that seems to confirm this view, but there is also much irrationality and unthinking acceptance of dogma.

Modernist arguments for the rationality of Buddhism — as well as for its supposed endorsement of free inquiry — invariably rely on the *Kesamutti Sutta* (also known as *Kālāma Sutta*) in which the Buddha advises:

> Do not go by oral tradition, by lineage of teaching, by hearsay, by a collection of scriptures, by logical reasoning, by inferential reasoning, by reasoned cogitation, by the acceptance of a view after pondering it, by the seeming competence [of a speaker], or because you think: "The ascetic is our guru." But when you know for yourselves: "These things are wholesome; these things are blameless; these things are praised by the wise; these things, if accepted and undertaken, lead to welfare and happiness," then you should live in accordance with them.[88]

And similarly, when

> you know for yourselves: "These things are unwholesome; these things are blameworthy; these things are censured by the wise; these things, if accepted and undertaken, lead to harm and suffering," then you should abandon them.[89]

These passages are interesting for a number of reasons. First, they remind of epistemological debates in Indian philosophy about the proper sources of knowledge. Most schools of Indian philosophy recognized three such *pramāṇas* (sources of knowledge): perception (*pratyakṣa*), inference (*anumāna*), and *śabda*, which includes reliable textual sources and things learned from reliable experts. (Śabda is close to what in Western epistemology is called "testimony.") The list of candidate pramāṇas that the Buddha rejects in these passages are all variants of inference (the 5th to 8th) and śabda (the 1st to 4th and the last two).

Second, the pramāṇa debates in Indian philosophy emerged mostly in response to the Buddhist challenge to Vedic orthodoxy, and thus started centuries after the

---

87 Mark Siderits, "The Case for Discontinuity," in *Madhyamaka and Yogācāra: Allies or Rivals?*, eds. Jay Garfield and Jan Westerhof (Oxford: Oxford University Press, 2015), 111–26, and Dan Lusthaus, *Buddhist Phenomenology: A Philosophical Investigation of Yogācāra Buddhism and the Ch'eng Wei-shih lun* (London: RoutledgeCurzon, 2002).
88 AN 3.65, 281.
89 Ibid., 280.

events recounted in the *Kesamutti Sutta*. This might seem to suggest that the text was redacted in response to the pramāṇa debates, but that is actually quite unlikely. In those debates the Buddhist position was that perception and inference are the only two pramāṇas, but in this sūtra the Buddha rejects inference (as well as śabda, which was recognized as a pramāṇa by most schools of what later would be called Hindu philosophy). Hence, this sūtra conflicts with later Buddhist epistemological orthodoxy. If it had been redacted in response to the pramāṇa debates it would surely have been redacted to match orthodoxy.

Third, while these passages *might* be read as supporting free inquiry, they most certainly do not support rationality. In the contrary, the Buddha's explicit rejection of variants of inference is a rejection of the use of reason as a tool to gain knowledge. The passages are decidedly anti-rational.

Fourth, if inference and śbada are rejected as sources of knowledge, then it seems that only perception is left, but these passages do not explicitly endorse perception. Instead they tell you to accept or reject "when you know for yourself" (*attanāva jāneyyātha*) that some practice leads to welfare or suffering and so forth. What the passages fail to tell is how one gets to know something "for oneself." It could be by empirical means, but considering that the passage does not advocate to *find out* for oneself, but instead assumes that one already somehow knows, a more plausible interpretation is that knowing something "for oneself" refers to something like gut-feeling or intuition, the very opposite of rational inquiry.

Furthermore, it is not clear what the criteria for acceptance of rejection mean exactly either. The first passage quoted above instructs to reject a practice if "you know for yourself" that "these things, if accepted and undertaken *by you*, lead to harm and suffering." The italicized words "by you" are missing in the otherwise excellent translation quoted above but are implied by the phrase in Pāli: *ime dhammā samattā samādinnā ahitāya dukkhāya saṃvattantī'ti*.[90] What is unclear is whose suffering or happiness the phrase refers to. Do these passages recommend to establish in some unspecified way whatever makes you happy or unhappy and then stick to that? Or do they recommend to accept or reject what leads to happiness or suffering in general?

Regardless of the answers to these last questions, this sūtra does not endorse rationality. While it is undeniable that rationality and logic played a central role in many schools and currents of Buddhism, especially those with strong philosophical inclinations,[91] it is equally undeniable that there have been and continue to be many forms of Buddhism, especially those focused exclusively on ritual, in which rationality plays no important role at all. Furthermore, there is no evidence that the Buddha endorsed rationality. In the contrary, the *Kesamutti Sutta*, which is often quoted in this regard, actually suggests the opposite.[92]

---

90 *Samādinnā* derives from *samādiyati*, meaning "to take upon oneself," "to undertake (by oneself)," "to accept (oneself)," and so forth.
91 According to Johannes Bronkhorst, the rational element was introduced to Buddhism by the Sarvāstivāda school in the third or second century BCE, possibly under Greek influence. See Bronkhorst, *Buddhist Teaching in India*, 114.
92 Dale Riepe has argued that intuition, especially the intuition of the Buddha, is the highest source of knowledge in Buddhism. Indeed, more often than not, the criterion to accept something as true in the Pāli canon is that the proposition in question was set forth by the Buddha on the basis of his intuition. Hence, rather than free inquiry, the canonical texts appear to advocate uncritical acceptance of the Buddha's authority. Dale Riepe, *The Naturalistic Tradition in Indian Thought* (Delhi: Motilal Banarsidass, 1961).

Meditation, Pacifism, and Dependent Origination

The pattern that has been emerging in the preceding sections is probably best described as a lack of pattern. Of the candidates for inclusion in a definition of Buddhism considered thus far, none appears to be universal and univocal, and most fail in both respects. Although this suggests that this approach to defining Buddhism is probably misguided, there a few more candidates that deserve attention, either because they are often considered to be a fundamental element of Buddhist philosophy, or because they are emphasized by many Buddhist modernists and engaged Buddhists.

The two most important philosophical doctrines that have not been mentioned yet are impermanence and dependent origination. According to the first, everything is impermanent, and this is a cause of more subtle forms of suffering (dukkha). Outside Buddhist *philosophy* this doctrine plays no important role or is even denied. As already mentioned above, most Buddhists believe in personal survival after death and in immortality — and thus in permanence — of whatever survives. The doctrine of dependent origination plays no significant role outside philosophy either, but this doctrine is not an acceptable defining element of Buddhism for another reason: it was most likely not taught by the Buddha himself, but dates to a later period in which early Buddhists started to develop a Buddhist response to the Vedic/Brahmanic doctrine of liberating knowledge.[93]

Two supposed aspects of Buddhism that are often emphasized by engaged Buddhists and Buddhist modernists, respectively, are pacifism and meditation. According to the early and very influential Sarvāstivāda school, liberation or awakening does not require meditation,[94] and meditation plays no important role in Pure Land Buddhism and in many other historical and current schools and sects of Buddhism. Furthermore, there is probably no concept in the Buddhist tradition that is as vague and polysemous as "meditation." The category includes zazen (sitting Zen meditation), Tibetan visualization practices,[95] Buddhaghosa's meditation on death,[96] and much more. There is little that these and the hundreds of other practices called "meditation" have in common. Significantly, in his *Visuddhimagga*, a "meditation manual" and one of the most influential texts in Theravāda Buddhism, Buddhaghosa wrote that meditation "is of many sorts and has various aspects" and refused to define meditation because any attempt to define it would only "lead to distraction."[97]

Pacifism, finally, can hardly be a defining element of Buddhism. It is too peripheral for that and has not been universally adhered to by Buddhists either. From Japanese temple armies to South-Asian Buddhist kings spreading Buddhism through war, there is much in the history of Buddhism that contradicts the idea that Buddhism, in practice, must be pacifist. And neither is there consistent support for the idea that it should be pacifist in theory. According to Iselyn Frydenlund, the idea that Buddhism is pacifist is a relatively recent, modernist construction resulting from a kind of "positive Orientalism." She points out that "political paradigms

---

93 Bronkhorst, *Buddhist Teaching in India*, 44.
94 Ibid., 106.
95 Donald *Buddhism & Science*, 197–207, spends ten pages giving a detailed description of the visualizations in this kind of meditation.
96 Buddhaghosa, *Visuddhimagga* (5th c.), trans. Bhikkhu Nyanamoli (Onalaska: BPS Pariyatti, 1999), VIII.1–41. See also the section "Suffering, Shock, and Intoxication" in chapter 13.
97 Ibid., III.2.

in the Pāli canon all accept the institution of war, in that they regard it as being within the jurisdiction of the state," and that canonical sources apply the principle of non-violence (ahiṃsā) to individuals only, further making exceptions for soldiers and kings.[98]

Defining "Buddhism" and "Buddhist"

A definition should neither be too broad, nor too narrow. It should not exclude what should be included because it falls under the term defined or include what should be excluded because it does not. Definitions of Buddhism focusing on philosophical doctrines violate this criterion because doctrines like no-self or dependent origination are not universally (or even widely!) understood and accepted. But even much more basic ideas turn out to be problematic in this respect. If the core doctrines of the Four Noble Truths and the badness of suffering are interpreted too broadly, then medicine, for example, would be included in the definition. If, on the other hand, they are interpreted too narrowly, then the definition might even exclude the Buddha himself.

A second criterion is that a good definition captures essential or core characteristics rather than peripheral ones. Plato's not entirely serious definition of "human" as "featherless biped" violates this criterion and so do several of the candidates discussed above. Even if the supposed penchant for pacifism would be universal among Buddhists and Buddhisms, it would not be a likely element of a definition of Buddhism for this reason. And rationality, the rejection of caste, or metaphysical quietism are too peripheral — in addition to other problems mentioned in preceding sections — to define Buddhism as well.

The point of a definition is to improve clarity, and not reduce it, and for this reason, definitions should not be vague, obscure, or ambiguous. Most importantly, a definition should not rely on terms that are themselves ambiguous or polysemous. As an illustration of a violation of this criterion, consider a stipulative definition of *bwonk* as "a bow on a bank." The supposed category of bwonks, then, includes ships' bows on river banks, violin bows on arrays of switches, certain projectile weapons on financial institutions, and much more. These things have absolutely nothing in common, except that they can all be described as "bows on banks," and consequently, the concept of *bwonk* is utterly useless, except as an illustration of utterly useless concepts. Meditation practices and interpretations of the notion of the (or a) Middle Way vary as much as ship's bows and violin bows, or river banks and financial banks, and are, therefore, not useful elements in a definition of Buddhism. Like bwonks, all that some practices called "meditation" share is a label.

When applied to "Buddhism," the second of these criteria may be the most controversial. Of the fourteen candidates for inclusion in a definition of Buddhism considered in the preceding sections, there are two that are uncontroversially core features — the closely related doctrines of the Four Noble Truths and the badness of suffering or dukkha — and four that are probably uncontroversially peripheral, namely, the rejection of caste, metaphysical quietism, rationality or free inquiry, and non-violence. For any of the remaining eight, it is debated whether they are core

---

98 Iselin Frydenlund, "'Buddhism Has Made Asia Mild': The Modernist Construction of Buddhims as Pacifism," in *Buddhist Modernities: Re-Inventing Tradition in the Globalizing Modern World*, eds. Hanna Havnevik et al. (New York: Routledge, 2017), 204–21, at 208.

characteristics of Buddhism or not. However, any of those eight — the doctrines of karma, rebirth, no-self, impermanence, and dependent origination, the notions of nirvāṇa and the Middle Way, and the practices of meditation — violates at least one of the other two criteria.[99] And as already mentioned a few paragraphs back, the two uncontroversial core features are too vague or ambiguous to define Buddhism as well.

This does not mean that Buddhism cannot be defined, however. What is means is that Buddhism has no clear and univocal defining *essence*, but considering that most Buddhist philosophies are anti-essentialist — they hold that *nothing* has an essence,[100] that there are no essences — this seems a very appropriate conclusion.[101]

The main alternative to an essentialist definition is analogous to the definition of a family: the defining criterion is descendance or ancestry. Contrary to the originalist approach, which identifies Buddhism with its founder (or, actually, with a reconstruction thereof), this approach defines Buddhism as what descends from that founder. Mere descendance is insufficient as a defining criterion, however. If mere descendance was sufficient to define a family, then you and I would be family because if we could trace our ancestry far enough, we'd surely find a shared ancestor that both of us descend from. In case of families, we tend to draw a fuzzy boundary between the inside and the outside on the basis of the number of discrete steps of direct descendance — that is, parent-child relations — but here the analogy stops being useful: there are no discrete steps in genetic trees of doctrines, ideas, and -isms.

The most obvious alternative is to require a sufficient degree of similarity. This is more or less the approach of Wittgenstein's famous idea of "family resemblances."[102] There is no single characteristic that all of the members of a family share, but there is a pool of characteristics, and every family member has a number of the characteristics in that pool. In case of Buddhism it would be hard to define that pool of characteristics, however. The Four Noble Truths should be in it, of course, but in which form and interpretation? Including only one would surely make the definition too narrow, but including all of them would make the definition unmanageable and probably also too broad.[103] Similar problems apply to many of the other defining elements considered above. The family resemblance approach, then, does not look promising either.

The most common type of definition is called "definition by genus and difference." This kind of definition specifies a larger category, the genus, and what sets

---

[99] In summary: Karma — too narrow; does not play a role in all schools and variants of Buddhism. Rebirth and nirvāṇa — too broad; also found outside Buddhism, although usually as *mokṣa* rather than *nirvāṇa*. No-self, impermanence, and dependent origination — too narrow; play no role in non-philosophical Buddhism. The Middle Way and meditation — polysemous; refer to several very different and unrelated things.

[100] This is just a generalization of the doctrine of no-self. The self is the essence of a person. Persons do not have an essence or self, but other things do not have an essence or "self" either. See the section "Realism (1) — Universals and (Anti-)essentialism" in chapter 7.

[101] This anti-essentialism cannot be part of the defining "essence" of Buddhism either for the same reason that other philosophical doctrines cannot be: the resulting definition would exclude non-philosophical Buddhism and thus be too narrow.

[102] Ludwig Wittgenstein, *Philosophische Untersuchungen* (1953; Frankfurt a.M.: Suhrkamp, 1975), §§65–71.

[103] The easiest way to include all interpretations, which would also avoid making the definition unmanageable, is to have "some version of the Four Noble Truths" in the pool of defining characteristics, and to take a similar approach in case of other ambiguous or polysemous elements. The resulting definition would be far too broad, however. It would almost certainly include medicine and many kinds of therapy, and possibly even some political ideologies.

the thing defined apart from that larger category, the difference. Plato's definition of "human" as "featherless biped" is an example of this type. "Biped" is the genus; "featherless" is what makes humans different from other bipeds. Whether Buddhism can be defined in this way is an open question, but even if no exact specification of the difference can be given, it would be helpful to at least know the genus. Here we stumble upon a problem immediately: while most people would say that Buddhism is a religion, some Buddhist modernists and secular Buddhists deny that and maintain that Buddhism is a philosophy instead.

The German language has two words that are closely related to both "religion" and "philosophy": *Weltanschauung* and *Lebensanschauung*. The first can be translated literally as "worldview," but the second has no English equivalent, though a literal translation would be "life-view." A life-view is close to what is sometimes called someone's "philosophy" in colloquial language. It includes views on life and what makes life valuable, on appropriate life goals and the meaning of life, on how to properly live one's life, on the good life and the bad, and so forth. The notion of a *Lebensanschauung* or life-view overlaps with ethics and social philosophy, with philosophy of life, with folk psychology, and so forth, but also with the notion of a *Weltanschauung* or worldview. The latter is more focused on ideas about the nature of reality and the world around us, about how the world works, about what exists and what does not; and overlaps with metaphysics and the natural sciences. There is no sharp boundary between the notions of a life-view and a worldview, and often they come together in one larger package, a life/world-view that includes a broad, more or less integrated array of views on life, the nature of reality, the good and the bad, and so forth.

Religions are life/world-views, and so are some but not all philosophies. Marxism, for example, can be considered a life/world-view, while Utilitarianism cannot.[104] Buddhism-as-philosophy would be a life/world-view as well, so regardless of whether Buddhism is (taken to be) a religion or a philosophy, it is a life/world-view. Hence, that's our genus.

Life/world-views are not singular ideas, doctrines, or theories, but collections thereof. They are too broad and multifaceted to be singular "things." Given that individual doctrines and ideas, that is, the elements of such collections, can be "Buddhist" as well, this suggests a different approach to defining Buddhism:

> A life/world-view is Buddhist (and thus a variety of Buddhism) if most of the ideas, doctrines, theories, and so forth that make up that life/world-view are Buddhist.

By this definition, a Marxist Buddhism that consists mostly of Buddhist doctrines with some Marxism mixed in would be a kind of Buddhism, while a Buddhist Marxism that is mostly Marxist with some Buddhist ideas added to the mix would not. While this seems right, there are at least two problems with this definition.

The first and most obvious issue is that this suggestion does not solve the problem of definition but only pushes it down the road. Saying that a collection is Buddhist if most of its elements are Buddhist is meaningful only if there is a good way to

---

104 Utilitarianism is (roughly) the view that an act is right if (of all available acts) it is the act that leads to the greatest happiness for the greatest number of people. Utilitarianism is not a life/world-view because it is far too narrow and specific.

tell whether such elements are Buddhist, and consequently, the suggestion is helpful only if we can define what makes ideas, doctrines, and so forth "Buddhist." This might seem as hard as defining Buddhism itself, but here we may be able to make the family-descendance analogy work.

Descendants mix and recombine the genetic material of their ancestors, but also mutate it and mix it with external influences. Similarly, descendant ideas mix, recombine, reinterpret, and extend ancestor ideas. What makes Dharmakīrti's ideas "Buddhist" is that he built on and remixed ideas that were themselves "Buddhist." But Dharmakīrti was also influenced by the world around him, and consequently, he responded to and incorporated ideas with different, non-Buddhist origins. In the family tree of ideas and doctrines that descend from whatever the Buddha originally taught new ideas were introduced at many points, while old ideas "mutated" into entirely new forms.

The problem for the descendance analogy mentioned above applies here as well: the "genetic" relation may be too distant and too diluted to consider two people to be part of the same family, and the same applies to doctrines and ideas. At what point is an idea or doctrine that is derived from Buddhist ideas no longer "Buddhist"? Would a doctrine (A) that holds that physicians should first diagnose a disease, then identify its cause, and then decide on and implement treatment be Buddhist if the person introducing that doctrine claimed that she based it on the Four Noble Truths? Would a doctrine (B) claiming that what makes an act bad is that it leads to more pain and suffering be Buddhist if the person advocating that doctrine based it on Śāntideva's *Bodhicaryavatara*? Would a doctrine (C) that holds that reality as I experience it is a mental construction be Buddhist just because it was influenced by Yogācāra?

If these doctrines would be embedded in broader life/world-views that are unambiguously Buddhist, then I'm inclined to say that these doctrines are Buddhist as well, but that turns around the order of explanation. We need a criterion to decide whether these doctrines are Buddhist regardless of whether they are advocated or held by someone with a Buddhist life/world-view. Obviously, the descendance/ancestry criterion would imply that these three doctrines are Buddhist, but as already explained above, that criterion is insufficient. By that criterion, if someone would come up with a new doctrine (D) that is loosely based on (B), but that makes no reference whatsoever to Śāntideva, then (D) would be Buddhist because (B) would be Buddhist. And the same applies to a doctrine (E) that is based on (D), and so forth.

Going for the other, hyper-purist extreme does not work either because, if no "mixing in" of new materials and no "mutation" of ideas is allowed, the only Buddhist doctrines are those that were held by the Buddha himself. I hope that the preceding sections have made sufficiently clear that this could (or would?) have the unacceptable implication that almost all of the doctrines, ideas, and practices that we recognize as "Buddhist" turn out not to be Buddhist after all. Clearly, here we need a middle way between hyper-purism and an unrestricted descendance/ancestry criterion.

If someone would hold a doctrine (F) that is identical to (C) except that it is based on Berkeley or some other Western Philosophers rather than on Yogācāra, then, according to an unrestricted descendance/ancestry criterion, (C) would be Buddhist and (F) would not, even though they make the exact same claims. But why would a doctrine or theory be called "Buddhist" if it could just as well be based on or derived from other, that is, non-Buddhist, sources? Notice that in case of (F) and (C) what they are derived from, or their "ancestry," is the *only* difference, and we have already found that that criterion is insufficient. By implication then, if (F) is not "Buddhist," then neither is (C), but this conclusion implicitly gives us an additional criterion: a doctrine is not Buddhist if it could *just as well* be based on other sources.

Inserting this new criterion into the descendance-based definition results in the following:

> A theory, doctrine, practice, or idea is Buddhist if most of what it is based on or derived from is Buddhist and if it could not just as well be based on or derived from non-Buddhist sources.

By this definition, none of the three doctrines suggested above would be "Buddhist." (A) can just as well be based on medical ideas developed by the ancient Greeks or Romans. (B) could just as well be based on a suggestion by Karl Popper.[105] And (C) could just as well be based on Western philosophy. On the other hand, by this definition, *all* of the doctrines, theories, ideas, and practices discussed in previous sections of this chapter are Buddhist. In some cases, similar doctrines can be found elsewhere — Heraclitus also appears to have said that everything is impermanent, for example — but in all such cases there are significant differences in substance besides the difference in ancestry.

Above, I mentioned that there were two problems for the definition of Buddhism as a life/world-view that is made up mostly of Buddhist ideas, doctrines, theories, and so forth, and unfortunately, this only solves the first problem. The second problem concerns the word "most" or "mostly." There is no meaningful way to count doctrines, ideas, practices, and so forth, or even to separate them into discrete individuals. And lacking a way to count doctrines there is no way to say whether most doctrines that make up a life/world-view are Buddhist or not.[106] On the other hand, sometimes you do not need to count. If a glass jar is filled with an uneven mix of white and black beads you might be able to spot immediately that its content is mostly black or mostly white. The need for counting or other exact measures only arises in a gray zone where it is not immediately clear what there is most of. And since it is only to be expected that there is such a gray zone of life/world-views for which we are not exactly sure whether they are Buddhist or not, this second problem may not be a big problem after all.

A similar problem affects the boundary between Buddhist and non-Buddhist doctrines, practices, and ideas, however. The cannot-be-based-just-as-well-on-other-sources criterion does not result in a sharp boundary line either, as there doubtlessly are cases where it is debatable whether a doctrine could be based on other sources *just as well*; not in the least because it is not perfectly clear what "just as well" means. Hence, there also is a gray zone for doctrines.

But why should these gray zones be a reason for concern? Wittgenstein once asked the rhetorical question: "If the border between two countries would be disputed, would it follow that the citizenship of all of their inhabitants would be put

---

105 Karl Popper, *The Open Society and Its Enemies*, Vol. 1 (London: Routledge, 1947). Therein, see note 6 to chapter 5 and note 2 to chapter 9.
106 Actually, this is not exactly right. What is needed is a way of measuring, and counting is just one way of measuring. If I pour 30ml of whisky in a glass, and fill it up with 120ml of water, then my glass would be filled with mostly water (and I would have wasted my whisky). I would not be able to count the whisky and water, but I have already mentioned their measures.

in question?"¹⁰⁷ Obviously the answer to that question is "no." Ambiguity due to gray zones only arises if we find ourselves *in* a gray zone, and since such gray zones are probably unavoidable anyway, this should be taken as an injunction to steer free of those gray zones as much as possible rather than as a problem of definition.

While the foregoing provides definitions of "Buddhism" and "Buddhist" that are applicable to the problem at hand — a naturalist and sociopolitically radical philosophy that is recognizably and defensibly Buddhist — one may wonder whether the radical Buddhists discussed in chapter 3 would approve. Since few of them addressed the questions of what Buddhism is or what makes something Buddhist explicitly, this is not an easy question to answer.

What can be easily observed, on the other hand, is the sharp division between secular Buddhists and Theravāda Buddhist modernists with originalist inclinations on the one hand, and Mahāyāna reformers who strongly reject originalism on the other. That Theravāda tends towards originalism is not surprising, of course, as it is one of the most central dogmas of that sect that their version of Buddhism is what the historical Buddha taught, but originalism is also a common feature of Protestant Buddhism and Western Buddhist modernism.¹⁰⁸ Typically, adherents of those attempt to reconstruct the original teachings of the Buddha, but such reconstructions are sometimes quite idiosyncratic and tend to be heavily influenced by the cultural context in which that reconstruction takes place.¹⁰⁹ In the same way that original Theravāda was a product of fifth century Sinhalese culture, modernist and secular Buddhisms are products of their cultural contexts. And because of that, these reconstructions can often tell us more about the context in which they were created than about the historical Buddha.

Mahāyāna modernism started in Japan with the writings of Inoue Enryō 井上圓了, who rejected originalism and was not troubled by the inauthenticity of Mahāyāna texts,¹¹⁰ or even by claims that the Buddha did not exist.¹¹¹ Inoue's influence was deep, and the next generation of Buddhist reformers in Japan included several of his students. Some of them wrote in the first issue of the journal *New Buddhism* 新佛教 that "when we see people trying to bring back the old faith of [the historical Buddha …] all we can do is laugh at such a stupid and worthless idea," and that religions necessary evolve in response to changing circumstances and conditions.¹¹² And similar sentiments were expressed some time later by Senoʼo Girō 妹尾義郎, probably the most radical among radical Buddhists.¹¹³ Significantly, this evolutionary

---

107 Ludwig Wittgenstein, *Zettel* (Berkeley: University of California Press, 1967), §556.
108 See the introduction and first two sections of chapter 3.
109 Stephen Batchelor, the most influential Western "secular Buddhist," for example, reconstructs the Four Noble Truths as an injunction to embrace dukkha, which he interprets as "whatever situation life presents," to let go of "the grasping that arises in reaction to it," to stop reacting to that grasping, "so that one can act unconditioned by reactivity" ("A Secular Buddhism," *Journal of Global Buddhism* 13 [2012]: 87–107, at 101). On the influence of culturally hegemonic ideas, such as narcissistic individualism, on Batchelor's "Buddhism 2.0," see the section "secular Buddhism" in chapter 3.
110 "Inauthentic" here meaning that Mahāyāna sūtras do not record actual teachings by the historical Buddha.
111 See the section "realism and reform in Japan — Inoue Enryō" in chapter 3.
112 For the full quote and its context, see the beginning of the section "Uchiyama Gudō and early Buddhist socialism" in chapter 3.
113 See the section "Senoʼo Girō and the Youth League" in chapter 3. The qualification "possibly the most radical among radical Buddhists" is based on figure 4.1 in chapter 4.

view fits much better with the definitions of "Buddhism" and "Buddhist" suggested above than with an essentialist approach.

Uchiyama Gudō 内山愚童 and early Taixu 太虛 were also keenly aware how Buddhism was used as a tool to keep the masses in check and thereby adapted to changing circumstances,[114] but I have not seen anything in their writings (or those that I can access at least) that suggests a particular definition of Buddhism. Among the radical Buddhists, only Ambedkar seems to approach something like originalism. At least, his book *The Buddha and His Dhamma* is presented as a reconstruction of the taught and life of the historical Buddha.[115] To what extent he really believed that he was just describing historical fact, I do not know, but it is hard to believe that he was not aware of the eccentricity of his interpretation.

What Is a Buddhist?

The question what it means for someone rather than something to be a Buddhist is of limited relevance here, but because the question was important to some of the radical and engaged Buddhists discussed in chapter 3, and because it is closely related to the topic of this chapter, it deserves some attention.

Perhaps, the most widespread understanding of what it means to be a lay Buddhist is to have taken refuge in the three jewels and to have taken the five precepts,[116] but this cannot possibly be what defines a Buddhist for a number of reasons. Firstly, it is doubtful that everyone who is considered a Buddhist by herself or others has actually taken the five precepts in a ceremony or otherwise. Secondly, lay Buddhists drink alcohol,[117] which is forbidden by the fifth precept.[118] And thirdly, the notion of taking refuge in the three jewels, often considered to be the core of Buddhist identity, is much too vague and flexible to be a meaningful criterion.

The three jewels are the Buddha, the Dharma, and the *saṃgha*. A Buddhist is supposed to *take refuge* in these three,[119] but interpretations of what that means differ widely. For Buddhadāsa it means attaining and abiding in the Buddha "in our heart and mind in every moment,"[120] for example, while for Seno'o Girō its meaning differs from jewel to jewel. Taking refuge in the saṃgha is striving for an ideal society, taking refuge in the Dharma is basing one's views on relevant knowledge, and taking refuge in the Buddha is revering the historical Buddha.[121] What is even more problematic than the ambiguity of "taking refuge" is the ambiguity of the three jewels themselves. For Seno'o, the Dharma is not just Buddhist doctrine, but all true and relevant knowledge, and he was hardly unique in this respect. (Many centuries earlier, Nichiren 日蓮 seemed to have advocated a similar view, for example.) Similarly, interpretations of the notion of the saṃgha as a jewel vary from the monastic community, to all Buddhists, or even all of society, among others. And even the jewel of

---

114 See the sections "Uchiyama Gudō and Early Buddhist Socialism" and "China/Taiwan — a Pure Land in the Human World" in chapter 3.
115 See the section "Ambedkar and the 'New Vehicle' in India" in chapter 3.
116 The five precepts are no killing, no stealing, no lying, no improper sexual conduct, no intoxicants.
117 And monks or priests in Japan drink alcohol as well.
118 And eat meat and fish, which is forbidden by the first.
119 The Pāli phrase *saraṇaṃ gacchati* literally means "going for shelter, protection, refuge."
120 Donald Swearer, "Bhikkhu Buddhadāsa's Interpretation of the Buddha," *Journal of the American Academy of Religion* 64, no. 2 (1996): 313–36, at 326.
121 See the section "Seno'o Girō and the Youth League" in chapter 3.

the Buddha is ambiguous. For Nichiren Shōshū 日蓮正宗 (the "Orthodox School of Nichiren"), for example, Nichiren, rather than the historical Buddha, is the Buddha that one takes refuge in.

It appears, then, that the notion of taking refuge in the three jewels is almost infinitely reinterpretable, making it meaningless as a defining criterion. I do not think that there is another objective criterion either, or at least none that would not exclude significant numbers of people who consider themselves Buddhists or who are considered Buddhists by others.[122] And it is the latter what matters most. What makes one a Buddhist is not some formal criterion but recognition and self-recognition. A Buddhist is someone who considers herself to be a Buddhist and who is recognized as a Buddhist by a significant number of other Buddhists, who are Buddhist by this same, rough definition.

An implication of this definition is that you can fully accept a Buddhist philosophy and still not be a Buddhist either because you do not think of yourself as a Buddhist or because others do not consider you a Buddhist, or both. It is for this reason that I do not consider myself a Buddhist even though I accept the variety of Buddhism advocated in this book. Of course, I have not explained what that variety is yet, nor have I shown that it is a variety of Buddhism indeed. That's what the rest of this book are about. I do not call myself a "Buddhist" because that would only lead to misunderstanding. My Japanese friends and acquaintances would probably think that I believe that I go to Amitābha's Pure Land when I die, while my Western friends and acquaintances would probably think that I practice some kind of mindfulness meditation. All of them would be completely wrong. And for roughly similar reasons I do not think that many Buddhists will call me a "Buddhist" either, so I fail both criteria for the "Buddhist" designation. Hence, I'm not a Buddhist, even though I adhere to a variety of radical Buddhism.

There is, furthermore, a third, albeit not entirely unrelated, reason to be hesitant about the "Buddhist" self-identification: it appears to conflict with the acceptance of Quinean, pragmatist naturalism.[123] A key aspect of the latter is the recognition that the acceptance of any view, theory, or idea is provisional because everything is open to counter-evidence and revision. The "Buddhist" identification is a religious identification, however, and religious identifications are never provisional. To be a Muslim is not to accept Islam *as long as* it is better supported by evidence than any alternative, but to accept Islam *unconditionally*. Similarly, to call oneself a "Buddhist" is to accept some variety of Buddhism unconditionally, but that is something I can never do because naturalism trumps everything else.[124]

Postscript

I suppose that some Buddhists could consider this chapter an attack on some of their deepest held beliefs. It is not intended as such. I'm merely trying to figure out how to

---

122 A *possible* candidate could be the following: A Buddhist is someone who aims for awakening and thereby becoming an arhat or boddhisattva, either in this life or in some future life after many rebirths (through accumulation of good karma or merit). I think that this (rough) definition might include all practicing Buddhists, but I'm not sure that many of them would recognize this as a definition of "Buddhist."
123 See the section "Naturalism" in chapter 1 as well as the section "Perspectives and Science" in chapter 9.
124 We'll return to this problem in the section "Labels, Hesitations, and Rafts" in chapter 17.

decide whether the radical Buddhism developed in this book can indeed be considered a variety of Buddhism. However, I'm doing so guided by a naturalist methodology which is an inherent part of *radical* Buddhism,[125] but which may conflict with more traditional Buddhisms.

Perhaps, my rejection of essentialist definitions of "Buddhism" and "Buddhist" is controversial as well, but I want to emphasize here that my rejection of the Four Noble Truths, in whatever form, and other core doctrines of Buddhism *as defining elements* does not in any way imply that I think that these are not important, or in some sense even essential to Buddhism. All that I have tried to point out above is that they are too ambiguous or insufficiently universal to *define* Buddhism because either they would exclude some varieties of Buddhism or they would include some "things" that are not Buddhism. Nevertheless, I cannot really imagine a variety of Buddhism without some form of the Four Noble Truths, but I cannot imagine a human being without a brain either, and in the same way that having a brain is not what defines a human being, including some form of the Four Noble Truths is not what defines Buddhism. Things called "Buddhism" or "Buddhist" are more like parts of a tree: what groups them together is not some clear and objective defining similarity, but that they are all part of this great flourishing organism that grew from one tiny seed.[126]

---

125 See chapter 1.
126 In a sense, the definitions proposed above are merely intended to recognize theory-oriented branches as branches of that tree.

6

Radicalizing Radical Buddhism

The term "radical Buddhism" was introduced about a decade ago as a container for a number of mostly early-twentieth-century currents and thinkers within the Buddhist tradition that were politically engaged and that opposed the dominant sociopolitical or economic ideology of their time.[1] As explained in chapter 1, secularization forces religions, as well as all political ideologies other than hegemonic neoliberal capitalism, outside the public sphere, and radical Buddhists and their neighbors, engaged Buddhists, reject this secularization-as-privatization. At the same time, radical Buddhists and Buddhist modernists accept another dimension of secularization, namely, the turn away from the mythical and supernatural and towards a form of naturalism. The aim of this book is to radicalize radical Buddhism by pushing it towards the appropriate extremes on both of these dimensions of secularity: towards the anti-secular extreme on the sociopolitical dimension (i.e., secularity-as-privatization), and toward the secular extreme on the secularity-as-naturalism dimension. In other words, the goal is a theory that is (1) radically naturalist; (2) politically radical; (3) recognizably and defensibly Buddhist; and (4) radical in the sense of being uncompromising, rigorous, and consistent.

The main purpose of part I of this book, which is now finally approaching its conclusion, is to clarify what this means and thereby laying much of the groundwork of this project. Toward this end, chapter 3 introduced more than twenty radical, engaged, modernist, and secular Buddhists. What many of them have in common — and what characterizes the more radical among them especially — is a this-worldly focus, social engagement, and a tendency to prioritize reason over tradition. These are not alien to Buddhism, as chapter 2 has shown — on the contrary, social engagement, this-worldliness, and rationalism have been part of the Buddhist tradition for at least two millennia, and possibly from its start. Chapter 4 further explored and commented on some of the patterns and trends in the thought of the Buddhist thinkers and activists introduced in chapter 3, focusing on their complex relations with materialism (or physicalism) and Marxism, the predominance of moralistic critique and common lack of systemic critique, and the role of ideology.

These chapters were mainly aimed at clarifying the notion of radical Buddhism and its relation with the broader Buddhist tradition, as well introducing the context and part of the groundwork for parts II and III of this book. There are, however, several other key notions in the statement of this book's goal that require clarification

---

[1] See the introduction to chapter 1 for further details about the term's introduction and original definition, but note that I am not using the term in exactly the same way.

as well. What does "naturalism" mean here? What does it mean to be "politically radical"? And what makes some theory or ideas "recognizably and defensibly Buddhist"?

The first of these questions was addressed in the section "naturalism" in chapter 1. I argued there that the most pertinent variety of naturalism is a version of methodological naturalism based on the thought of W.V.O. Quine and, through him, on pragmatism. The two most important aspects of this naturalism are, first, that it holds that theories and ideas should be provisionally accepted if and only if they are supported by the best available evidence, recognizing that tradition, scripture, or authority do not count as evidence, and that they always remain open to refutation by counter-evidence. And second, methodological naturalism requires clarity and takes exception to ambiguity and obscurity. Importantly, methodological naturalism implies a weak form of metaphysical naturalism, which rejects supernatural entities and causes, because appeals to those, and supernatural explanations in general, conflict with the best-evidence requirement and usually also with the clarity requirement.

The second question — what it means to be "politically radical" — was also addressed in chapter 1, albeit only in passing. In the section "A Guide to This Book," it was suggested that radicality is a spectrum and that a Buddhism or Buddhist is more politically radical if it or they demand(s) more sweeping reform, more explicitly or more prominently reject(s) capitalism, or demand(s) or allows a greater political role for Buddhism.[2] No more exact definition was provided and does not really need to be provided either. Political radicality is a criterion in the final evaluation of the theory developed in the remainder of this book,[3] but not a guiding principle in the development thereof. This book succeeds — at least, by the standard I'm adopting here — if that theory rejects capitalism and demands sweeping sociopolitical or economic reform. Nevertheless, chapter 4 identified one key idea shared by the most radical Buddhists that ties their radical sociopolitical engagement to their roughly naturalist attitude: a strong this-worldly focus rooted in a kind of metaphysical realism that recognizes that there is only this world and, therefore, that a utopian Pure land can only be realized in this world, if it can be realized at all.

Of the three questions mentioned three paragraphs back, the third — What makes some theory or ideas "recognizably and defensibly Buddhist"? — received by far the most attention. Chapter 5 was devoted in its entirety to answering this question. The reason for this is twofold. First, whether this book succeeds in reaching its goal is impossible to judge if there is no clear criterion of what makes a theory or idea "Buddhist." And second, such a criterion is likely to be controversial, and consequently, it needs to be well-supported.

Chapter 5 argued that there is no hope for an inclusive, essentialist definition of "Buddhism" because for any proposed essential element there is at least one school, current, or variety of Buddhism that would fall outside the definition. One could, of course, adopt an exclusivist attitude and argue that whatever falls outside one's preferred definition is not "Buddhist" (and many Buddhist modernists and Orientalists have taken that attitude indeed, calling what they exclude "corruptions" of the "true" doctrine), but this is an arrogant attitude. It implies that one believes to

---

2   See also the section "Locating Radical Buddhism" in chapter 1, which explained the goal of this book and which more or less defined "politically radical" as "rejecting neoliberal capitalism and the hegemony of psychopathy."
3   See chapter 17.

have the authority to decided what is "Buddhist" and what is not while denying this authority to many millions of believers and adherents of Buddhism. I do not claim such authority, which leaves me no choice but to take an inclusivist approach to defining "Buddhist" and "Buddhism," an approach that does not exclude anyone or anything that is commonly called "Buddhist." Lacking a defining essence, this means that Buddhism can only be defined genetically or historically. The most important definition, given the purpose of this book, is not one of Buddhism as a whole, but is a criterion to decide whether some theory, doctrine, practice, or idea can be properly called "Buddhist." That criterion is that most of what a theory (etcetera) is based on or derived from is Buddhist and that it could not just as well be based on or derived from non-Buddhist sources.[4]

Sources and Schools

The fourth criterion in this book's goal is that the radicalization of radical Buddhism proposed is "radical in the sense of being uncompromising, rigorous, and consistent." This point is closely related to the adoption of methodological naturalism, but it also cautions against unbridled eclecticism. While eclectic patchworks of theories and ideas may be fascinating at first sight, they rarely turn out to be consistent upon a closer look. This does not imply that ideas from different sources and backgrounds should not be combined at all, or course, but it does counsel restraint and a critical attitude in assessing whether what is combined is really compatible. For this reason, a secondary aim of part I of this book was to put a spotlight on the schools and currents of thought that are most likely to play a central role in parts II and III, thereby preventing random eclecticism and consequent inconsistency.

One way of narrowing the selection of primary sources is by looking at the sectarian affiliations of the five radical Buddhists identified in chapter 4, Uchiyama Gudō 内山愚童, early Taixu 太虛, Lin Qiuwu 林秋梧, Seno'o Girō 妹尾義郎, and B.R. Ambedkar. Of those five, four belong to East-Asian Mahāyāna, while the fifth, Ambedkar, constructed his own idiosyncratic hybrid of Mahāyāna and early Buddhism.

Three of the four Japanese and Chinese Buddhists on this list had Zen/Chan 禪 affiliations. Uchiyama belonged to Sōtō 曹洞 Zen and Lin Qiuwu was ordained at Kaiyuan Temple in Tainan, which was originally also affiliated to Sōtō Zen, but which had switched to Rinzai 臨濟 Zen some time before Lin's ordination.[5] Nevertheless, he studied at Komazawa University in Japan, which is the university of the Sōtō Zen sect, suggesting a continuation of Sōtō influence, both on that temple and on Lin. Taixu was ordained at Xiao Jiuhua Temple in Suzhou, which was affiliated with the Linji Chan sect (Japanese: Rinzai Zen), but his thought was based mostly on his reading of a number of Yogācāra texts. And Seno'o was a follower of Nichiren 日蓮 Buddhism, but was also influenced by Pure Land Buddhism, among others. The philosophical roots of these affiliations can traced a bit further, as illustrated in figure 6.1.[6]

---

4 See the section "Defining 'Buddhism' and 'Buddhist'" in chapter 5 for further explanation.
5 Pei-ying Lin, "A Survey of the Japanese Influence on Buddhist Education in Taiwan during the Japanese Colonial Period (1895–1945)," *Religions* 11, no. 2 (2020): art. 61.
6 See the 3rd to 7th sections of chapter 3 for further details.

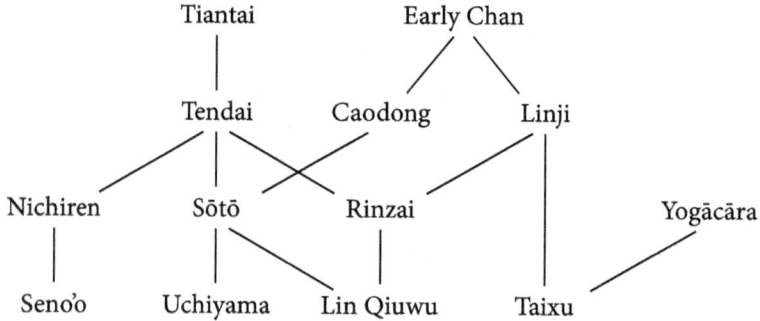

Fig. 6.1. Sectarian influences on East-Asian radical Buddhists.

The Nichiren, Sōtō, and Rinzai sects were founded by Nichiren, Dōgen 道元, and Eisai 栄西, respectively. All three of them were originally Tendai 天台 monks, and all three remained heavily influenced by Tendai thought, as is the case for virtually all Japanese Buddhism from roughly the eleventh century onward. Tendai itself was the Japanese version of Chinese Tiantai, founded by Zhiyi 智顗 several centuries earlier.⁷ Sōtō and Rinzai are Japanese offshoots of the Chinese Caodong and Linji Chan sects, but it can be argued that the Japanese sects are closer to Tendai philosophically than to their Chinese parent Zen/Chan sects. To varying extent all four East-Asian radical Buddhists were also influenced by Pure Land Buddhism, which is not shown in the figure, but this is true for East-Asian Buddhism in general and especially for Chinese Buddhism, which developed into a hybrid of Chan and Pure Land Buddhism. And as mentioned, a key influence on Taixu both early and late was Yogācāra.⁸ The latter school is also important for another reason: much early engaged and radical Buddhism in Japan was strongly influenced by Inoue Enryō's 井上圓了 realist interpretation of Yogācāra philosophy.⁹

Pure Land influence was probably mostly indirect. A few decades before the emergence of radical Buddhism, Japanese Buddhist modernism originated in the Pure Land school, and it was the same school that promoted research on Yogācāra thought. As pointed out by Rainer Schulzer, especially in Shinran's 親鸞 True Pure Land sect 浄土真宗 (to which Inoue Enryō, the father of Buddhist modernism in japan, belonged), a Buddhist is only obliged to have faith in the saving grace of Amītabha, and consequently, there do not have to be any religious dogmas that stand in the way of accepting a scientific worldview.¹⁰ It must be noted, however, that this is a very different approach to modernizing Budhism than that of the "radicals." The latter attempted to ground a modern and radical worldview in Buddhism rather than to "shrink" Buddhism to make place for a secular worldview *next* to it. This difference is a variant of the secularity-as-privatization dimension mentioned in chapter 1: Pure Land modernism limits the role of Buddhism to part of the private sphere, thus making space for a separate, secular worldview outside that small sphere, while radical Buddhism expands Buddhism into a comprehensive worldview.

---

7 See the sections "From Nāgārjuna to Zhiyi" and "From Saichō to Nichiren" in chapter 2.
8 For the early, radical Taixu, this Yogācāra influence was probably mostly indirect through the thought and writings of Zhang Taiyan 章太炎. See the section "China/Taiwan — a Pure Land in the Human World" in chapter 3.
9 See the section "Realism and Reform in Japan — Inoue Enryō" in chapter 3.
10 Rainer Schulzer, *Inoue Enryō: A Philosophical Portrait* (New York: SUNY Press, 2019).

A second way of narrowing this project's focus is by selecting the schools and thinkers that seem most likely to provide important building blocks for the philosophical foundations of a radicalized radical Buddhism. As mentioned in chapter 4, almost all radical, engaged, and modernist Buddhists emphasized that Buddhism should not simply be about death and rebirth but should be relevant in this world and this life. Tanaka Jiroku 田中治六 called this this-worldly orientation *genseshugi* 現世主義, or "this-world-ism." Although Tanaka's genseshugi was practical more than philosophical, its foundation was a realist metaphysics,[11] and much of the same was true for the more radical among the Buddhist reformers of the early-twentieth century.[12]

For an austere realist, only this world is real, and consequently, this life and this world are all there is. But this has important implications. Then, there are no Buddha lands, Pure lands of bliss, paradises, or heavens, and aspiring for a rebirth in Amitābha's Pure land is a delusion. Then, suffering cannot be rewarded or compensated in future lives and cannot be punishment for bad deeds in past lives either, and consequently, suffering is nothing but injustice. Then, if we want to escape or alleviate suffering, we have to do so *in this life*. Then, if we aspire for a Buddha land, we have to realize it *in this world*. In other words, realism makes the problem of suffering and its solution more urgent and thereby radicalizes genseshugi, and for this reason realism is a key component of radical Buddhism.

Realism is not a univocal notion, however. The term is used to name theories that assert the reality of a number of different things and there are subtle but important variations within all of those "realisms." An attempt at clarification will have to wait until chapter 7, but there is a different problem that needs to be addressed here.

A metaphysical foundation for genseshugi requires a realism that affirms the reality of this world and denies the reality of other worlds, but this may seem to be incompatible with the common Buddhist doctrine of the distinction between ultimate and phenomenal reality and the more or less illusory nature of the latter. What is incompatible with this doctrine indeed, is a naive realism that rejects this distinction and holds that the way we experience and describe the world (i.e., phenomenal reality) is the one and only true way to experience and describe the world and thus is not illusory. But a realist does not need to be a *naive* realist. She can also opt for perspectival realism, for example. According to perspectival realism, phenomenal reality is like a perspective on ultimate reality — it is partial, incomplete, and possibly distorted, and therefore, illusory (in some sense or to some extent) but not independent from ultimate reality and thus not wholly illusory.[13] Hence, perspectival realism is not incompatible with the aforementioned doctrine, and perhaps more importantly, it is not alien to Buddhism either. In the contrary, the metaphysics of Tiantai/Tendai and some related schools and thinkers — such as Dōgen, the founder of Sōtō Zen — looks very much like perspectival realism.[14] Furthermore, I have argued before that a constructive engagement between some Yogācāra thinkers like

---

11 Specifically, Inoue Enryō's realist interpretation of Yogācāra mentioned above.
12 See the section "Uchiyama Gudō and Early Buddhist socialism" in chapter 3.
13 The term "perspectival realism" is not standard terminology. Rather, there is no standard term in this respect and similar ideas are advocated under different names. See the last section of chapter 7 on perspectivism and perspectival realism, and chapter 10 on related and similar theories and ideas.
14 See the last three sections of chapter 2.

Dharmakīrti and Dignāga on the one hand and the American philosopher Donald Davidson on the other leads to something like perspectival realism as well.[15]

Hence, it turns out that the two approaches to narrowing the selection of sources are converging. The sectarian roots of four of the five radical Buddhists mentioned[16] — Tiantai/Tendai, Zen/Chan, Yogācāra, and to a lesser extent Pure Land Buddhism — largely overlap with the schools of thought that seem most promising sources for a metaphysical foundation for radical Buddhism. Missing in the latter is Pure Land Buddhism, for obvious reasons, as the belief in the possibility of rebirth in an other-worldly Pure Land is the very essence of Pure Land metaphysics. Aside from that, Pure Land Buddhism makes few philosophical claims at all. Missing in the former, for equally obvious reasons, is Donald Davidson. Davidson was a student of W.V.O. Quine, and the two agreed in many respects,[17] including much of what matters here. As mentioned in the previous section, the naturalism adopted here is Quine's pragmatist naturalism, and consequently, Quine's philosophy is already one of this project's sources. Davidson is, of course, a new addition, but "new" only in the same sense that adding another Yogācāra philosopher would be new. Davidson belongs to the admittedly small Quinean school of Western, analytic philosophy in roughly the same way that that philosopher belongs to the Yogācāra school.

It seems, then, that I can limit my main sources for part II of this book to just three: Tiantai/Tendai, Yogācāra, Quine and Davidson, and some other, closely related philosophers.[18] But this does not seem to help much with part III. That part is concerned with aspects of ethics and social philosophy rather than with metaphysics or epistemology. Mahāyāna ethics is typically focused on the bodhisattva ideal, and this appears to be the case for most radical and engaged Buddhists as well. The main sources for bodhisattva ethics are Śāntideva's *Bodhicaryāvatāra* and Asaṅga's *Bodhisattvabhūmi*. Asaṅga was the founder of the Yogācāra school, but Śāntideva belonged to the rivaling Mādhyamaka school. The differences between Asaṅga's and Śāntideva's moral theories are mostly insignificant, however.[19] Unfortunately, there is another problem: while these texts suggest a theory of normative ethics, that is, a theory that explains how to decide what is right or wrong, they do not answer a

---

15 Lajos Brons, "Dharmakīrti, Davidson, and Knowing Reality," *Comparative Philosophy* 3, no. 1 (2012): 30–57, and "Meaning and Reality: A Cross-Traditional Encounter," in *Constructive Engagement of Analytic and Continental Approaches in Philosophy*, eds. Bo Mou and R. Tieszen (Leiden: Brill, 2013), 199–220.
16 The fifth, Ambedkar, probably had no sectarian roots at all. His Navayāna Buddhism seems to be the product of his own ideas and predispositions more than anything else. See the section "Ambedkar and the 'New Vehicle' in India" in chapter 3.
17 They did not agree about everything, of course. Rather, there are important, albeit often subtle, differences between their philosophies, although some apparent differences appear to be mostly verbal. The two most interesting comparisons of Quine and Davidson are by Hans-Johann Glock, *Quine and Davidson on Language, Truth and Reality* (Cambridge: Cambridge University Press, 2003) and Gary Kemp, *Quine versus Davidson: Truth, Reference, and Meaning* (Oxford: Oxford University Press, 2012). The former puts more emphasis on the similarities between the two and rejects both. Kemp puts more emphasis on their differences and endorses Quine.
18 Zen/Chan was also mentioned above, but here relevant metaphysical ideas from those schools (such as Dōgen's) appear to be influenced more by Tiantai/Tendai than by anything else. See chapter 8.
19 The main differences are in their applied ethics, not in their normative ethics (i.e., moral theory). Asaṅga makes more positive prescriptions and shows more concern for this-worldly suffering than Śāntideva, and consequently, Asaṅga's bodhisattva might be a more engaged Buddhist than Śāntideva's. Additionally, there is also a meta-ethical difference, or more specifically, there is a meta-ethical problem for Śāntideva as a Mādhyamika that Asaṅga as a Yogācārin avoids. See chapters 12 to 14 for further details.

more fundamental question: Why is that theory of normative ethics right? This question belongs to meta-ethics, a branch of philosophy that is virtually absent in Indian thought and that has a history of little more than a century in Western thought.[20] Answering this question will not require adding new schools of thought as further sources, however. Meta-ethics is located between metaphysics and epistemology on the one hand, and normative ethics on the other, and consequently, part of the materials necessary to answer this question will be provided by part II, and some of what is missing to bridge the remaining gap can be found in Davidson's philosophy.

A Very Sketchy Overview of Parts II and III

Having somewhat clarified this book's goal and sources, I can now briefly sketch its remainder. Parts II and III are titled *sat* सत् and *dao* 道, respectively. *Sat* is a Sanskrit root word meaning both "truth" and "reality." *Dao* is a classical Chinese philosophical term meaning something like social conventions, but also a moral theory. These two short words cover much of what those two parts are about, and I'll return to their relevance in the introductions of parts II and III, respectively.

Part II is concerned with metaphysics and epistemology and, to a lesser extent, with philosophy of language, or with what is called "theoretical philosophy" in parts of Europe. Its aim is to lay the theoretical foundations for a radicalized radical Buddhism: to present a theory of the nature of reality, truth, and justification that is simultaneously naturalist and "recognizably and defensibly Buddhist." As explained, the latter means that the theory must be based mostly on Buddhist sources, and that it cannot be based on non-Buddhist sources *just as well*. The most important Buddhist sources are Yogācāra and Tiantai/Tendai, supplemented by Quine, who also provided the relevant kind of naturalism, and his student Donald Davidson. The second criterion requires an assessment of the possibility of constructing with sufficient ease a sufficiently similar perspectival realism on non-Buddhist sources. (The two "sufficient" clauses translate the "just as well" clause in the criterion.) This is the topic of chapter 10, the final chapter of part II.

Part III focuses on ethics and social philosophy, or "practical philosophy." Building on the epistemology developed in part II, as well as on important ideas found in Śāntideva's *Bodhicaryāvatāra* and Asaṅga's *Bodhisattvabhūmi*, part III argues for a theory of normative ethics focused on universal compassion and the prevention and alleviation of suffering. On the basis of this moral theory, it argues against capitalism, thereby giving shape and content to the sociopolitically "radical" aspect of radical Buddhism, but also discusses problematic aspects of utopianism.

Between Science and Religion

A legitimate worry at this point is whether the result of all of this can *really* be called "Buddhist." This issue has already been addressed in the previous chapter, of course, but there is one remaining problem and that problem has broader implications for this book and project. Supposedly, Buddhism is a religion. But where is that *religion* in the foregoing? One possible answer to this question is to deny that Buddhism is a religion. This is a common idea among Buddhists modernists and especially among

---

20 There is something like meta-ethics in classical Chinese thought. For more about that, see the introduction of chapter 11.

secular Buddhists. According to them, Buddhism is a philosophy, or even a science, rather than a religion, but this only raises further questions: What exactly distinguishes religion from philosophy? What is a religion? What is a philosophy? How are both related to science? And where exactly does radical Buddhism fit into all of that?

In chapter 5, I suggested that religions and some philosophies are life/world-views.[21] A life/world-view is a combination of a *Lebensanschauung* or "life-view" and a *Weltanschauung* or "worldview." The distinction is related to that between practical and theoretical philosophy mentioned in the previous section, but is not as academic — it concerns popular views and ideas as much as philosophical theories. When someone is talking about their "philosophy" in English, they are probably referring to their life-view or some specific part thereof. Someone's life-view includes their ideas and perspectives on what makes life valuable, on life goals and the meaning of life, on how to live one's life, on the good life and the bad, and so forth. The notion of a life-view overlaps with that of a worldview, but the latter is more focused on ideas about the nature of reality and the world we live in, about how that world works, about what exists and what does not, and so forth. Hence, while a life-view is closer to practical philosophy (e.g., ethics, social philosophy), a worldview is closer to theoretical philosophy (e.g., metaphysics, epistemology) but overlaps with science as well.[22] There is no sharp boundary between the two and often they come together in one larger package: a life/world-view that includes a broad, more or less integrated array of views on life, the nature of reality, the good and the bad, and so forth.

Religions are life/world-views, and consequently, the question what a religion is can be answered by determining what exactly sets religious life/world-views apart from non-religious ones. That, unfortunately, is not so easy. There is no single uncontroversial definition of religion. The concept itself is a relatively recent, Western invention, and most traditional definitions apply to the three monotheistic religions but become strained when they are used to describe practices or ideas in South or East Asia. Nevertheless, several scholars of religion have made helpful suggestions. According to Antoine Vergote, for example, religion is

> the whole of language, sentiments, behaviors, and signs that relate to a supernatural being (or beings). "Supernatural" means that which does not belong to natural forces or human agency, but which transcends those.[23]

The supernatural indeed seems to play an important role in religious life/world-views, but the mere inclusion of something supernatural is probably not sufficient to differentiate religious from non-religious life/world-views. Beliefs in ghost or spirits, or even in the existence of non-physical minds would then be religious beliefs. Many people who do not consider themselves religious, perhaps even most of them, have some supernatural beliefs, and consequently, if mere inclusion of supernatural elements would make a life/world-view religious, then non-religious life/world-views might be exceedingly rare.

---

21 See the section "Defining 'Buddhism' and 'Buddhist'."
22 By implication, it can be said that part II of this book is about the *Weltanschauung* of radicalized radical Buddhism, and part III about its *Lebensanschauung*.
23 La religion [...] est l'ensemble de langage, des sentiments, des comportements et des signes qui se rapportent à un être (ou à des êtres) surnaturel(s). «Surnaturel» signifie ce qui n'appartient ni aux forces naturelles ni aux instances humaines, mais ce qui transcende celles-ci. — Antoine Vergote, *Religion, foi, incroyance: Étude psychologique* (Brussels: Pierre Mardaga, 1983), 9–10.

Vergote does not claim that mere inclusion is enough. He writes that religion is a whole of things that *relate to* supernatural beings. Hence, the supernatural must not just be included, but play a central role — if not *the* central role — in a life/world-view. And consequently, the supernatural must not just be accepted as existent and thus be part of one's worldview, but must in some way or other matter to one's life and thus be part of one's life-view as well. While I think that this captures something important about the notion and phenomenon of religion, I doubt that it can provide a clear and unambiguous boundary between the religious and the non-religious. For that purpose, we would need to specify how central exactly the role of the supernatural must be, and we would need an unambiguous threshold between sufficiently central and not central enough. I do not think that there is such a threshold, which means that either there is a gray zone between religious and non-religious life/world-views, or that the religiosity of life/world-views is a spectrum rather than a dichotomy. But in any case, a radicalized radical Buddhism that denounces all supernatural elements would be a non-religious life/world-view by this standard.

All life/world-views are knowledge claims. Adherence to a life/world-view is claiming to have some kind of knowledge about the good life and the world around us. But not all knowledge claims are the same. As already pointed out in chapter 1, religions claim certain and final knowledge, and most of philosophy aims for certain and final knowledge as well, while scientific knowledge claims are provisional; that is, they are open for revision once contrary evidence is found. Consequently, religion involves dogmas, beliefs that must be uncritically accepted, while science and philosophy are (in theory!) critical and anti-dogmatic.

The reason why religion is dogmatic and why philosophy and science also can be in practice even if they are supposed not to be in theory, is related to a key function of religion. Religion can be said to have several functions, of course, depending on the perspective one takes. Shared religious beliefs may be an essential element in forging the bonds between people that make societies larger than bands or tribes possible, for example. But the most important function of religion and life/world-views in general is denying death.

In *The Denial of Death*, Ernest Becker argued that humans and other animals need an instinctive fear of death but that we need to control this fear to avoid being consumed by it.[24] The terror of death is a potentially debilitating fear, and our most important tools to control or suppress that terror are our belief systems, that is, our life/world-views. Our belief systems allow us to participate in "immortality projects" and thereby to "deny death." One of the terms Becker used in reference to such immortality projects is "heroism." In an interview with Sam Keen, a few days before his death, Becker explained that "to be a hero means to leave behind something that heightens life and testifies to the worthwhileness of existence."[25]

Becker's ideas lead three social psychologists, Jeff Greenberg, Tom Pyszczynski, and Sheldon Solomon, to develop Terror Management Theory (TMT) in the early 1980s. To a large extent, TMT is a more systematic and testable version of Becker's ideas, and many of the central hypotheses of TMT and thus of Becker's theory have been tested extensively and confirmed repeatedly. In 2015 the three published a book reviewing almost three decades of research. In that book they summarized the core

---

24 Ernest Becker, *The Denial of Death* (New York: Simon & Schuster, 1973).
25 Sam Keen, "The Heroics of Everyday Life: A Theorist of Death Confronts His Own End," *Psychology Today*, April 1974, 71–80, at 72.

idea of Becker and TMT as follows: "the awareness of death gives rise to potentially debilitating terror that humans manage by perceiving themselves to be significant contributors to an ongoing cultural drama," and "reminders of death increase devotion to one's cultural scheme of things."[26] While Becker and TMT almost completely agree in their main claims, they differ in their terminologies, and I'll more or less adopt the TMT terminology here.

A key element in TMT is self-esteem. Jeff Greenberg and Jamie Arndt wrote that "effective terror management is faith in a meaning providing cultural worldview and the belief that one is a valuable contributor to that meaningful world."[27] Self-esteem is that belief. To have high self-esteem is to believe that one is a valuable contributor to the world according to one's belief system or cultural worldview, or to be a "hero" in Becker's sense of that term. Since we rely on our worldviews and our self-esteem to control or manage the fear of death (i.e., for "terror management"), reminders of death (i.e., increases of "mortality salience") lead to "worldview defense," that is, they lead people to bolster their worldviews, but also to strengthen their self-esteem either by self-deception or by trying to contribute more to the world according to their worldview. (Note that the TMT notion of a "worldview" is more or less what I have been calling a "life/world-view.") This hypothesis is called the "Mortality Salience Hypothesis," and is the most extensively tested part of TMT.[28] The converse relation also holds — that is, strengthening someone's self-esteem leads to less subconscious thoughts about death. The negative corollary is that weakening someone's self-esteem by marginalization, for example, leads to more death-related thoughts, increasing mortality salience and thus necessitating more worldview defense, often resulting in a radicalization of that worldview or the subject's attempts to contribute to the world according to that view.

Because reminders of death raise mortality salience requiring worldview defense, it is less stressful for the unconscious mind to just avoid reminders of death. Unfortunately, there are too many potential death reminders. One of the most fundamental is what Becker called our "creatureliness," the fact that we are a creature or animal (among many other things). Anything that reminds us of our animal status or creatureliness indirectly reminds us of the fact that animals die, and thus that we die. It is for this reason that all cultures conceptually separate humans from animals, and it is for the same reason that many cultures repress our bodily natures. Our spirits are what make us human, while our bodies are our animal parts. Reminders of our bodies are, therefore, reminders of our creatureliness and thus of death. Thus, the body must be covered up or decorated; it must be brought under control. And sex, if seen as a mere bodily act, must be hidden and plastered over with taboos. In the aforementioned interview with Keen, Becker explained: "all humanly caused evil is based on man's attempt to deny his creatureliness, to overcome his insignificance.

---

26 Sheldon Solomon, Jeff Greenberg, and Tom Pyszczynski, *The Worm at the Core: On the Role of Death in Life* (New York: Random House, 2015), 211.
27 Jeff Greenberg and Jamie Arndt, "Terror Management Theory." In *Handbook of Theories of Social Psychology*, Vol. 1, eds. Paul A.M. Van Lange, Arie W. Kruglanski, and E. Tory Higgins (London: Sage, 2011), 398–415, at 403.
28 A meta-analysis covering 164 articles on 277 experiments concluded that the Mortality Salience Hypothesis "is robust and produces moderate to large effects." See Brian L. Burke, Andy Martens, and Erik H. Faucher, "Two Decades of Terror Management Theory: A Meta-Analysis of Mortality Salience Research," *Personality and Social Psychology Review* 14, no. 2 (2010): 155–95, at 187.

All the missiles, all the bombs, all human edifices, are attempts to defy eternity by proclaiming that one is not a creature, that one is something special."[29]

Becker and TMT argued that because we depend on our worldviews for "terror management," awareness of death raises religious and other cultural identification and strengthens belief in or consent to religious doctrine, but also increases negativity and even hostility toward other religions and cultures. But this is not just true for religious life/world-views. Non-religious views also tend to radicalize under the influence of mortality salience. There is one important exception to this general rule: if tolerance is a key value in a worldview, then an increase in mortality salience leads to an increase in tolerance rather than to an increase in hostility among the adherents of that worldview.[30] The other side of the coin is that if a worldview is already intolerant, competitive, or aggressive, mortality salience (i.e., awareness of death) will make it even more hostile and intolerant.

The last few paragraphs provide a brief sketch of what in TMT is called "symbolic immortality." One important form of symbolic immortality is the attempt to live on in one's culture or society by strongly identifying therewith. The stronger that identification, the stronger the subconscious conviction that as long as the society or culture you identifies with survives, you survive, at least in some sense. Mark Johnston made a similar argument in *Surviving Death* but attempted — unsuccessfully, I think — to broaden the scope: by genuinely identifying with the whole of mankind, one could survive personal death.[31] "Symbolic immortality" contrasts with "literal immortality," which is the most literal form of death denial. This kind of denial of death can take different forms: from treating death as an extension of life (as in ancient Egypt and ancient China), to postulating an immortal soul (common in almost all religions), or even attempts to "cure" death (as in ancient Chinese alchemy).

Religious life/world-views generally involve both literal and symbolic immortality. They promise an afterlife, or rebirth, or some other way of "surviving" death, and provide cultural worldviews people can strongly identify with. Non-religious life/world-views, in contrast, rarely involve literal immortality but can still provide symbolic immortality, and usually they do. All that is needed is "a meaning providing cultural worldview and the belief that one is a valuable contributor to that meaningful world," and almost anything can be such a "cultural worldview" as long as it "provides meaning." One way to provide meaning is providing an overarching view or narrative that helps make sense of the world around us and our place in it, which is exactly what a life/world-view does. But meaning can be derived from many kinds of "things," practices, and beliefs. What provides meaning is something a person can strongly identify with, get attached to, become fanatical about; something that gives a person a sense of purpose or self-worth; something so important to that person that they feel personally threatened or attacked when that thing is perceived to be under threat or attack.

So, for example, if you adhere to and identify with a scientific and atheist life/world-view, it is that view that provides you with meaning and thereby unconscious-

---

29 Keen, "The Heroics of Everyday Life," 71.
30 Jeff Greenberg et al., "Terror Management and Tolerance: Does Mortality Salience Always Intensify Negative Reactions to Others Who Threaten One's Worldview?" *Journal of Personality and Social Psychology* 63, no. 2 (1992): 212–20.
31 Mark Johnston, *Surviving Death* (Princeton: Princeton University Press, 2010). About why I believe Johnston's attempt to be unsuccessful, see Lajos Brons, "The Incoherence of Denying My Death," *Journal of Philosophy of Life* 4, no. 2 (2014): 68–89.

	literal immortality	supernatural	dogmatic	symbolic immortality
traditional Buddhism	+	+	+	+
Buddhist modernism	+/−	+/−	+/−	+
Marxism, neoliberalism	−	−	+	+
radical Buddhism	−	−	−	+
ideal science	−	−	−	−

Table 6.1. Between science and religion.

ly gives you symbolic immortality. Your unconscious terror management or control of the fear of death depends on your belief in the truth of your life/world-view and your belief that you are a valuable contributor to the world according to that view (i.e., your self-esteem). And because you need terror management to function, you will defend your life/world-view against perceived threats or attacks. Consequently, a non-religious person may respond very similarly to a religious person if they feel that their life/world-view is threatened. And for the same reason, non-religious life/world-views can be as dogmatic or fanatic as religious views.

Four characteristics of religious life/world-views have been mentioned thus far. (1) They award a central role to the supernatural; (2) They involve dogmatic elements that are exempt from criticism or counter-evidence; (3) They provide "literal immortality" by promising an afterlife, or rebirth, or some other kind of life after death; and (4) They provide "symbolic immortality" by helping adherents to make sense of the world and their place in it. There are, of course, other characteristics of religion, but these four are probably the most important and they suffice here. Table 6.1 compares a number of Buddhisms and other ways of looking at the world and our place in it with respect to these four characteristics.

Traditional Buddhism has all the characteristics of a religion, or at least all four distinguished here: it includes supernatural beliefs (e.g., gods, hell-beings, substance dualism,[32] and so on), it offers literal immortality through rebirth,[33] it involves many ideas that must be accepted by the believer and that are exempt from counter-evidence (i.e., it is dogmatic), and given that it is a life/world-view, it provides symbolic immortality because that is what life/world-views do. Buddhist modernism, Protestant Buddhism, secular Buddhism, engaged Buddhism, and radical Buddhism are all life/world-views as well and thus also offer symbolic mortality but differ from traditional Buddhism and each other in other respects. Some variants of Buddhist modernism are more dogmatic than others — Protestant Buddhists tend to be dogmatic believers in the reliability of the Pāli canon, for example. And some include supernatural elements or a belief in rebirth, while others, such as secular Buddhism, do not or do to a lesser extent.

Marxism is usually not considered to be a religion but is undeniably a life/world-view and certainly one people can get strongly attached to, and as such it offers symbolic immortality. Furthermore, Marxism can be as dogmatic as religion and

---

32 See the section "Physicalism" in chapter 4.
33 See the section "Karma, Rebirth, (No-)Self, and Nirvāṇa" in chapter 5.

often is. The preferred kind of "evidence" for many Marxists is a quote by Karl Marx or Vladimir Lenin, for example. "Neoliberalism" here refers to the conglomerate life/world-view consisting of neoclassical economics, advocacy of neoliberal capitalism, and associated views on human nature, ethics, and so forth. Neoliberalism or its components — neoclassical economics, especially — are sometimes called a religion,[34] but like Marxism, it does not have all four characteristics. Neither Marxism nor neoliberalism involve central supernatural beliefs, although the belief in an invisible hand can sound very much like one, and neither promises an afterlife. Like Marxism, neoliberalism is dogmatic, perhaps, even more so. It includes many ideas that have been proven false again and again, but believers continue to hold on to anyway.[35]

Ideal science is what science is supposed to be. Ideal science is anti-dogmatic and anti-supernatural and rejects beliefs in some kind of afterlife. Furthermore, ideal science is not a life/world-view. It is too incomplete and too fragmentary for that, and it is not something that is supposed to provide meaning or that one gets overly attached to. Ideal science does not exist. It is an idealization. Actual science rarely functions like the ideal. Instead, people can get as attached to scientific views as they get to religious views, identify with them as strongly, and feel as threatened when they perceive them to be under attack. Hence, there are science-based life/world-views, often called "scientism," and even fanatical apostles of those. (Richard Dawkins might be a good example of the latter.) Furthermore, the response to a perceived threat or attack is no different either. Core beliefs must be defended and are thus effectively exempt from counter-evidence and revision. Hence, the psychological necessity of worldview defense leads to some form of dogmatism, albeit probably in a much weaker form than religious dogmatism, and therefore, if real science would be added to the table, it would have "+/−" in the last two columns.

Importantly, if even strong attachment to scientific views tends to lead to some kind of dogmatism, it may very well be the case that a "+" in the fourth column automatically leads to a "+" in the third, or in other words, that any life/world-view will lead to dogmatism, simply because, as a life/world-view, it is too important for adherents to *not* defend its core beliefs, which thereby effectively become something like dogmas. If this is right, then the project of this book can never be more than a theoretical exercise. The radical naturalism requirement implies that a radical Buddhism taken to its logical extreme cannot be dogmatic. But because any radical Buddhism would be a life/world-view, it would automatically tend towards some dogmatism and thereby negate or at least undermine its own radicality. Therefore, radicalized radical Buddhism is inherently unstable.[36]

This does not mean that the answer to the question I asked in chapter 1 — whether a radicalized radical Buddhism is possible — is "no." But it might mean that such a Buddhism is *practically* impossible; it might mean that no one can remain in that

---

34   Robert Nelson, *Economics As Religion: From Samuelson to Chicago and Beyond* (University Park: Pennsylvania State University Press, 2006), and John Rapley, *Twilight of the Money Gods: Economics As Religion and How It All Went Wrong* (London: Simon & Schuster, 2017).
35   Important examples include the efficient markets hypothesis, the notion of trickle-down economics, the NAIRU, and austerity. All of these ideas are "zombies" — they have been killed, or proven false, repeatedly, but they stumble on and continue to misguide policy anyway. See, for example, John Quiggin, *Zombie Economics: How Dead Ideas Still Walk among Us* (Princeton: Princeton University Press, 2010). See also chapter 15.
36   See also the section "A Buddha Land in This World" in chapter 16, as well as chapter 17.

position because the psychological need of worldview defense would drive one away from anti-dogmatic radical naturalism. Unless perhaps, if anti-dogmatic naturalism is the most central value in one's life/world-view. (Perhaps, it could be said that someone with such a view would be dogmatically anti-dogmatic, but I'm not sure whether that actually makes sense.) But that would reduce the other elements of radicalized radical Buddhism — Buddhism and sociopolitical radicality — to mere accidental elements, raising doubts about how appropriate it is to call such a view "radical *Buddhism*."

It seems, then, that there is something contradictory about the aim of this book. The question whether a radicalized radical Buddhism, something located at the position marked with "★" in figure 1.1, is possible can only be a mere academic puzzle, because no one could remain in that position. But at the same time, it cannot be a mere academic puzzle because the very reason that no one could remain in that position is that the result would be a life/world-view. Moreover, given that I accept the naturalistic principles that guide this inquiry, if I succeed in developing that position in the remainder of this book, I would have to accept it as right, and it would thus become *my* life/world-view.[37] But if it becomes my view, then I'm bound to somehow betray its anti-dogmatism and exempt some principles or beliefs from scrutiny. What's most worrying about that, however, is that I might unconsciously already do that during this inquiry, thereby undermining the very project of this book. There is no way out of this conundrum, unfortunately. The best I can do is to approach my question with as much detachment as possible and treat it as nothing but an interesting academic puzzle indeed.

For now, let's ignore this problem and return to the questions that this section set out to answer: Is Buddhism a religion? Or is it a philosophy? There can be little doubt that traditional Buddhism is a religion, but less traditional forms — from Buddhist modernism to radical Buddhism — are not as easy to classify. They fall somewhere in between traditional religion and science. If anything between those two extremes is called "philosophy," then such Buddhisms would be philosophies indeed, but such a classification of "philosophy" is itself controversial.[38] If a philosophy refers to a life/world-view, then Buddhisms would be philosophies as well but so are religions. Perhaps, the best answer is that Buddhism is a philosophy with religious elements or a religion with philosophical elements, but I doubt that this is an answer that would satisfy many.

---

37 See the section "Naturalism" in chapter 1.
38 Quine would not accept it. For Quine, philosophy was part of science, not apart from it.

PART II

SAT

Sat सत् or *satya* is a Sanskrit root word meaning both truth and reality. It occurs in many compound terms, including *paramārthasat* and *saṃvṛtisat*, meaning "ultimate truth or reality" and "conventional truth or reality," respectively. Sat is more or less what part II of this book is about: truth and reality.

In *Engaging Buddhism* Jay Garfield suggested that the polysemy of certain philosophical terms in Pāli and Sanskrit like *sat* or *satya* offer important philosophical insights and should therefore be taken seriously. Terms like *sat* or *satya*, karma, dharma, and many others all have many different meanings. "Each draws together what appears from a Western point of view to be a vast semantic range into what appears from a Buddhist perspective to be a semantic point."[1]

I'm not convinced by Garfield's argument. If a language makes more fine-grained distinctions than English — and there are plenty of languages that do, as English is a more blunt and more exotic tool for philosophical analysis than many Western philosophers seem to realize — then switching to that language, even occasionally, may result in valuable philosophical insights,[2] but I doubt that, as Garfield is suggesting, the reverse is true. Switching to a language that makes fewer fine-grained distinctions is more likely to produce confusion and fallacious arguments through equivocation than to evoke insight.

The polysemy of *sat/satya* does not suggest anything philosophically interesting. That the notions of truth and reality are closely related is obvious without having a single word for them, while having a single word may lead to the false conclusion that they are the same. That they are not should be obvious by taking into consideration that their predicate forms take different subjects: "true" is predicated over sentences, propositions, beliefs, or something similar, while "real" is predicated over objects, events, and so forth. That is a fundamental metaphysical distinction, and brushing it under a terminological carpet can only lead to confusion. That said, I'm not sure whether the polysemy of *sat/satya* indeed caused serious philosophical

---

1 Jay L. Garfield, *Engaging Buddhism: Why It Matters to Philosophy* (New York: Oxford University Press, 2015), 331.
2 In "Dry Dust, Hazy Images, and Missing Pieces: Reflections on Translating Religious Texts," in *In Search of Clarity: Essays on Translation and Tiantai Buddhism* (Nagoya: Chisokudō, 2018), 213–32, Paul Swanson, who is fluent in both English and Japanese and whose academic output mainly consists of translations from classical Chinese, has written down some interesting observations about switching between languages. One thing he observes is that one cannot give the same talk in two different languages, but he also points out that there are no one-to-one correspondences between words in different languages.

mishaps in the Indian tradition. The Western notion of truth, on the other hand, continues to confuse many.

In the paper "Recognizing 'Truth' in Chinese Philosophy," I argued that the ancient Chinese did not have theories of truth but had theories of *justification* that, due to terminological obscurities, may look like theories of truth to an insufficiently careful observer.[3] There is no single unambiguous equivalent of the English word "truth" in Classical Chinese (although 然 *ran* comes close), and, partially because of that, it is not always immediately clear what exactly a philosopher is theorizing about. The situation is not really that different in Western philosophy, however. That two philosophers are both writing about "truth" does not necessarily imply that they are writing about the same thing. Moreover, the most common confusion about "truth" in Western thought is also the most common confusion in interpretations of Chinese philosophy about truth and adjacent notions. Alexus McLeod's otherwise excellent book about "theories of truth" in Chinese philosophy is not really about theories of truth,[4] but it is mostly about theories of *justification*, and while justification is very close to truth, the two notions are *not* the same. Perhaps, the most obvious example of the same mistake in Western thought is the oversimplified characterization of pragmatist theories of truth as whatever works, or whatever scientist agree about, or something similar.[5] But even a closer look at what pragmatists like Peirce, James, and Dewey actually held suggests — as Bertrand Russell already pointed out in 1910 — that they sometimes confused truth with criteria for assigning "truth" status, or in other words, with justification.[6]

Some explanation is in order here, so let's start with the notion of truth. What does it mean, and what does it *not* mean, to say that some statement or belief is "true"? The answer to that question may seem ridiculously obvious, but sometimes it is worth stating the obvious. According to Alfred Tarski's famous *t schema*, a sentence or proposition p (or belief described as p) is true if and only if whatever p describes is the case: "p" is true if and only if p.[7] Thus, "grass is green" is true if and only if grass is green. W.V.O. Quine called this "disquotation."[8]

Importantly, this really is all that "true" means. There are philosophical debates about what, if anything, makes a statement true, but those debates are about theories of truth, not about what "truth" and "true" *mean*. To say that something is true is just to say that it is the case. So, to say that something is true is not to say or even imply that someone actually believes it, or that there is evidence for it, or that many people believe it, or that it is generally accepted. All of those things may be important, but they are not "truth." Truth is just being the case, and something may be true even if no one believes it and there is no evidence for it.

Justification, on the other hand, has to do with evidence and arguments. A statement or belief p is justified if it follows from solid evidence or an irrefutable argu-

---

3 Lajos Brons, "Recognizing 'Truth' in Chinese Philosophy," *Logos & Episteme* 7, no. 3 (2016): 273–86. See also "Postscript: Reply to McLeod," in *Philosophy of Language, Chinese Language, Chinese Philosophy: Constructive Engagement*, ed. Bo Mou (Leiden: Brill, 2018), 364–70.
4 Alexus McLeod, *Theories of Truth in Chinese Philosophy* (London: Rowman & Littlefield, 2015).
5 These are really beyond oversimplification and are, perhaps, better qualified as parodies, but that's beside the point here.
6 Bertrand Russell, "William James's Conception of Truth," in *Philosophical Essays* (Cambridge: Cambridge University Press, 1910).
7 Technically this is not entirely correct because the "…" device only applies to some kinds of truth-bearers.
8 W.V.O. Quine, *Philosophy of Logic*, 2nd edn. (Cambridge: Harvard University Press, 1986).

ment or something close enough. Or in other words, a statement or belief is justified if it passes the accepted criteria to be accepted as truth, or the criteria for assigning "truth" status. But justification does not guarantee truth. A statement may be true and not justified, but the reverse can also happen. Given all the evidence we had, our belief in classical, Newtonian mechanics was entirely justified *until* we found contrary evidence that proved that belief unjustified and the content of that belief probably false.

Truth and justification are often considered to be properties of beliefs. Traditionally, beliefs that were both true and justified were considered knowledge, but Edmund Gettier showed in the 1960s that there are cases in which beliefs are true and justified without being knowledge.[9] Since then, much of epistemology has been an attempt to find a new definition of knowledge. We will ignore this problem here and will assume that knowledge is something very similar to justified true belief. Two of the three terms in that definition have been discussed in the foregoing, but I have not said anything yet about "belief."

To believe something is to hold it true. Believing that p is to hold true that p. To believe that p is to believe that whatever p describes is the case. So, if p is a true belief, then the believer holds p true and is right in doing so because p actually is true. And, if p is a justified belief, then the believer holds p true and is justified to do so because she has solid evidence or an irrefutable argument for p, or something else that is close enough to qualify as justification.

It is this latter notion especially, that can be a source of confusion. To have a justified belief that p is to be justified to believe that p, which is to be justified to hold p true because that is what believing means. But if one is justified to hold something true, then one is justified to call that "thing" true. In other words, justification entitles one to say that p is true. And because some justified beliefs turn out to be false, this implies that we are sometimes entitled to call things true that are actually false.

The key point here is not that this implies that truth really is like justification but rather that we sometimes use words like "true" or "truth" when we are really talking about justification (and not out of sloppiness but because of what those words mean). And consequently, when one encounters writings or sayings about "truth" the first question should always be: *Is this really about truth? Or is it about justification?*

The confusion of truth and justification is expressed in many forms, but there is also a closely related confusion that is worth mentioning here, namely, the distinction between "truth" with a lowercase *t* and "Truth" with a capital *T*. In an attempt to limit the confusion, I'll write the former in italics here and the latter in small caps. Supposedly, TRUTH is being the case (and thus "truth"), while *truth* is something like "socially accepted as true" or "commonly believed to be true." A related distinction is that between *knowledge* and KNOWLEDGE — the latter is justified TRUE belief (i.e., knowledge in a strict sense of that term), while *knowledge* is something like "socially accepted *as* knowledge." All of this is rather confusing, of course, but the confusion is easily avoided, at least in philosophy. Truth is being the case — nothing more, nothing less. Being socially accepted, being called "true," being generally believed, and so forth — and thus *truth* with a small *t* — is not "truth."

Nevertheless, confusions like these are quite understandable given how we use words like "truth" and "true." If justification entitles us to call something true, and if social acceptance of some idea counts as sufficient justification, then social ac-

---

9   Edmund Gettier, "Is Justified True Belief Knowledge?" *Analysis* 23 (1963): 121–23.

ceptance is sufficient to *call* that idea true. But this implies that when we say that something is true we almost always mean that it is justified and that we, therefore, believe that it is true. What must be realized, however, is that this does not imply that that statement, belief, or idea *is* true. Again, justification to assign "truth" status (and thus, to call something "true") is justification, not truth.

What probably makes the problem worse is that while we are often entitled to *call* something "true" (because we have justification) we can never do more than that. It can, perhaps, be argued that such "calling true" is a mere rhetorical use of "true," but that would imply that all attribution of "truth" is rhetorical in exactly this sense. This point was made most emphatically, albeit not in these terms, by Donald Davidson in a reply to Pascal Engel. Davidson wrote that "[t]here are times when we are certain that something is the case; we have excellent, even overwhelming, evidence, subsequent events bear us out, and everyone comes to agree with us. I have no doubt that very often what we believe in such cases is true."[10] But even then, strictly speaking, we do not know with absolute certainty, and cannot know with absolute certainty that what we believe is true — all we have is justification, not truth.

> When we say we want our beliefs to be true we could as well say we want to be certain that they are, that the evidence for them is overwhelming, that all subsequent (observed) events will bear them out, that everyone will come to agree with us. It makes no sense to ask for more. Of course, if we have beliefs, we know under what conditions they are true. But I do not think it adds anything to say that truth is a goal, of science or anything else. We do not aim at truth but at honest justification. Truth is not, in my opinion, a norm.[11]

So when we say that we want our beliefs or theories to be true, that may very well be what we really want, but all that we can actually aim for is justification. I think this matters in at least two ways. Firstly, it should instill a kind of humility. We can aim for the best evidence, the best arguments, and so forth, but the fact that we can never achieve more than that — more than justification — implies that we can always turn out to be wrong. Truth is fixed, but justification is not. A belief that is justified today may become unjustified tomorrow and the other way around. In other words, we should only accept "things" as true provisionally, but this is not a new point, of course; on the contrary, it is a crucial element of the Quinean, pragmatist naturalism adopted here.[12]

Secondly, there may be areas of thought where aiming for truth seems impossible for entirely different reasons, or where aiming for truth and aiming for justification would suggest different approaches. If justification is all we can aim for anyway, then this would greatly matter in those areas. One such area is ethics. (And it might actually be the only one.) Aiming for moral truth raises many more troubling questions than aiming for moral justification, and if the latter is all we can do anyway, then we can and should avoid those troubling questions. We'll return to this issue when we turn to meta-ethics in chapter 11.

---

10 Donald Davidson, "Reply to Pascal Engel," in *The Philosophy of Donald Davidson*, ed. L.E. Hahn (Chicago: Open Court, 1999), 460–61, at 461.
11 Ibid.
12 See the section "Naturalism" in chapter 1.

One may wonder whether "truth" and "true" are more than rhetorical devices if we often mean something else, namely justification, when we use those terms, and if we cannot really aim for truth. Perhaps it can be said that in daily use they are mere rhetorical devices indeed, but this is certainly not the case in a more philosophical context. As an abstract, philosophical notion, "truth" is a very precise and unambiguous notion. To say that p is true is to say that whatever p describes is the case. And even if we cannot really aim for truth or particular truths, we certainly can talk and think about this abstract notion — about the idea, concept, or phenomenon of truth, and about what, if anything, makes something true. Furthermore, we can also talk and think about justification, and when we do so, we are talking and thinking about something else.

Unfortunately, there are many other terminological ambiguities in philosophy that are equally confounding. "Philosophical problems arise when language goes on holiday," wrote Wittgenstein,[13] but this is a kind of philosophical problem that can and should be avoided. For this reason, before proceeding to more substantial matters, the next chapter will focus on conceptual issues. As explained in chapter 6 and elsewhere in part I, radical Buddhism is built on realist metaphysical foundations, but the term "realism" is used in many different ways within and outside philosophy, and it is not equally clear in all of these uses what the term exactly means. In addition to "realism," there are a number of other terms that will be discussed in chapter 7: "idealism," "perspectivism," "mysticism," and more. Additionally, the chapter will also discuss the related topic of (anti-)essentialism.

Based on this terminological groundwork, chapter 8 will attempt to clarify relevant aspects of Yogācāra and Tiantai/Tendai 天台 philosophy and, with a bit of help from Donald Davidson, bridge the gap between the two. The focus of chapter 8 is on the overlap between metaphysics and the philosophy of language. One of its main claims is that what follows from the Yogācāra views on conceptual construction and concept formation is a moderate kataphasis, similar to that advocated by Zhiyi 智顗. Chapter 9 builds on the foundations laid in chapter 8 to explore its epistemological implications. It argues for a coherence theory of justification and applies this approach to argue for the this-worldly or austere realism (according to which there is just this world and just this life) that characterizes radical Buddhism.

Chapter 10, finally, proposes a label for the view developed in chapters 8 and 9, "post-Yogācāra realism," and turns to the not-just-as-well criterion in the definition of "Buddhist" proposed in chapter 5:

> A theory, doctrine, practice, or idea is Buddhist if most of what it is based on or derived from is Buddhist and if it could not *just as well* be based on or derived from non-Buddhist sources.[14]

This is a rather vague criterion, however, and partially for that reason there is no perfectly clear and definite answer to the question whether the view advocated here is "Buddhist" in this sense. Surely, it is possible to construct a similar view out of other source materials, but probably not "just as well" or just as easily. Chapter 10 also has another closely related goal, which is to map some of the adjacent terrain. Parts of the view presented here have been advocated in other philosophical traditions as

---

13   Ludwig Wittgenstein, *Philosophische Untersuchungen* (1953; Frankfurt a.M.: Suhrkamp, 1975), §38.
14   See the section "Defining 'Buddhism' and 'Buddhist'" in chapter 5.

well, and there undoubtedly is much to be learned from comparison and constructive engagement. That comparative project itself cannot be part of this book, of course, it is already thick enough, but I believe it is worthwhile pointing out a few important or interesting connections.

7

Conceptual Matters

As a colloquial term, "realism" refers to an attitude towards problems and solutions that is not influenced by ideals, values, or emotions. It is often contrasted to "idealism," which from a "realist" perspective advocates ideal solutions while disregarding whether those are actually possible. Closely related are political realism and idealism. According to the former, politics is and should be just about power; according to the latter, politics should aim for a better society. In art and literature, "realism" refers to styles that aim for an unembellished depiction of reality, while "idealism" aims for unreal standards of beauty and perfection. None of these uses of the terms "realism" and "idealisms" are relevant here, but in philosophical terminology some kinds of "realism" tend to be opposed to "idealism" as well. And consequently, if Yogācāra advocates a kind of idealism, it cannot be realist, or at least not in the relevant senses of "realism" and "idealism." It is debatable whether Yogācāra metaphysics is idealist, but before we turn to that topic in the next chapter, we first need to have a clearer view of what terms like "realism" and "idealism" exactly mean and whether they really are mutually exclusive indeed.

Furthermore, "realism" and "idealism" are not the only ambiguous or polysemous terms that play important roles in following chapters. The common Buddhist distinction between ultimate reality and conventional or phenomenal reality has produced a variety of views on how these two are related and how and whether we can know ultimate reality. According to *apophatic* views, the ultimate is fundamentally inexpressible. According to *kataphatic* views this is too negative or even nihilist; while we may not be able to fully and completely describe the ultimate, language is not entirely arbitrary and deceptive either. A number of terms have been used to describe various positions that take the distinction between ultimate and phenomenal reality seriously. "Mysticism," "relativism," and "perspectivism" are the most important. Unfortunately, like "realism" and "idealism," these terms too are polysemous or ambiguous and have additional, mostly unrelated meanings outside philosophy. Hence, these terms are in need of clarification as well. A further topic that is directly or indirectly related to almost all these other -*isms* and what they refer to are (anti-) *essentialism* and the related notion of natural kinds.

Realism (1) — Universals and (Anti-)Essentialism

In philosophy, the term "realism" refers to theories that claim that something exists, and consequently, the term is meaningful only if it is clear what kind of thing it claims to exist. According to "moral realism," for example, there are moral facts (i.e., moral facts exist), and those moral facts are what make moral statements true. This example of a realism reveals an important ambiguity, namely, that the claim that facts exist might mean two very different things. Recall Tarski's *t schema* introduced in the introduction to part II: "*p*" is true if and only if *p*; or "grass is green" is true if and only if grass is green. Another way to read this is: "'grass is green' is true if and only if *it is a fact* that grass is green," but there are at least two ways to understand the latter sentence: the fact-as-truthmaker reading and the truth-as-factmaker reading. According to the first, there exists a fact that grass is green independent from and prior to the statement "grass is green," and it is that fact that makes the statement true. This is usually called the "correspondence theory of truth." Consequently, facts are a kind of thing that exist independent from us, which is what the truth-as-factmaker reading denies. According to that second interpretation, saying that "grass is green" is true just means the same thing as saying that it is a fact that grass is green. There is no independent, prior fact, but rather saying that "grass is green" is true assigns "fact" status to the greenness of grass. Thus, according to the second view, true statements do not literally *create* facts, all they do is assign "fact" status. A moral realist understands the sentence in the first way: there are moral facts that exist independently. Correspondingly, realisms hold that something exists *independently* and not as a mere conceptual or mental construction.

While the term "moral realism" at least gives a hint about what kind of things it claims to exist, there are two uses of the term "realism" in metaphysics that lack any further specification but that are very different.[1] These are realism about universals and realism about external reality.

The debate whether universals exist is probably the longest running debate in Western philosophy. It started with the ancient Greeks and still we are nowhere near a consensus. It is also a debate with equivalents in the Indian and Chinese traditions. In metaphysics, a universal is what particular things have in common. The term contrasts with "particular." The strawberry I ate with breakfast this morning is a particular; its redness is a universal. According to nominalists, only particulars exist. According to realists, universals also exist, so redness exists in addition to red things. Both nominalism and realism are problematic but for very different reasons.

According to realism, the strawberry I had for breakfast this morning *exemplifies* redness, so the particular strawberry stood in an *exemplification relation* to the universal redness. But then, what is this exemplification relation? If it is a relation, then it must itself be a universal because there are not just universals for characteristics of singular things but relational characteristics as well, like "being south of …" or "being in between … and …." But if the exemplification relation is a universal, then the particulars in this case must somehow exemplify that relation: "the strawberry and redness exemplified the exemplification relation," or something like that. This, of course, just gives us a further exemplification relation, which adds a further universal, and so forth, *ad infinitum*. It seems that the only way out of this infinite regress is to deny that the exemplification relation is a relation. Then what is it? Some primitive feature of reality that cannot be further explained.

Another problem for realism is that if there is a universal for any characteristic things have, including relational characteristics, then there might be infinitely many universals. Hence, realism leads to a rather extravagant ontology. Furthermore, there

---

1 Other examples of realisms with an explicitly specified subject matter (like moral realism) include modal realism, which holds that possible worlds are real, mathematical realism, which holds that numbers are real, and logical realism, according to which logical principles are mind-independent.

might even be paradoxical universals, and that cannot be right: something that is self-contradictory cannot possibly exist. An example of such a paradoxical universal can be based on Russell's paradox. Recall that my strawberry *exemplified* redness. Universals are abstract objects, and consequently they have neither shape, nor color, nor location. Thus, the universal redness is not itself red. Or in other words, redness does not exemplify redness. But the universal colorlessness does exemplify colorlessness because as a universal it is colorless. Hence, colorlessness exemplifies itself. Now, imagine a universal "does not exemplify itself." Does that universal exemplify itself? If it does, it does not; and if it does not, it does. The universal "does not exemplify itself" is self-contradictory, so it cannot possibly exist, but that means that a realist must have some criterion to exclude problematic universals like these, and that criterion cannot be some kind of ad hoc fix that tries to fix the damage after it is done.

One way to avoid some problems like these was suggested by Aristotle, who held that universals do not exist outside the things that exemplify them, but rather *in* them. This is sometimes called "immanent realism." Paradoxical universals, then, do not exist, because nothing exists that exemplifies those. Immanent realism faces other problems, however. Imagine that due to some freak glitch in the fabric of the universe tomorrow all red things suddenly turn green. Then, with the disappearance of red things, so does the universal redness because it only exists in the things that exemplify it. A few days later, however, somewhere suddenly a red flower blooms. Does redness then reappear? Or is it a different redness? Can something disappear and reappear? How would we know whether the two rednesses are the same or different? There do not seem to be good answers to these questions, but without answers, the idea of immanent realism does not make much sense.

The main problem for nominalism is of a very different nature. Consider the sentence "the strawberry I had with breakfast and the tomato I had with lunch had the same color." For a realist this sentence is entirely unproblematic — she can analyze it as saying that there is (or there exists) a color such that the strawberry and the tomato both exemplified it. But that is not an option for a nominalist because this analysis implies that that color (i.e., that universal) exists, which is exactly what a nominalist denies. Another problem for nominalism is a sentence like "red is a color," which again is no problem for a realist. The latter just reads it as "the universal redness is a color universal" or something like that, but that obviously is not an option for a nominalist.

Rudolf Carnap tried to solve the latter problem by claiming that sentences like "red is a color" are about the way we use language rather than about things in the world.[2] This is called "meta-linguistic nominalism." Carnap's solution did not really work. Wilfred Sellars's might,[3] but that solution is much too technical to discuss here. An entirely different solution for the problem posed by the first sentence is denying it — that strawberry and that tomato did not have the same color. Nothing has. Rather, every shade is unique. Perhaps the most basic problem for nominalism is how to explain that things appear to have characteristics in common, but this variant of nominalism denies that. Everything is unique. There are no shared characteristics. The appearance of shared characteristics is mere appearance. It is due to us, to our classification of things under the same conceptual umbrella. This kind of

---

2   Rudolf Carnap, *Logische Syntax der Sprache* (Vienna: J. Springer, 1934).
3   Wilfrid Sellars, "Abstract Entities" (1963), in *In the Space of Reasons* (Cambridge: Harvard University Press, 2007), 163–205.

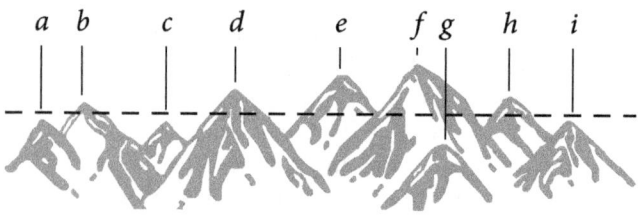

Fig. 7.1. A mountain landscape.

nominalism is uncommon in Western philosophy but not in Buddhist philosophy. It was advocated by Yogācāra philosophers like Dignāga and Dharmakīrti, for example.

Buddhist nominalism is motivated by anti-essentialism. Realism about universals holds that redness and other universals exist, but if universals exist independently, then when we perceive a strawberry to be red, all we do is discover some fact of nature, some thing that was already out there, namely redness, and that redness is just part of the nature or essence of that strawberry. This may not sound particularly problematic, but consider another example, the mountain landscape depicted in figure 7.1.

In the same way that the universal redness suggests that red is a *natural kind* that is somehow *given* by the way things are, the universal mountain (or mountainhood) suggests that there is a natural kind called "mountain" and a corresponding mountain essence. But it does not take very deep reflection to realize that this suggestion does not make much sense. Mountains have vague boundaries in three different ways. (And so does redness, by the way.)

First, there is a vague boundary between mountains and non-mountains, such as hills. One could, of course, draw a line somewhere, like the dashed line in the figure. Then, *b, d, e, f,* and *h* are mountains, but *a, c, g,* and *i* are not. But any such line is completely arbitrary — there is nothing in nature that compels us to draw that line at a certain height. In practice, where the line is drawn often depends on local custom. In the Netherlands, for example, it is drawn at 300 meters because otherwise the country would not have a single mountain (and even then, it shares its only mountain with Belgium and Germany). Furthermore, such a boundary raises various other questions: should it be a certain height above sea level or above the surrounding landscape? In the first case, a molehill in Mongolia or Tibet would be a mountain, which is obviously absurd. In the second case, you'd need a way to decide that level of the surrounding landscape, which is bound to be just as arbitrary. And what to do with ice? What if *b* is just above the line because its top is a huge chunk of permanently frozen ice? Does that count towards it height or not; that is, does only rock count?

Second, there is a vague boundary between mountains and not-yet-mountains or not-mountains-anymore. Mountains are created through orogeny or volcanism, and grind down due to erosion. In the beginning there is no mountain, but then very slowly[4] the land rises and a mountain is formed, which gradually is eroded until there is no mountain anymore. The whole cycle takes hundreds of millions of years. At some point in that slow and gradual process there is a mountain, and at another, much later point there is no mountain anymore. But any way to fix those two points is completely arbitrary. This arbitrariness is exactly the same as that in case of the

---

4 Or sometimes very quickly in case of a volcano.

first vague boundary, however, so it could be argued that this *diachronic vagueness* is just a special case of the *synchronic vagueness* with regards to the boundary between mountains and non-mountains.

The third kind of vagueness is of a different nature: it concerns the vague boundary between a mountain and not-(that)-mountain. Let's say that there is a valley between *d* and *g* in the figure. It gently slopes upwards towards *f* and curls to the left in the direction of *e*; somewhere in both directions the valley ends. The third vague boundary is that between the mountain — *d*, for example — and that valley. Where is that boundary? Is it a certain gradient in the slope? Where the slope is shallower than that threshold you are in the valley; where it is steeper you are on the mountain. Or is it a certain height? Again, wherever this boundary is drawn, it is completely arbitrary.

W.V.O. Quine rejected the positing of abstract entities, such as universals, on the ground that they do not have clear identity criteria. This principle is captured in the slogan "no entity without identity."[5] It turns out that mountains do not have clear identity criteria either, that is, there are no unambiguous criteria to decide what is a mountain and what is not and to decide where a mountain begins and ends. By the same standard we should then refrain from positing mountains. Perhaps, that is an overreaction, but we'll turn to that issue below.[6] A more moderate conclusion would be that mountains are not a *natural kind*; that the category of mountains is not given by reality but created by us; that there is no essence or *svabhāva* (Sanskrit; literally "self-being") of mountainhood, that is, there is no clear and unambiguous set of features that make something a mountain.

Anti-essentialism rejects natural kinds and essences or svabhāvas. Buddhist philosophy is anti-essentialist, while Western philosophy is predominantly essentialist. There have been some notable anti-essentialists in Western philosophy as well, including Quine. Other philosophers, such as John Dupré and Samuel Wheeler, have argued against natural kinds and have shown that supposed paradigm cases of natural kinds do in fact suffer from some of the same kinds of vagueness as mountains in the example above.[7] Biological species were long a favorite, but species have very vague diachronic boundaries.[8] Chemical elements have also been suggested, but any element has isotopes and some properties of particular isotopes are due to the exact properties of that isotope rather than the element, suggesting that elements do not have essences. Sex or gender are further candidates, but there is a whole collection of conditions that can result in intermediates between male and female. Gender, it turns out, is a socially constructed spectrum, even if many humans are close to the extremes on that spectrum. And so forth. The only plausible essences Wheeler could find are of things made by us: things that are patented or trademarked. Coca-Cola has an essence, but none of its main ingredients does. But we would not normally consider Coca-Cola a *natural* kind.

---

5   W.V.O. Quine, "Speaking of Objects" (1969), OROE: 1–25, at 23.
6   In the section "Apophasis, Kataphasis, Relativism, and Mysticism" and in chapter 8.
7   John Dupré, *The Disorder of Things: Metaphysical Foundations of the Disunity of Science* (Cambridge: Harvard University Press, 1993), and Samuel Wheeler, *Neo-Davidsonian Metaphysics: From the True to the Good* (New York: Routledge, 2014).
8   Individual animals, such as individual humans, have birthdays, but species do not. Species evolve in a gradual process and there is no sharp, diachronic boundary between a species and its parent species.

Under Aristotle's immense influence, essentialism has been the default in Western philosophy, and its hegemony was strengthened by Saul Kripke's *Naming and Necessity*.[9] Kripke argued that proper names, like "Kripke," are *rigid designators,* which means that they refer to the same "thing" in all possible worlds. Largely based on this idea he developed a forceful argument for natural kinds and essentialism that is accepted by mainstream analytic philosophy, but not by Quine and Davidson.[10] Wheeler's most original contribution to the debate about essences and natural kinds is his attempt to find some kind of middle path between Quine's and Davidson's anti-essentialism and Aristotle's and Kripke's essentialism.[11] This middle path, *relative essentialism,* rejects absolute essences and natural kinds but holds that things have essences relative to what they are called. Hence, a red strawberry is essentially red relative to its designation as a red strawberry and only relative to that designation. Given that essentialism assumes that essences are absolute, that is, they are not dependent on what things are called, Wheeler's relative essentialism is a variety of anti-essentialism but one that is considerably more hospitable to essentialist intuitions.[12]

Realism (2) — External Reality

The other kind of realism that is usually not further qualified is external world realism, and this is the kind of realism that the unqualified term to refers to in this book. John Searle has defined this kind of realism as "the view that the world exists independently of our representations of it."[13] Importantly, this is all that this kind of realism holds. Unfortunately, realism in this sense is sometimes confused with realism about universals, and there are a number of views that are commonly associated with external world realism that are sometimes put under the same terminological umbrella.[14] This is a bit like calling cheese a kind of wine because many wine drinkers also eat cheese. Often, such a lack of terminological hygiene is attributed to Hilary Putnam, and Putnam is indeed a prime target of Searle's denunciation of such confusions, but this is not entirely fair. Putnam distinguished externalism (or external realism) from internalism (or internal realism), and his description of externalism, which is just one particular variety of realism, is often interpreted as his view of realism *simpliciter*. That description is the following:

> The world consists of some fixed totality of mind-independent objects. There is exactly one true and complete description of "the way the world is." Truth

---

9   Saul Kripke, *Naming and Necessity* (Cambridge: Harvard University Press, 1972).
10 Quine rejects rigid designators because the notion depends on modality, which he rejects. (For a good introduction to Quine's views on modality, see Dagfinn Føllesdal, "Quine on Modality," in *The Cambridge Companion to Quine,* ed. Roger Gibson [Cambridge: Cambridge University Press, 2004], 200–213.) Davidson once remarked that he does not know a rigid designator when he sees one ("Knowing One's Own Mind" [1987], SIO: 15–38, at 29).
11 Quine was a much more consistent anti-essentialist than Davidson was. As Wheeler is well aware, there are persistent elements of essentialism in Davidson's thought.
12 Essentialist intuitions appear to be innate to humans. Susan Gelman has argued that essentialism is a cognitive bias that has its origins in very early childhood. Susan Gelman, *The Essential Child: Origins of Essentialism in Everyday Thought* (Oxford: Oxford University Press, 2003).
13 John Searle, *The Construction of Social Reality* (London: Allen Lane Penguin, 1995), 153.
14 Some of these confusions may be caused by a mix-up of external world realism and realism about universals, but it cannot be emphasized strongly enough that these two realisms make very different claims. To say that there is an external, mind-independent world is not to say that universals (or natural kinds, etc.) exist or vice versa.

involves some sort of correspondence relation between words or thought-signs and external things and sets of things. I shall call this perspective the *externalist* perspective, because its favorite point of view is a God's Eye point of view.[15]

In contrast, in the internalist perspective, the question "what objects does the world consist of? is a question that [...] only makes sense [...] *within* a theory or description," and there is or can be "more than one 'true' theory or description of the world."[16] Because both the externalist and the internalist view hold that there is an independent or external reality, both are forms of realism. Unfortunately, Putnam later sometimes called externalism "realism" *simpliciter*,[17] thus contributing to the terminological confusion.

To clarify what realism is, it may be useful to discuss what it is not, and toward that end the above quote by Putnam is quite useful. The first claim Putnam attributes to external realism is that "the world consists of some fixed totality of mind-independent objects," but even this claims too much. A realist does not need to hold that mind-independent reality is fixed, nor that it consists of discrete objects. All she holds is that there *is* a mind-independent reality.

The second attribution is that there is "exactly one true and complete description of 'the way the world is'." Searle vehemently disagrees with this and argued that it is consistent with realism that "different and even incommensurable vocabularies can be constructed for describing different aspects of reality for our various purposes."[18] Quine similarly rejected the idea that there is just one correct description of reality and argued that from the multiple possible descriptions, in a given context, we should choose the one that best fits our interests and purposes.[19] Realism, importantly, is not a view about *how* things are, but it is the view that there is a way that things are, independently from all human views about how things are.

Putnam's third attribution is the correspondence theory of truth, the view that truth is the right kind of correspondence between statements or beliefs and mind-independent facts, but as Searle rightly pointed out, "realism is not a theory of truth and it does not imply any theory of truth" and "it is thus possible to hold [realism] and deny the correspondence theory."[20]

In *Realism with a Human Face,* Putnam elevated the fourth attribution in the quote above to the defining element of realism: "the whole content of Realism lies in the claim that it makes sense to think of a God's-Eye View (or, better, of a 'View from Nowhere')."[21] I agree with Putnam that such a claim makes no sense, but I disagree that this has anything to do with realism, and so does Searle. Again, realism claims that there is an independent reality, not that it can be viewed from anywhere, let alone from nowhere. "The whole idea of a 'view' is already epistemic and [realism] is

---

15 Hilary Putnam, *Reason, Truth and History* (Cambridge: Cambridge University Press, 1981), 49.
16 Ibid.
17 See, for example, Hilary Putnam, *Representation and Reality* (Cambridge: MIT Press, 1988), 107 and *Realism with a Human Face* (Cambridge: Harvard University Press, 1990), 23.
18 Searle, *The Construction of Social Reality,* 155.
19 W.V.O. Quine, "On What There Is" (1948), FLPV: 1–19; *Word and Object* (Cambridge: MIT Press, 1960); and "Ontological Relativity" (1969), OROE: 26–68.
20 Searle, *The Construction of Social Reality,* 154.
21 Putnam, *Realism with a Human Face,* 23.

not epistemic," wrote Searle, and consequently, "it would be consistent with realism to suppose that any kind of 'view' of reality is quite impossible."[22]

In his history of anti-realism in continental philosophy, Lee Braver based his definition of realism mostly on Putnam, but he added a few more elements of his own.[23] These additional elements are (1) bivalence, or the idea that statements are either true or false; (2) the idea that "there must be a way for the mind to reach reality as it is"[24] and that there is a kind of passive knowledge of reality that requires no interpretation; and (3) the anti-relativist idea that knowing subjects are all more or less the same and unchanging. Graham Harman added one more element in his review of Braver's book: (4) "most anti-realists do not think philosophy has anything to tell us about the collision of two inanimate objects if this collision is not somehow encountered by humans — whereas most realists do."[25]

Like Putnam's suggestions, even if many realists hold these, they are not parts of realism itself. They are not what realism *is*. The first, bivalence, is a principle of classical logic, which a realist might accept or reject, but she would be wise to accept it as it has been shown repeatedly that rejection of this principle causes serious problems. The second is another epistemic claim, while realism is not epistemic, as pointed out by Searle. The third, anti-relativism, is explicitly rejected by Searle who advocates a kind of relativistic realism, as well as by Quine, Wheeler, and several other realists including myself. This point is really a restatement of the second attribution by Putnam discussed above. And lastly, Harman's addition is meta-philosophical rather than metaphysical — it is about the nature and scope of philosophy rather than about reality — and thus has little if anything to do with realism. A realist can hold that philosophy is just concerned with the world as it is experienced by or otherwise relates to humans, or she may place herself in the opposing camp. If one, like Quine, holds that philosophy is part of science, then it makes no sense to assume that philosophy must necessarily be anthropocentric in this way, but it is not this view that makes Quine a realist.

After rejecting some of the confusions about "realism," Searle revised his provisional definition as follows:

> *Realism is the view that there is a way that things are that is logically independent of all human representations. Realism does not say how things are but only that there is a way that they are.* And "things" in the previous two sentences does not mean material objects or even objects. It is like the "it" in "It is raining," not a referring expression.[26]

And this, indeed, is all that "realism" means. While Putnam and Braver are right that many realists have several other views, those views are logically independent from realism and should not be confused with it.

That said, there are varieties of "realism" that claim more than just the existence of some kind of external, mind-independent reality. Usually these are prefixed with

---

22 Searle, *The Construction of Social Reality,* 154.
23 Lee Braver, *A Thing of This World: A History of Continental Anti-Realism* (Evanston: Northwestern University Press, 2007).
24 Ibid., 21.
25 Graham Harman, "A Festival of Anti-Realism: Braver's History of Continental Thought," *Philosophy Today* 52, no. 2 (2008): 197–210, at 198–99.
26 Searle, *The Construction of Social Reality,* 155. Italics in original.

some kind of descriptive term, but that is sometimes forgotten. Perhaps, the most important is naive realism, which denies the distinction between external or noumenal reality and phenomenal reality and thus holds that the phenomenal is ultimately real. According to *naive realism*, the world as we experience it is just the world as it really is. Other qualified realisms that I have mentioned in part I of this book are "this-worldly realism" and "austere realism."[27] Both terms referred to a combination of realism, naturalism, and other unidentified elements that only recognizes this world as real, without accepting naive realism, and that rejects supernatural, other worlds.[28]

Idealism

The term "idealism" often contrasts to "materialism" but often also to "realism." Three kinds of materialism and three corresponding idealisms were distinguished in chapter 4.[29] Firstly, metaphysical materialism or physicalism holds that reality is physical (or material, originally), and thus that the mental somehow depends on, or emerges from the physical.[30] *Metaphysical idealism*, in contrast, maintains that apparent material or physical reality is really in the mind, and thus that everything that exists is mental. Secondly, according to economic materialism, certain economic or "material" aspects of society determine or strongly influence certain other "ideal" aspects of society; according to economic idealism it is the other way around.[31] And thirdly, axiological materialism, which is closely related to the colloquial use of the term "materialism," prioritizes wealth and other material goals, while axiological idealism prioritizes immaterial goals like justice and fairness. The second and third of these idealisms are irrelevant here.

Metaphysical idealism is anti-realist. If all of reality is in the mind, then there is no external, mind-independent reality, and as the defining thesis of realism is that there is a mind-dependent reality, metaphysical idealism opposes realism. However, this does not necessarily imply that realism is materialist or physicalist. Again, all that realism claims is that there is an external reality; not that is of a certain kind or nature. Materialism or physicalism is a variety of realism but not the only variety. Substance dualism, for example, is another.

In addition to metaphysical idealism and the other two idealisms mentioned above, there are further varieties of idealism that are sometimes confused with metaphysical idealism, even though they make quite different claims. These further varieties are mostly forms of *epistemological idealism*.[32] According to epistemological idealism, all of our experience of reality is necessarily mediated by the mind. Linguistic idealism, for example, holds that the world of our experience is created by the categories given in our languages.

Contrary to metaphysical idealism, epistemological idealism is compatible with realism, and indeed many idealist philosophers in the Western tradition were realists. By far the most influential realist idealist was Kant, who distinguished "things-

---

27 In chapters 4 and 6.
28 More about this in chapter 9.
29 See the section "The Problem(s) with Materialism(s)" in chapter 4.
30 See the section "Physicalism" in chapter 4.
31 See the sections "The Problem(s) with Materialism(s)" and "Economic Materialism" in chapter 4.
32 The distinction between metaphysical and epistemological idealism was also briefly addressed in the section "From Nāgārjuna to Zhiyi" in chapter 2.

in-themselves" from their appearances.³³ The Kantian distinction between noumenal reality (i.e., the things-in-themselves) and phenomenal reality (i.e., appearances) itself is not unique. It has ancient roots in Western thought and more or less corresponds to the distinction between ultimate and conventional reality in Buddhist philosophy, but Kant made some important innovations. He argued that we can only know things as we experience them and not as they really are. The thing-in-itself is beyond or before our experience, and because all we can know is based on our experience, the thing-in-itself is largely outside the scope of knowledge. The realization of the latter leads to a kind of epistemological humility: we cannot nearly know as much as we'd like to know.

Nevertheless, while noumenal reality is *largely* outside the scope of knowledge, we are not doomed to complete ignorance. Appearances are not independent from the things-in-themselves. The phenomenal and the noumenal are not two different worlds but two different aspects of reality, and appearances (i.e., how we experience things) are grounded in or caused by the things-in-themselves. This necessary relation between the noumenal and the phenomenal opens the door to a method to gain some knowledge of noumenal reality: the transcendental method.

Transcendental arguments have the following form: (1) x is the case; (2) x cannot possibly be the case unless y is the case; (3) Therefore, y is the case. Kant uses transcendental arguments to show, among others, that space is noumenally real and, contra metaphysical idealism, that there must be objects in space. Like the distinction between noumenal reality and phenomenal reality, transcendental arguments were not invented by Kant and are not unique to the Western tradition either. A fascinating, albeit not very explicit, example can be found in the *Discourse on the Perfection of Consciousness Only* 成唯識論 written by Xuanzang 玄奘 (seventh century), mostly based on Dharmapāla's³⁴ commentary on Vasubandhu's *Triṃśikāvijñaptimātratā*.³⁵ Xuanzang wrote:

> There are three kinds of *dharmas* (things) that exist. The first are *dharmas* that can be known through perception, such as form/matter and mind. The second are *dharmas* that reveal themselves in their uses, such as jugs and clothes. [...] The third are *dharmas* that are used actively, such as eyes and ears. Because of their uses, one realizes and knows that they exist.³⁶

The existence of eyes and ears can be inferred from their uses. The form of this argument may not be immediately obvious, but it appears to be that we know that we can see and hear, which would be impossible without eyes and ears. Therefore, eyes and ears exist. That is a transcendental argument.

While the term "transcendental idealism" is usually associated with Kant, other transcendental idealisms have been proposed but are rarely called such due to the

---

33 Immanuel Kant, *Kritik der Reinen Vernunft* (1781/1787; Hamburg: Felix Meiner, 1998).
34 This Dharmapāla was a sixth-century Indian monk and student of Dignāga and should not to be confused with the nineteenth and twentieth century Sinhalese Buddhist reformer of the same name, discussed in the section "Sri Lanka — Dharmapāla and Ariyaratne" in chapter 3.
35 Vasubandhu's *Triṃśikāvijñaptimātratā* (*Thirty Verses on Consciousness Only*) is one of the most influential texts of Yogācāra, which was cofounded by Vasubandhu. Likewise, Xuanzang's commentary became one of the most influential texts in Chinese Yogācāra.
36 且定有法略有三種。一現所知法。如色心等。二現受用法。如瓶衣等。…三有作用法。如眼耳等。由彼彼用證知是有。— Xuanzang 玄奘,《成唯識論》(7th c.), T31n1585, 6b.

strong Kantian association. A *transcendental idealism*, in a general sense, is just an epistemological idealism that holds that external or noumenal reality cannot be experienced but that we can nevertheless make some inferences about it based on our phenomenal experience. There is a further position that, like transcendental idealism, grants a kind of extraordinary access to external reality and that I shall call "quasi-idealism." While according to transcendental idealism we can gain some inferential knowledge about external reality, *quasi-idealism* maintains that we can — under certain, extraordinary circumstances — experience external or noumenal reality directly. According to quasi-idealism, all ordinary experience of reality is necessarily mediated by the mind, but this means that it is not a variety of epistemological idealism, strictly speaking, because that omits the "ordinary" qualification. The most common kind of quasi-idealism is a variety of mysticism that will be discussed below.

The "Noumenal"

Thus far I have used the adjective "noumenal" as if that term is unproblematic, but unfortunately that is not the case either. The Greek νοούμενον derives from the verb νοέω, which means, among other things, "to perceive by the mind." In Platonic philosophy, noumena are contrasted to phenomena — the latter are perceived directly, while noumena are inferred by the mind. The distinction is more often associated with Kant. According to Kant, external reality or the thing-in-itself is mostly unknowable, but we can infer some things about it from the forms of our phenomenal experience through transcendental reasoning. What we can infer in that way is noumenal, and thus the terms "thing-in-itself" and "noumenon" usually co-refer in Kant's writings. Nevertheless, from a historical perspective they are not identical, and the terms "noumenon" and "noumenal" are potential sources of confusion. Among analytic philosophers they are typically used to refer to external, mind-independent reality (i.e., the thing-in-itself), while among continental philosophers they are sometimes used in their Platonic, and perhaps etymologically more correct, sense of objects perceived, apprehended, or inferred by the mind, in other words, a kind of mental object. In this book, I only use the term in its more or less Kantian sense, as referring to external or ultimate reality.

The Kantian distinction between things-in-themselves and phenomenal appearances itself is, as already mentioned above, much older and widespread. Aristotle made a distinction between real and apparent colors in his discussion of rainbows, for example.[37] But the main impetus for the prominence of the reality-appearance distinction in early modern Western thought is Galileo's and Descartes's distinction between primary and secondary qualities — the former are independent of the observer and thus noumenal in the Kantian sense, while the latter are more like phenomenal effects. That the reality-appearance distinction is as widespread as it is, should probably not be a surprise. Psychological research has shown that the development of something like this distinction is a normal step in children's cognitive development between the ages of 3 and 4½.[38]

---

37 Zed Adams, *On the Genealogy of Color: A Case Study in Historicized Conceptual Analysis* (New York: Routledge, 2016).
38 See, for example, John Flavell, "The Development of Children's Understanding of False Belief and the Appearance-Reality Distinction," *International Journal of Psychology* 28, no. 5 (1993): 595–604.

Apophasis, Kataphasis, Skepticism, and Mysticism

As mentioned in the section on external world realism, it is sometimes assumed that realism entails some kind of view on reality or the possibility of having such a view. It was explained there that this confuses realism with other -isms and ideas, but that does not make those other -isms and ideas any less relevant here.

Kant advocated humility about our epistemic access to noumenal reality, but he did not completely deny the possibility of gaining knowledge of what lays beyond or before the world of appearances. It is sometimes mistakenly assumed that realists believe that it is possible to have such knowledge, while anti-realists believe this to be impossible, but that is just another example of an epistemic interpretation of "realism," while it was repeatedly pointed out above that external-world realism is not epistemic. Hence, it is not "anti-realist" to deny that we can have knowledge of ultimate or noumenal reality. Rather, denying that we can have a certain kind of knowledge is a variety of local skepticism — it is *noumenal skepticism*, although this use of the term "noumenal" seems rather odd given its etymology. Importantly, realists can be noumenal skeptics; that one believes that there is an external, mind-independent reality does not imply that one believes that we can know anything about that reality.

Closely related to skepticism versus anti-skepticism about ultimate or noumenal reality is the apophasis-kataphasis distinction explained in chapter 2.[39] While noumenal skepticism holds that we cannot have knowledge about the ultimate, the apophatic attitude denies that we can talk about or describe the ultimate, and thus that ultimate or noumenal reality is beyond language. Anti-skepticism and kataphasis are the respective opposing points of view. A corollary of the apophatic, negative attitude towards language is a devaluation of that what can be described and that what depends on language, namely, conventional or phenomenal reality. From the kataphatic point of view, on the other hand, language is not wholly deceptive, leading to a much more positive view of the conventionally real.

According to Robert Gimello, Mādhyamaka was apophatic, which lead to a kataphatic reaction in Yogācāra and Chinese Buddhism.[40] I'm not sure to what extent Yogācāra was really kataphatic, but we'll turn to that question in the next chapter. The Chinese progression from apophatic to kataphatic discourse was a very slow and gradual process. For example, Sengzhao 僧肇 (fourth to fifth century), an influential early Chinese Buddhist, wrote in his *Treatise on the Emptiness of the Unreal* 不真空論 (chapter 2 of the *Zhaolun* 肇論):

> A thing is not identical with its name, which does not approach/capture the [ultimately] real thing; a name is not identical with a thing, and thus does not lead to [ultimate] truth. And this being so, ultimate truth remains in silence, beyond description/elucidation by names. How could spoken or written words even recognize/distinguish it?[41]

---

39 See the section "From Nāgārjuna to Zhiyi."
40 Robert Gimell, "Apophatic and Kataphatic Discourse in Mahāyāna: A Chinese View," *Philosophy East and West* 26, no. 2 (1976): 117–36.
41 是以物不即名而就實, 名不即物而履真。然則真諦獨靜於名 教之外, 豈曰文言之能辨哉？— Sengzhao 僧肇,《肇論》(5th c.), T45n1858, 152a.

This is a clear expression of apophasis. A more kataphatic discourse only started to develop later in Tiantai 天台 and especially its Japanese offshoot, Tendai.[42]

Apophasis is closely related to *mysticism*, but the term "mysticism," like all of the key terms discussed in this chapter, has many different meanings. It is often understood as referring to the practice of using alternative states of consciousness such as meditation to achieve extraordinary experiences. In the present context, the most relevant notion of mysticism is a corollary of apophasis. It holds that ultimate reality is inexpressible and — because ordinary experience is always and perhaps necessarily mediated by language — inaccessible to the ordinary mind, but can be known or experienced non-conceptually or non-linguistically in some extra-ordinary mental state.

Much Buddhist thought is (or appears to be?) mystical in this sense: meditation supposedly gives access to a kind of non-conceptual knowledge or experience of non-conceptual ultimate reality. Such mysticism is realist because it claims that there is a mind-independent, external and non-conceptual reality. That reality is inexpressible, however, and thus this kind of mysticism is an apophatic realism. Furthermore, while it may seem that such mysticism is epistemologically idealist because it claims that phenomenal reality is mediated by the mind, it really is not. According to epistemological idealism all experience of reality is necessarily mediated by the mind, and mysticism denies the latter claim — the whole point of such mysticism is to experience unmediated reality. Hence, this is an example (and possibly the only example) of what I called "quasi-idealism."

To what extent unmediated experience of external reality is possible, and thus whether this mysticism makes sense, is questionable. Wilfrid Sellars has famously called the idea that we can have experiences of reality that are unmediated by our concepts the "myth of the given" and argued against this "myth."[43] Many Buddhists, of course, claim that non-conceptual awareness in meditation is possible, but such claims are anecdotal and impossible to verify.[44] Furthermore, introspective accounts of our mental states and experiences are notoriously unreliable.[45]

Relativism, Pluralism, and Perspectivism

If reality as we experience it (i.e., phenomenal reality) is mediated or constructed by the mind, then it is relative to whatever guides that construction or mediation. This is the most basic claim of *relativism*, but beyond this, there is not much that the many doctrines and ideas called "relativism" have in common. Attempts to define relativism generally settle on two key principles: first, what is true, right, or beautiful, or what can be said to exist, is relative to a frame of reference or scheme; and second,

---

42 See the last three sections of chapter 2 as well as chapter 8.
43 Wilfrid Sellars, "Empiricism and the Philosophy of Mind" (1956), in *Science, Perception and Reality* (London: Routledge and Kegan Paul, 1963), 127–96.
44 There is a burgeoning neuroscience of meditation, but there is no way to use neuro-imaging to look into the meditator's mind. That is, we cannot see what and how the meditator is experiencing during meditation, only which parts of her brain she is using.
45 Eric Schwitzgebel, "The Unreliability of Naive Introspection," *Philosophical Review* 117, no. 2 (2008): 245–73; Peter Carruthers, *The Opacity of Mind* (Oxford: Oxford University Press, 2011); Eric Schwitzgebel, "Introspection, What?" in *Introspection and Consciousness*, eds. Declan Smithies and Daniel Stoljar (Oxford: Oxford University Press, 2012), 29–47.

there are no objective standards to choose between schemes.[46] Hence, relativisms differ in what they consider to be relative and in what they consider it to be relative to. Especially with regards to the latter there is a bewildering variety: frames of references or schemes can be cultures (or sub-cultures), communities, languages, theories, paradigms, scientific disciplines, purposes, contexts, ideologies, and much more. Moreover, there are other ways in which relativisms and adjacent -isms and ideas vary as well.

Let's call whatever is relative a "view." A view, then, is a collection of beliefs about what some part of the world is like (i.e., an account of phenomenal reality), or of what is good or right or beautiful, and so forth.[47] That a view is relative to or constructed by a scheme only implies a multiplicity of views if there are multiple relevant schemes, but one could hold that there is just one scheme. This would be some kind of *monistic* relativism or monistic constructionism, depending on whether one wants to emphasize the relative or the constructive aspect. Paradigmatic relativism assumes that there are multiple views. Relativists typically hold that there is exactly one view per scheme and that one cannot easily switch between schemes. *Pluralists*, on the other hand deny one or both of these claims, most commonly the second. Hence, Quine's argument that if we can describe some event in physical or psychological terms, we should choose the description that fits our purpose, is pluralist and not relativist because, even though both descriptions are relative to schemes, we can switch between them and understand both. The idea found in a few Buddhist texts that hungry ghosts (*pretas*) see pus or blood where humans see water, is a kind of relativism, on the other hand, because it is normally impossible for a human to perceive the world the way a hell-being does or the other way around.[48]

Relativism comes in stronger and weaker forms. One way to draw the distinction is Maria Baghramian's suggestion that according to *strong* relativism there are no universal, scheme-transcendent truths — or in other words, there is nothing shared by all views — while according to *weak* relativism there may be some things that are universal.[49] A related distinction is that between philosophical relativisms that make overt metaphysical, epistemological, meta-ethical, or other philosophical claims, and applied relativisms that are not concerned with philosophy, but that are anthropological, sociological, or hermeneutical, for example.[50] The former are typically strong, while the latter tend to be weak. Many famous examples of relativism, including Whorf's, Kuhn's, and Gadamer's, belong to the latter kind (but unfortunately, philosophers often mistaken them for metaphysical theories).

According to *perspectivism* (or sometimes "perspectivalism"), every view is, by necessity, from a point of view, and the idea of a view from nowhere, or a God's-Eye point of view as Putnam called it, makes no sense. Perspectivism can be strong or weak and can be pluralist or relativist. It is pluralist (rather than relativist) if it as-

---

46 See, for example, Michael Krausz, "Introduction," in *Relativism: A Contemporary Anthology*, ed. Michael Krausz (New York: Columbia University Press, 2010), 1–10, at 1.
47 Recall that beliefs, by definition, are held to be true by the person having that belief. See the introduction to part II of this book.
48 Asaṅga, *Mahāyānasaṃgraha* (4/5th c.), II.14; Vasubandhu, *Viṃśatikākārikā* (5th c.), 3b–c; and Candrakīrti, *Madhyamakāvatāra* (7th c.), VI.71. See also the section "Relativism and Perspectivism in Yogācāra and Tiantai" in chapter 8.
49 Maria Baghramian, *Relativism* (New York: Routledge, 2004), 9.
50 Lajos Brons, "Applied Relativism and Davidson's Arguments against Conceptual Schemes," *The Science of Mind* 49 (2011): 221–40.

sumes that one can switch between perspectives. And it is weak (rather than strong) if there may be things shared in or by all perspectives. Furthermore, perspectivism can be realist or anti-realist, and a realist perspectivism can be apophatic or kataphatic.

This threefold distinction of anti-realist, apophatic, and kataphatic perspectivism is closely related to Bo Mou's distinction between *subjective* and *objective* perspectivism. Mou describes the subjective variety as "a radical 'anything goes' version of conceptual relativism," while "objective perspectivism bases the eligibility of a perspective [...] on whether the perspective points to some aspect that is really or objectively possessed by the object of study."[51] In other words, in subjective perspectivism, perspectives are groundless, and therefore, incapable of revealing anything about external or ultimate reality. Hence, subjective perspectivism is apophatic unless it is anti-realist — in that case perspectives would also be groundless but due to the lack of a ground. (Brook Ziporyn attributes such a groundless, "anything goes" perspectivism to Zhiyi 智顗,[52] but for reasons explained in the next chapter, I doubt that this is an accurate interpretation.[53]) In contrast, objective perspectivism holds that perspectives are grounded in external or ultimate reality and, therefore, tell us at least something about that reality.[54] What we can learn about external or ultimate reality is still, and by necessity, perspectival, of course, but that does not make it inherently false; only partial, one-sided, or incomplete. This is a kataphatic version of perspectivism.

In this book I will defend a version of perspectival realism that is realist, anti-essentialist, moderately kataphatic, weak, and pluralist, and that could be called "quasi-perspectivist." Perspectival realism holds that views on reality are dependent on or constructed in accordance with conceptual schemes, which are, roughly, sets of conceptual categories used to perceive, understand, and talk about the world but that are also formed in interaction with the world. The perspectival realism defended here is *quasi*-perspectivist because it is agnostic with regards to the possibility of non-conceptual access to ultimate reality,[55] while according to a corresponding perspectivism or epistemological idealism, all experience and description of external or ultimate reality would be scheme-mediated.[56]

---

51 Bo Mou, "Searle, Zhuang Zi, and Transcendental Perspectivism," in *Searle's Philosophy and Chinese Philosophy*, ed. Bo Mou (Leiden: Brill, 2008), 405–30, at 406.
52 Brook Ziporyn, *Emptiness and Omnipresence: An Essential Introduction to Tiantai Buddhism* (Bloomington: Indiana University Press, 2016).
53 See the section "Relativism and Perspectivism in Yogācāra and Tiantai" in chapter 8, but see also the section "From Nāgārjuna to Zhiyi" in chapter 2.
54 Objective perspectivism is perspectivism in the most literal sense of "perspective." It is largely analogous to the ordinary situation of different people looking at the same thing from slightly different points of view and thus seeing a slightly different side of that thing.
55 Nevertheless, even if non-conceptual access to ultimate reality is possible, it plays no epistemological, soteriological, moral, or other role in the view proposed and defended in this book and is thus largely irrelevant.
56 If the notion of a perspective is understood broader, that is, as any point of view, rather than just a conceptual scheme, then non-conceptual access (if it exists) would also be a perspective, and the variety of perspectival realism proposed in this book would be perspectivist (rather than quasi-perspectivist) and non-Kantian transcendental idealist.

Fig. 7.2. A photograph as noumenal reality.

An Analogy

Many of the -isms discussed in this chapter can be further illustrated by means of an analogy. Figures 7.2 and 7.3 represent noumenal or external reality and phenomenal or conventional reality, respectively. The photograph in figure 7.2 is analogous to the world as it really is; the labeled sketch in figure 7.3 is analogous to our conceptually determinate experience of the world. As in that picture, we cut up the world into bits that correspond to our words, and label these bits accordingly. Hence, we see some parts of the world as houses, others as trees, or mountains, or cars, or goats,[57] and so forth.

According to metaphysical idealism, the photograph does not exist and only the sketch is real. Realism, in the sense of external world realism and not in the sense of realism about universals, disagrees and claims that the photograph is real. Naive realism maintains that figure 7.3 is the photograph rather than figure 7.2, and thus denies that there is a difference between the sketch and the photograph.

Epistemological idealism holds that we can only see the sketch and never the photograph, but according to transcendental idealism, we can infer some things about the photograph on the basis of our experience, that is, on the basis of the sketch. Mysticism claims that, although we can normally only experience the sketch, there is a special kind of perception or awareness, such as meditation, that allows us to see the photograph as well.

Relativists, perspectivists, and pluralists usually hold that there are many different sketches, and thus that figure 7.3 is merely one among the possibilities. These positions are not necessarily mutually exclusive, although some variants are, but they focus on different things. The key point for relativism is that the sketch is relative to something. Similarly, constructionism holds that the sketch is constructed by something. In case of the analogy, that "something" is language, but other constructionisms are possible. Because the sketch is, thus, dependent on something that is outside

---

57 No, there are no goats in the picture.

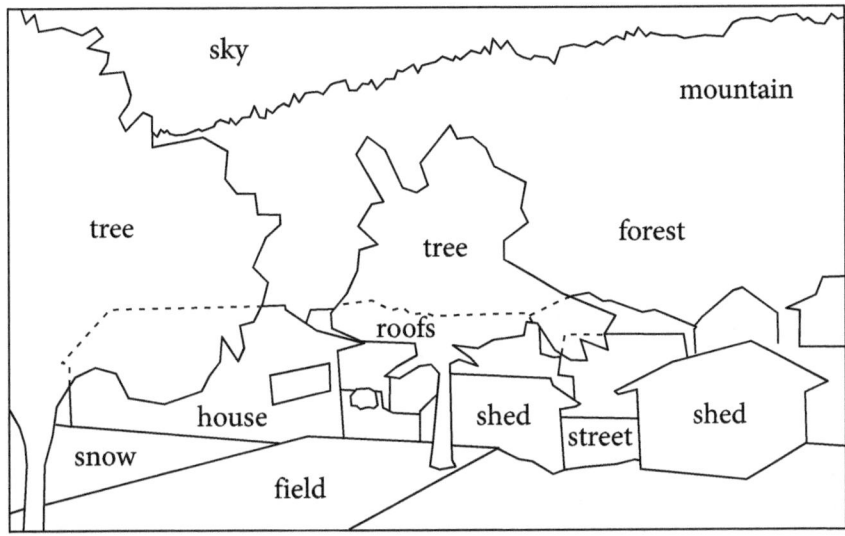

Fig. 7.3. A labeled sketch as phenomenal reality.

one's control, one cannot normally voluntarily switch to seeing a different sketch based on the same photograph, or at least not without considerable effort. Pluralism differs in this respect — according to pluralism we can switch between sketches.

Perspectivism claims, like epistemological idealism, that we can only see the sketch and never the photograph. According to subjective perspectivism, there is no relation between the sketch and the photograph or the photograph does not exist at all. Objective perspectivism, on the other hand, holds that the sketch is based on the photograph but does not completely and accurately represent it.

8

Realism and Reality in Yogācāra and Tiantai

The variety of realism at the foundation of radical Buddhism is not the minimal realism defined in the previous chapter. It does not just claim that there is an external, mind-independent reality, but that, in some sense, that is the *only* reality. "In some sense," because it does not deny the distinction between phenomenal or conventional and external or ultimate reality (i.e., it is not naive realism), but it takes the non-dualist position that these kinds of "realities" are more like different facets of, or perspectives on the same world. Only this world is real, even though this one real world can be and is experienced very differently by different people (and other creatures). And because only this world and only this life are real, there are no Pure lands or heavens, and suffering cannot be compensated in future lives or be a punishment for bad deeds in past lives. Consequently, if we want to escape or alleviate suffering, we have to do so *in this life*, and if we aspire for a Buddha land or other kind of utopian or better society, we have to realize it *in this world*.[1]

On the surface, the goal of the present chapter is to mine the most promising Buddhist traditions, identified in chapter 6 as Yogācāra and Tiantai, for raw materials to construct this metaphysical and epistemological foundation for a radicalized radical Buddhism, as well as to start laying that foundation. Obviously, one cannot mine what is not there in the first place, but that observation raises a question: to what extent does it even makes sense to say that something is or is not there? Jan Westerhoff has pointed out that, from a Buddhist perspective, the answer might be that it does not.[2] Among the reasons he mentions for this negative answer, the following two are the most interesting.

Firstly, the idea of there being "a way it really was" or "a way it really was meant" depends on realism about the past, that is, on the idea that the past exists. But some Buddhist schools, such as Sautrāntika, denied the latter, while others, such as Sarvāstivāda, accepted the existence of the past but held it to be causally inefficient, which implies that there is little we can know about it.[3]

---

1 About this austere or this-worldy realism and why it matters for radicalized radical Buddhism, see also chapters 4 and 6.
2 Jan Westerhoff, *The Golden Age of Indian Buddhist Philosophy* (Oxford: Oxford University Press, 2018), 24ff.
3 The relation of the past to the present in this perspective is somewhat like the relation between noumenal and phenomenal reality in transcendental idealism: by necessity we can only experience the phenomenal and the present, but based on that experience we can make some inferences about the noumenal and the past. See the section "Idealism" in chapter 7.

Secondly, several Yogācāra and later Mādhyamaka texts express the view that experiences of reality differ between observers. In the previous chapter, I gave the example of hungry ghosts (*pretas*) seeing pus or blood where humans see water,[4] but there are other examples as well. Typically, what is taken to determine these different perspectives is karma. For example, Vasubandhu explained in his own commentary on his *Twenty Verses* that "because pretas are in the same situation due to their karma, all and not just one of them see rivers filled with pus."[5]

Regardless of whether different perspectives are due to karma or other factors, we cannot step outside of them and observe the world, or history, or some text from nowhere — all experience and all interpretation is perspectival. That is the most fundamental insight of perspectivism. Hans-Georg Gadamer famously applied this insight to hermeneutics. He pointed out that "wanting to avoid one's own concepts in the explanation [of a historical text, etc.] is not just impossible, but manifest nonsense. Rather, explanation is bringing one's own preconceptions (*Vorbegriffe*) into the game, and thereby really bring the meaning of the text to speak for us."[6] Gadamer called this a "fusion of horizons."[7] To a large extent, fusing horizons is what this chapter aims for.

For Vasubandhu, disagreement between perspectives, such as that between humans who see water where pretas see pus, appears to be an argument for the irreality of the object. If this interpretation is right, there are only perspectives, and nothing that those perspectives are perspectives on. There are no rivers seen differently by humans and pretas; there are just these different perceptions. Similarly then, the lack of agreement about the interpretation of Vasubandhu's writings and Yogācāra or any other Buddhist school in general, indicates that there are just interpretations and nothing those interpretations are interpretations of. Or in other words, there is no "real" or "objective" meaning of the text, no intention of the author, and perhaps even no author or no text. And therefore, there are no "right" interpretations, which obviously means that this interpretation cannot be right either.

The main alternative is to read Vasubandhu's argument epistemologically, that is, as claiming that the thing-in-itself is unknowable rather than non-existent, but that's not an unproblematic reading either. The very first line of the *Twenty Verses* holds that "all is just consciousness only because of the appearance of *non-existing objects*,"[8] which seems to support an ontological rather than epistemological reading. Other translations are possible, and there are other texts that need to be taken into account as well.

Mining for raw materials is a rather questionable analogy if it is uncertain whether those "raw materials" can be identified or even exist at all. Furthermore, aside from the more fundamental problems raised in the preceding paragraphs, there are other obstacles. The primary sources tend to be rather obscure and can be interpreted in

---

4 See the section "Relativism, Pluralism, and Perspectivism."
5 tulyakarmavipākāvasthā hi pretāḥ sarve 'pi pūyapūrṇāṃ nadīṃ paśyanti naika eva — Vasubandhu, *Viṃśatikāvṛtti* (5th c.), ad Vk §3c.
6 Die eigenen Begriffe bei der Auslegung vermeiden zu wollen, ist nicht nur unmöglich, sondern offenbarer Widersinn. Auslegen heißt gerade: die eigenen Vorbegriffe mit ins Spiel bringen, damit die Meinung des Textes für uns wirklich zum Sprechen gebracht wird. — Hans-Georg Gadamer, *Wahrheit und Methode: Grundzüge einer philosophischen Hermeutik*, 2nd edn. (Tübingen: J.C.B. Mohr, 1965), 374–75.
7 Ibid., 289.
8 vijñaptimātram evedam asadarthāvabhāsanāt — Vasubandhu, *Viṃśatikākārikā* (5th c.), §1. Emphasis added.

many different ways, and the secondary sources disagree about almost everything. But perhaps, all of these "obstacles" are mere nuisances rather than insurmountable barriers. My aim in this chapter is not to reconstruct Vasubandhu's, or Dignāga's, or Zhiyi's 智顗 philosophy, but to build on interpretations thereof. For that purpose, I do not really need "correct" interpretations, if those even exist, but *plausible* interpretations.[9] The aim of this chapter is not only interpretation, moreover, but to bring Yogācāra and Tiantai closer together, with a little help from Donald Davidson, in order to lay the foundations of a this-worldly realism for radical Buddhism, a project that will continue in the next chapter.

A Bit of Historical Context

Yogācāra was founded by Asaṅga and his younger half-brother Vasubandhu in late-fourth to early-fifth century, but key ideas of the school almost certainly circulated earlier. Among the most important sūtras for the school are the *Ārya-saṃdhinirmocana Sūtra* and the *Laṅkāvatāra Sūtra*, both of which were compiled from much older fragments in the late-third or early-fourth century. The central Yogācāra doctrine that all is just consciousness or mind only is already found in the *Laṅkāvatāra Sūtra,* and other important ideas such as "storehouse consciousness" and the "three natures" are mentioned in the *Ārya-saṃdhinirmocana Sūtra,* for example.

While Yogācāra is classified as a Mahāyāna school, it was closely affiliated with the "mainstream" Abhidharma Sautrāntika school.[10] Vasubandhu was originally a mainstream Buddhist. His most important Abhidharma text, the *Abhidharmakośabhāṣya,* mostly defended Sautrāntika doctrines. After his older brother Asaṅga converted him to Mahāyāna, he wrote several of the most important Yogācāra treatises. To what extent it is appropriate to speak of "conversion" is debatable, however, as Mahāyāna and the mainstream probably had not really separated at the time.

After Asaṅga and Vasubandhu, the most important Yogācāra philosophers are Dignāga (ca. 480–540) and Dharmakīrti (sixth or seventh century). Dignāga is credited for founding the "logico-epistemological" tradition within Buddhist philosophy, and Dharmakīrti was probably the greatest philosopher in that tradition. The two obviously never met, but allegedly, there may have been a link through Dharmapāla (530–61) who was, supposedly, a student of Dignāga and who was, according to Tibetan sources, in contact with Dharmakīrti later. However, Dignāga died when Dharmapāla was still a child or young teenager, and Dharmapāla probably died before Dharmakīrti was even born. Significantly, both Dignāga's and Dharmakīrti's logico-epistemological writings appear to take a Sautrāntika point of view mostly, confirming the continuing connection between the two schools.

The Chinese monk Xuanzang 玄奘 (ca. 602–64) traveled extensively through India from approximately 630 until his return in China in 645. Among others, he visited

---

9   The case of Zhiyi's interpretation of Nāgārjuna (see next section) also illustrates that accuracy in interpretation is not always necessary. Sometimes interesting or useful interpretations are preferable to accurate ones.
10 The term "mainstream" here denotes what Mahāyāna disparagingly called "Hīnayāna." At the time, the mainstream really was the mainstream, but it was overtaken by Mahāyāna later. The only surviving mainstream school is Theravāda. On the relation between Yogācāra and Sautrāntika, see Robert Kritzer, *Rebirth and Causation in the Yogācāra Abhidharma* (Vienna: Arbeitskreis für Tibetische und Buddhistische Studien, 1999), and Johannes Bronkhorst, *Buddhist Teaching in India* (Boston: Wisdom Publications, 2009).

Nālandā, the great Buddhist university where Dignāga, Dharmapāla, Dharmakīrti, and many other famous Buddhist scholars taught and studied. Of all the Buddhist schools he encountered, Xuanzang was most interested in Yogācāra. His *Discourse on the Perfection of Consciousness Only* 成唯識論 is a commentary on Vasubandhu's *Thirty Verses* (*Triṃśikāvijñaptimātratā*) based mostly on Dharmapāla's commentary on the same text. Xuanzang's *Discourse* would become one of the most influential texts in Chinese Yogācāra or *Weishi* 唯識 (consciousness/mind only).

Buddhism came to China in the first century but was confused with and influenced by Daoism for a long time. Initially, Buddhist texts where translated in largely Daoist Chinese terms, but this changed after Kumārajīva (344–413), a Buddhist monk from Kucha in present-day Xinjiang, produced a great number of translations of sūtras and commentaries that set a new standard, and that were rarely eclipsed by later translations, even if those might have been more accurate.

Foreign monks continued to bring new texts and schools, but the schools that flourished in China are quite different from those that are prominent in histories of Indian Buddhism. Pure Land teachings entered China in the second century leading to the establishment of the Pure Land school in 402 by Huiyuan 慧遠 (334–416). A meditation school, influenced by the aforementioned *Laṅkāvatāra Sūtra* became Chan 禪 (Japanese: Zen) in the fifth century. Earlier, Mādhyamaka had established itself as Sanlun 三論, but like many other sects and schools, it would not survive as an independent sect.

While these and other schools were more or less transplanted from India, Zhiyi 智顗 (538–97) founded an entirely new school of Buddhism: Tiantai 天台, named after the mountain where Zhiyi lived. A problem for Chinese Buddhism was to make sense of the contradictions between the various texts imported from India. The typical solution to that problem was to rank teachings into provisional and final teachings, with many different grades of provisional teachings and usually a single sūtra at the top. For Tiantai, that single sūtra was the *Lotus Sūtra* (*Saddharma Puṇḍarīka Sūtra*), and for the Huayan 華嚴 school, which was founded around the same time, it was the *Flower Garland Sūtra* (*Avataṃsaka Sūtra*).

Aside from the *Lotus Sūtra*, the most important influence on Zhiyi was his misinterpretation of Nāgārjuna's famous doctrine of the emptiness of emptiness in *Mūlamadhyamakakārikā* 24.18 based on Kumārajīva's Chinese translation.[11] The original Sanskrit is:

yaḥ pratītyasamutpādaḥ śūnyatāṃ tāṃ pracakṣmahe
sā prajñaptirupādāya pratipatsaiva madhyamā.

which was translated by Mark Siderits and Shōryū Katsura as:

Dependent origination we declare to be emptiness.
It (emptiness) is a dependent concept; just that is the middle path.[12]

---

11 Paul Swanson, "Zhiyi's Interpretation of Jñeyāvaraṇa: An Application of the Threefold Truth Concept," in *In Search of Clarity: Essays on Translation and Tiantai Buddhism* (Nagoya: Chisokudō, 2018), 45–62.

12 Mark Siderits and Shōryū Katsura, *Nāgārjuna's Middle Way: Mūlamadhyamakakārikā* (Boston: Wisdom, 2012), 277.

and from the Tibetan by Jay Garfield as:

> Whatever is dependently co-arisen | That is explained to be emptiness.
> That, being a dependent designation, | Is itself the middle way.[13]

Kumārajīva's translation is:

> 眾因緣生法 我說即是無
> 亦為是假名 亦是中道義[14]

which can be translated into English as:

> The arising from causes and conditions of all dharmas [is what] I explain as emptiness.
> It is a (conventional) designation. It is the meaning of the Middle Way.

What Nāgārjuna claimed is that the dependently arisen, or phenomenal reality, is empty and that this doctrine is "the Middle Way." However, Zhiyi read Kumārajīva's translation as implying that reality has three different aspects: emptiness 空 (無 in Kumārajīva's translation, but more commonly 空), the conventional 假, and the middle 中. While for Nāgārjuna "the Middle Way" is not a third element but just a name for the doctrine of the identity of emptiness and the phenomenal, for Zhiji "the middle" refers to a third truth — in addition to conventional truth and ultimate truth (i.e., the truth of emptiness) — that expresses that identity. In other words, the third truth (i.e., the middle 中) is the non-dualistic affirmation that conventional or phenomenal reality is ultimate reality, and therefore, that there is just one world.

Due to the rise of Huayan and Yogācāra, especially after Xuanzang's *Discourse*, Tiantai soon experienced a decline but was revived briefly in the eight century by Zhanran 湛然 (711–82). In 806 its Japanese branch, Tendai, was established by Saichō 最澄 (767–822). Tendai, however, incorporated elements of Huayan/Kegon, Chan/Zen, and esoteric Buddhism and differed from Zhiyi's Tiantai in many, but mostly subtle, ways. At first, its main opponent in doctrinal matters was the Hossō 法相 (Chinese: Faxiang) sect, the Japanese branch of Chinese Yogācāra (which was known as *Faxiang* in addition to *Weishi*) but eventually it got involved so deeply into politics that the sect became its own enemy, and new sects branched off in the twelfth and thirteenth century. Those new branches flourished, while Tendai gradually declined.

Most of the sects that split off from Tendai were not really new. Rather, they were — nominally at least — Japanese branches of Chinese sects that had little to do with Chinese Tiantai, even though all of these branches where founded by Tendai priests in Japan and where heavily influenced by Tendai thought. Sōto 曹洞 Zen came from Caodong; Rinzai 臨濟 Zen from Linji; and the Pure Land 浄土 sects from Chinese Pure Land Buddhism. The one exception was the Nichiren 日蓮 school, named after its founder, Nichiren (1222–82). With some justification, Nichiren though of himself as following in Saichō's footsteps. He opposed the strong influence of esoteric Buddhism and other "corrupting" influences in Tendai and

---

13 Jay L. Garfield, *The Fundamental Wisdom of the Middle Way: Nāgārjuna's Mūlamadhyamakakārikā* (Oxford: Oxford University Press, 1995), 69.
14 T30n1564, 30b.

wanted to return to the *Lotus Sūtra*. He may have gone a bit overboard in his reduction of Buddhist practice to ritually chanting of that sūtra's title, but it does not seem unreasonable to say that Nichiren was much closer in spirit to original Tendai (and perhaps to Tiantai) than the Tendai sect itself.[15]

Although we now can fill whole libraries with books about Buddhist philosophy and celebrate the tradition's great thinkers, philosophy never played a central role in the religious lives of the vast majority of monks and other followers. Most Buddhists were more concerned with relatively practical or soteriological matters than with the abstruse questions that philosophers like to ponder. In Japan this relatively practical and soteriological orientation seems to have been particularly strong. The metaphysical or epistemological views of key thinkers such as Saichō, Nichiren, and Dōgen 道元 (1200–53; founder of Sōtō Zen) can often only be gleaned from scattered remarks in polemical texts expounding the benefits of one sect versus others or in texts about entirely different topics, such as meditation. This, unfortunately, makes interpreting the metaphysical views of Japanese Buddhists even harder than those of their Indian and Chinese intellectual ancestors.

Yogācāra Realism

Does Yogācāra deny external or mind-independent reality? Although the most common answer to this question appears to be "yes," it is actually not that easy to answer, and it is also possible that there is not a single answer or that the answer differs for different Yogācāra philosophers.[16]

Above I quoted Vasubandhu's claim that "all is just consciousness only because of the appearance of non-existing objects," which opens the *Twenty Verses*, one of his most influential texts. This quote seems as clear a denial of the existence of an external reality as one could find. In the *Mahāyānasaṃgraha*, Asaṅga also appears to claim literally that external objects do not exist. Furthermore, that text also gives the example of pretas seeing the world differently as an argument in support of this claim.[17]

So, that settles it, it seems — Yogācāra denies external reality. But that conclusion would be premature.

Yogācāra philosophers distinguished three aspects of the experience of reality, the "three natures" (*svabhāvas*). (1) *Parikalpita-svabhāva*, the "fully conceptualized" or (conceptually) constructed nature: the experience of things as conceptual constructs, or the appearance; (2) *Paratantra-svabhāva*, the "other-dependent" nature: the complex of causes that bring about the thing's constructed nature, or the process and causes of bringing forth that appearance; (3) *Pariniṣpanna-svabhāva*, the "perfected" nature: the true nature of things, namely, emptiness, which can only be experienced in meditation that entirely transcends language.

In the *Trisvabhāvanirdeśa*, Vasubandhu wrote that the constructed nature, that is, the thing as is appears does not exist, that the other-dependent exists but not

---

15 See also the section "From Saichō to Nichiren" in chapter 2, and the section "Sources and Schools" in chapter 6.
16 It is significant that Inoue Enryō, the father of Japanese Buddhist modernism, answered "no" to this question. His interpretation of Yogācāra was realist and strongly influenced the this-worldly realism that motivated early Japanese engaged and radical Buddhism. See the section "Realism and Reform in Japan — Inoue Enryō" in chapter 3.
17 Asaṅga, *Mahāyānasaṃgraha* (4–5th c.), II.14. But what is "seen differently" if the world doesn't exist?

constructed (*parikalpita*)	elephant	duality (*dvaya*)
other-dependent (*paratantra*)	elephant's appearance	discrimination (*vikalpa*)
perfected (*pariniṣpanna*)	elephant's absence / piece of wood	suchness (*tathatā*)

Table. 8.1. The magical elephant.

in the form that it appears, and that the perfected exists as non-duality.[18] He then proceeded by comparing perception to a magic show in which the magician makes a piece of wood (*kāṣṭha*) look like an elephant: "The constructed nature is the elephant; the other-dependent is its appearance; and the absence of the elephant is considered to be the perfected."[19] But then he added three more concepts: duality (*dvaya*), discrimination (*vikalpa*), and suchness (*tathatā*), and compared those with the elephant, its appearance, and the piece of wood, respectively.[20] Table 8.1 summarizes these associations and identities.

The concept of "suchness" (*tathatā*; also translated as "thusness") is more or less the Buddhist equivalent of Kant's "thing-in-itself,"[21] although it differs in its connotations — it refers to the ultimately real ground or nature of phenomenal appearances — and consequently, to recognize the existence of suchness is to accept realism. This becomes even more evident in the indirect equation of the perfected with the piece of wood. The perfected as the elephant's absence can easily be understood as metaphysical idealism, but that interpretation no longer makes sense if the elephant's absence is equated to the presence of something else, and the text is quite explicit that there is something else, namely, the piece of wood. That piece of wood is the real form appearing as elephant. Similarly, suchness is not just the absence of appearances or of things as they appear, but also the presence of those appearances' ultimately real ground. Suchness is not nothing, and suchness is not in the mind. Hence, this is realism, not metaphysical idealism.

The text continues by asserting that the penetration of the real objects or true reality (*arthatattva*) results in the knowledge of the constructed appearance, the abandonment of the other-dependent as constructing the appearance, and the attainment of non-conceptual perception of suchness, presumably through meditation. With that attainment, the appearance of duality disappears and non-duality is realized.[22] The result is compared to breaking free from the illusion of the magic show. The elephant is no longer perceived, the process that created that false perception is terminated, and instead, one sees the piece of wood for what it is.[23] The goal of practice, then, is to see reality (i.e., suchness, or the piece of wood) as it is, but that objective makes sense only if reality is assumed to exist. Hence, again, this is realism not idealism.

18 Vasubandhu(?), *Trisvabhāvanirdeśa*, §§11–13.
19 svabhāvaḥ kalpito hastī paratantras tadākṛtiḥ | yas tatra hastyabhāvo 'sau pariniṣpanna iṣyate — Ibid., §28.
20 Ibid., §30.
21 See the section "Idealism" in chapter 7.
22 Vasubandhu(?), *Trisvabhāvanirdeśa*, §§31–33.
23 Ibid., §34.

The arguments in the *Trisvabhāvanirdeśa* raise a question: would it be possible that apparent arguments for idealism are also merely denying the object-as-it-appears and not its ultimately real ground? Re-reading the opening statement of the *Twenty Verses* certainly suggests a positive answer to that question. "All is just consciousness only because of the appearance of non-existing objects," wrote Vasubandhu. Indeed, that what appears, or the object-as-it-appears, does not exist *as such*, but that does *not* imply that nothing exists outside the mind. But then, why is this doctrine called "mind only" or "consciousness only" (*vijñaptimātra* or *cittamātra*), suggesting the opposite, namely, that nothing exists outside the mind? Perhaps, it is a mistake to think that is what the term implies. Dan Lusthaus pointed out that -*mātra* (only) does not appear to have metaphysical implications in other uses, and there is no good reason to assume why this case is different.[24] Furthermore, *vijñaptimātra* cannot mean that nothing exists outside a single mind because Yogācāra recognizes the existence of other minds that exist outside that mind.

There is another problem, however. The *Trisvabhāvanirdeśa* probably was not written by Vasubandhu, or at least not by the Vasubandhu who co-founded Yogācāra and wrote the *Twenty Verses*. Mathew Kapstein argues convincingly that for linguistic, stylistic, and historical reasons, it is very unlikely that *that* Vasubandhu authored the text.[25] More likely, it was an anonymous text that was later attributed to Vasubandhu.[26] Nevertheless, it has terminological similarities to the *Laṅkāvatāra Sūtra* and other important Yogācāra texts such as the *Mahāyāna Sūtrālamkāra Kārikā*, and its content is undeniably Yogācāra as well. Still, if the *Trisvabhāvanirdeśa* is not by Vasubandhu, we are back at square one with regards to his position.

Although I wrote above that the logico-epistemological school was founded by Dignāga, Vasubandhu also wrote a work about reasoning and perception, the main topics of that school, the *Vādavidhi*. That text is lost, but fragments remain in quotes by other authors, including Dignāga. In one remaining fragment, Vasubandhu wrote that "a direct perception is a consciousness through the object [*artha*] itself only."[27] *Artha*, here appears to refer to the external, mind-independent object. Dignāga used the same word in the same sense and argued that "(direct) perception is free from conceptual construction."[28] What is perceived in that direct perception (*pratyakṣa*) is the thing (*artha*) itself.[29] Massaaki Hattori explains that

> According to Dignāga, a thing, which in itself is essentially inexpressible, comes to be expressed by a word only when it is associated with a name (*nāman*) and

---

24   Dan Lusthaus, *Buddhist Phenomenology: A Philosophical Investigation of Yogācāra Buddhism and the Ch'eng Wei-shih Lun* (London: RoutledgeCurzon, 2002), 534.
25   Matthew Kapstein, "Who Wrote the *Trisvabhāvanirdeśa*? Reflections on an Enigmatic Text and Its Place in the History of Buddhist Philosophy," *Journal of Indian Philosophy* 46 (2018): 1–30.
26   It is for this reason that I placed a question mark after "Vasubandhu" when mentioning the author of the *Trisvabhāvanirdeśa* in footnotes above.
27   Vasubandhu, *Vādavidhi* (5th c.), §9, trans. Stefan Anacker, *Seven Works of Vasubandhu: The Buddhist Psychological Doctor*, rev. edn. (Delhi: Motilal Banarsidass, 2005), 40. Anacker indicates that "object" here translates *artha* (76).
28   pratyakṣaṃ kalpanāpoḍham — Dignāga, *Pramāṇasamuccaya* (6th c.).
29   On Dignāga's recognition of the existence of an external reality, see also Shōryū Katsura, "Dignāga and Dharmakīrti on Apoha," in *Studies in the Buddhist Epistemological Tradition*, ed. Ernst Steinkellner (Vienna: ÖAW, 1991), 129–46, at 138.

other factors. Conceptual construction (*kalpanā*) means nothing other than this process of associating a name, etc. with a thing.[30]

What these passages imply is not that external reality does not exist, but that it cannot be expressed in language — is ineffable, and thus that the object-*as-it-appears* does not exist. The same view is expressed by Asaṅga in his *Bodhisattvabhūmi*: "the essential nature of entities does not exist in the way it is described in words.[31] However, it is also not the case that it is completely and totally nonexistent."[32] Rather, "all entities possess an essential nature that is ineffable."[33] He explicitly rejected the idea that there are no ultimately real underlying substances,[34] which he ascribed to Mādhyamaka, because nominal designations of things or people would be invalid if there are no underlying substances (i.e., suchness).

> As long as the bare [underlying] substance of the entities of form, etc., does exist, then the application of designating assertions to the entities of form, etc., is valid. It would not be [valid] if [the bare underlying substance of form and the rest] did not exist, [because in that case] the application of designating assertions would be [an act] that is not related to a [real substance].[35]

The ineffable, real nature of things cannot be experienced by the ordinary mind but only by an extraordinary kind of non-conceptual knowledge or experience called *pṛṣṭhalabdha-jñāna*. In the *Trisvabhāvanirdeśa*, this transcendence of conceptually conditioned ordinary consciousness of things (i.e., seeing the wood rather than the elephant) is presented as the goal of Buddhist practice.[36] This is mysticism as defined in chapter 7: an apophatic realism that holds that ultimate reality can only be experienced through extraordinary, non-conceptual means.[37] The purpose of achieving this extraordinary knowledge is overcoming attachment or craving. We become attached to things-as-they-appear, and supposedly, by seeing them as they really are we can dispel that attachment. Xuanzang warns in his *Discourse on the Perfection of Consciousness Only* that we should not substitute one kind of attachment for another, however,

> [b]ecause the mind and mental conditions arise in dependence on others, they are like magic and not [things that] really exist. To eliminate the false attachment to what is projected by the mind and mental conditions as existing in external, ultimate reality, [we] say that there is only consciousness (*vijñāna*). [But]

---

30 Massaaki Hattori, *Dignāga, On Perception, Being the Pratyakṣapariccheda of Dignāga's Pramāṇasamuccaya from the Sanskrit Fragments and the Tibetan Versions* (Cambridge: Harvard University Press, 1968), 83n127.
31 Similarly, Dharmakīrti argued that due to obscuring cognitions things are commonly said to exist, but they do not really or ultimately exist in the way that they are conceptually constructed by that cognition. Dharmakīrti, *Pramāṇavārttika* (6th/7th c.), §§1.69–70. See also John Dunne, *Foundations of Dharmakīrti's Philosophy* (Boston: Wisdom, 2004), 339.
32 Asaṅga, *The Bodhisattva Path to Unsurpassed Enlightenment: A Complete Translation of the Bodhisattvabhūmi* (4–5th c.), trans. Artemus Engle (Boulder: Snow Lion, 2016), 77.
33 Ibid., 79.
34 On Asaṅga's realism or non-idealism, see also Janice Dean Willis, *On Knowing Reality: The Tattvārtha Chapter of Asaṅga's Bodhisattvabhūmi* (Delhi: Motilal Banarsidass, 1982).
35 Asaṅga, *The Bodhisattva Path to Unsurpassed Enlightenment*, 81.
36 Asaṅga's *Mahāyānasaṃgraha*, especially chapter 8, also explains in detail how and why such non-conceptual knowledge or wisdom should be achieved.
37 See the section "Apophasis, Kataphasis, Skepticism, and Mysticism" in chapter 7.

if one becomes attached to mind-only as ultimate reality, then that is [just like being attached to] the external world of objects — it is [just] an attachment to the Dharma [i.e., an unhelpful dogma].³⁸

According to the second Noble Truth, suffering is caused by attachment or craving.³⁹ For that reason, Buddhist practice aims at overcoming attachment, and as Xuanzang points out, an attachment to a view, even if it is a right view, is still an attachment, and therefore unhelpful or even harmful. Based on this passage among others, Dan Lusthaus argues that for Yogācāra, ontology or metaphysics is itself the problem because it feeds the craving for some kind of (knowledge of) external reality. Yogācāra makes "no ontological claims," he argues, "except to question the validity of making ontological claims"⁴⁰ because "questions about the ultimate reality of non-cognitive things are simply irrelevant and useless for solving the problem of karma."⁴¹ While this reminds of the metaphysical quietism mentioned in chapter 5, and thus has ancient roots in the Buddhist tradition,⁴² Lusthaus's claim that Yogācāra rejects metaphysics and simultaneously adopts the realist view that there is an external reality is a contradiction as the latter is a metaphysical view. A more plausible, or more charitable at least, interpretation is that Yogācāra philosophers held the apophatic position that nothing more can be said about external or ultimate reality than that it exists, and thus that trying to do so anyway is unhelpful.

Apophasis becomes a problem when there is a need to talk or write about things or stuff in external or ultimate reality — for example, when theorizing about perception, one of the most important topics in the logico-epistemological tradition. Dignāga and Dharmakīrti solved this problem by provisionally adopting a language and ontology borrowed from mainstream Buddhism. They ultimately rejected that ontology, but that rejection should not be taken to imply a rejection of ultimate reality itself; it is merely an apophatic rejection of the possibility of describing ultimate reality. If the goal of practice is overcoming attachment by seeing beyond the ordinary, then ultimate reality itself *cannot* be rejected because, without it, that goal would make no sense. The key point of Yogācāra, then, is not that the external world does not exist, but that we should not mistake our conceptual projections of the world for the world itself. This idea was echoed centuries later in Europe when Nietzsche wrote that

> in language, man posited an own world next to the other [world], a place that man held to be so solid to, from it, lift the other world from its hinges and make himself its lord. In so far as man throughout long periods of time believed in the concepts and names of things as *eternal truths*, did he develop the pride with which he lifted himself above the animals: he really thought to have knowledge of the world in language.⁴³

---

38 諸心心所依他起故。亦如幻事。非真實有。為遣妄執心心所外實有境故。說唯有識。若執唯識真實有者。如執外境亦是法執。— Xuanzang 玄奘,《成唯識論》(7th c.), T31n1585, 6c.
39 See the section "Early Buddhism" in chapter 2 as well as the first three sections of chapter 5.
40 Lusthaus, *Buddhist Phenomenology*, 535.
41 Ibid., 536.
42 See the section "Metaphysics, Rationality, and Free Inquiry" in chapter 5.
43 Die Bedeutung der Sprache für die Entwicklung der Cultur liegt darin, daß in ihr der Mensch eine eigne Welt neben die andere stellte, einen Ort, welchen er für so fest hielt, um von ihm aus die übrige Welt aus den Angeln zu heben und sich zum Herren derselben zu machen. Insofern der

Significantly, metaphysical idealism makes the opposite move: by eliminating the external world, it leaves *nothing but* our projections. Furthermore, the goal of an unmediated, non-conceptual experience of reality implies that Yogācāra does not involve a kind of epistemological idealism either, because that is defined as holding that all of our experience of reality is *necessarily* mediated by the mind.[44]

So, does this, then, settle it? Can it now be concluded that Yogācāra was realist and not idealist?

Perhaps. Perhaps, not. There is still plenty of room for further arguments for and against either position. Lambert Schmithausen has pointed out, for example, that Xuanzang argued against the Abhidharma view of external matter and speculates that the same argument applies to the positing of anything outside the mind.[45] But I want to emphasize once more that my goal here is not to determine the one and only correct and final interpretation of Yogācāra, if that is even possible. My aim is much more modest; it is to show that a realist interpretation of Yogācāra is *plausible*, and I think that the foregoing is sufficient to establish that.

Tiantai/Tendai Non-dualism

In case of Tiantai/Tendai, metaphysical questions are almost inseparable from soteriological questions,[46] and both have their doctrinal roots in the *Lotus Sūtra*. As explained in chapter 2 of this book, the two most important passages can be found in chapters 2 and 16 of that sūtra. Its second chapter suggests that we are all destined to become Buddhas, and that, therefore, we are in a sense bodhisattvas already, which in Tiantai/Tendai and much of the rest of East-Asian Buddhism is interpreted as implying that we all have the Buddha-nature.[47] In chapter 16, the Buddha says that this world is the Buddha's Buddha land, which implies that this world cannot just be a phenomenal deception or magic show. Rather, this world is ultimately real.[48] These two doctrines, Buddha-nature and non-dualism, would become increasingly intertwined. "The world of Buddha-nature" is ultimate reality, and non-dualism implies that everything has Buddha-nature. So, Zhanran, for example, wrote:

> A perfected person knows the ins and outs of the principle of non-dualism, and that there are no things outside the mind corresponding to our mental projections. [What does it matter] who is sentient or insentient? In the meeting of the

---

Mensch an die Begrifffe und Namen der Dinge als an aternae veritates durch lange Zeitstrecken hindurch geglaubt hat, hat er sich jenen Stolz angeeignet, mit dem er sich über das Thier erhob: er meinte wirklich in der Sprache die Erkenntnis der Welt zu haben. — Friedrich Nietzsche, *Menschliches Allzumenschliches* (1878), *Digital Critical Edition (eKGWB)*, http://www.nietzschesource.org/#eKGWB/MA-I, §I.11.

44 See the section "Idealism" in chapter 7.
45 Lambert Schmithausen, *On the Problem of the External World in the "Ch'eng wei shih lun"* (Tokyo: International Institute for Buddhist Studies, 2015), 24.
46 According to Hans-Rudolf Kantor, "Dynamics of Practice and Understanding — Chinese Tiantai Philosophy of Contemplation and Deconstruction," in *Dao Companion to Chinese Buddhist Philosophy*, eds. Youru Wang and Sandra Wawrytko (Dordrecht: Springer, 2018), 218–92, this is an inherent part of the Tiantai conception of "contemplation" 觀, which is the most central notion in Tiantai practice.
47 See the section "Mahāyāna" in chapter 2.
48 See the section "From Nāgārjuna to Zhiyi" in chapter 2.

Lotus Sūtra nothing is discriminated. What difference is there between the plants and trees, the earth, and the four elements?⁴⁹

Everything was (or all kinds of things were) in attendance when the *Lotus Sūtra* was preached. Therefore, everything is part of the Buddha's Buddha land, everything has Buddha-nature, and everything is ultimately real. In medieval Japan, the Tiantai/Tendai notion of universal Buddha-nature fused with the doctrine of "original enlightenment" 本覺, the idea that everyone is in some sense already awakened or enlightened, which developed in Chinese Buddhism and was especially influential in Huayan.⁵⁰ Because of this fusion, there is very little explicit metaphysics — the focus is always on soteriological issues of Buddhahood and awakening.

While the increasing entanglement of metaphysics and soteriology tends to obscure both in later Tiantai/Tendai thought, there are plenty of unambiguous metaphysical claims in Zhiyi's thought. For example, in *The Great Calming and Contemplation* 摩訶止觀, a series of lectures written down by his disciple Guanding 灌頂, Zhiyi proclaims:

> Dharma nature (i.e., ultimate reality) and all the phenomena are non-dual and non-distinct. [...] To seek the ultimate nature of things beyond the ordinary phenomena is like leaving this emptiness to seek for emptiness elsewhere. The ordinary phenomena are the same as the ultimate nature of things. There is no need to abandon the ordinary and turn toward the sacred/noble.⁵¹

Or as JeeLoo Liu puts it: "there is no need to find a reality beyond this reality — there is no other reality."⁵² For Zhiyi, "the (ultimately) real is identical with the conventional, and the conventional is identical with the (ultimately) real."⁵³ This is the essence of Zhiyi's non-dualist identification of the ultimate and the phenomenal, and that identification is what he called the "middle."⁵⁴

In case of Saichō, the founder of Tendai, is is not that easy to extract a clear and unambiguous metaphysical position, partially because of the aforementioned entanglement with soteriology, and partially because Saichō was concerned more with sectarian politics than with philosophical doctrine. For example, one of the most explicit metaphysical remarks in his *Essay on Protecting the Realm* 守護國界章 can be found in a comparison of the benefits of Tendai and other sects, particularly Yogācāra/Hossō, with regard to the topic of the essay's title. Saichō argues that

---

49 圓人始末知理不二。心外無境誰情無情。法華會中一切不隔。草木與地四微何殊。— Zhanran 湛然,《金剛錍》(8th c.), T46n1932, 785b.
50 Jacqueline Stone, *Original Enlightenment and the Transformation of Medieval Japanese Buddhism* (Honolulu: University of Hawai'i Press, 1999).
51 法性與一切法無二無別。...離凡法更求實相。如避此空彼處求空。即凡法是實法。不須捨凡向聖。— Zhiyi 智顗,《摩訶止觀》(594), T46n1911, 6a-b.
52 JeeLoo Liu, *An Introduction to Chinese Philosophy: From Ancient Philosophy to Chinese Buddhism* (Malden: Blackwell, 2006), 287.
53 真即是俗；俗即是真。— Zhiyi,《妙法蓮華經玄義》(6th c.), T33n1716, 703b. See the section "From Nāgārjuna to Zhiyi" in chapter 2 for a longer quote including this sentence.
54 Haiyan Shen summarizes Zhiyi's theoretical philosophy as "everything can be understood as an expression or revelation of the ultimate truth, and the ultimate truth is the essential substance or basic principle behind all things." Haiyan Shen, "Tiantai Integrations of Doctrine and Practice," in *The Wiley Blackwell Companion to East and Inner Asian Buddhism*, ed. Mario Poceski (Malden: Wiley Blackwell, 2014), 127–44, at 131.

Yogācāra/Hossō teaches that "because that what the conditionally generated creates is other-dependent, there is only deception and no actuality." On the other hand, Tendai teaches that "because that what the dependently arisen creates [i.e., phenomenal reality] is in accordance with the [ultimately] real, there is only actuality and no deception."⁵⁵

In his private notes on the Tiantai/Tendai practice of "threefold contemplation" 三觀, he also wrote about the relation between the phenomenal and the real. The context here is meditation, or "contemplation," and not metaphysics, but despite that, the following passage clearly expresses Saichō's adoption of Zhiyi's non-dualist three truths doctrine:

> At first, the practitioner of calming and contemplation may calmly dwell in the basic understanding [that a]ll the *dharmas*, like particles of dust, are simultaneously empty, conventionally real, and the middle. When the profound truth of the threefold contemplation is clearly understood, completely separate from emotional thought, then [one understands that] there is nothing to be practiced and nothing to be realized. [...] The internal [phenomena] and the external [things] are equally obscure; the conditioned [things] and [internal] contemplation are all quiet. All thought arises due to mental projection which must not be clung onto. [He who] continues to dwell in the threefold contemplation without a second thought is a true practitioner of calming and contemplation.⁵⁶

This realist and non-dualist orientation was further strengthened in later Tendai under the aforementioned influences, but it was rarely expressed in unambiguous terms. Probably, the clearest affirmation of phenomenal reality can be found in the writings of Dōgen, the founder of Sōtō Zen, who was originally a Tendai priest. As mentioned in chapter 2, Dōgen considered dualism "foolishness."⁵⁷ Awakening is not learning to see some other world but learning to see clearly that there is just one world. And a thought or perception before awakening "is not a wrong thought; it is just a thought at the time before clarification/enlightenment; and at the time of clarification it is not discarded."⁵⁸

Hee-Jin Kim once called Dōgen a "mystical realist,"⁵⁹ but while Dōgen certainly was a realist, at least in the sense that he recognized a mind-independent reality, it is quite debatable whether he adhered to a form of mysticism as defined here.⁶⁰ In his second book about Dōgen, Kim points out that according to the prevalent conception of Zen, which is largely due to the influence of D.T. Suzuki, "the essence of Zen consists in the unmediated enlightened experience (or state of consciousness), totally untainted by ideational and valuational mediations as well as by historical and so-

---

55 依他緣生所造作故。唯假不實。...眞如緣起所造作故。唯實不假。— Saichō 最澄,『守護國界章』(818), T74n2362, 206c.
56 謂止觀行者。先可安住本解。法法塵塵即空假即中。全離念慮。三觀妙理分明之時。無所行無所證。...內外並冥。緣觀俱寂。諸心歷境起更勿執。二念不續住三觀。是眞止觀行者。— Saichō,『修禪寺相傳私注』(9th c.), in『傳教大師全集』, Vol. 3 (Tokyo: 天台宗宗典刊行会, 1912), 661–81, at 663.
57 See the section "From Saichō to Nichiren" in chapter 2.
58 ソレ邪思量ナルニアラス。タタアキラメサルトキノ思量ナリ。アキラメントキ。コノ思量ヲシテ失セシムルニアラス。— Dōgen 道元,「法性」,『正法眼藏』(1231–53), T82n2582, 202b.
59 Hee-Jin Kim, *Eihei Dōgen: Mystical Realist* (1975; rpt. Boston: Wisdom, 2004).
60 See the section "Apophasis, Kataphasis, Skepticism, and Mysticism" in chapter 7.

cial conditions."⁶¹ But "such a Zen," in Kim's view, and mine as well, "is not Dōgen's." For Dōgen, awakening is not associated with a mystical view from nowhere. Rather, as Bret Davis points out, "it involves an ongoing nondual engagement in a process of letting the innumerable perspectival aspects of reality illuminate themselves. Enlightenment thus entails an egoless and nondual perspectivism."⁶²

Relativism and Perspectivism in Yogācāra and Tiantai

Dōgen is not the only philosopher in the broader Tiantai/Tendai tradition whose thought has been described as perspectival or perspectivist. In the contrary, JeeLoo Liu and Brook Ziporyn, two philosophers with very different backgrounds and orientations, have argued that something like perspectivism is a basic feature of Tiantai thought in general.⁶³ Furthermore, closely related relativisms have been advanced in Yogācāra texts as well.

The most obvious variety of relativism in Yogācāra is the aforementioned example of pretas seeing rivers of pus or blood where humans see flowing water. As far as I know, the earliest mentions of this idea are by Asaṅga and Vasubandhu.⁶⁴ It was mentioned a few centuries later by the Mādhyamaka commentator Candrakīrti, who extensively commented on Yogācāra thought,⁶⁵ but it was not discussed much, or at least not in surviving texts, until several centuries later in Tibetan Buddhism. The key idea here is that karma determines rebirth as a preta (hungry ghost), human, god, and so forth, and thus that karma indirectly determines one's perspective. That is, humans and pretas have different perspectives on water *because* of their different karmas.

The second relativism in Yogācāra is a kind of monistic conceptual constructionism. Phenomenal reality (i.e., the world as is appears to us) is the product of conceptual construction (*kalpanā*). Raw, uninterpreted perception (*pratyakṣa*) is reorganized and interpreted through our conceptual categories, and because of this, we see cows as cows, tables *as* tables, and weddings as weddings. (More about this in the next sections.) This constructionism is monistic, however, as the Yogācāra thinkers do not seem to consider the possibility of different conceptual schemes resulting in different phenomenal realities. Rather, our shared karma as humans guarantees that we all share the same phenomenal reality.⁶⁶

It is possible that these two Yogācāra relativisms are really the same. If pretas see pus or blood where humans see water due to different conceptual schemes and

---

61   Hee-Jin Kim, *Dōgen on Meditation and Thinking: A Reflection on His View of Zen* (Albany: SUNY Press, 2007), 35.
62   Bret Davis, "The Philosophy of Zen Master Dōgen: Egoless Perspectivism," in *The Oxford Handbook of World Philosophy*, eds. Jay L. Garfield and William Edelglass (Oxford: Oxford University Press, 2011), 348–60, at 349–50.
63   Liu, *An Introduction to Chinese Philosophy*, and Brook Ziporyn, *Emptiness and Omnipresence: An Essential Introduction to Tiantai Buddhism* (Bloomington: Indiana University Press, 2016). On Dōgen's perspectivism, see Kim, *Dōgen on Meditation and Thinking*; Davis, "The Philosophy of Zen Master Dōgen"; and Lajos Brons, "Meaning and Reality: A Cross-Traditional Encounter," in *Constructive Engagement of Analytic and Continental Approaches in Philosophy*, eds. Bo Mou and R. Tieszen (Leiden: Brill, 2013), 199–220.
64   Asaṅga, *Mahāyānasaṃgraha* (4–5th c.), II.14, and Vasubandhu, *Viṃśatikākārikā* (5th c.), 3b–c.
65   Candrakīrti, *Madhyamakāvatāra* (7th c.), VI.71.
66   Roy Tzohar, "Imagine Being a 'Preta': Early Indian Yogācāra Approaches to Intersubjectivity," *Sophia* 56 (2017): 337–54, at 347–48.

conceptual construction, then the two are the same indeed, but the source texts are insufficiently clear about this. In the first relativism, different views depend on different kinds of being; in the second, the human view depends on conceptual construction. But these two relativisms are never linked to each other.[67]

As mentioned, the first and possibly second relativism became a topic of debate in Tibetan Buddhism. In addition to the example of the river, a second simile of uncertain origin occurred in those debates. José Cabezón summarizes it as follows:

> Imagine a cup full of what human beings call "water." When "hungry spirits" (pretas) see this, they do not see water, but rather pus and blood; when hell beings see it, they may see molten metal. Gods see nectar, and so forth. The beings in each realm see what it is their karmic predisposition to see.[68]

In reference to this simile, Gorampa, a fifteenth-century, Tibetan Buddhist philosopher, wrote that

> [Tsong kha pa claims][69] that when the six eye consciousnesses of the six classes of beings look at [the object found] at the site occupied by a full cup of water, all six eye consciousnesses are equally nonerroneous [...,] and that hence their six objects must be accepted as equally existent [therein].[70]

Gorampa rejected this idea because

> [i]t would [...] follow that a human [being] drinks all six substances — ambrosia, pus and blood, and so forth — when it is only the human drinking a cup full of water, so long as that cup of water is being watched by the six eye consciousnesses of the six classes of beings, for all six substances would exist in the space of that cup of water [at that time]. Therefore, who but those who have an inflated sense of their own powers would dare maintain that six separate, real, and tangible substances exist in a single location?[71]

The objection is interesting because it depends on the assumption of identity between being something and being non-erroneously perceivable as something. however, this identity is not self-evident. Consider Heraclitus's famous example of seawater being "both pure and defiled: pleasant or drinkable and safe to fish, [but] undrinkable and deadly to humans."[72] In the same way that seawater is pleasant-to-fish and deadly-to-humans,[73] whatever fills the cup might be water-to-humans and pus-to-pretas, but that does not imply that seawater is simultaneously pleasant and deadly *simpliciter* or

---

67 The first relativism is mentioned in passing by Asaṅga and Vasubandhu; the second is developed by Dignāga and Dharmakīrti. Hence, they do not occur in the writings of the same thinkers.
68 José Cabezón and Geshe Lobsang Dargyay, *Freedom from Extremes: Gorampa's "Distinguishing the Views" and the Polemics of Emptiness* (Boston: Wisdom, 2006), 314n223.
69 I have not been able to find this claim in Tsong Khapa's writings, but I must admit that I am not well acquainted with those.
70 Translation from Cabezón and Lobsang Dargyay, *Freedom from Extremes*, 139–41.
71 Ibid., 143.
72 Θάλασσα ὕδωρ καθαρώτατον καὶ μιαρώτατον, ἰχθύσι μὲν πότιμον καὶ σωτήριον, ἀνθρώποις δὲ ἄποτον καὶ ὀλέθριον. — Heraclitus, Fragment DK B61/Byw. 52 (~6–5th c. BCE).
73 This may not be Heraclitus's intended interpretation. See the section "Classical Perspectives — Zhuangzi, Heraclitus, and Epicurus" in chapter 10.

that the cup's contents are simultaneously water and pus *simpliciter*. It might be neither. Instead, what fills the cup might be some unnameable ultimately real substance that has the causal capacity of being non-erroneously perceived as water by humans, as pus or blood by pretas, as nectar or ambrosia by gods, and so forth. This, I think, is closer to the Yogācāra view, at least. It also appears closer to Dōgen's view, as we'll see below. Furthermore, co-location is not inherently problematic, as Gorampa suggests, either. If I shape a chunk of clay into a statue, then that statue and the clay are two "separate, real, and tangible substances [that] exist in a single location."

The most fundamental distinction between varieties of perspectivism is Bo Mou's distinction between subjective and objective perspectivism.[74] The latter assumes that different perspectives on something are somehow grounded in or caused by aspects of the ultimately real nature of that "thing," and thus that perspectives are one-sided, partial, and incomplete, but not untrue. Subjective perspectivism, on the other hand, assumes that "anything goes," that there is no consistent relation between the perspectival perception and the real thing, or even that there is no underlying real thing at all (i.e., that there are just perspectives and nothing those perspectives are perspectives on). JeeLoo Liu interprets Tiantai perspectivism as objective; Brook Ziporyn interprets it as subjective.[75]

Ziporyn locates the origin of Tiantai perspectivism in a passage about the Buddhas' knowledge of reality in the second chapter of the *Lotus Sūtra*, "Skillfull Means." In Kumārajīva's Chinese translation:

唯佛與佛乃能究盡諸法實相[76]

This is translated by Ziporyn as "[o]nly a Buddha together with a Buddha knows the ultimate reality of all things."[77] Key to his perspectivist interpretation is the first part, "only a Buddha together with a Buddha," 唯佛與佛,[78] which in his interpretation

> has an enormous hidden significance, because it hints at one of the main themes of the *Lotus Sūtra*: that real wisdom is no one's possession; that no single viewpoint — not even that of a Buddha, a single Buddha — can ever encompass the ultimate reality of all things; that there is always "more to know" than any one perspective of knowing, however vast and exalted, can encompass.[79]

---

74   Bo Mou, "Searle, Zhuang Zi, and Transcendental Perspectivism," in *Searle's Philosophy and Chinese Philosophy*, ed. Bo Mou (Leiden: Brill, 2008), 405–30, at 406. See the section "Relativism, Pluralism, and Perspectivism" in chapter 7.
75   On Liu versus Ziporyn's interpretations of Zhiyi, see also the section "From Nāgārjuna to Zhiyi" in chapter 2.
76   T9n262, 5c.
77   Ziporyn, *Emptiness and Omnipresence*, 88.
78   Other translations do not feature this expression, which Ziporyn also points out in a note (ibid., 288n4), as well as on 89. For example, Gene Reeves has: "only among Buddhas can the true character of all things be fathomed" (*The Lotus Sutra* [Boston: Wisdom, 2008], 76) and Tsugunari Kubo and Akira Yuyama: "No one but the buddhas can completely know the real aspects of all dharmas" (*The Lotus Sūtra* [Berkeley: Numata Center for Buddhist Translation and Research, 2007], 23). It seems to me that the most literal translation is "only a Buddha with a Buddha can examine/know the ultimate nature of all dharmas," which largely corresponds to Ziporyn's translation.
79   Ziporyn, *Emptiness and Omnipresence*, 89.

According to Tiantai perspectivism, "to see something is to see 'not-all' of it. We are always seeing a little fragment of the world, but every bit of the world is changed by the fact that it is a part of the world,"[80] and, because of that, no thing has a "single consistent noncontradictory identity."[81] In Ziporyn's view, if something can be made to look in a certain way, even for just a moment and even to just a single observer, then that is a perspective on that thing and "'what something is' is nothing more and nothing less than 'how something is seen — by someone or other, from some perspective.' 'What it is' simply has no other coherent meaning."[82] And while in apophatic Buddhism all such perspectives are deceptive or false, in Ziporyn's Tiantai *all* such perspectives are true.[83]

According to Ziporyn, emptiness in Tiantai means ambiguity, specifically, the ambiguity resulting from differences in perspective. He explains, summarizing his view on Tiantai metaphysics:

> What is illusory is not that there is something there or even that there are differences in the world. What is illusory is that there are distinct things that are *one way or another*, definitively. In reality, everything can be seen in the way it appears and *also always in at least one other way*. Since it can always be seen in at least one other way, it can be seen in *infinite ways*. Outside of these infinite ways of seeing, however, there is no "it." These ways of seeing it are not added to the one way — the one way of seeing it — that is really it. There is no privileged perspective on it that reveals the "real" qualities it has, as opposed to the other, "distorted" appearances. Appearing with certain features and attributes is one way it appears. Imagined as actually being featureless is another way it appears. Neither is more true than the other.[84]

While I agree with some, perhaps even much, of this, it seems to me that there are three serious problems here. First, the claim that "since [something] can always be seen in at least one other way, it can be seen in *infinite ways*" is a non sequitur — that supposed implication just does not follow. That I have at least one other coin in my wallet (besides the five-yen coin I just put in there) does not imply that I have infinitely many coins in my wallet either.

Second, the claim that "outside of these infinite ways of seeing [...] there is no 'it'" appears to be an anti-realist rejection of the existence of the ultimately real thing or suchness underlying or causing the ways it appears, and that cannot possibly be right. It was already pointed out above that Tiantai is realist, and it is not particularly difficult to substantiate that characterization with further textual evidence. For example, in *The Great Calming and Contemplation*, Zhiyi appeals to what is seen by Buddhas to argue that the objects we perceive must be ultimately real.

> If the objects projected by the mind were non-existent [in the sense of] the Middle [truth of non-dualism] then there would be nothing to be known through wisdom and nothing to be seen with the eyes. Thus it should be known that there

---

80 Ibid., 150.
81 Ibid., 151.
82 Ibid., 170.
83 Ibid., 147.
84 Ibid., 193.

are objects perceived by the Buddha eye. [...] If there were no ordinary objects, then this [Buddha] eye would not [be able to] see the Buddha land(s).[85]

Third, and most importantly, I'm rather skeptical about Ziporyn's thesis that Tiantai perspectivism is subjective, that is, that it holds that all perspectives are equally true. Such "anything goes" perspectivism has the uncharitable implication that a mistaken perception of a rope as a snake would be just as valid as recognizing it as a rope, and I'm not convinced that Zhiyi held that view. On the other hand, Dōgen, who is also part of the broader Tiantai tradition, seems to have argued for exactly that when he suggested that what is experienced in dreams or what is seen with eyes clouded by cataracts is equally ultimately real.[86]

Ziporyn quotes very little textual evidence to support his subjective perspectivist interpretation. I'm not sure whether there is unambiguous textual evidence for the opposing point of view either, but there are clues scattered in various places. One important clue can be gleaned from the *Lotus Sūtra* passage quoted above, for example. That short fragment is part of a longer sentence:

> Only a Buddha and/with a Buddha can examine/know the ultimate nature of all *dharmas*: their appearances, their natures, their essences/substances, their (causal) powers/capabilities, their functions, their causes, their destinies, their consequences, their (indirect) effects, all of their aspects from beginning to end.[87]

These appearances, natures, causal powers, and so forth are all aspects of the ultimately real thing, or suchness. In Ziporyn's interpretation, if a drunk sailor briefly sees a walrus as a mermaid, then the mermaid-hood of the underlying suchness would be as real as its walrus-hood; and if someone during a psychotic episode sees the stains on her wallpaper as giant crawling ants, then their ant-ness would be as real as their stain-ness. One might wonder, however, whether this really is what the phrases "their appearances" or "their effects" in the *Lotus Sūtra* passage mean. Perhaps, we should make a difference between an appearance *of* something and an appearance that is merely *triggered by* something. More problematic, however, is that a drunk or madman can see anything as anything, or as Ziporyn put it, anything "can be seen in *infinite ways.*" If anything can be seen as anything, and all those infinite ways are inherent aspects of the underlying ultimately real thing or suchness, then every suchness has all possible characteristics, which means that they all have exactly the same characteristics and are, therefore, indistinguishable, even to Buddhas. But that cannot be right.

The sūtra passage, as well as the quote by Zhiyi a few paragraphs back, make clear that appearances of things are not just loosely associated with or triggered by ultimately real things but are connected to them in a much more direct way. That is, ordinary views are not true because they are one among infinitely many possible views but because they reveal something about the ultimately real things that they are caused by and are views on.

---

85 若無中境智無所知眼無所見。當知應有佛眼境也。…若無俗境此眼不應見於佛土。— Zhiyi, 《摩訶止觀》(594), T46n1911, 26b.
86 In Muchū Setsumu 夢中說夢 and Kuge 空華, respectively. Both are chapters from 正法眼藏, T82n2582.
87 唯佛與佛乃能究盡諸法實相,所謂諸法如是相,如是性,如是體,如是力,如是作,如是因,如是緣,如是果,如是報,如是本末究竟等。— T9n262, 5c.

Furthermore, if any perspective would be equally true, as Ziporyn suggests, then that would imply that there are no mistaken views. The fact that Zhiyi and other Tiantai thinkers made much effort to correct views that they considered to be mistaken in their lectures and writings strongly suggest that they did not believe that. In the contrary, there surely are mistaken views, which raises the question how we can distinguish right views from mistaken views, but that is a topic for the next chapter.

Above, I suggested that Dōgen sometimes appeared to argue for a subjective perspectivism, but Dōgen's ideas are not that easy to classify. The two main sources for his perspectivism are a short passage in the *Genjōkōan* 現成公案 chapter from the *Shōbōgenzō* 正法眼藏 and much of the *Sūtra of Mountains and Water* 山水經 from the same book. In the former, Dōgen stated:

> Either in dust [as layman, seeing nothing but the ordinary phenomena] or outside the frame [as an accomplished monk, seeing beyond the ordinary], of all the numerous aspects [of things], we can see and understand only those that we have developed eyes of learning [i.e., capability] for.[88]

Significantly, in this passage different perspectives are acquired — what we (can) see does not depend on karma or on some kind of innate capacity but on our "eyes of learning" 學眼.[89] Furthermore, the passage also suggests that we can learn more and thus learn to see things in different ways and that indeed is an important aspect of Dōgen's philosophy.[90] In the *Sūtra of Mountains and Water*, however, Dōgen argues for a perspectivism in which perspectives are determined by kinds of beings, similar to the first Yogācāra relativism mentioned above.

> Generally, the way of seeing mountains and water differs in accordance with the kind of being. There are creatures that see as jeweled necklace(s) the so-called water that we see, but it is not that they see [what we see as] a jeweled necklace as water. Something that we see in some form, they see as water. Their jeweled necklace is what we see as water. There are [beings] that see water as miraculous flowers, but it is not that [they] use [what we see as] flowers as water. Demons [i.e., pretas] see water as raging flames; [they] see [it] as pus and blood. Dragons and fish see [it] as a palace; [they] see [it] as a tower. Some see [it] as the seven jewels or a jewel; some see [it] as a forest or a wall; some see [it] as the pure liberation of dharma-nature; some see [it] as true human reality; some see it as [the non-duality of] physical appearance and mental nature. Humans see [it] as water, the cause and condition of death and life. Thus, views differ in accordance to kind. For now, we should be suspicious about this. Are there many ways of seeing one object? Are many phenomena mistakenly assumed to be one thing? On top of [our] spiritual effort, we should make further effort. But if the foregoing is the case, then the way of practice and realization [i.e., our effort] should not be singular or dual either. Ultimate reality may also involve thousands of kinds and manifold forms. Furthermore, reflecting on this doctrine, even though there are

---

88 塵中格外。オホク樣子ヲ帶セリトイヘトモ。参學眼力ノオヨフハカリヲ見取會取スルナリ。— Dōgen,『正法眼藏』,「現成公案」, T82n2582, 24b.
89 The idea of acquired perspectives is not entirely new of course. Since Buddhahood is also an acquired state, the multi-perspectival view of collective Buddhas in the *Lotus Sūtra* fragment quoted above, and thus all the individual perspectives involved are also acquired.
90 See the quote by Bret Davis at the end of the previous section.

many kinds of water, there is no original water, and there is no water of many kinds. But even then, the many waters [as seen] according to the [various] kinds do not depend on the mind, do not depend on the body, do not arise from karma, are not self-dependent, and are not other-dependent, but are the liberated/awakened [form] depending on water itself.[91]

The passage reminds of the *Lotus Sūtra* fragment. Therein the various perspectives on some thing are also implicitly assumed to be somehow dependent on the underlying suchness, and Dōgen here makes the same point.[92] The ways of seeing depend on the suchness we see as water itself, but our way of seeing that suchness, *as* water, is just one of many ways of seeing it, and we should not fall into the trap of believing that our way of seeing it is inherently better or more true than others.

[Water] is not [just] flowing and falling. If we recognize it only as flowing, the word "flowing" slanders water. It is like forcing [it] to be non-flowing, for example. Water is just the suchness of its real form. Water is the virtue of water. [It] is beyond flowing. When [the understanding of] the flow and non-flow of a single [instance of] water is mastered, then a complete understanding of the manifold dharmas is realized at once.[93]

Hence, while water can be seen in many ways, in some sense it is none of them. Rather, it is the underlying form that makes all those ways of seeing (i.e., all those perspectives) possible. But this also means that those perspectives are not arbitrary; they are part of the ultimately real nature of whatever it is that we see as water, or mountains, or whatever.

The latter suggests an objective perspectivist interpretation of Dōgen's philosophy, which contradicts the subjective perspectivist suggestions mentioned above. This is, moreover, not the only inconsistency. The nature of perspectives in *Genjōkōan* and the *Sūtra of Mountains and Water* is very different as well; the former appear to be human perspectives, while the latter are associated with different kinds of beings. And while different perspectives in the *Genjōkōan* are acquired, all that must be acquired and understood according to the *Sūtra of Mountains and Water* is the

---

91 オホヨソ山水ヲミルコト種類ニシタカヒテ。不同アリ。イハユル水ヲミルニ瓔珞トミルモノアリ。シカアレトモ瓔珞ヲ水トミルニハアラス。ワレラカナニトミルカタチヲカレカ水トスラン。カレカ瓔珞ハ。ワレ水トミル。水ヲ妙華トミルアリ。シカアレトモ華ヲ水トモチキルニアラス。鬼ハ水ヲモテ猛火トミル。濃血トミル。龍魚ハ宮殿トミル。樓臺トミル。アラヒハ七寳摩尼珠トミル。アルヒハ樹林牆壁トミル。アルヒハ清淨解脱ノ法性トミル。アルヒハ眞實人體トミル。アルヒハ身相心性トミル。人間コレヲ水トミル。殺活ノ因縁ナリ。ステニ隨類ノ所見不同ナリ。シハラクコレヲ疑著スヘシ。一境ヲミルニ。諸見シナシナナリトヤセン。諸象ヲ。一境ナリト誤錯セリトヤセン。功夫ノ頂顙ニ。サラニ功夫スヘシ。シカアレハスナハチ修證辨道モ。一般兩般ナルヘカラス。究竟ノ境界モ。千種萬般ナルヘキナリ。サラニコノ宗旨ヲ憶想スルニ。諸類ノ水タトヒオホシトイヘトモ。本水ナキカコトシ。諸類ノ水ナキカコトシ。シカアレトモ隨類ノ諸水。ソレ心ニヨラス。身ニヨラス。業ヨリ生セス。依自ニアラス。依他ニアラス。依水ノ透脱アリ。— Dōgen,『正法眼藏』,「山水經」, T82n2582, 64b–c.

92 Significantly, the passage from *Genjōkōan* about developing new ways of seeing quoted above depends on the same assumption. The aspects seen through new "eyes of learning" are caused by real aspects of the thing or suchness perceived.

93 流落ニアラス。流ノミナリト認スルハ。流ノコトハ水ヲ謗スルナリ。タトヘハ非流ト強爲スルカユヱニ。水ハ水ノ如是實相ノミナリ。水是水功徳ナリ。流ニアラス。一水ノ流ヲ參究シ。不流ヲ參究スルニ。萬法ノ究盡。タチマチニ現成スルナリ。— Dōgen,『正法眼藏』,「山水經」, T82n2582, 66c

meta-perspectival view that there are multiple perspectives.⁹⁴ Solving such inconsistencies is not an aim of this inquiry. What matters most here is the point made in the *Sūtra of Mountains and Water* that perspectives are not arbitrary or groundless and that there always are other perspectives, and the suggestion in *Genjōkōan* that we can learn to see from new perspectives, although the latter suggestion is of greater relevance in the next chapter.

Apoha and Its Implications

The non-arbitrariness of perspectival views is also a key point in Yogācāra constructionism, that is, the second kind of Yogācāra relativism mentioned in the previous section. According to Dignāga and Dharmakīrti, "thought and language are causally related to our experiences of things and hence are grounded in reality."⁹⁵ Concept formation and conceptual construction (*kalpanā*) play key roles in the grounding of our phenomenal experiences in real things (*artha* or *svārtha*). Georges Dreyfus summarizes and clarifies Dharmakīrti's account of reality-based concept formation as follows:

> Our starting point is our experience of things and their mutual resemblances. These experiences give rise to a diffuse concept of similarity. To account for this sense of similarity, we construct a more precise concept by correlating conceptual representations with a single term or sign previously encountered. This creates a more precise concept in which the representations are made to stand for a commonality that the objects are assumed to possess. [...] In this way experiences give rise to mental representations, which are transformed into concepts by association with a linguistic sign. The formation of a concept consists of the assumption that mental representations stand for an agreed on imagined commonality. Two points must be emphasized here regarding concept formation. First a concept, which is nothing but an assumption of the existence of a fictional commonality projected onto things, comes to be through the conjunction of two factors: the experience of real objects and the social process of language acquisition. Hence, the process of concept formation is connected with reality, albeit in a mediated way. Second, a concept is mistaken.⁹⁶

There are interesting similarities and differences between this account and ideas defended by Donald Davidson and W.V.O. Quine. The first half of this quote is strikingly similar to Davidson's assertion that "all creatures classify objects and aspects of the world in the sense that they treat some stimuli as more alike than others. The criterion of such classifying activity is similarity of response."⁹⁷ And the quote's conclusion reminds of Davidson's theory of *triangulation* (which was also endorsed

---

94 If the perspectives in the *Sūtra of Mountains and Water* are inherently inaccessible to other kinds of beings, then it might be more appropriate to use the term "relativism" rather than "perspectivism" for the ideas expressed in that text.
95 Georges Dreyfus, "Apoha As a Naturalized Account of Concept Formation," in *Apoha: Buddhist Nominalism and Human Cognition*, eds. Mark Siderits, Tom Tillemans, and Arindam Chakrabarti (New York: Columbia University Press, 2011), 207–27, at 209.
96 Georges Dreyfus, *Recognizing Reality: Dharmakīrti's Philosophy and Its Tibetan Interpretations* (Albany, SUNY Press, 1997), 227.
97 Donald Davidson, "Three Varieties of Knowledge" (1991), SIO: 205–20, at 212.

in some form by Quine[98]), the core idea of which is that concepts and the possibility of communication and thought depend "on the fact that two or more creatures are responding, more or less simultaneously, to input from a shared world, and from each other."[99] The most obvious difference concerns the last sentence in the quote, "a concept is mistaken," which reflects the apophatic attitude of Yogācāra, while especially Davidson tended to go to the other extreme, almost approaching a form of naive realism.

According to the Yogācāra three-natures theory, the perfected nature (*pariniṣpanna-svabhāva*) of things, that is, emptiness, cannot be described.[100] As explained above, such apophasis becomes problematic when there is a need to talk or write about ultimately real things, and when theorizing about perception and other topics in epistemology, there often is such a need. Dignāga and Dharmakīrti solved this problem in two ways. First, they provisionally adopted an ontology as a way of speaking about ultimate reality but ultimately rejected that ontology. Second, they avoided making positive or kataphatic claims about things in ultimate reality by means of their *apoha* theory, according to which the conceptual construction and classification (*kalpanā*) of phenomenal appearances proceed by means of exclusion (*anyāpoha*).

Dignāga argued that there are only two instruments or sources of knowledge (*pramāṇa*): perception (*pratyakṣa*) and inference (*anumāna*).[101] Perception, in his definition, is free from (or prior to) conceptual construction (*kalpanāpoḍha*). Our conscious awareness of things, however, is of phenomenal conceptual constructs. Such verbal cognition (*śabda*) is not pratyakṣa by definition, because pratyakṣa is non-conceptual, but is not a separate pramāṇa either. Rather, it is a kind of inference. In *Pramāṇasamuccayavṛtti* 5.1, Dignāga states that "verbal cognition is not a means of cognition separate from inference. That is, a [word] denotes its own referent (*svārtha*) by exclusion (*anyāpoha*) of other [referents]."[102]

Direct perception gives rise to a *pratibhāsa*, a pre-conscious mental response to the object. According to Dignāga, every pratibhāsa necessarily accords with its object because it is, and can only be, caused by that object. Dharmakīrti, who further developed Dignāga's logic and epistemology,[103] disagreed. Sometimes, due to various circumstances and disturbances, an object can fail to cause a genuine pratibhāsa. Only a non-contradictory or coherent (*avisaṃvādin*) pratibhāsa is genuine.[104] Consequently, non-contradictoriness became an important topic in Yogācāra epistemology after Dharmakīrti. We'll return to that topic in the next chapter.

A pratibhāsa, genuine or not, is the raw material for a *pratibhāsa-pratīti*, the conscious and conceptual experience of a thing as something. The unconscious cognitive process in which a pratibhāsa-pratīti, a determinate perception, is produced out of the raw data of the pratibhāsa is conceptual construction, or kalpanā. This

---

98 See, for example, W.V.O. Quine, "I, You, and It: An Epistemological Triangle," in *Knowledge, Language and Logic: Questions for Quine,* eds. Alex Orenstein and Peter Kotatko (Dordrecht: Springer, 2000), 1–6.
99 Donald Davidson, "Indeterminism and Antirealism" (1997), SIO: 69–84, at 83.
100 See the section "Yogācāra Realism" in this chapter.
101 Dignāga, *Pramāṇasamuccayavṛtti* (6th c.), Chapter 1.
102 Translation, with minor changes: Ole Holten Lind, *Dignāga's Philosophy of Language: Pramāṇasamuccayavṛtti Von Anyāpoha* (Vienna: ÖAW, 2015), 2.
103 Mainly in his *Pramāṇavārttika* and especially his own commentary thereon.
104 See, for example, S.R. Bhatt and Anu Mehrotra, *Buddhist Epistemology* (Westport: Greenwood, 2000), 20.

conceptual construction, according to Dignāga and Dharmakīrti, proceeds through exclusion, *apoha* or *anyāpoha*. In an unconscious inferential process, the raw data of the *pratibhāsa* is compared with the conceptual categories in our memory, but rather than fitting the raw data into any of those categories, we exclude it from all but one of them. We recognize something that is not a non-cow, or not a non-table, or not a non-tree, and so forth.

This idea may not make much sense at first, and unsurprisingly, there is an ongoing debate on how to understand the *apoha* theory. One key notion needed to understand the theory and its purpose is Quine's "ontological commitment." An ontological commitment is an implication of a view or theory that something exists. As Quine explained:

> We commit ourselves to an ontology containing numbers when we say there are prime numbers larger than a million; we commit ourselves to an ontology containing centaurs when we say there are centaurs; and we commit ourselves to an ontology containing Pegasus when we say Pegasus is. But we don not commit ourselves to an ontology containing Pegasus [...] when we say that Pegasus [...] is not.[105]

Similarly, the recognition that "something is a cow" would ontologically commit us to cows, that is, it would imply that cows exist *as cows*, and that is not an acceptable implication from a Yogācāra point of view. In that view, any conceptually determinate ontological commitment must be avoided because such a commitment would imply that we can describe something in ultimate reality, which is exactly what Yogācāra denies. This is the point of *apoha*: explaining conceptual construction and classification without ontological commitments to conceptually determinate ultimately real things. Unfortunately, how it is supposed to do so is less clear.

According to the theory, when we see something *as* a "cow," what we really recognize is that something is not a non-cow. Obviously "not non-" cannot be a double negation because then "not non-X" means the same thing as just "X," and therefore, "something is not a non-cow" is equivalent to "something is a cow," and the latter, again, is what Dignāga and Dharmakīrti aimed to avoid.

In Western classical logic "non-X" refers to a class complement (i.e., the class or collection of things that are not X), and consequently, "something is not a non-cow" can be read as involving a negation ("not") and a class complement ("non-"). Unfortunately, if "non-" is understood this way, the sentence is logically equivalent to "something is a cow" again,[106] so this interpretation cannot be right either.

An apparent third option is that "non-" refers to an open class of alternative classifications. Hence, "non-cow" means "horse, or pig, or flower, or ...." Obviously, such a class of alternative classifications would be extremely large, much larger than what our limited mental processing capacity can handle in the short time we need to classify something as a "cow." But there is an even more serious problem: "non-cow" interpreted like this does not ontologically commit us to cows, but it does commit us to horses, pigs, flowers, and so forth instead. One could try to avoid this by defining the class of alternative classifications without mentioning specific examples — by appealing to the set of properties that no cow has, for example — but this leads to

---

105 W.V.O. Quine, "On What There Is" (1948), FLPV: 1–19, at 8.
106 Technically, "something is not a non-cow" is the obverse of "something is a cow."

other problems. Then non-dragons are non-unicorns because the set of properties no dragon has is identical to the set of properties no unicorn has, namely, all properties. But even more problematic is that "something is a non-cow" would then mean "something has a property that no cow has," which would ontologically commit one to properties or universals, while Yogācāra is nominalist (i.e., it rejects the existence of properties or universals).[107]

These problems for the third interpretation are related to the assumption that "non-cow" must exclude all possible alternatives, but the exclusion of the "flower" classification probably rarely plays a role in recognizing something as a "cow," even if it might matter in some exotic cases. Instead of referring to all possible alternative classifications, "non-cow" could also be understood as referring just to the contextually subjectively salient alternative classifications. To say that something is "not a non-cow," then, is to say that it is not a horse, or a pig, or anything else that crosses one's unconscious mind when looking at the thing in question or when processing its pratibhāsa. This still implies an ontological commitment to horses and pigs, and so forth, but that is a consequence of a mistake this interpretation inherits from the third interpretation.

Apoha does not proceed by comparing the pratibhāsa to actual things out there but by comparing it to memories of previous word use connected to previous sensory data. Hence, to say that something is "not a non-cow" is not to say that it is not a horse and so forth, but that it is not *like things one remembers to have classified as not a non-horse before*, and so forth. This final interpretation is only ontologically committed to memories of horses but not to the horses themselves, but that is a commitment a Yogācārin accepts.[108]

Whether this interpretation is right is hard to say—neither Dignāga nor Dharmakīrti is sufficiently clear. Because of that, there is little certainty about how the apoha theory is to be understood and many interpretations have been put forward. Mark Siderits, for example, has proposed an interpretation based on Bimal Matilal's distinction between "nominally" and "verbally bound negation" found in Hindu philosophy,[109] but as Siderits admits himself,[110] there is no clear evidence for that distinction in Buddhist philosophy. Moreover, it is not immediately clear either how Siderits's two kinds of negation relate to "exclusion" and "difference." *Anyāpoha* literally means exclusion (*apoha*) of what is different (*anya*), and any plausible interpretation of the theory should take this term seriously. What it should explain is how conceptual construction or concept formation works by excluding what is different.

The "final" interpretation given above succeeds in this respect, I think.[111] According to that interpretation, "something is not a non-cow" means that that thing is not like things one remembers to have classified as a horse before,[112] nor like things one remembers to have classified as a pig before nor like anything else that is contextu-

---

107 See the section "Realism (1) — Universals and (Anti-)Essentialism" in chapter 7.
108 In any sensible interpretation, the apoha theory is also ontologically committed to an external, ineffable cause of the *pratibhāsa*, which implies that the theory is realist.
109 Mark Siderits, *Indian Philosophy of Language* (Dordrecht: Kluwer, 1991), and Bimal Matilal, *Epistemology, Logic, and Grammar in Indian Philosophical Analysis* (The Hague: Mouton, 1971).
110 Mark Siderits, "Śrughna by Dusk," in *Apoha*, eds. Siderits, Tillemans, and Chakrabarti, 283–304.
111 No explanation is ever final, of course. It is just the final interpretation given here. Hence, the scare quotes.
112 Or as not a non-horse, strictly speaking.

ally and subjectively salient. Hence, conceptual construction and classification is exclusion of what one believes to be different in that context.

Furthermore, this interpretation has some important implications. First, conceptual classification depends on memory; to interpret some raw sensory data as a "cow" involves the largely unconscious recognition that that data "is not like things one remembers to have classified as (not non-)Φ before," where "Φ" stands for all the things or classifications that are contextually and subjectively salient.

Second, and closely related to this first implication, because everyone has different memories of cows, horses, or whatever else is salient to a person in some situation and because different memories affect what exactly is salient in the first place, there are subtle differences in the classifications by different people of something as a (not non-)"cow." And therefore, what one person means with the word "cow" is subtly different from what another means. As Davidson put it,

> what a person's words mean depends in the most basic cases on the kinds of objects and events that have caused the person to hold the words to be applicable; similarly for what the person's thoughts are about. [… W]hatever she regularly does apply them to gives her words the meaning they have and her thoughts the contents they have.[113]

An implication hereof is what Davidson called the "primacy of the idiolect": what people mean does not depend on some thing called "a language" but on their own individual experiences with word use. And consequently, languages depend on idiolects (personal ways of using language) and not as it usually assumed the other way around. Or more provocatively:

> There is no such thing as a language, not if a language is anything like what many philosophers and linguists have supposed. There is therefore no such thing to be learned, mastered, or born with. We must give up the idea of a clearly defined shared structure which language-users acquire and then apply to cases.[114]

Third, in conceptual construction and classification, whatever is salient in the pratibhāsa is compared to whatever is or becomes salient in memory,[115] and salience is likely to be determined partially by the kind of being. Dōgen was almost certainly right when he pointed out that fish and other non-human creatures see and remember water differently than how we see it. And if pretas or dragons exist, they'll see water differently as well. Because of this, two similarly intelligent creatures belonging to very different species living in very different circumstances might never be able to communicate with each other because what is salient to them differs so much that they can never know whether they are talking about the same thing.

---

113 Donald Davidson, "Knowing One's Own Mind" (1987), SIO: 15–38, at 37.
114 Donald Davidson, "A Nice Derangement of Epitaphs" (1986), TLH: 89–107, at 107. Davidson's argument for the primacy of the idiolect in this paper does not start from the same premise. Rather, he argues that we do not need pre-existing linguistic conventions, or languages to make ourselves understood but can always create new temporary and local conventions on the spot. Davidson's quote and the relevance of its point for moral theory are discussed in the section "Maps *for* and *of* Behavior" in chapter 14.
115 Some thing, property, or memory is salient if it catches the person's or animal's attention.

Fourth, if we can only classify something as (not non-)"cow" by excluding what is different, then we can only have a concept of "cow" if we have concepts of at least some of those different but related things. Hence, we cannot have isolated concepts; we cannot have a concept "red" and no other color concepts; we cannot have a concept "warm" without having a concept "cold"; and so forth. Davidson made a very similar point, albeit not for exactly the same reasons.[116]

Fifth, this interpretation blurs or even erases the line between conceptual construction and concept formation, which is significant as both are assumed to be based on apoha. If conceptual classification of perceptual stimuli depends on one's memories of previous word use in relation to previous stimuli, then new experiences change future conceptual classifications and constructions, provided that those new experiences are remembered, and thereby the meaning of one's words. Similarly, when a child learns a word, and thereby a conceptual classification, the word's meaning is increasingly refined in response to the child's observations and experiences of the word's use, which will be observations of word use by others at first. In this way, the child gets gradually attuned to the conceptual constructions, and thus the phenomenal world, of its language teachers. This is more or less how I understand Dharmakīrti's rather underdeveloped theory of concept formation. But this is also one of the key points of Davidson's theory of triangulation.

Triangulation, *Kalpanā*, and Kataphasis

Donald Davidson introduced the notion of triangulation as an analogy in lieu of a theory in a lecture given in 1981,[117] but it has precursors in his theory of radical interpretation and in Quine's notion of radical translation and related ideas, which date to the 1960s and which employ the same *triangle of interpretation*.[118] From the end of the 1980s, this analogy developed into a picture of the linguistic interaction between two or more speakers in a shared environment, which would become the central idea in much of Davidson's later philosophy. In different forms and applications, the idea is used to help explain how we get the notions of truth and objectivity, how we learn a first language or radically interpret a second, how we get to mean anything by our words, why private first languages are impossible, how we proceed from no thought to thought, why skepticism cannot get of the ground, how our beliefs are connected with reality, and more. Obviously, not all of these extensions and applications are relevant here. I'll just focus on how the theory helps to clarify the connections between words and things suggested by Dignāga and Dharmakīrti and on what follows therefrom.

In its most basic from, triangulation is a singular occasion of pointing out some object by one communicating creature to another by means of some ad hoc sign.

---

116 See, for example, Donald Davidson, "Interpretation: Hard in Theory, Easy in Practice," in *Interpretations and Causes*, ed. Mario De Caro (Dordrecht: Kluwer, 1999), 31–44, at 32.
117 Donald Davidson, "Rational Animals" (1982), SIO: 95–105.
118 W.V.O. Quine, *Word and Object* (Cambridge: MIT Press, 1960), and Donald Davidson, "Truth and Meaning" (1967), ITI: 17–36. Davidson himself mentions Quine's thesis of radical translation as a precursor of triangulation in "Externalisms" in *Interpreting Davidson*, eds. Petr Kotatko, Peter Pagin, and Gabriel. Segal (Stanford: CSLI, 2001), 1–16. In the same paper he also suggests that all the key elements of his theory of triangulation were already present in "Truth and Meaning." In "Epistemology Externalized" (1990), SIO: 193–204, he also claimed that the main ingredients of his philosophical ideas all date to the early 1960s.

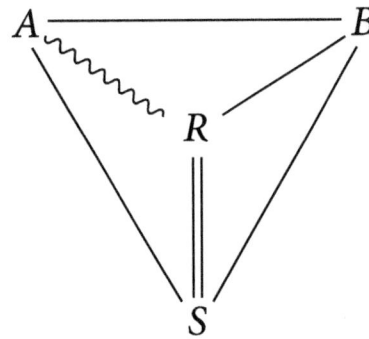

Fig. 8.1. The triangle of interpretation.

These two creatures and the shared stimulus are the three vertices of the triangle. Many of Davidson's papers employ a less basic form of triangulation; in those the term denotes a model of a process of word learning by means of repeated similar signs in the repeated presence of similar stimuli.[119] In some of these papers the notion of ostensive learning appeared as a variant denotation of such triangulatory word learning,[120] and in that form the idea made its final appearance in the last pages of the posthumously published *Truth and Predication*.[121]

Figure 8.1 shows what I call "the triangle of interpretation," the basic figure that underlies Davidson's theory of interpretation as well as its direct precursors in his and Quine's philosophy. It is this triangle that "models the primitive situation in which we take the first steps into language, or begin decoding a totally alien language."[122] Creature *A* responds with response *R*, which may be a linguistic sign but also some other kind of behavior, to stimulus *S*, and creature *B* observes all of that. The different kinds of lines in the figure represent different kinds of relations: observation (simple lines), reference (double line), and utterance or action (wavy line). If the response *R* is a more or less linguistic one — say, uttering the word "table" — and *S* is a table, then what the figure shows is that *A* says "table" in response to observing a table, and *B* observes *A*, the table, and the word "table" (but *B* probably sees the first two and hears the third). From her observations, *B* might infer that *R* refers to or is a response to *S*, but this leaves still lots of room for ambiguity, as Quine stressed in his theory of the indeterminacy of translation,[123] and is insufficient for learning a first language.

---

119 The most important are the following: Donald Davidson, "The Conditions of Thought," in *The Mind of Donald Davidson*, eds. Johannes L. Brandl and Wolfgang L. Gombocz (Amsterdam: Rodop, 1989), 193–200; "Epistemology Externalized"; "The Second Person" (1992), SIO: 107–22; "The Social Aspect of Language" (1994), TLH: 109–25; "The Emergence of Thought" (1997), SIO: 123–34; "Seeing through Language" (1997), TLH: 127–41; "The Irreducibility of the Concept of the Self" (1998), SIO: 85–91; "Interpretation"; and "Externalisms."

120 An early example of the identification of the two notions can be found in "Meaning, Truth and Evidence." Much later, in "Comments on Karlovy Vary Papers," Davidson wrote that the importance of ostensive learning was his original inspiration for the idea of triangulation. Donald Davidson, "Meaning, Truth and Evidence" (1990), TLH: 47–62. Donald Davidson, "Comments on Karlovy Vary Papers" (2001), in *Interpreting Davidson*, eds. Kotatko, Pagin, and Segal, 285–308.

121 Donald Davidson, *Truth and Predication* (Cambridge: Belknap, 2005).

122 Donald Davidson, "Locating Literary Language" (1993), TLH: 167–81.

123 Quine, *Word and Object*, and "Ontological Relativity" (1969), OROE: 26–68.

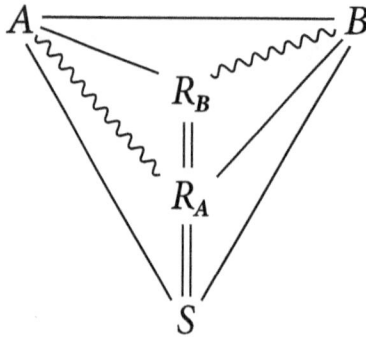

Fig. 8.2. Advanced triangulation.

In the end of the 1980s Davidson started to distinguish this "primitive learning situation" from the more advanced version of triangulation involved in concept formation and language learning.[124] This version depends on a repetition of the more complex situation depicted in figure 8.2. Each repetition of a similar situation is assumed to involve the same two creatures, A and B (but in principle only the language learner or interpreter B needs to be constant and the teacher or interpretee A can vary), different but similar stimuli S_1, S_2, and so forth, and different but similar responses $R_{A,1}$, $R_{A,2}$, and so forth. The indexed numbers represent the different occasions of similar situations. Advanced triangulation involves the following seven steps or aspects, numbered (a) to (g):

(a) A finds certain stimuli S_1, S_2, and so forth similar. For example, A finds a number of flat-topped objects that we would call "tables" similar. (And as it will turn out, A calls those things "tables" as well.)

(b) B finds the same stimuli S_1, S_2, and so forth similar, although possibly not at first. That is, B also finds tables similar, but does not know yet that they are tables and that they are called "tables."

(c) B finds A's responses $R_{A,1}$, $R_{A,2}$, and so forth to those stimuli similar. For example, A responds to the tables by uttering something involving the word "table" every time, and B picks up on that similarity, that is, B recognizes the word "table." It should be noted here that, in apparent deviation from (b), B does not necessarily have to pick up on the subjective similarity between stimuli S_1, S_2, and so forth prior to the triangular learning situation but may develop this awareness of subjective similarity in response to the observed similarity in A's responses $R_{A,1}$, $R_{A,2}$, and so forth to those stimuli.

(d) A finds B's responses $R_{B,1}$, $R_{B,2}$, and so forth to its own (A's) responses $R_{A,1}$, $R_{A,2}$, and so forth similar. B responds to A's utterances of the word "table" in similar ways; by parroting that word, for example. Note that without this step (d) A would never realize that B is actually learning the word "table," and thus that there would be no reason to assume that B has indeed learned the word. This is an application of the more general point that without similarity in responses there is no reason to assume that the creature recognizes a similarity between stimuli.

---

124 In "The Conditions of Thought" and "The Second Person," presented in conferences in 1988 and 1989, respectively, but published in 1989 and 1992.

(e) *B* assumes (a) to explain (c). In other words, *B* (unconsciously) assumes that *A* finds tables similar, or that they are similar, to explain the observed similarity in responses (i.e., the repeated utterance of "table").
(f) *A* assumes (b) and (c) to explain (d). That is, *A* assumes that *B* finds tables similar and that *B* finds her utterances of the word "table" similar because otherwise the similarity in *B*'s responses would make no sense.
(g) Both *A* and *B* are aware of (a) to (g), either directly or by assumption.[125]

In this way, in a process of triangulation, a concept and a phenomenal appearance emerge together in mutual dependence. Without the concept of a "table" one cannot see tables as tables, and without perceptions of tables one cannot form the concept of "table." It seems to me that Dignāga made a similar point in his *Ālambanaparīkṣā* and its commentary when he argued that the perceived phenomenal object and the capacity to see that object cause each other.[126]

These seven steps, (a) to (g), are not so much a description of how we actually learn words and concepts but an investigation into what is necessary for it to be possible to learn words and concepts. Davidson's point is that without this triangular arrangement, we would not be able to have language and to communicate at all. Hence, the triangulation thesis can be understood as a transcendental argument.[127] In "Three Varieties of Knowledge," for example, Davidson argues that the thesis helps solve "three basic problems: how a mind can know the world of nature, how it is possible for one mind to know another, and how it is possible to know the contents of our own minds without resort to observation or evidence."[128] Thus, the fact that we can communicate with each other proves among other things that there must be other minds that we are communicating with and that there is a shared external world that we are communicating about.[129]

In this form and application, triangulation eclipses earlier arguments by Davidson with partially similar premises and conclusions. For example, in "The Method of Truth in Metaphysics," he wrote that "successful communication proves the existence of a shared, and largely true, view of the world."[130] And in "A Coherence Theory of Truth and Knowledge," he argued that

> we must [...] take the objects of a belief to be the causes of that belief. And what we, as interpreters, must take them to be is what they in fact are. Communication

---

125 This explanation is a lot clearer (I hope, at least) than Davidson's own. (His style of writing is rather obscure, unfortunately.) Nevertheless, in "The Second Person," (a) to (c) can be found on 119, (d) is added on 120, and (e) to (g) on 121.
126 Dignāga, *Ālambanaparīkṣā* and *Ālambanaparīkṣāvṛtti* (4–5th c.), §§7–8. This text and its commentary are extremely terse and hard to understand, but it seems to me that Vinītadeva's commentary supports my interpretation. Vinītadeva, *Ālambanaparīkṣāṭīkā* (8th c.). Translations of all three of these texts with further commentaries etc. can be found in Douglas Duckworth et al., *Dignāga's Investigation of the Percept: A Philosophical Legacy in India and Tibet* (Oxford: Oxford University Press, 2016).
127 Nevertheless, Davidson sometimes expressed doubt that his argument really was a transcendental argument. See, for example, Donald Davidson, "Reply to A.C. Genova," in *The Philosophy of Donald Davidson*, ed. Lewis E. Hahn (Chicago: Open Court, 1999), 192–94.
128 Donald Davidson, "Three Varieties of Knowledge" (1991), SIO: 205–20, at 208.
129 See also Davidson, "Epistemology Externalized"; "Meaning, Truth and Evidence"; and Ernest Sosa, "Knowledge of Self, Others, and World," in *Donald Davidson*, ed. Kirk Ludwig (Cambridge: Cambridge University Press, 2003), 163–82.
130 Donald Davidson, "The Method of Truth in Metaphysics" (1977), ITI: 199–214, at 201.

begins where causes converge: your utterance means what mine does if belief in its truth is systematically caused by the same events and objects.[131]

In these arguments, as well as in triangulation as transcendental argument, the most basic premise is that there is communication, and therefore, that communication is possible. Significantly, as Dan Lusthaus has pointed out, Yogācāra also "rests on both the necessity and possibility that there be communication between distinct minds."[132] Where Davidson and Yogācāra differ is in what is supposed to follow from this basic premise. Probably, the most fundamental differences are related to the question of what exactly is located at S in the triangle depicted above: what is the shared stimulus that both A and B respond to?

From a Yogācāra perspective, an external object (svārtha) causes a pratibhāsa, which triggers a process of conceptual construction (kalpanā) resulting in a determinate cognition (pratibhāsa-pratīti), which in turn triggers response R. Hence, the direct cause of the response R is this determinate cognition, and therefore, that is the stimulus S. (Except in case of reflexes and some unconscious responses; then the stimulus is a pratibhāsa and no pratibhāsa-pratīti comes into play.) This is also, more or less, Quine's point of view,[133] but Davidson disagreed.[134] Concept formation, language, and communication in general require that the stimulus S is shared, but whatever is in the mind is private. The only possible shared cause is what is located at the very start of the causal chain, that is, the external object or ground.

Davidson's argument that it must be this distal cause that is the stimulus because the proximal cause is not shared makes sense, but one may wonder whether there is a genuine disagreement here — Quine and the Yogācārin are not likely to deny that what set the causal chain in motion is indeed the distal cause, or the external object. Technically, Davidson was right when he pointed out that what is located at S in the triangle must be the distal cause, but Quine and the Yogācārin where also right that what *directly* causes the awareness of the stimulus in A's and B's minds is some intermediary proximal cause. Davidson, however, seemed to want to eliminate such proximal intermediaries altogether.

The triangle of interpretation implies that "in the simplest and most basic cases, words and sentences derive their meaning from the objects and circumstances in whose presence they were learned."[135] Davidson repeated this point in many of his writings,[136] but he did not always clearly distinguish weaker from stronger versions of this externalism. Weaker versions just hold that "what a speaker means is not determined solely by what is in the head; it depends also on the natural history of what is in the head."[137] According to the strongest version of Davidson's externalism, what is in the head plays no role at all, and the contents of beliefs and the meanings of words are their unintermediated causes. In his famous "Swampman" thought experiment, for example, he argues that if a freak incident would simultaneously

---

131 Donald Davidson, "A Coherence Theory of Truth and Knowledge" (1983), SIO: 137–53, at 151.
132 Lusthaus, *Buddhist Phenomenology*, 489.
133 Quine, *Word and Object*.
134 Donald Davidson, "The Inscrutability of Reference" (1979), ITI: 227–41; "Meaning, Truth and Evidence"; and "Pursuit of the Concept of Truth" (1995), TLH: 63–80.
135 Donald Davidson, "The Myth of the Subjective" (1988), SIO: 39–52, at 44.
136 See, for example, Davidson, "Knowing One's Own Mind," 37, and "The Conditions of Thought," 195. See also the block quote from "A Coherence Theory of Truth and Knowledge," above.
137 Davidson, "The Myth of the Subjective," 44.

kill him and create an exact replica, then that replica, Swampman, would not mean anything by his words because those words were not learned in a context that would give them a meaning.[138]

This strong version of externalism has rather implausible implications. Consider the fictional case of Hans. Hans grew up in a Swiss mountain village surrounded by St. Bernard dogs. In his early twenties, he moved to Japan and had an accident that made him forget all about his youth in Switzerland. In a conversation, some time after he recovered, Hans remarked that dogs are about the same size as cats, thinking about the tiny dogs that are most common in Japanese cities. According to Davidson, however, because Hans learned the word "dog" in the presence of St. Bernard dogs, when he remarked that dogs are about the same size as cats, Hans meant that St. Bernard dogs are about the same size as cats. Hence, Hans does not just mean something else than what he thinks he means, there even is a difference in truth value between the two. This makes no sense, and Davidson would agree. In one of the papers in which Davidson seems to appeal to strong externalism at one point, he also claims that "the presumption that I am not generally mistaken about what I mean is essential to my having a language."[139] And in the paper that introduced Swampman he also argues that

> it doesn't follow, simply from the fact that meanings are identified in part by relations to objects outside the head, that meanings aren't in the head. To suppose this would be as bad as to argue that because my being sunburned presupposes the existence of the sun, my sunburn isn't a condition of my skin.[140]

Davidson's (unconscious?) slide from weaker to stronger versions of externalism and back again is probably partially due to an oversight and partially due to his rejection of mental intermediaries between the world and our minds. The oversight is memory. The noun "memory" and the verb "to remember" occur a few times in Davidson's writings, but never in a relevant sense. This is odd, given that the recognition of similarity between stimuli S and responses R in repetitions of the triangular situation described above depends on memory. Without memory, triangulation does not make much sense. (Notice also that in the theory of apoha — or at least in the interpretation presented in the previous section — memory plays a key role.)

Davidson objected to intermediaries between the mind and the world because they create space for skepticism. If what triggers our responses is something in the mind like sense data rather than the external causes of that sense data, then it is conceivable that the way that sense data represents or shows the world to us is radically different from the way the world really is. And if that is a possibility indeed, then it follows that we cannot know anything about the external world. However, according to Davidson, this skeptical conclusion only follows if the supposed intermediary plays an epistemic role. "Skepticisim rests on the [...] idea that empirical knowledge requires an epistemological step between the world as we conceive it and our conception of it."[141] Starting with "The Myth of the Subjective," Davidson repeatedly argued against the idea of a kind of non-conceptual mental content that justifies

---

138 Davidson, "Knowing One's Own Mind," 19.
139 Donald Davidson, "What Is Present to the Mind?" (1989), SIO: 53–67, at 66.
140 Davidson, "Knowing One's Own Mind," 31.
141 Davidson, "Meaning, Truth, and Evidence," 56–57.

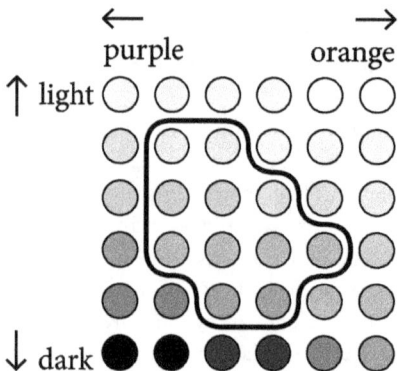

Fig. 8.3. A collection of "red" things.

our conceptual beliefs about the world.[142] In Yogācāra terms, what he rejected was the (non-Yogācāra!) idea that a pratibhāsa *justifies* the pratibhāsa-pratīti it gives rise to. What he did not object to, however, is the idea that the former somehow *causes* the latter.[143]

Pratibhāsa is a causal intermediary. If Davidson is right and causal intermediaries are relatively innocent, then the apoha theory should not imply that we are massively mistaken about the external world. However, as pointed out by Dreyfus in the long quote in the beginning of the previous section, the Yogācāra point of view is that concepts and conceptual perception orcognition are systematically mistaken.

In Dharmakīrti's perspective, there are two possible distortions between the world and our conscious minds. The first, relatively innocent distortion is between external things (svārtha) and pratibhāsa. Due to darkness or an eye defect, for example, the object may fail to produce a genuine pratibhāsa. The second is kalpanā, the process of conceptual construction and classification (through apoha), which results in the determinate cognition (pratibhāsa-pratīti). Kalpanā seems to be capable of producing the kind of systematic deception that Davidson rejects, and Yogācārins certainly tend to think of it as such, which raises the question: how deceptive can kalpanā really be if both its raw material (i.e., pratibhāsa) and the concepts involved are grounded in or caused by external reality?

In a social process that works something like triangulation, based on real similarities and differences between things, we form concepts, a concept of "red," for example. About this Dharmakīrti and Davidson are in agreement. Then, we apply those concepts when we encounter something new. We unconsciously compare it with our concepts and previous experiences and if it is not non-red, then we conclude it is red. Neither the concept of "red" nor our later conclusion implies that all the things we call "red" have something in common. There is no universal redness that all so-called "red" things share. (Here Dharmakīrti and Quine agree, but Davidson's position is less clear.) Rather, according to Dharmakīrti, all things are unique, and therefore,

---

142 "The Myth of the Subjective" is the earliest clear expression of this line argument. The most important precursor is: Donald Davidson, "On the Very Idea of a Conceptual Scheme" (1974), ITI: 183–98. The most important papers in which Davidson argues against skepticism aside from these two are: "Meaning, Truth and Evidence"; "Epistemology Externalized"; "Three Varieties of Knowledge"; and "Reply to A.C. Genova."

143 See, for example, Davidson, "A Coherence Theory of Truth and Knowledge," 144.

subsuming all these different things under one single header "red" is misrepresenting them.

Consider, for example, the 6 × 6 = 36 "things" in figure 8.3, sorted in a grid from light to dark and from purple to orange. (You'll have to imagine the colors, as the image is here printed in black-and-white.) One might call the eleven things surrounded by the thick black line "red," but aside from that classification, they have nothing in common and their actual shades are all subtly different. So, does that mean that these things really are not red? Does it mean that we are being deceived when we think of them as red?

Perhaps. But look back at the mountain landscape in figure 7.1. By the same standard we would have to say that the peaks above the dotted line in that figure really are not mountains either, and that conclusion seems absurd.[144]

What these examples illustrate is that we are or can become quite aware that not all red things have the same shade, that not all mountains are of the same height, and that were we draw the line between red and non-red or between mountain and non-mountain is somewhat arbitrary. And as long as we are aware of that, in what sense are we deceived by our constructs "red" and "mountain"? What these examples seem to confirm is Zhiyi's point that language may not be technically correct but is not entirely mistaken either, and that, anyway, we cannot avoid it; we do need language, and as long as we are aware of its limitations, we do not have to be deceived by it.[145] What these examples do *not* suggest is massive deception.

One might (and should) start to wonder at this point whether massive deception is even intelligible. Given the Dharmakīrtian framework explained above, there are two possible sources of such deception, or two possible distortions: one is between the external object and the pratibhāsa, the other is kalpanā, between pratibhāsa and pratibhāsa-pratīti. While it seems likely that two creatures with very different sense organs perceive the world quite differently, I'm not sure whether it makes sense to say that a dog is deceived because it sees fewer colors than a mantis shrimp.[146] The more important source of distortion or deception is kalpanā, conceptual construction and classification, which raises the question of how our conceptual classifications map to the real world characteristics of things, and how deceptive such classifications can be. There are three possibilities, illustrated in figure 8.4.

The rightmost part of the figure shows a "crisp" classification. The things on the right of the class boundary — the thick black line — are included in one class and the things on the left of the line are included in another class. Let's call these two classes "dark" and "light," respectively. Obviously, if our classification would be crisp, then our class boundaries would exactly track real boundaries between things or their

---

144 Well... technically they are not mountains, of course. They are drawings of mountains at best, but that is beside the point here.
145 About Zhiyi, Paul Swanson wrote that "affirmation of the use of language tempered by the awareness of its limitations is exactly the position taken by [Zhiyi], who is constantly re-affirming the inadequacy of language to describe reality, yet immediately affirms the necessity to use language in the attempt to describe the indescribable and conceptualize that which is beyond conceptualization" (*Foundations of T'ien-T'ai Philosophy: The Flowering of the Two Truths Theory in Chinese Buddhism* [Berkeley: Asian Humanities Press, 1989], 23, also quoted in chapter 2).
146 Nevertheless, similarity between creatures matters in triangulation, as Davidson occasionally observed (e.g., "The Second Person," 121), because otherwise the creatures might be unable to perceive the same stimulus. The same point was also made in relation to apoha and Dōgen's kind-specific perspectivism in the *Sūtra of Mountains and Water* above. Very different creatures might have very different pratibhāsa, and therefore, perceive the world very differently.

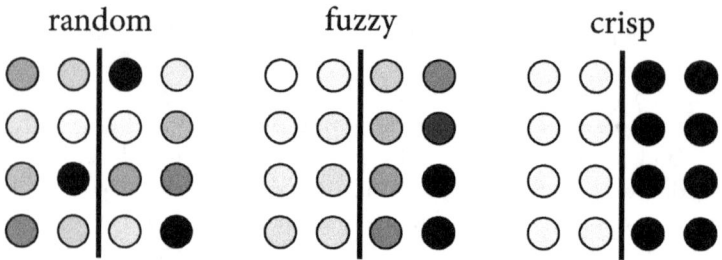

Fig. 8.4. Three kinds of conceptual classification.

properties in the external world. The cases of colors and mountains illustrate that many of our conceptual classes do not work like that.

Randomness, on the left, is the other extreme. If our conceptual classifications would be completely random, they would lack any externally real ground or basis. What we would call "dark" or "light" would be completely arbitrary. What we'd see as dark or light would indeed be dark or light to us, but there would be nothing in external reality resembling or grounding that perception. The most important implication of the theory of apoha or Davidson's triangulation argument is that this is impossible. Conceptual classes are formed in social processes based on real similarities and differences between things — about this key point Davidson and Dharmakīrti agree — and consequently, we cannot form completely random conceptual classes. Conceptual classes must be based on real properties of real things.

This then, leaves only the third, or middle, option: fuzzy classification, the kind of conceptual classification illustrated by the examples of "red" above and "mountain" in chapter 7, but as explained before, there are more vague or fuzzy boundaries between mountains and non-mountains than figure 8.4 suggests.[147]

The realization that kalpanā involves conceptual classes with somewhat arbitrary boundaries (as in the "fuzzy" picture in figure 8.4) can lead to two responses. One can look at the middle picture in figure 8.4, compare it to the picture on the right, and say, *"conceptual classes are not crisp, and therefore, language is deceptive and what we say about reality is false"*; or one can look at the middle picture, compare it to the picture on the left, and say *"conceptual classes are not random, and therefore, language is not completely deceptive and what we say about reality is at least partially true."* The first is apophasis; the second is kataphasis. This is all that the apophasis-kataphasis contrast amounts to — it is a difference in attitude not a substantial difference.[148]

Not all attitudes are equally suitable or productive, however. The apophatic attitude demands more from language than it can possibly deliver — a perfect match with independent/external reality — and then, because it cannot meet that impossible demand, rejects language as a tool to describe reality altogether. The problem is not language, the world, or the mismatch between the two, but that impossible demand. Giving up that impossible demand opens up a path to the realization of what

---

147 See the section "Realism (1) — Universals and (Anti-)Essentialism" in chapter 7.
148 In terms of the analogy at the end of the previous chapter, apophasis is saying that the sketch in figure 7.3 is a deception because it is different from the photograph in figure 7.2, while kataphasis is saying that the sketch is partially true because it is based on, grounded in, or a representation of the photograph.

language can do, and what it cannot. Hence, what is more deceptive than language itself, is the apophatic claim that language is deceptive.

While our concepts and conceptual boundaries do not neatly match external reality, language is not completely deceptive either. And moreover, in at least some cases, perhaps even many, we can become aware of the relative arbitrariness of our conceptual boundaries, such as those between "red" and "orange" or "mountain" and "hill." Language is a tool, and as long as we are aware of its limitations, it does not *need* to deceive us. This is, more or less, Zhiyi's view on language. It is a moderately kataphatic view. But the arguments that got us here are mostly based on Yogācāra.

9

Epistemic Justification, Science, and Austere Realism

One cannot have a language unless one shares a world and interacts with other creatures similar to oneself. This is one of the versions or implications of Donald Davidson's triangulation argument, but it also follows from Dharmakīrti's picture of concept formation.[1] The possibility of learning a language, and therefore the possibility of there being language, requires a second person that one can interact with and that is sufficiently similar to the learner, and a shared stimulus. A shared stimulus can only be an external stimulus. Hypothetically, the shared stimulus could be a delusion created in the minds of multiple creatures simultaneously by some evil demon, mad scientist, or computer program, but such a stimulus would still be external, that is, outside a single creature's mind.

Davidson refined his argument for the claim that a second person is necessary under the influence of Wittgenstein. Without a second person to correct the learner, the learner would be unable to distinguish a correct classification from a mistake, and without the ability to recognize mistakes, she would not be able to learn conceptual classes, and therefore a language, at all.[2] One could object against this Wittgensteinian argument that there may be other feedback mechanisms by means of which the learner could distinguish mistakes, but it is far from clear what those mechanisms could be, aside from further designs by an evil demon or mad scientist. It is important to realize that memory by itself is not sufficient because it is the reliability of memory itself that is in question here.

According to the Yogācāra philosopher Dharmakīrti, concepts are formed "through the conjunction of two factors: the experience of real objects and the social

---

1   See the last two sections of the previous chapter.
2   Donald Davidson, "The Second Person" (1992), SIO: 107–22; "The Social Aspect of Language" (1994), TLH: 109–25; "The Emergence of Thought" (1997), SIO: 123–34; "Interpretation: Hard in Theory, Easy in Practice," in *Interpretations and Causes*, ed. Mario De Caro (Dordrecht: Kluwer, 1999), 31–44; and "What Thought Requires" (2001), PoR: 135–49.
    In his "Intellectual Autobiography," Davidson suggested that he may have gotten the idea for his Wittgensteinian argument from Kripke. See Donald Davidson, "Intellectual Autobiography," in *The Philosophy of Donald Davidson*, ed. Lewis E. Hahn (Chicago: Open Court, 1999), 3–70, at 65–66, and Saul Kripke, *Wittgenstein on Rules and Private Language* (Cambridge: Harvard University Press, 1982). See also Ludwig Wittgenstein, *Philosophische Untersuchungen* (Oxford: Blackwell, 1953), and Claudine Verheggen, "Language, Thought and Knowledge," in Robert Myers and Claudine Verheggen, *Donald Davidson's Triangulation Argument: A Philosophical Inquiry* (New York: Routledge, 2016), 11–115.

process of language acquisition."³ In other words, concepts are formed in social interactions directed to shared, external stimuli, that is, in triangulation. What Davidson added to this fundamental insight is that concepts cannot be formed in any other way, and that, therefore, the fact that we have concepts proves the existence of other minds and a shared, external world.

This conclusion conflicts with the traditional interpretation of Yogācāra as idealist, but as argued in the previous chapter, most Yogācāra philosophers explicitly recognized external reality and only rejected the existence of things-as-they-appear, that is, they apophatically rejected the possibility of accurate *description* of ultimate or external reality, but not its existence.⁴ Furthermore, Yogācāra also emphatically rejected solipsism, and consequently, something like Davidson's conclusion should be acceptable to a non-dogmatic Yogācārin.

In Western philosophy, Davidson's conclusion has been rejected on grounds similar to the evil demon or mad-scientist "possibilities," but more often it is ignored or misunderstood. Supposedly, the argument fails to prove what it purports to prove because alternative explanations can be given. That these alternative explanations are exceedingly exotic does not matter in a widely shared view on philosophical methodology.

Davidson once remarked that "Rorty sees the history of Western philosophy as a confused and victorless battle between unintelligible skepticism and lame attempts to answer it."⁵ This is only a slight exaggeration both of much of mainstream Western philosophy and of Richard Rorty's view thereon.⁶ Indeed, a common strategy to refute one opponent's point of view (or to test one's own!) has always been to come up with some exotic skeptical "possibility," such as evil demons, brains in vats, and so forth. But the hypothetical skeptic can always come up with some extravagant story, some hypothetical possibility, and consequently, nothing survives the skeptical onslaught.

But this is exactly the approach to philosophy that pragmatism and Quinean naturalism reject.⁷ Philosophy is not a substitute for religion, aiming to provide new absolute truths, but rather one of the sciences, provisionally accepting the explanations that are best supported by evidence, and only until counter-evidence forces their rejection. Davidson rejected the label "pragmatist," which Rorty attributed to him, but his reflex to "tell the skeptic to get lost" is a very pragmatist one.⁸

The point is that, unless we have good reasons to believe that we are being deceived by evil demons or that we are brains in vats hooked up to computers delivering artificial stimulations, there is no reason to take such skeptical "possibilities" seriously. Given that we have language, and that by far the most plausible and par-

---

3   Georges Dreyfus, *Recognizing Reality: Dharmakīrti's Philosophy and Its Tibetan Interpretations* (Albany, SUNY Press, 1997), 227.
4   See the section "Yogācāra Realism" in chapter 8.
5   Donald Davidson, "Afterthoughts" (1987), SIO: 154–57, at 157.
6   Richard Rorty, *Philosophy and the Mirror of Nature* (Princeton: Princeton University Press, 1979). Considerably more subtle than Davidson's sketchy attribution, Rorty wrote that "Philosophy and the principal genre of modern philosophy have a symbiotic relationship. They live on another's death, and die on another's life" (114).
7   See the section "Naturalism" in chapter 1.
8   Davidson, "Afterthoughts," 157. For Rorty's characterization of Davidson as pragmatist, see Richard Rorty, "Pragmatism, Davidson and Truth" (1986), in *Objectivity, Relativism, and Truth: Philosophical Papers*, Vol. I (Cambridge: Cambridge University Press, 1991), 126–50.

simonious explanation we have for that fact is that we share a world outside our minds, we must accept that implication.

Yogācārins may have agreed up till this point, but Davidson went further. He argued that triangulation and other related arguments proved that most of our beliefs are true. According to Yogācāra, on the other hand, we are systematically mistaken. In the last pages of the previous chapter, I argued that what follows from triangulation and the Yogācāra theory of *apoha* is that, because our concepts are necessarily grounded in reality, we can only be mistaken in a limited sense. That is, we can mistake the conceptual boundaries we draw for real boundaries. We can be deluded to believe that our concepts "carve nature at is joints," to use a beloved metaphor of Western philosophy. But in many cases we can also learn to recognize that the conceptual boundaries between thisness and thatness (i.e., between red and orange, between mountain and hill, between tree and shrub, etc.) are often or even always arbitrary. They are not "given" by nature, but constructed by us in a social process by means of apoha.[9]

There are two ways of looking at this. We can take a negative, apophatic attitude and point out that language does not neatly map to external reality and, therefore, that we cannot describe reality. This is the approach of Yogācāra and much of Indian Buddhism in general. Or we can take a positive, kataphatic attitude and point out that because language is necessarily grounded in reality it is at least partially correct, and therefore, as long as we are careful, we can (and must!) use language to talk about external reality. This approach is characteristic for much of Chinese Buddhism and especially for Zhiyi 智顗 and the broader Tiantai/Tendai 天台 tradition he founded.[10]

Apophasis rejects language as a tool to describe reality because it cannot deliver what is demanded, namely, a perfect match with external reality. It is that demand that is the problem, however, and giving up that impossible demand allows a more balanced view of what language can do, and what it cannot. The apophatic claim that language is deceptive might be more deceptive than language itself, and consequently, we should side with Zhiyi's moderate and careful kataphasis. As explained before, language is a tool, and as long as we are aware of its limitations, it does not *need* to deceive us.

However, Davidson's claim that most of our beliefs are true goes much further than this. It goes, in fact, about as far as the this-worldly, *austere* realism of radical Buddhism, and consequently, what needs to be assessed is whether the view developed in the last sections of the previous chapter does lead us there indeed.

Avisaṃvāda

Our starting point is what follows from apoha and triangulation, namely, that when I believe that the flower I'm looking at is red, there is usually something there that can be more or less accurately described as a flower and as red. However, there may be, and almost certainly are, other, equally accurate and equally partial descriptions of whatever I am seeing as a red flower, that is, there are different perspectives on the same thing or suchness. Dōgen 道元 would have pointed out that a bee would be seeing something quite different if he would have used this example, but he also

---

9 See the section "*Apoha* and Its Implications" in chapter 8.
10 See chapter 8 and the section "From Nāgārjuna to Zhiyi" in chapter 2.

suggested that we can acquire some new and different perspectives (but probably not the bee's).¹¹

Furthermore, it is only usually the case that my red flower perception is really caused by something that is indeed in some sense a red flower. My determinate perception of the red flower as red flower is constructed out of *pratibhāsa* — unprocessed, indeterminate sensory impression — but not all pratibhāsa is genuine. A genuine pratibhāsa is caused by the external object that it is a pratibhāsa of, but Dharmakīrti argued that, sometimes due to darkness, eye defects, or other relevant circumstances, an object can fail to cause a genuine pratibhāsa. Only a non-contradictory or coherent pratibhāsa is genuine, which raises the question of how to distinguish false from genuine perceptions.

Dharmakīrti's answer to that question is not entirely clear, however. In the chapter on pramāṇas (sources or instruments of valid knowledge) of his *Pramāṇavārttika*, he wrote:

> A source/instrument of knowledge (*pramāṇa*) is uncontradicted (*avisaṃvādin*) acquaintance (*jñāna*). Non-contradictoriness [of the knowledge of a thing] is [that] thing's constant action (i.e., constant effect). [Non-contradictoriness also occurs when] verbal expressions communicate the intention [of the speaker].¹²

The key term in the passage is the adjective *avisaṃvādin*, which contrasts with *visaṃvādin* (the *a-* prefix means "not," like "un-" in English). *Visaṃvādin* means "contradictory," "disagreeing," "inconsistent," "incoherent," and so forth, and consequently, the most literal translations of *avisaṃvādin* are "uncontradicted," "non-contradictory," or "coherent."¹³

In the quoted passage, Dharmakīrti defines *pramāṇa* as avisaṃvāda, and the latter in turn as constancy of effect or successful communication of intention. The second criterion appears to apply to the interpretation of others; a valid cognition in such cases arises when one understands what the interpreted other means. The first criterion — constancy of effect — is less specific but also less obvious. In one of the earliest and most influential commentaries on Dharmakīrti's *Pramāṇavārttika*, Devendrabuddhi explained that sometimes

> one may not be certain of the difference between a [genuine] perception and a spurious perception when they occur; in such cases the actual perceptual awareness is known to be trustworthy [*avisaṃvādin*] through the engagement of a subsequent instrumental cognition.¹⁴

---

11   See the section "Relativism and Perspectivism in Yogācāra and Tiantai" in chapter 8.
12   pramāṇam avisaṃvādi jñānam [;] arthakriyāsthitiḥ | avisaṃvādanaṃ [;] śabde'py abhiprāyanivedanāt — Dharmakīrti, *Pramāṇavārttika* (6th/7th c.), §2.1.
13   *Avisaṃvādin* is translated by Vittorio van Bijlert, *Epistemology and Spiritual Authority: The Development of Epistemology and Logic in the Old Nyāya and the Buddhist School of Epistemology with an Annotated Translation of Dharmakīrti's Pramāṇavārttika II (Pramāṇasiddhi) Volumes 1–7* (Vienna: ATBS, 1989) and John Dunne, *Foundations of Dharmakīrti's Philosophy* (Boston: Wisdom, 2004), as "trustworthy" and by Dreyfus, *Recognizing Reality*, as "nondeceptive"
14   Devendrabuddhi, *Pramāṇavārttikapañjikā* (7th c.), trans. Dunne, *Foundations of Dharmakīrti's Philosophy*, 377.

In other words, we can trust that a perception of a thing is genuine if it coheres with subsequent perceptions or other cognitions, such as inference. Devendrabuddhi also suggested that the same criterion does not apply to inferential knowledge, which makes sense given that valid inference is already coherent by definition. An impression, then, cannot be taken at face value but must be examined and tested before accepting it.

While this may not sound like a particularly exotic idea, it contrasts sharply with the traditional conception of the aims and scope of epistemology in the West. Devendrabuddhi's interpretation of Dharmakīrti reminds more of scientific practice — examining and testing — than of Western epistemology. The aim in the latter has typically been to identify an infallible foundation for knowledge, but in Dharmakīrti's view there is no such infallible foundation. Uninterpreted perception (pratibhāsa) can *always* be wrong, and the only way to find out whether it is genuine or spurious in some particular case is to test whether it coheres with other cognitions, that is, with what else we already know or can find out.

The comparison with scientific practice may appear somewhat anachronistic, but the point is not that Dharmakīrti (or Devendrabuddhi) advocated what we now consider to be the scientific method. Rather, the point is that, contrary to mainstream Western epistemology, he did not separate epistemic justification from how a serious scholar (such as a philosopher or monk, scientist, and so forth) gains knowledge in practice; he did not look for firmer foundations. Furthermore, what Dharmakīrti or Devendrabuddhi taught about the practical, scholarly project of gaining knowledge is quite similar to the most general principles of scientific methodology. Theodor Stcherbatsky (Фёдор Щербатской), the father of Western academic study of Buddhist logic and epistemology, reached a similar conclusion.

> The Buddhists insist that if an idea has arisen it is not at all enough for maintaining that it is true and that it agrees with reality. There is as yet no necessary connection between them and a discrepancy is possible. At this stage cognition is absolutely unreliable. But later on, when its origin has been examined, when it has been found to agree with experience, when its efficacy has been ascertained, only then can we maintain that it represents truth and we can repudiate all objections to its being correct.[15]

Hence, a belief is not justified until "its origin has been examined," until it has been tested and "found to agree with experience," and until we know its effects and causes. In very general terms, these are what we now consider to be standard scientific procedures and criteria. Although Stcherbatsky was probably influenced by the demythologized and rationalized Buddhism common in academic circles around that time,[16] his interpretation should not be dismissed as an example of this rationalist bias. Dharmakīrti did indeed recommend to "examine origins" to see whether a source is reliable; "agreement with experience" is one way of putting Devendrabuddhi's interpretation of avisaṃvāda; and causal efficiency or having effects was for

---

15 Theodor Stcherbatsky, *Buddhist Logic*, Vol. 1 (Delhi: Motilal Banarsidass, 1993), 67. Originally published in Russian as *Теория Познания и Логика по Учению Позднейших Буддистов* in 1903. The first English edition, translated by himself, was published in 1930.

16 See the introduction to chapter 2. See also the section "Metaphysics, Rationality, and Free Inquiry" in chapter 5.

Dharmakīrti the most important criterion to decide the reality or unreality of something. Furthermore, "constancy of effect" was also explicitly mentioned as a mark of avisaṃvāda in the passage from the *Pramāṇavārttika* quoted above.[17]

Like Dharmakīrti, Quine did not separate epistemic justification from scholarly knowledge acquisition. He repudiated "the Cartesian dream of a foundation for scientific certainty firmer than scientific method itself."[18] Instead of this "Cartesian dream," which he attributed to "the old epistemologists," he argued for a naturalized epistemology[19] that does not seek "a firmer base for science than science itself" but that instead models itself after science. Doing naturalized epistemology is just doing science, and "so we are free to use the very fruits of science in investigating its roots."[20]

Western theories of epistemic justification have been predominantly foundationalist: they claim that there is some kind of foundational mental content that justifies our beliefs, but that does not require any epistemic justification itself. According to rationalist foundationalism, that foundational mental content consists of self-evident a priori truths. There are few plausible candidates for the status of self-evident a priori truth,[21] however, and surely not enough to build a solid foundation for the rather large structure of human knowledge, and because of that (among other reasons), rationalist foundationalism is generally rejected in favor of empiricist foundationalism. According to the latter, the foundational mental content that justifies our beliefs is something that represents or mirrors reality, something like sense data.[22] The foundational mental content itself usually plays no active role in the foundationalist picture; it merely (re-)presents the world to us, and our beliefs are justified in as far as they match that (re-)presentation, and thus, reality itself.

Philosophers associated with the Quinean naturalist or (neo-)pragmatist tradition (such as Davidson, Rorty, and Hilary Putnam) have argued that foundationalism is incoherent. Putnam, for example, wrote that "the notion of comparing our systems of beliefs with unconceptualized reality to see if they match makes no sense,"[23] and similarly, Davidson called the idea of "a confrontation between what we believe and reality" "absurd."[24] Their point is that we cannot get outside our beliefs to compare those with reality; rather, "nothing can count as a reason for holding a belief except another belief."[25] Or as Rorty put it, "nothing counts as justification unless by reference to what we already accept, and there is no way to get outside our beliefs and our language so as to find some test other than coherence."[26]

---

17   For translations of the most important passages of Dharmakīrti's *Pramāṇavārttika* and some commentaries, see Van Bijlert, *Epistemology and Spiritual Authority*, 115–68, and Dunne, *Foundations of Dharmakīrti's Philosophy*, 374–90. For more extensive discussion on Dharmakīrti's and his commentators' ideas on epistemic justification, see Dreyfus, *Recognizing Reality*, chapters 16 and 17.
18   W.V.O. Quine, *Pursuit of Truth*, rev. edn. (Cambridge: Harvard University Press, 1992), 19.
19   W.V.O. Quine, "Epistemology Naturalized" (1969), OROE: 69–90.
20   W.V.O. Quine, *From Stimulus to Science* (Cambridge: Harvard University Press, 1995), 16.
21   According to Quine there are none.
22   As mentioned before in chapter 8, pratibhāsa may seem superficially like sense data, but contrary to most conceptions of sense data, pratibhāsa is indeterminate and non-conceptual, and even more importantly, it does not justify beliefs.
23   Hilary Putnam, *Reason, Truth and History* (Cambridge: Cambridge University Press, 1981), 130.
24   Donald Davidson, "A Coherence Theory of Truth and Knowledge" (1983), SIO: 137–53, at 137.
25   Ibid., 141.
26   Rorty, *Philosophy and the Mirror of Nature*, 178.

To Dharmakīrti the idea of comparing beliefs to reality would probably have sounded even crazier than it did to Putnam, Davidson, or Rorty. Ultimate reality is by definition beyond language, and consequently, there is no way a conceptual belief can "match" to anything in reality. As far as I can see, Dharmakīrti did not explicitly infer from this premise that coherence is the only possible criterion of epistemic justification, but he did argue for something very much like that criterion anyway. *Avisaṃvāda* means "coherence," or "non-contradictoriness." In Devendrabuddhi's interpretation, avisaṃvāda is coherence with further cognitions. And in Stcherbatsky's summary, justification depends on coherence with the results of further examination and experience and on coherent effects.

Objections to the Coherence Principle

According to coherence theories of justification — not to be confused with coherence theories of truth[27] — what justifies a belief is coherence with a larger set of beliefs. The main argument for such coherentism is that, if there can be no direct confrontation between beliefs and reality, this is the only other option. There are, however, several counterarguments and objections, as is usually the case in philosophy.

One might object, for example, that beliefs do not justify anything and that only "evidence" justifies, but that objection would miss the point, as evidence consists itself of beliefs. The evidence for my belief that the weather is nice is not that the sun is shining, but my *belief* that the sun is shining; without the latter belief, I would have no evidence. Someone else might have evidence, of course, but that only means that that someone else has an appropriate belief.

Another objection against coherentism is that, if all that justification requires is that a belief does not conflict with other beliefs the believer holds, then different believers may have justified but contradictory beliefs. To illustrate this, consider the following scenario:

> John believes that cats are robots carefully crafted by aliens to spy on us. Xiuying believes this is not true. John's belief (which I'll call "*C*") does not conflict with any of his other beliefs and neither does Xiuying's belief conflict with any of her other beliefs. Consequently, John's belief that *C* is justified, and so is Xiuying's belief that not-*C*. But *C* and not-*C* are contradictory (and thus incoherent) beliefs and therefore cannot both be justified.

The most obvious response to this scenario is to relativize justification. Then, *C* is justified for John and not-*C* is justified for Xiuying. However, that is not the response that most coherentists would give because this objection to coherentism rests on a mistake: it is not coherence with some of the beliefs someone happens to have that make some specific belief justified, but coherence with *justified* beliefs. In other

---

27 According to the coherence theory of truth, coherence makes a statement or belief *true*. Whether that idea makes sense is quite debatable (I think it does not), but more important is that it is a very different idea from what is discussed here. A coherence theory of justification merely claims that coherence with other beliefs, such as evidential beliefs and perceptual beliefs, gives one justification, or the right kind of reasons, to believe that some specific belief is true. One can, however, have the right reasons to believe that something is true, while that something unbeknownst to the believer is actually false. On the distinction between truth and justification, see the introduction to part II.

words, a belief is justified if it does not conflict with any other justified belief a believer holds. John probably has some unjustified beliefs about animal physiology, robotics, exobiology, and so forth, and those unjustified beliefs cannot justify his belief *C*.

However, coherence with *un*justified beliefs does not make a belief *un*justified, so this response leaves the door open for another objection: *C* might not conflict with any of John's remaining *justified* beliefs because he has no justified beliefs about cats, robots, and aliens. This objection is also illustrated in the following scenario:

> Sandeep believes that 65,537 is the largest prime number.[28] Sandeep has no other beliefs about 65,537 or about prime numbers. Therefore, Sandeep's belief does not conflict with any of his other beliefs, and is thus, justified.

Davidson's response to this kind of objection was that this scenario is impossible, and the same response is available to a Yogācārin. There are no isolated beliefs. It is not possible to have a single belief about 65,537 or about prime numbers or about anything. To believe anything at all about prime numbers — or to even have the concept of a prime number — one must have very many related beliefs. And many of these beliefs and the concepts that figure in them arise together in mutual dependency. This follows as much from Davidson's theory of triangulation as it does from Dignāga's and Dharmakīrti's theory of apoha.[29]

A closely related objection to coherentism was put forward by Moritz Schlick in response to Otto Neurath. Like Davidson, Putnam, and Rorty, Neurath had argued several decades earlier for a coherence theory of justification on the ground that the only evidence for a belief could be other beliefs. In "Sociology in Physicalism" he wrote:

> *Statements are compared with statements,* not with "experience," not with a "world," nor with something else. [...] Every new statement is confronted with the totality of available statements that have already been brought into harmony with each other. *A statement is called correct when it can be incorporated* [into this totality]. What cannot be incorporated is rejected as incorrect.[30]

Schlick interpreted Neurath's coherentism as a coherence theory of truth, rather than justification, and argued that

> [a]nyone who is serious about coherence as the sole criterion of truth must believe that some fairy tale that has been imagined is just as true as a historical report or the sentences in a chemistry textbook, if only the fairy tale is devised so well that there is no contradiction anywhere. I can paint a grotesquely adventurous

---

28 It is not, but it is probably the largest Fermat Prime.
29 On apoha, see the section "*Apoha* and Its Implications" in chapter 8. For Davidson's arguments, see Donald Davidson, "The Problem of Objectivity" (1995), PoR: 3–18; "Interpretation"; and "What Thought Requires."
30 Aussagen werden mit Aussagen verglichen, nicht mit "Erlebnissen," nicht mit einer "Welt," noch mit sonst etwas. [...] Jede neue Aussage wird mit der Gesamtheit der vorhandenen, bereits miteinander in Einklang gebrachten, Aussagen konfrontiert. Richtig heißt eine Aussage dann, wenn man sie eingliedern kann. Was man nicht eingliedern kann, wird als unrichtig abgelehnt. — Otto Neurath, "Soziologie im Physikalismus," *Erkenntnis* 2 (1931): 393–431, at 403. Italics in original.

world with the help of [my] imagination — the coherence philosopher must believe in the truth of my description if only I ensure the mutual compatibility of my claims, and as a precaution, avoid any collision with the common description of the world by moving the setting of my story to a distant star where no observation is possible.[31]

In Schlick's view, this reveals the "logical impossibility of the coherence theory," "because with it, I can arrive at any number of consistent systems of sentences that are incompatible with each other."[32] However, according to Davidson, Schlick's objection makes no sense for reasons that are available to the Yogācārin as well. Davidson writes that "it's not clear what it means to say I could 'arrive' at various systems, since I do not invent my beliefs; most of them are not voluntary."[33] This is a key point: we do not choose most of our beliefs.[34] Rather, our most basic beliefs are caused by the world. Things in the world may not *justify* my beliefs, but they certainly *cause* them, and about this Davidson and Yogācāra agree. And consequently, in normal circumstances I cannot genuinely believe a fairy tale I knowingly devised myself.[35]

The insight that our most basic beliefs, like my belief that it is nice weather when I am writing this sentence, are caused by the world also plays a key role in a response to the last objection to coherentism considered here. This objection, which is best known in its presentation by Erik Olsson, is rather more technical than the previous ones.[36] The argument follows C.I. Lewis, the most influential mid-twentieth century pragmatist and a teacher of Quine, in conceiving of coherence in probabilistic terms, but the kind of coherentism it refutes is not Lewis's.[37] Olsson's objection depends on a specific conception of the distinction between foundationalism and anti-foundationalism and on the assumption that that form of anti-foundationalism is an essential element of coherentism.

According to foundationalism, evidence justifies a proposition or belief. In probabilistic terms, the probability that A is the case given evidence E is larger than the

---

31 Wer es ernst meint mit der Kohärenz als alleinigem Kriterium der Wahrheit, muß beliebig erdichtete Märchen für ebenso wahr halten wie einen historischen Bericht oder die Sätze in einem Lehrbuch der Chemie, wenn nur die Märchen so gut erfunden sind, daß nirgends ein Widerspruch auftritt. Ich kann eine grotesk abenteuerliche Welt mit Hilfe der Phantasie ausmalen: der Kohärenzphilosoph muß an die Wahrheit meiner Beschreibung glauben, wenn ich nur für die gegenseitige Verträglichkeit meiner Behauptungen sorge und zur Vorsicht noch jede Kollision mit der gewohnten Weltbeschreibung vermeide, indem ich den Schauplatz meiner Erzählung auf einen entfernten Stern verlege, wo keine Beobachtung mehr möglich ist. — Moritz Schlick, "Über das Fundament der Erkenntnis," *Erkenntnis* 4 (1934): 79–99, at 86.
32 Damit zeigt sich die logische Unmöglichkeit der Kohärenzlehre; sie gibt überhaupt kein eindeutiges Kriterium der Wahrheit, denn ich kann mit ihr zu beliebig vielen in sich widerspruchsfreien Satzsystemen gelangen, die aber unter sich unverträglich sind. — Ibid., 87.
33 Donald Davidson, "Empirical Content" (1982), SIO: 159–75, at 173.
34 Some people claim that we can choose religious beliefs. Regardless of whether that is true, the notion of belief here is not that notion. To believe something just means to hold it true. (See the introduction to part II.) And one cannot hold true what one knows to be false.
35 The phrase "in normal circumstances" must be emphasized here, because there certainly are scenarios in which people come to believe in their own stories. Nevertheless, the reason why people sometimes accept a story as true is that they come to believe that it coheres with a substantial subset of their other beliefs.
36 Erik Olsson, "What Is the Problem of Coherence and Truth?" *The Journal of Philosophy* 99 (2002): 246–72, and *Against Coherence: Truth, Probability, and Justification* (Oxford: Clarendon, 2005).
37 C.I. Lewis, *An Analysis of Knowledge and Valuation* (LaSalle: Open Court, 1946). Lewis used the term "congruence" rather than "coherence."

probability that A is the case without that evidence. This can be represented formally as follows:

[FJ] $P(A|E) > P(A)$

Coherentists reject foundationalism, defined as [FJ], and the rejection of [FJ] implies that a single piece of evidence E does not increase the probability of A being the case, that is,

[AF] $P(A|E) = P(A)$

What increases the probability of A, according to coherentism (in this interpretation), is not a single piece of evidence but coherence between multiple pieces of evidence. Thus, if there are two pieces of evidence for A, such as two witness reports E_1 and E_2, then the probability that A is the case given these two witness reports is larger than the probability of A by itself, that is, without these witness report:

[CJ] $P(A|E_1, E_2) > P(A)$

The supposed problem for coherentism arises from the fact that these two witness reports must be independent from each other. If the two witnesses align their stories *before* they report them, then there effectively is just one witness report.[38] However, if E_1 and E_2 are indeed independent from each other, meaning that

$P(E_1|E_2, A) = P(E_1|A)$ and $P(E_2|E_1, A) = P(E_2|A)$

and the same for not-A; then it follows therefrom, together with [AF] and Bayes's theorem,[39] that

$P(A|E_1, E_2) = P(A)$

which contradicts [CJ] and thereby shows that coherentism is incoherent.

The problem in this argument is its definition of anti-foundationalism as [AF]. That definition, together with Bayes's theorem, implies that

$P(E|A) = P(E)$

or in words, that the probability of the "evidence" E given that A is the case is identical to the probability of E even if A would not be the case. Hence, the so-called "evidence" is independent from whatever it is supposed to be evidence for. That, obviously, makes no sense.

---

38 This problem was mentioned before in the context of attempts to reconstruct the "original" teachings of the historical Buddha. See the section "The Idea of an 'Original Buddhism'" in chapter 5.
39 $P(A|E) = [\,P(A) \times P(E|A)\,] / P(E)$

Indeed, few coherentists have accepted [AF].[40] They typically argue for some form of "weak foundationalism" that accepts [FJ] and thus rejects [AF].[41] According to Lewis, for example, the individual witness reports E_1 and E_2 must have some credibility by themselves.[42] Davidson and Putnam go further than that: the credibility of the individual witness reports is not a requirement but a natural necessity. Because our perceptions and perceptual beliefs are caused by things in the world, most of our most basic beliefs are true.[43] A Yogācārin would not, and should not, follow Davidson and Putnam all the way.

Davidson's claim is that most of our most basic beliefs are true, but this notion of basic beliefs presupposes that there also are other, non-basic beliefs. There is no sharp boundary between these categories and neither are they separable in practice. My beliefs that it is nice weather outside or that I am sitting at a table when writing this are at the basic end of the spectrum, but both beliefs involve very many other beliefs that are far less basic. I see the table I'm sitting at as table because I have a concept "table," but that concept is not an atom. It follows from the theories of apoha and triangulation that it is inherently part of a network of associated concepts and beliefs.[44] This network includes beliefs about what kinds of things tables are and what other things belong to that kind and how to distinguish them, beliefs about how tables are used and where they are typically found, how they are made and what they are made of, and so forth. All of these associated beliefs give meaning to my concept of table. Without a rather large collection of such associated beliefs, I could not have a concept of "table" at all.

Quine sometimes used the metaphor "web of belief" to describe how our beliefs hang together.[45] Some beliefs are closer to the center of that web; others are closer to the edges. The beliefs furthest at the edges are what connects the web to the outside world. Those are what Davidson called our most basic beliefs. My belief that I'm sitting at a table right now is such a basic belief. My belief that tables are a kind of furniture is a little bit closer to the center. And my belief that tables have a flat surface larger than a square foot and between one and three-and-a-half feet high is a bit closer still. There is a kind of hierarchy in our beliefs from very basic to increasingly abstract and theoretical beliefs. Ideas that are closer to the center are not just further removed from the world; they are also more widely connected. The more central a

---

40 The only *possible* exception I am aware of is Laurence BonJour, *The Structure of Empirical Knowledge* (Cambridge: Harvard University Press, 1985), but he did not explicitly endorse [AF] either.

41 In addition to C.I. Lewis and Davidson, two other interesting examples are Susan Haack, *Evidence and Inquiry: A Pragmatist Reconstruction of Epistemology* (New York: Prometheus, 2009) and Paul Thagard, *Coherence in Thought and Action* (Cambridge: MIT Press, 2000). Not coincidentally, both are heavily influenced by pragmatism.

42 Lewis, *An Analysis of Knowledge and Valuation*. It is also on this ground that Lewis rejected objections like Schlick's. He wrote, "[i]f [...] there were no initial presumption attaching the mnemically presented; no valid supposition of a real connection with past experience; then no extent of congruity [...] would give rise to any eventual credibility. The coherence of a novel, or of the daydreams we are aware of fabricating as we go along, can never have the slightest weight toward crediting the content of them as fact, no matter how detailed and mutually congruent such items may be" (357).

43 Hilary Putnam, *The Threefold Cord: Mind, Body, and World* (New York: Columbia University Press, 1999). For Davidson's arguments and references, see above as well as the last section of chapter 8. For a comparison of Davidson's and Putnam's coherentism, see Lajos Brons, "Putnam and Davidson on Coherence, Truth, and Justification," *The Science of Mind* 54 (2016): 51–70.

44 See the last two sections of chapter 8.

45 Most famously in the title of W.V.O. Quine and J.S. Ullian, *The Web of Belief*, 2nd edn. (New York: Random House, 1978).

belief in the web, the greater the number of other beliefs that somehow depend on it. The belief that 1 + 1 = 2 is a very central belief. Almost everything else we believe is directly or indirectly connected to that belief. (Every belief that involves quantity depends on the belief that 1 + 1 = 2, for example.) Quine appealed to the web of belief mostly to explain that when counter-evidence forces us to revise our beliefs, we start close to the edges of the web and never at the center, but there is another important aspect of the web metaphor that matters here.

The more central a belief in the web of belief, the more other beliefs will depend on it, but this also implies that it is explicitly tested for coherence on a very regular basis. Beliefs that are not as central but are not on the edge of the web either are not as well-connected, however. This is the zone of more or less theoretical beliefs that are not as abstract and general as the belief that 1 + 1 = 2 and that are not as practical and specific as my belief that I'm sitting at a table right now — they are somewhere in between. They are relatively specific and, therefore, not as often appealed to as "1 + 1 = 2" and the like. Because of that, they are not tested for coherence with other relatively specific beliefs as frequently either. Consequently, this middle zone between abstract central beliefs and basic perceptual beliefs is the weakest part of our webs of belief. Because the beliefs that populate it are not supported as well as those in the center or at the edges, if there are incoherences in our webs of belief, this is where most of them will be found.

Most of the beliefs I rely on in my attempts to makes sense of, and understand the world around me are located in this intermediary zone. And because they are located in this zone, they are not directly grounded in external reality like basic, perceptual beliefs and rarely if ever tested for coherence with more distant parts of the web of belief. Consequently, while the basic conceptual classifications made by a perspective or conceptual scheme are at least somewhat reliable due to their grounding through apoha in reality, there is no ground to make the same assumption about further, associated beliefs about the things that belong to those classes. Or in other words, the fact that my having the concept of "mountain" precludes the possibility that there is nothing in external reality resembling mountains at all does not imply that my further, associated beliefs about mountains are trustworthy as well.

Perspectives and Science

The limited reliability of our less basic beliefs makes Lewis's approach to coherentism as something like "congruence" between witness reports particularly relevant. In Lewis's example, there are several "relatively unreliable witnesses who independently tell the same circumstantial story."

> For any one of these reports, taken singly, the extent to which it confirms what is reported may be slight. And antecedently, the probability of what is reported may also be small. But congruence of the reports establishes a high probability of what they agree upon, by principles of probability determination which are familiar: on any other hypothesis than that of truth-telling, this agreement is highly unlikely; [...] And the one hypothesis which itself is congruent with this agreement becomes thereby commensurably well established. It is the possible

role of congruence in the determination of empirical truth which is dramatized in detective stories and mystery tales.[46]

Our situations are much like any single one of these witnesses. The extent to which our perspectives accurately "report" independent or ultimate reality may be slight, but it is not zero because perspectives are not arbitrary. And the congruence of perspectives "establishes a high probability of what they agree upon." However, as in Lewis's example, this is only the case if the perspectives are independent from each other. And as in that example, the more we would want to know about what the witnesses or perspectives are reporting about, the further removed those should be from each other. Two witnesses perceiving the same scene from very different points of view, with very different backgrounds and interests, and differing in other relevant ways will tell us more about what really happened than two very similar witnesses standing close to each other. Similarly, two similar perspectives will give us less information about the real nature of some thing than two radically different perspectives.

This latter point reveals an important disanalogy. While we can measure the distance and differences between the points of view of two witnesses, we can not get outside our perspectives to measure the difference between two or more of them; there is no "God's Eye point of view."[47] But perhaps, we do not really have to. The witnesses could together construct a better but not perfect story of what happened than any one of their individual stories by comparing their accounts; they do not necessarily need a detective to do that for them. And similarly, we may be able to get a better, but not perfect, understanding of the world by comparing our perspectives and learning new ones.

"Of all the numerous aspects of things, we can see and understand only those that we have developed the capability for," wrote Dōgen.[48] We are not doomed to be constrained forever by our provincial schemes and perspectives; we can develop the capability for new ways of seeing and understanding. Nevertheless, there are limits to what and how we can learn to see. Dōgen also wrote that even though we believe that we "have a deep understanding of the substance that fills seas and rivers, we still do not know how dragons and fish understand and use water."[49] And we never will. As Thomas Nagel pointed out, the only way to understand what it is like to be a bat is by being a bat, and that is not something we can do.[50] Similarly, the only way to understand what it is like for a fish to perceive water is by being a fish.

There are, then, limits to what we can learn to see. There are always further perspectives, and many of those are inherently out of our reach. This should give us reason for epistemological humility — for the acknowledgment that we can know far less than we might like to know and certainly far less than we like to think we know — but not for skepticism.

We may not be able to see the world as a fish or a *preta*, but we can learn other languages, for example. And if phenomenal or conventional reality is largely a conceptual or linguistic construction as Dignāga and Dharmakīrti suggest, then this

---

46 Lewis, *An Analysis of Knowledge and Valuation*, 346.
47 Putnam, *Reason, Truth and History*, 49.
48 See the section "Relativism and Perspectivism in Yogācāra and Tiantai" in chapter 8 for the full quote.
49 See the section "From Saichō to Nichiren" in chapter 2 for the full quote.
50 Thomas Nagel, "What Is It Like to Be a Bat?" *The Philosophical Review* 83, no. 4 (1974): 435–50.

would be an important means of acquiring new perspectives.⁵¹ In Western thought, linguistic relativism, the idea that the languages we speak strongly influence how we perceive the world around us, has precursors in the thought of early-nineteenth-century philosophers and scientists like Johann Gottfried Herder and Wilhelm von Humboldt, but it is most closely associated with the ideas of early-twentieth-century linguists Edward Sapir and especially Benjamin Lee Whorf. The latter wrote:

> We dissect nature along lines laid down by our native languages. The categories and types that we isolate from the world of phenomena we do not find there because they stare every observer in the face; on the contrary, the world is presented in a kaleidoscopic flux of impressions which has to be organized by our minds — and this means largely by the linguistic systems in our minds. We cut nature up, organize it into concepts, and ascribe significance as we do, largely because we are parties to an agreement to organize it in this way — an agreement that holds throughout our speech community and is codified in the patterns of our language. The agreement is, of course, an implicit and unstated one, *but its terms are absolutely obligatory*; we cannot talk at all except by subscribing to the organization and classification of data which the agreement decrees. This fact is very significant for modern science, for it means that no individual is free to describe nature with absolute impartiality but is constrained to certain modes of interpretation even while he thinks himself most free. The person most nearly free in such respects would be a linguist familiar with very many widely different linguistic systems. [...] We are thus introduced to a new principle of relativity, which holds that all observers are not led by the same physical evidence to the same picture of the universe, unless their linguistic backgrounds are similar, or can in some way be calibrated.⁵²

Much of what Whorf says in this quote is in agreement with what was concluded at the end of the previous chapter, although the expression "kaleidoscopic flux of impressions" claims more about *pratibhāsa* (unprocessed, indeterminate sensory impression), or what is causing it, than we may be able to know. Parts of this passage are quoted in almost every text that discusses Whorf or linguistic relativism, but a sentence that is nearly always omitted is also the sentence that is most relevant here: "[t]he person most nearly free [to describe nature with absolute impartiality] would be a linguist familiar with very many widely different linguistic systems."⁵³ This, more or

---

51 It is not one they consider, however. As mentioned in chapter 8, Dignāga and Dharmakīrti appear to assume that there is only one conceptual scheme, which is shared by all languages or, in other words, that all languages classify in the same way and merely differ in the labels they put on the various classes. Quine called this mistaken idea the "myth of the museum" ("Ontological Relativity" [1969], OROE: 26–68, at 27), but whether it really can be attributed to Dignāga or Dharmakīrti is unclear.
52 Benjamin Lee Whorf, "Science and Linguistics" (1940), in *Language, Thought, and Reality: Selected Writings of Benjamin Lee Whorf*, ed. John Carroll (Cambridge: MIT Press, 1956), 207–19, at 213–14. Italics in original.
53 Davidson omits this sentence in his influential "On the Very Idea of a Conceptual Scheme" (1974), ITI: 183–98, for example, most likely because he did not read Whorf and copied the quote from another source. Significantly, the omitted sentence conflicts with Davidson's interpretation of Whorf. See Lajos Brons, "Applied Relativism and Davidson's Arguments against Conceptual Schemes," *The Science of Mind* 49 (2011): 221–40.

less, follows from Lewis's analogy: the more perspectives you can combine, the more you know about what they are perspectives on.

Whorf assumed that natural languages are the only kinds of perspectives that matter, and implicitly also that different linguistic perspectives are independent from each other and that all languages together represent all possible perspectives. Without these assumptions of independence and universal coverage, there would be no reason to assume that knowing many languages would give one the ability "to describe nature with absolute impartiality." Unfortunately, these assumptions are groundless. Natural languages are the result of an evolutionary process — they mutate, spread, split up, merge, and die out. Many languages are related[54] and, thus, not independent, and there is absolutely no reason to assume that the five percent or so of all historical languages that are spoken today represent all possible variation. It is much more likely that they do not.[55]

Furthermore, as already pointed out above, natural languages are not the only perspectives — a fish's perspective is not a linguistic perspective. Natural languages are not even the only perspectives available to us. Perspectives are ways of seeing and understanding. As such, they do many things — they cut up and classify (as suggested by Whorf), they explain and relate, they enable us to see things that we otherwise would not or could not, or they enable us to see them in very different ways, and so forth. Natural languages do some of that, but not all. Life/world-views, such as religions and cultural worldviews, do some of that,[56] but not all. Various tools and instruments also do some of that, but again, not all, and so do measurement procedures, experiments, and much more. To measure is to classify, and new measurements classify in new ways, thus offering new perspectives. Experiments allow one to see things in different ways or from different perspectives or to see and understand something one could not see or understand before. The business of science, then, is to open up new perspectives. But science does more than that: it also combines and integrates perspectives, and spawns new ones.

Science is not a single perspective but a collection of perspectives most of which resulted from clashes between other, previous perspectives. Science continuously invents and adds new perspectives, new languages, new ways of seeing and understanding, and so forth. And it does so largely by applying standards of coherence. "Standards" is plural here, because there is more than one kind of coherence, as already illustrated but not yet made explicit in the foregoing.

Perhaps, the most fundamental distinction between kinds of coherence is that between internal and external coherence. Lewis's witness report analogy is concerned with external coherence, that is, the coherence of one story with other stories. However, as Lewis pointed out, the witness reports must have some individual credibility and for that they must be internally coherent as well. A witness who contradicts herself is not a credible witness. The difference between internal and external coherence, then, is the difference between contradictions within one witness report and contradictions between multiple witness reports, respectively. Because different wit-

---

54   Perhaps, all languages are related, but languages leave no fossil record, and because of that, we cannot track their history far enough back to get anywhere close to a single ancestor.
55   Lajos Brons, "Language Death and Diversity: Philosophical and Linguistic Implications," *The Science of Mind* 52 (2014): 243–60.
56   On the notion of a life/world-view, see the section "Between Science and Religion" in chapter 6.

ness reports are like different perspectives, external coherence can also be thought of as cross-perspectival coherence, that is, the coherence between perspectives.

In science, external coherence includes the coherence between different theories. A major criterion of good science is that theories should not contradict other accepted scientific theories. Another kind of external coherence is the coherence between a hypothesis and its empirical confirmation, in an experiment or subsequent experience. Devendrabuddhi's interpretation of Dharmakīrti as coherence with subsequent or other cognition(s) includes both of these kinds of external coherence. Dharmakīrti's assertion that coherence (*avisaṃvāda*) is constancy of effect can also be understood as referring to diachronic coherence, or coherence over time. If what is supposed to be the same cause has different effects at different times, then that is a diachronic incoherence, and it most likely means that there are possibly subtle differences between causes that were mistakenly believed to be the same.

All of these kinds of coherence matter in science, and to a large extent, science is driven by incoherence. Incoherence between theories or between theories and observations, diachronic incoherence, and other kinds of incoherence are what leads to new hypotheses, new experiments, new theories, and therefore, new perspectives. In as far as it follows the standards of coherence, science is the most coherent integration of all perspectives available to us. While this justifies us to accept the findings of science (again, in as far as it follows these standards), there are a number of important caveats.

First, as Dōgen pointed out, we do not and cannot know how fish perceive water. There are perspectives that are fundamentally out of our reach. And consequently, regardless of how much we think we know about something, there is always more to that "thing," more than we'll ever know, more than we can know, more than language can express.[57]

Second, while there are perspectives that are fundamentally out of reach, there are also many perspectives that are only contingently out of reach. Science keeps creating, adding, and integrating new perspectives. And because of that, scientific insights change. Scientific theories are always accepted provisionally and can in principle be refuted by counter-evidence. This, however, does not just apply to scientific knowledge, but to everything we think we know. There are no foundations, and therefore, coherence is the only possible criterion of justification. Because new beliefs, new experience, or new perspectives can always make incoherent what previously appeared to be coherent, nothing is immune from revision in principle. (Even though revision of some beliefs — like "1 + 1 = 2" — is very unlikely.)

Perhaps, you have noticed that this means that the argument has become circular here. I started by assuming methodological naturalism in chapter 1 and have now inferred such methodological naturalism from the metaphysics and epistemology built in part on that methodological foundation. There is a very similar circularity in Quine's appeal to science as a foundation for science. Quine accepted that circularity because it is not vicious,[58] and I'll follow his example. There is no real alternative anyway. Coherentism makes circularity unavoidable — if mutual coherence

---

57 This does not necessarily mean that any perspective that is out of reach would teach us anything relevant or interesting if it could be somehow brought within reach. I'm not sure whether we'd learn anything relevant or interesting if we'd be able to see water like fish, for example.
58 Peter Hylton, *Quine* (New York: Routledge, 2007), and Paul Gregory, *Quine's Naturalism: Language, Theory, and the Knowing Subject* (London: Continuum, 2008).

mutually justifies beliefs, then every justification is ultimately circular. And because circularity is unavoidable, we should not worry whether some argument is circular, but whether the circle is large enough. Furthermore, as Paul Gregory has pointed out, the foundationalist approach to epistemic justification involves some circularity as well,[59] and while circularity is not necessarily a problem for a coherentist, for a foundationalist it certainly is.

Third, as already mentioned in chapter 6,[60] not all science is "ideal." Not all science is coherent. Some theories may be held on to regardless of counter-evidence and conflicts with other accepted theories. Science is a human enterprise and humans are motivated by a variety of things, but one of our strongest motivations is to defend the stories we most firmly believe in, the life/world-views that help us to make sense of the world and that give meaning to our lives. If a scientific or pseudo-scientific idea plays a central role in someone's life/world-view, then she will protect that idea by turning a blind eye towards any incoherence, or even by explicitly denying it. It's easy to come up with various pseudo-scientific ideas (e.g., creationism, intelligent design, homeopathy, and so forth) that are fiercely defended by their believers, but not every pseudo-scientific idea that is incoherent but fiercely defended by its believers (because it plays a central role in their life/world-views) is commonly recognized as pseudo-science. Psychology has been plagued by theories that could not be confirmed (or refuted) empirically and has been particularly hard hit by the ongoing replication crisis,[61] but the most important offender, as we shall see in chapter 15, is mainstream, neoclassical economics. The implication of this is that scientific findings should not be *uncritically* accepted. As mentioned above, we are justified to accept the findings of science *in as far* as those satisfy the standards of coherence.

Fourth, we are justified to believe most scientific findings, but that does not necessarily imply that those are true.[62] Justification does not imply truth; all that justification means is that we have good reason to *believe* that something is true and thus to act *as if* it is true. Like the previous three caveats, this fourth leads to the same conclusion: epistemological humility. Truth and ultimate reality are fundamentally out of our reach. There may be many things we may be justified to believe, but we cannot reach out of our beliefs, and any belief can only be accepted provisionally.

Essences, Freedom, Paradise, and Other Incoherences

If we are justified to believe most of the findings of science and *not* justified to believe whatever is incoherent (regardless whether it is internally, externally, or otherwise incoherent), then this has some important implications. Some of those implications may be hard to swallow for traditional Buddhists, but most of them are embraced by radical and secular Buddhists.

---

59 What Gregory shows is that foundationalism is based on an antecedent commitment to a requirement he calls "linear propositional support," but what that requirement requires is that there are no antecedent commitments. See Gregory, *Quine's Naturalism,* chapter 4, and 124–25.
60 See the section "Between Science and Religion" in chapter 6.
61 The "replication crisis" is the rising awareness that very many scientific findings in certain fields have been impossible to reproduce in new tests or experiments.
62 In other words, the foregoing does not imply scientific realism, the idea that science is true or that science reveals truth.

As already pointed out in chapter 4,⁶³ substance dualism — the idea that the mental and the material are different substances and thus that minds are more or less independent from bodies — is not a coherent position. Metaphysical idealism, which holds that only the mental is real, is not a plausible position either. (As argued in chapter 8, it is doubtful that Yogācāra accepted metaphysical idealism anyway.) The only plausible and coherent theories in the philosophy of mind are variants of physicalism (or materialism, but that term is outdated).

The acceptance of some form of physicalism has further important implications. Minds are ontologically and otherwise dependent on the body or are even "embodied." While the details of the mind–body relation are quite fascinating, those are of limited relevance here.⁶⁴ What matters more is that this implies that when the body dies, the mind dies. There are no souls and there is no afterlife. When we die, there is nothing left to enter some afterlife. Neither is there anything left that could reincarnate.⁶⁵ Death is final.⁶⁶

Closely related to the denial of a soul or some other kind of immortal spirit is the rejection of a self-defining essence or fixed self. If there is some kind of self, then that self is an ever-changing composite, construction, or process, and not an unchanging essence or thing. This, or something very similar, has also been proclaimed by nearly all philosophical Buddhisms, but not necessarily by lay Buddhism.⁶⁷ It has also been

---

63 See the section "Physicalism."
64 My own position is related to the anomalous monism that was proposed by Davidson, and that was also endorsed by Quine and much earlier in some form by Spinoza, who wrote in his *Ethics* (1677) that "the Mind and the Body are one and the same thing, which is conceived now under the attribute of Thought [i.e., as mental], now under the attribute of Extension [i.e., as physical]" (in *The Collected Works of Spinoza*, Vol. I, ed. and trans. Edwin Curley [Princeton: Princeton University Press, 1985], 408–617, at III.2, 494). According to anomalous monism, mental events are brain events, although there probably are other bodily involvements, but this does not mean that there is an identity between types of mental events and types of brain events. The first clause is what "monism" refers to; the "but" is what is "anomalous" about it. Davidson claims that an a priori argument can be made that infers monism from strong anomaly, but I find that argument rather implausible. Instead, my argument is that the assumption of monism, on physicalist grounds, plus naturalism, of the kind derived above, lead to the acceptance of relevant neuro-scientific findings that imply weak anomaly. See Lajos Brons, "Patterns, Noise, and Beliefs," *Principia* 23, no. 1 (2019): 19–51; Donald Davidson, "Mental Events" (1970), EAE: 207–25. "Thinking Causes" (1993), TLH: 185–200; and "Laws and Cause" (1995), TLH: 201–19.
65 Some Buddhist theories of rebirth argue that the process is entirely causal and that there is nothing that transmigrates between lives. It is just one life causing another. (Like a flame lighting up another candle before going out.) Perhaps, the most obvious argument against this idea is population growth, but aside from that, a naturalist should also reject it because there is no scientific evidence whatsoever for such a causal process. It would, in fact, be quite unexplainable and thus incoherent.
66 In Mark Johnston's *Surviving Death* (Princeton: Princeton University Press, 2010), by far the most thorough study on the topic of the possibility of some kind of afterlife, he first discards all traditional "options," but then finally suggest one new possibility by redefining personal identity over time. If you could genuinely identify yourself with the whole of mankind, then you could live on in mankind (until mankind goes extinct, of course). The idea is interesting, but as I have shown elsewhere, there are some serious defects in Johnston's argument. See Lajos Brons, "The Incoherence of Denying My Death," *Journal of Philosophy of Life* 4, no. 2 (2014): 68–89.
67 In much of Buddhism, Abhidharma especially, composites, as well as constructions and processes, are not considered "things" that "exist," and consequently, if the self is a composite, then the self does not exist. The most famous argument along these lines can be found in the *Milinda Pañha* (*Questions of King Milinda*).

accepted in some form or other by many non-Buddhist philosophers and scientists working on the problem of "the self."[68]

In Buddhist philosophy, the term for "essence" is *svabhāva*, literally "self-being," and it is not just the essential self that is rejected, but essences or svabhāvas in general. Nothing has an essence, and consequently, there are no natural kinds and neither are there universals.[69] The essence of a thing is the set of properties a thing must have to be the kind of thing it is, but if kinds are not given and we create kinds and classify things according to those created kinds, then this notion of essence makes no sense. John Dupré has offered some strong arguments against the idea of essences and natural kinds, but one of the most interesting studies on the topic is Samuel Wheeler's *Neo-Davidsonian Metaphysics*.[70] Wheeler discusses the typical candidates for natural kinds (e.g., species, atoms, and so on) and finds all of them lacking. The only kinds that have a defining essence are, in fact, artificial kinds — the kinds of things created by us that must satisfy certain strict criteria to belong to that kind, such as Coca-Cola. Nevertheless, based on influential essentialist arguments by Aristotle and Saul Kripke, Wheeler argues against a complete rejection of the notion of essences: things do have essences but only relative to their designations. Hence, a table does not have an essence in itself, but it does have an essence *as table*. Or in Yogācāra terms, our *pratibhāsa-pratīti* (conceptually determinate awareness) of the table as table has an essence (i.e., a set of properties that make it that kind of pratibhāsa-pratīti), but the underlying suchness that indirectly caused the table-awareness does not.[71]

The Buddhist rejection of selves and essences is also related to its rejection of permanence. There are no permanent, fixed selves or other kinds of essences, but nothing else is permanent either. Given available scientific knowledge, this doctrine of impermanence appears to be justified — indeed, nothing lasts forever. The rejection of essences, selves, and permanence are closely related in the Buddhist view because they are all part of a therapeutic response to craving or attachment. The prospect of death is a form of suffering (dukkha) because we crave continued existence (i.e., immortality).[72] Craving continued existence is craving for a permanent self, and thus for the existence of a self (which is a kind of essence) as well as for permanence. Hence, our beliefs in selves, essences, and permanence is motivated by a craving for immortality. According to Ernest Becker and Terror Management Theory,[73] we do have such a craving indeed — we would not even be able to function without it — so much of this argument makes sense. Nevertheless, whether giving up our instinctive beliefs in selves, essences, and permanence (if even psychologically possible) can relieve the suffering associated with this craving is an open question.

With the rejection of rebirth (or reincarnation), the theory of karma has to go as well, because that no longer makes sense. According to Buddhist views on karma, good intentions or volitions (*cetanā*) lead to good rebirths and bad intentions or

---

68 For a good recent overview of the topic of non-self theory in Buddhism and science, see Evan Thompson, *Why I Am Not a Buddhist* (New Haven: Yale University Press, 2020), chapter 3.
69 See the section "Realism (1) — Universals and (Anti-)Essentialism" in chapter 7.
70 John Dupré, *The Disorder of Things: Metaphysical Foundations of the Disunity of Science* (Cambridge: Harvard University Press, 1993), and Samuel Wheeler, *Neo-Davidsonian Metaphysics: From the True to the Good* (New York: Routledge, 2014).
71 And neither does the intermediary pratibhāsa. Hence, the essential properties that make the pratibhāsa-pratīti a determinate awareness of some particular kind, like a table, are only essential properties of that pratibhāsa-pratīti.
72 See chapters 2 and especially 5.
73 See the section "Between Science and Religion" in chapter 6.

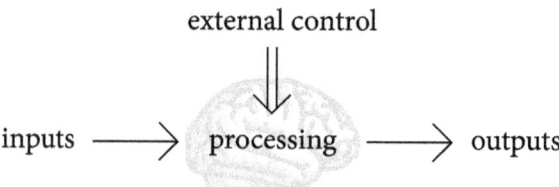

Fig. 9.1. Free will and external control.

volitions lead to bad rebirths. Without rebirth, karma would have no effect (unless it would have another effect, as in some naturalistic interpretations of karma[74]), and according to a common Buddhist ontological criterion, what lacks causal efficiency is not real. There is an even more fundamental problem for the theory of karma, however. Karma requires free will because volitional action is willed action — it is action due to free will.

The traditional view of free will contrasts with determinism. According to *hard* determinism there is no free will — everything is determined. In the same way that the planets move in their orbits due to physical laws and other particular circumstances, everything I do, say, or think results from natural processes and my particular circumstances. I do not type these words due to free will, but due to a combination of circumstances — things I learned or experienced in the past and remember now, things I'm experiencing right now, features of my brain's architecture and sense organs, and so forth. A few centuries ago, mechanical devices like clocks were the favorite analogies for determinists. The universe is like a clockwork, they believed, and so, in a sense, is the human mind. Nowadays, computers are the preferred analogues.

Quantum physics proved determinism false, but only on the micro scale.[75] To what extent that matters on the human scale is not clear, but it does not give us free will anyway. What quantum physics substitutes for determinacy is randomness. Some things — like the decay of radioactive isotopes — are not wholly determined but are partially random. Thus, the opposite of determinacy is randomness, but arguably, random actions are even less free than determined actions.

The traditional view of free will supposes that there is a third option besides determinacy and randomness. The idea is illustrated in figure 9.1. From a determinist point of view, there are certain inputs — perceptions, memories, and other circumstances — that are processed, leading to outputs, such as actions, thoughts, or utterances. The output is entirely determined by the inputs and features of the processing unit. If the process would be random instead, then the central processing unit would effectively ignore the inputs and just role dice, metaphorically speaking, to select an

---

[74] B.R. Ambedkar interpreted karma as the general principle that good deeds tend to have good effects and bad deeds tend to have bad effects, for example. See the section "Ambedkar and the 'New Vehicle' in India" in chapter 3.

[75] Actually, both parts of this sentence are controversial. Some interpretations of quantum mechanics, such as superdeterminism, disagree with the first part (i.e., they do not disprove determinism), while others disagree with the second. None of that controversy matters for the argument here, however.

action. The metaphysical libertarian desires a third option: external control.[76] In that view, the outputs are neither determined nor random but selected by some "thing," like a self or mind, that controls the decision-making process.

Now, the question is: How does that external controller make its decisions? The exact same figure applies in that case: the external controller (e.g., mind, self,[77] etc.) gets certain inputs, and then its output is to steer the central processing unit in figure 9.1 to make a decision. But the processing unit of the external controller, which controls the lower processing unit that makes the final decision for an output, itself makes its decisions either deterministically or randomly. This is, unless there is a higher-level external controller that controls the external controller, but then the same applies there and we need an even-higher-level external controller, and an even-even-higher-level external controller for that one, and so forth. (Hence, to have free will, I'd need more than one self. I'd need an infinite array of selves.)

The conclusion is obvious: the idea of a third option besides determinacy and randomness makes no sense. It is incoherent. And given that this implies that there is no third option, everything we do is either random or determined. Probably it is mostly the latter because randomness only occurs in processes at physical scales that are unlikely to play any significant role in our decision-making.

Metaphysical libertarianism, then, should be rejected and determinism mostly accepted, with the quantum caveat. According to soft determinism or *compatibilism*, this does not mean that we need to reject the notion of free will as well. Rather, we should redefine it. What makes an action free in the compatibilist view is not that it was the result of a decision by some external controller but just that it was the result of a decision.[78] If I could have decided to do otherwise then my action, and thus my will, was free. The most obvious problem for this idea was pointed out centuries ago by Spinoza:

> This is that human freedom, which all boast that they possess, and which consists solely in the fact, that men are conscious of their own desire, but are ignorant of the causes whereby that desire has been determined. Thus an infant believes that it desires milk freely; an angry child thinks he wishes freely for vengeance, a timid child thinks he wishes freely to run away. Again a drunken man thinks, that from the free decision of his mind he speaks words, which afterwards, when sober, he would like to have left unsaid. So the delirious, the garrulous and others of the same sort think that they act from the free decision of their mind, not that they are carried away by impulse.[79]

---

76 Metaphysical libertarianism should not be confused with political libertarianism, which strives for minimal states and unrestrained free markets.
77 In Buddhist philosophy, the desire for a self is sometimes understood as a desire for such an external controller. Hence, calling that "thing" (i.e., the external controller) the "self" seems appropriate. However, this would also suggest that, with the notion of the self, a Buddhist should also discard the libertarian notion of free will.
78 Thomas Hobbes was an influential, early compatibilist. He argued that you are free when you can do what you want to do. The version of compatibilism that relates freedom to decision is of more recent date. One of the most influential papers on this idea is: Harry Frankfurt, "Alternate Possibilities and Moral Responsibility" (1969), in *The Importance of What We Care About* (Cambridge: Cambridge University Press, 1988), 1–10.
79 Baruch Spinoza, "Letter LXII (LVIII): Spinoza to ..., the Hague, October 1674," in *Works of Spinoza*, Vol. 2 (1883; rpt. New York: Dover Publications, 1955), 389–92, at 390–91. For a more recent translation, see "Letter 58 (OP): To the Very Learned and Able Mr. G.H. Schuller, in *The Collected Works of*

A compatibilist could respond to this objection by revising her definition of a free action as one that is the result of a decision that was not influenced by forces outside the agent's control, or something similar, but such a response does not work. We do not create our own desires. Partially they are the product of our biology and psychology; partially they are due to culture or ideology (in the Marxian sense of "ideology"[80]); partially, they are shaped by advertisements; and so forths. Furthermore, not only desires are outside our control but beliefs as well. And because a rational decision to do X results from a belief that doing X is the best way to satisfy some desire, beliefs are as important in the decision-making process as desires. Consequently, any action is the result of a conscious or unconscious decision that is to a very great extent determined by forces outside the agent's control. We all think that we "act from the free decisions of our minds," but we're really not that different from "the delirious, the garrulous and others of the same sort."

A hard-nosed compatibilist may choose to stick to her definition — an action is free if it is the result of a decision, period — but that leads to another problem. Part of the reason why we want and need to believe in a free will is because responsibility, friendship, love, and many other things we value presuppose free will.[81] A genuine friend or lover freely seeks your company. And most people would say that you are not responsible for the consequences of an action if you could not have acted otherwise and thus that the action must have been free.[82] Mere decision is unlikely to be sufficient to qualify an action as free in the sense required. It is quite debatable, for example, whether a decision that was made due to brainwashing or manipulation makes the decider responsible for the consequences of her action. The problem is that we cannot draw a clear boundary between being manipulated or even forced to decide to do something and merely being compelled by the kind of forces mentioned in the previous paragraph. The compatibilist idea that decisions define freedom and responsibility depends on the assumption that we make relatively well-informed, rational decisions unaffected by culture, ideology, propaganda, advertisements, peer pressure, and so forth, but that assumption flies in the face of everything we know about human psychology.

The same problem applies to the theory of karma. If karma as volitional or freely willed action is simply action that is due to a decision, then being forced or manipulated to decide to do something bad will give you bad karma. But that is not what volitional action means. A volitional action is also a voluntary action, and an action resulting from coercion or manipulation is not voluntary. It seems then, that the theory of karma requires a stronger notion of free will than compatibilism can offer; it requires the incoherent notion of free will of metaphysical libertarianism.

Finally, if there is no rebirth or other kind of afterlife, then notions of heavens, hells, otherworldly paradises, or Buddha lands do not make much sense either. Sup-

---

Spinoza, Vol. II, ed. and trans. Edwin Curley (Princeton: Princeton University Press, 1985), 427–30, at 428. An almost identical statement can be found in the Ethics, III.2, 496.
80 See chapter 4.
81 The most influential paper making this point is Peter Strawson's "Freedom and Resentment." In that paper Strawson argues that, given the importance of love, friendship, responsibility, and so forth, we cannot possibly give up our belief that we have some kind of free will, regardless of whether that notion is coherent, and regardless of counter-evidence. Peter Strawson, "Freedom and Resentment" (1962), in Freedom and Resentment and Other Essays (London: Routledge, 1974), 1–28.
82 Frankfurt denies this. What makes one responsible for the consequences of X, in his view, is not having other options but having decided to do X. Frankfurt, "Alternate Possibilities and Moral Responsibility."

posedly, those are places we go to after death, but if we do not exist after death, we cannot go anywhere. This inability is a rather minor problem, as the concept of such supernatural heavens or Buddha lands is incoherent with the scientific understanding of our universe anyway. There are and can be no such places. For radical Buddhism, this implication of the acceptance of science and the principle of coherence is particularly important. If there are no heavens, paradises, Buddha lands, or Pure lands, then we cannot hope for a better existence in some other world and other life. If this world is the only world, and this life is our only life, then we can only create a better life for ourselves and for others in this world. Something like this this-worldly or austere realism has been a key motivation for Buddhist sociopolitical engagement since Nichiren 日蓮 at least.[83]

Posits and Phenomenal Reality

At the end of chapter 1, I suggested that radical Buddhism is "incomplete" because it is not concerned as such with personal liberation, death, or ritual, while those are core aspects of typical understandings of what Buddhism is about. Perhaps, radical Buddhism can be "completed" by combining it with more traditional practices and ideas, but the converse — a traditional Buddhism that is also radical — seems more problematic. At least, the preceding sections seem to throw cold water on the notion of combining radical and traditional Buddhism. If radical Buddhism rejects karma and rebirth, for example, then it appears to be incompatible with Buddhisms that consider those notions essential. Similarly, if scientific research would reveal that mindfulness does not have the effects it is supposed to have, then radical Buddhism might not be compatible with variants of modernist Buddhism that focus on mindfulness either.[84] But let's not jump to conclusions. Perhaps, a radical Buddhist could say that karma and rebirth are phenomenally real. This suggestion, however, raises two questions: first, what exactly does it mean to say that something is merely phenomenally real? And second, is phenomenal reality sufficient?

Phenomenal reality, by definition, is the way the world appears to us. It is the world or reality as we consciously experience it, but it is not a different world. Both Yogācāra and Tiantai/Tendai advocated varieties of non-dualism that include the idea that phenomenal or conventional reality and ultimate reality are not two different worlds or realities. Such non-dualism is one of the most central doctrines of Tiantai thought and is often referred to as the "middle" 中.[85] Yogācāra non-dualism is more commonly associated with the rejection of a dualism opposing the knowing or perceiving subject to the known or perceived object, but it also involves a

---

83 See the last two sections of chapter 2.
84 The efficacy of mindfulness meditation is a difficult question. Evan Thompson, *Why I Am Not a Buddhist*, has pointed out that most of the research on the topic is done by researchers who have already formed their conclusions in advance, which raises doubts about that research's credibility, and Nicholas van Dam et al., "Mind the Hype: A Critical Evaluation and Prescriptive Agenda for Research on Mindfulness and Meditation," *Perspectives on Psychological Science* 13, no. 1 (2018): 36–61, have identified a long list of methodological problems in mindfulness research. Furthermore, it has become clear that the effects of mindfulness meditation are not necessarily beneficial but can actually be quite harmful. See also Miguel Farias and Catherine Wikholm, *The Buddha Pill: Can Meditation Change You?* (London: Watkins, 2015).
85 See the sections "A Bit of Historical Context" and "Tiantai/Tendai Non-dualism" in chapter 8.

rejection of two-realities dualism.[86] An example of the latter can be found in the *Trisvabhāvanirdeśa* discussed in the previous chapter.[87] In that text, duality (*dvaya*) is associated with phenomenal appearances and non-duality with the realization of suchness (*tathātā*), the underlying real things or substances that indirectly cause the appearances. A phenomenon is ultimately real suchness seen in some conceptually determinate way, and by extension, phenomenal reality is the world seen, experienced, and understood in some conceptually determinate way. What is seen in this way is not a different world, however; it is just a mistaken or partial view on this one, non-dual world.[88] (Also recall the analogy at the end of chapter 7 that likened ultimate reality to a photograph and phenomenal reality to a labeled sketch based on that photograph.)

Different ways of seeing, experiencing, and understanding the world are different perspectives or (a consequence of) conceptual schemes. Perspectives more or less produce phenomenal realities. At the most basic level, they do this through conceptual construction (*kalpanā*). We see certain parts or regions of mind-external reality as tables, for example, because we have a concept "table." But as explained above, perspectives or schemes include more than just language. They also include beliefs about things and their relations: about what kinds of things tables are, how they are used, what they are made of, and so forth. These associated beliefs together give meaning to my concept of "table." And in the same way that some of these associated beliefs give meaning to my concept of "table," beliefs in karma or rebirth could play roles in some of my other concepts and meanings.

Furthermore, these associated beliefs are linked to other, more distant beliefs — about chairs, for example, or about tableware and what it is used for, about dinner, or about wood or other materials tables are made of, and so forth. And those beliefs have further links and associates. Directly or indirectly, the whole of our webs of belief is involved in a perspective, and therefore, in the phenomenal reality it constructs.[89]

There is a relatively inconsequential ambiguity in the notion of a perspective or conceptual scheme that I have glossed over thus far, but that needs to be addressed here. In the section "Perspectives and Science," I wrote that science is not a single perspective but a collection of perspectives most of which resulted from clashes between other perspectives. This suggests an interpretation of the notion of perspective as something close to a scientific theory — a way of seeing, understanding, and explaining some small part or aspect of the world around us. However, in the previous two paragraphs I used the term "perspective" to refer to something involving our whole webs of belief and not just small, topical parts thereof. Hence, a distinction should be made between local and global perspectives. The notion in the previous paragraphs is that of a global perspective: it is the whole of our concepts and beliefs

---

86 Since the object as it is conceptually determinately experienced is constructed as such by the mind (i.e., the subject), subject and object are inseparable. This, however, is not the same dualism as that supposing non-identity of the determinate experience and its ultimately real cause (i.e., the underlying suchness). Yogācāra rejects both of these dualisms but the first more obviously and explicitly than the second.
87 See the section "Yogācāra Realism" in chapter 8.
88 It is mistaken according to Yogācāra and partial according to especially later Tiantai/Tendai. See chapter 8.
89 The Quinean notion of a web of belief was introduced at the end of the section, "Objections to the Coherence Principle" in this chapter.

that determines how we see and understand the world around us. A local perspective is a part thereof, like a natural language, a scientific theory or discipline, and so forth.

The distinction matters because we can only (directly) change or replace local perspectives. We can learn new languages or adopt different scientific, local perspectives, but we cannot give up and replace all of our concepts and beliefs at once. The distinction is relatively inconsequential at the same time because the whole is defined by its parts,[90] and consequently, if I change a local perspective, my global perspective changes as well.

Adopting a different perspective is changing a relatively small part of my web of belief. Such changes can be close to the edge of the web, but the most important changes are in the middle zone between abstract central beliefs and the basic perceptual beliefs at the edges. A change in the center, however, is very unlikely; I do not see myself giving up the belief that 1 + 1 = 2, for example. Switching between natural languages changes the edges of the web, but such changes tend to be very subtle. Some natural languages classify colors subtly differently, for example, and other differences between languages may direct my attention at subtly different details of my perception. An example of a change in the middle zone is the choice to describe some human behavior in physical, biological, psychological, sociological, or other terms, or in a physical, biological, and so forth perspective. We choose perspectives in this sense depending on purpose and circumstances. A theory of karma and rebirth would likewise be located in this middle zone.

Different perspectives involve different set of *posits*. "Posit" is the term Quine used to refer to the things that exist according to some perspective or conceptual scheme. Any conceptually determinate thing is a posit in some perspective or scheme. Nevertheless,

> [t]o call a posit a posit is not to patronize it. A posit can be unavoidable except at the cost of other no less artificial expedients. Everything to which we concede existence is a posit from the standpoint of a description of the theory-building process, and simultaneously real from the standpoint of the theory that is being built.[91]

In "Posits and Reality," Quine argued that some posits, such as molecules, are useful because they help us explain and understand the world, while he was more skeptical about others.[92] Posits are real to the extent that they are useful, and they are useful if they are part of useful theories.[93] Dharmakīrti and Dignāga would probably have adopted a different criterion: something is to be considered real if it is causally efficient (i.e., if it has effects). But, perhaps, these two criteria are not as different as they may seem on the surface: posits that have no effects are unlikely to explain

---

90 Whether this is true for all "things," in the broadest possible sense of "thing," is debatable. All I'm claiming here is that it is true of global perspectives. That this is the case just follows from the rough definition of a perspective or conceptual scheme as the whole of concepts and beliefs that determine how I see and understand the world around me.
91 W.V.O. Quine, *Word & Object* (Cambridge: MIT Press, 1960), 22.
92 W.V.O. Quine, "Posits and Reality" (1955), WPOE: 246–54. See also "On What There Is" (1948), FLPV: 1–19, and *Word & Object*, 21–25.
93 W.V.O. Quine, "Two Dogmas of Empiricism" (1951), FLPV: 20–46, and "Posits and Reality." See also Hylton, *Quine*, 85–91.

anything, and posits that are theoretically useful are likely to be so because they have specific effects. Furthermore, these criteria are related to the coherence principle as well. Positing something "is good science insofar merely as it helps us formulate our laws — laws whose ultimate evidence lies in the sense data of the past, and whose ultimate vindication lies in the anticipation of sense data of the future."[94] Or in other words, posits are justified by something like constancy of effect, Dharmakīrti's main criterion of coherence (*avisaṃvāda*), or by coherence with other cognitions, as in Devendrabuddhi's interpretation of Dharmakīrti.[95]

The choice between different perspectives is a choice between different collections of posits or ontologies. It is a pragmatic choice: we choose the perspective that best fits our needs and purposes, and for Quine, those needs and purposes are primarily related to understanding and explaining the world around us.[96] Physical, biological, psychological, and so forth perspectives are complementary; they serve different explanatory purposes in the way that physics, biology, psychology, and so on explain very different things. Because of that, they are not obviously in conflict and we can freely switch between them.

The situation is different when two or more perspectives serve very similar or overlapping explanatory purposes, that is, if they aim to explain the same or very similar things. If two perspectives serve the same explanatory purpose, and purpose guides our choice between perspectives, then it seems that we cannot choose between those two perspectives;[97] but that is not exactly right. They might not differ in what they aim to explain, but two competing perspectives are likely to differ in how well they explain it. Aristotle and Newton gave very different explanations of why a stone falls to the ground if you lift it up and let it go. We do not freely switch between those two perspectives dependent on our needs and purposes. Rather, we discarded Aristotle's perspective and provisionally accepted Newton's, and more recently amended the latter.

Competing perspectives tend to involve contradictory ontological commitments (i.e., one posits something that the other explicitly denies), while this is rarely the case for complementary perspectives.[98] As an illustration of contradictory ontological commitments, consider the following two scenarios:

> According to perspective *1A* there is a color category "orange" in between red and yellow. Perspective *1B* denies this. According to *1B*, orange is just a variety of red. Hence, things called "orange" in *1A* are called "red" in *1B* (but not necessarily the other way around).

---

94 Quine, "Posits and Reality," 250. See also Hylton, *Quine*, 75.
95 See the section "Avisaṃvāda" in this chapter.
96 In case of languages, which are local perspectives closer to the edge of the web of belief, the purpose is not explanation, but communication, and we normally choose the language that best facilitates communication in a given situation.
97 Unless we have a very different kind of purpose, instead of explanation and understanding. More about that option below.
98 The main reason why this is the case is that complementary perspectives usually explain very different kinds of things and, because of that, have non-overlapping scopes. There is nothing that is explicitly affirmed as existing or posited according to psychology and explicitly denied by physics, for example. But there is much that is posited by one of these about which the other is agnostic because it lays outside that perspective's scope. Take electrons as an example, according to physics those exist, but psychology is agnostic.

According to perspective 2A there is a color category "gred," which is defined as "a greenish red or a reddish green." Perspective 2B denies this. According to 2B, gred does not exist and there are no things that are gred.

Both 1B and 2B deny the existence of something affirmed by 1A and 1B, respectively, but what is denied in the first scenario is a word, while what is denied in the second is what a word refers to. 1B does not deny that there is something that "orange" refers to; it simply refers to that "thing" with a different word (namely, "red"). But according to 2B, there is nothing that "gred" refers to. In other words, the disagreement between 2A and 2B is a disagreement about what there is, while the disagreement between 1A and 1B is merely a disagreement about how to talk about what there is. And while context and purpose determine the most appropriate way to talk about what there is, they do not determine what there is. Consequently, the choice between competing perspectives is not just a pragmatic choice. Rather, the main criteria for deciding between competing perspectives and their ontologies are coherence (with available evidence especially) and simplicity. According to Quine,

> [o]ur acceptance of an ontology is [...] similar in principle to our acceptance of a scientific theory, say a system of physics: we adopt, at least insofar as we are reasonable, the simplest conceptual scheme into which the discorded fragments of raw experience can be fitted and arranged.[99]

Karma and rebirth can be (re-)interpreted in various ways. The most obvious and most common interpretation is that they posit, and thus are ontologically committed to, some kind of entity that "carries" karma and that transmigrates from life to life. Another interpretation is that rebirth is just causal — a death causes a new life, but nothing transmigrates — and that karma is just something like a law of nature that determines that good deeds cause good new lives and bad deeds cause bad new lives.[100] The second kind of interpretation does not posit a carrier of karma or other kind of thing, but posits certain causal processes, laws, or forces. Regardless what exactly is posited, it should be clear that a perspective including karma and rebirth posits something that is explicitly denied by other plausible perspectives, by naturalistic or scientific perspectives, particularly. The choice between perspectives in this case, then, is not just a pragmatic choice but one that ought to be guided by coherence and simplicity, and as already explained in the previous section, those principles disqualify the karma/rebirth-based perspectives. In short, there can be no carrier of karma, there is no natural law of karma, and there is no causal process causing a new life upon the end of another.

But let's assume that some interpretation of karma and rebirth can be constructed that does not immediately stumble over this obstacle, that is, an interpretation that is not obviously incoherent and that might even cohere with everything else we know. Since it is practically impossible to test complete coherence of a web of belief, this is the best we can do anyway, which is one way of putting why any belief is only accepted provisionally. Then, we should accept the posits of this interpretation

---

99 Quine, "On What There Is," 16.
100 There are other options. B.R. Ambedkar, for example, held the view that karma is just the general principle that actions have effects, that good actions tend to have good effects and that bad actions tend to have bad effects. See the section "Ambedkar and the 'New Vehicle' in India" in chapter 3.

if they are causally efficient or if the interpretation is part of a useful theory. The problem is, of course, that we need some kind of evidence for causal efficiency and there is none, so by Dharmakīrti's criterion, we have no ground to believe that karma exists. And neither does the notion of karma pass the Quinean test as it is unclear what explanatory purpose it serves.

Not all of our purposes are explanatory, however. Our choice between languages, for example, is determined by purpose as well, but that purpose tends to be communication rather than explanation. Perhaps, there is another kind of purpose that justifies the acceptance of a karma/rebirth-based perspective. It could be argued, for example, that such a perspective gives people a reason to do the right thing and thereby creates better societies. Whether this is the case indeed is an empirical question, and the fact that caste systems, poverty, and this-worldly suffering are routinely excused or defended with an appeal to karma gives plenty of reason to be rather skeptical about this idea.[101] A more fundamental problem, however, is that what a perspective posits is not independent from its purpose. Karma as explanation posits certain things, causes, or processes, but karma as moral guide does not necessarily have the same ontological commitments. What is needed for the supposed beneficial effect on society, if there is such an effect, is that people *believe* in karma, and not that those beliefs are actually true, and consequently, all that karma as moral guide posits is beliefs in karma; that is, it does not posit carriers of karma, causal processes, and so on. Typically, theories of karma and rebirth are explicitly committed to much more than that. They are explicitly presented as having explanatory purposes and ontological commitments to carriers or causes. Consequently, adopting a different purpose cannot save traditional theories of karma and rebirth.

One way to respond to the incoherence of karma, rebirth, and related notions is to give them up, and that is indeed what many (but not all!) of the Buddhist thinkers mentioned in chapter 3 did, but there is another option, which is closely related to the suggestion in the previous paragraph. Early in the twentieth century, the now almost forgotten German philosopher Hans Vaihinger published *Die Philosophie des Als Ob* (*The Philosophy of "As if"*) in which he argued for something approaching global fictionalism.[102] In the preface to the second English edition of his book he wrote:

> The principle of Fictionalism [...] is as follows: "An idea whose theoretical untruth or incorrectness, and therewith its falsity, is admitted, is not for that reason practically valueless and useless; for such an idea, in spite of its theoretical nullity may have great practical importance."[103]

Fictionalism is the view that claims in some area of discourse are, despite contrary appearance, not really aiming at truth or truthful description but are, rather, "fictions." Or to put it somewhat differently: fictionalism with regard to some domain of knowledge holds that at least some of the most basic claims of or within that domain of knowledge are known to be false or unjustified, but should be accepted *as if* they were true or justified because it is useful to do so. An early example of

---

101 It is for this reason that several of the Buddhist thinkers mentioned in chapter 3 rejected the notion of karma.
102 For a good review of Vaihinger's philosophy, see Arthur Fine, "Fictionalism," *Midwest Studies in Philosophy* 18 (1993): 1–18.
103 Hans Vaihinger, *The Philosophy of "As If": A System of the Theoretical, Practical and Religious Fictions of Mankind*, 2nd edn. (London: Kegan Paul, 1935), vii.

something like fictionalism is Voltaire's famous statement that "if God did not exist, it would be necessary to invent him."[104]

Vaihinger's fictionalism was extremely broad. He was a fictionalist about mathematics, free will, physics, psychology, religion, and a whole lot more. This contrasts his fictionalism with more recent adoptions of that label. Contemporary fictionalism is nearly always local rather than global; it only applies to one narrowly defined area of knowledge. For example, Bas van Fraassen has argued for something like fictionalism about theories in the natural sciences; Hartry Field is a well known advocate of fictionalism about mathematics; Gideon Rosen argued for fictionalism about possible worlds, and there is a long list of philosophers that are something like fictionalists about moral discourse or free will.

The latter is especially useful to illustrate why fictionalism should be considered a genuine option. As explained in the previous section, the libertarian notion of free will is incoherent, which leaves only two options: accepting some kind of compatibilist redefinition of free will, or accepting that there is no free will in any relevant sense of the term. However, we need to believe in free will for reasons explained by Peter Strawson and others,[105] and it is unclear whether compatibilism can give us a notion of free will that satisfies Strawson's and others' requirements. Consequently, we probably do not have free will in any relevant sense of the term but need to believe we do anyway because without that belief, there cannot be love, friendship, responsibility, and so forth. That is fictionalism: the simultaneous acceptance that something is false and pretense that it is true anyway because we have no other option.

A Buddhist could be a fictionalist about karma and rebirth if she believes that it is useful to pretend that karma and rebirth are true or justified. A radical Buddhist, however, can only be a fictionalist about karma and rebirth if there actually is evidence that believing in karma and rebirth is useful. Perhaps such evidence can be found. Perhaps not. In any case, this is an empirical question, but one that has not been thoroughly researched yet, and not one that would be easy to test either. If there is an interpretation of karma or rebirth the adoption of which can be shown to have beneficial effects and be useful in that sense, then a radical Buddhist could be a fictionalist about karma or rebirth. Perhaps, in that case, she even *should* be a fictionalist about karma or rebirth, although this very much depends on the nature of the expected effects and on answers to questions in moral philosophy that will be discussed in part III of this book.

Summary of Chapters 8 and 9

The metaphysical and epistemological theory developed in the last sections of chapter 8 and the first sections of the present chapter is a variant of perspectival realism. "Perspectival realism" refers to a loose collection of theories that are realist, in the minimal sense of recognizing the existence of a mind-independent, external reality, but that also reject the idea that there is just one "right" way of describing reality. Rather, descriptions or understandings of or views on reality are perspectival, that is, they are views from particular perspectives, or constructions due to particular conceptual schemes. And because there is no view from nowhere or God's eye point

---

104 "Something like," because this statement does not actually state that God does not exist.
105 Strawson, "Freedom and Resentment."

of view, descriptions or understandings of reality are necessarily perspectival. A perspective is not a false view, however, but an incomplete or partial view; it does not and cannot radically misrepresent external reality because it is and can only be grounded therein.

The theory developed and defended here is not the only perspectival realism. Other perspectival realisms and related theories and ideas have been defended under a variety of names and guises in East and West. The next chapter will briefly discuss some of those. The remainder of this chapter summarizes the proposed metaphysical and epistemological underpinnings of a radicalized radical Buddhism.

Our conscious awareness of the world around us is mediated by language. We perceive tables *as* tables, cows *as* cows, and weddings *as* weddings. In other words, our conscious awareness is conceptually determinate. This conceptually determinate, conscious awareness (*pratibhāsa-pratīti*) is constructed (*kalpanā*) out of indeterminate, non-conceptual, and unconscious impressions (*pratibhāsa*) that are caused by external suchness (things or stuffs). Conceptual construction is not arbitrary, however. Our conceptual categories are themselves formed in a social process of interaction with other speakers and shared external "things." Both concept formation and conceptual construction proceed through an unconscious process of exclusion (*apoha*).[106]

All of this is standard Yogācāra. It may appear to deviate in its explicit admission of an external reality, but as explained in the section "Yogācāra Realism" in chapter 8, the interpretation of Yogācāra philosophy as metaphysical idealism is most likely mistaken. Yogācāra does not deny external suchness. What it denies is that our determinate awarenesses are real as such (i.e., in the specific conceptually determinate forms of our conscious experience). Where the view developed here does start to deviate somewhat from Yogācāra, is in some of the implications of the foregoing.

Yogācāra thinkers inferred from the constructedness of conscious experience that phenomenal reality is a deception, but that conclusion is too extreme. There is a middle path between the Scylla of apophasis and the Charybdis of naive realism, and the necessary grounding of our conceptual categories in external reality points at that middle path. Because kalpanā (conceptual construction) proceeds by applying categories that are necessarily based on real properties of things (because otherwise we could not have those categories), the resulting phenomenal appearances are simplifications or caricatures more than illusions or hallucinations. The relation between phenomenal and ultimate reality is a bit like that between a simple line drawing and the photograph it is based on as in figures 7.3 and 7.2. The drawing is neither a deception nor an accurate representation but somewhere in between.

This is, more or less, the view developed in the broader Tiantai/Tendai tradition. According to its founder Zhiyi, language misrepresents the world to some extent but is not entirely mistaken, and as long as we do not forget that, we do not have to let it deceive us. This is a moderately kataphatic approach: we can and need to use language to talk about external reality in the same way that we can use a drawing to depict something. Neither what we say nor what we draw is perfectly accurate but neither is a deception either. The problem with the apophatic rejection of language is that it demands too much. Like the skeptic who rejects all knowledge claims because there can be no absolute certainty, the Yogācārin rejects all conceptual cognition

---

106 See the last two sections of chapter 8.

because there can be no perfect accuracy.[107] Tiantai/Tendai corrects that; instead of giving up language, it gives up this craving for descriptive perfection.[108]

The broader Tiantai/Tendai tradition also placed greater emphasis on the perspectival implications of conceptual construction. According to Asaṅga and Vasubandhu, different kinds of creatures see the world differently dependent on karma — for example, *pretas* (hungry ghosts) see puss or blood where humans see water — but kalpanā implies that how a creature sees the world also depends on the language it speaks. If phenomenal reality is like a sketch produced by a particular set of conceptual categories, then different sets of conceptual categories produce different phenomenal realities. And while the perspective of pretas and other non-human perspectives are not available to us, Dōgen suggested that we can acquire some new perspectives. We can learn new languages, for example, but there are also other ways in which we can acquire a new way of seeing and understanding the world around us. This has an important epistemological implication: if a single perspective only gives us a partial view, then combining multiple perspectives gives us a better understanding of what we're looking at.

The theories of concept formation through exclusion (apoha) and conceptual construction of phenomenal reality have two further important implications. Firstly, if conceptual categories are not given by ultimate reality but are created by us in concept formation, then it makes no sense to assume that universals exist, in some meaningful sense of "existence." And based on what our various perspectives tell us about the world around us, there are no natural kinds or essences either.[109] Secondly, we cannot form or learn isolated concepts; rather, concepts are necessarily part of larger clusters that include other categories in the same domain and closely related concepts and beliefs. Because of this, all of our concepts and beliefs are directly or indirectly connected, and the content of a concept or belief is largely determined by its location in our webs of belief. What "book" means to me depends on my beliefs about books and how those beliefs are related to other beliefs.[110]

This inter-connectivity of our beliefs also plays an important epistemological role. We do not have direct access to ultimate reality, and therefore, we have no way to compare our beliefs with reality. All that can justify our beliefs are other beliefs. According to Dharmakīrti, the source of knowledge is coherent or uncontradicted (*avisaṃvādin*) cognition. Or in other words, a belief is justified in as far as it coheres with other justified beliefs. Truth is out of reach, however. We can aim for justification but never for truth. The more perspectives we learn to access or create, the more facets of reality we can see and the more evidence (or counter-evidence!) we can collect, but even coherence with all available evidence does not guarantee truth. All it does is tell us what we, collectively, are justified to believe. Furthermore, regardless

---

107 It must be emphasized here that Yogācāra rejected conceptual cognition, but not non-conceptual cognition, or something very similar: it aimed for a kind of non-conceptual awareness that reveals the true nature of suchness. Although, I doubt that such non-conceptual awareness is possible, the metaphysical and epistemological view advocated here is agnostic in this respect. It does not strictly follow that non-conceptual access to ultimate reality is possible or impossible, and there is no scientific and philosophical consensus about this either. Furthermore, nothing in this book depends on the possibility or impossibility of non-conceptual awareness.
108 This does not mean, of course, that Tiantai/Tendai rejected other perfections as well because that would have placed them outside the Mahāyāna tradition.
109 On universals and essences, see the section "Realism (1) — Universals and (Anti-)Essentialism" in chapter 7.
110 See the section "*Apoha* and Its Implications" in chapter 8.

of how many perspectives we manage to combine, there always are further perspectives, including inaccessible ones, such as those of fish or pretas, if those exist. And consequently, coherence is contingent: any belief that appears to be perfectly justified now can in principle turn out to be incoherent when we learn a new way to see. And because of that, any belief — even a belief as fundamental as "1 + 1 = 2" — can only be accepted provisionally.

This does not doom us to ignorance. It suggests epistemological humility, not skepticism. That we cannot know anything with absolute certainty does not mean that we cannot know anything at all. In the contrary, we know a lot, even if all of it is open to revision, and even if there is always more to know. Our most justified beliefs are the beliefs that result from the most rigorous testing for coherence with as many as possible different kinds of perspectives, including languages, theories, instruments, experiments, and so forth — in one word, science. What does not cohere with scientific findings, in as far those are coherent themselves, cannot be justified, and this has some important implications.[111] Traditional views on karma, rebirth, free will, Pure lands, heavens, and paradises cannot be accepted. There is only this world, and there is only this life. And consequently, as all radical Buddhists insisted, if we aim to alleviate suffering, we must do so here and now.

---

111 On scientific knowledge and its limitations, see the section "Perspectives and Science" in this chapter. On the implications of science, see the section "Essences, Freedom, Paradise, and Other Incoherences" also in this chapter.

10

Perspectives on Perspectival Realism

The philosophical theory summarized in the last section of the previous chapter is not the only version of perspectival realism, and other more or less similar ideas have been defended by philosophers from various backgrounds and traditions. What needs to be assessed is how similar those ideas really are. If the view outlined in the preceding has been advocated by non-Buddhists or could be constructed on the basis of non-Buddhist sources just as well, then, according to the rough definition of "Buddhist" proposed in chapter 5, it is not really a Buddhist view.

Strictly speaking, it is still too early to assess this not-just-as-well criterion. Whether a building is of a certain architectural type cannot be judged by its foundations alone, and thus far, the only aspect of a radicalized radical Buddhism outlined are its metaphysical and epistemological foundations. Nevertheless, the present chapter presents a partial assessment of similarities to adjacent views anyway mostly because it easier to judge whether the foregoing satisfies the not-just-as-well criterion while it is still fresh in your and my mind, rather than after many pages dealing with other topics. An assessment of this book's project as a whole will be the main topic of chapter 17.

There are, moreover, two other reasons for exploring adjacent views. First, there is undoubtedly much to learn from related ideas and the debates surrounding them. Problems not perceived from one perspective may be clearly perceived in another, for example, and a third could have a solution. The second reason is closely related to the perspectival coherentism implied in C.S. Lewis's witness accounts analogy.[1] Similar witness accounts by witnesses from very different perspectives strengthen each other. Similarly, similarities with views defended by others, especially by others with very different perspectives, strengthen the view defended here.

Nevertheless, while this comparative work is important, it is not the main goal of this chapter, and it would require another book, or several even. Hence, I will merely sketch a few connections that struck me as important or interesting and leave the real exploration for the future. The main purpose of this chapter is assessing whether the proposed metaphysical and epistemological foundations of a radicalized Buddhism can be called "Buddhist." As mentioned above, the yardstick for this assessment was proposed in chapter 5:

---

1   See the section "Perspectives and Science" in chapter 9.

> A theory, doctrine, practice, or idea is Buddhist if most of what it is based on or derived from is Buddhist and if it could not just as well be based on or derived from non-Buddhist sources.[2]

This rough definition mentions two requirements: (1) the theory must be mostly based on Buddhist sources; and (2) it could not just as well be based on other sources. Both requirements are rather vague, and consequently, using this yardstick is unlikely to result in a perfectly clear and unambiguous answer. The two requirements are also closely related; an assessment of the first results in the baseline for an assessment of the second. To judge whether something could be constructed just as well out of non-Buddhist sources, one first needs to know how easy it was to construct it out of Buddhist sources. So, before looking further into the not-just-as-well issue specifically, first I need to clarify this baseline.

The Baseline — Post-Yogācāra Realism

The sources on which the variety of perspectival realism presented in the previous two chapters is based can be divided into three groups:

1. Yogācāra: Asaṅga, Vasubandhu, Dignāga, Dharmakīrti, and a few related texts and commentaries.

2. The broader Tiantai/Tendai 天台 tradition, starting with Chinese Tiantai, and including Japanese Tendai and its thirteenth-century offshoots that remained strongly influenced by Tiantai/Tendai thought. Thinkers mentioned belonging to this broad tradition are its founder Zhiyi 智顗, Zhanran 湛然, Saichō 最澄, Dōgen 道元, and Nichiren 日蓮.[3] Of those five, Zhiyi and Dōgen received the most attention, but the strong this-worldly focus of Nichiren played a role in the background.

3. A nameless group of American philosophers with W.V.O. Quine at its center, including his teacher C.S. Lewis and his most influential students, Donald Davidson and Hilary Putnam, as well as Richard Rorty.[4] All except Davidson affiliated themselves more or less explicitly with pragmatism,[5] so they could, perhaps, be called "new pragmatists."[6] Of these five, Davidson was the most important, closely followed by Quine.

---

2 See the section "Defining 'Buddhism' and 'Buddhist'" in chapter 5.
3 Zhanran revived Tiantai after a period of decline that started soon after Zhiyi's death. Saichō introduced Tiantai/Tendai to Japan. Nichiren and Dōgen were thirteenth-century Japanese Tendai priests who split off and established separate sects — Nichiren Buddhism in case of the first, Sōtō Zen 曹洞 in case of the second. See chapters 2 and 8 for some further historical details.
4 Contrary to Davidson and Putnam, Rorty was never a "student" of Quine. Nevertheless, as Alan Malachowski observed, Quine "is central to Rorty's overall project" (*Richard Rorty* [Chesham: Acumen, 2002], 51).
5 Davidson rejected pragmatism because he identified it with a particular approach to defining truth, while he was a primitivist about truth, that is, he argued that truth cannot be defined. However, few pragmatists would have accepted Davidson's characterization of pragmatism. See, for example, Donald Davidson, "The Folly of Trying to Define Truth" (1996), TLH: 19–37.
6 Not to be confused with "neo-pragmatists." The term "neo-pragmatism" is used to refer to a "school" that overlaps with the "new pragmatists," but that is more strongly influenced by post-modernism

These three groups of sources played rather different roles in the argument. The starting point and all of the main building blocks were provided by Yogācāra: ultimate versus conventional or phenomenal reality, conceptual construction (*kalpanā*) and concept formation by *apoha*, the coherence (*avisaṃvāda*) criterion of knowledge, and so forth. Some of the connections between these building blocks, and some of the implications of the larger structure were in need of clarification, however, and that was the main role of sources (2) and (3).

Davidson's theory of triangulation was brought in to get a clearer picture of the details and implications of apoha. The main role of the other new pragmatists was to clarify the argument for and nature and implications of the coherence criterion. The moderately kataphatic conclusion that followed a rethinking of the Yogācāra theory of concept formation and conceptual construction was compared to, but not based on, Zhiyi. And Dōgen's perspectivism helped to clarify overlooked aspects and implications of Yogācāra constructionist relativism. However, none of these sources introduced fundamentally new elements.

Hence, while Quine, Davidson, Zhiyi, and Dōgen were instrumental in clarifying connections, implications, and arguments, the variety of perspectival realism advocated here is solidly based on Yogācāra. However, this does not mean that it is a Yogācāra view. A selection of Yogācāra doctrines was the starting point, rather than Yogācāra as a whole (further Yogācāra elements will be introduced in part III), and there may be significant distance between the point of departure (and certainly with Yogācāra as a whole) and the position arrived at.[7] For these reasons, it is more appropriate to call the view developed here "post-Yogācāra" than "Yogācāra."

My claim that the post-Yogācāra realism developed and defended in the previous chapters is almost entirely based on Buddhist sources and that non-Buddhist sources only played a role in clarification and explanation seems to indicate that it passes the first criterion in the definition of "Buddhist" mentioned above. That claim, and therefore this conclusion, may be met with skepticism, and for good reasons. An obvious and quite justified objection could be that my reading of Yogācāra philosophy might itself be influenced by Quine, Davidson, and other new pragmatists. If that is the case, then what I just called "post-Yogācāra realism" is really some kind of Quinean/Davidsonian/pragmatist view with Yogācāra window dressing.

There is undoubtedly some truth to this hypothetical objection, but reality is a bit messier and more complicated. In the introduction to chapter 8, I quoted Hans-Georg Gadamer, who pointed out that "wanting to avoid one's own concepts in the explanation [of a historical text] is not just impossible, but manifest nonsense. Rather, explanation is bringing one's own preconceptions into the game, and thereby really bring the meaning of the text to speak for us."[8] Any interpretation is inevitably colored by the philosophical biases and preconceptions of the interpreter. The

---

and other continental thought. Rorty is usually considered a (if not *the*) neo-pragmatist; Putnam is also sometimes included in the category.

7 How great this distance really is is hard to say. It seems to me that a fair comparison would not be one between the conclusions of the preceding chapters and Yogācāra as it was formulated one-and-a-half millennium ago but one with a hypothetical Yogācāra as it would have been created by its main thinkers if they would have known everything we know now. But that is obviously impossible, of course.

8 Hans-Georg Gadamer, *Wahrheit und Methode: Grundzüge einer philosophischen Hermeutik*, 2nd edn. (Tübingen: J.C.B. Mohr, 1965), 374–75. Quoted before in chapter 8. See there for the original German.

prevailing academic interpretation of Yogācāra thought in the West is heavily influenced by Tibetan Mādhyamaka, for example.[9] My own interpretation is certainly influenced by Quine and Davidson more than by Tibetan Mādhyamaka.[10] However, this is not a one-way street. On the contrary, my interpretation of Quine and Davidson is probably influenced as much by Yogācāra as the other way around. My first published paper about Davidson's philosophy, for example, was partially framed in terms of the Yogācāra distinction between *pratibhāsa* and *pratibhāsa-pratīti*.[11]

The fundamental building blocks of the view defended here were provided by an interpretation of Yogācāra. I do not have access to unmediated ultimate reality, but I do not have access to unmediated, uninterpreted Yogācāra either. And neither does anyone else. Any interpretation of Yogācāra is just that: an interpretation from a particular perspective. There are no uninterpreted, non-perspectival views. As Gadamer put it, "wanting to avoid one's own concepts in the explanation is not just impossible, but manifest nonsense." This itself follows from the perspectival realism expounded here: any interpretation is perspectival and there is no neutral, "objective," non-perspectival, "God's-eye" point of view.

Furthermore, what makes a theory or view "Buddhist" according to the rough definition provided is not (just) the perspective, but what it is a perspective on. Even if my perspective is partially informed by Quine and Davidson (but also by many other influences, not all of which I am aware of), it is still a perspective on Yogācāra and other schools of Buddhist thought. Consequently, given that it satisfies the first criterion, the question whether post-Yogācāra realism can be considered "Buddhist" is the question whether a similar view could be based on building blocks with different, non-Buddhist origins "just as well."

As mentioned before, this not-just-as-well criterion is rather vague and subjective, but it can be made a lot more useful by understanding it as comparing degrees of eclecticism. If a theory can be based either on a selection of sources *A* or on a selection of sources *B*, then it can be based just as well on *B* as on *A* if and only if selection of sources *B* is equally or less eclectic than selection of sources *A*; wherein one's own original contributions count as one of the sources. Or in other words, post-Yogācāra realism cannot be considered "Buddhist" if the same, or a very similar theory, could be based on an equally or less eclectic selection of non-Buddhist sources. Considering that the fundamental building blocks of post-Yogācāra realism are provided by a single school of thought, this means that any alternative, non-Buddhist foundation must be at least equally narrow to fail satisfaction of the not-just-as-well criterion. There is no "school" of new pragmatism in the same sense that there is a school of Yogācāra philosophy. There is much more disagreement between the philosophers I grouped under the "new pragmatism" label than between Yogācāra philosophers or almost any other school. And consequently, if an alternative, non-Buddhist foundation is to be sought in new pragmatism, "equally or less eclectic," or "at least equally

---

9 See, for example, Karl Brunnhölzl, "Preface," in *A Compendium of the Mahāyāna: Asaṅga's Mahāyānasaṃgraha and Its Indian and Tibetan Commentaries,* Vol. 1, trans. Karl Brunnhölzl (Boulder: Snow Lion, 2018), xv–xxiii. I have the impression that East-Asian interpretations of Yogācāra are much more heavily influenced by Chinese Pure Land Buddhism instead, and that the Tibetan influence there is (or was?) negligible.
10 Not in the least because I do not know much about Tibetan Buddhism at all.
11 Lajos Brons, "Applied Relativism and Davidson's Arguments against Conceptual Schemes," *The Science of Mind* 49 (2011): 221–40.

narrow," might require restriction to a single philosopher belonging to that loose collective.

New Pragmatism — Davidson, Putnam, and Quine

What I called "post-Yogācāra realism" is a variety of perspectival realism. Other varieties of perspectival realism or parts or elements thereof have been defended by a number of Western philosophers, including some of the new pragmatists. Putnam, for example, argued in some of his later writings for something like perspectival realism under a number of different labels including "sophisticated realism" and "pragmatic pluralism."[12]

> By "sophisticated realism" what I meant was a realism that accepts the idea that the same state of affairs can sometimes admit of descriptions that have, taken at face value, incompatible "ontologies," in the familiar Quinian sense of "ontology."[13]

And in *Ethics and Ontology* he wrote that "pragmatic pluralism" is

> the recognition that it is no accident that in everyday language we employ many different kinds of discourses, discourses subject to different standards and possessing different sorts of applications, with different logical and grammatical features — different "language games" in Wittgenstein's sense — no accident because it is an illusion that there could be just one sort of language game which could be sufficient for the description of all of reality![14]

Putnam's sophisticated realism or pragmatic pluralism differs significantly from post-Yogācāra realism with regards to its "naïveté" about perception.[15] Putnam argued for a kind of naive realism about perception according to which the world just is as we perceive it. Contrary to the (post-)Yogācāra view, he held that in perception we have direct and unmediated contact with the world, even if it is a conceptualized contact. Consequently, perspectives can only play a rather innocent role. We can choose to talk about the same things in physical or psychological terms, for example, but different perspectives do not produce different pictures of reality.

This reflects a more fundamental difference between the new pragmatists and much of the tradition of analytic philosophy they are affiliated with, on the one hand, and Yogācāra, Tiantai/Tendai, and much other Buddhist philosophy on the other. Yogācāra and Tiantai are non-dualist; they start from the given distinction between ultimate and conventional or phenomenal reality, and then they reason toward the non-dualistic idea that these are not two different worlds but that conven-

---

12 Throughout his long and tortuous career, Putnam has introduced a great number of -isms to describe his changing views. He is probably best known for the "internal realism" that he defended in the early 1980s and that is related to perspectival realism in many respects. Or, perhaps, for the functionalism in the philosophy of mind that he defended in the 1960s, but already rejected in the 1970s. But most of all, Putnam is famous for changing his mind.
13 Hilary Putnam, "Reply to Tim Maudlin," in *The Philosophy of Hilary Putnam*, eds. Randall Auxier, Douglas Anderson, and Lewis Hahn (Chicago: Open Court, 2015), 502–9, at 506.
14 Hilary Putnam, *Ethics without Ontology* (Cambridge: Harvard University Press, 2004), 21–22.
15 Hilary Putnam, *The Threefold Cord: Mind, Body, and World* (New York: Columbia University Press, 1999).

tional or phenomenal reality is a conceptually determinate perspective on ultimate reality. A comparison could be made with two kinds of interpretations of Kant's distinction between things-in-themselves, or noumenal reality, and phenomenal appearances.[16] According to the two-worlds interpretation, these are like two different realities. According to the two-aspects interpretation, they are merely two aspects of the same reality. The two-worlds interpretation is a dualist view; the two-aspects interpretation is a non-dualist view, albeit not the same non-dualist view as that of Yogācāra or Tiantai.

Most of analytic philosophy, however, rejected the Kantian distinction altogether, and the new pragmatists inherited that rejection. Putnam, Quine, Davidson, and so forth are not non-dualists, but anti-dualists. Phenomenal reality, for them, is not something like a perspective on ultimate or noumenal reality; rather, phenomenal reality is ultimate reality and the other way around. And by rejecting the distinction, the two terms become meaningless as well: there is just "reality" without any adjectives or other qualifiers. This anti-dualism motivates Putnam's naive realism about perception. It also motivates Davidson's arguments against conceptual schemes and conceptual relativism.[17] And, significantly, it leaves little room for conceptual construction, disregards unavailable and non-human perspectives, and downplays the role of perspectives in how we experience the world around us in general. But what is even more problematic from a Buddhist perspective is that this also means that there is nothing to realize, no illusion or deception to see through, and no special insights in the true nature of reality to be gained. What you see — *as you see it* — is all there is.

An obvious implication hereof is that anti-dualism is fundamentally incompatible with Buddhist thought in general and with Yogācāra or Tiantai non-dualism in particular. Consequently, it is very unlikely that anything like post-Yogācāra realism could be based on inherently anti-dualistic new pragmatism and certainly not "just as well." Nevertheless, the comparative project should not be terminated prematurely. If anti-dualism is the *only* real obstacle on the path to an alternative, non-Buddhist foundation for post-Yogācāra realism, then such a finding would still weaken the "Buddhist" credentials thereof. Furthermore, as mentioned above, comparison also matters for other reasons. Other perspectives may reveal unforeseen problems or solutions, for example, or in other ways help to improve a view.

Given the prominence of Davidson in both of the preceding chapters, Davidson's philosophy seems the best place to look for a non-Buddhist foundation for the kind of perspectival realism proposed here. Indeed, Samuel Wheeler has argued for a "neo-Davidsonian" variety of perspectival realism called "relative essentialism."[18] Wheeler's theory is based on a number of ideas he attributes to Davidson, including the following two:

(a) identity is always relative to a predicate; and
(b) there are no inherent joints in reality.

This attribution, however, is insufficiently supported in case of (a) and demonstrably false in case of (b). The latter is especially relevant here.

---

16 See the sections "Idealism" and "The 'Noumenal'" in chapter 7.
17 Brons, "Applied Relativism and Davidson's Arguments against Conceptual Schemes."
18 Samuel Wheeler, *Neo-Davidsonian Metaphysics: From the True to the Good* (New York: Routledge, 2014).

Wheeler's source for (a) is a remark that Davidson apparently made at some symposium "somewhere on the West Coast in the 1990s," and that serves as the epigraph of chapter 1 of his book. Although it may very well be the case that Davidson indeed said that "sameness is always relative to a predicate" in some symposium, I have been unable to find anything that is unambiguously similar to this quote in any of his published writings.

Attribution (b) is the real problem, however. Wheeler's single source for (b) is "On the Very Idea of a Conceptual Scheme," one of Davidson's best known but also one of his most obscure papers.[19] "On the Very Idea" appears to argue in favor of joints in reality more than against them, however. One of Davidson's arguments against conceptual schemes in this paper is that those "organize" what is already organized, but that argument only makes sense if it is interpreted as meaning that nature or reality provides that prior organization, and thus, that reality has "joints." His arguments in several of his papers on triangulation also seem to depend on the presupposition of an external reality consisting of, or pre-organized into, discrete objects and events,[20] and in one of his last papers Davidson argued for the existence of "divisions in nature" explicitly:

> Nature is pretty much how we think it is. There really are people and atoms and stars, given what we mean by the words. The infertility of hybrids defines real species, though this matters only to those interested in the relevant concepts. This explains why it is foolish to deny that these divisions exist in nature, whether or not anyone entertains the thought. Even if no one had ever had a concept, there would be species, though of course this is our concept and our word, born of our interests.[21]

Furthermore, Davidson's notion of causality as a law-like relation between kinds of events presupposes that events come in discrete natural kinds, and perhaps even kinds with causal essences.[22] And the fact that he called the irreducibility of kinds of mental events to kinds of brain events "anomalous monism" strongly suggests that he not just took natural kinds for granted, but their reducibility to more basic, physical kinds as well because otherwise there would not be anything "anomalous" about the mind,[23] and as John Dupré has shown, such reducibility requires natural kinds to have structural essences.[24]

On the other hand, Davidson did occasionally compare different conceptualizations to measurements of temperature in Celsius or Fahrenheit,[25] which implies that not every conceptual classification follows nature's presumed joints. However, he argued that this kind of jointlessness is of limited significance. "In the cases of Cen-

---

19 Donald Davidson, "On the Very Idea of a Conceptual Scheme" (1974), ITI: 183–98.
20 See, for example, Donald Davidson, "The Second Person" (1992), SIO: 107–22, and "Locating Literary Language" (1993), TLH: 167–81. On Davidson's theory of triangulation, see the section "Triangulation, Kalpanā, and Kataphasis" in chapter 8.
21 Donald Davidson, "Interpretation: Hard in Theory, Easy in Practice," in *Interpretations and Causes,* ed. Mario De Caro (Dordrecht: Kluwer, 1999), 31–44, at 38.
22 Donald Davidson, "Actions, Reasons, and Causes" (1963), EAE: 3–19.
23 Donald Davidson, "Mental Events" (1970), EAE: 207–25.
24 John Dupré, *The Disorder of Things: Metaphysical Foundations of the Disunity of Science* (Cambridge: Harvard University Press, 1993).
25 Donald Davidson, "Reality without Reference" (1977), ITI: 215–25, and "Reply to Simon J. Evnine," in *The Philosophy of Donald Davidson,* ed. Lewis E. Hahn (Chicago: Open Court, 1999), 305–10.

tigrade and Fahrenheit, nothing depends on whether we use one set of numbers or another."[26] And his use of this analogy suggests that he believed that this is the only kind of jointlessness or indeterminacy there is, and therefore, the only source of cross-perspectival difference. In other words, two perspectives or conceptual schemes can only differ from each other in relatively trivial and easily intertranslatable ways.

This is not Wheeler's view, however. Wheeler adopted Quine's term "posit," and indeed, some aspects of his brand of perspectival realism are Quinean more than Davidsonian (or "neo-Davidsonian" as he calls it himself). A posit, for Quine, is something that exists according to some perspective or conceptual scheme.[27] Wheeler explains his notion of posit by means of an analogy very similar to Davidson's Celsius-Fahrenheit case. A central metaphor in his book is a football field that can be measured in different units. The field is not intrinsically divided into meters or yards, and in that sense, there are no objectively real meters or yards as kinds of things, but those units or posits are based on something that is objectively real, and we need them to talk about that. And "just as space is not given in meters, so the physical world of objects is not given in chairs, squirrels, and hadrons."[28] All of these are posits, that is, all objects and events are posits. And because such posits are necessarily dependent on objective reality, they must have "essences" for reasons explained by Aristotle and Saul Kripke, but because per (b), there are no given essences or natural kinds in reality, these are "relative essences," that is, essences relative to a conceptual designation.[29]

While there is much to admire in Wheeler's view, it is not Davidson's. It is better described as an eclectic mix of Davidson and Quine with a sprinkling of Aristotle and Kripke. More importantly, perhaps, this brief review of the Davidsonian credentials of Wheeler's relative perspectivism shows that Davidson is not a likely source for an alternative foundation of something like post-Yogācāra realism. His view is too close to essentialism, which virtually all Buddhist philosophy rejects, too close to naive realism because it assumes that the world really is the way we think it is, and leaves too little space for conceptual construction and cross-perspectival difference.

Davidson's ambiguous views on essences and natural kinds sets him apart from the other new pragmatists: Quine, Putnam, and Rorty all explicitly rejected essentialism.[30] For, example, Putnam wrote that

> [t]he idea that the "non-psychological" fixes reference — i.e., that *nature itself* determines what our words stand for — is totally unintelligible. At bottom, to think that a sign-relation is *built into nature* is to revert to medieval essentialism, to the idea that there are "self-identifying objects" and "species" out there.[31]

---

26 Davidson, "Reply to Simon J. Evnine," 306.
27 See the section "Posits and Phenomenal Reality" in chapter 9.
28 Wheeler, *Neo-Davidsonian Metaphysics*, 64.
29 On Wheeler's "relative essentialism," see also the section "Realism (1) — Universals and (Anti-)Essentialism" in chapter 7.
30 W.V.O. Quine, "Three Grades of Modal Involvement" (1953), WPOE: 158–76; *Word & Object* (Cambridge: MIT Press, 1960); Hilary Putnam, *Reason, Truth and History* (Cambridge: Cambridge University Press, 1981); "Why There Isn't a Ready-Made World" (1981), in *Realism and Reason: Philosophical Papers*, Vol. 3 (Cambridge: Cambridge University Press, 1983), 205–28; Richard Rorty, *Contingency, Irony, and Solidarity* (Cambridge: Cambridge University Press, 1989). "A World without Substances or Essences" (1994), in *Philosophy and Social Hope* (London: Penguin, 1999), 47–71.
31 Hilary Putnam, "Introduction" (1983), in *Realism and Reason*, vii–xviii, at xii.

However, this does not mean that Quine, Putnam, or Rorty are closer to post-Yogācāra realism than Davidson. As already mentioned above, Putnam's naive realism about perception leaves no room for *pratibhāsa* as an intermediate, nor for any significant kind of conceptual construction, for example. And neither Rorty, nor Putnam developed a theory of concept formation similar to Davidson's theory of triangulation, which played a key role in chapter 8 in clarifying Dharmakīrti's theory of concept formation through apoha. Hence, while their non-essentialism might be a better fit, there are other key elements missing. (And Rorty would never have approved of the systematic ambitions of this project anyway.)

On the surface, Quine may seem the closest fit of all the new pragmatists. Like the Yogācāra philosophers, he was an anti-essentialist and nominalist, and his notions of posits and conceptual schemes are more congruent with the Yogācāra notions of conceptually determinate awareness (*pratibhāsa-pratīti*) and conceptual construction (*kalpanā*) than related ideas advocated by any of the other new pragmatists. Furthermore, Quine also advocated a rudimentary theory of concept formation similar to Davidson's triangulation.[32]

> There are two parts to knowing a word. One part is being familiar with the sound of it and being able to reproduce it. [...] The other part, the semantic part, is knowing how to use the word. [...] The word refers, in the paradigm case, to some visible object. The learner has now not only to learn the word phonetically, by hearing it from another speaker; he also has to see the object; and in addition to this, in order to capture the relevance of the object to the world, he has to see that the speaker also sees the object.[33]

There is, however, a fundamental difference between Quine's proto-triangulation and Davidson's more developed version of the idea: Quine's sketchy theory assumes realism — and not just the minimal variant — while the most interesting versions of Davidson's theory infer it. From a Yogācāra or related perspective, Quine's version assumes too much. At the same time, the only metaphysical assumption in the relevant variants of triangulation is that there is communication, and that assumption is shared by the Yogācārin. Moreover, it is Davidson's more developed version of the triangular learning situation that matters in clarifying the metaphysical and epistemological implications of Dignāga's theory of apoha and Dharmakīrti's rather underdeveloped theory of concept formation.[34]

It seems, then, that something like post-Yogācāra realism could at best be based on a more or less "eclectic" mix of Quine's and Davidson's ideas. "More or less," because the obstacle of anti-dualism remains. But what about Wheeler? His version of perspectival realism is based on an eclectic mix with Quine and Davidson as its main ingredients, but if Wheeler's philosophy could provide an alternative foundation for post-Yogācāra realism or something sufficiently similar, then that would still be a single, non-Buddhist source. It is not so much the number of sources that matters but the eclecticism of the sources, and a single source can be more eclectic

---

32 Considering that Davidson was heavily influenced by Quine, it was probably a predecessor of triangulation. In later writings, Quine adopted the term "triangulation," but what he meant with that term seems more in line with his own rudimentary theory than with Davidson's theory of triangulation.
33 W.V.O. Quine, "Ontological Relativity" (1969), OROE: 26–68, at 27–28.
34 See the last two sections of chapter 8.

than a collection of sources. However, if a source is eclectic just because it itself is based on multiple, unrelated sources, then every view is eclectic, because every view is ultimately derived from multiple sources. And this implication would make the equally-or-less-eclectic criterion meaningless.

The term "eclectic" does not denote a clearly defined category with crisp boundaries — instead, the notion is fuzzy, more or less subjective, and historical. Something is more or less eclectic largely to the extent that it is more or less easily *recognized* as eclectic, and this recognition is historically contingent. The passage of time results in a gradual congelation of what was once eclectic into something that is no longer recognized as just a mix of its ingredients, but as something quite separate therefrom. This process is similar to that of the mixing of languages resulting in a pidgin, which gradually develops into a creole, and then slowly into a wholly new language or even language family. Eclecticism is a spectrum ranging from the philosophical equivalent of a pidgin to that of a language. Wheeler's philosophy is still closer to the eclectic/pidgin end of the spectrum. Where exactly Quine and Davidson are located is debatable, but they are much further from the eclectic end. And Yogācāra is even closer to the other end.

The biggest obstacle to a new pragmatist foundation for something like post-Yogācāra realism is its anti-dualism, but even if that obstacle could be overcome, a new pragmatist foundation would almost certainly be more eclectic than the mostly Yogācāra foundation of the view developed in chapters 8 and 9. That view, therefore, satisfies the second criterion — it can *not* just as well be based on non-Buddhist sources — which means that by the standard proposed in chapter 5 and quoted above, post-Yogācāra realism is Buddhist.[35]

Classical Perspectives — Zhuangzi, Heraclitus, and Epicurus

Post-Yogācāra realism is, obviously, not the only version of perspectival realism.[36] Throughout history, apparently similar ideas have been suggested in all three great philosophical traditions, and it is worth making a quick inventory of some of these ideas to explore (in future work) how they may enrich and support the view presented here.

The earliest versions of something like perspectival realism can be found in the writings of Heraclitus (sixth to fifth century BCE) and Zhuangzi 莊子 (fourth century BCE). Both are very obscure; in the case of Heraclitus because only fragments remain, and in the case of Zhuangzi due to his style. And consequently, there are many competing interpretations of their thought. Zhuangzi, for example, has been interpreted as a skeptic, a relativist, or a perspectivist, and as a realist as well as an anti-realist. As Eric Schwitzgebel observed,

> [a] tension stands at the heart of the Zhuangzi. Sometimes Zhuangzi seems to advocate radical skepticism and relativism. [...] At other times, however, Zhuangzi

---

[35] Perhaps, at this point, you are wondering why this even matters. Recall that the goal of this book is a version of radical *Buddhism* that is radically naturalist, sociopolitically radical, and Buddhist. Given that goal, it matters a lot whether the philosophy proposed in the previous chapters is indeed Buddhist. Beyond that goal, it is quite irrelevant. All that ultimately matters is whether it is an acceptable and defensible theory. I think it is, but substantiating that opinion is not my main goal here.

[36] The most obvious reason why this should be obvious is that another version of perspectival realism was discussed in the previous section, namely Wheeler's.

seems to make a variety of factual claims and to endorse and condemn various ways of living, in apparent disregard of any skeptical or relativist considerations.[37]

According to Zhuangzi, everything can be looked at from multiple points of view:[38] what is beautiful from one perspective may be ugly from another, for example.[39] But the expressions of these different points of view are not groundless.

> Speech is not [just] puffing [out air]. The speaker has [a meaning in his] words — if what he said would not yet be determinate, would the result (i.e., what he said) [really] be speech or not? He believes that it is different from the sounds [made by] fledglings, but is there [really] a distinction or not?[40]

Words and the views expressed by them are not arbitrary but rooted in the use of things.[41] "A path is created by walking it, a thing is [called] as it is by it being called so."[42] Furthermore, Zhuangzi's distinction between the chirping of fledglings or mere puffing out air on the one hand, and meaningful speech on the other, depends on a distinction between truth and falsehood, which in turn depends on there being a way things are and, thus, on an external reality. On the other hand, he also wrote about dreaming of being a butterfly, and being uncertain whether it was really Zhuangzi dreaming of being a butterfly or a butterfly dreaming of being Zhuangzi.[43]

The text is unlikely to resolve the tension observed by Schwitzgebel, but perhaps that is intentional. An interesting suggestion by Mark Berkson is that the *Zhuangzi* should be seen as a kind of apophatic discourse.[44] If ultimate reality cannot be expressed in language, all we can do is point, allude, and defer. Berkson sees similarities in this respect with Jacques Derrida, who argued that if meanings cannot be directly grounded in ultimate reality due to it being out of our reach, then words and meanings can only point to other words and meanings.[45] Hence, meaning is deferred indefinitely into a network of differences, different words, different meanings: "[e]very concept is necessarily and essentially inscribed in a chain or in a system within which it refers to the other, to other concepts, by a systematic play of differences."[46] Derrida's theory of *différance* reminds of apoha,[47] but is so radically

---

37 Eric Schwitzgebel, "Zhuangzi's Attitude Toward Language and His Skepticism," in *Essays on Skepticism, Relativism, and Ethics in the Zhuangzi*, eds. Paul Kjellberg and Philip Ivanhoe (Albany: SUNY Press, 1996), 68–96, at 68.
38 Zhuangzi 莊子,《莊子》(4th c. BCE), §2.5.
39 Ibid., §2.11.
40 夫言非吹也。言者有言, 其所言者特未定也。果有言邪?其未嘗有言邪?其以為異於鷇音, 亦有辯乎, 其無辯乎? — Ibid., §2.4.
41 Ibid., §2.6.
42 道行之而成, 物謂之而然。— Ibid., §2.6.
43 Ibid., §2.14.
44 Mark Berkson, "Language: The Guest of Reality — Zhuangzi and Derrida on Language, Reality, and Skillfulness," in *Essays on Skepticism, Relativism, and Ethics in the Zhuangzi*, eds. Kjellberg and Ivanhoe, 97–126.
45 I am not following Berkson's view on Derrida and his similarities with Zhuangzi here but my own interpretation of Derrida. See Lajos Brons, "Meaning and Reality: A Cross-Traditional Encounter," in *Constructive Engagement of Analytic and Continental Approaches in Philosophy*, eds. Bo Mou and R. Tieszen (Leiden: Brill, 2013), 199–220.
46 Tout concept est en droit et essentiellement inscrit dans une chaîne ou dans un système à l'intérieur duquel il renvoie à l'autre, aux autres concepts, par jeu systématique de différences. — Jacques Derrida, "Différance" (1968), in *Marges de la philosophie* (Paris: Les Éditions de Minuit, 1972), 1–29, at 11.
47 About this connection, see also Brons, "Meaning and Reality."

apophatic that Derrida cannot even clearly express the theory itself. Différance is "neither a word nor a concept"[48] and Derrida's explanation alludes and illustrates more than that it clarifies or defines. Or in other words, it defers — it is différance applied to itself. An unfortunate consequence thereof is that the theory is not likely to be of much use in clarifying anything else either.

Among the attempts to resolve the aforementioned tension in the *Zhuangzi*, the most interesting are those that argue for a more or less perspectival realist interpretation. Bo Mou, for example, argues that Zhuangzi's view is

> a kind of objective perspectivism.[49] For, instead of "any perspective goes," Zhuang Zi bases relevance and eligibility of a perspective (given an object of study) upon whether it points to some aspect that is really or objectively possessed by the object of study.[50]

JeeLoo Liu similarly argues that Zhuangzi's perpectival view is not anti-realist.

> Zhuangzi certainly did not claim that reality is relative to perspectives or conceptual schemes, or that there is no fact of the matter with regards to reality in itself. We could probably say that Zhuangzi was skeptical about our linguistic ability to express the truth of reality, but he was not skeptical about the existence of this reality itself.[51]

In this quote Liu also affirms Berkson's suggestion that Zhuangzi's view was apophatic, but without using that term. If these interpretations are right, Zhuangzi's philosophy was a kind of apophatic perspectival realism.

Heraclitus, as mentioned, is at least as obscure as Zhuangzi but partially for a very different reason. Of Heraclitus writings only very short fragments remain. Furthermore, many of these fragments seem self-contradictory or are hard to understand for other reasons, earning Heraclitus the nickname ὁ Σκοτεινός, "the Obscure" or "the Dark," a few centuries after his death.

Among the seemingly self-contradictory fragments there are many that argue for some kind of unity of opposites. Famous examples include "[t]he road upward or downward are one and the same,"[52] and "seawater is both pure and defiled: pleasant/drinkable and safe to fish, [but] undrinkable and deadly to humans."[53] These fragments can be interpreted in numerous ways, but if interpretations that are contradicted by other fragments are ignored, only two plausible options remain. Either different qualifications or designations depend on or are relative to different perspectives; or different qualifications or designations are co-present potentialities or dispositions that realize in different circumstances. Edward Hussey, for example,

---

48 Derrida, "Différance," 2.
49 On Mou's notion of "objective perspectivism," and its opposite, "subjective perspectivism," see the section "Relativism, Pluralism, and Perspectivism" in chapter 7.
50 Bo Mou, "Searle, Zhuang Zi, and Transcendental Perspectivism," in *Searle's Philosophy and Chinese Philosophy: Constructive Engagement*, ed. Bo Mou (Leiden: Brill, 2008), 405–30, at 415.
51 JeeLoo Liu, *An Introduction to Chinese Philosophy: From Ancient Philosophy to Chinese Buddhism* (Malden: Blackwell, 2006), 165.
52 Ὁδὸς ἄνω κάτω μία καὶ ὠυτή. — Heraclitus, Fragment DK B60/Byw. 69 (~6–5th c. BCE).
53 Heraclitus, Fragment DK B61/Byw. 52 (~6–5th c. BCE). Previously quoted in the section "Yogācāra Realism" in chapter 8. See there for the original Greek.

argues for the second, while Catherine Osborne opts for the first.⁵⁴ I do not think the available fragments are sufficient to decide which of these interpretations is right, but the relativist or perspectivist (i.e., first) interpretation seems more charitable to me.

If Heraclitus was some kind of relativist or perspectivist, he probably was a perspectival realist. Many of the surviving fragments clearly presuppose a reality independent from our perceptions and designations, even though that reality may substantially differ from those perceptions and designations. "Nature likes to hide" or "the natures of things like to hide," he wrote.⁵⁵ The senses and our reasoning capacity are all we can go on, but because "nature likes to hide," we cannot trust them unconditionally. "Seeing, hearing, and learning — these I honor,"⁵⁶ but "eyes and ears are bad witnesses to men if they have souls that do not understand their language."⁵⁷ However, this did not lead Heraclitus towards an apophatic rejection of language and linguistic description. On the contrary, regardless of whether they are perspectival or dispositional, contradictory qualifications of things denote real qualities of those things. The potability and impotability of seawater are not deceptions — seawater really has both qualities. Hence, Heraclitus's view appears to be a kataphatic perspectival realism.

Epicurus, who lived two centuries after Heraclitus, was a prolific writer, but unfortunately, all of his books were lost until the middle of the eighteenth century. In 1752 charred remains of a Greek library were found in the "Villa of the Papyri" in Herculaneum, which was covered by meters of ash during the eruption of the Vesuvius in the year 79. Attempts to reconstruct the content of these scrolls with a variety of increasingly less damaging techniques have been ongoing ever since. The library appears to have belonged to a follower of Epicurus and included at least six and probably all of the thirty-seven volumes of his main treatise, Περὶ Φύσεως (*On Nature*). David Sedley estimates the length of individual volumes of the text at around 20,000 words, which would amount to well over 2,000 pages for the whole text if it would be printed as a book.⁵⁸ Very little of that is available now, however. The main sources on Epicurus's philosophy remain the same as what has been available for centuries — three long letters, a few fragments, and some descriptions of his ideas by later followers — but this may slowly change in the not-so-distant future.

In his *Letter to Herodotus*, Epicurus argues for a distinction between perception as a direct grasping of the thing perceived and the subsequent apprehension by the mind, which reminds of the Yogācāra distinction between *pratibhāsa* and *pratibhāsa-*

---

54   Edward Hussey, "Heraclitus," in *The Cambridge Companion to Early Greek Philosophy*, ed. A.A. Long (Cambridge: Cambridge University Press, 1999), 88–112, and Catherine Osborne, "Heraclitus," in *Routledge History of Philosophy*, Vol. I: *From the Beginning to Plato*, ed. C.C.W. Taylor (London: Routledge, 1997), 88–127.
55   Φύσις κρύπτεσμαι φιλεῖ. — Heraclitus, Fragment DK B123/Byw. 10 (~6–5th c. BCE). The term φύσις in this fragment can be translated as "nature," "the nature of things," "the natural qualities of things," "the real constitution of things," "the natural order," and so forth.
56   Ὅσων ὄψις ἀκοὴ μάθησις, ταῦτα ἐγὼ προτιμέω. — Heraclitus, Fragment DK B55/Byw. 13 (~6–5th c. BCE).
57   Κακοὶ μάρτυρες ἀνθρώποισιν ὀφθαλμοὶ καὶ ὦτα βαρβάρους ψυχὰς ἐχόντων. — Heraclitus, Fragment DK B107/Byw. 4 (~6–5th c. BCE).
58   David Sedley, *Lucretius and the Transformation of Greek Wisdom* (Cambridge: Cambridge University Press, 1998), 103. The original text of Περὶ Φύσεως was probably a lecture series, written between, roughly, 311 and 292 BCE (see ibid. 129ff).

pratīti.⁵⁹ The direct perception is always true to the object perceived and any error or falsehood in the apprehension by the mind can only be the result of the interference of belief or opinion (δόξα⁶⁰) in subsequent interpretation.⁶¹ Preconceptions (προλήψεις) play a key role in conceptually determinate awareness, but this is a much simpler and straightforward process than the Yogācāra theory of conceptual construction and concept formation through apoha.⁶² In his *Lives and Opinions of Eminent Philosophers*, Diogenes Laertius explained that for Epicurus, such preconceptions were like universal ideas stored in the mind, memories of things that had often appeared in external reality. Hence, no real "construction" takes place in this process — all that the mind does is name the direct perception and, thus, the things perceived. Or, in the words of Elizabeth Asmis: "there is an act of inference, but it consists of simply recognizing connections that are given," and "all preconceptions, even the most complex, are a record of appearances from outside, free of any added element of interpretation."⁶³

If preconception is little more than memory of things perceived and plays no active, constructive role in determinate perception, then those things and the kinds they belong to must more or less be given by mind-independent reality. Then it is reality that is determinate, rather than that we make it seem determinate, as in the Buddhist view. While this seems to leave little room for a distinction between appearance and reality or for any kind of relativism or perspectivism, Epicurus drew a distinction between things in themselves (καθ' αὐτό) and things in relation to us (πρὸς ἡμᾶς),⁶⁴ and suggested that appearances or perceptions differ between kinds of beings and between individuals. Such cross-perspectival differences are not the result of something like different conceptual schemes but of variations in and conditions of the relevant sense organs. Sense organs like the eyes and ears are adapted to certain kinds of physical signals, and therefore, different sense organs, or diseased sense organs, perceive differently.⁶⁵

Much of this is conjecture based on very limited available sources. If more of Epicurus writings are found and reconstructed the picture might change. According to Sedley, book 14 of *On Nature* deals with perception, the part of Epicurus's philosophy that seems the most relevant here, and a copy of that book has been found in Herculaneum. Unfortunately, the first part of the book is heavily damaged and the last part is about Epicurus's atom theory instead. The only recognizable fragment longer than a few words about perception is the following:

---

59 Epicurus, *Letter to Herodotus* (3rd c. BCE), in Diogenes Laertius, *Lives of Eminent Philosophers*, trans. R.D. Hicks, Vol 2., The Loeb Classical Library (London: William Heineman, 1925), Book X, §§35–83, at §50. See also ibid., Book X, §§31–34.
60 The Greek word δόξα, here translated as "belief or opinion," is associated with common belief or popular opinion and also has conceptual links to the notion of appearance as the opposite of reality.
61 See, for example, Elizabeth Asmis, "Epicurean Empiricism," in *The Cambridge Companion to Epicureanism*, ed. James Warren (Cambridge: Cambridge University Press, 2009), 84–104.
62 Nevertheless, the criterion to distinguish true from spurious perceptions is similar to Dharmakīrti's — coherence. See ibid., 103
63 Ibid., 90.
64 For example, Epicurus, *Letter to Pythocles* (3rd c. BCE), in Diogenes Laertius, *Lives of Eminent Philosophers*, trans. R.D. Hicks, Vol 2., The Loeb Classical Library (London: William Heineman, 1925), Book X, §§84–116, at §91.
65 Epicurus, *Letter to Herodotus*, §53. See also Elizabeth Asmis, "Epicurean Epistemology," in *The Cambridge History of Hellenistic Philosophy*, eds. Keimpe Algra et al. (Cambridge: Cambridge University Press, 1999), 260–94, at 271.

[...] τὸ θε]ωρούμεν[ον [...] | ... τὴ]ν αὐτὴν ἔχον | [...]στίαν φαίνεται|[...]ν αὔξης παραλ|[λάγμα]τα μείζω τ[ῶν | σωμάτω]ν ταῖς αἰσθή[σε|σι - - -[66]

Unfortunately, there are too many gaps for a reliable translation, but it seems to say something like "[...] what is perceived [...] reveals that it is the same [...] extent of variation is great of what is embodied in sense perception [...]"[67] This is obviously not enough to shed new light on Epicurus's theory of perception, but it does raise questions about the interpretation in the previous paragraphs. If the extent of variation in perception of the same thing is so great, is naming really all we do in sense perception? And is this "great variation" really just due to differences between sense organs? Or was Epicurus's theory really more constructive or more perspectival than the remaining letters suggest?[68]

Religious Perspectives — Ibn Rushd, Dooyeweerd, and *Anekāntavāda*

With the advent of the Dark Ages, philosophy died in Europe. It struggled on for a while in the remnants of Greek civilization in the Byzantine Empire until it was revived by Islamic scholars in the Middle East centuries later. Aristotle dominated Islamic philosophical thought, and when Europe finally reimported philosophy from the Muslim world, Aristotle became dominant there as well. Because of this, Aristotle's essentialism became a dogma of Western philosophy and remained unassailable until very recently.

In early Islamic thought, a major debate occurred between more philosophically oriented schools and more religiously oriented schools. Ultimately, the latter side won, thanks in part to the eloquence of Al-Ghazali. The last major contributions by the other side were made by Ibn Rushd (Averroes) in response to Al-Ghazali. Ibn Rushd lived on the far Western fringe of the Islamic Empire (he was born in Spain) and would be of greater influence on reemerging European philosophy than on Islamic thought.

Ibn Rushd's contribution to the debate between philosophers and religious thinkers was the rather deflationary idea that the two sides represented complementary more than contradictory points of view. Oliver Leaman explains:

> In Averroes' philosophy there is a continual contrast between different points of view. There is not just a distinction between God's point of view and the human point of view, but also a differentiation of the standpoints of a whole variety of different human beings based upon their reasoning.[69]

The *Faṣl al-Maqāl* (*On the Harmony of Religion and Philosophy*) is the main text in which Ibn Rushd developed this idea, but it is based on his views on language and real-

---

66 Giuliana Leone, "Epicuro, Della Natura, Libro XIV," *Cronache Ercolanesi* 14 (1984): 17–107, at 47.
67 Leone translates the fragment into Italian as "[...] cio che viene percepito [...] mostra di averse la stessa [...] maggiori variazioni di accrescimento dei corpi (percepiti) mediante i sensi [...]" (ibid.).
68 Considering the immense influence of Aristotelian essentialism, it is not at all impossible that Epicurus's ideas where interpreted as more essentialist than they really were.
69 Oliver Leaman, *Averroes and His Philosophy* (Richmond: Curzon, 1988), 194.

ity developed in his *Tahāfut al-Tahāfut* (*The Incoherence of the Incoherence*) and other texts.[70]

According to Leaman, for Ibn Rushd, "equivocation is an inevitable aspect of our language, since that language has to describe a wide gamut of views using the same name."[71] In the *Tahāfut al-Tahāfut*, Ibn Rushd asserted approximately thirty times that attributions of properties to God and other entities are equivocal. The words "cause," "will," or "eternal," for example, do not mean the same thing when we talk about God or about something else. Language abstracts from reality, but it can do so in different ways, corresponding to and reinforcing these different views. In his fourth proof "concerning the eternity of the world," Ibn Rushd wrote that

> knowledge is not knowledge of the universal concept, but it is a knowledge of individuals in a universal way which the mind attains in the case of the individuals, when it abstracts from them one common nature which is distributed among the different matters. [...] The universal [...] is not the object of knowledge; on the contrary through it the things become known, [...].[72]

Hence, things are recognized and known through our concepts or universals, but those concepts are themselves abstractions from external reality. (There can be little doubt that Ibn Rushd was a realist. He wrote, for example, that if there were nothing "outside the soul" "there would be no difference between reason and illusion."[73]) Because of this, a skillful doctor has different views on a disease and how to cure it than someone without a medical background.[74] In this example, the doctor's view is likely to be more advantageous to those suffering from this disease than the view of the medically ignorant, and other views may also be more or less fruitful or appropriate depending on context. Different people come to understand the truth (i.e., the meaning of scripture) by different means and through different views, and all of these views have their uses and value. In some sense, all views are true and complementary: if two views appear to contradict each other, at least one of the two needs to be interpreted metaphorically because "truth does not oppose truth but accords with it and bears witness to it."[75]

Like Ibn Rushd, Herman Dooyeweerd appealed to a kind of perspectivism to mediate a perceived conflict between scientific and religious points of view, but that is were the similarity ends. While Ibn Rushd was a Medieval Muslim judge, physician, and philosopher from Spain, Dooyeweerd was a twentieth-century Neocalvinist professor of law and philosopher from the Netherlands. One of the most important influences on his thought was the theologian and politician Abraham Kuyper who had founded Neocalvinism, leading to an important split in Dutch Protestantism in 1886. Kuyper had argued for "sphere sovereignty" (*souvereiniteit in eigen kring*), the

---

70 Ibn Rushd, *Faṣl al-Maqal fī ma bayn al-Hikma wa al-Shariah min Ittisal* [*On the Harmony of Religion and Philosphy*] (1179), trans. George Hourani, *On the Harmony of Religion and Philosophy* (Cambridge: Gibb Memorial Trust, 1961), and Ibn Rushd, *Tahāfut al-Tahāfut* [*The Incoherence of the Incoherence*] (1180), trans. Simon van den Bergh, *Averroes' Tahafut Al-Tafut* (Cambridge: Gibb Memorial Trust, 1954). References are to the standard Arabic edition by Bouyges shown in the margins of Van den Bergh's translation.
71 Leaman, *Averroes and His Philosophy*, 195.
72 Ibn Rushd, *Tahāfut al-Tahāfut*, B. 111–12.
73 Ibid., B. 113
74 Ibn Rushd, *Faṣl al-Maqāl*, 67.
75 Ibid., 50.

idea that each sphere of life was characterized by its own responsibilities, authorities, and so forth. A major effect of this idea on Dutch society was "pillarization" (*verzuiling*), a division of society along religious or political lines into more or less autonomous pillars that each had their own institutions and organizations ranging from newspapers to football clubs, from schools to hospitals, and from broadcasters to political parties.

Dooyeweerd turned the notion of sphere sovereignty from a sociopolitical into a metaphysical and epistemological theory. The world around us has a number of "modal aspects" (also called "modalities" or "aspects," among others) that are each characterized by their own laws. And like Kuyper's spheres, Dooyeweerd's modal aspects are part of the all-encompassing order designed and created by God. The modal aspects are ways of being of the world and the things in it, but also ways of seeing those, and thus, comparable but not identical to perspectives. Dooyeweerd distinguished fifteen modal aspects but did not exclude the possibility that there could be more.[76] The fifteen aspects are the following:

1. the quantitative aspect: concerning discrete amounts and numbers;
2. the spatial aspect: continuous extension, shape, and size;
3. the kinematic aspect: motion;
4. the physical aspect: energy, matter, force;
5. the biotic or organic aspect: life and organisms;
6. the sensitive or psychic aspect: feelings, sensitivity, and emotions;
7. the analytical aspect: distinction and conceptualization;
8. the formative aspect: construction, technology, and history;
9. the lingual aspect: language, symbols, and communication;
10. the social aspect: social roles and conventions, social interaction, and so forth;
11. the economic aspect: management of resources, (exchange) value;
12. the aesthetic aspect: beauty, harmony, enjoyment;
13. the juridical aspect: rights, responsibility, justice, retribution;
14. the ethical aspect: love, generosity, care; and
15. the pistic aspect: faith, religious commitment and belief.

The order of these modal aspects is not random — higher-numbered aspects presuppose lower-numbered ones. Thus, ethics (14) presupposes law (13), psychology (6) presupposes life (5), and everything presupposes number (1).[77] Religion (15) presupposes all other aspects, but Dooyeweerd's concept of religion is a bit broader than the ordinary conception. He claimed that every thinker is driven by an essentially religious idea because every system of thought has fundamental ideas that are impossible to prove by the standards of that system of thought itself. Thereby, such fundamental ideas go beyond reason and are accepted as articles of faith. It is exactly that what makes them religious.[78]

---

76 Herman Dooyeweerd, *A New Critique of Theoretical Thought*, Vol. 2: *The General Theory of Modal Spheres* (Amsterdam: Paris, 1955).
77 There is no temporal aspect. Rather, time is beyond reality as a whole; or the other way around: the whole of reality is embedded in time. The only "thing" that goes even beyond time is God.
78 Herman Dooyeweerd, *A New Critique of Theoretical Thought*, Vol. 1: *The Necessary Presuppositions of Philosophy* (Amsterdam: Paris, 1953). See also Marcel Verburg, "Inleiding," in *Herman Dooyeweerd: Grenzen van het theoretisch denken*, ed. Marcel Verburg (Baarn: Ambo, 1986), 11–50, at 18.

In the present context, what is most important about Dooyeweerd's ideas is that all of his modal aspects represent partial views on reality. Every thing can be seen from the perspective of multiple, if not all, aspects, and all of those perspectives together give the most complete view humanly possible. An obvious criticism of the fifteen aspects as a metaphysical theory is that the classification into these specific classes is itself a product of a particular cultural and conceptual perspective. Dooyeweerd's theory may be useful as a tool to systematically remind oneself of a variety of perspectives that might otherwise be overlooked, but for this reason, it is implausible as a metaphysical scheme.

A similar criticism can be leveled at any closed list of perspectives. Any theory that posits a certain fixed number of specific named perspectives implicitly assumes a non-perspectival position on a higher level. Perspectives cut up and classify, and a classification of and into perspectives is itself perspectival. In other words, a list of perspectives is itself the product of a higher-order perspective. But if that list of perspectives is given special status, especially if it is considered to be the one and only true and final list of perspectives, then that higher-order perspective is not recognized as a perspective and is implicitly assumed to be objective or absolute. Hence, closed-list perspectivism denies the perspectival nature of conceptual classification at the higher level. This is incoherent, except in two cases: (a) if the *apparent* perspectivism is really something else; or (b) in case of a weakly relativist perspectivism that assumes that the list of perspectives is universal.

According to weak perspectivism or weakly relativist perspectivism — in Maria Baghramian's sense of the strong-weak distinction[79] — there may be some things that all perspectives agree on and that are, therefore, universal. This does not mean that those "things" are non-perspectival but that they are pan-perspectival. If everyone would agree that Dooyeweerd's list of modal aspects is the way reality is divided into different spheres of being, then the higher-order perspective could be pan-perspectival and thus universal in that sense. However, Dooyeweerd himself expressed uncertainty about the list, there is ongoing debate in Dooyeweerdian circles about the modal aspects, and most importantly, it is rather unlikely that an inhabitant of North Sentinel Island, for example, would come up with the same list of perspectives. Furthermore, it seems improbable, to say the least, that there is another list of perspectives that would satisfy the universal agreement criterion. There may be things everyone agrees about,[80] but a division of reality into a specific, closed list of spheres of being is almost certainly not one of them. Option (b), then, turns out not to be an option at all.

The alternative, option (a), would be a view that is perspectivist on the lower level and absolutist on the higher level. Such a view might be defensible if there is a good argument why some classifications, namely those on the lower level, are perspectival while others, namely the higher-level lists of lower-level perspectives, are not. The

---

Dooyeweerd has a point here, but it can be argued that his claim is not true for pragmatism, and especially not for most of the "new pragmatists," because those reject the very idea of foundational ideas. A pragmatist does not non-provisionally accept anything, and for a pragmatist any idea (including pragmatism/naturalism itself!) is accepted or rejected on the basis of the same more or less naturalist standards.

79 Maria Baghramian, *Relativism* (New York: Routledge, 2004). See also the section "Relativism, Pluralism, and Perspectivism" in chapter 7.
80 Part III of this book explores universal agreement about certain aspects of moral thought, for example.

arbitrary positing of some specific classifications as non-perspectival in an otherwise perspectivist framework is incoherent. Perhaps, in case of a Dooyeweerdian theory, it could be claimed that the higher-level classification of and into modal aspects is given by God, but that claim would still have to be supported by a good argument. Since I doubt that there is a good argument for the positing of any perspective-transcendent list of perspectives, as part of an otherwise perspectivist theory, option (a) does not appear to be a real option either.

Closed-list perspectivism, then, is incoherent, which might be bad news for the final theory to be considered in this section, because the Jaina doctrine of *anekāntavāda* does not involve one, but two closed lists of perspectives. These two lists are the core teachings of *nayavāda* and *syādvāda* which are often considered the "wings" of anekāntavāda. What exactly this metaphor means and how the three are supposed to relate to each other differs between Jaina thinkers, but they all agree that the three come together, and often the term anekāntavāda is used both for that trio as a whole and for a specific part thereof. Anekāntavāda in the broad sense is usually translated as "non-absolutism." Satkari Mookerjee summarizes the core idea as follows:

> What is necessary is to recognize the metaphysical truth that things are possessed of an infinite plurality of attributes and the predication of one among these attributes is not false, though it is admittedly incomplete as a description of the nature of the subject.[81]

That "metaphysical truth" is the essence of anekāntavāda in the narrow sense. Its two wings are "logical" or "epistemological" tools or methods.[82] Often nayavāda is considered a method of analysis and syādvāda a method of synthesis, but it is not entirely clear what those qualifications are based on. Concerning the relation between the two wings and the bird (or building?) they are part of, Y.J. Padmarajiah writes that they "aid an apprehension of the complex structure of reality" (i.e., anekāntavāda in the narrow sense).[83]

The origin of anekāntavāda in the broad sense is the Jaina attempt to defend their views on soul, karma, and liberation against attacks from non-Jaina philosophers in the classical period of Indian philosophy.[84] According to Jainism, things are simultaneously permanent and impermanent, and non-Jaina philosophers argued that this is a contradiction and, therefore, that it cannot possibly be true. The Jaina defense was based on the idea that the universe and all things in it are indeterminate, that reality is "manifold or complex to its core,"[85] and that all things have infinite characteristics and are related to everything else.[86] Because it is impossible to grasp all of this

---

81 Satkari Mookerjee, *The Jaina Philosophy of Non-absolutism* (Delhi: Motilal Banarsidass, 1944), 143.
82 John Cort, for example, calls nayavāda and syādvāda "logical tools," but they are not really concerned with logic in a conventional sense of that term. Most Jaina authors who write in English seem to prefer the term "epistemological." This term does not seem exactly correct either, as there are also issues in the philosophy of language involved, but it is more appropriate than "logical." John Cort, "'Intellectual *Ahiṃsā*' Revisited: Jain Tolerance and Intolerance of Others," *Philosophy East and West* 50, no. 3 (2000): 324–47.
83 Y.J. Padmarajiah, *A Comparative Study of the Jaina Theories of Reality and Knowledge* (Delhi: Motilal Banarsidass, 1963), 381.
84 Cort, "'Intellectual *Ahiṃsā*' Revisited."
85 Padmarajiah, *A Comparative Study of the Jaina Theories of Reality and Knowledge*, 275.
86 Mookerjee, *The Jaina Philosophy of Non-absolutism*.

complexity, at least at once, any statement about some real thing or the universe as a whole expresses only a particular point of view or perspective (*naya*). Consequently, statements are contingent on perspectives, and no philosophical proposition can be true or false if it is asserted without some kind of implicit specification of that perspective.[87] Things, then, may be permanent from one perspective, and impermanent from another, and there is no contradiction.

Anekāntavāda in the narrow sense is this metaphysical theory that every real thing has infinitely many qualities and thus can never be wholly characterized. It would seem that this idea leads to an apophatic conclusion. Acharya Mahaprajña explains that the real nature of a thing or substance is inexpressible, for example, because "a substance is possessed of an infinite number of attributes" and it is "not possible to express in language those infinite number of attributes taking place at every moment."[88] Nevertheless, Jainism is not apophatic but moderately kataphatic. According to Padmarajiah, Jainism aims to strike a balance between the apophatic view that ultimate reality is absolutely beyond words, and its opposite, naive realist views that assume that our conceptual categories carve reality at its joints. "Reality is both expressible and inexpressible, and [...] there is no contradiction in holding this position since reality is so from different points of view."[89] Furthermore, anekāntavāda appears to strike a balance between apophasis and excessive confidence in language in an another sense: indeed, a thing cannot be expressed in all its aspects at once, but it is not wholly inexpressible either.[90] To call some concrete particular a "pot," for example, is not false, just perspectival and incomplete, and in that sense, the nature of this concrete particular is not wholly inexpressible.

This dialectic of expressibility and inexpressibility is the topic of syādvāda or *saptabhaṅgī*, the "doctrine of seven-fold predication." The core of syādvāda/saptabhaṅgī is a list of seven apparently existential statements, sometimes called "modes of predication," that all start with the prefix *syād-*, which is translated in a number of different ways by different interpreters. Most common translations are variants of "from some perspective," "in some sense," "under certain conditions," "relatively speaking," "seen in some way," and so forth. The seven modes of predication are the following:

1. *Syād-asti*: in some sense or perspective it is.
2. *Syād-nāsti*: in some sense or perspective it is not.
3. *Syād-asti-nāsti*: in some sense or perspective it is, and it is not.
4. *Syād-asti-avaktavyaḥ*: in some sense or perspective it is, and it is inexpressible (or indescribable, unspeakable, and so forth).
5. *Syād-nāsti-avaktavyaḥ*: in some sense or perspective it is not, and it is inexpressible.
6. *Syād-asti-nāsti-avaktavyaḥ*: in some sense or perspective it is, and it is not, and it is inexpressible.
7. *Syād-avaktavyaḥ*: in some sense or perspective it is inexpressible.

---

87 Bimal Matilal, *The Central Philosophy of Jainism (Anekānta-Vāda)* (Ahmedabad: LD Institute of Indology, 1981).
88 Acharya Mahaprajña, "The Axioms of Non-Absolutism" (1984), in *Facets of Jain Religion and Culture*, Vol. 1: *Anekāntavāda and Syādvāda*, eds. Rai A. Kumar, T.M. Dak, and Anil D. Mishra (Ladnun: Jain Vishva Bharati, 1996), 1–32, at 9.
89 Padmarajiah, *A Comparative Study of the Jaina Theories of Reality and Knowledge*, 353.
90 See, for example, Mookerjee, *The Jaina Philosophy of Non-absolutism*, 103

This inexpressibility, as explained above, is "due to the bewildering wealth of impressions directly pouring into the human mind whose limitations of powers are such that it cannot at once grapple with all the impressions by way of all-comprehending attention and precise expression."[91] Nevertheless, we are not "condemned to be cognitively overwhelmed and verbally dumb" according to Padmarajiah, and the inexpressible can eventually become expressible by paying attention to the "manifold features" of the real thing.

The main problem in interpreting this doctrine is not the notion of inexpressibility, however, but the pair *asti/nāsti*, "exists" or "does not exist."[92] (3) *Syād-asti-nāsti* appears to claim that something exists and does not exist from one and the same perspective, and that sounds rather paradoxical. It has been suggested that this is an example of a non-classical or deviant logic, which rejects the principle of the excluded middle,[93] but that is a controversial interpretation and it also has been pointed out that Jaina logicians were quite clear about their acceptance of the principles of classical logic.[94] Furthermore, no appeal to deviant logics is necessary to explain (3), and there is nothing paradoxical about that part of syādvāda either. What must be realized, however, is that syādvāda is a doctrine of seven-fold predication, not of seven-fold being or existence. Asti, here, is not "being" as existence per se, but "being" *something* or existence as *something*.

Moreover, as Thomas McEvilley pointed out, Jaina scholars typically do not interpret (3) *asti-nāsti* as meaning "that something is both A and not-A, but that it is A and is not B."[95] Using the conventional example of a pot or jar, (3) means that the pot "exists" (as pot) relative to its own nature but not (as pot) relative to another nature.[96] Or in other words, "non-existence is not related to the non-existence of the object itself but to its non-existence as another object. That is to say, a jar is not said to non-exist as a jar, but [to non-exist] as a piece of cloth."[97] Perhaps, the clearest explanation is given by Padmarajiah:

> Every entity comprises, within the fullness of its being, two constituent elements, both equally important, viz., what is *itself* (*svatattva*) and what is other-than-itself (*paratattva*). A jar (*ghaṭa*), for instance, is constituted not merely by all the traits entering into its making, but also by the numerous other traits which constitute entities like a cloth (*paṭa*), a fruit (*phala*) or a book (*pustaka*), which *are not*, or *are other than*, the jar. The former group of traits forms the positive element (*sat* or *vidhi*), that is, what the jar is per se, and the latter group the negative element (*asat* or *niṣedha*), or what-is-not (or what-is-other-than) the jar.[98]

---

91 Padmarajiah, *A Comparative Study of the Jaina Theories of Reality and Knowledge*, 306.
92 For a valuable discussion of various interpretations, see, for example, Arvind Sharma, "The Doctrine of Syādvāda: Examination of Different Interpretations" (1996), in *Facets of Jain Religion and Culture*, Vol. 1, eds. Kumar, Dak, and Mishra, 326–38.
93 See, for example, Filita Bharuch and R.V. Kamat, "Syādvāda Theory of Jainism in Terms of a Deviant Logic" (1984), in *Facets of Jain Religion and Culture*, Vol. 1, eds. Kumar, Dak, and Mishra, 339–44.
94 John Koller, "Syādvāda as the Epistemological Key to the Jaina Middle Way Metaphysics of Anekāntavāda," *Philosophy East and West* 50, no. 3 (2000): 400–407.
95 Thomas McEvilley, *The Shape of Ancient Thought: Comparative Studies in Greek and Indian Philosophies* (New York: Allworth, 2002), 337.
96 Mahaprajña, "The Axioms of Non-absolutism."
97 Sharma, "The Doctrine of Syādvāda," 336.
98 Padmarajiah, *A Comparative Study of the Jaina Theories of Reality and Knowledge*, 149.

The doctrine seems more paradoxical than it is due to the potential confusion of "being" something with "being" as existence (i.e., of predication with ontology), but it is also due to a second problem: we cannot refer to an object in a text without predication. The only way to introduce a pot as an example is by using the word "pot," but in doing so we are already calling the hypothetical example a "pot," thereby implying that it is a pot. If we, however, want to say that that thing is not a pot from another perspective, or is inexpressible from another perspective, then that sounds paradoxical as well.

To avoid this problem, whenever I write "this ⚱," imagine me standing in front of you pointing at some object that you and me might call a pot. Then, (1) *syād-asti* can be understood as "in some sense or perspective, this ⚱ is a pot." According to the interpretations quoted above, (2) *syād-nāsti* does not mean "in some other sense or perspective, this ⚱ is not a pot" but means that in some sense this ⚱ is not a piece of cloth, nor a frog, a rainbow, and so forth. If the class of things a pot is not is denoted as "non-pot," then (2) *syād-nāsti* means "in some sense or perspective, this ⚱ is not a non-pot."[99] And (3) *syād-asti-nāsti* means "in some sense or perspective, this ⚱ is a pot and not a non-pot." (3) is not contradictory because there certainly are many perspectives in which a pot is not simultaneously a piece of cloth, a frog, or a rainbow.

However, this does not solve the contradiction in (4) *syād-asti-avaktavyaḥ*; to say that "in some sense or perspective, this ⚱ is a pot and is inexpressible" is a contradiction. If in some perspective this ⚱ can be accurately described as a "pot" then, *in that perspective*, it is not inexpressible. None of the accounts of syādvāda I have seen offers a solution to this problem, however. Typically, it is not even recognized as a problem.

The second wing of anekāntavāda is nayavāda, which is often illustrated by means of the famous parable of the six blind men and an elephant.[100] In the story, six blind men encounter an elephant for the first time, so they decide to inspect it. One, touching its trunk, announces that it is like a snake. Another, touching a leg, says it is like a tree. A third, holding its tail, thinks it is like a rope. And so forth. All of the six men perceive only a small part of the elephant and base their judgment on that. Like the blind men, we also perceive any thing only partially or from a single perspective. That is what the word *naya* in *nayavāda* denotes: a particular perspective, point of view, or opinion.

Given that according to anekāntavāda in the narrow sense, real things have infinitely many qualities, there also are infinitely many ways of seeing a thing, and thus infinitely many naya. However, trying to look at something from infinitely many perspectives is "too broad or gross,"[101] and because we are limited beings, it is impossible anyway. For this reason, Jaina thinkers have classified the infinite perspectives into seven named naya. Hence, in some sense there are infinitely many naya, while in another sense there are just seven — or less than seven even, because these seven are further classified into smaller sets. There appears to be little agreement about those further classifications, however,[102] with one major exception. According to the fifth century monk Siddhasēna, one of the foremost authorities on anekāntavāda, the first

---

99 Notice that this is not the "not non-" of the apoha doctrine. See the section "Apoha and Its Implications" in chapter 8.
100 This parable almost certainly predates Jainism and also occurs in the other Indian religious traditions.
101 Padmarajiah, *A Comparative Study of the Jaina Theories of Reality and Knowledge*, 312.
102 Ibid., 324ff.

three concern the "substantial" (*dravyārthika* or *dravyāstika*) point of view while the last four are about the "modal" (*paryāyārthika* or *paryāyāstika*) point of view.[103]

In *Sanmati-tarka* I.7, Siddhasēna explains that the substantial perspective is really just concerned with "being" and, thus, with what the object really is, implying that the first naya on the list (*naigama-naya*) is the core of this subset, while the other two are elaborations or special cases. In I.5 he makes a similar claim about the modal point of view: the first naya of that subset (i.e., the fourth in the complete list: *ṛjusūtra-naya*) is the core thereof, while the remaining three are subtle varieties or "its branches and twigs." The first three naya, are *naigama-*, *saṃgraha-*, and *vyavahāra-naya*.

i. *Naigama-yana*: the "non-distinguished" or "undifferentiated" or sometimes "teleological" point of view. It is also considered the "ordinary" or "common" point of view and has two varieties or interpretations. According to the first it is the grasping of an object in its concrete unity and the ordinary description of this 🏺 as "pot." According to the second, it is concerned with the purpose of an action.
ii. *Saṃgraha-naya*: the "general" or "class" perspective. It describes this 🏺 in terms of the larger classes or categories it belongs to; for example, "container."
iii. *Vyavahāra-naya*: the "practical," "specific," or "particular" point of view. It focuses on what makes this 🏺 different from the other members of the larger classes or categories it belongs to.

The substantial perspective appears surprisingly essentialist or absolutist. (i) This 🏺 is a pot. (ii) It belongs to a larger class; for example, of containers; and (iii) it has certain characteristics that make it a pot rather than one of the other kinds of members of that larger class. That's all that the first three naya seem to state. But what does this have to do with the six blind men and the elephant? In that story, the elephant's trunk is perceived to be a snake from the perspective of one of the blind men, but neither the first three naya nor the remaining four allow for such a perspective. And neither does syādvāda. The first three naya say (i) that it is a trunk, (ii) that it is kind of proboscis, and (iii) that it is formed from the elephant's nose and upper lip, for example. According to syadvāda, (1) it is a trunk from some perspective, (2) not a non-trunk from some (other?) perspective, and so forth. Significantly, there is no perspective — neither in syādvāda, nor in nayavāda — in which the trunk is a snake or this 🏺 is not a pot. Despite the supposed inexpressibility and manifoldness of reality, the pot-hood of this 🏺 is apparently a real and undeniable feature of external reality, and thus part of this 🏺's essence.

While the substantial perspective focuses on the inherent qualities of the object, and is therefore often associated with noumenal reality, the "modal" perspective concerns its fleeting qualities, such as the context of its appearance and its verbal classification and is usually associated with phenomenal reality.

iv. *Ṛjusūtra-naya*: the "immediate" or "manifest" point of view. It considers the object in its spatial and temporal context and how the object appears at some particular moment.

---

103 Siddhasēna Divākara, *Sanmati-tarka* (5th c.), §§I.3ff.

v. *Śabda-naya*: the "verbal" perspective or the point of view of "synonyms," which puts the spotlight on the word (i.e., "pot") and its grammatical roles and functions.
vi. *Samabhirūḍha-naya*: the "subtle" or "etymological" point of view. It focuses on the etymology of the word (i.e., "pot") and its implications, and it clarifies subtle differences in the meaning of words that are commonly assumed to denote the same kind of thing. By implication, it rejects strict synonymy.
vii. *Evambhūta-naya*: the "thus-happened" or "such-like" perspective, which aims to restrict the word to a single use and meaning.

Supposedly, each of the seven naya is a one-sided (ekānta) and partial, imperfect point of view. Only a judgment that takes all seven naya into account is many-sided (anekānta, or literally, not-one-sided). Nevertheless, one-sided judgments are not false and reveal real aspects of the object.[104] Or, in the words of Siddhasēna:

> All nayas are true in their respective spheres, but when they [cross over into each other's spheres and] refute each other they are false. One who comprehends the many-sided nature of reality [i.e., anekāntavāda] never says that a particular view is just true or false.[105]

What is most puzzling about the doctrine of anekāntavāda is how this is supposed to work. It is hard even to conceive of the formulaic list of naya as different "spheres" of reality. (They are nothing like Dooyeweerd's spheres or modal aspects, for example.) And it is very unclear what these *seven* nayas have to do with the *infinite* nayas born from the manifoldness of ultimate reality. The basic idea of anekāntavāda — that reality is indeterminate and that there are, therefore, many different perspectives — sounds very much like a kind of perspectival realism, but its elaboration in syādvāda and nayavāda appears to have very little to do with that basic idea. Those "elaborations," in their essential affirmation of the pot-hood of this 🏺, appear to be antithetical to perspectivism or non-absolutism more than that they support it.

Perspectives in Modern Western Thought

In Western thought, perspectival views have been quite rare until the second half of the twentieth century and tended to gravitate towards anti-realist relativism. This is probably largely due to the dominance of Aristotelian essentialism, but a second factor explaining the late development of perspectival realisms may be that the term "perspectivism" is most often associated with Friedrich Nietzsche, whose philosophy is usually interpreted as anti-realist. Whether Nietzsche can be called a perspectival realist is debatable, but the common idea that he believed that there is no truth and that all our claims and theories are mere perspectival interpretations is almost certainly false.[106]

---

104 Narendra Bhattacharyya, *Jain Philosophy: Historical Outline* (New Delhi: Munshiram Manoharlal, 1999), 143–44.
105 ṇiyaya-vayaṇijja-saccā, savvaṇayā para-viyālaṇe mohā | te uṇa ṇa diṭṭhasamao, vibhayai sacce va alie vā — Siddhasēna, *Sanmati-tarka*, §I.28.
106 Brian Leiter, "Perspectivism in Nietzsche's Genealogy of Morals," in *Nietzsche, Genealogy, Morality: Essays on Nietzsche's Genealogy of Morals*, ed. Richard Schacht (Berkeley: University of California Press,

According to Steven Hales and Rex Welshon, Nietzsche claimed that "at the fundamental levels, there are nothing but logically atomic events of power,"[107] and because "there is an infinity of quanta and bundles of power, there is an infinity of perspectives."[108] The main target of Nietzsche's perspectivism was Kant's distinction between phenomenal appearances and things-in-themselves. Hence, Nietzsche was an anti-dualist in this respect. It appears that his main reason for rejecting the notion of things-in-themselves was a consequence of his idea that properties of things are their effects on other things and the assumption that things-in-themselves are relationless. By virtue of its lack of relations, a relationless thing has no effects on other things, and therefore, no properties, which Nietzsche considered absurd.[109] Since post-Yogācāra realism does not assume that ultimate reality consists of relationless, discrete things, this criticism does not apply here. Furthermore, Nietzsche's anti-dualism and ontology of bundles of force or power seems far removed from the view proposed in the previous chapters.

Because of the association of perspectivism with Nietzsche, philosophers defending some kind of perspectival view generally prefer a different term. John Searle has called his variant of perspectival realism "perspectivalism," for example. A second reason to avoid the term "perspectivism" is that that term is often taken to refer to the supposedly paradoxical claim that all statements are perspectival.

If all statements are perspectival then the statement that all statements are perspectival is also perspectival, implying that there is a perspective in which not all statements are perspectival, so the argument goes. But then that implication is also perspectival, which has the further implication that there is a perspective in which it is false that there is a perspective in which not all statements are perspectival. And so forth. The claim that all statements are perspectival, thus, leads to an infinite regress of incomprehensible nonsense or paradox, and therefore, that claim is false.[110]

There is, however, a fairly obvious way to block this infinite regress. That there is a perspective in which a statement p is true (or justified, but I'll ignore that distinction here) does not imply that there is another perspective in which the same statement p is false. That the statement F, "Fuji-san is a mountain in Japan," is true in at least some perspectives does not mean that the exact same statement F is false in some other perspectives. There may be a perspective in which there is no concept of mountain, but in that perspective F is not false but meaningless. And there may be another perspective V in which volcanoes are not classified as mountains, but then the sentence "Fuji-san is a mountain in Japan" is not a correct translation of F into the language of V. Rather, a correct translation of F would be: "Fuji-san is a volcano or mountain in Japan,"[111] and that statement would be true in V. But there is no reason why there would have to be a perspective in which F is false. And similarly, a statement that all statements are perspectival does not imply that there is a perspec-

---

1994), 334–57, and Steven Hales and Rex Welshon, *Nietzsche's Perspectivism* (Urbana: University of Illinois Press, 2000).

107 Hales and Welshon, *Nietzsche's Perspectivism*, 63.
108 Ibid., 75.
109 Ibid., 61.
110 For a more rigorous variant of this argument, see Rex Welshon, "Saying Yes to Reality: Skepticism, Antirealism, and Perspectivism in Nietzsche's Epistemology," *Journal of Nietzsche Studies* 37 (2009): 23–43, at 37.
111 Unless V distinguishes more things that are classified as mountains in the original perspectives as non-mountains. Then those would have to be added as further options.

tive in which that exact same statement is false and in which not all statements are perspectival.

Furthermore, while perspectival realists hold that classifications and descriptions of the world around us are perspectival, they typically do not claim that *all* statements are perspectival in the strong sense implied by the infinite-regress argument. That argument presupposes a kind of strong relativism in which there is and can be no agreement about anything between perspectives, but perspectival realism tends to be weakly relativist[112]; that is, perspectival realists typically hold that there are some "things" about which perspectives converge.[113]

The pull of the Scylla of anti-dualist, essentialist realism and of the Charybdis of anti-realist relativism is strong,[114] and it is not always easy to steer a safe course between those two. Perhaps, partially also for that reason, perspectival realists constitute a tiny minority among Western philosophers. In the past three decades several philosophers have proposed varieties of perspectival realism, however, and of those, five are worth mentioning here: John Searle, Maria Baghramian, Ronald Giere, Dave Elder-Vass, and Sally Haslanger. Samuel Wheeler could be added to this list but his "relative essentialism" was already discussed above.[115]

In *The Construction of Social Reality*, Searle argued that conceptual relativity of perspectives presupposes a mind-independent, external reality, and that "external realism allows for an infinite number of true descriptions of the same reality made relative to different conceptual schemes."[116] However, the extent to which different perspectives on reality can differ is rather limited in Searle's view.

After reviewing a variety of relativisms and related views in Western thought, Baghramian proposed a moderate pluralism in which conceptual schemes are likened to maps. In the conclusion of her book *Relativism*, she wrote,

> although the very idea of the world is already contaminated by our concepts; those concepts in turn are in a non-trivial way informed and constrained by the world. We cannot *talk* about that which our conceptual schemes map outside the parameters set by the maps we currently have at our disposal, but this does not mean that there is nothing outside our maps to speak of. [...] It may seem deeply paradoxical to claim that conceptual schemes are our different ways of mapping what there is [...], but we are not in a position to say what it is that we are mapping independently of such maps. But the paradox results in what is required of us by our opponents. Not one, not even the scientific realist, can step out of his conceptual skin what the world is like outside of all conceptions.[117]

---

112 Additionally, the infinite regress argument appears to assume an anything-goes subjective perspectivism, while perspectival realisms are varieties of objective (quasi-)perspectivism. On the distinction between strong and weak relativism, see Baghramian, *Relativism*, 9. On the distinction between objective and subjective perspectivism, see Mou, "Searle, Zhuang Zi, and Transcendental Perspectivism." On both, see the section "Relativism, Pluralism, and Perspectivism" in chapter 7.
113 This is certainly the case for the post-Yogācāra realism advocated here. In fact, the whole argument of part III depends on intersubjectivity; that is, on convergence or agreement between perspectives, or in other words, on there being some statements that appear to be universal or pan-perspectival.
114 The strongly relativist kind of perspectivism presupposed by the infinite-regress argument steers directly for the whirlpools of Charybdis.
115 See the section "New Pragmatism — Davidson, Putnam, and Quine" in this chapter.
116 John Searle, *The Construction of Social Reality* (London: Allen Lane Penguin, 1995), 165.
117 Baghramian, *Relativism*, 319.

This, indeed, could almost be a summary of the view advocated here.

Giere was one of the few philosophers who used the term "perspectival realism." He argued that "perspectival realism is as much realism as science can provide" and that "objectivist realism cannot even be an ideal goal."[118] His most important argument for this claim is that "a combination of perspectives remains perspectival" and does not become "objective in some stronger sense," and consequently, "the strongest possible conclusion is that some model provides a good but never perfect fit to aspects of the world."[119] This last conclusion is closely related to the pragmatist point that we aim for theories and explanations that work and not for some kind of ultimate truth. The quest for absolute certainty and ultimate truth is a religious quest, not a scientific one.

Both Giere and Elder-Vass proposed perspectival realisms that are science-based, but while Giere was focuses on the natural sciences, Elder-Vass is more concerned with the social sciences. His main claim is that moderate social constructionism is compatible with realism.[120] The ways we think and speak are influenced by social forces and alter the world in turn, but that insight does not contradict the idea that there is a world independent from us.

In *Resisting Reality*, Haslanger wrote that "what we *believe* to be real may be deeply conditioned by our point of view; but what is real is another matter."[121] Like Elder-Vass, she argued that social constructionism is "compatible with important forms of realism" including an affirmation of a non-essentialist notion of natural kinds or types that reminds of Wheeler's relative essentialism but that predates it by several years.[122] The kind of kinds she focused her attention on are social kinds, categories we use to capture and explain what goes on in parts of the social world. Kinds or types do not require essences or sharp boundaries — if some supposed social kind has enough unity to be explanatory useful, then it is an objective kind or type.[123]

Some Concluding Remarks

Doubtlessly, there are perspectival realisms that I have missed in this brief and sketchy overview, but completeness was not the point here. Rather, my aim in the preceding three sections was twofold. As mentioned in passing in the previous section, there is a common misconception that one either has to be an anti-realist relativist or an anti-dualist, essentialist realist, and that there is nothing in between. My first aim was to show that there actually are several paths between Scylla and Charybdis — paths that have been traveled by philosophers in all three of the great philosophical traditions, and that have seen a recent surge in interest in Western philosophy. Post-Yogācāra realism is one of these paths. It is neither exotic nor unique, but one version of perspectival realism among several others. And that's a good thing; if one witness would stand out because her story would be unique, that would not be a very credible witness.[124] Convergence increases credibility. Similarly,

---

118 Ronald Giere, *Scientific Perspectivism* (Chicago: University of Chicago Press, 2006), 16.
119 Ibid., 93.
120 Dave Elder-Vass, *The Reality of Social Construction* (Cambridge: Cambridge University Press, 2012).
121 Sally Haslanger, *Resisting Reality: Social Construction and Social Critique* (Oxford: Oxford University Press, 2012), 107.
122 Ibid., 183.
123 Ibid., 210.
124 See the section "Perspectives and Science" in chapter 9.

that many others managed to carve a similar path between Scylla and Charybdis increases the likelihood that those can be avoided indeed and that it is the right path.

My secondary aim was to invite further research into perspectival realism and its varieties (by myself and others), in the hope that those, and especially post-Yogācāra realism, will be strengthened by an exploration of links, similarities, differences, problems, and solutions. It is unlikely that all of the perspectival views mentioned in the preceding are equally useful in this respect. For example, Dooyeweerd's view is intriguing, but I doubt that the notion of a more or less closed list of perspectives makes much sense from a metaphysical point of view. And anekāntavāda was probably the most disappointing philosophical theory I ever encountered. Haslanger's *Resisting Reality*, on the other hand, is worthy of a much more in-depth treatment than what I could offer here, and the same is probably true for Wheeler's *Post-Davidsonian Metaphysics*. Surely, the view I am offering here can be strengthened and enriched through a serious engagement with the work of these and other philosophers.

PART III

DAO

After king You of Zhou fell in love with Bao Si, he exiled his wife, Queen Shen. The disgraced Shen family retaliated in 771 BCE by attacking and killing king You. The Zhou dynasty never recovered; although it remained nominally in power for another five centuries, this period was characterized by failing authority and nearly continuous war. Perhaps not coincidentally, this was also the most fruitful period in the intellectual history of China and is commonly recognized as the Golden Age of Chinese philosophy. Confucius 孔子, Mencius 孟子, Mozi 墨子, Laozi 老子, Zhuangzi 莊子, Xunzi 荀子, and many other of China's most famous philosophers lived in this period.[1] The "Hundred Schools of Thought" that they belonged to or founded fought over ideas as fiercely as others fought over influence and territory.

The main point of contention in the intellectual battle was the dao. The Chinese term *dao* 道 is interpreted differently in different schools of thought, and especially in the later development of Daoism — on the basis of the ideas of Laozi, Zhuangzi, and others — new layers of meaning were piled up on the concept. Nevertheless, there is a small number of closely related core meanings with deep historical roots. The concept's oldest known etymological root is following a path or road, and the plainest meaning of *dao* (as a noun) and its derivatives in other East-Asian languages is path, way, or road. However, the concept also has ancient normative connotations, and consequently, its etymological root is not just following some path, but following the right path.[2]

Dao as that what was fought over in the aforementioned intellectual battles is closely related to this last notion. In that context, and thus in the context of most of classical Chinese philosophy, *dao* has the primary meaning of the set or system of social conventions that provides the necessary guidance for people to lead virtuous lives. Dao is the set or system of morally right social conventions, a or the "public, guiding discourse."[3] In addition to this primary meaning, there is a secondary meaning in the same context of *dao* as the theory of some particular philosopher or school of what that public, guiding discourse ought to be.

---

1 Whether and when Laozi lived is actually a rather controversial issue. The name Laozi 老子 literally means "old master," and Bryan van Norden, *Introduction to Classical Chinese Philosophy* (Indianapolis: Hacket, 2011), suggested that that is what it literally means — that it is not a name but a reference to one or probably more old masters and their sayings.
2 Peter Boodberg, "Philological Notes on Chapter One of The Lao Tzu," *Harvard Journal of Asiatic Studies* 20, nos. 3–4 (1957): 598–618.
3 Chad Hansen, "Classical Chinese Ethics," in *A Companion to Ethics*, ed. Peter Singer (Oxford: Blackwell, 1993), 69–81, at 69.

The central concern of China's Golden Age philosophers, then, was to elaborate and defend theories of moral and social philosophy. This does not imply a lack of interest in questions that are nowadays typically classified as belonging to other branches of philosophy, however. For example, much effort was spent on problems of linguistic meaning and of the justification of beliefs. Nevertheless, such philosophical explorations into meaning, justification, and other topics outside the scope of moral and social philosophy in a strict sense, were almost always motivated by moral and sociopolitical concerns. And often these apparently much more esoteric topics were only a few small steps away from the more practical or ordinary questions that incited them.

For example, for the ancient Chinese, understanding a term meant having the ability to classify something as belonging (or not) to the kind of things picked out by that term. Thus, understanding *ma* 馬 and *wang* 王 is being able to classify things as (non-)horses and (non-)kings, respectively. However, while deciding whether something is a horse or not is a fairly innocent act, although the wrong classification may reveal ignorance, in case of terms with inherent moral or sociopolitical content such as "king" and other terms denoting social roles (e.g., "parent," "child," "ruler," "subject," "friend") classifying is also making a moral judgment. Calling someone a "friend" or a "king" while that person is not behaving in accordance with that term is misapplying the term. According to Confucius this sets a bad example and thereby erodes the moral and social content of that term, thus eroding the dao in turn.[4] By implication, the use and abuse of language can play a key role in regulating social behavior, and consequently, from questions about the dao, that is, moral questions, to questions about meaning and related technicalities of language was a small step indeed.

The ancient Greeks followed a different path from moral questions to other kinds of philosophical questions, but it was not much longer than the Chinese path. Near the end of the prologue of Plato's *Republic*, Socrates says to his opponent Thrasymachus that what they are discussing is "no ordinary/insignificant matter, but how we ought to live."[5] The real Socrates was Plato's teacher, but in many of Plato's writings he plays the role of Plato's mouthpiece, and indeed, "how we ought to live" was no insignificant matter for Plato, but the core concern of his philosophical investigations. Plato's attempts to answer the question how we ought to live started with inquiries into the nature of justice, goodness, and related notions, which often focused on questions about the meaning of "justice," "good," and so forth. And those questions lead to more fundamental questions about the nature of meaning in turn, but also to questions about the distinction of knowledge from mere opinion, about the nature of reality, and so forth.

Despite the obvious difference between these two philosophical traditions — the Greek/Western and the Chinese — there is a remarkable similarity in their origins: in both traditions it was critical reflection on relatively practical moral concerns that gave rise to the kind of investigations that we now tend to call "philosophy." However, despite this similarity in origins, there is a fundamental and important

---

4   But for Confucius and his followers that did not mean that a bad father should be called otherwise. Rather it meant that that bad father should start behaving like a real father, that is, like someone who would be properly called a "father."

5   οὐ γὰρ περὶ τοῦ ἐπιτυχόντος ὁ λόγος, ἀλλὰ περὶ τοῦ ὅντινα τρόπον χρὴ ζῆν. — Plato, Πολιτεία [*The Republic*] (4th c. BCE), trans. Christopher Emlyn-Jones and William Preddy, Vol. 1, Loeb Classical Library (Cambridge: Harvard University Press, 1937), 1.352d.

difference between these two traditions' guiding questions. Plato's question "How we ought to live" and the body of moral thought that developed to answer this question is inherently individualistic: it is about how *I* should live *my* life, or what kind of person *I* should try to become. It is fully answered by a specification of the principles that determine the rightness of an individual's life, and by implication that is all that many (but not all!) theories of Western moral philosophy aim for. The Chinese question, "What is the right dao?" (i.e., the set or system of social conventions that provides the necessary guidance for people to lead virtuous lives), on the other hand, is inherently social. It is about the right social conventions and how to establish them.

But there is a second fundamental difference: from the dao perspective, the Western approach is incomplete because it implicitly assumes that the principles that determine the rightness of a life are motivating reasons or, in other words, that knowing how one ought to live will lead one to live in accordance with that knowledge. This assumption was made explicit by Immanuel Kant in the eighteenth century, but it has been a guiding idea in Western moral thought since its inception.[6] Max Horkheimer saw in this idea an idealistic tendency permeating much of Western philosophy. He characterized it as the belief that "the world is already in order if everything is in order in the mind" and as a "lack of distinction between fantasy and reality in which idealist philosophy reveals itself as a refined form of a primitive belief in the almightiness of thought, that is, magic."[7] The dao approach makes no similar "magical" assumption, even if it makes other assumptions that are equally debatable. The quest is for guiding principles that actually lead people to live virtues lives. It could turn out that Kantian ethics is the dao that guides people toward virtue and society to harmonious order, but this is an open question. Finding the right principles is insufficient, and thus an approach that ends there is incomplete — the aim is to find something that actually delivers the good.

Decades of research in social and moral psychology have made it sufficiently clear that the Kantian assumption is an illusion: knowing the right thing does not automatically lead to doing the right thing. Psychopaths are the most obvious counterexample. But even among non-psychopaths the motivating force of moral principles is extremely weak. According to Daniel Batson we are "moral hypocrites" merely aiming to be seen as following moral principles by the people around us.[8] By implication, the individualistic approach to ethics is fundamentally flawed. For this reason, the first chapter of part III of this book will start with a closer look at the classical Chinese approach to ethics and social philosophy.[9] The topic of that chap-

---

6   Without that assumption the Western tendency to stop after determining moral principles just does not make sense. Moral principles are useful only if one assumes that moral principles will lead to moral lives, and that is exactly the assumption discussed here.

7   Bei Kant bildet dieser idealistische Zug, nach welchdem die Welt schon in Ordnung sein soll, wenn nur im Geiste alles in Ordnung sei, dieser Mangel an Unterscheidung zwischen Phantasie und Wirklichkeit, durch den die idealistische Philosophie sich als verfeinerte Form des primitiven Glaubens an die Allmacht der Gedanken, das heißt die Zauberei, erweist, bloß eine Seite seiner Lehre. — Max Horkheimer, "Materialismus und Moral" (1933), in *Gesammelte Schriften,* Band 3: *Schriften 1931–1936* (Frankfurt a.M.: Fischer, 1988), 111–49, at 122.

8   C. Daniel Batson, *What's Wrong with Morality? A Social-Psychological Perspective* (Oxford: Oxford University Press, 2016).

9   The contrast between classical Chinese and Western approaches suggested here should not be essentialized as there are exceptions in both traditions and Chinese philosophy later developed into new directions, mostly in response to Buddhism. The neo-Confucian philosopher Wang Yangming 王陽明 (16th c.), for example, argued that really knowing what is right will lead one to do what is right.

ter is meta-ethics, the branch of philosophy that investigates the metaphysical and epistemological foundations of ethics, and its main role in this book is to build on the foundations that have already been laid in part II. Hence, while chapter 11 begins with the dao approach to ethics and social philosophy, this is not the real starting point of the dao advocated here. That starting point is post-Yogācāra realism. Nevertheless, the notion of dao frames this part of the book.

Two key points made in part II are that we should aim for justification because truth is out of our reach, and that epistemic justification depends on coherence or convergence. After looking into the dao approach, chapter 11 will go over some of the arguments for convergence or intersubjectivity in meta-ethics. This convergence approach implies that the main aim should be to assess what, if anything, moral thought converges on, and this is what chapters 11 to 14 are concerned with. Specifically, what is needed for a solid foundation for ethics and social philosophy is convergence with regards to the kinds of things that are to be evaluated, and with regards to the methods of their evaluation. It may seem that there is no significant convergence in either respect; candidates for things to be evaluated include acts or actions, rules, and character traits, for example, and main candidates for the second are consequences and accordance with rules, with further disagreement about the kinds of consequences or the source and nature of those rules. I will argue, however, that much of this disagreement is illusory and that there actually is considerable convergence between views. Chapters 12 and 13 focus on aspects of the methods of evaluation, and chapter 14 looks into the metaphysics of the "things" that are to be evaluated (i.e., acts, rules, and so forth).

The remaining two chapters of this part of the book concern slightly more practical matters. One of the cornerstones of radical Buddhism is anti-capitalism, and chapter 15 discusses the case against capitalism (based on the moral/social-philosophical groundwork laid in chapters 12 to 14). The chapter after that broadens this discussion to offer some suggestions about how to think about and look for alternatives, focusing on the role of utopianism therein. After that, part IV, which only consists of one short chapter, returns to the question that guided this book — whether a radicalized radical Buddhism is possible — and summarizes its main findings.

This idea reminds of what I called the "Kantian assumption" above, but his argument for this claim is different from Kant's.

11

Intersubjectivity and Moral Epistemology

Throughout classical Chinese philosophy, two kinds of argument why a certain moral theory is the one and only right theory were especially common. One is an appeal to "heaven" *tian* 天, but this is not really the notion of heaven familiar from Western thought; that is, it is usually not a supernatural, godly, or personalized kind of heaven, and in many cases "nature" is a better translation of *tian*. Hence, this kind of argument is often best understood as an appeal to "natural" (i.e., "heavenly") preference.

An example of the second and much more interesting kind of argument can be found in the following quote by Confucius (or Kongzi) 孔子, who towers over all of Chinese philosophy:[1]

> If social/moral conventions (dao) are established by means of governance (i.e., laws and regulations), and punishment is used to maintain order, then people will [merely] avoid punishment and have no sense of shame. But if virtue is used to guide social and moral conventions, and ritual and tradition to maintain order, then there will be a [guiding] sense of shame as well as a standard.[2]

What matters here is not the claim that virtue and ritual or tradition will lead to the desired results but the kind of argument employed to argue for a particular moral theory (i.e., a dao 道).[3] Confucius argued that his ritual-and-virtue-based moral theory should be accepted because it will lead to the desired results. Or in other words, the expected consequences of adopting his dao are the desired consequences.

Consequences played an even more central role in the dao of Mozi 墨子, Confucius's main opponent in the early classical period. Mozi wrote, for example:

---

1. Alfred North Whitehead once remarked that Western philosophy "consists of a series of footnotes to Plato" (*Process and Reality* [1929], corr. edn. [New York: Free Press, 1978], 39). Similarly, much of Chinese philosophy could be considered a series of footnotes to Confucius.
2. 道之以政, 齊之以刑, 民免而無恥; 道之以德, 齊之以禮, 有恥且格。— Confucius 孔子,《論語》[*The Analects*] (5th c. BCE),〈為政〉, §3.
3. Notice the distinction between dao as moral theory and dao as (set or system of) social or moral conventions. (See the introduction to part III of this book.) The quote by Confucius uses the word *dao* in the latter sense but argues for his dao in the former sense.

> A wise man's business must be to plan [in accordance with] what leads to peace and order among the state's people (or for the state and people) and to avoid that what brings disorder.[4]

In other words, a wise man (especially one with public responsibilities) lets his actions and decisions be guided by their expected consequences. Mozi is usually classified as a consequentialist, while Confucius is not. The reason for this difference is that consequences play very different roles in their philosophies, and a much more obvious role in Mozi's.

Consequentialism is an approach to moral philosophy in which the consequences of some act or rule make that act or rule right or wrong. The most famous kind of consequentialism is the classical utilitarianism defended in the nineteenth century by Jeremy Bentham and John Stuart Mill. This theory is often summarized in the claim that the right act is the act that leads to the greatest happiness for the greatest number of people. Variants of consequentialism differ in the kind of consequences that matter (such as happiness or pleasure in classical utilitarianism and suffering in negative utilitarianism) but also in a number of other ways. For example, act-consequentialism is about the rightness of acts, while rule-consequentialism is about the rightness of rules. And objective consequentialism holds that only actual, realized, consequences matter and thus that rightness can only be determined afterwards, while subjective or prospective consequentialists argue that some kind of expected, foreseen, or foreseeable consequences determine the rightness of some act or rule.

While rule-consequentialism judges the rightness of individual rules, it is also possible to judge whole moral codes, systems of values and rules, or the theories they are based on on the basis of their actual or expected consequences. However, whether that still counts as "consequentialism" is not immediately clear, as illustrated by the following example.

Ethical egoism is the moral theory that holds that the right thing to do is always whatever is in one's objective, long-term self-interest (or something very similar). The most common argument for ethical egoism is that the common good is best served if everyone is selfish in this sense. Or in other words, if everyone always serves their own self-interest, they indirectly serve the interest of all. The idea is nonsensical — self-interest does not promote the common good — but that does not matter here.[5] What matters is that the moral code or theory of ethical egoism is defended by means of an appeal to the expected consequences of widespread adoption of that theory. This is a kind of *second-order* prospective consequentialism, but it does not imply that the *first-order* moral code or theory it recommends is consequentialist as well.

Classical Chinese approaches to moral philosophy tended to be second-order prospective consequentialist in this sense. The argument by Confucius quoted above is a good example: his dao (i.e., moral theory or approach to morality) should be accepted because it is expected to produce the desired results, or because it is expected to have the right consequences. Mozi's philosophy is both first and second-order

---

4 知者之事, 必計國家百姓所以治者而為之, 必計國家百姓之所以亂者而辟之。— Mozi 墨子, 《墨子》[*The Mozi*] (5th c. BCE), 〈尚同下〉, §1.

5 The idea that self-interest promotes the common good is usually defended by means of the doctrines of neo-classical economics. Why those doctrines are nonsensical is explained in the section "The Ideology of Supply and Demand" of chapter 15.

consequentialist. Although he also appealed to heavenly/natural preference, his most important and strongest argument for his first-order consequentialist moral theory was that adopting it will lead to harmonious order.[6] Mencius (or Mengzi) 孟子 argued against Mozi's first-order consequentialism on second-order consequentialist grounds. According to Mencius, talk of *li* 利 (utility/profit), Mozi's term for desirable consequences, would only undermine order and harmony, and therefore, adoption of something like Mozi's consequentialism will do nothing but "endanger the kingdom."[7] Hence, what makes first-order consequentialism a bad moral theory, according to Mencius, is that its adoption would have bad consequences. Other important philosophers from the classical period who adopted this second-order consequentialist approach include Xunzi 荀子 and Hanfeizi 韓非子.

While this type of argument is common in classical Chinese philosophy, the ancient Chinese did not have a monopoly. John Stuart Mill, for example, realized that in practice it is impossible to determine the consequences of everything one does before one decides to do or not do it. Most of the time we should, therefore, rely on guidelines or rules of thumb based on observed regularities. The mostly implicit argument for this approach is second-order prospective consequentialist: its adoption is expected to lead to the best results.[8]

In case of classical Chinese philosophy, the second-order prospective consequentialist approach is invited by the notion of dao itself. Recall that dao is, among other things, the set or system of social conventions that provides the necessary guidance for people to lead virtuous lives.[9] Finding the right dao or finding the right conventions is finding an approach to morality that actually guides people. And as guiding people to virtue is the ultimate aim of classical Chinese ethics and social philosophy, and thus the desired consequence, the right dao is the dao that follows from second-order prospective consequentialism.

John Searle once said that "as soon as we can revise and formulate a philosophical question to the point that we can find a systematic way to answer it, it ceases to be philosophical and becomes scientific."[10] An important advantage of second-order prospective consequentialism as a philosophical method is that it does exactly that to much of moral philosophy; that is, it changes part of ethics into an empirical science, namely, the science of figuring out what moral codes or theories to adopt and how to use them to promote the good. It does not completely lift ethics out of philosophy, however, as it leaves some questions for which there is no "systematic way to answer it" — questions like: what is the good? But also: should we accept second-order prospective consequentialism?

This and the next three chapters are concerned with questions like these. As mentioned before, the starting point is not second-order prospective consequentialism, but the post-Yogācāra realism developed in part II of this book. What follows from that starting point will end up quite close to the dao approach to ethics and social

---

6 For Mozi, who lived in a time of near constant war and disaster, harmonious order was the primary good, and the same was true for Confucius. Had Bentham and Mill lived in similar circumstances, they might also have preferred order to their primary good, happiness, or pleasure.
7 Mengzi 孟子,《孟子》[Mengzi] (4th c. BCE),〈梁惠王上〉, §1.
8 John Stuart Mill, *Utilitarianism* (1861), in *Collected Works*, Vol. X (Toronto: University of Toronto Press, 1969). See also the section "Consequences in Consequentialism" in chapter 12.
9 See the introduction to part III.
10 John Searle, "The Future of Philosophy," *Philosophical Transactions of the Royal Society of London B* 354 (1999): 2069–80, at 2069.

philosophy. Moreover, the notion of dao as a theory of ethics and social philosophy *and* as the collection or system of social conventions, moral codes, and other normative claims promoted by such a theory is much closer to what this part of the book is about than the Western term "ethics." If what is advocated in the following chapters would be given a name, it could be called "A Dao of Compassion."[11]

Three Arguments for Convergence

Why do we aim for objectivity or for solid evidence for our claims? Often the answer to that question is that we want to be able to silence our opponents; that we want to be able to prove that they are wrong and we are right; that we want to settle disagreement. But if there is no disagreement in the first place, none of that matters. If opinions converge already, there is little reason to search for further evidence or to desire a special kind of knowledge that transcends the consensus. This is a rather shallow argument for convergence as a criterion of epistemic justification, but there are at least two less shallow arguments, one of which was already hinted at in the introduction to part II and further explained in chapter 9, and will be recapitulated here. The other is an argument by Donald Davidson in his paper "The Objectivity of Values" that builds on some of the ideas that were presented in part II of this book.[12]

To say that a statement or belief is true is to say that its meaning or content somehow corresponds with the way things are. This correspondence *intuition* should not be confused with the correspondence *theory* of truth. According to the latter, statements or beliefs are made true by their correspondence to facts (or something relevantly similar). In contrast, the correspondence intuition is not a theoretical claim about the notion of truth but a key aspect of how we use the words "true" and "truth" and their functional equivalents in other languages. Contrary to the correspondence theory, the correspondence intuition is quite uncontroversial — practically everyone agrees that that is indeed what we mean when we say that something is true.

The correspondence intuition has an important epistemological implication: to know or test whether something is true, we have to compare or confront it with the way things are, that is, with the world outside our beliefs about it. This, according to Richard Rorty and Davidson among others, cannot be done. Rorty called this "the impossible attempt to step outside our skins" and argued that we cannot "say 'how language relates to the world' by saying what *makes* certain sentences true."[13] And Davidson pointed out that "when we say we want our beliefs to be true we could as well say we want to be certain that they are, that the evidence for them is overwhelming," and so forth. "It makes no sense to ask for more."[14]

If we cannot get out of our skins, or out of our beliefs, or out of our languages, to compare statements of beliefs with the world out there, then truth is out of reach, then we can only aim for justification. But as Davidson showed, we already do that anyway. Aiming for justification is exactly what "aiming for truth" means in practice.

---

11 See the section with this title in chapter 14. Elsewhere I use the more technical name "negative expectivism."
12 Donald Davidson, "The Objectivity of Values" (1995), PoR: 39–53.
13 Richard Rorty, *Consequences of Pragmatism* (Minneapolis: University of Minnesota Press, 1982), xix.
14 Donald Davidson, "Reply to Pascal Engel," in *The Philosophy of Donald Davidson*, ed. Lewis E. Hahn (Chicago: Open Court, 1999), 460–61, at 461. This is more fully quoted in the introduction to part II.

"We do not aim at truth but at honest justification." And consequently, "truth is not [...] a norm."[15]

Moral statements and beliefs are no different from other kinds of statements and beliefs in this respect. Moral epistemology has no special status or unique methods that sets it apart from epistemology in general. Regardless of whether moral facts exist, or whether there is something like moral truth, all we can and do aim for anyway is justification.[16] The moral statements and beliefs we should accept are the ones that are best justified. Furthermore, the criteria for justification are no different in moral epistemology either. As argued in chapter 9, if we cannot get out of our beliefs, then the only kind of justification available is coherence with our other justified beliefs. Moreover, because most of our most basic beliefs are caused by external reality, coherence is not some kind of cheap surrogate we have to resort to lacking access to "the real thing." Rather, in a sense, "coherence yields correspondence," as Davidson once put it.[17] Because most of our basic beliefs are necessarily true,[18] coherence implies a high likelihood of correspondence. What is coherent is probably true. And depending on the extent of coherence, that probability is more than sufficient to believe and say that the statement or belief in question *is* true.

Coherence is not really a singular criterion, however. Rather, as explained in chapter 9,[19] there are variants or aspects of coherence. The most important distinction is that between internal coherence and external coherence. The first is the coherence between different parts or aspects of the same view or theory; the second is the coherence with other accepted theories or between different views. The latter aspect of external coherence, which was explained by means of C.I. Lewis's converging witness accounts analogy, is also called "convergence" or "intersubjectivity" among other things.

Of all the kinds and aspects of coherence, intersubjectivity is the most demanding as a criterion for justification partially because it tends to be a good proxy for the others. If some idea is internally incoherent or if it contradicts other accepted ideas, then in all likelihood that idea will not be accepted by everyone, and thus fail the intersubjectivity or convergence test. A second reason why intersubjectivity is often the most important kind of coherence is related to the probabilistic nature of basic beliefs. Because our most basic beliefs are caused by the world, most of them must be true, and therefore, any individual basic belief is only probably true. The only way to test which ones are false is coherence, as was also pointed out by Devendrabuddhi in his explanation of Dharmakīrti's assertion that knowledge originates in uncontradicted or coherent (*avisaṃvādin*) acquaintance (*jñāna*).[20] In many circumstances the best or even only way to assess such coherence is to compare one's beliefs with the beliefs of others. Most of my most basic beliefs are true and so are most of yours; the beliefs we disagree about are the most likely candidates for falsehood, especially

---

15 Ibid.
16 A fortunate implication hereof is that inherently controversial answers to difficult metaphysical questions about moral facts and moral truth are effectively irrelevant.
17 Donald Davidson, "A Coherence Theory of Truth and Knowledge" (1983), SIO: 137–53. Davidson later came to regret this claim because it is somewhat misleading and, therefore, liable for misunderstanding. See Davidson, "Afterthoughts" (1987), SIO: 154–57.
18 Even if they are only partially or perspectively true. See the last sections of chapter 8.
19 See the section "Perspectives and Science."
20 Dharmakīrti, *Pramāṇavārttika* (6th/7th c.), §2.1. See the section "Avisaṃvāda" in chapter 9.

if more people, and therefore more points of view, are involved in the comparison than just you and me.

While the foregoing applies to any kind of statement or belief, in "The Objectivity of Values" Davidson sketched another argument for convergence or intersubjectivity that was specifically about moral claims. The argument is based on a point that Davidson repeated in many different forms throughout his writings, namely, that

> understanding [each other] depends on finding common ground. Given enough common ground, we can understand and explain differences, we can criticize, compare, and persuade. The main thing is that finding the common ground is not subsequent to understanding, but a condition of it. This fact may be hidden from us because we usually more or less understand someone's language before we talk with them. This invites the impression that we can then, using our mutually understood language, discover whether we share their view of the world and their basic values. This is an illusion. If we understand their words, a common ground exists, we already share their way of life.[21]

Moral or "evaluative" judgments are part of the package as much as non-evaluative judgments are (i.e., claims that appear to be factual rather than normative). If two people that are interacting understand each other, then this understanding implies that they are not just in agreement about many facets of the objects in the shared, external world around them, but also about normative aspects related to how to behave and how to interact in the given situation. Mutual understanding presumes evaluative convergence as much as it presumes non-evaluative convergence. And in both cases, the more basic the beliefs, the greater the convergence is expected to be.

> We should expect enlightened values — the reasons we would have for valuing and acting if we had all the (non-evaluative) facts straight — to converge; we should expect people who are enlightened *and fully understand one another* to agree on their basic values.[22]

There can be differences in norms between people who understand each other, of course, but "the more basic a norm is to our making sense of an agent, the less content we can give to the idea that we disagree with respect to that norm."[23] The point is related to the principle of charity that plays a central role in Davidson's and W.V.O. Quine's philosophy. "Serious deviations from fundamental standards of rationality are more apt to be in the eye of the interpreter than in the mind of the interpreted."[24] Or in other words, "finding a difference inexplicable is a sign of bad interpretation."[25] And consequently,

> [g]ood interpretation makes for convergence [...], and on values in particular, and explains failure of convergence by appeal to the gap between apparent values and

---

21 Davidson, "The Objectivity of Values," 51.
22 Ibid., 49.
23 Ibid., 50.
24 Donald Davidson, "Deception and Division" (1986), PoR: 199–212, at 204.
25 Davidson, "The Objectivity of Values," 51.

real values (just as we explain failure to agree on ordinary descriptive facts by appeal to the distinction between appearance and reality).[26]

Despite contrary appearances, the fallout of this argument is that we should expect basic moral beliefs to converge. What we do not know, however, is which moral beliefs are basic and which are not. My suggestion is that our most basic moral beliefs have to do with how and why we judge certain "things" to be good or bad, without appealing to explicit theories or principles. There is, I believe, sufficient convergence there, as well as sufficient convergence in this respect with all of the major moral theories, to serve as a foundation for an approach to ethics and social philosophy that extends the theoretical philosophy of part II in a more practical direction, and one that closely matches key insights by important Mahāyāna Buddhist thinkers about ethics such as Asaṅga and Śāntideva.

Moral Theory — A Primer

Moral theorists disagree about a lot of things, but the most fundamental difference is probably about what kinds of things are to be evaluated or what kinds of things are right or wrong. Throughout the Christian era, almost all Western ethics was about doing the right thing and thus about right and wrong acts or actions, but for the ancient Greeks, what mattered most was being the right kind of person, having the right character traits or virtues, and since the middle of the twentieth century, virtue ethics is making a comeback.

In contrast to the ethics of virtues, the ethics of acts has two main branches that disagree about what makes acts right. For the consequentialist branch only consequences matter; if an act has the right consequences, it is a good act. The other branch is nameless but could be called "motivationalism." For a motivationalist, what makes an act right is that it has the right kind of motives or motivations — the act is carried out for the right reasons. The dominant form of motivationalism in Western ethics is deontology, which selects a particular kind of motivating reasons: for a deontologist an act is right if it conforms to the applicable rule, or if it corresponds to the agent's duty. Usually, deontology is contrasted with consequentialism, and no other forms of motivationalism are recognized. This is a mistake, I think, regardless of whether other kinds of motivations played an important role in Western moral theory, it should be recognized that rule-following is not the only possible motivation or motivating reason.

The oldest form of consequentialism that we know of is Mozi's. For Mozi, something was right if it contributed to peace and harmony. Charles Goodman has argued that Śāntideva and Asaṅga were consequentialists as well.[27] Whether that qualification is accurate will be discussed in the next chapter.[28] The most famous consequentialists in the Western tradition were the utilitarians Bentham and Mill. They argued that an act is better to the extent that it contributes more to happiness or pleasure. We'll have a closer look at some of their ideas in the next chapter as well.[29]

---

26 Ibid., 50.
27 Charles Goodman, *Consequences of Compassion* (Oxford: Oxford University Press, 2009).
28 See the section "Consequences and Consequentialism in Mahāyāna" in chapter 12.
29 Ibid.

Simplifying a bit, classical utilitarianism, the paradigmatic form of consequentialism, makes three basic claims: (1) only consequences matter; (2) the only kind of consequences that matter are those that increase or decrease overall happiness or pleasure; and (3) everyone's happiness or pleasure counts equally. All three claims have been shown to be problematic. The absolute impartiality required by (3) would imply that a mother in a burning building, who rescues her own child while she could rescue two other children she does not know, does something morally wrong. The hedonism of (2) ignores that there are other things we value besides happiness — things like integrity, friendship, artistic achievements, and so forth.[30] None of those matter directly to utilitarianism, but they may matter indirectly if they have effects on happiness. And consequentialism itself — that is, (1) — is problematic because if only consequences matter, then justice, rights, promises, and contracts are all meaningless. Consequentialists have responded to these problems in a variety of ways, suggesting new theories that fix some of them but that have problems of their own. These debates continue and probably will continue for a while. Some of the arguments in the following chapters could be seen as a contribution to these debates.

Deontologists hold that rule-following makes acts right but disagree about the origins of those rules. For constructivists like Immanuel Kant and John Rawls, they follow from reason. According to contractarians, the rules are part of a real or hypothetical agreement between the members of a society, the *social contract*. There are some further varieties of rule-based moral theory that are not always categorized as deontologies, even though, in my opinion, they should be. These include cultural relativism, which holds that the rules derive from the tradition of a group of people; divine command theory, according to which the rules are given by God; and various theories that claim that the rules are somehow part of nature or the natural order, such as Vedic ethics, Laozi's 老子 Daoism, and natural law theory.

Some of these theories have been thoroughly discredited, although that has not necessarily affected their popular appeal. Divine command theory stumbles over a dilemma first formulated by Plato in the *Euthyphro*. According to this theory, doing the right thing is doing what God wants you to do, but this can be interpreted in two different ways: either an act is right because it is God's will, or it is God's will because it is right. The second horn of the dilemma implies that it is not God's will that makes the act right, but some other reasons, and if we know those other reasons, then God has no role to play. At best, then, God is some kind of messenger who tells us what is right and wrong but who does not decide or determine anything. The first horn of the dilemma is even worse for a theist: it implies that moral rules are completely arbitrary. If God would have reasons for his or her moral decisions, it would be those reasons that make things right or wrong (meaning that we'd end up at the second horn again), so the first horn implies that God cannot have any reasons; his will is utterly and completely arbitrary. So, either God is a mere messenger or God is a randomization device like a pair of dice or a magic eight-ball.

Neither horn of the dilemma was particularly attractive to Medieval Christian philosophers, and consequently, divine command theory was abandoned in Western thought quite early. It was replaced with natural law theory, which combines the idea of God as creator with Aristotle's ideas about physics and "natural" places and purposes of things. Advances in physics and biology in the seventeenth and

---

30 See chapter 13.

nineteenth century gradually undermined that foundation, however, until eventually they crumbled entirely.

While versions of divine command theory and natural law theory continue to appeal to followers of the Abrahamic religions, cultural relativism appears to attract many people with a more liberal or secular mindset. Probably, the greatest attraction of cultural relativism is its apparent tolerance of other cultures, but that impression is quite mistaken.

According to cultural relativism, right or wrong are relative to cultures or societies. What is right or wrong in one society is entirely determined by the norms and traditions of that society itself and has no validity outside it. Furthermore, there is no culture-external point of view to judge moral codes. The problem with this idea is that is makes sense only if we can actually say what is "inside" or "outside" one culture or society; that is, we need to be able to draw boundaries around and between cultures and societies. Or in other words, cultural relativism essentializes cultures or societies because it assumes that those are discrete, more or less clearly bounded, and internally homogeneous "things." But that assumption is nonsensical.[31]

In practice, there are two ways of defining cultures. The first is to choose some pre-defined social unit and declare that to be the relevant unit. For example, one could declare that the cultures or societies that matter for cultural relativism are countries. But countries are not internally homogeneous. If the moral standards of a country determine what is right or wrong within that country, then there will inevitably be people who have to submit to moral standards that differ from their own moral beliefs. Minorities are the most obvious example: if a minority in a country believes that X is morally wrong, but the moral standard of the country is that X is morally right (or the other way around), then according to cultural relativism, that minority is objectively wrong and has to conform.

The problem is actually even worse than that because it may even be the majority that deviates from the country's moral standards. The overt moral standards of a country are always the moral standards of its socially and politically dominant group. "The ideas of the ruling class are in every epoch the ruling ideas," wrote Karl Marx and Friedrich Engels, and there can be little doubt that they were largely right in this respect.[32] Hence, to say that what is right or wrong is determined by the moral standards of a country is to say that right and wrong are determined by the beliefs and interests of a country's elite, and the same is true for any other similarly arbitrary definition of a culture or society. If what is right or wrong for British Muslims is determined by the moral standards of British Muslims as a group, then it is the dominant sub-group within that group that decides what is right or wrong, and all other members of the group have to submit. And even if right and wrong could be decided democratically, there will always be many members of a group that have different moral beliefs.

Instead of promoting tolerance, this kind of cultural relativism declares the elites of arbitrarily defined "cultures" to be objectively right and tells everyone else to fall in line and shut up. If you are a woman in a male-dominated society, then according

---

31 See the section "Maps *for* and *of* Behavior" in chapter 14.
32 Die Gedanken der herrschenden Klasse sind in jeder Epoche die herrschenden Gedanken, — Karl Marx and Friedrich Engels, *Die deutsche Ideologie* (1846/1932), MEW 3: 9–530, at 46. See the section "Uchiyama Gudō and Early Buddhist Socialism" in chapter 3 for the rest of the quote. See also the section "Ideology" in chapter 4.

to this kind of cultural relativism, you are objectively wrong, or worse, if you complain about being discriminated. If you are a peasant in a (neo-)feudal society, then you are objectively wrong if you complain about oppression. And so forth. The only thing cultural relativism is tolerant of is discrimination and oppression.

As mentioned, there is another way of defining cultures or societies, which might seem to imply that there is a kind of cultural relativism that avoids these problems. That alternative to arbitrary definition is to define cultures or societies by their shared norms and values. This, however, would lead to a circularity that collapses cultural relativism into some kind of subjectivism. If what is right and wrong is determined by a culture and a culture is defined as a group of people that agree about what is right and wrong, then those groups or cultures are effectively irrelevant. Then, right and wrong for me are whatever I believe to be right and wrong, regardless of who, if anyone, agrees with me.

The vast majority of philosophers consider these and other problems for cultural relativism, natural law theory, and divine command theory to be fatal objections, leaving constructivism and contractarianism as the only plausible deontological theories. Those theories have their problems as well, but perhaps, those are not fatal. As is the case for consequentialism, there are many philosophers who believe that those problems can be fixed, and there is a lively, ongoing debate between adherents and detractors of varieties of constructivism and contractarianism.

There is also a sizable group of philosophers that have abandoned both consequentialism and deontology (because of these problems) in favor of virtue ethics. The paradigmatic theory of virtue ethics is Aristotle's, although other theories have been and continue to be proposed. A virtue is a commendable character trait, such as honesty, courage, loyalty, and so forth, and according to Aristotle, we should strive to develop such character traits because they contribute to εὐδαιμονία, which can be roughly translated as "flourishing" or "welfare." The main problem for virtue ethics is the *fundamental attribution error*. We are biased to attribute behavior to character and neglect situational circumstances, while social psychology has shown that in many cases our actions are influenced by circumstances more than by personality or dispositions.[33] What this research implies is that character traits such as virtues and vices in the sense required by virtue ethics probably do not exist.

Furthermore, the problem of the fundamental attribution error is also related to the pre-modern individualism and system blindness mentioned in chapter 4.[34] It was pointed out there that traditional Buddhists tend to blame suffering on individual moral defects, such as greed and selfishness, due to a lack of awareness or understanding of the role of social structures, circumstances, and systems. In the same way, virtue ethics makes individual characteristics the moral standard while ignoring situational factors such as the social, economic, and political environment.[35]

Virtues could also be conceived as hypothetical exemplars, however. Regardless of whether anyone can have a stable disposition to be honest, we can understand what

---

33 See, for example, Gilbert Harman, "Moral Philosophy Meets Social Psychology: Virtue Ethics and the Fundamental Attribution Error," *Proceedings of the Aristotelian Society, New Series* 99 (1999): 315–31.
34 See the section "Moralistic versus Systemic Critique" in chapter 4.
35 There is, moreover, a kind of double neglect involved because these situational factors influence behavior in two ways. Firstly, they influence behavior directly and probably more strongly so than any character trait or disposition. And secondly, they influence or even co-determine our character traits, dispositions, desires, and personalities.

such a disposition would be like, and we can strive to live up to a hypothetical ideal of honesty. Nevertheless, such hypothetical exemplars are not character traits one can have, and therefore, cannot be the kind of thing that is to be evaluated. What would be good or right in this interpretation is trying to live up to the ideal, trying to be honest, for example. But then what is evaluated is the trying, and regardless of whether one tries to be something or tries to do something, the trying itself is an action or multiple actions, and what makes that action or those actions right is that they are motivated by a desire to live up to the ideal. This interpretation of virtue ethics, then, would be another kind of motivationalism — a moral theory that evaluates acts by their motives or motivations. And if virtue ethics is defined as a moral theory based on the evaluation of character traits rather than acts (as suggested above), then this interpretation would not be a virtue ethic.

Finally, the ethics of care is often considered a variety of virtue ethics or at least to be closely related to virtue ethics, but is also better understood as a form of motivationalism. According to the ethics of care one ought to be motivated by care or empathy for the people and other creatures one has a personal relationship with.

Meta-ethical Convergence

It may seem that these moral theories have little in common, but a closer look will reveal that they share some fundamental ideas, and that the same ideas can also be found in pre-theoretical moral intuitions and ordinary, practical moral reasoning. Hence, much of the disagreement is verbal more than genuine and there is significant convergence.

Key claims of moral theories can be expressed in multiple, equivalent ways that differ merely in the terms and phrases used, and if claims in theories *A* and *B* can be accurately expressed by the same proposition, then disagreement between *A* and *B* is merely verbal with respect to those claims or that claim. The primary aim of the present section, then, is to rephrase relevant principles of moral theory and practical moral reasoning to reveal what they have in common. The account here will remain sketchy, and many of the details will have to be filled in in the next three chapters.

In the 1970s Lawrence Kohlberg published a number of famous papers in which he outlined his theory of moral development of children through a number of stages.[36] The idea that there is such a neat progression through stages is rather controversial and so is the idea that supposedly later stages are necessarily better than earlier stages. Neither controversy matters here. Kohlberg called his six stages "orientations," and the idea that these six orientations provide a fairly accurate map of the different ways that people, from children to adults, think about morality is far less controversial. The six orientations are the following:

> (POO) — *The punishment and obedience orientation.* Right and wrong are determined by physical consequences such as punishment and reward. "Good" is submission to authority and avoidance of punishment.

[36] Lawrence Kohlberg, "From Is to Ought: How to Commit the Naturalistic Fallacy and Get Away With It in the Study of Moral Development," in *Cognitive Development and Epistemology*, ed. Theodore Mischel (New York: Academic Press, 1971), 151–235, and "The Claim to Moral Adequacy of a Highest Stage of Moral Judgment," *Journal of Philosophy* 70, no. 18 (1973): 630–46.

- **(IRO)** — *The instrumental relativist orientation.* Right and wrong are determined by what satisfies one's needs and sometimes the needs of others. Fairness and reciprocity are thought of pragmatically, much like a marketplace.
- **(ICO)** — *The interpersonal concordance or "good boy–nice girl" orientation.* Right and wrong are determined by what pleases or helps relevant others and is approved by them. Much attention is being payed to conformity and trying to be "nice."
- **(LOO)** — *The "law and order" orientation.* Right and wrong are determined by duty, (dis-)obeying authority, and maintaining the given social order.
- **(SLO)** — *The social-contract legalistic orientation.* Right and wrong are thought of in terms of general individual rights and standards that have been agreed upon by society as a whole.
- **(UPO)** — *The universal ethical principle orientation.* Right and wrong are defined "by the decision of conscience in accord with self-chosen ethical principles appealing to logical comprehensiveness, universality, and consistency."[37] These ethical principles tend to be general and abstract.

These orientations are not mutually exclusive — on the contrary, they are likely co-present in most adults, although they will not all be equally important in all occasions. According to Kohlberg, SLO and UPO (i.e., the "highest" stages on his list) are relatively rare. The practical moral reasoning of most people appears to be influenced most strongly by the orientations in the middle and beginning on the list — IRO, ICO, and LOO, especially — and is often guided by intuition (at least) as much as by reasoning.

In the first four orientations, right and wrong are determined by (expected) consequences, but they differ in what kind of (expected) consequences matter. Punishment and reward in POO, satisfying one's needs in IRO, approval and conformity in ICO, and maintaining the social order, rather than undermining it, in LOO. Thus, in POO an act that lead to punishment was a wrong act, while an act that is expected to lead to a reward is probably a right act; in ICO an act that lead to approval was a right act; and in LOO an act that undermines the social order by going against it is a wrong act.

The remaining two (less practically important) orientations, SLO and UPO, are focused more on abstract principles, rules, and rights. What is in accordance with those is right; what breaks them is wrong. Consequences of acts play no obvious, direct role in these two orientations, but they do play an indirect role. The ethical principles in UPO and social contracts in SLO are strongly influenced by even more abstract principles of justice and reciprocity, among others, and those notions are inherently about consequences. Justice is (roughly!) getting what you deserve — the right kind of consequences for your actions; and reciprocity is about "repaying" in kind — the right consequences, again.

Hence, (expected) consequences play a central role in ordinary moral reasoning, especially if it is taken into account that IRO, ICO, and LOO tend to be much more influential than the other three orientations. (Very young children may be largely guided by POO, and while some people will make use of SLO or UPO in explicit moral arguments, these orientations tend to be rather inconsequential in daily, practical moral reasoning.)

---

37 Kohlberg, "From Is to Ought," 165.

The centrality of (expected) consequences in ordinary moral reasoning can also be illustrated in another way. Perhaps, you are a parent and have discussed issues of practical morality with your children, or perhaps you remember having such conversations with your parents when you were a kid. Imagine that you (as a parent) found out, for example, that your kid has been bullying other kids at school. How would your conversation with your child go? What would you say to her or him? Most likely, you would point out the devastating consequences that being bullied could have for the victims. You explain that bullying is bad because of its potentially terrible consequences.[38]

Right and wrong in ordinary moral reasoning, then, are largely determined by (expected) consequences. Much the same is true for the main moral theories mentioned in the previous section. In case of consequentialism this is obvious, of course, but (expected) consequences are as central in the other theories.

According to Kant one should "act only according to the maxim that one could want to become universal law."[39] Or in other words, you should only do X if you want it to be a rule that everyone is allowed to do X. There's no explicit mention of (expected) consequences, but "wanting to become universal law" is an implicit appeal to expected consequences, nevertheless. What Kant's principle means is that one should act according to the maxim that can be reasonably expected to have desirable consequences if it would be a universal law.

In Rawls's version of constructivism, the rules and institutions that we should accept are the product of a hypothetical agreement between all members in an equally hypothetical meeting in which everyone is ignorant about important aspects of their status and characteristics in the real world, due to the "veil of ignorance."[40] What, according to Rawls, would be decided in that hypothetical meeting, the "original position," would benefit everyone and harm no one[41] but would benefit those most in need more because everyone in the original position would realize that they might belong to the needy.[42] Hence, the crux of Rawls's theory is that we should accept the rules and institutions that we would agree upon behind the veil of ignorance because they are expected to have mutually beneficial consequences for all parties involved.

Hobbesian and game-theoretical contractarianism are quite similar in this regard, except that social contract theory assumes a more explicit contract. The right rules and institutions are those that are part of the social contract and the social contract is an agreement between the members of society based on the expectation of mutually beneficial consequences for all parties in the contract. We are or become parties in the contract by accepting those (expected) beneficial consequences, such as peace and order.

In all of these deontological theories expected consequences play an indirect role — the rules or institutions we should accept are the rules and institutions that

---

38 To illustrate how terrible these consequences can be: in Japan, where I live, there are many cases of schoolchildren being driven to suicide by bullying each year.
39 Handle nur nach derjenigen Maxime, durch die du zugleich wollen kannst, dass sie ein allgemeines Gesetz werde. — Immanuel Kant, *Grundlegung zur Metaphysik der Sitten* (1785; Frankfurt a.M.: Suhrkamp, 2019), §421.
40 John Rawls, *A Theory of Justice* (Cambridge: Belknap, 1971).
41 Unless you consider taxation a "harm."
42 As long as there are no gamblers in the original position this is quite plausible, but the outcome of the hypothetical meeting would depend completely on who or what exactly are participating (future people? animals? plants? ecosystems? mountains?) and what exactly is hidden from them by the veil of ignorance.

are expected to have the right kind of consequences. Earlier in this chapter, we saw that classical Chinese ethics tended to adopt a philosophical method in which expected consequences played a similarly indirect role: the right dao (i.e., a moral theory and the social conventions it advocates) is the dao that is expected to have the right kind of consequences. And in Aristotelian virtue ethics, expected consequences play a similar indirect role.

In Aristotelian virtue ethics, virtues are character traits that are believed, and thus expected, to have positive consequences for the agent's flourishing (εὐδαιμονία). Being virtuous makes one's live go better. The fifth century Theravāda monk Buddhaghosa made a similar point in his *Visuddhimagga*, and for this reason, his ethics is often understood as a variety of virtue ethics. For both Aristotle and Buddhaghosa, what defines a virtue, as virtue, is that it is a character trait that is expected to have certain beneficial consequences, but they differ greatly in the nature of those consequences. Flourishing in this life is the expected consequence that matters for Aristotle, but for Buddhaghosa, flourishing in this life is merely a nice bonus and useful means to lure people onto the path. What defines a virtue is that is expected to help achieve awakening and nirvāṇa.

Either directly or indirectly, (expected) consequences determine what is right or wrong. This does not mean that all theories and ordinary moral reasoning can be reduced to consequentialism, however. The reason for that is twofold: it is not exactly clear what consequentialism holds, and it is not exactly clear what expected consequences are. What these various views converge on is this:

> The right (or wrong) *X* are the *X* that have the right (or wrong) kind of (expected) consequences.

But this very general and abstract principle raises a number of important questions. What is the nature of (expected) consequences? Are expected consequences a kind of consequences (as the parentheses suggest)? What are the *right kind* (or wrong kind) of (expected) consequences? What makes them right or wrong? And what should be substituted for *X* (e.g., acts, rules, institutions, virtues, social conventions) and why?

Answering these questions is the goal of the next three chapters. Chapter 12 looks into the metaphysics of (expected) consequences and its implications for the interpretation of consequentialism. It also discusses the interpretation of Buddhist ethics, in particular Śāntideva and Asaṅga, as consequentialist. Chapter 13 is concerned with the question: what makes expected consequences right or wrong? As its chapter title suggests, it focuses on the wrongness of death and suffering. And chapter 14 investigates the metaphysics of acts, rules, social conventions, and related "things" (i.e., candidates for *X* in the abstract principle above).

12

Expected Consequences

Expected consequences determine the good. That, at least, is what most influential moral theories claim, albeit rarely explicitly. The only class of theories that explicitly define the good in terms of expected consequences (or intended consequences, foreseeable consequences, or something similar) consists of variants of so-called *subjective* or *prospective consequentialism*,[1] but as explained in the last section of the previous chapter, expected consequences play similar roles in variants of deontology and virtue ethics.

Nevertheless, this does not imply that all of these theories can be reduced to consequentialism. On the contrary, if consequentialism is understood as the family of moral theories that define the good in terms of consequences, then none of them can. By implication, subjective or prospective consequentialism is not consequentialism either. This may seem a surprising claim, but it also follows from the definition of subjective consequentialism in Elinor Mason's "Objectivism, Subjectivism, and Prospectivism" and from an enthymeme in the chapter on the same topic in Julia Driver's *Consequentialism*.[2]

Mason defines subjective consequentialism as the theory that claims that "the right action is the one that the agent believes is required by consequentialism."[3] However, if this is an accurate definition, then, on pain of vicious circularity, subjective or prospective consequentialism can not be a kind or variety of consequentialism; rather it would be some kind of derivative theory. Driver writes that "consequentialism is outcome-oriented, and procedures are evaluated in terms of their outcomes" and that "what subjective consequentialists do is place priority in the procedure itself completely independent of the outcome,"[4] which leads to the enthymematic conclusion that subjective consequentialism is not consequentialism. And elsewhere Driver pointed out explicitly that depending on a terminological choice, subjective consequentialism may turn out not to be consequentialism.[5]

---

1   The terms "subjective consequentialism" and "objective consequentialism" were introduced by Peter Railton in a very influential paper, but some authors prefer "prospective consequentialism" to refer to the former. Peter Railton, "Alienation, Consequentialism, and the Demands of Morality," *Philosophy & Public Affairs* 13, no. 2 (1984): 134–71.
2   Elinor Mason, "Objectivism, Subjectivism, and Prospectivism," in *The Cambridge Companion to Utilitarianism*, eds. Ben Eggleston and Dale Miller (Cambridge: Cambridge University Press, 2014), 177–98, and Julia Driver, *Consequentialism* (London: Routledge, 2012).
3   Mason, "Objectivism, Subjectivism, and Prospectivism," 178.
4   Driver, *Consequentialism*, 127–28.
5   Julia Driver, *Uneasy Virtue* (Cambridge: Cambridge University Press, 2001), 69.

Oddly, neither Mason nor Driver seems to endorse this conclusion. Perhaps, this is due to the ambiguous nature of expected consequences. And it may very well be the same ambiguity that prevents the notion from explicitly playing the central role in moral theory that it already plays implicitly. Furthermore, much of the same ambiguity also plagues other "consequentialisms." Resolving part of that ambiguity, and thereby clarifying one aspect of meta-ethical convergence, is the main aim of this chapter.

The Metaphysics of (Expected) Consequences

The notion of expected consequences is ambiguous in two different and unrelated ways. The first, and most obvious ambiguity can be expressed in question form: expected by whom? The second ambiguity is less obvious but much more fundamental.[6] That second ambiguity is metaphysical.

English grammar suggests that expected consequences are a kind of consequences, so the latter notion seems an obvious starting point for an analysis. Consequences are effects and are identified by their causes. Something is a consequence only if it is a consequence or effect *of* something else, and what identifies some particular consequence *as a consequence* and as *that* consequence is what it is a consequence of. Effects are usually held to be occurrent states of affairs or events rather than endurant objects, and by implication, so are consequences. Furthermore, at least in the world of medium-sized stuffs and objects like us, causes precede their effects or consequences, and thus a consequence at time t_0 entails the existence of a cause at an earlier time t_{-1}. From these considerations it can be inferred that

>(consequence) — x is a consequence at t_0 if and only if { x is a state of affairs or event, and there was another state of affairs or event y at t_{-1} such that y caused x, and t_{-1} was earlier than t_0 }.

Expectations are about the future, and therefore, if expected consequences are a kind of consequences, then they must have been expected at some time t_{exp}. t_{exp} must precede t_0, but does not have to be identical to t_{-1}. In other words, the time of expectation t_{exp} can be earlier or later than the time of the occurrence of the cause t_{-1}. Hence,

>(X-consequence) — x is an expected consequence at t_0 if and only if { x is a state of affairs or event, and there was another state of affairs or event y at t_{-1} such that y caused x, and it was expected at t_{exp} that y would cause x, and both t_{-1} and t_{exp} were earlier than t_0 }.

Expected consequences in this sense form a subset of actual consequences, namely those consequences that were expected to occur. There is a second understanding of the notion of expected consequences. In that second understanding expected consequences are not a kind of consequences but a kind of expectations.

As mentioned, expectations are about the future. More concretely, expectations are *beliefs* about the future — they are beliefs about what will be the case rather than about what is the case. Furthermore, because consequences conceptually imply

---

6   The first ambiguity will be addressed in the section "Problems for Subjective Consequentialism" below.

causes, a belief in a consequence is also a belief in a cause of that consequence, and therefore an expected consequence in this sense is a belief that a certain effect or consequence will occur if certain preconditions are met; that is,

(C-expectation) — x is an expected consequence at t_{exp} if and only if { x is the belief that { if there is or was a state of affairs or event y at t_0, then there will be another state of affairs or event z at t_{+1} such that y causes z } and both t_0 and t_{exp} are earlier than t_{+1} }.

There are several important differences between the two kinds or understandings of "expected consequences," and to avoid confusion, I will hereafter call the first "X-consequences" and the second "C-expectations" (as in the labels of their definitions above).

One of the most obvious differences between the two concerns time. In case of X-consequences, the expectations are in the past and the consequences are in the past or present. In case of C-expectations, the expectations are in the past or present and the consequences *may* occur in the future. This difference is related to a much more fundamental, metaphysical difference. X-consequences form a subset of states of affairs or events, and thus, are in, or part of the world — they are out there, and they are out there *now*. C-expectations, on the other hand, form a subset of beliefs. As such, C-expectations are in the mind, rather than in the world. (Although minds are part of the world, of course.)

Despite this fundamental difference in metaphysical kind, Quine's famous dictum "no entity without identity" implies that both are in trouble. Beliefs have notoriously murky identity conditions,[7] but consequences may be an even more problematic kind of entities.[8] Consequences lack clear boundaries (or even boundary zones) both with regards to depth and with.

The "depth" of consequences refers to their temporal depth; consequences and other effects are parts of causal chains without clear start and end points and without unambiguous "joints" dividing those chains in some kind of "natural" chunks. If I accidentally hit my cup of coffee, causing it to fall on the floor, and a student then slips in the puddle, falls and hits a bookshelf, resulting in Wittgenstein's *Tractatus* falling on the floor, opening on a page with a quote that gives another student, who picks up the book, an idea for a paper, which turns out good enough for an A; then, what exactly in that chain of events, which will undoubtedly continue in the future, is a consequence of what? Is all of it a single consequence of the first event? Or even of some earlier event because something caused me to hit my cup of coffee in the first place? Or is just the first event after the initial cause — if we take the hitting of the coffee cup to be the initial cause — the consequence? But what even is that "first event"? It is not the cup falling, because all kinds of things happen in between my hand touching it and it shattering on the floor, or even before it reaches the edge of the desk. The problem is that none of these questions have clear answers, and that

---

7 Donald Davidson once aptly remarked that "there is no useful way to count beliefs" ("A Coherence Theory of Truth and Knowledge" [1983], SIO: 137–53, at 138). It is also significant that Quine's notion of a "web of belief" (mentioned in chapter 9) uses the word "belief" as a mass term; it is not a "web of *beliefs*."

8 The remainder of the present section focuses on consequences; we'll turn to beliefs in the section "Problems for Subjective Consequentialism."

without clear answers, it is doubtful that the positing of consequences as discrete entities makes sense.

The "width" of consequences refers to their spatial width — causal chains branch out, and there is often no useful way to separate all co-occurring effects into discrete entities. The problems here are similar and related to those with regards to depth. The further a causal chain stretches into the future, the further it (usually) stretches out in space as well. And in the same way that we cannot meaningfully separate the chain of effects into discrete bits, we cannot draw spatial boundaries either. If the student hitting the bookshelf in the previous example causes *two* books to fall that are picked up by two different students, and the other book inspired the other student to write some truly dreadful prose that can only be awarded with an F; are the A and F grades then different consequences or the same? If they are different, then how do they relate to what happened until the moment those two students picked up those two books? Is that moment part of both consequences, and are those thus overlapping entities? And is that even possible? The list of questions can easily be extended, and as in case of depth, they lack clear answers.[9]

Any choice to identify a certain event or state of affairs as a, or even *the*, consequence of some cause is a choice made by us. We recognize consequences or effects to the extent that we have causal theories that identify them as such. Hence, consequences as discrete entities are social constructions, not things out there. That does not mean that the chains of effects are not out there,[10] but that we impose a classification on that spatio-temporally continuous (albeit possibly chunky) chain, drawing boundaries according to our more or less theoretically informed beliefs. This construction of consequences can only be based on beliefs and not on observation, moreover, as we cannot compare a world in which the supposed cause happened with another world in which it did not happen. The latter is an epistemological problem, of course, but epistemology and ontology are interwoven in social construction.

Furthermore, there are other epistemological problems for consequentialism that do not directly relate to the metaphysics of (expected) consequences. Perhaps, the most important is the so-called "epistemic objection" or "argument from cluelessness," which points out that in the long run, unforeseeable consequences vastly outnumber (or outweigh, if we cannot count) foreseen or expected consequences and thus that it is fundamentally unknowable what the actual consequences of an act would be.[11] Further epistemological problems are related to over- and underdetermination of effects by their supposed causes, and the problem of competing explanations.

---

9   The problem of "branching out" has a related problem in the opposite direction. What appear to be multiple causes may have an apparently single effect or consequences, and the interaction of these multiple causes can complicate their identification as causes. Brian Ellis, "Retrospective and Prospective Utilitarianism," *Noûs* 15, no. 3 (1981): 325–39, gives the example of two agents A and B who both can do two different things, *1* and *2*. The combination of A_1 and B_1 or A_2 and B_2 would have a good consequence, while the other two combinations would have a disastrous consequence. What then, is the single cause of the single consequence and who is responsible? Again, there is no clear answer, but consequentialism needs one.
10 Although the term "chain" might not be appropriate. It is too linear, suggesting that each event has a single cause and a single effect, while in reality there are always very many causes and very many effects.
11 James Lenman, "Consequentialism and Cluelessness," *Philosophy & Public Affairs* 29, no. 4 (2000): 342–70.

In short, consequences are metaphysically and epistemologically problematic entities, and any theory that ontologically depends on discrete, identifiable consequences is built on shaky foundations. This may seem to consign utilitarianism and many other supposed "consequentialist" theories to the dustbin but is is not perfectly clear whether all of those theories are actually committed to discrete consequences.

Consequences in Consequentialism

Expected consequences could either be decision criteria, evaluation criteria, or both. If expected consequences are decision criteria, then the decision concerns bringing about the state of affairs or event that will cause the consequence, and therefore, the decision must precede that consequence. By implication, only C-expectations can be decision criteria. If, on the other hand, expected consequences are evaluation criteria, then the time of evaluation must be after the occurrence of the basis of evaluation. That basis of evaluation could be the actual consequences, and thus X-consequences, but it could also be the expectations or intentions of the agent, and thus C-expectations. However, if expected consequences are supposed to offer moral guidance, they can only be C-expectations.

As far as I can see, proposals for subjective consequentialism are typically motivated by the fact that actual consequences cannot be decision criteria, and therefore, the expected consequences appealed to are C-expectations. C-expectations are not consequences, and therefore, if consequentialism is defined as a moral theory that defines the good as having the right (or best) consequences (or something similar), then subjective or prospective consequentialism is not consequentialism.[12]

If some things called "consequences" are supposed to provide decision criteria, then those things can only be C-expectations, meaning that they are not consequences at all. Furthermore, a true belief is still a belief, and a reliable expectation (i.e., a true belief about the future) is still an expectation, and therefore, even if one could predict the future with perfect certainty, a belief about future occurrences is an expectation, and any statement that some consequence "will" follow expresses a C-expectation. With this in mind, one may wonder what role *actual* consequences play in so-called "consequentialist" theories.

Classical utilitarians like Jeremy Bentham, John Stuart Mill, and Henry Sidgwick did not frame their theories in terms of consequences. Instead, they wrote about tendencies, about things that "will" happen, and about probabilities.[13] Bentham's "principle of utility" is

> that principle which approves or disapproves of every action whatsoever, according to the tendency which it appears to have to augment or diminish the happi-

---

12 Perhaps, consequentialism could be redefined disjunctively as a moral theory that defines the good as having good consequences *or* as being expected to have good consequences, but that would be very peculiar from a metaphysical perspective. It would be a bit like defining a class *belue* as consisting of all things that either are actually blue or are believed by someone to be blue. Such a notion of *belue* is unlikely to be very useful. Probably it will just cause confusion. And the same is true for a disjunctive understanding of "consequentialism."

13 Marcus Singer, "Actual Consequence Utilitarianism," *Mind* 86, no. 341 (1977): 67–77.

ness of the party whose interest is in question: or, what is the same thing in other words, to promote or to oppose that happiness.[14]

"Tendency" and "appears" are keywords here: they point at C-expectations. We form C-expectations on the basis of observed, or "appearing," tendencies relating certain kinds of actions to certain kinds of consequences, and it is those C-expectations that Bentham appeals to.

Tendencies play a similar key role in Mill's utilitarianism, which "holds that actions are right in proportion as they *tend* to promote happiness, wrong as they tend to produce the reverse of happiness."[15] An additional clue here is the present tense of the word "are." If actual consequences would determine the good, then this could only be determined afterwards, and one could only later find out whether actions were right. However, Mill writes about actions being right when they are performed, and that rightness is determined by their tendencies to have good consequences, that is, by their C-expectations. Or to put it in different terms, for Mill "consequences" are decision criteria (although he did not actually use the term "consequences") and are, therefore, really C-expectations.[16]

Sidgwick defined utilitarianism as "the ethical theory, that the conduct which, under any given circumstances, is objectively right, is that which will produce the greatest amount of happiness on the whole."[17] As mentioned above, "will" expresses expectation, but that Sidgwick's utilitarianism defines the good in terms of C-expectations becomes especially evident if one considers how much attention he pays to the problem of forming reliable expectations about probable consequences and that he laments the state of the social sciences (or "sociology" in his terms) for being insufficiently able to help in this respect. (The latter has not significantly changed since Sidgwick's time, unfortunately.) Sidgwick suggests that "Empirical Hedonism" is "the only method ordinarily applicable" for making moral decisions "at least until the science of Sociology shall have been really constructed,"[18] and that method of "Empirical Hedonism" he defines as that method

> according to which we have in each case to compare all the pleasures and pains *that can be foreseen as probable results* of the different alternatives of conduct presented to us, and to adopt the alternative *which seems likely* to lead to the greatest happiness on the whole.[19]

What matters for Bentham, Mill, and Sidgwick in moral theory is guidance: expected or intended consequences are decision criteria and, thus, must be C-expectations,

---

14 Jeremy Bentham, *An Introduction to the Principles of Morals and Legislation* (1789), rpt. of the 1823 edn. (Oxford: Clarendon, 1952), 2.
15 John Stuart Mill, *Utilitarianism* (1861), in *Collected Works*, Vol. 10 (Toronto: University of Toronto Press, 1969), 210. Italics added.
16 Mill seems to have changed his mind at some point about how reliable our expectations can be. The early Mill believed in certain knowledge, including certain inductive knowledge, which implies that we can have certain expectations; and if expectations are certain, then C-expectations realize as X-consequences. Later Mill was less confident, which is revealed by changes he made in the 1872 edition of his *A System of Logic*. Steffen Ducheyne, "J.S. Mill's Canon of Induction: From True Causes to Provisional Ones," *History and Philosophy of Logic* 29 (2008): 361–76.
17 Henry Sidgwick, *The Methods of Ethics*, 7th edn. (Indianapolis: Hacket, 1981, 1906), 411.
18 Ibid., 476.
19 Ibid., 460. Emphasis added.

and those expectations are based on "tendencies" and "probabilities." In classical utilitarianism, C-expectations rather than actual consequences determine the good. Similarly, more than two millennia earlier, Mozi 墨子 argued that

> [a] wise man's business must be to plan [in accordance with] what leads to peace and order among the state's people (or for the state and people) and to avoid that what brings disorder.[20]

Or in other words, a wise man lets his actions be guided by their expected consequences.

One may start to wonder at this point whether anyone actually defended or defends a moral theory that defines the good as being determined by actual consequences.[21] Such retrospective consequentialism is sometimes identified with objective consequentialism, but Peter Railton, who introduced the subjective-objective consequentialism distinction defines the latter a bit differently:

> *Objective consequentialism* is the view that the criterion of the rightness of an act or course of action is whether it in fact would most promote the good of those acts available to the agent.[22]

The key term is "would," which indicates that this is still a prospective consequentialism, albeit one that assumes perfect knowledge about the future consequences of one's actions. In *Uneasy Virtue*, Julia Driver distinguishes two kinds of such "objective consequentialism." The first kind "defines a right action as that which produces good actual consequences."[23] According to the second kind, "an agent's action could be deemed right/wrong, depending on the consequences of that act in normal circumstances, or what would have been normal circumstances."[24] The first of these kinds turns out to be a form of retrospective consequentialism, but the second is something quite different.

This second kind of "objective consequentialism" depends on a "robust modal realism"[25]: it defines the good in terms of counterfactuals, that is, as what would be the case in some possible world. If there are possible worlds and if the good in this world is determined by consequences in some possible worlds, then this would be a kind of genuine consequentialism indeed. (An eternalist in the metaphysics of time could even make a similar claim without an appeal to possible worlds.[26] Because future consequences exist according to externalism, something in the present could be right in the present if it has the right consequences in the future.) However, we have no telescope that lets us see possible worlds (if those exist;[27] or future worlds in case of the eternalist variant), and any claim about a possible world is a theoretical

---

20 Mozi 墨, 《墨子》 [*The Mozi*] (4/5th c. BCE), 〈尚同下〉, §1. Previously quoted in the introduction of chapter 11.
21 The answer is probably "yes." At least, G.E. Moore seems to have argued for something like that, but his retrospective consequentialism is widely considered incoherent.
22 Railton, "Alienation, Consequentialism, and the Demands of Morality," 152.
23 Driver, *Uneasy Virtue*, xiv.
24 Ibid., xix, 78.
25 Ibid., 78.
26 According to eternalism, not just present entities but also past and future entities exist.
27 The existence of possible worlds is itself a rather controversial claim.

claim. It is a claim about what would or could be, or in one word, an expectation. Even if counterfactual claims are theoretically informed expectations, they are still expectations. Consequently, calling this kind of theory "objective consequentialism" may be metaphysically correct in theory, provided that one accepts modal realism or eternalism,[28] but it is deceptive in practice, as determining what is right and wrong still depends on C-expectations. The labeling is particularly deceptive because it suggests that some C-expectations are "objective" while others are merely "subjective."

This latter problem becomes more obvious in another paper that skips the dubious metaphysics and just redefines "objective" as "well-motivated" and "fully informed" without taking into account that what counts as being well-motivated or fully informed is largely determined by the hegemonic values and beliefs in a society.[29] "Objective," thus understood, really means nothing but "in accordance with hegemony," which is a kind of Orwellian doublespeak that is interestingly similar to the Marxist-Leninist concept of "truth" that justified dictatorial one-party states.[30] (We'll return to the problematic role of ideology and hegemony in the next section.)

Driver's other, first kind of "objective consequentialism," which she does not endorse herself, depends on a distinction between rightness and praiseworthiness. Rightness is defined as having the right actual consequences and can thus only be determined afterwards, while praiseworthiness depends on C-expectations. An act is praiseworthy if the agent expects that the consequences will be good, and if it is found later that the consequences of that act were good indeed, then that act was right as well.

This is a peculiar idea. Bart Gruzalski has suggested that such praiseworthiness is a caricature of morality,[31] but there is a more fundamental problem: either the idea captures a common sense distinction, or it is a proposal for new terminology. If it is supposed to be the former, then it is based on a confusion of "right" and "turned out right." If I would hit a student, and as a result that student gets so angry at me that he storms out of the building, which is subsequently destroyed by an earthquake killing everyone inside; then my hitting that student *turned out right*, but that does not mean that it *was right*.[32] If it is a proposal for new terminology, on the other hand, then it effectively substitutes "praiseworthy" for what more commonly is thought of as "right" and "right" for what more commonly is thought of as "turned out right."[33]

---

28 Based on considerations in part II of this book, I think that we should probably reject both.
29 Julia Driver, "What the Objective Standard is Good for," in *Oxford Studies in Normative Ethics*, Vol. 2, ed. Mark Timmons (Oxford: Oxford University Press, 2012), 28–44, at 34.
30 Oversimplifying a bit, that understanding of "truth" is the following: "truth" is whatever is revealed in practice and especially in changing things, and therefore, social truths are revealed in revolutionary social practice (i.e., in changing things in society). And because the Party is the vanguard of social struggle, the Party is in the best position to realize and recognize truth. Therefore, truth is whatever the Party says that is true. And if that Party holds power, then this means that truth, by definition, is the hegemonic view. The first part of this argument is based mostly on Marx's *Feuerbach Theses* (MEW 3: 5–7), the second part is based mostly on Lenin's ideas about the communist party and its role.
31 Bart Gruzalski, "Foreseeable Consequence Utilitarianism," *Australasian Journal of Philosophy* 59, no. 2 (1981): 163–76, at 173.
32 I must admit that this is just my intuition and the intuition of everyone I ever asked about this (i.e., my students, mostly). Perhaps, some experimental philosopher should check how many people share this intuition, but I expect the percentage to be rather large.
33 Perhaps, the proposal also entails a suggestion that "turned out right" (i.e., the new "right") is the more important notion of the two, but that would have the implication that moral luck is better than trying to do the right thing.

We could just as well translate our moral terminology into Hindi or Korean: making moral decisions would still be guided by expectations. And whether the post-consequential evaluation adds anything morally relevant is not settled just by reapplying the term "right": that "turned out right" (i.e., the new "right") is morally relevant requires an independent argument.

Effectively then, virtually all "consequentialisms" are subjective or prospective consequentialisms because all "consequentialisms" maintain that we should let our moral decisions be guided by C-expectations. This has the obvious implication that "consequentialism" is a misnomer: consequences play no necessary or important role in the theories called "consequentialism."

Nevertheless, at least some of the moral theories called "consequentialism" are ontologically committed to consequences. The first of Driver's two varieties of "objective consequentialism" requires there to be consequences to evaluate actions (i.e., the supposed causes of those consequences), but it is not exactly clear what the moral relevance of such evaluations is. And the second variety requires there to be consequences in possible worlds, but in practice such unobservable entities cannot play any role. Less exotic versions of consequentialism — such as the classical utilitarianism of Bentham, Mill, and Sidgwick, and any other variety of subjective consequentialism — are not ontologically committed to consequences, and thus avoid the metaphysical and epistemological problems associated with such entities.

Problems for Subjective Consequentialism

C-expectations are a kind of beliefs and beliefs may face similar metaphysical difficulties.[34] It is unclear whether and how beliefs can be individuated — what passes through my mind when I am believing something or even several things might be a continuum without clear breaks or joints — and even if beliefs can be individuated, they may not be meaningfully separable from each other.[35] Donald Davidson has pointed out that the content of any belief depends on very many other beliefs.[36] My belief that there is a plant on the table I'm sitting at when writing this only makes sense against a background of other beliefs about tables and plants, which in turn involve further beliefs. But this implies that beliefs are part of much larger networks of beliefs from which they cannot be meaningfully isolated. Whether or to what extent subjective consequentialists need to worry about these metaphysical problems is not immediately clear, however.

Subjective consequentialism roughly holds that something (i.e., an act, rule, and so forth) is right if and only if (or to the extent that) it is believed (by whom?) that it will have good consequences (or better consequences than available alternatives). Perhaps, the most obvious ambiguity in this rough definition is the identity of the believers, that is, the person or persons who are expecting the good consequences. But before we can turn to that issue there is a more fundamental question that needs

---

34 For a review of the troubled metaphysics of beliefs, see Nikolaj Nottelmann, "Belief Metaphysics: The Basic Questions," in *New Essays on Belief: Constitution, Content, and Structure*, ed. Nikolaj Nottelmann (London: Palgrave MacMillan, 2013), 9–29.
35 The problem is aggravated by the opacity of mind: as Peter Carruthers has shown, most of the time we have no idea about what goes on in our minds. Peter Carruthers, *The Opacity of Mind: An Integrative Theory of Self-Knowledge* (Oxford: Oxford University Press, 2011).
36 See, for example, Donald Davidson, "The Emergence of Thought" (1997), SIO: 123–34. See also the last two sections of chapter 8.

to be answered first: what does it mean to say that someone believes something or has a certain belief?

Let us say that Jane believes that her friend owns a black cat. This can be an occurrent or a dispositional belief. If it is an occurrent belief, then Jane has this belief right now. If it is a dispositional belief, then Jane has the disposition to have an occurrent belief, in the right circumstances, that her friend owns a black cat. Even if it is an occurrent belief, Jane may not have the exact thought "my friend owns a black cat" — more likely she does not. That proposition is something like a summary of what passes through her mind mostly unconsciously when she occurrently believes that her friend owns a black cat. Her actual thoughts are almost certainly much more vague than the propositional summary in some respects and much more specific and detailed in others. Almost certainly, she'll think of some specific, named friend rather than of the generic "my friend" and of some specific cat, for example. And this is not the case just when we form beliefs about named particulars we are familiar with: according to Lawrence Barsalou even abstract concepts evoke simulations of specific examples in our (unconscious) minds.[37] In other words, the real contents of our beliefs — what passes through our minds when we are occurrently believing something — is richer, more detailed, more multifaceted, more embedded, and more vague than any proposition can express. Summarizing a belief by means of a proposition is like drawing a sketch or map. It may be perfectly accurate given its purpose and context but may be misleading in another.[38]

Even good, non-misleading maps or sketches are simplifications, but that does not make them false, and consequently, belief attributions can be true, even if they only sketch or summarize the belief attributed. It is true that Jane believes or has a belief that her friend owns a black cat if and only if, in the given context, the proposition that her friend owns a black cat is a sufficiently accurate summary of what Jane believes. Nevertheless, that Jane believes that her friend owns a black cat does not imply that she at any time had a discrete, individual belief with a propositional content identical or similar to the proposition that her friend owns a black cat. All it implies is that this proposition, in the given context, accurately summarizes what she actually believed.[39] And similarly, Jane's belief (or C-expectation) that pulling at her friend's sleeve will prevent him from being hit by a truck does not imply that she had or has a discrete, individual belief with more or less that propositional content.

Importantly, when we attribute a C-expectation, we attribute a conditional belief about the future, but we are not making claims about the exact mental contents of the person having that expectation. We are merely claiming that in the given context, our propositional summary of that person's beliefs is sufficiently accurate. But that means that we are bypassing the metaphysical problems hinted at above. Those apply to what happens in people's minds and not to the rough sketches we draw to make sense thereof. So, with that problem out of the way, let's turn to the other issue identified above.

---

[37] Lawrence Barsalou, "Situating Concepts," in *The Cambridge Handbook of Situated Cognition*, eds. Philip Robbins and Murat Aydede (Cambridge: Cambridge University Press, 2009), 236–63.
[38] Mark Richard, *Propositional Attitudes: An Essay on Thoughts and How We Ascribe Them* (Cambridge: Cambridge University Press, 1990); Kent Bach, "Do Belief Reports Report Beliefs?" *Pacific Philosophical Quarterly* 78 (1997): 215–41; Lajos Brons, "Patterns, Noise, and Beliefs," *Principia* 23, no. 1 (2019): 19–51.
[39] For a much more detailed argument for this point, see Brons, "Patterns, Noise, and Beliefs."

Expectations do not float around; *people* have expectations,[40] but varieties of subjective consequentialism differ with regards to the identity of those people relative to the agents. Borrowing and slightly stretching Driver's distinction between evaluational internalism and externalism,[41] we can distinguish *internalist* from *externalist* consequentialisms. In the first, the C-expectations that matter are the ones the agent happens to have or had. Hence, as long as *I* believe that my action will have good consequences, I am doing the right thing. In externalist consequentialism, on the other hand, whether what I do is right depends not just on what *I* believe.

From a commonsense point of view, internalist consequentialism seems to mistake "*trying* to do the right thing" for "doing the right thing" but more problematic is that it makes ignorance a valid excuse in every case actual consequences turned out worse than expected by the agent. And even worse, since there is no way to determine what someone really believed at the time of acting,[42] the agent can always claim afterwards to have acted on the expectation of good consequences.

Externalist consequentialism either requires specification of the "expecter(s)" whose expectations matter or a procedure by which the expectations that matter are or should be formed. These two options are not as different as they may seem. Plausible candidate procedures are very similar to scientific procedures and those involve consensus formation among scientists or other knowledgeable people, and thus implicitly determine whose expectations matter; and the other way around, plausible candidate expecters, such as scientists or other particularly well informed people, are largely defined or identified by the procedures they follow in arriving at their expectations.

It is important to realize that externalism is not any more objective than internalism.[43] Expectations are beliefs, and therefore, subjective by definition, and even in the unlikely case that everyone shares the same expectation, it is still only intersubjective. Calling externalism "objective," therefore, would be deceptive. It can even be a kind of Orwellian Newspeak in the case of hegemonic falsehoods, which are probably the biggest problem for externalism.

A hegemonic falsehood is a socially dominant or consensual belief that is actually false. Such a belief can be disseminated through religion, ideology, or cultural hegemony, and may find almost universal acceptance in some relevant community. There was a consensus in European medicine that bloodletting was a beneficial procedure (i.e., had good consequences) for almost two millennia, for example, but in most cases the practice is actually harmful. Bloodletting went out of fashion, but there is an analogue that has only gained strength over the past few decades. According to its detractors, mainstream, neoclassical economics is a religion or an ideology rather than a science.[44] It is a closed system that is almost completely detached from

---

40 And sometimes some other animals appear to have expectations as well, but I'll ignore that possibility in the following.
41 Driver, *Uneasy Virtue*.
42 The agent might not even know or remember herself.
43 Even the best expectations are unlikely to be true in detail or in the long run. This problem is a corollary of the "epistemic objection" mentioned in the section "the metaphysics of (expected) consequences" above: in the long run, unforeseen consequences vastly outnumber or outweigh expected ones.
44 On economics as a religion, see Robert Nelson, *Economics as Religion: From Samuelson to Chicago and Beyond*, rev. edn. (University Park: Penn State University Press, 2014), and John Rapley, *Twilight of the Money Gods: Economics as Religion and How It All Went Wrong* (London: Simon & Schuster, 2017). Comparisons of economists to high priests are too numerous too list, but the introduction in Yanis

empirical reality, and that is, moreover, littered with mathematical and conceptual errors and contradictions.[45] Its predictions consistently fail.[46] Where it predicted economic growth it brought economic destruction,[47] and even suffering, death, poverty, and starvation.[48] These are probably controversial claims,[49] but they are controversial exactly *because* mainstream economics is hegemonic. It is almost universally adhered to within the economics profession and the financial sector and provides the justification of most economic policy, but it is also widely accepted as the one and only true view of "economic reality" outside those areas. However, the hegemony of neoclassical economics is not complete, even though economists are revered in the mainstream press as sages, their preferred recipes often differ from popular preferences.[50] For a believer, that can only mean that ordinary folk are wrong and should

---

Varoufakis, *Economic Indeterminacy: A Personal Encounter with the Economists' Peculiar Nemesis* (London: Routledge, 2014) is particularly noteworthy. An early study of the role of political ideology in economics is Gunnar Myrdal, *The Political Element in the Development of Economic Theory* (London: Routledge, 1953). Among recent denouncements of mainstream economics as ideology, some of the more interesting include David Orrell, *Economyths: Ten Ways Economics Gets It Wrong* (Ontario: John Wiley, 2010); John Weeks, *Economics of the 1%: How Mainstream Economics Serves the Rich, Obscures Reality and Distorts Policy* (London: Anthem, 2014); and Michael Hudson, "Economic Methodology is Ideology, and Implies Policy." In: *J Is for Junk Economics: A Guide to Reality in an Age of Deception* (Dresden: Islet, 2017), 291–304. See also Norbert Häring and Niall Douglas, *Economists and the Powerful: Convenient Theories, Distorted Facts, Ample Rewards* (London: Anthem, 2012), as well as chapter 15.

45 By far the most rigorous analysis of mathematical errors, contradictions, and other methodological flaws in mainstream economics is Steve Keen's *Debunking Economics: The Naked Emperor Dethroned?*, rev. and exp. edn. (London: Zed, 2011). See also the section "The Ideology of Supply and Demand" in chapter 15.
46 Mainstream economists predicted around 2007 that there would be no more economic crises because we had entered "the great moderation," for example. Only a handful of economists predicted the 2008 financial meltdown and resulting economic crisis, and none of those belonged to the neoclassical mainstream. (The most prominent was Steve Keen — see previous footnote.) On the strange fate of the idea of "the great moderation" as well as several other ideologically motivated "zombie ideas" in economics that keep being revived after being proven wrong, see John Quiggin, *Zombie Economics: How Dead Ideas Still Walk Among Us* (Princeton: Princeton University Press, 2010).
47 On the economic destruction resulting from the enforced application of mainstream economic dogma in the "developing" world, see Mike Davis, *Late Victorian Holocausts: El Niño Famines and the Making of the Third World* (London: Verso, 2001); Ha-Joon Chang, *Kicking Away the Ladder* (London: Anthem, 2002); *Bad Samaritans* (London: Random House, 2007); Erik Reinert, *How Rich Countries Got Rich... and Why Poor Countries Stay Poor* (London: Constable, 2007); and Naomi Klein, *The Shock Doctrine: The Rise of Disaster Capitalism* (New York: Henry Holt, 2007). On similar processes and effects in the EU, see, for example, Servaas Storm and S.W.M. Naastepad, "Europe's Hunger Games: Income Distribution, Cost Competitiveness and Crisis." *Cambridge Journal of Economics* 39, no. 3 (2015): 959–86. See also the section "Free Trade Ideology" in chapter 15.
48 See especially: Davis, *Late Victorian Holocausts*, and Klein, *The Shock Doctrine*.
49 Which is the reason for all the footnotes and references in this paragraph.
50 According to Bryan Caplan the policy preferences of economic laymen tend to be closer to "Mercantilism" than to mainstream economics. What might be most interesting about this is that Mercantilism is relatively similar to variants of Listian National Systems approaches that virtually every developed country used to get rich (see, e.g., Chang, *Kicking Away the Ladder*, and Reinert, *How Rich Countries Got Rich*), suggesting that, contrary to Caplan's conclusion, the "general public" may actually have more sensible economic policy preferences than mainstream economists. See Bryan Caplan, *The Myth of the Rational Voter: Why Democracies Choose Bad Policies* (Princeton: Princeton University Press, 2006).

be silenced by denying them any voice in formulating economic policy,[51] or even by abolishing democracy.[52]

Perhaps, some readers are unwilling to accept my quick sketch of mainstream economics as a source of false expectations that are nevertheless widely accepted,[53] but they'll have to admit the *possibility* of something like that occurring. Consensual expectations *can* be false. There is no guarantee that even the "best" science available is right in its expectations — it may even be consistently wrong in some areas. There is no infallible community of expecters and no infallible procedure: expectations can be wrong, not just because of bad luck, but because of social, psychological, ideological, and other reasons. And some of these factors make it even possible for expectations to be systematically wrong.

There is a second problem for externalism: while internalism is too easy, externalism is too hard.[54] If doing the right thing depends on expectations informed by scientific knowledge and procedures or provided by the right community of expecters, then most people never do anything right. I cannot act on the basis of what I do not know, and therefore; if externalism is to provide moral guidance rather than just evaluation, which is the very point of subjective consequentialism, then it requires me to inform myself of these "external" expectations (which might coincide with my own expectations, but I cannot know that beforehand) *every time* I contemplate doing something that may have morally relevant effects (but I cannot know that beforehand either, so effectively this includes all of my actions). That is demanding too much.

For subjective consequentialism to work, some kind of compromise between internalism and externalism would be needed, then; some kind of mechanism that pushes the agent toward externalism when more is at stake and toward internalism in case of relatively trivial decisions. The most obvious way to achieve that is by means of some kind of *principle of prudence*, something like the following:

> The more serious the expected consequences, the better supported one's expectations have to be.

Although common sense morality actually appears to involve a principle somewhat like this, there are two problems for this suggestion. First, the principle suggested here is very vague: it is insufficiently clear what makes an expected consequence more or less serious. One could, of course, say that an expected consequence is more serious if more people will or could be affected, or if the effects are more far-reaching,

---

51 Wolfgang Streeck, *How Will Capitalism End? Essays on a Failing System* (London: Verso, 2016), 74, points out that "mainstream economics has become obsessed with the 'irresponsibility' of opportunistic politicians who cater to an economically uneducated electorate by interfering with otherwise efficient markets." Indeed, mainstream economists have been very suspicious of democracy for many decades (see also Klein, *The Shock Doctrine*). It is for that reason that economic decision-making had to be "saved" from democracy and brought under the control of "independent" technocrats, such as central bankers. Because of this, in most countries democratically elected politicians, and the people who elect them, can have no significant influence on economic policy anymore.
52 Among mainstream economists, one of the most outspoken enemies of democracy is Jason Brennan, *Against Democracy* (Princeton: Princeton University Press, 2016).
53 Chapter 15 might change their minds.
54 Rather aptly, Peter Galle, "Gruzalski and Ellis on Utilitarianism," *Australasian Journal of Philosophy* 59, no. 3 (1981): 332–37, at 333, has suggested that something like externalism would "make stupidity a crime."

or if there is a greater chance of bad (side-)effects or of irreversible bad effects, or if there is a higher risk of things turning out badly, and so forth, but this list of criteria may very well be open-ended and virtually any item on the list is itself rather vague. The principle resists precising, which is probably partially due to the second, more fundamental problem: any criterion that determines how far one should move toward externalism (i.e., to "better supported" expectations) is itself an expectation. A principle of prudence appeals to expectations about the seriousness of consequences, and these expectations too can be either internalist or externalist, but if they are internalist then ignorance is an excuse for abstaining from further research, and externalism requires one to already know everything there is to know about the risks and possible consequences involved, and another compromise between internalism and externalism on this level will lead to an infinite regress.

Despite these serious problems, at least two arguments can be made in favor of a principle of prudence. First, it is probably much easier to predict in most cases *that* some action might have far-reaching consequences than what exactly those consequences will be. And second, assuming that this is the case indeed, one would expect that, everything else being equal, the moral decisions of an agent operating with a principle of prudence have on average better consequences than those of an agent without such a principle. Or in other words, if one is not afraid of a bit of circularity, a principle of prudence can be defended on subjective consequentialist grounds.

Foreseeable and Intended Consequences

The focus in the preceding has been on C-expectations mostly, but not all varieties of subjective consequentialism are defined in terms of "expected consequences." Some refer to "intended consequences" or "foreseeable consequences" instead. Both notions are very similar to "expected consequences," but only the first shares its metaphysical ambiguity.

If something is foreseeable then it has not occurred yet, and therefore, foreseeable consequences cannot be a subset of consequences. (The analogue of X-consequences would be "consequences that *should* have been foreseen.") To foresee is to expect, and something that is foreseeable is something that can, could, or should be expected. A foreseeable consequence is, therefore, a C-expectation that the agent could or should have, or should have had. The expectations that an agent should have or should have had are the most reliable expectations available — "external" expectations — and consequently, foreseeable consequences are external C-expectations. Or perhaps, in a more lenient interpretation of "should," foreseeable consequences are a compromise between internal and external expectations by means of some principle of prudence.

Contrary to foreseeable consequences, intended consequences are metaphysically ambiguous: they could be consequences that were intended, analogous to X-consequences, or they could be analogous to C-expectations. If intended consequences are evaluation criteria then the subset of actual consequences of an action that was intended determines the rightness of that action. If intended consequences are to play a role as decision criteria, then they cannot be a subset of actual consequences; rather, in that case they are a subset of expectations. To intend to cause an effect is to expect to cause an effect, although possibly with a lower probability, but not necessarily the other way around. Therefore, intended consequences are a subset of C-expectations, namely those C-expectations that are intended.

The idea that there is a morally significant difference between what it intended and what is expected or "merely foreseen" is an old idea and is best known as the *doctrine of double effect*. One of the examples Alison McIntyre gives in a rather thorough review of this doctrine is the following:

> A doctor who intends to hasten the death of a terminally ill patient by injecting a large dose of morphine would act impermissibly because he intends to bring about the patient's death. However, a doctor who intended to relieve the patient's pain with that same dose and merely foresaw the hastening of the patient's death would act permissibly.[55]

While this example might have some intuitive plausibility, it is easy to come up with scenarios in which intended consequences would be a rather dubious criterion of rightness.

> At a busy pedestrian crossing, Jane pulls at her friend's sleeve with the intention of preventing him from being hit by a truck. She expects that by pulling his sleeve, he will probably stumble and push a young mother and her two children in front of that truck. She does not *intend* the latter to happen, however — even though she *expects* both consequences, she only *intends* the first (i.e., saving her friend).

It seems outrageous that Jane's action of pulling at her friend's sleeve in this case would be morally right, but that is exactly what defining right actions in terms of intended consequences would imply.

The doctrine of double effect and intended consequences consequentialism, then, would require some restrictions that specify when exactly intended consequences outweigh expected or merely foreseen consequences. McIntyre discusses six such restrictions. The nature of those restrictions matter little here, but what does matter is their combined effect: *even if* there might be cases in which the distinction between intended consequences and merely expected consequences is morally significant, such cases would be very rare and in the vast majority of cases *all* expected consequences matter. And if in most cases *all* expected consequences matter, then intended consequences consequentialism, which holds that only intended consequences matter, is false. The next section will suggest another, less problematic understanding of intentions, however.

Consequences and Consequentialism in Mahāyāna

According to the coherentism that is part of the post-Yogācāra realism proposed in part II, convergence justifies the acceptance of beliefs. The previous chapter claimed that moral thought converges on the idea that right and wrong are determined by expected consequences. Let's call this general idea "expectivism." Given that post-Yogācāra realism is Buddhist (see chapter 10), it could be argued that an expectivist moral theory that is explicitly built on post-Yogācāra realist foundations is Buddhist as well, but that would be a bit too easy. What is needed to support the "Buddhist" credentials of an expectivist moral theory is expectivist Buddhist moral thought.

---

55 Alison McIntyre, "Doing Away with Double Effect," *Ethics* 111, no. 2 (2001): 219–55, at 219.

Not all Buddhist moral thought is equally relevant here, given the focus on Yogācāra, Tiantai/Tendai 天台 and related schools, but we cannot ignore the Mādhyamaka scholar Śāntideva for at least two reasons. Firstly, his *Bodhicaryāvatāra* is probably the best known and certainly one of the most influential Buddhist texts with a significant focus on moral philosophy. And secondly, Śāntideva is often interpreted as a consequentialist — most influentially by Charles Goodman[56] — and if that interpretation is right and Śāntideva's consequentialism turns out to be a variety of subjective consequentialism, then that would support an expectivist interpretation of Mahāyāna ethics.[57] Nevertheless, there are other thinkers and sources that need to be taken into account as well, not in the least the *Bodhisattvabhūmi* by the founder of Yogācāra, Asaṅga.

The central figure in Asaṅga's *Bodhisattvabhūmi*, Śāntideva's *Bodhicaryāvatāra*, and Mahāyāna ethics in general is the bodhisattva — Mahāyāna ethics is bodhisattva ethics. In the *Vimalakīrti Sūtra* Mañjuśrī asks, "how does the bodhisattva follow the wrong way?" Vimalakīrti answers:

> Even should he enact the five deadly sins, he feels no malice, violence, or hate. Even should he go into the hells, he remains free of all taint of passion. [...] He may follow the ways of desire, yet he stays free of attachment to the enjoyments of desire. He may follow the ways of hatred, yet he feels no anger to any living being. [...] He may follow the ways of immorality, yet, seeing the horror of even the slightest transgressions, he lives by the ascetic practices and austerities. He may follow the ways of wickedness and anger, yet he remains utterly free of malice and lives by love. [...] He may show the ways of sophistry and contention, yet he is always conscious of ultimate meanings and has perfected the use of liberative techniques.[58]

The passage illustrates a common idea in Mahāyāna thought: a bodhisattva can do anything provided that he does so without negative afflictions (*kleśas*) and with good intentions, and those good intentions are generally related to his raison d'être, saving every sentient being from suffering. Variants of this idea can be found in the writings of both Asaṅga and Śāntideva, and in both cases it is phrased in terms that suggest a consequentialist interpretation. For example, in his *Śikṣā-samuccaya*, Śāntideva wrote:

> If a bodhisattva does not make a sincere, unwavering effort in thought, word, and deed to stop all the present and future pain and suffering of all sentient beings, and to bring about all present and future pleasure and happiness, or does not seek the collection of conditions for that, or does not strive to prevent what is opposed to that, or does not bring about small pain and suffering as a way of preventing great pain and suffering, or does not abandon a small benefit in order to accom-

---

56 Charles Goodman, *Consequences of Compassion: An Interpretation & Defense of Buddhist Ethics* (Oxford: Oxford University Press, 2009).
57 Charles Goodman was by no means the first to associate Mahāyāna ethics with consequentialism. Probably, that honor goes to Inoue Enryō 井上圓了, who already suggested something like this in 1887. Inoue Enryō, 『仏教活論序論』 (1887), in 『井上円了選集』, vol. 3 (2003): 327–93, at 379. See also Rainer Schulzer, *Inoue Enryō: A Philosophical Portrait* (New York: SUNY Press, 2019), 269–72.
58 Robert Thurman, *The Holy Teaching of Vimalakīrti: A Mahāyāna Scripture* (University Park: Pennsylvania State University Press, 1976), 64.

plish a greater benefit, if he neglects to do these things even for a moment, he undergoes a downfall.⁵⁹

Especially the demand to "bring about small pain and suffering as a way of preventing great pain and suffering" appears to express a very consequentialist idea, and indeed, Goodman identifies this passage as "the heart" of Śāntideva's consequentialism.⁶⁰ By far the most widely quoted passage from Śāntideva's writings in support of a consequentialist interpretation is a verse from the *Bodhicaryāvatāra*: "[i]f the suffering of one ends the suffering of many, then one who has compassion for others and himself must cause that suffering to arise."⁶¹

In both of these passages, preventing great suffering appears to be something a bodhisattva should do, implying that it is a decision criterion and not an evaluation criterion. This suggests that Śāntideva's consequentialism is subjective or prospective, which seems to be confirmed by another passage from the *Bodhicaryāvatāra*:

> If the perfection of generosity consisted in making the universe free from poverty, how can previous Protectors [i.e., Buddhas] have achieved it, when the world is still poor, even today? The perfection of generosity is said to result from the mental attitude of relinquishing all that one has to all people, together with the fruit of that act. Therefore, the perfection is the mental attitude itself.⁶²

The crux of this argument is that it is not success that determines the rightness of an act or the achievement of a virtue (i.e., the perfection of generosity) but intention. In other words, it is not the actual consequences of one's actions that matter but the intended consequences, which are a subset of expected consequences.

The idea that intention is what matters most is not an innovation by Śāntideva. On the contrary, it goes back to the Buddha, who is recorded as saying that "it is volition [*cetanā*] [...] that I call *kamma*. For having willed, one acts by body, speech, or mind."⁶³ Cetanā (intention or volition) determines karma (Pāli: *kamma*) and thus the moral quality of an act. A significant difference between the two passages, however, is that while the Buddha used the word *cetanā*, Śāntideva used *citta*. *Cetanā* means something like "impulse," "intention," or "volition." According to Peter Harvey "it is the impulse that immediately leads to action," and "cetanā is not 'intention' in the sense of a plan, a resolve to do something."⁶⁴ *Citta*, on the other hand, is often translated as "mind" or "thought" and here refers to exactly such a resolve to do something. The perfection of generosity is the resolve (citta).

If Śāntideva was a consequentialist, then he was a subjective consequentialist, but before accepting that conclusion, let us put the *Bodhicaryāvatāra* verse about the suffering of the one and the many in its context. Adding some of the surrounding verses, the textual context is as follows:

---

59 Śāntideva, *The Training Anthology of Śāntideva: A Translation of the Śikṣā-samuccaya* (8th c.), trans. Charles Goodman (Oxford: Oxford University Press, 2016), §15, 17.
60 Goodman, *Consequences of Compassion*, 89.
61 Śāntideva, *The Bodhicaryāvatāra* (8th c.), trans. Kate Crosby and Andrew Skilton (Oxford: Oxford University Press, 1995), §8.105.
62 Ibid., §§5.9–10.
63 Chakkanipāta, AN 63.5/III.415, 963.
64 Peter Harvey, "Karma," in *The Oxford Handbook of Buddhist Ethics*, eds. Daniel Cozort and James Mark Shields (Oxford: Oxford University Press, 2000), 7–28, at 9.

> You may argue: compassion causes us so much suffering, why force it to arise? Yet when one sees how much the world suffers, how can this suffering from compassion be considered great? | If the suffering of one ends the suffering of many, then one who has compassion for others and himself must cause that suffering to arise. | That is why Supuṣpacandra, though undergoing torture at the hands of the king, did nothing to prevent his own suffering out of sacrifice for many sufferers. | Those who have developed the continuum of their mind in this way, to whom suffering of others is as important as the things they themselves hold dear, plunge down into the Avīci hell as geese into a cluster of lotus blossoms.[65]

The *social* context of the passage is at least as important to understand it. "You" and "us" in the first sentence refer to the community consisting of the audience and the speaker or writer, that is, the community of monks and aspiring bodhisattvas at Nālandā. Śāntideva was not just speaking to aspiring bodhisattvas but also about bodhisattvas. "One who has compassion" and "those who have developed the continuum of their mind" refer to a bodhisattva and bodhisattvas, respectively, and he mentions one famous bodhisattva, Supuṣpacandra, by name. Furthermore, the second verse is the beginning of the answer to the question in the first verse: "how can this suffering [by us, aspiring bodhisattvas] be considered great?" Hence, what the second verse in this passage means is that

> (B) — If the suffering of a bodhisattva ends the suffering of many others, then a bodhisattva who has compassion for others and himself must cause that suffering for himself to arise.

This does not conflict with the consequentialist interpretation, but it is worth pointing out that (B) is very different from utilitarianism. Utilitarianism is impartial and agent-neutral, but (B) is neither. Impartiality means that everyone's interests, and thus everyone's suffering, count equally, but according to (B), the suffering of a bodhisattva, if brought on by himself to avoid the suffering of others, is less important than the suffering of others. Agent-neutrality means that the same rules or principles apply to everyone, but the principle that appears to be implied by (B) applies only to bodhisattvas. Hence, if (B) is to be interpreted as a precept, then it advocates self-sacrifice and extreme altruism and not utilitarianism or anything like it.

It is that interpretation as precept which is most problematic, however. At no point in this passage and the following verses does Śāntideva say what a bodhisattva *should* do. He does not prescribe; he *describes*. He explains to his audience of aspiring bodhisattvas what it is like, or what it means, to be a bodhisattva. He does not specify principles or precepts but describes virtues. Extreme altruism is a defining virtue of a bodhisattva. And in this respect, the *Bodhicaryāvatāra* reminds of a similar extreme altruism in many of the Jātaka tales.

Furthermore, from a Mādhyamaka perspective, (B) *could* not express a precept or rule because Mādhyamaka rejects ultimate truths, and if there are no ultimate truths, then there are no ultimate moral truths, and thus no ultimately true moral principles either. If (B) would be a principle, then bodhisattvas would realize that it is not ultimately true. If Bodhisattvas act according to (B) anyway, that must mean that it is not a principle. Goodman realizes part of the problem. His solution is that

---

65 Śāntideva, *The Bodhicaryāvatāra*, §§8.104–7.

bodhisattvas who have fully realized emptiness "do not believe any ethical theory at all; indeed they are not committed to any theory about anything. Spontaneously, and without any need for deliberation or practical reasoning, they behave as if they were act-consequentialists."[66] This reminds of Confucius's famous saying:

> At fifteen, I was determined to study. At thirty, I stood firm. At forty, I had no doubts. At fifty, I knew what heaven/nature commanded. At sixty, my ears were obedient. At seventy, I could follow what my heart desired, without transgressing the rules.[67]

With sufficient training, virtue becomes automatic. For a bodhisattva (B) is not a principle or rule; rather, a bodhisattva acts in accordance with (B), "without transgressing the rules," automatically. It has become a character trait, that is, a virtue.

This, however, is only part of the problem. As Gordon Davis has pointed out, even if (B) is not a principle for a bodhisattva, it is still used as a standard.[68] If bodhisattvas spontaneously "behave as if they were act-consequentialists" and that behavior is what makes them bodhisattvas, then that standard is not *just* conventionally true. It does not matter that they are unaware of the standard and follow it "spontaneously" (or that they "follow what their hearts desire, without transgressing the rules"); what matters is that there *is* an independent standard. Furthermore, in the verses directly preceding the block quote above, Śāntideva does argue for a principle or rule, namely, that all suffering should be prevented. The problem for a Mādhyamika is that if there are no ultimate truths, then there cannot be such a standard or such a principle either. Then even the bodhisattva perfections are merely conventionally true. Then everything sinks into a nihilistic morass, which is exactly the main Yogācāra objection to Mādhyamaka.

Ultimately, then, Śāntideva's moral theory appears to be incoherent because it aspires for or even claims ultimate truths in the moral sphere, while for a Mādhyamaka there are no ultimate truths at all. This problem is only of limited relevance here, however.[69] First, because the arguments in this book build upon a mostly Yogācāra foundation rather than on Mādhyamaka. And second, because we do not need moral truth anyway but justification.[70]

There is another apparent, and much more interesting, incoherence in the *Bodhicaryāvatāra*. In the passage about the perfection of generosity, Śāntideva defined virtue as intention, but in the passage following the verse about the suffering of the one and the many, the virtues of bodhisattva are presented by sketching what they actually do. The latter reminds of the Aristotelian conception of virtue as a character trait manifested in habitual behavior, but the former does not. This might suggest a contradiction or equivocation — a mix-up between two notions of virtue in the *Bodhicaryāvatāra* — but I do not think that interpretation would be right. Actual behavior illustrates or even proves intention, and thus virtue, but it does not

---

66 Goodman, *Consequences of Compassion*, 6
67 吾十有五而志于學, 三十而立, 四十而不惑, 五十而知天命, 六十而耳順, 七十而從心所欲, 不踰矩。— Confucius 孔子,《論語》[*The Analects*] (5th c. BCE),〈為政〉, §4.
68 Gordon Davis, "Moral Realism and Anti-realism Outside the West: A Meta-ethical Turn in Buddhist Ethics," *Comparative Philosophy* 4, no. 2 (2013): 24–53.
69 But this problem will receive some further attention in chapters 13 and 14.
70 See the section "Three Arguments for Convergence" in chapter 11.

define virtue, and ultimately, it is intention that matters. Consequently, there is only one notion of virtue in play here: virtue as intention or resolve (citta).

For Aristotle, what makes a character trait a virtue is that it contributes to flourishing. For Śāntideva, what makes an intention or resolve a virtue is that it would alleviate suffering, which is a subjective consequentialist criterion. It is not direct or act-consequentialism because what is defined is the nature of virtues and not the rightness of acts, and consequently, it could be argued that Śāntideva was an indirect subjective consequentialist. However, the notion of virtue in the *Bodhicaryāvatāra* blurs or even erases the boundary between subjective consequentialism and motivationalist virtue ethics.

Someone who has a genuine intention or resolve (citta) to try to alleviate suffering, will, in the right circumstances, try to do what they expect to alleviate suffering *because* they expect it to alleviate suffering. And conversely, if someone tries to do what they expect to alleviate suffering *because* they expect it to alleviate suffering, then they have the intention to alleviate suffering. This is more or less what it means to have an intention or resolve and thus a virtue. In other words, having an intention to do what one expects to have a certain consequence is being motivated by that expectation and the other way around. Intentions in this sense,[71] then, are motivating expectations. And therefore, to say that someone has a virtue (i.e., intention, or resolve) is to say that they are motivated by expected consequences, and to recommend to develop an intention or resolve (i.e., virtue) is to recommend being motivated by expected consequences.

Traditional virtue ethics assumes the existence of virtues as more or less stable character traits, but as mentioned in the previous chapter,[72] psychological research has put this assumption into doubt. Śāntideva's moral theory can be interpreted as being committed to the existence of more or less stable intentions, which are a weaker and probably less controversial type of mental entity, but an even more austere interpretation could even dispense with those. Rather than assuming that virtues are a kind of thing people can have, all that such an interpretation would be committed to is virtues as hypothetical exemplars. In that reading, it does not matter whether anyone ever had some kind of virtue of compassion. Assuming that this virtue is defined as the intention/resolve to alleviate suffering, what matters is that one is motivated to do whatever one expects to alleviate suffering. A bodhisattva, then, is someone who is motivated to do whatever he expects to alleviate suffering, meaning that he is guided by a subjective act-consequentialist principle. The virtue as intermediary entity has effectively dropped out of the equation, except perhaps as a rhetorical device, which leads us back to something like Goodman's act-consequentialist interpretation but with one important difference: bodhisattvas follow a principle. Given his Mādhyamaka affiliation, the latter would probably have been an unacceptable implication for Śāntideva, and for that reason this is probably not an accurate interpretation of his moral thought, but it would be much less problematic for a Yogācārin.

Like Śāntideva, Asaṅga held that expected consequences determine what is right or wrong, but contrary to the Mādhyamika, he did not hesitate to posit principles or rules. The closest equivalent to the verse about the suffering of the one and the many in the *Bodhicaryāvatāra* is the following passage from Asaṅga's *Bodhisattvabhūmi*:

---

71 In contrast to the notion of "intended consequences" discussed in the previous section.
72 See the section "Moral Theory — A Primer."

If a bodhisattva sees that using some abrasive or severe means would benefit sentient beings, but does not use it to guard against unhappiness, he commits an offense. [...] But there is no offense if he sees that the present benefit would be small and that great unhappiness would be caused [by those means].[73]

The two quotes may seem similar, but the differences are significant. While Śāntideva merely describes what a bodhisattva is like, Asaṅga specifies a rule they must follow on pain of "committing an offense."

As Goodman has pointed out, there is an important ambiguity in the quote by Asaṅga: are "abrasive or severe means" to be used if this would benefit sentient beings collectively or distributively?[74] In the former case, the improvement of the aggregate well-being of all people involved outweighs the harm caused by the "abrasive or severe means." In case of a distributive benefit, the improvement of each individual's well-being outweighs the harm to that individual. Or in other words, in case of a distributive interpretation, a bodhisattva is not allowed to use "abrasive or severe means" if there is at least one individual, other than the bodhisattva himself, who would be harmed more than helped by those means.

The ambiguity is resolved in favor of the distributive reading in another passage. Asaṅga suggests that a bodhisattva would kill "a thief or robber who is intent upon killing many hundreds of living beings [...] for the sake of a small amount of material wealth" thinking that

[e]ven though I shall have to be reborn in the hells for depriving this living being of his or her life, it is better that I should be reborn in a hell than that this sentient should end up in the hells because of having committed an immediate misdeed.[75]

Hence, even that thief's best interests are being served by getting killed, and thus, in a sense, no one (except the bodhisattva himself) is harmed. Of course, this argument entirely depends on a belief in hell and karma, but it is the general point that matters here: a bodhisattva does not cause harm to others unless the benefits outweigh the harm even for the persons who are harmed, and in the latter case, he may even be obliged to cause that harm.

Either in case of Śāntideva's Mādhyamaka ethics or in case of Asaṅga's Yogācāra ethics, Mahāyāna ethics is bodhisattva ethics. It may seem that this rather drastically limits its scope and relevance, but from a Tiantai/Tendai perspective, that conclusion would be mistaken. Mahāyāna ethics is not just ethics for bodhisattvas but for everyone. Or more precisely: it is ethics for everyone *because* it is ethics for bodhisattvas.

The most important scripture for Tiantai is the *Lotus Sūtra*, which states in its second chapter that "the Buddha-tathagatas only teach and transform bodhisattvas" and that "their one purpose is to demonstrate the Buddhas' insight to all beings and

---

73 bodhisattvo yena kaṭuka-prayogeṇa tīkṣṇa-prayogeṇa sattvānām-arthaṃ paśyati taṃ prayogaṃ daurmanas-ārakṣayā na samudācarati. sāpattiko bhavati (sātisāraḥ) akliṣṭām-āpattim-āpadyate. an-āpattir-yat parīttam-arthaṃ dṛṣṭa-dhārmikaṃ paśyet prabhūtaś-ca tan-nidānaṃ daurmanasyam. — Asaṅga, *Bodhisattvabhūmi* (4–5th c.), I.10.2.10.16.
74 Goodman, *Consequences of Compassion*, 79.
75 Asaṅga, *The Bodhisattva Path to Unsurpassed Enlightenment: A Complete Translation of the "Bodhisattvabhūmi"* (4–5th c.), trans. Artemus Engle (Boulder: Snow Lion, 2016), 279.

have them apprehend it."⁷⁶ As pointed out in chapter 2,⁷⁷ this passage only makes sense if "only bodhisattvas" in the first sentence and "all beings" in the second co-refer or, in other words, if we are all destined to become Buddhas and are in some sense bodhisattvas already. Indeed, that is exactly what Tiantai/Tendai thinkers commonly held.

From a Tiantai perspective, we are all bodhisattvas, whether we realize it or not, and consequently, bodhisattva ethics applies to all of us. It is for this reason that many East-Asian Buddhists take a version of the four bodhisattva vows phrased by Zhiyi 智顗, the founder of Tiantai, the first of which is the vow to liberate or save all sentient beings.⁷⁸ Reading Asaṅga through Lotus glasses, universal bodhisattva-hood means that we are all obliged to save all sentient beings and to alleviate suffering, including to cause small suffering for ourselves to prevent greater suffering (with the mentioned conditions and restrictions). Bodhisattvas are guided by a principle commanding them to do what is expected to have the desired consequences — alleviating suffering first of all — and therefore, *we all are*.

Expectivism and Free Will

Virtually all defensible variants of consequentialism are subjective consequentialisms — that is, they define the good in terms of expected consequences. In the previous chapter,⁷⁹ I argued that the main moral theories can all be (re-)phrased as defining the good in terms of expected consequences as well. This could be taken as an argument for the claim that virtually all moral theory is consequentialist, but I want to resist that claim because I think it is misleading. Expected consequences are expectations and not consequences, while consequentialism is usually understood as defining the good as whatever has the right consequences. Saying that all plausible moral theories are consequentialist would, therefore, suggest that what matters most in all moral theories are consequences. What I have argued in this chapter is something entirely different: what matters most in all moral theories are expectations, including in so-called "consequentialism" and in Mahāyāna ethics. For this reason, I think it is more appropriate to say that all plausible moral theories are *expectivist*.

Nevertheless, that expectivism is not consequentialism does not imply that actual, realized consequences do not matter at all. One reason why actual consequences matter, albeit indirectly, is that if certain realized consequences could reasonably have been expected, then whatever caused those consequences was right or wrong, depending on the nature of those consequences, which may be a reason to hold something or someone responsible. There is a problem with the notion of responsibility, but we'll turn to that shortly. A second, and more important reason why actual, realized consequences matter, is that they are usually good reasons to expect that the same or similar causes will have similar effects in the future. Expectations are often based on known past consequences, and for this reason, in practice, actual consequences can be as important in expectivist judgment as in consequentialist judgment.

---

76 Translation: Gene Reeves, *The Lotus Sutra* (Boston: Wisdom, 2008), 83.
77 See the section "Mahāyāna."
78 Zhiyi 智顗,《釋禪波羅蜜次第法門》(6th c.), T46n1916, 476b. See the end of the section "Mahāyāna" in chapter 2 for a translation of Zhiyi's complete, four-part bodhisattva vow.
79 See the section "Meta-ethical Convergence" in chapter 11.

The aforementioned problem with responsibility has to do with free will. On the basis of an epistemology derived from Yogācāra metaphysics and Dharmakīrti's notion of *avisaṃvāda* (coherence or non-contradictoriness), it was argued that a radicalized radical Buddhist should reject free will.[80] Or more specifically, she should be a fictionalist about free will,[81] meaning that a radicalized radical Buddhist holds that there is no such thing as free will, but acts as if there is free will anyway because we need the pretense of free will to be able to believe in love, friendship, responsibility, and so forth.

It is debatable whether this is sufficient for moral theory. Most deontological theories, such as Kantian constructivism, depend on free will, for example. According to Kant one can only do the right thing if one does so autonomously and freely. If there is no free will, then from a Kantian perspective, one can never do the right thing. The question is whether giving up the incoherent belief in free will is equally problematic for expectivism. Rightness itself does not seem particularly troubling. An act is right if it is expected to have the right kind of consequences, and whether the act in question is "free" does not matter. The problem is responsibility.

The common notion of responsibility implies freedom: we only hold someone responsible if they could have done otherwise (i.e., were free to do otherwise). Unless we would redefine responsibility,[82] it seems that if there is no free will, then there is no responsibility either, but giving up on responsibility seems rather irresponsible from a moral point of view. The solution is similar to the solution of the problem of free will itself, however, and that solution, fictionalism, is supported by expectivism. Like free will, responsibility is a useful fiction. We should hold someone or something responsible if or to the extent that holding that person or thing[83] responsible is expected to have the right kind of consequences. Strictly speaking, there is no such thing as responsibility, but that does not prevent us from holding people or things responsible, which really is the only facet of responsibility we need anyway, and which fits perfectly in an expectivist framework.

Consequently, contrary to many other moral theories, expectivism does not depend on the metaphysically dubious or even incoherent assumption of the existence of free will; it is consistent with fictionalism in this respect and with fictionalism about responsibility. This is a fortunate finding because if expectivism would simultaneously follow from the epistemological considerations of chapter 9 and conflict with another implication thereof (i.e., the rejection of free will), then that would mean that the view advocated here is incoherent, and thus should be rejected by its own standards. Instead, we can (provisionally, as always) conclude that expectivism follows from and coheres with the post-Yogācāra realism outlined in part II of this book.

---

80 See the section "Essences, Freedom, Paradise, and Other Incoherences" in chapter 9.
81 See the section "Posits and Phenomenal Reality" in chapter 9.
82 According to many compatibilists, for example, we should hold someone responsible if their action is the result of a conscious decision.
83 In the widest possible sense of "thing," including ideas, institutions, ideologies, systems, and so forth. See the section "Moralistic versus Systemic Critique" in chapter 4. In the case of the responsibility of things in this wide sense, free will is irrelevant, of course, as no one claims that ideas, institutions, and so forth have free will anyway.

13

The Badness of Death and Suffering

In what is probably the most discussed passage in the *Bodhicaryāvatāra*, Śāntideva argues that all suffering should be prevented.[1] The argument appears to be that, because persons or selves are not ultimately real, there are just experiences of suffering and no persons experiencing that suffering. For that reason, it makes no sense to merely try to prevent some suffering that "I" mistakenly believe to be "mine." There is no "I" and "mine," there is just suffering, and because it is undisputed that suffering must be prevented, this implies that all suffering must be prevented.

This interpretation cannot be right, however, because according to the Mādhyamaka school to which Śāntideva belonged, experiences of suffering are not ultimately real either. A sizable literature has sprung up trying to disentangle this problem.[2] Perhaps, this interpretation is less problematic for a Yogācārin due to differences in ontological commitments, but what's more important here than the argument itself is one of Śāntideva's premises: "if one asks why suffering should be prevented, no one disputes that!"[3] The question is whether there is such a convergence indeed. Is there near universal agreement that suffering is bad and that it, therefore, should be prevented?[4]

That, roughly, is the topic of this chapter: the question whether there is a universally agreed upon intrinsic good like happiness or bad like suffering. Or, to phrase this question somewhat differently: what kind of expected consequences matter? The utilitarian answer is happiness or pleasure. The negative utilitarian answer is suffering or pain. The classical Chinese answer was typically something like peace and harmony.[5] Aristotle's answer was εὐδαιμονία (flourishing). And so forth. *Prima facie*, there appears to be little convergence, but perhaps, there is more agreement below the checkered surface.

---

1 Śāntideva, *The Bodhicaryāvatāra* (8th c.), trans. Kate Crosby and Andrew Skilton (Oxford: Oxford University Press, 1995), §8.103.
2 The three main interpretations are discussed in Jay Garfield, Stephen Jenkins, and Graham Priest, "The Śāntideva Passage: Bodhicaryāvatāra VIII.90–103," in Cowherds, *Moonpaths: Ethics and Emptiness* (Oxford: Oxford University Press, 2016), 55–76.
3 Śāntideva, *The Bodhicaryāvatāra*, §8.103.
4 Nevertheless, we'll return to Śāntideva's argument, if it is one, in the section "A Dao of Compassion" in chapter 14.
5 See the introduction of chapter 11.

Instrumental and Intrinsic Goods

Not all goods and evils advocated by the various views are equally important. What matters is whether there is convergence with regards to *intrinsic* goods or evils, and an important way in which the apparent lack of convergence could be merely apparent would be that the various views advocate different instrumental goods or goals that are all supposed to lead to the same intrinsic goods or ultimate goals. The difference between an instrumental goal and an ultimate goal is that the first is an intermediate step on the way to something else, while an ultimate goal is the end of the line and does not lead to any further goals. Many people think of happiness as their ultimate life goal, for example, and health, wealth, love, and so forth as instrumental goals on the way to that ultimate goal. Similarly, an instrumental good is good because it contributes to something even better, while an intrinsic good is good in itself.

The classical utilitarians argued for happiness as the intrinsic good. If they were right, then it should be possible to explain that the other goods are merely instrumental goods needed to achieve happiness or that some of the supposed other goods are mistaken and are really not good at all. Do we want to flourish because it makes us happy? Or do we want to be happy because it makes us flourish? Do we want peace and harmony because it is necessary to achieve happiness? Or the other way around? Do we only care about the happiness of loved ones because their happiness makes us happy? Or is their happiness an ultimate goal in addition to our own happiness? Some of these and many similar questions seem relatively easy to answer; others are much harder. That peace and harmony,[6] for example, is an instrumental good is quite plausible, but whether it is flourishing or happiness that deserves the top spot is far less clear. And similarly, while pleasure is often considered an instrumental good because it contributes to our happiness, according to Kataryna De Lazari-Radek and Peter Singer it is the other way around:

> Happiness is instrumentally good, not intrinsically good. Pleasure, in the sense of being in a positive hedonic state, is intrinsically good, and happy people are more likely to experience this positive hedonic state than unhappy people. That is why happiness matters, even if it is not an intrinsic value.[7]

In addition to such problems of priority, there are also other reasons to doubt that happiness is the one and only intrinsic good. Many critics of utilitarianism have created scenarios showing that in certain circumstances there are things we value more than happiness. One of the best known such scenarios is the following story by Bernard Williams:

> Jim finds himself in the central square of a small South American town. Tied up against the wall are a row of twenty Indians, most terrified, a few defiant, in front of them several armed men in uniform. A heavy man in a sweat-stained khaki shirt turns out to be the captain in charge, and, after a good deal of questioning of Jim which establishes that he got there by accident while on a botanical

---

6 The good in Mozi's 墨子 consequentialism.
7 Kataryna De Lazari-Radek and Peter Singer, *The Point of View of the Universe: Sidgwick and Contemporary Ethics* (Oxford: Oxford University Press, 2014), 251–52.

expedition, explains that the Indians are a random group of the inhabitants who, after recent acts of protest against the government, are just about to be killed to remind other possible protesters of the advantages of not protesting. However, since Jim is an honoured visitor from another land, the captain is happy to offer him a guest's privilege of killing one of the Indians himself. If Jim accepts, then as a special mark of the occasion, the other Indians will be let off. Of course, if Jim refuses, then there is no special occasion and Pedro here will do what he was about to do when Jim arrived, and kill them all. Jim, with some desperate recollection of schoolboy fiction, wonders whether if he got hold of a gun, he could hold the captain, Pedro and the rest of the soldiers to threat, but it is quite clear from the set-up that nothing of that kind is going to work: any attempt of that sort of thing will mean that all the Indians will be killed, and himself. The men against the wall, and the other villagers, understand the situation, and are obviously begging him to accept. What should he do?[8]

The utilitarian answer to this question is that Jim should kill one of the Indians, but many people disagree; sometimes integrity, or following one's consciousness, or something similar, outweighs happiness. Other scenarios appear to reveal that we sometimes prioritize loyalty, fairness, artistic achievement, autonomy, knowledge, or various other goods over happiness. And psychological experiments have shown that we sometimes care more about the happiness of others than about our own.[9] A utilitarian might respond to these challenges by claiming that all of these are instrumental goods — we desire integrity, loyalty, fairness, and so forth because they tends to contribute to happiness — but that response is not equally credible in all cases.

One may also wonder to what extent happiness as a goal is really universal rather than the product of cultural conditioning.[10] Do all people in all cultures now and in the past strive for happiness? Is there even a word for "happiness" in all languages? It is often assumed that the answer to the second question is "yes," but that affirmative answer brushes significant differences in meaning and associations between these supposed equivalents of English "happiness" under the carpet. There is quite a collection of words in Chinese, for example, that can be used as translations of "happiness," but all of these words have subtly different meanings and can be translated into English with different words or expressions.[11] 幸福 means "good fortune," 喜悅 is "joyfulness," 樂 could be translated as "cheerfulness" or "ease," and so forth. Furthermore, there even are significant differences in use and associations of supposed equivalents of "happiness" in European languages.[12] If this linguistic variation is taken into account, it seems very unlikely that all cultures strive for what is called "happiness" in English.

---

8   Bernard Williams, "A Critique of Utilitarianism," in J.J.C. Smart and Bernard Williams, *Utilitarianism: For and Against* (Cambridge: Cambridge University Press, 1973), 75–150, at 98–99.
9   C. Daniel Batson, *Altruism in Humans* (Oxford: Oxford University Press, 2011).
10 Personally, if I would be given the choice between happiness and knowledge (for me personally, and everything else being equal), I would probably pick knowledge. I doubt that I am the only one.
11 Zhengdao Ye, "Why Are There Two 'Joy-like' 'Basic' Emotions in Chinese? Semantic Theory and Empirical Findings," in *Love, Hatred, and Other Passions: Questions and Themes on Emotions in Chinese Civilization*, eds. Paolo Santangelo and Donatella Guida (Leiden: Brill, 2006), 59–80.
12 Anna Wierzbicka, "'Happiness' in Cross-Linguistic & Cross-Cultural Perspective," *Daedalus* 133, no. 2 (2004): 34–43.

Could all of these goods be reduced to another intrinsic good then? Of the candidates mentioned, flourishing appears to be the most promising candidate. Perhaps, we desire happiness because we need it to flourish. And similarly, we need peace and harmony, loyalty and friendship, fairness, autonomy, and so forth to flourish. But what does it mean to flourish? Most likely, different people will give very different answers to this question. One might say that it means to be happy; another that it means to live in peace in harmony; a third that it means to be free and autonomous; and so forth. Nothing has been reduced. All that has been done is that we have hidden the diversity behind equivocation.

An option that has been ignored thus far is that there is not one, single, universal good but that there are multiple. Perhaps, all the conceptions of the good can be reduced to a small set of universal goods. This might seem a more promising approach, but it is hard to say what exactly that list of universal goods would include. Furthermore, it is not just the items on the list that must be universal, but there must be agreement about their order as well. If it could be shown that everyone agrees that happiness and loyalty should be on the list, for example, but some people believe that happiness almost always outweighs loyalty while for some others it is the other way around, then these two groups of people would disagree which kind of expected consequences matter most.

An interesting example of something like this is provided by Jonathan Haidt, who claims to have found six universal "foundations" of morality.[13] Although these moral foundations are supposedly universal, people differ with regards to their priorities, and there are patterns in these priorities or rankings. One of the clearest and most important patterns relates the ranking of moral foundations to political orientation. Haidt and colleagues have found that people on the left of the political spectrum value compassion and the avoidance of harm and suffering, as well as fairness higher than the other foundations, while people on the right of the spectrum often prioritize tradition, authority, chastity, purity, loyalty (including patriotism), and similar values over fairness and compassion.

It is starting to look increasingly unlikely that there is significant convergence with regards to the good. Perhaps, it is delusional to expect otherwise. According to Bernard Gert, "everyone agrees that death, disability, and pain are evils or harms" and "evil or harm is best defined as that which all rational persons avoid unless they have an adequate reason not to."[14] The good could be thought of as the mirror image of the bad or evil — as that which all rational persons desire unless they have an adequate reason not too — but this is ambiguous because there are different kinds of desires. The most important distinction here is that between rationally *required* and *allowed* desires. "All that is rationally required is to avoid the evils,"[15] and consequently, rationally required desire is just the desire for the absence of evils such as death, disability, and pain. Rationally allowed desire, on the other hand, cannot possibly result in a universal list because there is no reason why desires, other than the desire to avoid harm and so forth, would be shared by all rational individuals.

---

13 Jesse Graham, Jonathan Haidt, and Brian Nosek, "Liberals and Conservatives Rely on Different Sets of Moral Foundations," *Journal of Personality and Social Psychology* 96 (2009): 1029–46; Jonathan Haidt, *The Righteous Mind: Why Good People Are Divided by Politics and Religion* (New York: Pantheon, 2012); Ravi Iyer et al., "Understanding Libertarian Morality: The Psychological Dispositions of Self-Identified Libertarians," *PLOS One* 7, no. 8 (2012): e42366.
14 Bernard Gert, *Morality: Its Nature and Justification* (Oxford: Oxford University Press, 2005), 91.
15 Ibid., 93.

If this is right, then there are no universal intrinsic goods. Rather, there are two kinds of goods. The first and most important kinds are the goods that derive from the avoidance or absence of evil. If evil is universal, then those goods are universal as well. However, they would be derivative and, therefore, instrumental rather than intrinsic goods. The other kinds of goods are related to our desires beyond the avoidance or absence of evil. Perhaps, these goods are intrinsic goods. Perhaps, they are instrumental goods serving to increase our happiness or flourishing or something else. But regardless, they are not universal, because there is no limit to the things a rational individual can desire after the rational requirement of avoiding evil is met. Furthermore, such merely allowed goods would always be outweighed by the avoidance of evil.

Universal Intrinsic Evil

According to Bernard Gert, all moral agents

> agree that killing, causing pain or disability, or depriving of freedom or pleasure any other moral agent is immoral unless there is an adequate justification for doing such an action. Similarly, they all agree that deceiving, breaking promises, cheating, breaking the law, and neglecting duties also need justification in order not to be immoral. There are no real doubts about these matters.[16]

However, even if all of these ten evils are indeed universally agreed upon, they may not all be *intrinsic* evils. Killing is evil because it causes death, and death is probably an intrinsic evil. The next four evils in this quote — pain, disability, loss of freedom, and loss of pleasure — appear to be evils because they are forms or causes of suffering. The remaining five transgressions undermine society or violate trust. Arguably, what makes these transgressions evils is that humans as social animals need society, and therefore trust, to be able to live well. A breakdown of the social norms that hold society together could lead to societal collapse involving significant suffering, but even relatively minor transgressions of rules against deception, promise breaking, cheating, law breaking, and the neglect of duties are likely to cause some suffering, barring exceptional circumstances. Hence, like most of the other evils on Gert's list, the intrinsic evil lurking in the background appears to be suffering.

If this is right, then death and suffering are the ultimate evils. The badness of suffering is, of course, a core assumption of Buddhism,[17] but according to John Bowker, suffering is a problem in all other religions as well: "indeed, it is often said that suffering is an important *cause* of religion, since the promises held out by religion represent a way in which men can feel reassured in the face of catastrophe or death."[18]

> To talk about suffering is to talk not of an academic problem but of the sheer bloody agonies of existence, of which all men are aware and most have direct

---

16 Bernard Gert, *Common Morality: Deciding What to Do* (Oxford: Oxford University Press, 2004), 9.
17 See the section "Suffering" in chapter 5.
18 John Bowker, *Problems of Suffering in Religions of the World* (Cambridge: Cambridge University Press, 1970), 1. Bowker adds that it "is an inadequate or immature way of seeking reassurance, because it rests in illusion: it is an attempt to control the real world by means of the wish-world" (ibid.).

experience. All religions take account of this; some, indeed, make it the basis of what they have to say.[19]

Nevertheless, the badness of suffering is not a religious idea per se. According to Gert it is inherently bad or evil because it would be irrational not to try to avoid suffering,[20] and consequently, universal agreement about the badness of suffering has little to do with religious sensitivities.

Universal agreement about the badness of suffering is often assumed or proclaimed but rarely explicitly argued for or demonstrated. For example, Derek Parfit claimed that "the double badness of suffering" is universally accepted but did not offer any real evidence to support that claim. Suffering is doubly bad because it is both bad for the sufferer and unqualified bad. At the very least, undeserved suffering is bad — bad *period* and not just bad for the sufferer — but according Parfit no one ever deserves to suffer, and consequently, "all suffering is in itself both bad for the sufferer and impersonally bad."[21] Parfit's defense of his claim of the universality of the double badness of suffering does not amount to much more than that he knows "of no one who has both understood the claim that suffering is doubly bad [...] and in an undistorted and unbiased way rejected this claim" and that he believes that "the double badness of suffering is already [...] very close to being a universally recognized truth."[22]

A question that needs to be asked, however, is what would count as evidence for this claim, because affirmative universal claims are notoriously hard to prove, as are negative existential claims. All that one could establish is that apparent counter-evidence is not really counter-evidence at all, and that is exactly what Parfit did. The only case of someone who appeared not to hold that suffering is bad that he could think of was Nietzsche, and in a careful analysis, he showed that this appearance was mistaken. There may be other cases. For example, Wayne Hudson mentioned that "some American Indian societies [...] took great pleasure in torturing captives to death and regarded such practices as central to their honour code."[23] Examples like this are easy to come by, and many people seem to approve of or even rejoice in the suffering of some others, such as outsiders and criminals. Apparently suffering is not always bad; it can even be good if it happens to the other.

It can be shown quite easily that this is incoherent. Imagine two neighboring tribes — let us call them the Fulang and the Wahala.[24] The Fulang and the Wahala hate each other, but they are culturally very similar. One shared aspect of their cultures is that they believe that suffering of their enemies pleases their gods and is, therefore, good. However, in all other cases, suffering is bad. Consequently, the Fulang believe that the suffering of Fulang is bad, while the suffering of Wahala is good; and the Wahala believe that the suffering of Wahala is bad, while the suffering of Fulang is good. The only way these contradictory beliefs could be coherent is if the badness of suffering is relative, that is, if suffering would never be just bad but would

---

19 Ibid., 2.
20 Gert, *Morality*.
21 Derek Parfit, *On What Matters,* Vol. 2 (Oxford: Oxford University Press, 2011), 569.
22 Ibid., 568.
23 Wayne Hudson, "Historicizing Suffering," in *Perspectives on Human Suffering,* eds. Jeff Malpas and Norelle Lickiss (Dordrecht: Springer, 2012), 171–79, at 172.
24 These fictional tribe names are terms for "suffering" in Scots Gaelic and Hausa, respectively.

only be bad for some people.[25] This would imply that for the Fulang, the suffering of Fulang is bad-for-Fulang and the suffering of Wahala is good-for-Fulang; and the other way around for the Wahala. But that is not what the Fulang and Wahala believe. They believe that the suffering of the other is good *simpliciter*, and that the suffering of members of the in-group is bad *simpliciter*. And that is incoherent — both tribes cannot be right. Or actually, both tribes are half right — the Fulang and Wahala agree that suffering is bad. What they disagree about is the exception.

Intersubjectivity generates justification. If different people agree about the badness of suffering but disagree about exceptions, then the belief in the badness of suffering is a justified belief, but the beliefs in exceptions are not. Paraphrasing Śāntideva: if suffering is bad, then all of it is.

Much of the same applies to beliefs about the badness of death. Arguably, death is "doubly bad" as well, and as in the case of suffering, beliefs in the goodness of the death of others are incoherent. If death is bad, then all of it is. Nevertheless, in case of the badness of death there are two arguments for universality that have no exact parallels for suffering. The first is an argument from evolution; the second is psychological. The argument from evolution is simply this: imagine two humanoid species, Lhumans and Dhumans. Lhumans believe that death is bad; Dhumans do not. Because they do not believe that death is bad, Dhumans are violent, take great risks, do not care for the sick and elderly, and have high suicide and murder rates. Slowly, but surely, the Dhumans will be out-competed by the more numerous Lhumans, and eventually, the Dhumans will go extinct.

A belief in the badness of death is a biological necessity and so is a fear of death.[26] Indeed, psychologists have found evidence for the universality of certain mechanisms to repress that fear. This so-called "terror management" was explained in chapter 6.[27] The important point here is that Terror Management Theory has shown that we all believe that death is so bad that we spend much unconscious effort denying it.

This denial of death reveals an important ambiguity: "death" is equivocal. The denial of death is rarely the denial of biological death; rather, it is a denial of death as an absolute endpoint. In other words, the denial of death is the idea that in some way or form we survive our biological deaths. What it denies is *annihilation*. That such a denial of annihilation is incoherent and that biological death inevitably involves annihilation does not matter here.[28] What matters is that the two notions are conceptually different and are indeed distinguished by many (and probably even most) people. And what matters is that while both are bad, they are not equally bad: annihilation is (almost!) the ultimate evil. Nevertheless, biological death is intrinsically bad as well. It would be merely instrumentally bad if everyone believed that it necessarily leads to the ultimate evil of annihilation, but that is exactly what all religions, and the denial of death in general, deny.

For very different reasons and in very different ways, suffering is not univocal and unambiguous either. Unlike death, suffering comes in degrees,[29] ranging from severe

---

25 It would not be bad just for the sufferer as in Parfit's argument, however. The suffering of a Wahala would be bad for all Wahala.
26 Ernest Becker, *The Denial of Death* (New York: Simon & Schuster, 1973).
27 See the section "Between Science and Religion" in chapter 6.
28 Lajos Brons, "The Incoherence of Denying My Death," *Journal of Philosophy of Life* 4, no. 2 (2014): 68–89. See also the section "Essences, Freedom, Paradise, and Other Incoherences" in chapter 9.
29 The "unlike" clause is is not entirely correct because even death can be said to have degrees, although they are more appropriately called "stages." Dying is not like switching off the lights. Different parts

suffering worse than death, or even worse than annihilation, to minor dissatisfaction that probably would not be called "suffering" anyway. A closely related problem is that it is not perfectly clear what exactly falls in the category of suffering and what does not. And a third issue is that "suffering" is not a linguistic universal — words in different languages that superficially seem equivalents of "suffering" often have sometimes subtly different meanings. It was already pointed out in the section "On Suffering" in chapter 5 that *dukkha* and "suffering" do not express the exact same concept but neither do Spanish *sufrimiento* or Japanese 苦しみ (*kurushimi*).

What is universal is the concept of "pain,"[30] and "suffering" and "pain" are closely related. What is probably also universal is that pain is not necessarily morally bad, either because it is expected to have beneficial effects that outweigh the pain, or because it is in some relevant sense voluntary. The pain involved in getting a tattoo is rarely considered morally wrong and is rarely considered a kind of suffering.[31] It is this latter aspect that is key: suffering is a kind of *involuntary* physical or mental pain.[32] Even if the concept denoted by English "suffering" is not universal, the concept of involuntary physical or mental pain can be expressed in any language.[33] Furthermore, it is suffering in this quite minimal sense that matters here; the claim that suffering is a universal, intrinsic evil is the claim that there is universal agreement that involuntary physical or mental pain is intrinsically bad.[34]

Further criteria could be added to a definition of "suffering" to distinguish it from minor dissatisfaction or discomforts. Most famous and influential is Eric Castell's definition of suffering "as the state of severe distress associated with events that threaten the intactness of a person,"[35] discussed in chapter 5. However, in the present context that is not really necessary because suffering is a spectrum anyway, and even what falls on the minor extreme on the spectrum is still considered bad — just less

---

of the body shut down at different times and some shut down gradually. Where exactly in that process we say that someone is dead is a choice, and consequently even death is, to some extent, socially constructed.

30 Strictly speaking this is not entirely correct either because, as Anna Wierzbicka points out, not all languages have a word that exactly corresponds to English "pain." Nevertheless, all languages do have a concept that corresponds to the core meaning of "pain" as "feeling something bad in one's body" ("'Pain' and 'Suffering' in Cross-Linguistic Perspective," *International Journal of Language and Culture* 1, no. 2 [2014]: 149–73, at 156).

31 Sometimes it is also suggested that pain of the mother in childbirth is not a case of suffering either for similar reasons. However, that women choose (or are pressured to) have children does not imply that they choose to endure pain while giving birth. (And I suspect that this argument has been made only by men.)

32 On involuntariness as a key aspect of suffering, see also Thomas Metzinger, "Suffering," in *The Return of Consciousness: A New Science on Old Questions*, eds. Kurt Almqvist and Anders Haag (Stockholm: Axel and Margaret Ax:son Johnson Foundation, 2017), 237–62.

33 Assuming that the universal linguistic primitives listed by Natural Semantic Metalanguage are really universal. See, for example, Anna Wierzbicka, *Semantic Primitives* (Frankfurt: Athenäum, 1972). *Semantics: Primes and Universals* (Oxford: Oxford University Press, 1996).

34 Nevertheless, there may be cultural and other differences in how bad various kinds or aspects of suffering are considered to be. Lucy Tatman has suggested that suffering feminizes the sufferer, and if that is the case indeed, then masculine cultures may consider suffering even worse than feminine cultures. (Although, the care- or empathy-focus of feminine cultures may have the opposite effect.) And Wayne Hudson has pointed out that there are significant historical differences in responses to suffering. Lucy Tatman, "The Other Thing about Suffering," in *Perspectives on Human Suffering*, eds. Malpas and Lickiss, 43–48. Hudson, "Historicizing Suffering."

35 Eric Castell, "The Nature of Suffering and the Goals of Medicine," *The New England Journal of Medicine* 306, no. 11 (1982): 639–45, at 640; *The Nature of Suffering and the Goals of Medicine* (Oxford: Oxford University Press), 33.

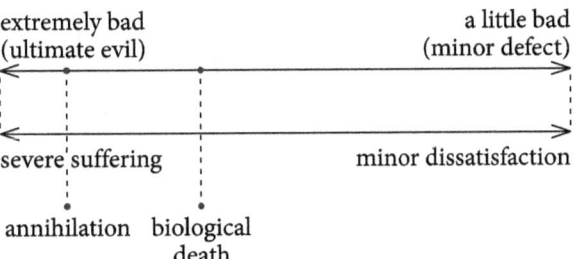

Fig. 13.1. The spectrum of evil.

bad. In other words, the spectrum from severe suffering to minor dissatisfaction corresponds with the spectrum from ultimate evil to minor nuisance. On that same spectrum we find the two deaths: annihilation, which is close to ultimate evil but not as bad as the worst kinds of suffering (and thus not the ultimate evil after all), and biological death, which is not as bad as annihilation, but still far, far worse than minor dissatisfaction. Figure 13.1 summarizes this in graphical form.

What this figure represents is universal, I think. What differs between people and cultures concerns details: how bad suffering has to be to be worse than annihilation, how much worse annihilation is than biological death,[36] and so forth. There is, however, universal agreement that death and suffering are evil, and that they are intrinsically evil. Below I will consider a few important objections against this claim and what it might imply, but first I will briefly examine some relevant Buddhist perspectives on the badness of death and suffering.

Suffering, Death, and Bodhisattva Ethics

Engaged and radical Buddhism are more or less defined by the claim that all suffering, including this-worldly suffering, is bad.[37] Dharmapāla, one of the first modern engaged Buddhists wrote, for example, that "the basic doctrine of Buddhism is to relieve human suffering,"[38] and according to B.R. Ambedkar, "the world is full of suffering and [...] how to remove this suffering from the world is the only purpose of [the Buddha's] Dhamma."[39] Somewhat similarly, for Buddhadāsa the aim of Buddhism is twofold peace: inner peace resulting from overcoming dukkha and worldly peace resulting from the mitigation of this-worldly suffering.

In Japan, early engaged and radical Budhists like Tanaka Jiroku 田中治六, Watanabe Kaikyoku 渡辺海旭, and Uchiyama Gudō 内山愚童 saw the alleviation of all suffering as the goal of Buddhism. Tanaka coined the influential term *genseshugi* 現世主義, "this-world-ism," to refer to this this-worldly orientation.[40] Rather than focusing on death and rebirth, Buddhism should be concerned with suffering in this world (*gense*) and this life. A few decades later, Seno'o Girō 妹尾義郎, probably

---

36 Not any worse if you, like me, believe that they are the same, of course.
37 See chapter 3.
38 Anagarika Dharmapāla, "The World's Debt to Buddha" (1893), in *Return to Righteousness: A Collection of Speeches, Essays and Letters of the Anagarika Dharmapala*, ed. Ananda Guruge (Colombo: Ministry of Education and Cultural Affairs, 1965), 3–22, at 20.
39 B.R. Ambedkar, *The Buddha and His Dhamma* (1957), in *Writings and Speeches*, Vol. 11 (New Delhi: Dr. Ambedkar Foundation, 1979), 121.
40 On *genseshugi*, see also the section "Sources and Schools" in chapter 6.

the most radical among the radical Buddhists, founded the Youth League for New Buddhism 新興仏教青年同盟, which proclaimed in its founding meeting that "the suffering in present society is mainly caused by the capitalist economic system."[41]

Elsewhere in East Asia, Lin Qiuwu 林秋梧 and Thích Nhất Hạnh, among others, advocated a similarly broad view of suffering. According to the latter, "whatever we do to ease human suffering and create social justice can be considered practicing generosity."[42] And Lin argued that suffering is ultimately rooted in "the greed of a small part of mankind."[43]

For engaged and radical Buddhists, suffering is the ultimate evil, and not just suffering in some kind of narrow sense of dukkha-as-existential-dissatisfaction[44] but all suffering, explicitly including this-worldly suffering, such as poverty and the suffering caused by war and conflict. And consequently, mitigating all suffering is the first moral duty of an engaged or radical Buddhist. This idea is probably nowhere expressed as poetically and as humbly as in Miyazawa Kenji's 宮澤賢治 beloved poem *Undefeated by the Rain*.

> Undefeated by the rain
> Undefeated by the wind
> Undefeated by the snow or summer heat
> [...]
> If there is a sick child in the east
> going and nursing it
> If there is a tired mother in the west
> going and carrying her sheaf of rice
> If there is someone near death in the south
> going and saying "don't be afraid"
> If there is a quarrel or a lawsuit in the north
> telling them to stop because it's boring
> When there is drought, shedding tears
> When the summer is cold, wandering upset
> Called a nobody by everyone
> Without being praised
> Without being a burden
> Such a person
> I want to become[45]

---

41 新興仏教は、現社会の苦悩は、主として資本主義経済組織に基因することを認めて、これが根本的革正に協力して大衆の福利を保障せんとする。— 新興仏教青年同盟 (New Buddhist Youth League),『宣言』(*Proclamation*) (1931), rpt. in Inagaki Masami 稲垣真美,『仏陀を背負いて街頭へ—妹尾義郎と新興仏教青年同盟』(Tokyo: 岩波新書, 1974), 3-6, at 4.

42 Thich Nhat Hanh, "Commentary," in *The Sutra on the Eight Realizations of the Great Beings*, trans. Diem Thanh Truong and Carole Melkonian (Loubès-Bernac: Dharma Books, 1987), 10-25, at 19.

43 一小部分的人類之貪欲 — Lin Qiuwu 林秋梧,〈階級鬥爭與佛教〉,《南瀛佛教》7, no. 2 (1929): 52-58, at 55.

44 See the section "Suffering" in chapter 5.

45 雨ニモマケズ|風ニモマケズ|雪ニモ夏ノ暑サニモマケヌ|[...]|東ニ病氣ノコドモアレバ|行ッテ看病シテヤリ|西ニツカレタ母アレバ|行ッテソノ稻ノ束ヲ負ヒ|南ニ死ニサウナ人アレバ|行ッテコハガラナクテモイヽトイヒ|北ニケンクヮヤソショウガアレバ|ツマラナイカラヤメロトイヒ|ヒデリノトキハナミダヲナガシ|サムサノナツハオロオロアルキ|ミンナニデクノボートヨバレ|ホメラレモセズ|クニモサレズ|サウイフモノニ|ワタシハナリタイ — Miyazawa Kenji 宮澤賢治,「雨ニモマケズ」1931, in『【新】校本・宮澤賢治全集』, Vol. 13 (Tokyo: 筑摩書房, 1997).

There are many different ways in which Miyazawa's poem can be read, but given its context — the writer, his background, and his social and intellectual surroundings — it seems most appropriate to me to read it as a kind of modernized version of the bodhisattva vow.[46] Miyazawa was a follower of Nichiren 日蓮, the thirteenth-century monk who aimed to return Tendai 天台 to it *Lotus* roots but ended up splitting off a new sect in the process.[47] For Nichiren the kind of suffering that needed to be addressed most urgently was entirely this-worldly: it included famine, disease, poverty, and so forth.[48] The cause of that suffering was that the people and the state had turned their backs to the *Lotus Sūtra*, and that was what needed to be corrected, but more important than Nichiren's proposed cure was his practical, this-worldly focus, which later followers like Miyazawa and Seno'o inherited.

Nichiren's intellectual background as a Tendai monk can be traced to Zhiyi 智顗, the founder of Tiantai (the Chinese mother sect of Tendai) and the author of the most famous version of the bodhisattva vow. The first of four parts of that vow pledges that "[e]ven though sentient beings are unlimited [in number], I vow to liberate/save [them all]."[49] Since it follows from the *Lotus Sūtra* that everyone is already a bodhisattva, at least potentially, this is a commitment that everyone should make to realize that potentiality.[50] We should all aim to save all sentient beings and alleviate all suffering. We should all "want to become such a person" as in Miyazawa's poem.

That bodhisattvas are not just concerned with spiritual suffering but with this-worldly suffering as well is also evident in Asaṅga's *Bodhisattvabhūmi*. The morality chapter of that book lists the duties of a bodhisattva, as well as "extreme forms of defeat" and "minor offenses." Among the duties we find that a bodhisattva

> takes care of those sentient beings who are ill, leads those who are blind and shows them to a road, causes the deaf to understand meanings with a [form of] sign language that represents words through symbols, and transports those whose limbs are deficient by carrying them [bodily] or by means of a vehicle.[51]
> [...] protects sentient beings who are frightened from the objects that they fear.[52]
> [...] dispels the sorrow of sentient beings who are in [various] states of distress.[53]
> [...] furnishes the objects that are needed for subsistence to those who seek such objects[:] gives food to those who seek food; drinks to those who seek drinks; [...][54]

Furthermore, the second of "the four acts that represent an extreme form of defeat" (i.e., the greatest moral transgressions) is

> the refusal to give material objects, because of a greedy nature and hardheartedness, to petitioners who have approached in a correct manner, who are suffering,

---

46 See the section "Mahāyāna" in chapter 2.
47 See the section "From Saichō to Nichiren" in chapter 2.
48 Nevertheless, in Nichiren's thought this-worldly suffering may not have been an intrinsic evil; rather, it was evil mostly because it obstructed people's progress on the spiritual path.
49 亦云眾生無邊誓願度。— Zhiyi 智顗, 《釋禪波羅蜜次第法門》(6th c.), T46n1916, 476b.
50 See the sections "Mahāyāna" in chapter 2 and "Consequences and Consequentialism in Mahāyāna" in chapter 12.
51 Asaṅga, *The Bodhisattva Path to Unsurpassed Enlightenment: A Complete Translation of the Bodhisattvabhūmi* (4–5th c.), trans. Artemus Engle (Boulder: Snow Lion, 2016), 250.
52 Ibid., 252.
53 Ibid., 253.
54 Ibid.

miserable, and impoverished, and who lack a protector and someone to rely upon [...]⁵⁵

And listed among the "minor offenses" are failing to care for the sick, to assist those who are suffering,⁵⁶ to dispel grief, to provide food to those who need it,⁵⁷ and so forth.

There is, however, an important difference between Asaṅga and radical Buddhists like Lin Qiuwu, Seno'o, and early Taixu 太虛. Due to what I called "system blindness" in chapter 4, Asaṅga was limited to individualistic diagnoses and solutions and blind to systemic causes of suffering.⁵⁸ This system blindness, which permeates almost all Buddhist thought, is not an inherent feature of Buddhism itself but of premodern worldviews. It could only be overcome after the invention of the concept of "society" and related concepts, which took place in Europe around the turn of the nineteenth century (and in Asia about a century later) and which allowed new ways of seeing and thinking. Without a concept of "society" there can be no notions of social systems and systemic causes of social problems. The radical Buddhists were the first to fully realize the importance of a systemic, rather than individualistic, view on suffering and its causes. With the blinkers of system blindness removed, it is no longer sufficient for an aspiring bodhisattva to be "such as person" (as in Miyazawa's poem); rather, an aspiring bodhisattva must be sociopolitically engaged as well.

According to radical Buddhists, that Buddhism should be concerned more with this life and this world than with death and the afterlife does not imply that death was considered less evil. On the contrary, the traditional focus on death and the afterlife effectively devalues this life and thereby its termination in death, while the radical Buddhist this-worldly focus implies that the termination of this life (i.e., death) is one of the greatest evils.

It could, perhaps, even be argued that death, in some sense, is not an evil at all for traditional Buddhism, which would refute the universality claim made in the previous section. But that would be a mistake. Such an argument would only make sense if it would equate nirvāṇa with annihilation, and would infer that because nirvāṇa is the supreme good, it follows that annihilation is the supreme good. There are two ways to respond to this argument. The first would be by pointing out that in the Pāli canon, nirvāṇa is not equated with annihilation. Rather, as pointed out in chapter 5, in the *Ariyapariyesanā Sutta* it is associated with immortality,⁵⁹ in the *Nidānavagga* section of the *Connected Discourses* and elsewhere, the doctrine that equates nirvāṇa with annihilation is explicitly rejected,⁶⁰ and in many Buddhist texts, nirvāṇa is associated with a state of bliss.⁶¹ Hence, like all religions, Buddhism appears to deny annihilation because it is almost (!) the greatest imaginable evil.

The second response is philosophical more than textual. Even if nirvāṇa would imply annihilation, this does not imply that annihilation is good. Rather, it means that annihilation is the lesser evil. Nirvāṇa is escape from saṃsāra, the cycle of death and rebirth. If life inherently involves suffering, then an infinite chain of lives — an

---

55 Ibid., 267.
56 Ibid., 294.
57 Ibid., 296.
58 See the section "Moralistic versus Systemic Critique" in chapter 4.
59 See the section "The Idea of an 'Original Buddhism'" in chapter 5.
60 See the section "The Middle Way" in chapter 5.
61 See the section "Karma, Rebirth, (No-)Self, and Nirvāṇa" in chapter 5.

infinity in *saṃsāra* — implies infinite suffering. Such infinite suffering is the greater evil, and being preferable to infinite suffering does not mean that annihilation is good in itself.

Some Objections

Perhaps the most obvious objections to my claim that there is universal agreement about the badness of death and suffering, as graphically summarized in figure 13.1, is that religion, including Buddhism, typically denies annihilation. How could something be considered an ultimate evil if that something is not believed to exist? This objection ignores *why* annihilation is denied. As Ernest Becker and Terror Management Theory forcefully argued, annihilation is denied *because* it is an ultimate evil, or very nearly so.[62]

A related objection would be that annihilation is *the* ultimate evil, which would be an objection against the supposedly universal ranking of evils. But this objection would be a mistake as well, I believe. From a Christian or Muslim perspective, for example, annihilation is surely preferable to an eternity in hell.

Another possible objection would be to point out that ascetics seem to indulge in their own suffering. Hence, to the ascetic, suffering is good rather than evil. This too, would be a mistake. An ascetic values suffering in this life because he, or rarely she, believes that this will lead to less or even no suffering in an or the afterlife. In other words, it is precisely because the ascetic believes that suffering is evil that he chooses the lesser suffering in this life to avert greater suffering later on.

A more profound kind of objection does not focus on the evils and their ranking but takes issue with the kind of moral theory the foregoing might seem to imply instead. The most clear-cut examples of moral views based on the idea of the badness of suffering are negative utilitarianism and empathy-based or compassion-based versions of virtue ethics or ethics of care. Negative utilitarianism is a version of utilitarianism that strives to minimize suffering instead of maximizing happiness. The idea was first suggested (albeit, as a social philosophy more than as a moral theory) by Karl Popper in *The Open Society and Its Enemies*.[63] While classical utilitarianism aims for the greatest happiness for the greatest number of people, negative utilitarianism aims for "the least amount of suffering for anybody."[64]

The best known objection to negative utilitarianism is usually called "the benevolent world-exploder," or something similar, and was first put forward by Ninian Smart.[65] "Suppose that a ruler controls a weapon capable of instantly and painlessly destroying the human race." Given that this would end all human suffering, according to negative utilitarianism that ruler would be morally obliged to use the weapon. And because "we should assuredly regard such an action as wicked," negative utilitarianism is wrong.[66]

It might seem that Smart's argument could be blocked easily by means of an appeal to the badness of death. In the view defended here, right and wrong are

---

62 See the section "Universal Intrinsic Evil" above, and the section "Between Science and Religion" in chapter 6.
63 Karl Popper, *The Open Society and Its Enemies*, Vol. I: *The Spell of Plato* (1943; London: Routledge, 1947). See especially note 6 in chapter 5 and note 2 in chapter 9.
64 Ibid., 241: note 2 in chapter 9.
65 Ninian Smart, "Negative Utilitarianism," *Mind* 67, no. 268 (1958): 542–43.
66 Ibid., 542.

determined by the expected suffering *and death* resulting from something. (What kind of thing that "something" is is the topic of the next chapter.) However, such a response would fail. Human extinction would not necessarily have to result from excess deaths, but could also be the consequence of insufficient births as in Thomas Metzinger's "benevolent anti-natalist robot" scenario.[67] In that scenario, a future artificial intelligence programmed to minimize suffering decides that the best way to achieve this goal is by making sure no more human children are born.

The crux of Smart's argument is in his premise that "instantly and painlessly destroying the human race" is "wicked." However, by assuming that causing human extinction is inherently evil, he is begging the question against negative utilitarianism. It is significant that Smart does not defend this key assumption; rather, he appears to take it for granted. Undoubtedly, Smart is not alone in taking the badness of causing human extinction for granted, but it is worth disentangling the notion to assess what exactly, if anything, is bad about it and why.

First of all, there is the issue of the difference between human extinction and *causing* human extinction. Arguably, if human extinction is bad, then causing human extinction is bad as well, and if human extinction is morally neutral, then so is causing human extinction, which suggests that the "causing" part is morally neutral, but that is not exactly right. Human extinction due to natural causes, such as a giant meteor strike, might be bad but would not be *morally* bad. Without human agency, there is no moral value. Nevertheless, the supposed moral badness of causing human extinction derives entirely from the supposed badness of human extinction itself.

Probably, one of the main reasons why most people take the badness of human extinction for granted is a conscious or unconscious religious belief in mankind as the pinnacle of creation. One of the most powerful arguments against that belief can be found in Robert Nozick's "The Holocaust."[68] According to Nozick, after the Holocaust "mankind has fallen" and "humanity has lost its claim to continue."[69] He imagines alien observers from another galaxy looking at human history:

> It would not seem unfitting to them [...] if that story came to an end, if the species they see with that history ended, destroying itself in nuclear warfare or otherwise failing to be able to continue. These observers would see the *individual* tragedies involved, but they would not see [...] any further tragedy in the ending of the species. That species, the one that has committed *that*, has lost its worthy status.[70]

Aside from the general point that humanity may not be the greatest thing ever and does not automatically deserve to continue, Nozick also makes another important point in this passage: there is a difference between the "individual tragedies" of people suffering or dying and the disappearance of the species *Homo sapiens*. The extinction of mankind would surely involve the suffering or death of very many individuals, even in the anti-natalist scenario, but the badness of the extinction of mankind

---

67 Metzinger, "Suffering." According to anti-natalism, suffering always outweighs anything that might offset it (like happiness or pleasure) in an individual's life, and therefore, it is always better not to be born. The best known anti-natalist is David Benatar, *Better Never to Have Been: The Harm of Coming into Existence* (Oxford University Press, 2006).
68 Robert Nozick, "The Holocaust," in *The Examined Life: Philosophical Meditations* (New York: Simon and Schuster, 1989), 236–42.
69 Ibid., 238.
70 Ibid., 238–39.

is not just the sum of the badness of the suffering and deaths of all those individuals. In thinking about the badness of human extinction, it may not be easy to separate these two, however; our intuitive assumption that human extinction is bad may be due, in large part, to the perceived badness of the individual tragedies involved. But if those are what make human extinction bad, then it is not intrinsically bad, and then greater suffering would outweigh the badness of human extinction.

Samuel Scheffler has suggested a third reason for the supposed badness of human extinction. This reason is that "the actual value of our activities depends on their place in an ongoing human history."[71] "Humanity itself as an ongoing historical project provides the implicit frame of reference for most of our judgments about what matters."[72] Scheffler argues convincingly that in a dying world "people would lose confidence in the value of many sorts of activities, would cease to see reason to engage in many familiar sorts of pursuits, and would become emotionally detached from many of those activities and pursuits."[73]

What would be the point of writing a book or composing a piece of music if humanity would be going extinct? A few people might read it or listen to it, but sooner rather than later it would be lost, and all my hard work would be in vain. What would be the point of raising and educating children if humankind would be doomed? It is easy to come up with other examples. The point is that without a future for humankind, almost everything that matters to us loses its value. It is for this reason that Scheffler asserts that "the collective afterlife [i.e., the survival of humankind] matters more to people than the personal afterlife."[74]

However, that everything we value depends on the belief in a "collective afterlife" does not determine the nature of that collective. Scheffler assumes that it is the survival of humankind that gives value to our activities, but most of his argument only suggests that it is the survival of people that are sufficiently *like us* that matters. He more or less acknowledges this in a footnote,[75] but that acknowledgment never plays a part in his argument, which remains naively cosmopolitan. This may be due to a kind of blindness that permeates his argument, a blindness that is rather common among Western philosophers. The nature of this blindness is a lack of recognition of the fact that Western civilization is not universal, that there are other civilizations or cultures, other ways of seeing things, other communities and frames of reference that give meaning in different ways to the actions of their members and adherents.[76] If Scheffler's argument is adjusted for this oversight, then we end up with something very similar to what Ernest Becker argued more than forty years ago in *The Denial of Death*. It is not the survival of humankind that we rely on to give value to our actions, and thereby control our fear of death, but the survival of people *like me*, people I identify with and that I largely share a cultural worldview with.

Human extinction, then, is bad because it leads to extinction of people like me, thereby eliminating the source of all value to me and obliterating my source of control over the fear of death (i.e., my "terror management"). But this means that it is not bad in itself, that is, not intrinsically bad. Rather, it is merely instrumentally

---

71 Samuel Scheffler, *Death and the Afterlife* (Oxford: Oxford University Press, 2013), 54.
72 Ibid., 60.
73 Ibid., 44.
74 Ibid., 72.
75 Ibid., 49n13.
76 About this blind spot in contemporary Western philosophy, see Bryan van Norden, *Taking Back Philosophy: A Multicultural Manifesto* (New York: Columbia University Press, 2017).

bad. And if it is not intrinsically bad, then there may be greater evils than the extinction of mankind.

Given that suffering is intrinsically bad, if mankind would continue forever there would be an infinite amount of human suffering, and an infinite amount of evil would surely outweigh the evil involved in causing human extinction. But nothing lasts forever, and consequently, the comparison is not between an infinite evil and a finite one but between two finite evils. Even then it might seem that this finite sum of future suffering is greater than the suffering that would result from causing human extinction, but that conclusion would depend on a number of assumptions and predictions with very high degrees of uncertainty. It's very hard to estimate how much death and suffering exactly would result from causing human extinction and even harder to estimate how much death and suffering there is in humanity's future otherwise. For all we know, that future might not be as long as we hope it is anyway.[77] And taking drastic, irreversible measures based on uncertainty is rarely a good idea.[78]

Nevertheless, if, as in Smart's scenario, there would be some kind of trick to instantly and painlessly destroy all of mankind and all other suffering beings,[79] then the badness of suffering would morally justify that. Perhaps, this conclusion is hard to accept because it is not easy to detach oneself from sentimental beliefs in human greatness or human achievements. But the question that needs to be asked is whether those achievements really outweigh the sum of human suffering. Is preserving the *Mona Lisa* or Darwin's theory of evolution, for example, worth the suffering of an innocent child dying of thirst and hunger in a climate-change-related disaster?

The actions of most people suggest that the answer to this question is "yes." Even though we all agree about the badness of suffering, we tend to close our eyes for actual suffering. Perhaps, this is the main reason why it is so hard to accept that the badness of suffering may outweigh the badness of causing human extinction: it is too easy for us to ignore the suffering of others, while human extinction would directly affect ourselves. However, this is a psychological problem, and not a moral one. That we cannot accept that causing human extinction might be right does not mean that it is wrong, it might mean that there is something wrong with us.

Our proclivity to prioritize the suffering of some and ignore the suffering of many others is also key to the most important objection against empathy- or compassion-based versions of care or virtue ethics. Compassion literally means to suffer with someone. The notion is usually considered to be synonymous with the more technical term "empathic concern," one of eight kinds of empathy distinguished by Daniel Batson.[80] Empathic concern is feeling for the other who is suffering and being motivated thereby to alleviate that suffering. Empathic concerns are always directed at some specific other — it is partial, as opposed to "impartial," and it is this partiality that is the problem. As Paul Bloom put it in *Against Empathy*, the effect of partial

---

77 See the section "Mappō" in chapter 16.
78 The principle of prudence suggested in the previous chapter even seems to forbid this.
79 This is another obvious, but thus far ignored, defect in Smart's and similar arguments: human beings are not the only creatures that suffer, and if suffering is bad, then the suffering of other creatures is bad as well.
80 C. Daniel Batson, "The Things Called Empathy: Eight Related but Distinct Phenomena," in *The Social Neuroscience of Empathy*, eds. Jean Decety and William Ickes (Cambridge: MIT Press, 2009), 3–15.

empathy is that it is likely that "our feeling for the suffering of the few leads to disastrous consequences for the many."[81]

In *Altruism in Humans*, Batson discusses several "liabilities" of empathy-induced altruism like these.[82] Good intentions can lead to very bad results and empathy can easily lead people to act unfairly or even immorally. Furthermore, we empathize more with some kinds of needs than with others, and more with some kinds of people than with others, which adds another element of unfairness. Because of this, while wanting to alleviate suffering certainly seems a good thing, our partiality may cause more suffering rather than less if we let ourselves be lead by empathy.

For this reason, Bloom argues for "rational compassion" instead of empathy. Such rational compassion is a more detached and less emotional attitude, similar to Peter Singer's "effective altruism,"[83] but it seems to leave out something important. Compassion, again, is suffering with the other, and by suffering with the other we come to better understand the nature and badness of suffering, which is probably important as a moral motivation. This consideration raises the question whether there could be another option besides rational compassion or effective altruism.

In a chapter on empathy in relation to politics, Bloom writes that "political debates typically involve a disagreement not over whether we should empathize, but over *who* we should empathize with."[84] Given the foregoing, the obvious answer to the question, "who should we empathize with?" is "everyone," but that answer raises another question: can we actually do that?

Suffering, Shock, and Intoxication

Although Śāntideva's *Bodhicaryāvatāra* is by far the most quoted text in discussions of Mahāyāna ethics, it is not actually about ethics, or at least not explicitly. Rather, it is about the bodhisattva perfections, and the topic of the most relevant chapter is the perfection of meditation. That chapter's most important recommendation is to "practice the supreme mystery: exchange of self and others."[85] The exchange of self and other, which is to be achieved through meditation, is the exchange of self-interest and the interests of others as motivating reasons. Hence, it is a self-less devotion to others.

> If one does not let go of self one cannot let go of suffering, as one who does not let go of fire cannot let go of burning. | Therefore, in order to allay my suffering and to allay the suffering of others, I devote myself to others and accept them as myself.[86]

Given that altruism is a defining feature of Śāntideva's conception of bodhisattvahood,[87] acquiring and nurturing this virtue of self-less devotion to others is the key to *bodhicitta*, the awakening mind of a bodhisattva.

---

81 Paul Bloom, *Against Empathy: The Case for Rational Compassion* (London: Bodley Head, 2016), 127.
82 Batson, *Altruism in Humans*, chapter 8.
83 Peter Singer, *The Most Good You Can Do: How Effective Altruism Is Changing Ideas about Living Ethically* (New Haven: Yale University Press, 2015).
84 Bloom, *Against Empathy*, 122. Emphasis added.
85 Śāntideva, *The Bodhicaryāvatāra*, §8.120.
86 Ibid., §8.135–36.
87 See the section "Consequences and Consequentialism in Mahāyāna" in chapter 12.

Meditation and ethics are also closely related in Buddhaghosa's *Visuddhimagga*, the most influential text of Theravāda moral thought. The *Visuddhimagga* is a "meditation manual" and mainly discusses meditation subjects and techniques. It recommends two meditation subjects that are "generally useful" and that everyone should meditate on. These two are lovingkindness (*mettā*) and death.[88]

The Pāli word *mettā* (Sanskrit: *maitrī*) is often translated as "lovingkindness" or "benevolence." In older Vedic texts maitrī is associated with love and sympathy, and as lovingkindness is assumed to imply the desire to alleviate suffering, the notion is also related to compassion. Usually, another word, *karuṇā*, is translated as "compassion," however, and mettā and karuṇā are indeed not identical. Buddhaghosa's explanation of the difference is that karuṇā is concerned with alleviating the suffering of others, while mettā is concerned with their general well-being.[89] However, this seems to make compassion (karuṇā) a special kind or aspect of mettā, as concern for the well-being of those who suffer is concern with the alleviation of that suffering, and it makes no sense to say that mettā only applies to concern for the well-being of non-suffering beings. Perhaps, on the same grounds, the positive counterpart of karuṇā, *muditā* could also be considered a special kind or aspect of mettā. Muditā, which is sometimes translated as "sympathetic joy," is not sharing in the suffering of others like compassion, but sharing in their joy or fortune. It is genuine happiness due to the other's happiness.

It seems to make most sense, to me at least, to think of mettā as a virtue related to compassion, and of karuṇā and muditā as emotional attitudes that motivate and support that virtue. This virtue of mettā is the genuine desire for the well-being of all sentient beings, for the alleviation of their suffering, and for the enhancement of their happiness and joy. Mettā is a kind of target-less, universal compassion. Unlike empathy, which is always aimed at a specific other, mettā is impartial compassion for everyone.

Mettā or lovingkindness is cultivated, according to Buddhaghosa, in a meditation exercise that gradually extends the scope of one's concern for the well-being of others.[90] At first, one might only have compassion, or sympathetic joy, for those close to oneself, but in meditation this circle is to be extended further and further until it includes all sentient beings.

The other meditation subject recommended to everyone by Buddhaghosa is death. In the section on death as a meditation subject,[91] he describes a number of meditation exercises focusing on the absolute unavoidability, finality and irreversibility of death. The aim and purpose of these exercises is to bring about a state of shock called *saṃvega*.[92] Saṃvega is a religiously and morally motivating state of shock that is explicitly associated with awareness of death or suffering.[93] According to Buddhaghosa, the experience of saṃvega decreases attachments and increases lovingkindness and vigor.[94] Similarly, Śāntideva wrote that "the virtue of suffering

---

88 Buddhaghosa, *Visuddhimagga* (5th c.), §III.57.
89 Ibid., §§IX.108–9.
90 Ibid., §III.58.
91 Ibid., §§VIII.1–41.
92 Ibid., §§VIII.5–6.
93 On the nature of saṃvega and how it could do the work it is supposed to do, see Lajos Brons, "Facing Death from a Safe Distance: *Saṃvega* and Moral Psychology," *Journal of Buddhist Ethics* 23 (2016): 83–128.
94 Buddhaghosa, *Visuddhimagga*, §III.58, §XIII.35, and §XIV.137, resp.

has no rival, since, from the shock [saṃvega] it causes, intoxication falls away and there arises compassion for those in cyclic existence, fear of evil, and a longing for the Conqueror [i.e., the Buddha]."[95]

It is important to realize that Buddhaghosa's two generally beneficial meditation subjects are not unrelated and are not some kind of sectarian idiosyncrasy either. The meditation on death is intended to promote the genuine understanding of the badness of death and suffering, an understanding that can only be achieved through a state of shock; and by promoting this understanding, it is intended to strengthen the meditator's commitment to impartial compassion, that is, lovingkindness or mettā. Hence, the purpose of this kind of meditation — and it is worth noting once more that this is arguably one of the most important kinds of meditation within the Buddhist tradition — is not some kind of stress-reduction, as in the image of meditation promoted by the mindfulness industry, but its very opposite. The goal of the most important forms of Buddhist meditation is stress *induction*,[96] or as Paul Williams remarked, "the spiritual path is not one of comfortable feelings and acceptance. It is deeply uncomfortable."[97]

For those who aim to let "intoxication fall away," there are, of course, many different ways one could meditate on death, suffering, and lovingkindness or universal compassion. Buddhaghosa suggests, for example, to go into retreat and repeat "death, death,"[98] but aside from not being very subtle, I'm not convinced that this is the best way of going about it either. It is probably much more useful to meditate on a stanza from Thích Nhất Hạnh's famous poem *Please Call Me by My True Names*.

I am the twelve-year-old girl,
refugee on a small boat,
who throws herself into the ocean
after being raped by a sea pirate.
And I am the pirate,
my heart not yet capable
of seeing and loving.[99]

I suppose that it is relatively easy to meditate on the fate of that twelve-year-old refugee girl, but it is not so easy to *really* feel her terror and understand her suffering, and it is even less easy to identify with the sea pirate and understand the suffering that made him who he is. That, however, is what the meditation on death, suffering, and lovingkindness is about: feeling and understanding the suffering and terror of death of *everyone* involved. And as Buddhaghosa pointed out, such meditation is not successful unless it results in saṃvega, a state of severe distress and shock. It is that state of distress and shock that makes intoxication fall away and opens the mind to the realization of the true evil of all suffering and death.

---

95 Śāntideva, *The Bodhicaryāvatāra*, §6.21.
96 Donald Lopez, Jr., *The Scientific Buddha: His Short and Happy Life* (New Haven: Yale University Press, 2012), 108.
97 Paul Williams, "General Introduction: Śāntideva and His World," in Śāntideva, *The Bodhicaryāvatāra*: vii-xxvi, at xxv.
98 Buddhaghosa, *Visuddhimagga*, §VIII.4.
99 Thich Nhat Hanh, *Being Peace* (Berkeley: Parallax, 1987), 67.

14

The Metaphysics of Acts and Rules

The previous chapters argued that right and wrong are determined by the suffering and death that is expected to result from something but left open what that "something" is. That is the topic of the present chapter. The main candidates are acts and rules, but other possibilities include virtues and whole moral codes.[1] As more or less stable character traits or dispositions, virtues in the traditional sense do not seem to exist.[2] This could be a reason to exclude them from the list of candidates, but virtues as hypothetical exemplars could be said to exist in some sense, and if the promotion of such exemplars is expected to have relevant effects, then this needs to be taken into consideration here. However, acts of promotion are acts, and therefore, if what matters about virtues is their promotion (because they do not really exist as anything but hypothetical exemplars) then this option can be reduced to acts.

The main argument in this chapter is that something similar applies to rules. In some sense, rules do not really exist, and in as far as they can be considered to exist — in some other, looser sense — they can be reduced to acts. An argument to this conclusion can be made largely parallel to the case of the promotion of virtues: like promoting a virtue, instituting a rule is an act and so is breaking and thereby weakening it, for example. If the expected effects of a rule are good, then establishing that rule is good and breaking that rule is (usually) bad. Furthermore, the rule itself is meaningless, or is not even a "rule," if it has not been put into effect by the right kind of act. Hence, rules can be reduced to acts. However, while this argument may have some force, I think a better argument is needed to support the metaphysical claims that rules in some relevant sense do not exist independently and can be reduced to acts.

Maps *for* and *of* Behavior

In philosophy the notion of a rule is usually associated with language, especially since Ludwig Wittgenstein. Languages could be thought of as systems of rules, and some philosophers associate linguistic meaning with rule-following. However, Donald Davidson was rather skeptical about these ideas.

---

[1] As explained in the introduction of chapter 11, in classical Chinese philosophy, whole moral codes or moral theories (dao 道) were often defended on the ground that they would establish peace and harmony.
[2] See the section "Moral Theory — A Primer" in chapter 11.

Throughout his career, Davidson made a number of controversial claims that sent opponents into a frenzy. Ranking first among these is probably his claim that nonhuman animals do not think, closely followed by the assertion that "there is no such thing as a language." The first of these claims becomes a lot less extravagant if one realizes that "thinking" for Davidson nearly always meant propositional thought and that he also remarked that "something much like thinking is going on, and we often have no alternative explanation available of what [animals] do."[3] The second also becomes a lot less outrageous if it is not taken out of context. What Davidson wrote is that

> there is no such thing as a language, not if a language is anything like what many philosophers and linguists have supposed. There is therefore no such thing to be learned, mastered, or born with. We must give up the idea of a clearly defined shared structure which language-users acquire and then apply to cases.[4]

To a large extent, this is what I will be claiming in this section, but my line of argument will be different from Davidson's. The perspective adopted here is based on social science rather than on philosophy, although I do not think there is a sharp boundary between those two. Language is an aspect of culture, and if it is understood as such, much of what Davidson claims in this quote should be or become more obvious than controversial.

On the face of it, considering that few concepts are as ambiguous as the concept of "culture," the idea of looking at language and rules through the lens of culture may not seem particularly helpful at all. In 1952, Alfred Kroeber and Clyde Kluckhohn described thirty-five different interpretations of the concept of "culture" and listed 176 definitions and 130 other statements on the word's meaning, and this was decades before "culture" became a buzzword in the social sciences and before the number of definitions and interpretations exploded.[5] I tried to make sense of this conceptual mess before, with very limited success.[6] Much of the problematic ambiguity of the "culture" concept results, however, from asking the wrong question. What culture is, is not a question that is likely to get a satisfactory answer. Culture somehow relates to what people do, to behavior, and therein lies the key: the question that needs be asked, and answered of course, is how culture relates to behavior.

In a paper about the development of the concept of "culture," Richard Peterson wrote that while culture "was once seen as a map *of* behavior it is now increasingly seen as a map *for* behavior."[7] The map-*of*/map-*for* metaphor itself is apt, but I doubt that the shift was as pronounced as he suggests. Rather, it seems to me that both aspects or interpretations have coexisted for quite some time.[8] Key to the issue is not whether such a conceptual shift has taken place but that culture plays both these two roles: it is both a map *of* and a map *for* behavior.

---

3 Donald Davidson, "Reply to Simon J. Evnine," in *The Philosophy of Donald Davidson*, ed. Lewis E. Hahn (Chicago: Open Court, 1999), 305–10, at 305.
4 Donald Davidson, "A Nice Derangement of Epitaphs" (1986), TLH: 89–107, at 107. Previously quoted in the section "Apoha and Its Implications" in chapter 8.
5 Alfred Kroeber and Clyde Kluckhohn, *Culture: A Critical Review of Concepts and Definitions* (Cambridge: Peabody Museum of American Archaeology and Ethnology, 1952).
6 Lajos Brons, *Rethinking the Culture-Economy Dialectic*, PhD Thesis, University of Groningen, 2005.
7 Richard Peterson, "Revitalizing the Culture Concept," *Annual Review of Sociology* 5 (1979): 137–66.
8 Brons, *Rethinking the Culture-Economy Dialectic*.

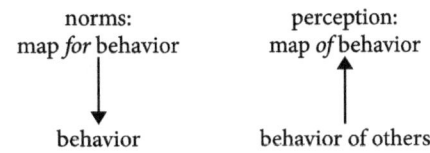

Fig. 14.1. Maps for and of behavior (1).

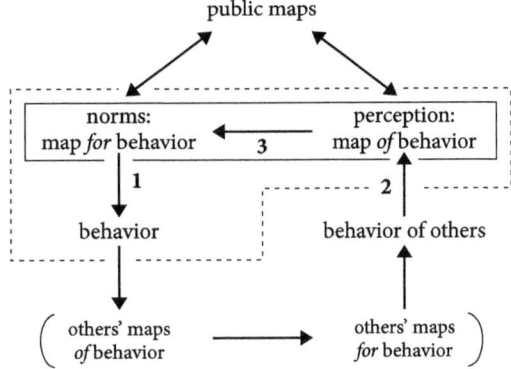

Fig. 14.2. Maps for and of behavior (2).

Maps for behavior are sets of norms influencing actual behavior; maps of behavior are more or less abstracted and systematized subjective impressions of actual behavior. My map for behavior tells me how I think that I should behave; my map of behavior tells me how I think others usually behave. There is an obvious asymmetry between the two notions, which is expressed by the different prepositions "for" and "of," and which is illustrated by the differing directions of the arrows in figure 14.1: maps for behavior influence behavior, while maps of behavior are influenced by behavior. Furthermore, my map for behavior influences my behavior, while my map of behavior is based on observed behavior of others. The same applies to these others and their maps, of course, but with "self" and "other" mirrored.

The "maps" in figure 14.1 are private, that is, they are in the agent's mind, and largely unconscious. Due to the opacity of our minds,[9] neither the kind of abstracting or systematization involved in the creation and updating of maps of behavior nor the processes that determine our acts and desires involving maps for behavior are fully conscious. On the contrary, they are mostly unconscious. Furthermore, these private, largely unconscious, and ever-changing maps are created and continuously transformed in response to a subject's unique experiences, brain architecture, and so forth.

In addition to these private maps, there also appear to be some kind of public maps, which are added in figure 14.2 along with some missing relations. The various relations are all represented by arrows, but this similarity in symbols does not imply a similarity in what these arrows represent. The relation between a map for behavior and actual behavior, arrow 1, is some kind of conscious or (usually) unconscious in-

---

9   Peter Carruthers, *The Opacity of Mind: An Integrative Theory of Self-Knowledge* (Oxford: Oxford University Press, 2011).

fluence or guiding relation. Arrow 2 represents the selective observation and induction that produces maps of behavior. And from these maps of the behavior by others, guidelines for appropriate behavior are inferred (arrow 3) that become part of my map for behavior. Again, most of this takes place unconsciously.

In addition to these arrows, figure 14.2 shows two boxes. The smaller box enclosing maps for and of behavior marks their essentially private nature. As mentioned, these maps are in the mind of the agent rather than in the outside world. The larger, tilted-L-shaped box with the dashed outline shows the part of the diagram that "belongs" to a single individual. This includes the two private maps but also that individual's behavior.

Public maps, shown at the top of the figure, can be both maps for and of behavior, and are related to private maps in a number of ways. Furthermore, public maps can take many different forms: they can be spoken or written, for example, and they can be reports of observed behavior (i.e., maps of) or propagations of particular norms (i.e., maps for). These public maps may include preachers, police officers, and politicians telling us what to do; journalists and scientists telling us what we or many of us are actually doing; self help guides and etiquette books; and much, much more. What all of these have in common is that they are public representations of some individual's or individuals' maps for or of behavior, although often for a very small audience. Mediated by our individual, subjective interpretations, these public maps influence our individual observations (i.e., maps of) and our individual norms (i.e., maps for), and conversely, our interpretations of the public maps we are exposed to are also influenced by our private maps for and of behavior. Hence, public and private maps continuously interact. I'll return to public maps and their problematic nature in the next section.

With this in mind, it can be asked again: what is culture? Is it maps for behavior? Maps of behavior? Public maps? And regardless of, or in addition to, the choice between these alternatives: which ones? Whose maps for behavior count? Whose maps of behavior count? Which public maps count? Arguably, the answer should be "all of them," but even that answer is not broad enough as it does not take into account that most of these maps change continuously. New observations change maps of behavior and thus often indirectly also maps for behavior, and both are influenced by new exposures to new or different public maps. Culture as phenomenon, then, is not just the collection of maps at some point in time, or even all points in time, but also the collection of processes of the (re-)production of these maps.

It is not primarily the general concept of "culture" as phenomenon or category that matters here but the concept of "a culture." The quote by Davidson above is about "a language," not about language in general — it is about French, Swahili, and Korean; not about the phenomenon of language. Supposedly, a culture, like a language, is some kind of "thing" or entity.

W.V.O. Quine famously argued that there is "no entity without identity."[10] What he meant is that we can only justifiably speak of a thing or entity if there are identity conditions specifying what that thing or entity is and what it is not, and where the boundaries between that-thing and not-that-thing are. So, how do we draw a boundary line around a culture, or between two? What are the identity conditions of a culture? And what are the identity conditions of a language? Or, in terms of the

---

10 W.V.O. Quine, "Speaking of Objects" (1969), OROE: 1–25, at 23.

above, which private and public maps and which processes count as belonging to or constituting one and the same culture?

The problem is that whatever answer we would give to these questions, we would be drawing boundaries rather than finding them, and drawing some more or less arbitrary boundaries does not magically change the collection of maps and processes that fall inside them into a "thing." They remain a collection, a rather loose collection, lacking clear and sharp boundaries both in space and time.[11] There is no exact day, minute, or second when a culture came into existence (but there may be exact times when they disappeared in some cases), and neither are there exact spatial boundaries between one culture and its neighbors.[12]

Language is linguistic culture. All of the above applies to language and languages if the adjective "linguistic" is added in the appropriate places. A language is a loose collection of maps for and of linguistic behavior, more or less heaped together by relations of similarity and history. There is, by implication, no such "thing" as a language. But this does not mean that we cannot speak of "the English language." It merely implies that in doing so, we need to realize that there is no *thing* called "English," but simply a collection of maps that are similar enough for some observers to group them together under that heading.

However, something seems to be wrong here. I do not only speak English but a few other languages as well (although most of them badly), and I can keep those languages apart. It is especially the latter that stands in need of explanation. Maps for and of linguistic behavior are maps for and of *specific* languages. Public maps are dictionaries, phrase books, grammar books, lessons by language teachers, and so forth, of English, Russian, Tagalog, or any other specific language. And similarly, maps *for* are my ideas about how to speak a specific language, and maps *of* are my observations about common ways a specific language is spoken. How is all of that possible if those languages do not exist to begin with?

It seems that I need prior notions of English and Japanese to be able to classify certain collections of private and public maps as, respectively, maps for and of English and maps for and of Japanese, but this is not right. Most conceptual classes are not formed prior to classification, but through classification. I do not have to learn a concept "table" first and then apply it to the world around me, but instead, as argued in chapter 8,[13] I form a concept of table in response to social interactions focused on saliently similar or non-different (*apoha*) stimuli in a shared world. In fact, I would not even be able to learn most basic concepts first and then apply them to

---

11 This problem, if it is one, is closely related to the more general problem of drawing conceptual boundaries addressed in the last sections of chapter 8.
12 Conceiving of cultures as sets rather than collections does not help either. A set is conceptually similar to a collection, but a set is generally considered to be an entity (i.e., a "thing") in addition to its members. If a culture would be considered a set of maps and processes, then it would be a thing. The identity of a set is wholly determined by its members, which implies that a culture-as-set goes out of existence immediately, because most of its members change continuously. and that any given culture would be different from a culture one second later involving all and only the same people. This implication could be avoided by adopting the eternalist view that not just present things exists but past and future things as well. A culture then, could be defined as a certain set of past, present, and future maps. This does not solve the problem of arbitrary boundaries and might even make it worse: I now would have to fix a sharp boundary determining when some culture came into existence, a culture's birthday. And such a birth *day*, or birth *second* even, would be a sharp boundary between one culture and another preceding it.
13 See the last two sections of chapter 8.

the world. Concept formation depends on social interaction in a shared reality. Concepts emerge from classification; they do not precede it. And the same is true here: I do not need a prior concept of my first language before learning it, but a concept of that language will emerge in linguistic interaction with speakers around me whom I gradually learn to understand — that is, in my formation of maps of linguistic behavior — and in my interactions with speakers who appear not to conform to those maps at all (i.e., speakers of "other languages"). As Davidson put it, "we must give up the idea of a clearly defined shared structure which language-users acquire and *then apply* to cases" (emphasis added).

A language is something like an apparent, local convergence of maps for and of linguistic behavior, and this convergence, as well as the divergence between languages, is easily explained by arrow 3 in figure 14.2: I base my map for my linguistic behavior on my map of the linguistic behavior of the people around me, the people I interact with. What the figure does not show, however, is that there is an important feedback loop: because I am more likely to interact more intensively and more frequently with people whom I understand and who are in relevant ways similar to me, barring exceptional circumstances, most of my interactions will be with people who mostly conform to my maps of linguistic behavior, because conforming to my map of linguistic behavior means understanding someone. And the more I interact with people like me, the more I will become like them in my linguistic behavior. Hence, social interaction intensifies convergence, and at the same time, the preference for interaction with similar people creates the conditions for divergence between different languages or cultures.

All of this can be simulated on a computer quite easily. Robert Axelrod did something like this with interesting results.[14] His model population was a set of 100 "cultures" in a 10-by-10 grid, where each culture was defined as having one of ten values on a number of different dimensions. His model showed that in interaction, these cultures slowly start to converge. There are a few important aspects missing in Axelrod's model, but taking inspiration from his approach, a simulation model can be built that takes much of the foregoing into account.

As in Axelrod's model, in my model there are 100 communities or individuals[15] in a 10-by-10 grid. There are ten cultural dimensions, each with ten values. This is an absurdly small number, considering that two languages can differ in tens of thousands of ways (because a language has tens of thousands of words and a smaller but still substantial number of grammatical rules) and that there are many more than ten possible values on any of these tens of thousands "dimensions." But modeling that extent of variation is not practically feasible, or at least not with the tools and skills available to me.

In each time step in the model, every community interacts with one of its neighbors. Which of its neighbors a community selects to interact with depends on similarity, randomness, and geographical features. Similarity is defined as the number of features two communities have in common (i.e., the same values on the same dimensions). The effect of randomness can be varied by means of a model parameter.

---

14 Robert Axelrod, "The Dissemination of Culture: A Model with Local Convergence and Global Polarization," *Journal of Conflict Resolution* 41, no. 2 (1997): 203–26.
15 It does not make a significant difference here whether the model simulates 100 interacting communities or 100 interacting individuals, so where it says "community" in the following, one could read "individual" instead.

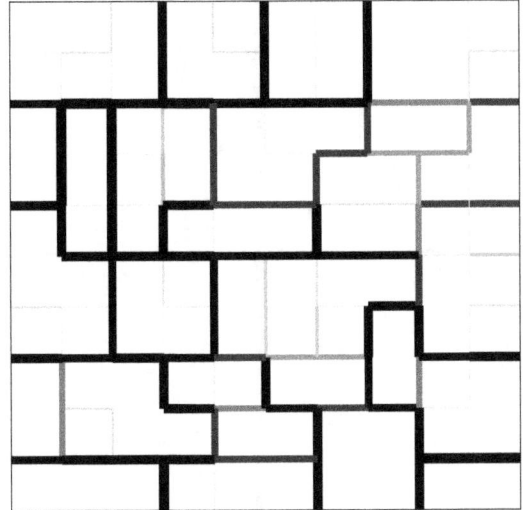

Fig. 14.3. A simulation of cultural convergence and divergence (1).

Geography can introduce barriers like rivers and mountain ridges, but this is not necessary. Communities have a preference to interact with other communities that are similar to them, but geographical barriers or random events can override this preference.[16]

In each interaction, a community randomly copies one cultural trait (i.e., a value on one of the ten dimensions) from the neighbor it is interacting with, but the more the two interacting communities have in common, the greater the chance that it will copy a trait it already has, and thus does not change. This models what is represented by arrows 2 and 3 in figure 14.2: the community or individual observes the others' behavior and adapts its maps *of* behavior on the basis of that observation (arrow 2). From that map of behavior, it consciously or unconsciously infers guidelines for proper behavior, thus adapting its own maps *for* behavior (arrow 3).

This is the main engine of cultural or linguistic change, but there is another effect that is missing in Axelrod's model: languages or cultures change due to all kinds of processes and events and not just because of interaction. To simulate this, the model also includes random "mutations." Because languages or cultures are defined by just ten dimensions in the model, one mutation implies that suddenly 10 percent of a language or culture is different. That is unrealistic, of course, but it is unavoidable if random mutations are taken into account, and it would be even more unrealistic to not take those into account. However, the chance of a random mutation occurring at any time step is quite low, to compensate for the size of the effect. In most model runs it was 1 percent or 2.5 percent at most. The effect of these mutations was, moreover, quite predictable. If it was very low, the results were similar to Axelrod's, that is, there was a gradual convergence of communities into a very small number of stable, unchanging large cultures (sometimes only one). If it was higher, there was little stability and the number of cultures formed was much higher.

---

16 In case two or more neighbors are equally close in terms of culture and geography, the choice between them is random as well.

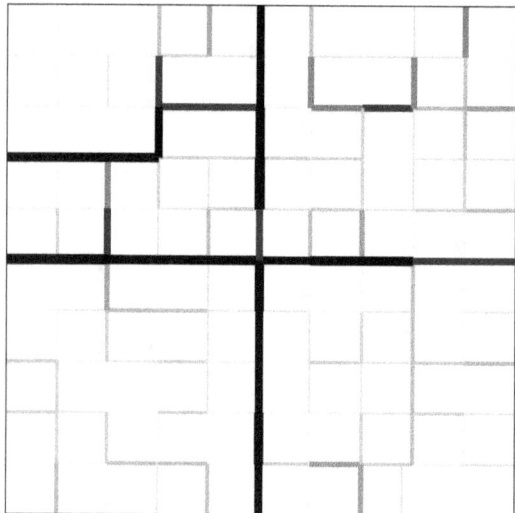

Fig. 14.4. A simulation of cultural convergence and divergence (2).

Figure 14.3 shows a fairly typical situation after 600 time steps in the model. The lines between cells are thicker and darker if two adjacent communities have *less* in common. Hence, very thick lines can be thought of as cultural boundaries. If there is no line between two cells, then these two communities have the same value on each of the ten dimensions. The thickest and darkest lines represent situations where two adjacent communities differ in all of the ten dimensions. In this particular simulation run, all 100 cells started out with identical values,[17] there were no geographical features, random events trumped the preference for interaction with the most similar neighbor in only 17 percent of cases, and the mutation rate was set at 2.5 percent. The result of these settings, as shown in the figure, is a large number of small cultures that greatly differ from each other but that are internally very homogeneous.

An area without geography is called an "isotropic plain" in the field of geography. The real world is not an isotropic plain but has geographical features — some of those are physical like mountain ridges, others are social like country borders — and a more realistic simulation should take that into account. Figure 14.4 shows the result of a typical simulation run with geography, also after 600 steps. There were two minor geographical barriers in this simulation — one running from top to bottom throughout the middle of the area, the other running from left to right also through the middle of the area. Hence, the two geographical features together make a very large "plus" sign with the same size as the whole area. The direct effect of geography was very minor; it effectively added 1 to the perceived difference between interacting communities in their choice for interaction partners. Or in other words, if a cell next to a geographical barrier had two candidates for interaction — one on the other side

---

17   Other simulation runs began with a random starting situation, but that did not significantly change the outcomes, although it did sped up the process a bit. In contrast, in Axelrod's model all simulation runs had to start with random numbers because the model did not include cultural change, and consequently, nothing would happen if cultures were all identical at the start.

of the barrier and one on the same side — then the barrier would only have an effect if these two candidates were identical in all other respects.

A second difference with the previous simulation run is that there was a 31-percent chance of randomness overriding similarity in the choice of interaction partners here rather than 17 percent, which has the result of creating larger, less internally homogeneous cultures. This can be easily seen in figure 14.4 by comparing it to the previous figure. The effect of geography is even more easily discernible in the figure, and despite their very minor effect in any individual step, the geographical barriers emerge as the main cultural boundaries,[18] splitting the area into four quadrants, only one of which, the top left, has clear internal subdivisions.

What is shown by these simulations is that cultures or languages do not depend on prior concepts or conventions, and that — under plausible assumptions, namely, a preference for interaction with similar communities or individuals, and a propensity to (unconsciously) adapt oneself to one's interaction partners — a patchwork of alternative sets of linguistic or cultural conventions will emerge from normal processes of human interaction. The processes that produce divergence between these larger multi-cellular linguistic or cultural communities also produce convergence within. Furthermore, the same processes are at work in many different kinds of social interaction and convention formation. Scientific communities develop their own jargon, for example, and electronic communication spawned an abundance of new abbreviations and terms that are near incomprehensible to n00bs (i.e., the uninitiated).

What emerges from these processes is what we call languages, dialects, cultures, and so forth, and their relative stability deludes us into thinking of (at least some of) them as singular entities — as *things* — but all they really are are emergent, local, and temporary convergences in the maps for and of (linguistic or other) behavior of different people. A culture or language is nothing but a fleeting speck in an ever-changing patchwork created by human interaction. It only looks like one homogeneous thing if we ignore time and change and zoom out enough to blur its internal heterogeneity.[19]

There is, moreover, another reason to say that cultures in some sense do not exist, or that there are no such "things." Supposedly, languages and cultures are shared, which means that they must consist of shared maps for and of behavior. However, there are no shared maps. Private maps are just that, private, but they are also largely unconscious and unique. As mentioned above, private maps are created and continuously transformed in response to a subject's unique experiences, brain architecture, and so forth. There is no way in which such maps, or even substantial parts thereof, could be shared. And public maps are not really shared either but for a different reason: public maps are not real.

Public Maps and Rules

Maps for and of behavior are collections of rules. Conversely, a rule can be defined as an element of a map for or of behavior. In ordinary language the word "rule" is

---

18 They are already quite obvious after two hundred steps.
19 It is mostly for this reason that cultural relativism does not make sense: it assumes something that does not exist, namely, cultures as a fixed, homogeneous, clearly defined things. See the section "Moral Theory — A Primer" in chapter 11.

mostly used in a prescriptive sense, that is, as an element of a map *for*; but in philosophical jargon it is also used in a descriptive sense, that is, as an element of a map *of*. Nevertheless, the prescriptive sense is more important here because moral rules are prescriptive by definition. Moral rules are normative, that is, they specify what you should or should not do. Hence, they are elements of maps *for* behavior. Furthermore, rules are generally assumed to be public and shared, and consequently, they must be the constitutive elements of public maps. But if public maps are not real, as I claimed in the previous paragraph, then that means that rules are not real either. Of course, dictionaries, anthropological studies, and law books are real, but those are mere physical expressions of maps. They are not the maps themselves. Public maps of and for behavior are something like their content, and it is that content that does not really exist.

Let's take a law as an example. A physical law book is not a law, but then, *what* is a law? Supposedly, it is whatever that law proclaims: the collection of rules that constitute its content. This collection of rules is not a physical object, which raises the question of how we decide the reality of non-physical objects. Buddhist philosophers like Dignāga and Dharmakīrti asserted that the criterion of reality of some supposed entity is causal efficiency: something can be considered real only if it has causal effects. In case of non-physical entities this seems a particularly useful criterion. If some supposed entity has no effects whatsoever, and is thus not observable or detectable in any way either, what reason do we have to assume it exists? Quine suggested another criterion: if our best scientific theories and explanations are ontologically committed to an entity, then we should assume it exists. The point of this criterion is that if our best theories imply the existence of some kind of thing and that kind of thing cannot be explained away or reduced to something else that we have already accepted as existing, then, and only then, we should accept that kind of thing in our ontology.[20]

Public maps and rules, such as laws, fail by either criterion. A law has no causal effects and there is no good reason to believe that we are necessarily ontologically committed to laws either. Perhaps, these claims seem absurd. Surely, laws have causal effects, you might object, and surely we are ontologically committed to laws, but this objection would be mistaken.

Laws are not themselves causally efficient, but they do have causally efficient counterparts. Those causally efficient counterparts are *interpretations* of the law (which are a kind of beliefs) in the minds of law-givers, law-followers, law-breakers, police officers, judges, lawyers, and so forth. Those interpretations have effects and are thus, by that standard, real. Similarly, our explanations of the role of laws in human behavior are ontologically committed to interpretations of laws in people's minds and not to some kind of mind-and-world-transcendent object out there that constitutes the law. Interpretations are real, but laws, or rules in general, are not. If a law or rule can be said to exist at all, then it exists as a fictional object. A law or rule is as real as Sherlock Holmes.

Private maps for behavior are causally efficient and therefore real. Whatever influences those private maps is, by virtue of that influence, causally efficient as well

---

20 I think that these two criteria are really the same criterion but will not give an extensive argument for that idea here. Briefly: if some entity is not causally efficient it is very unlikely to play such an essential role in our best theories that they are ontologically committed to it. And if an entity is causally efficient, then it must pop up in our best theories somewhere.

and thus also real. Interpretations of laws or other kinds of public maps and the rules that constitute them are an important influence on private maps *for*, albeit probably not as important as the observed behavior of others mediated by private maps *of*. These interpretations of public maps are themselves the effect of contact with their expressions, resulting from acts of publication, promotion, or other forms of dissemination. These acts and their results are real; indirectly they cause a change in people's private maps for behavior and thereby in behavior itself. And as mentioned before,[21] without such acts, a rule is nothing.

However, in a sense, even with such acts, a rule is nothing. Interpretations of a rule are not like perspectives on the same thing: in case of rules there are only interpretations and nothing, or no thing, these interpretations are interpretations of.[22] Even at the time of a law's drafting or enactment, there is no thing that *is* the law. There are only interpretations of the law in the minds of the drafters and legislators.[23] But this realization suggests a looser understanding of the notion of a rule. If there are no rules in a strict sense and only interpretations, then we could understand a rule as something like an average of more or less converging interpretations — as an average of converging but not strictly identical elements in the private maps of or for behavior of different people. Of course, rules in this looser sense are not real either for the same reason that the average Frenchman is not real. The notion of the average Frenchman does not refer to an actual person but to an idea or an abstraction, and as such, it is a fiction, and the same is true for rules in this loose sense.

Furthermore, like rules in the strict sense, rules in the loose sense are not evaluable for their consequences, albeit for a different reason. Rules in the strict sense cannot be evaluated because they do not exist; rules in the loose sense cannot be evaluated because they are unobservable. If rules in the loose sense would be what is morally evaluated, then right and wrong would be determined by the consequences of something like the average map for behavior of a group of people, but maps for behavior are private. All that can be observed is the behavior guided by those maps, but evaluating behavior is evaluating acts.

Nevertheless, neither the fact that rules in this loose sense are fictional nor the fact that they are unobservable makes them any less important. In the same way that the notion of the average Frenchman can be a convenient shortcut to say things that would otherwise be overly complicated, the notion of a rule in the loose sense can be quite useful as well. (Unless explicitly stated otherwise, the word "rule" will refer to this looser notion of rules in the following.) Rules matter because they influence what we do, and therefore, good rules have positive effects, and bad ones have negative effects. But this is not a one-way road: acts influence rules as well. Any act affects some rules. In case of some kinds of acts this is obvious. The act of enacting a law, for example, quite obviously changes, however subtly, at least some people's maps for behavior. However, breaking a law or unwritten rule also affects private maps, provided that such an act is observed, because any observed act will affect someone's map *of* behavior, and thus indirectly, that person's map *for* behavior. Usually, such

---

21 See this chapter's introduction.
22 On perspectives and perspectivism, see the section "Relativism, Pluralism, and Perspectivism" in chapter 7 and the section "Perspectives and Science" in chapter 9.
23 Assuming that moral principles are more or less abstracted rules, this implies that moral principles cannot be true if truth is defined as correspondence. It does not affect epistemic justification, however, and it strengthens the case for the approach adopted in this book: to aim for moral justification rather than moral truth. See the introduction to part II and chapter 11.

effects will be very subtle, but they do not have to be, and even subtle effects can be important. Breaking a rule signals that that rule can be broken, thereby weakening it. And for the opposite reason, following a rule strengthens it, because rule-following underlines the rule's importance in the observer's map of behavior.

Much the same applies to virtues. As more or less stable dispositions or character traits, virtues probably do not exist. What we do is often influenced by situational circumstances more than by our characters or dispositions.[24] But regardless of whether such virtues exist, virtues in a looser sense as exemplars of moral behavior can be promoted, and a successful act of promoting a virtue changes people's maps for behavior. And in the same way that rule-following and rule-breaking affects maps of behavior, and thereby indirectly maps for behavior, virtuous or vicious behavior also affects maps of behavior.[25]

The fallout of all of this, is that rules and virtues can be reduced to acts. There are no rules and there are no virtues in a strict sense, but everything we do leads to changes in people's maps of and for behavior, however small, and thereby affects rules and virtues in a looser sense, and those rules and virtues (or what they represent) affect what we do in turn.

A possible, and perhaps even obvious, objection to the view advocated in this and the previous chapters is that the argument against the reality of public maps and rules in this section undermines that view itself. If rules and principles do not really exist, then the principles that suffering and death are bad and that right and wrong depend on expected consequences do not exist in that sense either. That indeed follows, but I have never claimed that such principles "exist" — merely that convergence or intersubjectivity justifies the acceptance of these principles as true. The requirement of "existence" of these principles as some kinds of moral "facts" matters only if one aims for truth rather than justification and if one accepts the correspondence theory of truth, But as explained in part II,[26] it makes no sense to aim for truth; we can only aim for justification, and I see no reason to accept the correspondence theory of truth either.

A more important objection is that the foregoing seems to undermine the notions of convergence and intersubjectivity and thereby undermines epistemic justification. In the same sense that there are no rules and only interpretations of rules, there are no principles and only interpretations of principles; and like the interpretations of rules, the interpretations of these principles differ between people (and continuously change, moreover). The problem is that this might make one wonder whether two or more people can agree about some principle if they do not even interpret it in the same way?

This objection is mistaken, however. It assumes that agreement about something requires perfect correspondence, but such a requirement would make agreement impossible. You and I might agree that cherries are delicious, for example, but that does not imply that the content of your belief about the deliciousness of cherries is the same as mine. On the contrary, given our different experiences with cherries, we cannot even have the exact same beliefs about the deliciousness of cherries, or any other belief about cherries for that matter, and the same is true for any other

---

24 See the section "Moral Theory — A Primer" in chapter 11.
25 Alternatively, the notions of virtues and vices could also be reinterpreted as those maps for behavior themselves.
26 See the introduction to part II and chapter 9.

kind of mental content.²⁷ Hence, if agreement between beliefs would require their identity, there could never be any agreement at all. What agreement or convergence requires instead, is significant similarity. This is a rather vague criterion, of course, but that is probably unavoidable and moreover not necessarily a problem. The desire for clear-cut criteria is born from a craving for absolute certainty and final answers, but that craving can rarely if ever be satisfied and the most fundamental precept of the pragmatist (or Quinean naturalist) approach adopted here is to give up that craving.²⁸ There are no final answers to our questions, only provisionally better and worse answers; and from the answers available to us we should choose the ones that are best supported by the available evidence, while recognizing that both the available answers and the available evidence are likely to change.

A Dao of Compassion

The previous chapter opened with a very brief discussion of an argument in Śāntideva's *Bodhicaryāvatāra*. According to that argument, from the two premises that persons are not ultimately real and that suffering must be prevented, it follows that experiences of suffering do not belong to anyone, and therefore, that all suffering must be prevented. This, however, is inconsistent with Mādhyamaka doctrine, because according to that school, experiences of suffering are as ultimately unreal as persons. But perhaps, pointing out inconsistencies like this is missing the point. Arguably, Śāntideva was not advocating a moral theory but promoting an exemplar of virtue, thereby aiming to change his audience's maps for behavior (regardless of whether he'd ever have phrased it in these terms). And because he was not advocating a moral theory, it would be a mistake to interpret him as if he was arguing for one.

However, even if Śāntideva was not advocating a moral theory in the *Bodhicaryāvatāra*, he must have had one, at least implicitly, because without a theory, his moral ideas would be groundless. His promotion of the bodhisattva ideal as an exemplar of virtue presupposes a theory explaining why those virtues should be promoted or why they are right. A theory like the one proposed here could do that but could not have been accepted by Śāntideva. As a Mādhyamika he was committed to the doctrine that nothing is ultimately true and, consequently, that there is no ultimately true moral theory explaining the rightness of the bodhisattva path.²⁹ This, of course, put Śāntideva in a rather awkward position, regardless of whether he realized that: he needed a theoretical foundation for the moral message of the *Bodhicaryāvatāra*, but the Mādhyamaka doctrines he subscribed to did not allow him one.³⁰

Fortunately, a Yogācārin is not burdened by the Mādhyamika's nihilistic rejection of ultimate truth. For the Yogācārin there are ultimate truths, including moral

---

27 Lajos Brons, "Patterns, Noise, and Beliefs," *Principia* 23, no. 1 (2019): 19–51.
28 See the section "Naturalism" in chapter 1, as well as the section "Perspectives and Science" in chapter 9.
29 This point was made before in the section "Consequences and Consequentialism in Mahāyāna" in chapter 12. On the other hand, the theory defended here doesn't claim ultimate truth either (because truth is fundametally out of reach from a pragmatic/naturalist point of view). Rather, the claim is merely that given all we know, it is the most justified theory.
30 An open question is whether Śāntideva could do without a foundation if he would accept a version of naturalism similar to that adopted in this book. See previous note.

truths, and therefore a Yogācārin could accept a moral theory that would make the moral views expressed in the *Bodhicaryāvatāra* or similar Yogācāra texts consistent. Whether Yogācāra actually included an explicit moral theory is another matter.

Attributions of moral theories to Buddhist schools or thinkers are always based on indirect textual evidence. Buddhist philosophers did not explicitly advocate moral theories but professed various rules, principles, precepts, and virtues. What moral theory a philosopher may have implicitly held is inferred by modern philosophers from those rules. Such inferences are always speculative because there are usually multiple theories that could justify the same rules and principles, and there are few clues as to the right theory because key rules and principles were never defended on theoretical grounds, if they were defended at all. Rather, their rightness is just taken for granted, as something that does not need much further argument or theoretical foundation.

Besides Asaṅga's recommendation to bring about small suffering to avert greater suffering,[31] there is little textual evidence for any underlying moral theory. The principle is consistent with some forms of consequentialism, but virtue-ethical and even deontological readings are also possible. In chapters 11 and 12 I argued that all of these theories converge on the centrality of expectations, and the same appears to be true for Asaṅga and Śāntideva. It is not consequences that matter but *expected* consequences, and expected consequences are a variety of expectations rather than a variety of consequences. Because convergence or intersubjectivity yields epistemic justification as argued in chapter 9, we are justified to believe that rightness and wrongness depend on expected consequences. To avoid confusion with consequentialism, and to avoid the interpretation that all moral theories are "merely" varieties of consequentialism, I suggested to call this "expectivism" in the end of chapter 12. Such expectivism is consistent with what we know about Yogācāra ethics, but considering that I argued that all plausible moral theories are essentially varieties of expectivism, that conclusion is hardly surprising. Nevertheless, the specific variety of expectivism advocated here appears to fit with Asaṅga's moral views as well.

According to that variety, the kind of expected consequences that matter are those related to death and suffering, and the kind of things that are evaluated for their expected consequences are acts. In chapter 13 I argued that there is little agreement about the good but that everyone agrees that death and suffering are bad and, consequently, that right and wrong are determined by the suffering and death that are expected to result from something. And in the present chapter I tried to show that that "something" can only refer to acts, because of the available options — acts, rules. virtues, and so forth — only acts are real, and because what matters about the other options can be reduced to acts.

Something like the latter point can also be observed in arguments by Confucius 孔子 and Mencius 孟子 mentioned in the introduction of chapter 11. Mencius objected to Mozi's 墨子 emphasis on utility (*li* 利) because promoting utility would undermine peace and harmony, and Confucius asserted that (only) if virtue is used to guide people, there will be order. What matters is not the notion of utility itself but its promotion, that is, the act of promotion. And what matters is not virtue itself but its use to guide people.

These arguments also illustrate another point made above: irreality does not imply irrelevance. That rules, virtues, moral codes, and so forth do not really exist does

---

31 See the section "Consequences and Consequentialism in Mahāyāna" in chapter 12.

not make them any less important. Because people's interpretations of rules influence their maps for behavior, these interpretations can have very real effects. And consequently, if we think of rules not as real things, but as convenient designators for converging interpretations of maps of and for behavior in people's minds, then the resulting notion refers to something that is phenomenally very real. Rules, virtues, moral codes, and so forth in that sense matter. However, what matters about them, again, is their promotion, implementation, and so forth.

The classical Chinese notion of dao 道 referred to a set of conventions to guide people's virtue (*de* 德) or virtuous behavior, or to a theory providing such a set of conventions. Hence, a dao is a guide, and as such it is not fundamentally different from other guides. Promoting a single virtue or rule differs from promoting a dao only in scale. The moral theory I am arguing for here (i.e., that I am promoting) is a dao of universal compassion. It puts suffering with the other and the understanding of and (appropriate!) response to that suffering in the center. From a dao perspective, it is just another guide, and in the same way that an act or rule or virtue is morally justified to the extent that is expected to deliver the good and limit the bad, so is this dao of compassion as a whole.

A dao perspective also puts a spotlight on two related issues, one more practical and one more fundamental. The practical issue has to do with a problem pointed out in chapter 12:[32] the more serious the expected consequences, the better supported one's expectations should be; but to expect serious consequences in the first place, one might already need to have relatively well-supported expectations. I doubt that there is a solution to this problem — at least if one hopes for something like a final solution — but the dao perspective suggests a way to deal with it. The right dao as guide is the dao that is expected to lead to the best results, and that means that the right dao is probably one that includes some kind of *principle of prudence*, a principle that the more serious the expected consequences, the better supported those expectations should be. That such a principle is not a strict solution to the problem of deciding whose expectations matter due to circularity does not matter. What matters is whether it works.

The "more fundamental" corollary hereof is that the dao perspective changes much but not all of ethics into an empirical science.[33] The rules, virtues, principles, systems, guidelines, and so forth that should be promoted are those that can be expected to deliver the good and avoid the bad as much as possible. This *might* imply that the dao of compassion advocated here is not the dao that should be promoted, but this is an empirical question.[34] What I aimed to show in these last chapters is that right and wrong are determined by the death and suffering that can be expected to result from some act, taking into account that effects can be very indirect and often involve complex interactions. *How* to best minimize death and suffering — including how to organize our societies, what to teach, and what ideas to promote towards that end — is an empirical question.

A similar point was made by Max Horkheimer in several of his writings of the 1930s.[35] Suffering is the ultimate evil, and therefore the aim and purpose of the social

---

32 See the section "Problems for Subjective Consequentialism" in chapter 12.
33 See also the last paragraphs of the introduction of chapter 11.
34 And the same applies to the argument for a principle of prudence .
35 Max Horkheimer, "Die gegenwärtige Lage der Sozialphilosophie und die Aufgaben eines Instituts für Sozialforschung" (1931), in *Gesammelte Schriften,* Band 3: *Schriften 1931–1936* (Frankfurt a.M.: Fischer, 1988), 20–35, and "Materialismus und Moral" (1933), in *Gesammelte Schriften,* Band 3: 111–49.

sciences should be to figure out how to abolish suffering. However, like the radical Buddhists writing and working on the other side of the planet around the same time, he was also well aware that the world had been moving in the opposite direction — toward more suffering — and was continuing to do so.

> Never stood the poverty of people in more blatant contrast to their possible wealth as nowadays; never were all strengths more cruelly tied [down] as in these generations, where the children are starving and the hands of the fathers make bombs.[36]

And like the radical Buddhists, Horkheimer saw capitalism as the main culprit. The question that needs to be answered next, then, is whether they were right in this assessment: is capitalism the main source of evil — that is, of death and suffering — in this world?

---

36 Nie stand die Armut der Menschen in schreinderem Gegensatz zu ihrem möglichen Reichtum als gegenwärtig, nie waren alle Kräfte grausamer gefesselt als in diesen Generationen, wo die Kinder hungern und die Hände der Väter Bomben drehen. — Horkheimer, "Materialismus und Moral," 135.

15

The Case against Capitalism

In its mission statement, the Youth League for New Buddhism 新興仏教青年同盟, founded by Seno'o Girō 妹尾義郎 in 1931 in Japan, declared that "the capitalist economic system goes against the spirit of Buddhism and obstructs the livelihood and welfare of the general public."[1] Indeed, if there is one thing all of the radical Buddhists and many of the engaged Buddhists discussed in chapter 3 have in common, it is their opposition to capitalism. Uchiyama Gudō 内山愚童, early Taixu 太虛, Lin Qiuwu 林秋梧, and Seno'o identified capitalism as the primary source of human suffering in modern society, and B.R. Ambedkar rejected capitalism on very similar grounds.[2] Less radical but still "engaged" Buddhists that explicitly rejected or reject Buddhism include Watanabe Kaikyoku 渡辺海旭, U Nu, Buddhadāsa, Sulak Sivaraksa, the 14th Dalai Lama, and, perhaps, Dharmapāla.[3]

The list becomes considerably longer if the capitalist *ideology* that underlies capitalism as political-economic system, as well as the pre-modern system blindness and moralistic pre-modern individualism that continue to permeate much of Buddhism are taken into account.[4] A.T. Ariyaratne, for example, interpreted the second of the Four Noble Truths as claiming that suffering is caused mainly by egoism, competition, and greed. Significantly, these are "qualities" that are worshiped by capitalism — egoism, competition, and greed are the very core of capitalism as ideology. Consequently, if one identifies selfishness and greed as a key source of suffering — as all of the Buddhist thinkers and activists mentioned in these paragraphs did and most if not all other Buddhists discussed in this book did as well — then one should also reject the ideology promoting those. Given that greed is a form of craving and that selfishness is rooted in mistaken views about permanence and the self, one may even wonder whether *any* form of Buddhism is compatible with capitalism at all.

---

1   現資本主義経済組織は仏教精神に背反して大衆生活の福利を阻害するもの... — Kashiwahara Yūsen 柏原祐泉,『日本仏教史　現代』(Tokyo: 古川弘文館, 1990), 214.
2   Ambedkar did not explicitly criticize capitalism in his main work *The Buddha and His Dhamma*, but he did so in a memorandum about the draft constitution of India that was later published as *States and Minorities*, in *Writings and Speeches*, Vol. 1 (New Delhi: Dr. Ambedkar Foundation, 1979), 381–449, as well as in other writings. His critique was focused on exploitation, inequality, and injustice but did not mention suffering explicitly. For example, he blamed capitalism for inequality in Europe (408) and about the capitalist understanding of "liberty," he wrote that "what is called liberty from the control of the State is another name for the dictatorship of the private employer" (410).
3   For relevant quotes, see the sections about the Buddhist thinkers and activists mentioned here in chapter 3.
4   On pre-modern idealism and system blindness, see the section "Moralistic versus Systemic Critique" in chapter 4.

It is only system blindness (i.e., the pre-modern lack of understanding of the role played by social systems and structures) that prevents some from realizing that "the capitalist economic system goes against the spirit of Buddhism" indeed.

For the radicalized radical Buddhism that is the topic of this book, this kind of argument does not necessarily have much force. The previous chapters argued that in that view, what makes something morally wrong is that it causes or is expected to cause death and suffering,[5] and the more death and suffering something is responsible for, the worse it is. Hence, an assessment of the anti-capitalist element in radicalized radical Buddhism depends on an assessment of the extent to which capitalism is indeed responsible for much of the suffering in this world. But before proceeding to assess the case against capitalism, there are two issues that require some attention first: one is the case *for* capitalism, and the other is the question of what exactly capitalism is.

The distinction between capitalism as ideology and capitalism as political-economic system was already made above. The former is the collection of values and ideas that promote and support the latter. The latter, capitalism as system, is often defined as a simple sum of private ownership plus markets, but Geoffrey Hodgson has pointed out in *Conceptualizing Capitalism* that both of these features of capitalism actually predate it, and therefore, cannot be sufficient to define it.[6] Instead, Hodgson offers the following definition:

> Capitalism is defined [...] as a system of production with the following six characteristics:
> 1. A legal system supporting widespread individual rights and liberties to own, buy, and sell private property
> 2. Widespread commodity exchange and markets involving money
> 3. Widespread private ownership of the means of production by firms producing goods or services for sale in the pursuit of profit
> 4. Much of production organized separately and apart from the home and family
> 5. Widespread wage labor and employment contracts
> 6. A developed financial system with banking institutions, the widespread use of credit with property as collateral, and the selling of debt.[7]

The first three items in this definition also capture key elements of capitalism as ideology: the idealization of economic freedom and private property and an insistence to leave as much as possible to "the market." The remaining three seem more practical than ideological, but item number 6 is a key aspect of capitalism that will be discussed in the section "Playing with FIRE" below.

Of the six items in Hodgson's definition, five include the rather ambiguous term "widespread," which raises the question of how widely spread exactly these aspects have to be to qualify. "Capitalism" does not denote a natural kind with sharp and unambiguous boundaries. There is a gray zone between systems that are obviously capitalist and those that are obviously not, and there may be little agreement about

---

5   Strictly speaking, that something already has caused death or suffering is only relevant in the moral framework suggested in the previous chapters if this is reason to believe that it will continue to do so. See the section "Expectivism and Free Will" in chapter 12.
6   Geoffrey Hodgson, *Conceptualizing Capitalism: Institutions, Evolution, Future* (Chicago: University of Chicago Press, 2015).
7   Ibid., 259.

how to classify what falls in between. There is no neutral or "objective" way to decide how far an economic and political system can deviate from the libertarian ideal to still count as "capitalist," and a largely capitalist system may have elements that are fundamentally non-capitalist or even anti-capitalist. Of course, if such elements become dominant, then the system in question can no longer be called "capitalist." What's more important than the labeling of such ambiguous cases, however, is the recognition of the existence of non- or anti-capitalist elements in most capitalist systems, especially in the assessment of arguments for or against capitalism.

Defenders of capitalism often point at its supposed achievements: a decline in poverty, increases in literacy and life-expectancy, and so forth. Such arguments are conveniently forgetting two things. First, they confuse correlation with causation: that several indicators of progress have improved during the two or more centuries that capitalism ruled a substantial part of the planet does not automatically imply that it caused that progress. It may be the case that progress was made in spite of rather than thanks to capitalism. Second, much of that progress was due to social currents and organizations such as labor unions who were often opposed to capitalism or to other non- or anti-capitalist elements within largely capitalist systems. Capitalism did not lead to improved living conditions for the working class, for example; pressure by labor unions and other social organizations did.

Furthermore, since the kind of free-market fundamentalism that is often called "neoliberalism" became hegemonic in the 1970s and many but not all non-capitalist elements have been purged from the economic and political systems of most countries, socioeconomic progress has stalled almost everywhere. There has been little real wage growth in most industrialized countries since the 1970s, for example, and neither has there been substantial progress in the "developing" world. (More about this in the section "Free Trade Ideology" in this chapter.) Global poverty did decline, but virtually all of the global decline in poverty of the last half century has been in China, which introduced capitalist elements into its planned and state-controlled (i.e., fundamentally anti-capitalist) economy at the end of the 1970s and which has seen spectacular economic growth ever since.

China indeed managed to lift half a billion people out of poverty, but it is debatable whether capitalism can be credited for that. First, China's spectacular growth may have been caused by other factors.[8] Second, China's system is far removed from the capitalist ideal; the state remains in control of key parts if not most of the economy. And third, even if it is the case that it was the adoption of capitalist elements into its economic system that lead to an increase in wealth, this does not imply that the *distribution* of that wealth in such a way that it resulted in poverty alleviation can be credited to capitalism as well. On the contrary, it seems that remnants of socialist policy — that is, fundamentally anti-capitalist elements in China's system — should be credited for that.

Historical evidence more strongly suggests that the non- or anti-capitalist elements within many capitalist systems were or are the drivers of socioeconomic progress rather than capitalism itself. Or even that progress was made in spite of capitalism and not because of capitalism indeed.

Capitalism is often contrasted with socialism (as if feudalism never existed), but whether an argument against capitalism is an argument for socialism or the other way around should be an open question. (The focus in this chapter is on capitalism;

---

8 This is the issue of confusing causation and correlation mentioned in the previous paragraph.

the next chapter will discuss some aspects of the quest for an alternative.) A good example of the common capitalism-socialism contrast in the polemics for and against capitalism is Frank Brennan's *Why Not Capitalism?* which was written in response to G.A. Cohen's *Why Not Socialism?*[9] In the introductory chapter of his book, Brennan wrote:

> Socialism seems to answer to a higher moral calling. Perhaps the best evidence of this is that socialists so often defend their view in moral terms, while capitalists defend their view in economic terms.[10]

This statement corresponds to a rather widespread idea: socialism is based on ethics while capitalism is based on economics and therefore on science. Brennan is too much of a philosopher to accept this simplistic view and argues that capitalism is morally superior as well. And so did most other philosophers who defended some form of libertarian capitalism.[11] Furthermore, Marxist socialism tends to be supported by its own economic theory in addition to moral arguments. Nevertheless, the basic idea that the argument for socialism is moral while the argument for capitalism is scientific is widespread and very influential.

The idea is doubly nonsensical. First, it is nonsensical because the underlying idea that capitalism provides a more efficient path towards material well-being implicitly assumes a moral claim, namely that we *should* aim for the kind of material well-being that capitalism might provide. In other words, capitalism is as morally grounded as socialism; it just differs in its moral preferences and priorities. The second reason why the idea is nonsensical is much more important because virtually all arguments for capitalism depend on the pervasive idea that science, economics in particular, somehow proves that capitalism is right. It is for this reason that an assessment of capitalism must start with an investigation into its supposed scientific foundations, and therefore, into mainstream, neoclassical economics.

There are two other reasons to spend a large part of this chapter on mainstream economics. First, it was mentioned in chapter 9 that not everything that passes for "science" actually satisfies scientific criteria of coherence, and mainstream economics is probably the best example thereof.[12] And second, because the idea that right and wrong are determined by expected consequences requires a more or less reliable way of forming expectation, especially if much is at stake, it is essential to be able to distinguish real science from ideology, as argued in chapter 12.[13] Mainstream economics is the best (but probably not only) example of an ideology masquerading as "science," and thereby disrupting rather than enabling the formation of reliable expectations.

This, then, is the topic of the first few sections of this chapter — scrutinizing the alleged "scientific" foundation of capitalism — though in the course of those sections, the lines between mainstream economics and capitalism as both ideology and system and between scrutiny and critique will gradually be erased.

---

9 G.A. Cohen, *Why Not Socialism?* (Princeton: Princeton University Press, 2009).
10 Jason Brennan, *Why Not Capitalism?* (New York: Routledge, 2014), 5.
11 The most influential example is probably Robert Nozick. See his *Anarchy, State, and Utopia* (Oxford: Blackwell, 1974). Unsurprisingly, Nozick's and Brennan's moral views are rather different from those advocated in this book.
12 See the section "Perspectives and Science" in chapter 9.
13 See the section "Problems for Subjective Consequentialism" in chapter 12.

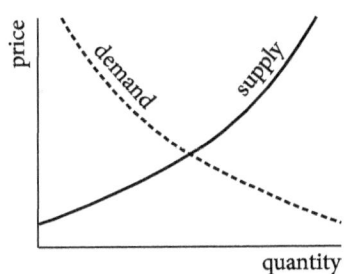

Fig. 15.1. Supply and demand curves (1).

The Ideology of Supply and Demand

Mainstream, neoclassical economics is built on a model of individual economic decisions by consumers and producers. The ideological core of that model is a set of curves that relate demand for some commodity by consumers and supply by producers to price, shown in figure 15.1. These supply and demand curves are used by economists to make economic predictions and give advice, and to argue against government intervention in the economy, among other things.

The model and its two curves are derived by a number of steps from certain assumptions about human economic behavior, preferences, production costs, and so forth. Most of those assumptions are patently false and many are even absurd, and some of the steps in the argument are dubious at best. By far the most rigorous analysis of these problems can be found in Steve Keen's *Debunking Economics*,[14] but given the central role of figure 15.1 in mainstream economics and capitalist ideology, as well as for reasons mentioned above, I believe it is essential to spend a few pages scrutinizing the ideas behind it.

The theory starts with a model of an individual consumer. That individual consumer is perfectly rational, perfectly informed, and perfectly selfish. Furthermore, if that consumer derives satisfaction or "utility," measured in "utils," from the consumption of one unit of some good, then he will get more satisfaction and thus more utils from consuming more, but for every additional good the increase of satisfaction will be smaller. This is called "marginal utility." Thus, consuming one piece of cheesecake will produce, for example, 10 utils, the second piece 8, the third piece 6, and so forth. And by implication, consuming one piece produces 10 utils in total, consuming two pieces 10 + 8 = 18 utils, three pieces 10 + 8 + 6 = 24, and so forth.

This is, of course, absurd. Consuming many pieces of cheesecake will make the consumer feel sick, resulting in dissatisfaction (i.e., negative utils). If nausea starts to kick in after the fourth piece and overwhelms the enjoyment of eating cheesecake by the fifth, then the fifth piece would carry a satisfaction or utility of approximately −25 or even lower because that piece would cancel out all previous enjoyment, and every next piece would just lead to more nausea and thus more negative utils (but not as low as −25 as these following pieces would only increase nausea and not cancel out the previous enjoyment because the fifth piece already did that). Figure 15.2 compares the utility curve according to orthodoxy, the dotted line, with a corrected, more realistic utility curve, the continuous line.

---

14 Steve Keen, *Debunking Economics*, rev. and exp. edn. (London: Zed Books, 2011).

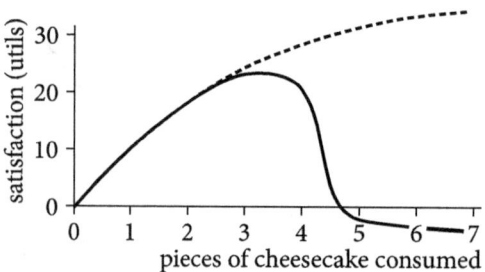

Fig. 15.2. Cheesecake utility.

Utility curves can have considerably more irregular shapes than the cheesecake curve in this figure, however. Let's assume that some consumer's utility of one new, white car of some particular brand "Acme" and model "Coyote" is a certain number of utils.[15] Owning another white Acme Coyote would not increase the consumer's satisfaction by much, however, and might actually decrease it if parking space would be rare or costly, which it is in many cities. From the third, white Acme Coyotes may very well start becoming a nuisance. Having to own three of them might, especially in a city, be so expensive and troublesome that it would be better to own none at all. Consequently, the utility curve for white Acme Coyotes looks somewhat similar to that of pieces of cheesecake, but with two important differences. First, the line for cars peaks and sinks much earlier than that for pieces of cheesecake and its peak is (probably) much higher. Second, and much more importantly, half a piece of cheesecake will produce some satisfaction (or some nausea), but half a car is most likely just an annoyingly big piece of trash. Therefore, while the line for cheesecake is smooth, the line for white Acme Coyotes will be flat or even decreasing until the first whole car where it peaks, after which it sinks because of the increasingly large part of unusable half-a-car, and suddenly peaks again at the second whole car, and then sinks below zero because of the trouble and expenses associated with owning too many (pieces of) cars.[16]

The important point here is that utility curves do not have the shape mainstream economists suppose they have. They will not continue to rise infinitely and they may have flat starts, valleys and peaks, and other odd and irregular features. And therefore, the "law of diminishing marginal utility," which holds that all utility curves have shapes like the dotted line in figure 15.2 is false.[17] Furthermore, the theory cannot be rescued by claiming that this single consumer could sell off the additional pieces of cheesecake or the additional white Acme Coyotes, and that this would cause the curve to continue to climb. This is a model of a *single consumer*. He is a consumer, and not a supplier or trader, and moreover, if he is single (not in the sense of

15 And let's assume that Acme Coyotes do not explode and actually do have a positive utility.
16 Utility curves with a flat start or peaks and valleys can also occur for other kinds of commodities. Let's say that our consumer plays a 47-string concert harp. He's been using strings of type A, but now wants to try strings of type B. He needs to replace all of the strings to do that, however, so the utility of 1 to 46 strings is pretty much zero. Then, at 47 strings the utility suddenly jumps, after which it continues to climb very gradually because it is nice to have a few spare strings, until the number of strings gets so large that issues of storage start to play a role and utility starts decreasing again.
17 More accurately, the "law of diminishing marginal utility" holds that every next unit of a commodity will have a positive value in utils but a smaller value than the previous unit. But it is still false.

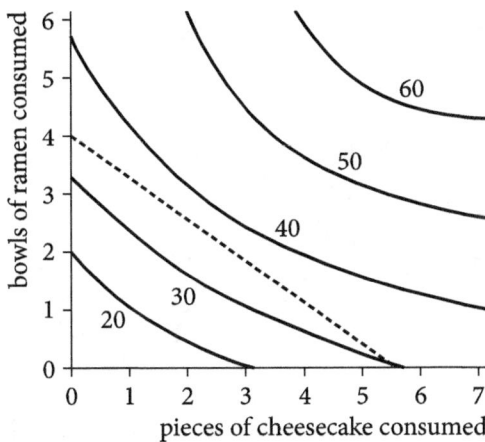

Fig. 15.3. Indifference curves (1).

"unmarried" but in the sense of "alone"), then there is no one else to buy the surplus from him. But even if that is ignored, it does not really change much. There is a limit to how many pieces of cheesecake this consumer or trader could sell. One million pieces of cheesecake would quickly turn into a rotting mess with a very large negative utility, and thus the utility decline would merely be postponed. And half cars are still useless, so the utility curve for Acme Coyotes would still have peaks and valleys. In other words, the "law of diminishing marginal utility" is still false. But let's ignore this, and move on.

Let's say that the same consumer likes bowls of ramen slightly more than pieces of cheesecake. Every combination of pieces of cheesecake and bowls of ramen also gives him a certain satisfaction or utility, shown in figure 15.3. The lines in the figure are called "indifference curves." They connect all combinations of goods with the same total utility. The line marked "30" in the figure marks all combinations that add up to 30 utils: 5.6 pieces of cheesecake and no ramen, 4 pieces and half a bowl, 3 pieces and 1 bowl, and so forth.

If bowls of ramen cost 550 yen each and pieces of cheesecake cost 400 yen, and the consumer has 2200 yen in his pocket, then he can buy either 4 bowls of ramen or 5.5 pieces of cheesecake or any other combination of ramen and cheesecake on the dotted line or below in figure 15.3. The highest total satisfaction the consumer can reach with his money is the point closest to the 40 utils line. And because our consumer is perfectly rational, perfectly informed, and perfectly selfish, he will try to achieve that maximum satisfaction by purchasing approximately 2.4 pieces of cheesecake and 2.25 bowls of ramen.

By varying the price of ramen and adding a few more indifference curves in between 30 and 40 to the diagram, the effect of price on the consumer's consumption can be shown. The thick black lines in figure 15.4 show the amounts of ramen and cheesecake available for different prices of ramen. Because the price of cheesecake is constant, all of these lines go through the same point on the *y*-axis: 0 bowls of ramen and 5.5 pieces of cheesecake.

The thick black line crossing the *y*-axis just below 5 is the line for a ramen price of 450 yen per bowl. At that price, and a fixed price of cheesecake, the highest indifference curve he can reach is 40 utils. That point corresponds to 3.3 bowls of ramen and 1.9 piece of cheesecake, so at a price of 450 per bowl, the consumer would buy

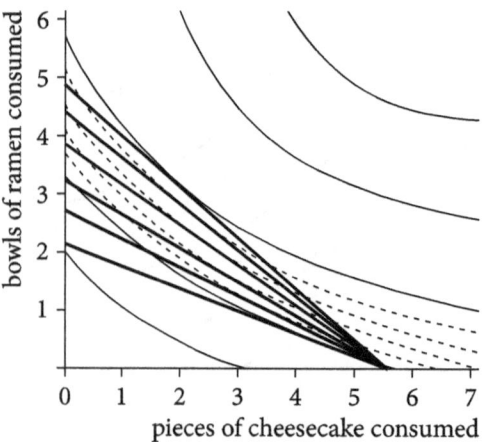

Fig. 15.4. Changing the price of ramen.

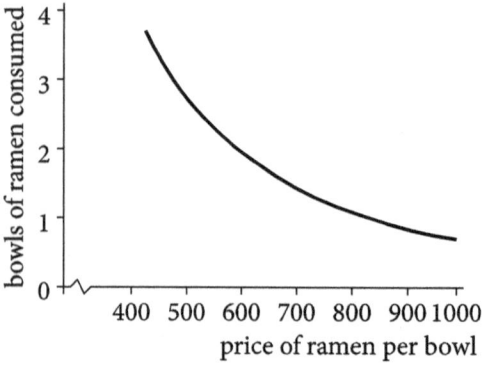

Fig. 15.5. The demand curve of ramen for a single consumer.

3.3 bowls of ramen. Similarly, at a price of 500 yen per bowl, he would buy 2.7 bowls, at a price of 580 2.1, and so forth. With this data a new diagram can be drawn that shows the relation between price and consumption. This is the "demand curve" for an individual, single consumer in figure 15.5.

The demand curve in figure 15.5 looks much like the one in figure 15.1 (with the axes switched!), but remember that it depends on fictional utility curves and several other assumptions. That utility curves do not have the shape they are supposed to have was already shown above, but many of these other assumptions are almost equally nonsensical. For example, the consumer must always be able to make a choice between different combinations of goods or commodities. And his preferences must be transitive — if he prefers A over B and B over C, then he must prefer A over C. Both these assumptions may be acceptable for an idealized, perfectly rational consumer, but psychologists and experimental economists have shown that they do not always apply to real people. And the assumption that a consumer can always compare all possible combinations of goods in terms of their utility becomes especially ludicrous if it is taken into consideration that real consumers do not compare two commodities but possibly thousands.

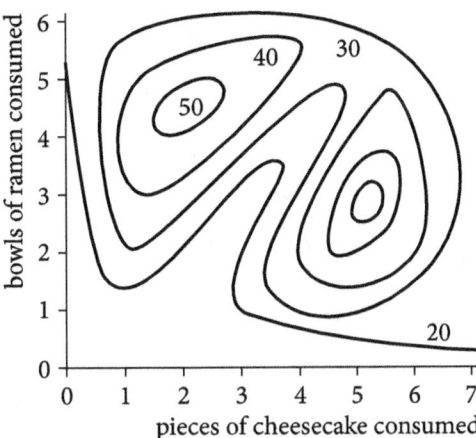

Fig. 15.6. Indifference curves (2).

It is further assumed that the satisfaction derived from consuming one good is completely independent from the satisfaction derived from consuming any other good and that there are no interaction effects between consumption of various goods. However, it might be the case that the consumer is fine if he eats lots of ramen and a little cheesecake or the other way around, but gets sick if he eats roughly equal amounts of both, for example. If this kind of interdependencies are not ignored, and if it is also taken into account that eating too much ramen or cheesecake also makes our consumer nauseated and thus leads to dissatisfaction, the picture starts to change rather drastically. Then, even with all of the other aforementioned assumptions, a rational consumer's indifference curves would look something like figure 15.6.

Obviously, this seriously messes up the demand curve. Now, at some price levels, there is not a single point at which this consumer can maximize his utility, but two, which means that the supposed "curve" is not a curve at all. Furthermore, if some of the other aforementioned assumptions are relaxed as well, indifference curves cannot be drawn anymore at all, not even weird or irregular ones, and thus, no demand curve could be derived either. But, again, let us ignore all that and move on.

Thus far, it was assumed that the consumer's budget is fixed at 2200 yen, but obviously, if his income rises or falls, so does the budget he has available for ramen and cheesecake. With a smaller budget he would end up with a different combination of goods to maximize his utility. Keeping prizes constant, a number of different lines can be drawn in figure 15.3 parallel to the dotted line to represent different budgets. These lines each touch different indifference curves. Connecting the points at which such budget lines reach maximum utility results in the thick black line in figure 15.7. This line is called an "Engel curve." It has a slightly peculiar shape in the figure, which is largely due to the fact that the indifference curves in my figures are not as nice and smooth as the indifference curves of a perfectly rational, perfectly informed, and perfectly selfish consumer that can (and prefers to) consume infinite amounts of anything are supposed to be. On the other hand, as Steve Keen pointed out, "Engel curves can take almost any shape at all,"[18] so there is no reason why this oddly shaped

---

18 Keen, *Debunking Economics*, 50.

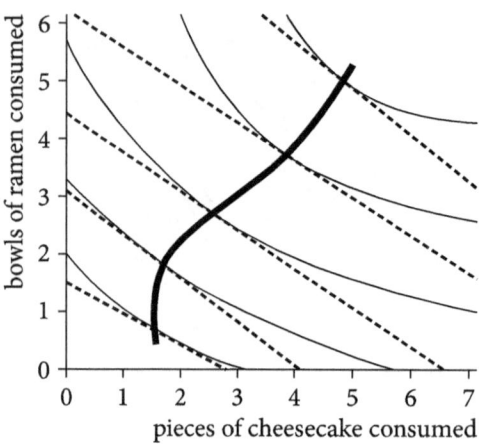

Fig. 15.7. Indifference curves and the Engel curve.

curve would be impossible. And besides, the Engel curve in this figure is rather pedestrian compared to what you'd get if you'd try to fit an Engel curve into figure 15.6.

An Engel curve shows how a consumer's spending pattern changes with a change in income. For reasons to be explained below, mainstream economists assume that Engel curves are straight lines unlike the line in the figure, which implies that spending patterns do not change when income changes. If the consumer gets richer, he just gets more of the same things and in the exact same proportion (and he gets less, but still in the same proportion, if he gets poorer). This is obviously absurd — spending patterns change very much with a change in income or budget, but this too we will have to ignore to move on.

No economy consist of a single consumer, so a demand curve for a single consumer is rather useless. We need a demand curve for an economy as a whole, or in other words, for all the consumers in that economy together. To get that demand curve, you would have to find the individual demand curves of all consumers in the economy, and add up the total number of bowls of ramen consumed at each price level. If there are a thousand consumers in the economy and they have similar preferences, then the market demand curve could, supposedly, look something like figure 15.8.

There is a rather nasty complication, however. The derivation of the individual demand curve depends on a fixed price of cheesecake and a fixed budget. Regardless of the price of ramen, the single consumer still has only 2,200 yen to spend. That is fine in the single-consumer model, but that becomes very implausible in the case of whole economies. If the price of ramen goes up or down or if the consumption of ramen rises or falls, that will influence the income, and thus the budget, of some people in the economy and those people are consumers too. In other words, changes in price and changes in consumption change the incomes and budgets of some consumers, and therefore, in an economy with multiple consumers, budgets *cannot* be fixed.

Furthermore, there is another kind of income effect that comes into play when three or more commodities are taken into account. For example, if the consumption of one of those three commodities cannot easily change but its price can, then a change in the price of that commodity will effectively raise or lower the consumer's income, and thereby his budget available for the other two commodities. Think of a raise in rent, for example. Moving house may not be a short-term option, so such a change would effectively just decrease a consumer's remaining income and budget.

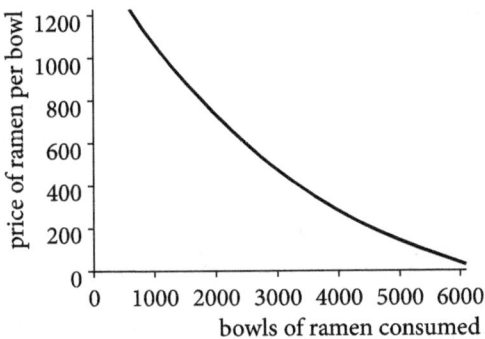

Fig. 15.8. The demand curve of ramen.

Or if a commodity takes up much of a consumer's budget but is really considered inferior by that consumer, then a decrease in the price of that commodity may make it possible for the consumer to buy better alternatives and thus lead to a decrease in consumption of the inferior good. For example, if due to poverty all you can afford is one kind of bread, if that bread becomes cheaper, you have to spend less on it, but because of that you can buy less of it and spend what you save on better food. Hence, while a demand curve is supposed to slope downwards (i.e., rising prices mean falling consumption and falling prices mean rising consumption) it can be the other way around.

When such effects and the role of income are properly taken into account it turns out that a demand curve "can take any shape at all — except one that doubles back on itself."[19] In a paper published in 1953, W.M. Gorman proved that the only way to get demand curves with the shape mainstream economists believe they have — downward sloping lines similar to the curve in figure 15.8 — is by assuming that the Engel curves of all consumers are parallel, straight lines.[20] This is an interesting assumption. As mentioned above, assuming that Engel curves are straight lines is assuming that spending patterns do not change with income, which really only could be the case if there is just one commodity available. Assuming that they are parallel for all consumers is assuming that all consumers have identical preferences, which really only could be the case if there is just one consumer. These are obviously absurd assumptions. If the only way a continuously downward sloping demand curve or line can be derived is by assuming that an economy consists of a single consumer consuming as single commodity, then this demand curve has little if anything to do with a real economy. Even ignoring most of the problems mentioned in previous sections, in a real economy, a demand curve can have almost any shape. But let us ignore all that as well and move on.

Assuming a downward sloping demand curve, if there is only one producer, then there are only two things that matter: the market demand curve for whatever it is producing and the costs of production per unit. (But keep in mind that every step in the derivation of that demand curve turned out to be invalid and that every important assumption it is based on is false.)

19 Ibid., 52.
20 W.M. Gorman, "Community Preference Fields," *Econometrica* 21, no. 1 (1953): 63–80.

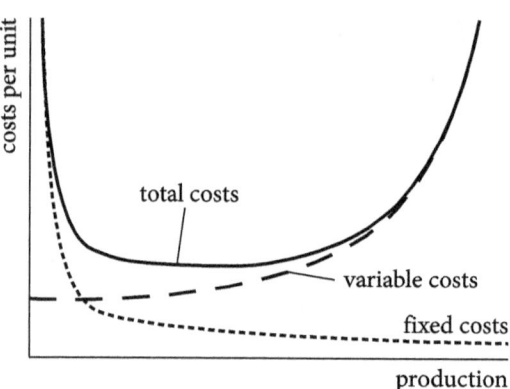

Fig. 15.9. Production costs.

Economists divide production costs into two different kinds: fixed costs and variable costs. Fixed costs do not depend on how many units are produced. They include the costs of buildings, machinery, tools, and so forth. Variable costs depend on the level of production and include labor and resources. It is assumed that variable costs rise with the level of production: the more units one attempts to produce at the same fixed costs, the more labor or other variable cost factors are needed. Therefore, the curve of variable costs per unit of production rises. The curve of fixed costs, on the other hand, starts very high, then drops steeply, and almost flattens out. The first units (bowls of ramen, pieces of cheesecake, cars, or whatever) are expensive to make due to fixed costs (buildings, machinery, and so forth), but the more units are made, the less these fixed costs matter. In figure 15.9, the dotted line represents fixed costs, the dashed line variable costs, and the continuous line the total average costs of production per unit.

It was already shown in the 1950s, however, that this figure does not look anything like a real average cost curve.[21] 95 percent of managers reported that there is no significant rise in the variable costs. In fact, for the vast majority of firms, the variable cost curve appears to be nearly or completely flat. This will turn out to have important implications.

Profits are total income minus total costs. Total costs are obtained by multiplying the number of units produced with the average production costs (represented by the continuous line in figure 15.9). Total income is the number of units produced multiplied by the price at which they can be sold. In case of the demand curve of ramen derived above, if the producer sets the price at 900, it can sell 1,000 units. The more units are produced, the lower the price has to be to sell all of them. Figure 15.10 shows total costs (thick dotted line) and total income (very thick gray line). The difference between those two is total profit (continuous black line). The two thinner lines show what happens if the nonsensical assumption of rising average variable costs is discarded. Then total production costs (thin dashed line) are more or less linear and the profit peak (thin continuous line) occurs later (i.e., at a higher level of production).

Supposedly, the situation changes drastically if there are many producers of the exact same good. Economist assume that in typical markets there will be very many producers, and that, because of that, none of them can influence the total supply or

---

21 W.J. Eiteman and G.E. Guthrie, "The Shape of the Average Cost Curve," *American Economic Review* 42, no. 5 (1952): 832–38.

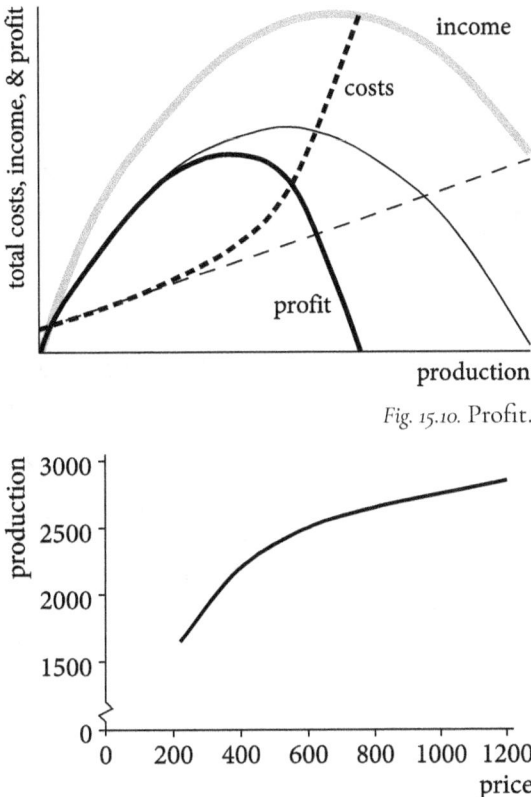

Fig. 15.10. Profit.

Fig. 15.11. Supply curve for a single producer.

price. All of them, therefore, have to accept the market price, because if one of them would sell above the market price, it would lose all its customers to its competitors and consequently, go bankrupt. And if it would sell below the market price it would decrease its own profits. (There's something very fishy about this, but we will get to that soon.) If the production cost curves for ramen would be like figure 15.9 with the y-axis (i.e., costs per bowl) ranging from 0 to 1,000 and the x-axis (production) from 0 to 4,000, then the maximum profits a producer can reach can be calculated for every price level. Figure 15.11 shows these maximum profits. This is the supply curve for an individual producer. If the market price is 600, the producer can reach the maximum profit by producing and selling 2,458 units. The supply curve starts at a price of 230. Below that price, the producer cannot make a profit at any production level.

To derive this supply curve, it is essential to assume that the producer can sell everything it makes because that is what calculated income depends on. This assumption is defended in the same way as the assumption that individual producers cannot influence price or total supply: there are so many producers in the market that the production of each of them is just a drop in the ocean of total supply, and therefore, every firm can sell everything without influencing prices or total supply. This assumption is absurd from a mathematical point of view, but we'll get to that shortly.

The total supply is simply the sum total of individual supply curves of all producers in the market, which obviously implies that total supply at each price level depends on the number of producers. In fact, given that it is assumed that all pro-

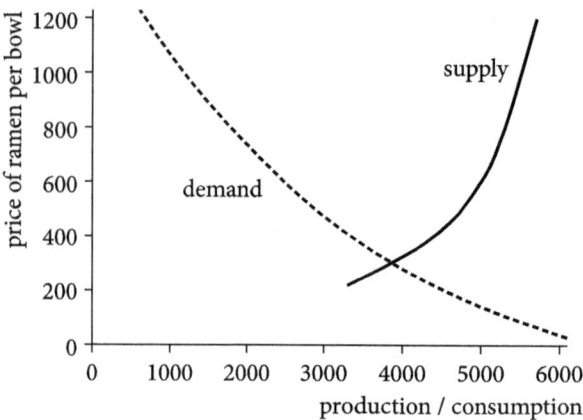

Fig. 15.12. Supply and demand curves (2).

ducers are identical, the total supply at each price level is just the individual supply multiplied by the number of producers. Hence, the total supply curve for a market with 10 producers would look exactly like figure 15.11, but with one zero added to each number on the *y*-axis.

If the total supply curve is added to figure 15.8, which showed the demand curve, then the result is figure 15.12 (but note that the axes in figure 15.12, relative to 15.11, are switched). The point where the two lines cross is where the market is in equilibrium. At that price level all units produced will indeed be sold. According to the figure, slightly less than 4,000 units will be produced and sold at a price of 327 each.

What the figure does not show is the number of producers in this market. That number is 2. If there would be 3 producers, then the two lines would not cross, because the three of them would together produce almost 5,000 units, which would reduce the market price to well below the minimum they need to cover their costs.

Recall that there were supposed to be many producers in this market. Two is not very many. This is an obvious problem for the theory indeed, but there is an easy way to address this problem, just lower fixed costs. If fixed costs are extremely low, then even small production volumes relative to the market are profitable and there is room for very many producers. Unfortunately, for the vast majority of industries, the fixed costs are much larger (rather than smaller) than in the example thus far, so we would have to, again, sacrifice realism to save the theory.

The assumption, then, that there are very many producers is not a plausible assumption in most industries. (And keep in mind that they must be producers of the *exact* same commodity.) But the derivation of the total supply curve depended on some other assumptions as well: because of the large number of producers, none of them can influence price or total supply, and rising average variable costs of production apply. The importance of the latter assumption cannot be overstated. If it is assumed that a producer can sell whatever it produces, then there is a maximum profit only if average production costs rise and at some point overtake income. If average production costs flatten out — as they do in reality; see above — then profits keep rising with production. And if there are no maximum profit levels at various price levels, then there is no supply curve. Then, regardless of the price level and still under the assumption that all production is sold, the profit-maximizing producer sets its production level at *infinite*. This is obviously absurd.

Furthermore, even if there are very many producers, it is mathematically impossible that a change in production level of one of them without compensation by the others would not affect total supply and price. Even if there are 100 producers, and one of them increases its production only slightly, that changes total supply by a tiny little bit, and thereby price by a tiny little bit, and that tiny little bit affects everyone in the market. Economists argue that these "tiny little bits" are in fact so tiny that they can be ignored, but that is a rather dubious claim (and mathematical nonsense), especially if it is taken into consideration that in most markets there will not be very many producers.

Given the model we have now it is rather easy to simulate the effect a single producer could have on the market. Let's assume that in this market somehow a situation has evolved in which there are 10 producers, each making 250 units (2,500 total) and selling them for 585 per unit, which is the price level at which all 2,500 units will be sold according to the demand curve. All 10 of them make a rather modest profit of 8,850 (or 8,710 if rising average variable costs are assumed). Now, if one of them would suddenly decide to quadruple its production, then total supply would rise from 2,500 to 3,250, which would reduce the price to 458. The firm that raised its production now makes a profit of 208,000 (or 203,000 if rising average variable costs are assumed), but the other 9 firms (that did not change their production level but that are affected by the same change in price) now *lose* approximately 23,000 each. (And even a much smaller production increase would increase profits of that firm, while reducing profits of all others.) Hence, a perfectly rational and omniscient, profit-maximizing firm would raise its production to put all of its competitors out of business and then establish a monopoly in which it could have maximum profits. But because, supposedly, all firms in the market are perfectly rational, omniscient, and profit-maximizing, they will all try to do that, leading to massive overproduction, a collapse of the price, and all of them going bankrupt. Except, of course, if they all predict that consequence as well.

That's not what happens, however, and the main, but not only, reason for that is that production costs work a little bit differently; or actually, not a *little* bit. Variable costs are more or less flat, but fixed costs are not as "fixed" as they are supposed to be either. So-called fixed costs are the costs of buildings, machinery, and so forth needed for a certain maximum production level, that is, fixed costs are related to a certain production capacity. If a producer runs at 100 percent capacity, it produces the maximum number of units that can be made with the buildings, machinery, and so forth available. There is no point in adding more labor if you are at 100 percent capacity because those extra workers would just stand by and watch.[22] And there is no point in trying to put more resources or inputs in the machines if those are already at 100 percent capacity either — you cannot make a machine run faster than its maximum speed. Typically, fixed costs are very high and are not earned back until a producer is well over 50 percent capacity, and it may be much closer to maximum capacity, and because of that, the vast majority of firms run at capacities between 80 percent and 100 percent. If you are already close to 100 percent capacity, then

---

22 Recall that it is assumed that variable costs rise with the level of production because if one tries to produce more units at the same fixed costs, more labor or other variable cost factors are needed. This effectively means adding more labor (etc.) to a machine or process that already runs at (close to) full capacity, which is useless. This just is not how production works and it is a mystery to me how mainstream economics can seriously believe that their conception of production costs makes sense.

a production expansion is possible only by spending "fixed costs" to open another production line, which also would have to run at close-to-full capacity immediately to be profitable. That means that increasing production requires a large investment, which can be earned back only if the full jump in production can be profitably sold. Profit levels are generally insufficient to make such investments, and banks and investors are only willing to lend the money if they are sufficiently confident that the production expansion will pay off (or even not at all; see the section "Playing with FIRE" below).

There are various other complexities and complications, but those matter little right now. The important thing is that every assumption that underlies the derivation of a supply curve has been shown to be false. Production curves are not even remotely similar to what economists imagine them to be. There is not enough room for many producers in most markets. And even if there would be many producers, the actions by any one of them would affect total supply and price. The implication is that there is no way to derive supply from price, and therefore, that there is no such thing as a supply curve. But let us ignore all of that and move on.

So here we are. We have consistently ignored reality by making absurd assumptions, by confusing small amounts with zero (in the derivation of the supply curve), and by making one invalid step after the other (in the step-wise derivation of the demand curve, especially),[23] but it has paid off: we now have our two curves. So, what can we do with them? *Nothing*, seems to be the obvious answer, as these curves have nothing to do with reality, but economists see things a bit differently.

Faced with criticism like the foregoing, many economists would protest and claim that their "science" is really much more sophisticated than the sketch I'm providing here, which to some extent is true. However, as David Orrell pointed out, "what counts is less what economists say — they are skilled at deflecting criticism, and have plenty of practice — than what kinds of calculations they actually perform."[24] Economists might accept that some of their assumptions are false and point out that there are sophisticated theories and models taking this into account, but in practice, all of their calculations and all of their predictions and recommendations remain based on the same problematic assumptions. Hence, even if the problem is recognized, that recognition is mere empty rhetoric and does not lead to any significant change. More often the problem is brushed aside. It does not matter that all of the assumptions that the theory is based on are false because all scientific theories are based on false assumptions, the argument goes, and all that matters is whether the resulting theory is a useful tool. This is really mainstream economics' last line of defense, and it fails as miserably as everything that came before.

A physicist might assume that friction does not matter when predicting the effects of gravity on a cannon ball. In that case, she is making two kinds of assumptions at once. First, she restricts her theory to cannon balls and similar objects. And second, she assumes that for those objects the effects of friction are negligible. Economists make similar assumptions, but what they do not seem to realize is that those assumptions imply that its theories only apply to perfectly rational, perfectly informed, and perfectly selfish, profit-utility-maximizing beings (in the same way

---

23 Presumably, you have noticed the tally marks in the margins. They count variants of the phrase "but let us ignore that and move on." The tally mark on this page shows that reality had to be ignored in order to accept a bunch of absurd assumptions five times to get to the point where we are now.
24 David Orrell, *Economyths: Ten Ways Economics Gets It Wrong* (Ontario: John Wiley, 2010), 6.

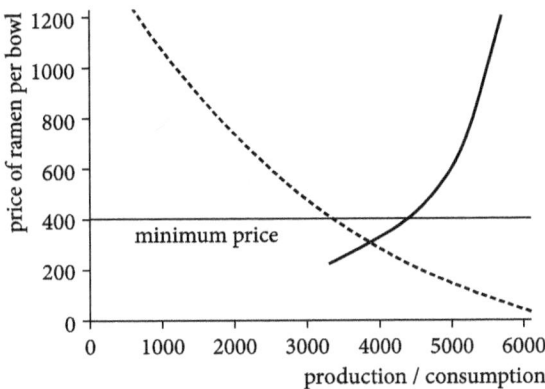

Fig. 15.13. Effects of a minimum price.

that the physicist's theory is restricted to cannon balls), and that for such beings certain effects can be ignored (like friction for cannon balls). But perfectly rational, perfectly informed, and perfectly selfish, profit-utility-maximizing beings do not exist (while cannon balls do), and economists thus restrict the domain of their theories to *nothing* — their theories have no application.[25]

Whether mainstream economic theories are useful is debatable as well. They are not useful to understand how an economy works because they assume things that do not and cannot exist in a real economy, such as a supply curve. And neither are they useful as tools for prediction, as the predictions of mainstream economists are consistently wrong. For example, the consensus among mainstream economists just a few months before the Great Recession of 2007 to 2009 erupted was that there would be continuous economic growth and no more crises. Economic theories may be "useful" in another way, but let us return to our question first: what can we do with these theories? What can we do with our fictitious supply and demand curves?

Rather neat stuff, supposedly. We can "prove," for example, that the market is always right and that governments can only get it wrong. Here is how that is supposed to work. Suppose that the government decides that ramen shops need to be supported and towards that end implements a minimum price for ramen of 400 yen per bowl. If the supply and demand curves in the previous figure apply to the ramen market, then we can add a third line to that figure showing this minimum price, as in figure 15.13. The total supply is where that line crosses the supply curve: 4370 bowls of ramen. The total demand is where the minimum price line crosses the demand curve: 3600 bowls of ramen. Hence, we now have an overproduction of 770 bowls (if those extra bowls are actually produced). Consumers have to pay more for their ramen than before and are thus unhappy. The two producers see their profits rise from 183 thousand to 306 thousand each and are very pleased. But because there are very many more consumers than producers, overall welfare decreases. The same applies to virtually any other kind of government interference in the market: whatever the government does, it will decrease overall welfare. By treating labor as a commodity,

---

[25] There are other major disanalogies between abstraction in economics and abstraction in physics, as I pointed out in *The Hegemony of Psychopathy* (Earth: punctum books, 2017), 46ff. See also the section "Ideal Theory, Utopia, and Ideology" in chapter 16.

specialization and trade		no		yes	
		A	B	A	B
labor	corn	10	10	6	14
	cars	10	10	14	6
production	corn	40	45	24	63
	cars	40	35	56	21
trade	corn			17	−17
	cars			−15	15
consumption	corn	40	45	41	46
	cars	40	35	41	36
	total	80	80	82	82

Table 15.1. The supposed benefits of free trade.

for example, it can be shown in the same way that a minimum wage increases unemployment. And so forth.

All of this is nonsense, of course. It depends on fictitious supply and demand curves that bear little if any resemblance to reality. But this also reveals why these fictitious curves are so pervasive anyway: they serve an ideological agenda. They serve a pro-market and anti-government agenda that favors deregulation and small governments. They serve an agenda that benefits the financial sector (FIRE; see below) and large corporations and that harms almost everyone else. It is in this sense — and only in this sense — that mainstream economic theories are "useful": they are useful to serve the interests of the global financial and industrial elite, the Transnational Capitalist Class.[26]

Free Trade Ideology

Free market ideology often comes together with free trade ideology. According to conventional "wisdom" free trade leads to prosperity. There are various more or less sophisticated theories making this claim, but they all go back to David Ricardo's theory of "comparative advantage."[27] There is a fundamental problem with that theory, as was shown by Frank Graham in 1923, but unfortunately, that problem tends to be ignored.[28]

Assume a world with two countries, A and B, and two commodities, corn and cars. Both country A and country B produce corn and cars, and both have a labor force of 20 "units." These units might be 10,000 workers or 1 million work hours — this does not matter. In both countries, half the labor force produces corn and the other half

---

26 Leslie Sklair, *The Transnational Capitalist Class* (New York: Wiley, 2000), and William Robinson, *Global Capitalism and the Crisis of Humanity,* new edn. (Cambridge: Cambridge University Press, 2014). See also the section "Ideology" in chapter 4.
27 David Ricardo, *On the Principles of Political Economy and Taxation* (London: Murray, 1817).
28 Frank Graham, "Some Aspects of Protection Further Considered," *The Quarterly Journal of Economics* 37, no. 2 (1923): 199–227.

produces cars. All of the production is consumed at home; there is no trade between A and B, and there are no other countries and no other commodities. There is one important difference between countries A and B, and that is that in country A, 10 units of labor produce 40 units of corn, and 10 units of labor produce 40 units of cars; while in country B, 10 units of labor produce 45 units of corn, and 10 units of labor produce 35 units of cars. As in the case of labor, it does not matter what exactly these "units" stand for. For convenience, I will omit the word "unit" in the following and will just write "cars" and "corn" rather than "units of cars" and "units of corn."

Country B is slightly better at producing corn, while country A is slightly better at producing cars; that is, country B has a *comparative advantage* in corn and country A has a comparative advantage in cars. Ricardo showed that in such a situation both countries will benefit from specialization and trade. (As mentioned, there is something wrong with his argument, but we will turn to that below.)

If in country A 14 units of labor produce cars and 6 produce corn, and country B does the opposite, then the total production of cars and corn increases, and if the two countries trade their surpluses then both will get richer. Table 15.1 shows why this is supposedly the case.

Productivity is assumed to be unchanged. In country A, each unit of labor produces 4 units of a commodity. So, if 10 units of labor produce 40 corn, then 6 produce 24 corn. The ratios are slightly different for country B — productivity of corn there is 4.5 units per unit of labor and that of cars 3.5. Consequently, in B 6 labor produces 21 cars after specialization. The total world production of corn is 87 units (up from 85) and that of cars is 77 units (up from 75). The ratio of corn to car production is approximately 1.1, and if the two commodities are traded, one would expect them to be traded at approximately that ratio. If the two countries trade 15 cars for 17 corn (according to the approximately 1.1 ratio) then, as shown in the table, country A ends up with 41 corn and 41 cars (up from 40 and 40), and country B ends up with 46 corn and 36 cars (up from 45 and 35). Consequently, both countries benefit from specialization and trade indeed. Free trade makes everyone richer. Or does it?

It should, perhaps, be noted here that the model thus far assumes specialization *followed* by free trade, but that this order is by no means necessary. Rather, free trade may lead to specialization because if country A and B open up their borders without prior specialization, then the more expensive cars and cheaper corn from country B will effectively force that country to specialize in corn, while the reverse applies to country A.

This is not what is wrong with Ricardo's model, however. Rather, the problem is that the standard model assumes that productivity is constant, while Ricardo was actually well aware that it is not. Elsewhere Ricardo argued that farmers always use the most fertile land first and that if they are for some reason forced to expand and make use of less fertile land, then productivity declines. This is nowadays usually called "diminishing returns to scale." The opposite effect, called "increasing returns to scale" also occurs: it requires less labor per car to produce 1,000 cars than to produce only one car. This is the reason why most commodities are mass-produced.

Agriculture, fishing, mining, and several other mostly primary industries are characterized by diminishing returns. The best land, best fishing waters, best ore layers, and so forth are always used first, and expansion to lesser land, lesser waters, and lesser ore layers will reduce the overall productivity. Conversely, reducing production will generally increase productivity because the least productive land, waters, and ore layers will be taken out of production first.

increasing/diminishing returns		no		yes	
		A	B	A	B
labor	corn	6	14	6	14
	cars	14	6	14	6
production	corn	24	63	27	58
	cars	56	21	61	18
trade	corn	17	–17	16	–16
	cars	–15	15	–15	15
consumption	corn	41	46	43	42
	cars	41	36	46	33
	total	82	82	89	75

Table 15.2. The effect of increasing/diminishing returns.

Manufacturing industry, on the other hand, is characterized by increasing returns. Mass producing things is almost always cheaper in manufacturing. The extreme case is probably software: the first copy of a new computer program or application costs a lot to produce, but producing additional copies costs almost nothing. In case of national economies rather than single factories, increasing returns are a bit more complicated and are mostly driven by feedback loops between industry, supply chains, education, and spill-overs.

What Frank Graham showed is that these effects need to be taken into account when modeling the effects of free trade. If country A specializes in cars, then its productivity in cars will increase because car production has increasing returns. And its productivity in corn production will also increase because corn production, as an agricultural sector, has diminishing returns, and therefore focusing production and concentrating on the most fertile land increases the average productivity. Hence, county A will not produce 24 corn (with 6 labor) and 56 cars (with 14 labor) as suggested above, but 27 corn and 61 cars, for example. If country B specializes in corn, then its productivity in corn will decrease because corn production has diminishing returns, and its productivity in cars will also decrease because car production has increasing returns. Hence, country B will not produce 63 corn (with 14 labor) and 21 cars (with 6 labor) as above, but 58 corn and 18 cars, for example.[29] Table 15.2 compares these numbers with those in the previous, Ricardian example.

The ratio of total world production of corn and cars in this scenario (85/79) is still close to 1.1, but a little bit lower than before, and the two countries could trade 15 cars for 16 corn. The result is that country A ends up with 43 corn and 46 cars (up from 40 and 40) or a total of 89 units of consumed commodities (up from 80), and country B ends up with 42 corn and 33 cars (down from 45 and 35) or a total of 75 units of consumed commodities (down from 80). In other words, while country A

---

[29] Increasing and diminishing returns are here modeled as $L^{1+R} \times F$ (rounded to the nearest integer) in which L is units of labor, R is –0.25 for corn and 0.25 for cars, and F is the value that results in the formula returning the same numbers as in the first example in case of a 10/10 division of labor.

benefits from specialization and trade, country B does not. On the contrary, country B gets poorer rather than richer.

Different numbers lead to the same conclusion: if one country specializes in commodities with increasing returns, and another country specializes in commodities with diminishing returns, then the first country gets richer and the second gets poorer. Of course, there are two other possible combinations. If both countries specialize in commodities with increasing returns, then both countries will benefit from specialization and trade.[30] If both countries specialize in commodities with diminishing returns, then, unless specialization is extreme, positive and negative effects more or less cancel each other out, and the effects on the two economies are negligible.[31]

The conclusion from all of this is obvious: a country should not open to free trade before it has the capability of specializing in an industry (or preferably in multiple industries!) with increasing returns, because specializing in diminishing returns industries will make it poorer rather than richer. This is hardly a new insight. In fact, it was well known to Mercantilist economists and related schools of thought, such as National System economics and the German Historical school, from the sixteenth century onward. Ricardo's argument was intended to prove the Mercantilists wrong. But they were not wrong, or at least not in this respect.

That the Mercantilist emphasis on building up a competitive industry before opening up to trade works is also shown by economic history. Under the influence of variants of Mercantilist economics, Great Britain closed its borders to trade and built up its own manufacturing industry. Only after British manufacturing had grown to become sufficiently large and competitive did trade policy change and did the government promote mostly free trade. Significantly, Adam Smith and David Ricardo — two of the most influential enemies of Mercantilism and defenders of free trade — were British economists living and working in this transitional period from Mercantilist protectionism to free trade ideology. That they became so influential is largely because Great Britain's economy was then sufficiently developed to profit from free trade. In other words, Smith's and Ricardo's ideas were useful to the economic elite to "scientifically" defend their material interests. The United States, under the influence of Friedrich List's and Alexander Hamilton's National System economics, which was closely related to Mercantilism, followed a similar path. Protectionism reigned until a sufficiently competitive manufacturing industry had established itself, after which free trade ideology was adopted.

In Ricardo's original example, the two countries were England and Portugal (rather than A and B), and trade between those two in the commodities of his example was almost free (i.e., there were low tariffs). The results were disastrous for Portugal because it killed off Portugal's small manufacturing industry, while it gave an economic boost to England. In other words, in actual, historical practice, Ricardo's example followed the third scenario, and free trade made Portugal poorer.

When Great Britain took control of India, it destroyed Indian manufacturing industry and forced India to focus on much more primitive diminishing return industries. The products thereof where then transported to Great Britain, where they

---

30 For example, if corn would have the same increasing returns as cars, both countries would increase their total consumption to 84 or 85 units.
31 But if the two countries have 3/17 divisions of labor, rather than 6/14 as in the above examples, then the negative effects are stronger, and both countries get poorer.

were the inputs for England's burgeoning manufacturing industry, which sold some of its products back to India, products that Indians used to make themselves. While England benefited greatly from this arrangement, India, being forced to give up what little manufacturing industry it had, involuntarily steered a course for poverty and underdevelopment. Other colonial powers followed the British lead and forced their colonies to focus on diminishing return industries such as agriculture and mining, and the International Monetary Fund (IMF) and World Bank continue this policy until this day. The motivation has changed, however. While colonial powers denied their colonies a manufacturing industry for entirely selfish, Mercantilist reasons, the IMF and World Bank enforce free trade and government austerity on the developing world because they believe in the mainstream economic dogma that free trade makes everyone richer.

The effects are the same; the former colonies — now "developing countries" — are not allowed to actually develop. They are effectively forced to be like country B in the third example above (or even to be extreme variants thereof, committing their full labor force to the equivalents of corn), while the rich, industrialized countries are more like country A. And as in that example, the rich countries benefit from free trade while the poor countries do not. If colonialism is defined by denying the colonies a manufacturing industry and independent economic policy, then the world-order is now more colonial than ever. The hypocrisy is stunning. The West does not allow the "developing world" to use the exact same policies that they used to get rich themselves.[32]

According to Ricardo's pseudo-scientific theory, everyone benefits from free trade. This idea became a dogma of mainstream economists and their political allies (e.g., centrists, neoliberals, and many other liberals and conservatives). But the dogma is false, and this has been shown in actual practice over and over again. In the countries where IMF and World Bank took over after the fall of "communism," for example, de-industrialization lead to economic decline and poverty. In the European Union, similar things happened, albeit on a slightly less devastating scale. Dictated by Germany mostly, neoliberal free trade ideology reigned, and continues to reign, and countries were and are forced to specialize in their comparative advantages, either directly or by "the market." For Germany, with its strong and advanced manufacturing industry, this worked out great. For Southern Europe, not so much. Spain, Portugal, Italy, and Greece de-industrialized, and their governments — having their hands tied behind their back by EU-enforced austerity and free trade rules including restrictions on subsidies and other kinds of interference with the economy — could not do anything about it.[33]

The term "ideology" is used with at least two different meanings. It can refer to a more or less coherent set of beliefs about how society should be organized and what the scope and aims of government should be. "Ideology" in this sense is often called "political ideology." And it can refer to the set of values and beliefs adhered to and defended by a social class — in the broadest sense of "class" — and that serves the

---

32 For a much more thorough and detailed account of the topic addressed in this and the surrounding paragraphs, see Ha-Joon Chang, *Kicking Away the Ladder* (London: Anthem, 2002); *Bad Samaritans: Rich Nations, Poor Policies, and the Threat to the Developing World* (London: Random House Business, 2007); and Erik Reinert, *How Rich Countries Got Rich... and Why Poor Countries Stay Poor* (London: Constable, 2007).

33 Servaas Storm and C.W.M. Naastepad, "Europe's Hunger Games: Income Distribution, Cost Competitiveness and Crisis," *Cambridge Journal of Economics* 39, no. 3 (2015): 959–86.

interests of that class. This second notion of ideology was discussed before in chapters 3 and 4.[34] Usually, the unqualified term "ideology" (in the second sense) refers to the values and beliefs that serve the interests of the socio-economic or political elite or "ruling class." Free trade ideology and free market ideology are ideology in both senses of the term, but it is the second sense that is most important.

In the third example above, country A benefits from free trade, while country B gets poorer. This is because country A focuses on the production of cars and country B focuses on the production of corn. In other words, the industrialized country benefits from free trade, while the agricultural country does not. It works the same way in the real world. If all the countries involved in free trade would be industrialized countries, then — assuming that the model is right — they would all benefit from free trade, but countries that have no competitive manufacturing industries and that are forced to focus on sectors with diminishing returns do not. In other words, free trade makes rich countries even richer and poor countries even poorer. The interests that are being served by free trade ideology are the interests of rich countries and particularly of the rich and powerful in those countries, the Transnational Capitalist Class. That is the very definition of ideology.

As is the case with most ideologies, not everyone adheres to free trade ideology. While the insight that a manufacturing industry with increasing returns is essential for economic prosperity seems to be forgotten by most late-twentieth and twenty-first-century economists, it is not completely forgotten by politicians and by the general public, much to the chagrin of mainstream economists. Many governments that officially adhere to free trade ideology simultaneously use various policies to protect infant industries and other sectors of the national industry that politicians and governments consider vital to national interests, except when they are not allowed to by international agreements, the World Bank, or the IMF.

According to Bryan Caplan, most citizens of democratic countries have "systematically biased beliefs about economics," that is, most citizens favor Mercantilist or Mercantilist-like economic policies rather than the policies prescribed by mainstream economics.[35] Because Caplan uncritically subscribes to mainstream economic dogma, his conclusion is that the public is ignorant and wrong or "systematically biased." However, given that mainstream economics is completely and disastrously wrong about the effects of free trade and Mercantilism is at least partially right, it turns out that the general public actually favors more sensible economic policies than professional economists do. Ha-Joon Chang also argued that you do not need economists to have sensible economic policies.[36] It turns out that he is right.

Jason Brennan, who we have met before as a defender of capitalism, builds on Caplan's flawed analysis to argue against democracy and for "epistocracy," a political system in which only the most knowledgeable have the right to vote or otherwise influence policy.[37] Caplan's and Brennan's books fit in a long tradition of mainstream economists arguing against democracy, partially because it is not enough like a market for their preferences and partially because it is "irrational" by their standards. Like Caplan, Brennan uncritically accepts mainstream economics, and completely

---

34 See the section "Uchiyama Gudō and Early Buddhist Socialism" in chapter 3 and especially the section "Ideology" in chapter 4.
35 Bryan Caplan, *The Myth of the Rational Voter: Why Democracies Choose Bad Policies* (Princeton: Princeton University Press, 2006).
36 Ha-Joon Chang, *23 Things They Don't Tell You About Capitalism* (London: Penguin, 2010).
37 Jason Brennan, *Against Democracy* (Princeton: Princeton University Press, 2016).

ignores the fact that the people he considers most "knowledgeable" are actually completely wrong. More importantly, he also ignores that something very much like the system he prefers is already in effect.

As shown by Wolfgang Streeck and others, since neoliberalism took over in the 1970s,[38] political power over many aspects of the economy has gradually been transferred from parliaments (and thus indirectly from the public) to institutes outside democratic control.[39] "Independent" central banks were the keystone in this process, but international agreements and various other legal and institutional changes also took away more and more power from parliaments to implement economic policy. In the current situation, there are very few, if any, countries in which the parliament has any significant power left to make or change economic policy. Economic policy has been transferred to institutes outside democratic control, institutes controlled by mainstream economists, neoliberals, and other believers in the pseudo-scientific dogmas of free markets and free trade. In other words, when it comes to economic policy, something much like Brennan's vision has already been realized.

Unfortunately, the results have been disastrous. If the public favors Mercantilist policies indeed, then they are more knowledgeable about sensible economic policy — perhaps because they are less influenced by economic ideology — than those who are supposed to be, and a more democratic approach to economic policy would have resulted in a very different world with less poverty and less economic disaster (and perhaps, with less environmental disaster as well).

The consequence of the gradual retraction of the economy from democratic control is that free trade ideology has become virtually untouchable. It has been embedded in institutions on which politicians and citizens have hardly any influence, and it is defended by layers of ideologically motivated obfuscation and pseudo-science that are continuously reinforced by mainstream economics (which works more like a religious sect than like a science[40]) and the perverted "common sense" they have managed to create.

Playing with FIRE

The power base of mainstream economics and neoliberal capitalist ideology is the financial industry and the institutions it has infiltrated. In *Giants*, Peter Phillips names the 389 most powerful people in global capitalism, mostly white men.[41] A significant number of them work for, or have close ties with Goldman Sachs and other investment banks. During the Great Recession, Matt Taibbi wrote about Goldman Sachs that "[t]he world's most powerful investment bank is a great vampire squid wrapped around the face of humanity, relentlessly jamming its blood funnel into anything that smells like money."[42] The statement is rather unfair to vampire squids,

---

38 The term "neoliberalism" refers to the kind of capitalism as ideology and system that became dominant from the 1970 onward. It differs from other earlier forms of capitalism in its more fundamentalist adherence to free market and free trade ideology.
39 Wolfgang Streeck, *How Will Capitalism End?: Essays on a Failing System* (London: Verso, 2016).
40 On mainstream economics as a religion, see, for example, Robert Nelson, *Economics as Religion: From Samuelson to Chicago and Beyond,* rev. edn. (University Park: Penn State University Press, 2014), and John Rapley, *Twilight of the Money Gods: Economics as Religion and How It All Went Wrong* (London: Simon & Schuster, 2017).
41 Peter Phillips, *Giants: The Global Power Elite* (New York: Seven Stories, 2018).
42 Matt Taibbi, "The Great American Bubble Machine," *Rolling Stone,* April 5, 2010, https://www.rollingstone.com/politics/politics-news/the-great-american-bubble-machine-195229/.

but aside from that detail, the characterization is quite appropriate and, moreover, equally applicable to the finance, insurance, and real estate industry — usually abbreviated FIRE — as a whole.

In *Killing the Host,* Michael Hudson describes FIRE as parasitic. He writes that "instead of creating a mutually beneficial symbiosis with the economy of production and consumption, today's financial parasitism siphons off income needed to invest and grow."[43] To understand FIRE's parasitic nature it needs to be separated from other industries in a four-sector model of the economy. Between all of these four sectors there are flows of money in both directions, as shown in figure 15.14.

The term "industry" in this figure refers to all other industries — manufacturing, agriculture, mining, trade, and so forth — hence, everything that is not covered by FIRE, households, and the state. Separating FIRE from industry, or "other industries," in this way is somewhat uncommon in mainstream, *neo*classical economics for reasons that will be explained below, but was more or less standard in *classical* economics, although the labels differed. The classical distinction was between production (here "industry") and rent extraction, which is now mainly (but not exclusively) the domain of FIRE.

"Rent" is a key term here. As a colloquial term it refers to the (usually periodic) payments owed to the owner of some property one rents, such as house rent, but the term has a different, albeit related, meaning in classical economics. In that context rent is price minus value. Or in other words, rent is income that has no counterpart in necessary production costs. The most common kind of rent discussed by classical economists such as Adam Smith was land rent, which is similar to house rent. Landlords own soil or buildings which farmers and others rent. The landlord's costs for providing that soil or building, and thus its value,[44] are negligible or even zero. Consequently, the landlord's income consists almost entirely of rent. Other kinds of rent are monopoly rents, interests on loans, and patents, for example. If a producer has a monopoly on some good in a market and uses this to sell for a price well above the production costs of that good, then the difference is rent. Typically, rent is income that is generated just by ownership or control of something (such as real estate, money, economic rights, a market, and so forth) rather than by producing something.

Adam Smith and other classical economists considered rent extraction parasitic.[45] Rent extraction does not contribute to the economy but rather damages it, and a healthy economy must be protected from the economic damage done by rent extraction. For them, a "free market" was a market that is free from excessive rents, such as monopoly rents, but neoclassical economists have corrupted this idea and changed the concept of a free market into one in which rentiers (i.e., owners or controllers of rent-producing privileges) are free to extract as much rent as they want, effectively creating a "toll-booth economy."

As mentioned, the arrows in figure 15.14 represent flows of money. The dark gray, dashed arrows represent payments by FIRE, industry, and households to the state. These are taxes mainly, but also include much smaller payments for specific

---

43 Michael Hudson, *Killing the Host: How Financial Parasites and Debt Bondage Destroy the Global Economy* (Dresden: Islet, 2015), 15.
44 This is its value for classical economists but not for neoclassical economists. For neo-classical economists, value equals price and thus there is no such thing as rent by its classical definition.
45 Most of them did not use that term, however. The main exception is Karl Marx, who on several occasions used terms like "parasitic" to describe usury and other forms of rent extraction.

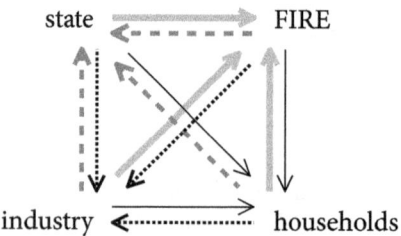

Fig. 15.14. Money flows.

goods and services provided by the state. Thin continuous arrows are payments to households such as salaries and welfare benefits. The arrow from state to households also includes other benefits that the state provides to households such as education, health care, infrastructure, and so forth. Dotted arrows are payments to industry. This is sales income mostly, but it also includes state subsidies, for example, as well as other benefits, such as infrastructure and education, insofar as those apply to industry. The thick, light gray arrows, finally, are payments to the FIRE sector such as interests on loans, insurance premiums, house and land rents, and so forth. Arrows could be added to the figure to represent sector-internal payments — from company to company or from household to household and so forth — but I will ignore those as they are largely irrelevant here.

Ideally, the system as a whole is in balance. That does not mean that the dotted arrow from households to state and the continuous arrow in the opposite direction should represent roughly equal amounts of money, but that for each of the four sectors the sum of the three incoming flows should be roughly equal to the sum of the three outgoing flows, at least in the long term. Unfortunately, the system is not in balance. It almost never is because rents by their nature are mostly extractive: rentiers suck wealth out of the system without giving much if anything back. A few centuries ago, feudal landlords were the main rent extractors. In the modern world FIRE has taken their place. Unless heavy restrictions are in place, incoming money flows are substantially larger in case of FIRE than outgoing flows, which is exactly why most classical economists argued for restrictions on banking and other rent-extracting activities.[46] For this reason, the financial relations between FIRE and the other three sectors deserve some closer attention.

The main money flow between households and FIRE consists of the payment of interests on loans, followed by amortization (paying back loans) and insurance premiums. The main reverse flow consists of insurance benefit payments (which are always delayed as much as possible). There also is a reverse flow of money in the form of salaries to FIRE employees, but aside from money transfers to the managerial elite, this flow is negligible. Moreover, because that managerial elite behaves more like an integral part of the FIRE sector than like a part of the households sector,[47] payments

---

46 Rather unsurprisingly, the main exception were economists like David Ricardo that were closely affiliated with banking.
47 Most of this "household" income of the financial elite is spent in a way that is more typical of the FIRE sector than that of households, that is, it is invested in real estate and other rent-extracting privileges, rather than used for consumption.

to that elite are better thought of as a sector-internal flow than as a flow from FIRE to households.

Payments to FIRE are almost unavoidable for the vast majority of people in industrial societies. Few people wholly own their house — they either rent it or financed its purchase with a mortgage in which case the house is collateral in case of a default, meaning that the bank will become the owner of the house. Consequently, the vast majority of people pay a substantial part of their income to FIRE, and FIRE does not given them anything back for those payments. In case of a rented house, the owner is responsible for maintenance, of course, but typically that represents around 10 percent of the rent paid to the owner. And in the case of a mortgage, the inhabitant of the house gets nothing for her interest payments at all. Hence, these are big one-way flows from households to FIRE, and it should not come as a surprise that FIRE does everything it can to increase these flows. The more mortgages it can "sell," the more money FIRE makes, and if someone lured in with false promises and shiny brochures can no longer satisfy their financial obligations, the bank can always foreclose and sell the house.

The maximum a household can pay in interests and amortization or as rent is whatever is left after daily necessities and other obligations, such as taxes and other debts, are taken care of. The financial sector aims to siphon off that surplus income, and the lower taxes, the more FIRE can siphon off. Market prices for houses and other real estate are determined by this ability to pay. Lowering taxes on real estate, for example, thus increases the prices of real estate because households will have more to spend on their mortgages.[48] But if there is an unexpected rise in other household costs (e.g., food, taxes, other debts) or a fall in household income, then the mortgage becomes a millstone around the debtor's neck. Somewhat similarly, the lower the interest rates, the larger the sum of money that can be borrowed relative to the household's available income, but if interests rise, so do the financial obligations of the debtor, regardless of whether she can actually pay.

In addition to mortgage debts, many households also have credit card debts or personal loans or study debts, as well as various insurances. All of these together assure that there are massive rivers of money flowing from households to the FIRE sector, and very little trickling down in the opposite direction.

The textbook story about the relation between FIRE and industry is that FIRE provides industry with the loans to invest and grow. This is a myth. Investment in facilities, machines, research and development, and so forth is almost always financed out of a company's cash flow or current assets, or by issuing stocks. If companies borrow money from banks it is almost never to invest in new production facilities, but it is either to take over already existing production facilities that are owned by other companies or to buy back stocks. Historically, banks have never played a significant role in productive investment. Business loans were for bridging temporal gaps between expenses and expected income — between sowing and harvesting, for example, or if there is a large distance between the places were goods are bought and were they are sold — and banks remain largely unwilling to lend money for investment in new production. The myth that banks provide the capital needed for growth is nothing but propaganda for banks. It is an attempt to make banks seem beneficial.

---

48 Mortgage-related tax reductions and exemptions have the same effect. By increasing real estate prices, they increase mortgages, and thus the flow of money from households to FIRE. Consequently, such policies are really nothing but state subsidies to FIRE.

In reality they are not. The relation between banks and industry is parasitic rather than beneficial.

One of the ways in which FIRE sucks money out of industry is by forcing companies to buy back stocks. The financial sector "invests" in stocks of asset-rich companies and then forces those companies to sell assets or to borrow money to buy back stocks. Buying back stocks reduces the total number of stocks in that company but does not change the perceived value of the company. Thus, the value of the company *per stock* increases if there are fewer stocks, and therefore, the stock price rises, making stockholders richer.

The ideal scenario for a bank is the following. (1) Buy stocks in some company. (2) Force the company to sell its assets to buy back stocks and to pay large dividends to its stockholders. (And thus to receive increased dividend payments.) (3) After all assets are sold and the company is "asset-stripped," force the company to borrow money to buy back more stocks. (4) Sell stocks for the increased stock price — making a big profit on that price increase in addition to the dividend payments and the profit from the loan to the company for buying back the stocks — and leave the company without much of its prior assets and with a big loan, requiring it to pay interest to the bank out of the cash flow it could have used for investment in production otherwise. This is not the only way in which banks extract money from industry, and it is probably not even the most nefarious, but it nicely illustrates the real relation between FIRE and industry. That relation, again, is parasitic rather than beneficial. As is the case for households, there is a large flow of money to FIRE but merely a trickle in the opposite direction.

The main money flow from FIRE to the state consists of taxes, but FIRE has managed to make most of its activities tax-exempt or subject to very low tax rates. Conversely, money flows from the state to FIRE in the form of interest payments on bonds and loans. And FIRE has been as successful in increasing this money flow as it has been in decreasing its tax payments.

The main taxes that affect FIRE are taxes on property, especially real estate, and on rent. If these are lowered or even abolished then the state needs to find alternative sources of revenue or cut its expenses. In theory, a state could just print some of the money it needs, but in practice that is never an option as FIRE has effectively taken this power out of the hands of states and reserved it for itself. It is now FIRE that creates money, but with a few computer keyboard strokes rather than by printing it.[49] The only source of structural alternative revenue is raising other taxes. The prime candidates for taxes to be raised are taxes on labor and consumption. The effect thereof is to increase the costs of production for industry and the costs of living for households. If households have less to spend due to a tax increase this also affects industry because the less consumers buy, the less industry sells. Consequently, raising taxes on labor and consumption beyond a certain level hurts the economy.

Incidental, rather than structural, alternative revenue can be raised either by borrowing money from FIRE or by selling off state assets, that is, privatization. Either source of revenue is limited, however. Banks will not lend a state infinite amounts of money and states do not have infinite supplies of assets they can sell either. Fur-

---

49 Every time someone takes out a loan, the bank creates money out of thin air because banks are only required to have a tiny percentage of the money they lend. This is the main process of money-creation. The idea that states create money is largely a myth perpetuated by FIRE and its allies to mask the fact that *they* are the ones who are in control of the money supply.

thermore, privatization is rarely an important source of revenue. Privatization is the social and political equivalent of the asset-stripping mentioned above, but is done mainly for ideological reasons. It is motivated by the hegemonic belief that "the market" can run the privatized operations and services more efficiently than the state.[50] This, however, is a false belief, as the "customers" of privatized public transport, mail, and utilities in most countries can testify — privatization almost always raises costs rather than that it reduces them. The main reason for this is that as soon as a business becomes privatized, FIRE starts extracting money from it in the form of interest payments, dividends, and so forth. And because of that, FIRE profits much more from privatization than the state or its citizens (i.e., households). The other and more important source of incidental revenue, borrowing money, also primarily benefits FIRE, but that should be obvious: the more the state borrows, the more interests it has to pay to FIRE.

If a state refuses to tax FIRE or taxes it insufficiently it can raise the financial burden on households and industry instead or increase incidental revenue, but there are limits to both. Sooner or later there is nothing left to privatize, there is insufficient revenue to be able to get more loans, and taxes on labor and consumption become an obstacle to economic growth and, therefore, start generating less rather than more revenue. At that point only the last tool in the toolbox, cutting costs or austerity, remains. But austerity only further hurts the economy by further reducing the money that households and industry can spend and by slowly crippling the infrastructure needed for the economy to function efficiently.[51] Austerity can be very profitable to FIRE, on the other hand, as it may push the state to privatize what was previously never considered as a possible candidate for privatization.

All of this has the combined effect of creating a large flow of money from the state to FIRE and only a trickle from FIRE to the state, but the Great Recession of 2007 to 2009 has revealed that this imbalance is actually even worse. Most of the profits of the FIRE sector are made in activities that are euphemistically called "investment banking" but that really are not investments (or at least not investments in industry or productivity growth in general) and that have fairly little to do with banking in a traditional sense. Investment banking is really a mix of gambling, ponzi schemes, and other deceptions hidden behind layers of obscure terminology and esoteric and often nonsensical mathematics. The main problem with investment banking, however, is that while FIRE takes all the profits, in the Great Recession the state became responsible for the losses. Imagine going to a casino — if you win, the winnings are yours; if you lose, the state covers your losses. That is really what the bank bailouts of the Great Recession were: the state covering the gambling losses of FIRE. And the excuse for that was that otherwise the financial system would collapse and the world economy would go down in flames, but that is an ideologically motivated lie. The rest of the economy — or the real economy — is not dependent on the "financial system." On the contrary, the "financial system" is a parasite sucking money and energy out of it.

---

50 See the section "The Ideology of Supply and Demand" in this chapter.
51 That austerity does not work has been shown again and again, but it is one of many zombie ideas in mainstream economics that, regardless of how often it is killed, just does not seem to die. Trickle-down economics is another example of such a zombie idea. See John Quiggin, *Zombie Economics: How Dead Ideas Still Walk Among Us* (Princeton: Princeton University Press, 2010).

Money flows from industry, states, and households to the finance, insurance, and real estate (FIRE) sectors with little flowing in the opposite directions. But this cannot continue forever. Debts have a tendency to increase (often exponentially), and consequently, interest payments also increase; which would not be a problem if they would increase slower than the inflation rate, but that is almost never the case. The growth of debt is the main but not the only cause of the continuous growth of the river of money flowing toward FIRE. The main secondary cause is "investment" by FIRE of some of its profits in other kinds of rent-producing privileges such as real estate, thus continuously increasing its potential for rent extraction.

At some point, payments to FIRE become so large that industry can no longer invest in productivity growth, households can only afford the bare necessities because much of their income goes straight to FIRE, and the state no longer has sufficient revenue to invest in infrastructure, to stimulate growth, to alleviate poverty, and so forth. At that point, the real economy (i.e., everything but FIRE) can no longer grow. But rent extraction relative to the size of the real economy continues to increase (either due to a further growth of debts, or because of economic contraction due to declining consumption, or both), and consequently, from this point onward, financial obligations to FIRE exceed the ability to pay. Industry no longer has sufficient revenue to pay their workers and suppliers *and* to pay FIRE; and households no longer have sufficient income to buy daily necessities *and* what they owe to FIRE, which further reduces the revenue of industry. This is when the economy collapses. When the sum of debts of households and industry is approximately 150 percent or more of GDP, crisis is almost inevitable,[52] although it can be postponed by the state at considerable costs. Usually the crisis starts a little bit earlier. Already before industry and households owe more to FIRE than they can pay, the growth of FIRE itself starts to slow down because the number of new loans starts to fall. And because FIRE is used to almost exponential growth rates and may even depend on it for its profits, such a slow-down leads to a panic, which spreads to the rest of the economy.

The result of economic collapse or crisis is a very large and growing number of debts that cannot be repaid. The only real solution for that is debt cancellation, either by means of a wave of bankruptcies, as in the Great Depression in the 1920s, or a "debt jubilee," which is a cancellation of some or all debts by the government. A debt jubilee is really only possible if the state owns or controls FIRE, which was the case throughout most of financial history. And consequently, throughout much of that history, debt jubilees were common occurrences. In the Great Recession, bankruptcies in the financial sector were avoided as much a possible by means of cash gifts from the state to FIRE totaling trillions of dollars. Due to that, most of the debts of households, industries, and states to FIRE remained in place. This turned several economies into what Steve Keen calls "debt Zombies."[53]

A debt zombie economy is characterized by economic stagnation because households and industry have no or very little money left after paying FIRE. Without consumption and investment an economy cannot grow, and thus, a debt zombie is kept in limbo at the edge of economic collapse. As long as the state is willing and able to keep the national economy in limbo, mainly by subsidizing FIRE, it can stay there, although it is not impossible that continuing economic stagnation leads to a gradual

---

52 Richard Vague, *A Brief History of Doom: Two Hundred Years of Financial Crises* (Philadelphia: University of Pennsylvania Press, 2019).
53 Steve Keen, *Can We Avoid Another Financial Crisis?* (Cambridge: Polity, 2017).

breakdown of civic society and to destabilizing violence or even revolt. In the short term, stagnation leads to growing inequality, unemployment, and poverty, to a further deterioration of public services and of trust in the government, and to a rise of (usually far-right) populist movements preying on insecurity and fear.

At this point, one might start to wonder: how does FIRE get away with this? The answer is fairly simple: power. FIRE controls much of the economic decision making by means of direct and ideological power. Michael Hudson partially explains this power/control by comparing "investment banking" to parasitism:

> Modern biology provides the basis for a [...] social analogy to financial strategy, by describing the sophisticated strategy that parasites use to control their hosts by disabling their normal defense mechanisms. To be accepted, the parasite must convince the host that no attack is underway. To siphon off a free lunch without triggering resistance, the parasite needs to take control of the host's brain, at first to dull its awareness that an invader has attached itself, and then to make the host believe that the free rider is helping rather than depleting it and is temperate in its demands, only asking for the necessary expenses of providing its services. In that spirit bankers depict their interest charges as a necessary and benevolent part of the economy, providing credit to facilitate production and thus deserving to share in the surplus it helps create.[54]

The main source of FIRE's *direct* power is personal. In most industrialized countries, and probably also in many other countries, the people in charge of economic decision making — ministers of finance, central bank presidents, top bureaucrats, and so forth — all have close links to FIRE. Goldman Sachs has been particularly successful in getting its former managers in top government positions. And many CEOs and business leaders also have close ties to the financial sector. In this way, FIRE directly controls much economic decision making — it is their pawns and associates who make all the important decisions.[55]

Ideological power may be even more important. Ideological power is, as Hudson phrases it, "making the host believe that the free rider is helping rather than depleting it." Ideological power is making the state, industry, and households believe that FIRE is beneficial rather than parasitic, and therefore, that FIRE should not be hindered by regulation or political interference. FIRE has been incredibly successful in this respect. Its main tool of ideological power is mainstream, neoclassical economics, which is ideology (or religion) posing as science. It has chosen to ignore economic reality and to leave debts and the financial sector out of their models. (And in addition to that, their models are incoherent, based on obviously nonsensical assumptions, empirically false, and practically useless, *except as ideological tools*, which is, of course, exactly what they are.[56]) FIRE and mainstream economics have been so successful in spreading their self-serving ideological dogmas that almost everyone believes in them — the "free" press uncritically repeats all the propaganda they produce and politicians of all major parties in all so-called "democracies" are devout

---

54 Hudson, *Killing the Host*, 15–16.
55 As mentioned above, Peter Phillips has done a very thorough job at digging up who exactly are at the top of this pyramid of direct power. See Phillips, *Giants*.
56 See previous sections. It is, by the way, no coincidence that almost all prominent mainstream economists are also on the payroll of FIRE.

believers in the religion of neoclassical economics (and its political arm, neoliberal capitalism).

As mentioned above, classical economists made a distinction between industry and rent-extraction. This distinction underlies the four-sector model, but by refusing to make this distinction and grouping industry and FIRE together, the parasitical nature of FIRE is completely hidden. Similarly, by ignoring the classical distinction between industry and rent-extraction in measuring Gross Domestic Product (GDP), an economy can seem to grow when its productive industry is really deteriorating and it is only the financial sector that grows by preying on the real economy. But such growth is fake growth: it is not the economy that is growing but merely the parasite that is sucking the life out of it.

When a mainstream economist mentions debt and loans, it is always to claim that loans allow companies to invest in new production, which as mentioned above, is a blatant lie — it is propaganda intended to make banks look useful. As mentioned, banks almost never lend money for this kind of investment, and never have. Furthermore, by ignoring debt, the models of mainstream economics cannot predict economic crises. The handful of economists who predicted the Great Recession, for example, were all non-mainstream economists that awarded a key role to debt in their models and theories. All that the models and theories of mainstream economics are "good" for, is, again, "making the host believe that the free rider is helping rather than depleting it."

Part of the solution to the problems sketched in this section is obvious: FIRE should be controlled by the state. As mentioned above, throughout much of financial history — the part of human history during which something like money, loans, and debts existed — the state either directly or indirectly controlled banking. Often it was not the state itself that functioned as bank, but religious institutions (including Buddhist monasteries), but those were usually also ultimately controlled by the state, unless they effectively *were* the state. And consequently, if debts started to weigh too heavily on the economy, the state could cancel them in a debt jubilee. Until fairly recently, important parts of FIRE remained under government control and those that were not were limited by laws and regulations. But FIRE has managed to turn the economic world upside down: it is now FIRE that controls the state instead of the state controlling FIRE, and that is a recipe for economic disaster.

FIRE has no interest in limiting debt and rent extraction. On the contrary, it depends for its profits on continuous growth thereof. That is impossible, of course, leading to crisis or stagnation, at which point through direct and ideological power, FIRE lets the state pick up the bill. Ultimately, it is industry and households who are paying. To avoid economic crisis or stagnation, the sum of private debt (i.e., debts of industry and households) needs to be well below 150 percent of GDP and probably even below 100 percent.[57] Debt and rent extraction cannot grow infinitely and must be restrained. And when debts can no longer be repaid, they must be canceled. The only way to realize this is by bringing banks under state control. Furthermore, state control is also the only way to make banks play their supposed beneficial role: lending money for productive investment.

Nationalizing FIRE is insufficient if other kinds of exploitative rent-extraction are left in place. Private monopolies should be brought under democratic control (i.e., nationalized), patent laws should be revised and limited to short periods, and

---

57 Vague, *A Brief History of Doom*, and Keen, *Can We Avoid Another Financial Crisis?*

to avoid exploitation through ownership of real estate it may be necessary to regulate or even nationalize real estate as well. Of all measures, bringing the financial sector under democratic control (or state control, assuming that the state is at least somewhat democratic) is by far the most important. A free economy — as the classical economists, including Adam Smith, were well aware — is an economy free of excessive rent extraction. Realizing that requires restraining or preferably even nationalizing the finance, insurance, and real estate (FIRE) sector. Private banks cannot be trusted, because their interests and the interests of the rest of the economy — that is, the *real* economy — are diametrically opposed. And given that a large private financial sector is a defining element of capitalism,[58] this means that capitalism must be abolished.

Misery for the Many

The previous sections illustrated how capitalism enriches the rich and impoverishes the poor, while masking that with layers of ideological obfuscation presented as "science." What makes capitalism morally evil, however — at least by the standard developed in previous chapters — is the death and suffering it is responsible for. Some of that death and suffering has already been mentioned or hinted at in the foregoing, but unfortunately, there is much more.

Perhaps, the most fundamental problem for capitalism is economic growth. This problem is closely related to the central role of the financial sector (FIRE). To a large extent, capitalism is funded by means of debt; it *depends* on debt-funded growth. But with debts come interest payments. If some household, company, or state borrows a sum of money x, and needs to pay interests y, then it can only do so if it expects to have $x + y$ at some later date, or in other words, if it expects to have more money later than it has now. If it fails to gather $x + y$ in time, it cannot pay what it owes to FIRE and will go bankrupt. The problem is that this does not apply to a single economic actor, but to very many at the same time, and consequently, all of those together must have more money later than now, which can only be the case if the economy grows (i.e., if there is more money in the economy as a whole later than now). Without economic growth, debtors can no longer pay what they owe to FIRE and go bankrupt.

Since the 1970s there has been a fringe movement within economics advocating "degrowth," that is, reducing the size of mainly Western, industrialized economies to create more sustainable societies. Mainly because of the climate crisis, this movement has become slightly less "fringe" in the last two decades, leading to a significant increase in research on the idea of degrowth and the related but older idea of a steady-state economy, an economy that does not grow. The most important conclusion that can be drawn from that research is that "recession and depression are possible within capitalism; degrowth is probably not."[59] The reason why capitalism and degrowth are incompatible is debt. Without interests a steady-state economy might be possible, but without interests and other kinds of rent-extraction FIRE cannot survive and an economy without FIRE is not a capitalist economy.

---

58 See this chapter's introduction.
59 Giorgos Kallis et al., "Research on Degrowth," *Annual Review of Environment and Resources* 43 (2018): 291–316, at 300.

That capitalism needs economic growth would not be a problem if economic growth would be benign and could continue forever. Mainstream economists believe that it can continue forever, because their models assume that resources are more or less unlimited,[60] and that even if some resource runs out, thanks to human inventiveness an alternative will be found and growth can continue. Thus far, this seems to have worked indeed, but it is worth paying closer attention to the nature and sources of economic growth.

Economic growth is an increase in the GDP of an area, usually a country, and GDP is the sum total of all final goods and services produced in that area measured by their market value. So, economic growth is an increase in production in terms of market value. This implies that if market value is kept constant an economy can grow in two, and only two ways: either by making more people produce things or by making people produce more things per person. The former requires population growth or the entrance of previously non-working groups into the labor force. From an economic point of view (but probably not *only* from an economic point of view), one of the most important inventions of the twentieth century was the washing machine because it allowed women to start working outside the house.[61] Although this made an important contribution to economic growth in the second half of the twentieth century, the second source of economic growth, an increase in "productivity," is by far the most important.

Productivity growth is an increase in the total market value of goods and services produced per producer or worker. Or to put it the other way around, it is producing the same amount of things measured by their market prices with fewer people. In the short term, productivity can increase and decrease for all kinds of reasons. If a product suddenly becomes fashionable and consumers are willing to pay more for it, then the market price of that product rises and its producers, therefore, become more "productive." In the longer term there is really just one source of productivity growth: a substitution of energy for labor. If you own a shoe factory and you want to produce more shoes, then you can either hire more workers or buy some machines to do part of the work. However, running those machines requires energy. That is the main reason why productivity growth is really a substitution of energy for labor.

Almost all historic productivity growth has depended on cheap energy. We burned coal to allow workers to use machines to produce more, and when oil became cheaper, we switched to oil. While there have been and continue to be changes in the sources of energy, one thing has remained the same: to produce more with fewer workers, you need more energy as an input in the production process. Most of that energy comes from fossil fuels. An increasing but comparatively very small part comes from nuclear energy and other alternative sources, but fossil fuels — coal, oil, and gas — remain the dominant sources of energy. Current productivity levels as well as further growth thereof, and thus the current economic state as well as further economic growth, are almost completely dependent on fossil fuels. The world floats on oil. Drain away that oil, and everything runs aground.[62]

---

60 But also because they hide FIRE's destructive role, explained in the previous section, by refusing to distinguish it from productive industry. A consequence thereof is that in the fictional world of mainstream economics — contrary to the real world — FIRE cannot possibly strangle economic growth
61 Chang, *23 Things They Don't Tell You About Capitalism*.
62 The relatively new field of biophysical economics gives up the mainstream-economic assumptions of infinite resources and non-existence of pollution in favor of a more realistic approach. Probably,

The consequences of capitalism's fossil-fuel addiction have unfortunately become blatantly obvious, except perhaps, to mainstream economists. Pollution does not exist in mainstream economic models, but in the real world it certainly does. CO_2 emissions from our fossil fuel use have already warmed up the planet by more than 1°C and even if we stop burning fossil fuels right now, the planet will continue to warm to 1.5 or possibly even 2°C above pre-industrial levels.[63] That may not seem like much, but it is already causing droughts, floods, stronger storms, and all kinds of other mayhem and this will only get worse.[64] How bad it might get is a topic for next chapter,[65] but even the best case scenarios imply hundreds of millions refugees, widespread famine, and a sharp increase in violent conflict over increasingly scarce resources. The mainstream economic assumption that we'll always find a replacement before a resource runs out might be right — perhaps, fusion energy becomes a reality within the next decades[66] — but it will be too late for the very many victims of climate breakdown and its consequences that are dying and suffering right now and in the decades to come.[67]

Climate breakdown is likely to become the biggest disaster caused by capitalism, and even the biggest disaster in the history of mankind, certainly in terms of death and suffering involved; but capitalism's association with disaster, death, and suffering has a much longer history. In the nineteenth century, economic ideology motivated a liberalization of grain markets and grain trade with disastrous consequences. According to Mike Davis, between 30 and 60 million people died in famines in China, India, and Brazil alone, but famines even hit the poor in the heartland of capitalism, Great Britain. He writes that "the route to a Victorian 'new world order' was paved with bodies of the poor,"[68] and that

---

the most important conclusion of that approach is that there really is no alternative to fossil fuels if we want to maintain the present levels of energy consumption. See Charles Hall and Kent Klitgaard, *Energy and the Wealth of Nations: An Introduction to Biophysical Economics,* 2nd edn. (Berlin: Springer, 2018).

63 We're expected to reach 1.5°C around the year 2030 and 2°C in the middle of the 2040s. Wangyang Xu, Veerabhadran Ramanathan, and David Victor, "Global Warming Will Happen Faster than we Think," *Nature* 564 (2018): 30–32.

64 The Intergovernmental Panel on Climate Change (IPCC) published a special report on the disastrous effects of 1.5°C of warming in comparison with the even more disastrous effects of 2°C: IPCC, *Global Warming of 1.5°C* (Geneva: IPCC, 2018).

65 See the section "Mappō" in chapter 16.

66 This is extremely unlikely, unfortunately. Proponents of nuclear fusion tend to claim that we are almost at "break-even," the point at which the system produces more energy than we put into it, but this is not actually true. We are getting closer to Q=1 ("Q" is energy output divided by energy input), but only if you focus on Q of the most central part of the fusion reactor. If you focus on Q of the fusion power plant as a whole, then we are closer to 0.01, and even the most advanced planned reactors are not expected to exceed Q=0.1 (again, for the plant as a whole, rather than just part of the reactor). For nuclear fusion to become economically viable, Q needs to be around 10. (Hall and Klitgaard, *Energy and the Wealth of Nations.* Their notion of EROI is largely analogous to Q.) Given that progress in the field is excruciatingly slow, the probability of jumping from Q=0.1 to Q=10 in the near future is close to zero. And even if we could do it in 20 or 30 years from now (which still seems optimistic), it will take decades more before any significant number of fusion plants could be built and running.

67 On the relation between capitalism and climate breakdown, see also Naomi Klein, *This Changes Everything: Capitalism vs. the Climate* (New York: Simon & Schuster, 2014), and Bill McKibben, *Falter: Has the Human Game Begun to Play Itself Out?* (New York: Henry Holt, 2019).

68 Mike Davis, *Late Victorian Holocausts: El Niño Famines and the Making of the Third World* (London: Verso, 2001), 10.

[m]illions died, not outside the "modern world system," but in the very process of being forcibly incorporated into its economic and political structures. They died in the golden age of Liberal Capitalism.[69]

This, however, was just the beginning. Free market and free trade fundamentalism has caused and exploited disasters ever since, as documented by Naomi Klein and John Rapley among others.[70] From the late 1970s onward the World Bank and IMF forced the developing world to adopt economic policies based on mainstream economic dogma, often with the help of dictatorial, brutally repressive regimes in developing countries themselves. As already explained above,[71] these policies destroyed infant industries and decimated real wages and economic growth. Nowhere in the developing world did capitalist "liberalization" reduce poverty. Countries that did develop quickly, like the East-Asian "tigers," did so mostly because they protected their industries, against economic dogma.

More than 7 million children die each year from poverty, hunger, and preventable diseases. They die in countries that could have seen economic growth, food security, and better medical institutions if it was not for the economic destruction that was forced upon them. Probably not all developing countries could have followed the same path as South Korea, for example, but with more sensible economic policies — like most developing countries had before they were forced to abolish them — most of them would have had industrial growth and economic growth, enabling better health care, better education, better infrastructure, starting a virtuous cycle of growth and development.[72] It's difficult to give an exact number, but it seems a very conservative estimate to say that in such a scenario the yearly number of children dying from poverty, hunger, and preventable diseases would be much less than half of what it is now. And that would imply that capitalism is responsible for the death of at least 100 million children since 1980 alone.[73]

Capitalism does not just kill in the developing world but in rich countries as well. For example, according to a meta-analysis by Sandra Galeo and colleagues, in the year 2000 more than 800,000 Americans died of poverty-related causes.[74] Moreover, capitalism does not just *kill*. In addition to the millions of people that have died because of capitalism, there are many millions more that have survived the suffering brought upon them by that same system and ideology. Additionally, capitalism also promotes suffering indirectly by promoting egocentricity, greed, and cultural psychopathy, and by undermining compassion, care, and trust and thereby destroying

---

69 Ibid., 9.
70 Naomi Klein, *The Shock Doctrine: The Rise of Disaster Capitalism* (New York: Henry Holt, 2007) and Rapley, *Twilight of the Money Gods*.
71 See the section "Free Trade Ideology" in this chapter.
72 Ha-Joon Chang compares the cases of Mozambique and South Korea in *Bad Samaritans*. In the 1960s, both countries has similar levels of wealth and growth. Mozambique was forced to implement policies based on mainstream economic dogma, while South Korea chose a path of rapid industrialization, state involvement in the economy, and protection of domestic industry, against economic dogma. Mozambique saw hardly any growth and is still one of the poorest countries in the world. South Korea is one of the richest.
73 This paragraph, as well as parts of the preceding and following paragraphs, are copied with minor changes from Brons, *The Hegemony of Psychopathy*, 51–53.
74 Sandra Galeo et al., "Estimated Deaths Attributable to Social Factors in the United States," *American Journal of Public Health* 101, no. 8 (2011): 1456–65.

the bonds between people.[75] Capitalism, as Marx and Engels wrote more than 170 years ago, has "left no other bond between man and man than naked (self-)interest,"[76] but humans are social creatures and depend for their well-being on the communities and social networks they are part of.

All that capitalism has to offer — *if it would work* — is material wealth, but human well-being mostly depends on less tangible factors like community, and it actively undermines those. What capitalism promises, wealth, "freedom," and material progress, it only delivers to the few — what it produces in bulk is destruction and misery.

A Cautious Conclusion

That capitalism only offers its supposed advantages to the few and has little else in store but misery for the many does not imply that every aspect of capitalism is equally harmful, or that all of the six items in Hodgson's definition quoted in the beginning of this chapter should be turned into their opposites. Markets are not the panacea libertarians and mainstream economics believe them to be, but that does not mean that there is no place for markets at all, for example — not in the least because the main alternative, socialist-style planning, is unlikely to result in anything approaching efficiency in large and complex economies.[77] However, this latter point should not be taken to imply that there is no place for economic planning at all either. Perhaps, there is a middle path, and perhaps, that middle path is preferable to either extreme. At least, historical evidence suggests that mixed economies combining capitalist and non-capitalist elements have been more successful in many relevant respects.[78]

Similarly, that individual rights to own, buy, and sell private property may have to be limited in certain additional ways,[79] does not mean that private property has to be abolished altogether. And that it is almost certainly necessary to bring some means of production under democratic control, does not mean that they should *all* be state-owned either. Nevertheless, there probably is no place for rent extraction, investment banking, and much of the present financial industry in an ethical and sustainable society, and that alone implies that it cannot be a capitalist society (by Hodgson's definition). Furthermore, the dependence of capitalism on fossil-fueled economic growth is causing a climate breakdown that, unless we manage to sufficiently alleviate it in time, will cause more death and suffering than any other event in human history. Hence, for the sake of the planet and almost everything that lives on it, capitalism has to go.

---

75 Brons, *The Hegemony of Psychopathy*.
76 Karl Marx and Friedrich Engels, *Manifest der Kommunistischen Partei* (1848), MEW 4: 459–93, at 464. See the section "The Problem(s) with Materialism(s)" in chapter 4 for a longer quote that this phrase is part of.
77 Geoffrey Hodgson, *Is Socialism Feasible? Towards an Alternative Future* (Cheltenham: Edward Elgar, 2019).
78 See this chapter's introduction. Perhaps this implies that a radicalized radical Buddhist would or should be politically closer to Ambedkar's more or less social-democratic views than to, for example, Uchiyama's utopian, primitivist anarchism, but this is an open question. See also the next chapter, "The Other Side of Utopia."
79 In addition to already existing limitations, such as the ban of owning and trading nuclear weapons (in case of individuals).

16

The Other Side of Utopia

There is a common assumption that rejecting capitalism means accepting socialism, but that is a mistake for two reasons. First, the choice between capitalism and socialism is a false dilemma; there are and have been other alternatives, from feudalism and tribal societies to wholly new kinds of arrangements that have not been tried yet. And second, any social, political, and economic system needs to be judged on its own merits and demerits and not on what it opposes. Given the framework presented in chapters 12 to 14, this means assessing its (expected) consequences with regards to death and suffering. Hence, the radical Buddhists discussed in chapter 3 *may* have been right in their advocacy of some form of socialism, but this does not just follow from the rejection of capitalism.[1]

Assessing the various possible and impossible alternatives to capitalism is not my aim in this chapter. That might require a book at least as thick as this one. Instead, this penultimate chapter explores some of the implications of the methodological constraints that follow from the epistemological considerations of chapter 9.[2] Coherence yields epistemic justification, but such justification is always provisional. There is always a chance that we learn something new, showing that we were wrong, implying that what was a justified belief is no longer justified. This applies to social, political, and economic ideas as much as to any other kind of belief, and this has important implications.

Ideal Theory, Utopia, and Ideology

Most political and economic thought is "ideal theory," meaning that arguments are based on an idealized world in which important aspects of reality are abstracted away. Abstraction is not necessarily a bad thing. On the contrary, it is often necessary in science, but it is not self-evident that the results of abstractions and idealizations are always applicable to the real world, and if theory does not descend from the ideal world to reality it turns into an intellectual game without practical relevance, or worse, as the case of neoclassical economics illustrates.[3] In that case abstraction

---

[1] Whether socialism actually can be an appropriate alternative to capitalism is quite debatable, although this depends on what exactly "socialism" is supposed to mean. Geoffrey Hogdson, *Is Socialism Feasible? Towards an Alternative Future* (Cheltenham: Edward Elgar, 2019), has presented some strong arguments against the feasibility of a system that is simultaneously democratic, benign, and "socialist."
[2] See especially the section "Perspectives and Science" in chapter 9.
[3] See much of the previous chapter.

and idealization resulted in a "theory" that explains nothing,[4] but that is extremely useful as a tool to serve the interests of the ruling financial, industrial, and political elite. In such a case, ideal theory turns into *ideology* in the Marxian sense of that term: a collection of values and ideas that serve the interests of a ruling class, and that spread throughout society because of the dominance of that class.[5]

Ideal theory in social and political philosophy, as well as in economics, tends to involve three kinds of abstractions.[6] First, it assumes ideal agents. That is, it assumes that all members of a society have certain characteristics that real people do not. What these characteristics are differs a bit from theory to theory. Most theories assume that all agents are rational, and many assume egoism (i.e., that people are only motivated by their own self-interest), but the most important and most common assumption is that of compliance: most theories assume that people comply to the ideal. This idealization is closely related to an idea that permeates Western moral philosophy and that became most explicit in Kant; namely, that the task of ethics is just to figure out what is right because when people know what is right they will act accordingly.[7] This is a nonsensical assumption, of course. Real people do not always comply. Real people do not always do what is right and most certainly not what is best. Real people are not ideal actors.[8]

Second, ideal theory is utopian in the sense that it describes and argues for ideal situations and ideal solutions without seriously considering whether those are actually achievable. Almost all political thought, both left and right, is "guilty" of ideal theory in this sense, but this kind of utopianism also influences more practical political decision-making. In a situation where there really are only two options that are both bad but to different extents, refusing to support the less bad option because it is not ideal or not good enough is an example. However, refusing to support the lesser evil when there really are better options available is a different situation,[9] and unfortunately it is not always clear what is realistically possible and what not. Nevertheless, a principled rejection of every policy and every solution because it is not ideal or not good enough is utopianism, and if it too often leads to the adoption of the greater evil, it is a rather counter-productive form of utopianism.

Third, ideal theory is utopian in a second sense in focusing on ends rather than means, or in end results rather than intermediate stages. This kind of utopianism is rather obvious in neoclassical economics and its political arm, neoliberal capitalism, for example. The free market is supposed to make everyone more prosperous in the

---

4   The word "theory" is in scare quotes here, because strictly speaking, neoclassical economics has no theory. In the context of science, "theory" usually refers to well-confirmed hypotheses, but the hypotheses of neoclassical economics have only been dis-confirmed.
5   On neoclassical economics as abstraction and ideology, see also Lajos Brons, *The Hegemony of Psychopathy* (Earth: punctum books, 2017), esp. 45–55. On ideal theory as ideology, see Charles Mills, "'Ideal Theory' as Ideology," *Hypatia* 20, no. 3 (2005): 165–84. On ideology in general, see the section with that title in chapter 4.
6   Laura Valentini, "Ideal vs. Non-ideal Theory: A Conceptual Map," *Philosophy Compass* 7, no. 9 (2012): 654–64. Mills, "'Ideal Theory' as Ideology."
7   See the introduction to part III. As mentioned there, Max Horkheimer made a very similar point about Kant and Western ethics in his "Materialism and Morality," calling this kind of ideal theory "idealism." Max Horkheimer, "Materialismus und Moral" (1933), in *Gesammelte Schriften,* Band 3: *Schriften 1931–1936* (Frankfurt: Fischer, 1988), 111–49.
8   Real people are not "ideal" agents in the other senses mentioned either; that is, human beings are neither perfectly rational nor perfectly selfish.
9   In such a situation, "lesser-evilism" becomes an ideological tool to coerce people into accepting the status quo.

long run, and poverty in the short run is ignored. That in reality only the rich get richer in a free market because trickle-down is a myth is also ignored,[10] of course, but that is mostly due to the first kind of idealization mentioned above. On the other end of the political spectrum, the same kind of end-state utopianism can be found among political ideologies that reject small, incremental improvements on the ground that only wholesale, revolutionary change is acceptable.[11]

One implication of the focus on ends and end-states rather than means and the present is that it tends to change utopias into ideological justifications for their present opposites. All too often, utopia serves to justify dystopia. One example hereof was already alluded to in the previous paragraph: the capitalist or libertarian utopia promises material wealth and freedom for all (in the future), and that utopia "justifies" poverty, inequality, and injustice in the present. The same utopia "justified" the tens or even hundreds of millions of deaths due to famine and preventable disease mentioned in the previous chapter.[12] By focusing on the ideal, utopian end-state, the suffering and death on the path towards that ideal are brushed aside or judged to be necessary sacrifices at best.

And of course, it isn't not just capitalism that is guilty of this kind of murderous utopianism, but socialism as well. In the nominally socialist and communist states that existed throughout much of the twentieth century and in those that have managed to persist until this day, millions of deaths and massive suffering have been excused by appeals to lofty ideals like Lenin's sketch of the utopian future in *State and Revolution*. Using some rather creative accounting, Stéphane Courtois claimed in the introduction of the *Black Book of Communism*, which he edited, that "communism" was responsible for at least 100 million deaths.[13] Noam Chomsky has pointed out that by the same standards, capitalism would be responsible for more deaths in India alone,[14] but while these numbers are debatable, what cannot be denied is that nominally socialist or communist regimes — regardless of whether they really are or were socialist or communist — have been responsible for very many deaths and very extensive suffering.

While ideal theory is dangerous, it can also be very useful. Science without abstraction and idealization is impossible. Any law in physics or chemistry, for example, is an idealization that abstracts away whatever is contextually irrelevant. In political thought ideal theory can also be useful in other ways. The ideal, especially in its utopian sense, can serve as a benchmark: it makes it possible to assess how good or bad real societies are, relative to the ideal.[15] And the ideal can serve as a myth

---

10 On the myth of trickle-down economics, see, for example, John Quiggin, *Zombie Economics: How Dead Ideas Still Walk among Us* (Princeton: Princeton University Press, 2010). See also David Hope and Julian Limberg, "The Economic Consequences of Major Tax Cuts for the Rich," LSE International Inequalities Institute Working Paper #55, 2020, https://eprints.lse.ac.uk/107919/. On free market ideology, see the section "The Ideology of Supply and Demand" in chapter 15.
11 I'm explicitly referring here to groups/ideologies that reject small improvements on this ground. Groups/ideologies that want revolutionary change but that do not reject small improvements are not (equally) "guilty" of ideal theory in this sense.
12 See the section "Misery for the Many."
13 Stéphane Courtois, ed., *Le livre noir du communisme: Crimes, terreur, répression* (Paris: Robert Laffont, 1997).
14 Noam Chomsky, "Counting the Bodies," *Spectre* 9 (2009), http://www.spectrezine.org/global/chomsky.html. On the (number of) victims of capitalism, see also the section "Misery for the Many" in chapter 15.
15 Unfortunately, while such "benchmarks" may be useful tools for one purpose, they may also lead to rather dubious claims when used inappropriately. For example, G.A. Cohen, *Why Not Socialism?*

empowering the disempowered. For example, Lenin's sketch in *State and Revolution* of communist society after "the dying away of the state" as a society that is characterized by freedom, equality, and lack of exploitation, and that is guided by the principle "from each according to his ability, to each according to his needs" is as appealing as it is utopian (even though Marxists tend to believe it is "scientific" rather than utopian). It has given generations of communists something to believe in and something worth fighting for.[16]

Nevertheless, ideal theory risks turning into ideology, making it harmful more than useful, except to those who benefit from that harm. All three kinds of idealization can have this effect. The first kind of idealization abstracts away reality and makes it possible to approach the subject matter with apparent mathematical precision, but that scientific appearance only obscures the fact that the "theory" is no longer about the real world and is an extremely useful tool in marketing the "theory" and its recommendations. The result is a mere appearance of scientific rigor masking political propaganda. Neoclassical economics is, of course, the best example of this, but due to "economic imperialism" (i.e., the infection of other sciences with mainstream economic concepts, methods, and assumptions) similar ideological nonsense has unfortunately become more common in social and political philosophy as well.

The second and third kinds of idealization can also turn ideal theory into ideology. If rejecting the lesser evil and rejecting small improvements only serve the interests of the rich, the powerful, or some other kind of privileged group, then any collection of values or beliefs that support that rejection is ideology. It is sometimes argued that the rejection of political violence by liberals, centrists, and other political moderates is ideology in this sense. A principled rejection of violence has the implication that political activism is no serious threat to the status quo and thus can be safely ignored by the ruling elite. By rejecting violence, activists take the moral high ground, but simultaneously give up their most powerful means of protest and resistance. Because this supposedly only serves the interests of those who profit from the status quo (i.e., the dominant class), the principled rejection of violence is ideology.

Violence is a complex topic, however, and although this argument certainly has some force, it also has its weaknesses. Most importantly, it depends on the assumption that non-violent protest is mostly ineffective. There may be historical support for this assumption, but even if non-violent protest has been mostly ineffective in most historical circumstances this does not imply that it is ineffective in all circumstances. There may be political fights in which non-violence is more effective. In other words, the effectiveness of violence versus non-violence is an open question.

Perhaps, the most fundamental problem with violence is that it is "monstrous." In *Beyond Good and Evil*, Nietzsche warned that "who is fighting monsters has to watch out that he does not become a monster oneself."[17] Taking inspiration from this quote,

---

(Princeton: Princeton University Press, 2009), compared real-world capitalism with ideal socialism and concluded (unsurprisingly) that the latter is superior. Responding to Cohen, Jason Brennan, *Why Not Capitalism?* (New York: Routledge, 2014), compared ideal capitalism with real-world "socialism" and concluded (again, unsurprisingly) that capitalism is superior.

16 Vladimir Lenin, *The State and Revolution* (London: G. Allen & Unwin, 1917), §V.4, "The Higher Phase of Communist Society." The slogan "from each according to his ability, to each according to his needs," which is quoted by Lenin, comes from Karl Marx's *Kritik des Gothaer Programms* (*Critique of the Gotha Program* [1875], MEW 19: 11–32, at 21): "Jeder nach seinen Fähigkeiten, jedem nach seinen Bedürfnissen!"

17 Friedrich Nietzsche, *Jenseits von Gut und Böse: Vorspiel einer Philosophie der Zukunft* (1886), Digital Critical Edition (eKGWB), http://www.nietzschesource.org/#eKGWB/JGB, §146. The fragment continues

I argued in *The Hegemony of Psychopathy* that in fighting cultural psychopathy — the pathologically egocentric worldview imposed by neoliberal capitalism and mainstream economics — one has to watch out not to become "psychopathic" oneself because then, rather than fighting the enemy, one becomes the enemy. Because the willingness to use violence is a willingness to dehumanize and objectify one's target, every act of violence is a kind of *psychopathy by choice,* and therefore, the willingness to use violence against others at least partially defines the enemy.[18]

However, this argument against violence concerns the use thereof in the fight against the hegemony of cultural psychopathy or similar enemies specifically, and it may not be applicable to other fights. Furthermore, it can be argued that the monstrosity objection is ideal theory itself, because it abstracts away a key aspect of the real world. It assumes that there is enough time for a protracted struggle by other means, but in our present situation, given what we know now about climate change, this assumption is becoming increasingly implausible.[19] The root of this idealization is the utopian assumption that success is defined by the achievement of the ultimate goal of replacing the hegemony of psychopathy with something more humane, but due to climate change, this may be a lost cause. If utopia is out of reach and all we can hope for is to avoid the hell of climate-breakdown-driven collapse, then we may need to rethink the appropriate means of struggle. Desperate times may call for desperate measures. And *perhaps,* then, Uchiyama Gudō 内山愚童 was right when he wrote that "the hand that holds the rosary should also always hold a bomb."[20]

Ideal theory cripples the opposition to the capitalist status quo in a much more important way than by denying it the use of violence, namely, by promoting sectarianism. While most people have very similar core values, they weigh those core values very differently.[21] Some people prioritize fairness or equity; others find freedom more important; yet others think purity or loyalty are the pre-eminent core values; and so forth. Moreover, different people have different ideas about how these values are best realized, what should be done if two values, or "sub-values" (i.e., specific variants of these core values) come in conflict, and so forth. And consequently, different people have very different ideas about the ideal society, and some of these different ideas evolved into different political ideologies (such as socialism and anarchism), each with their own utopia.[22] The ideal-theoretical focus on idealized end-states puts these utopias center stage, and thereby splinters the opposition to the capitalist status quo into a collection of tribes that each worship their own totem, their own vision of the ideal society.

---

with the much better known sentence: "[a]nd when you look in the abyss for too long, the abyss will look back into you."

18 This is a very short summary of the "monstrosity" argument. See pages 78 to 84 of *The Hegemony of Psychopathy* for the full argument.
19 More about this in the next section.
20 Fabio Rambelli, *Zen Anarchism: The Egalitarian Dharma of Uchiyama Gudō* (Berkeley: Institute of Buddhist Studies & BDK America, 2013), 24. See also the section "Uchiyama Gudō and Early Buddhist Socialism" in chapter 3.
21 Jesse Graham, Jonathan Haidt, and Brian Nosek, "Liberals and Conservatives Rely on Different Sets of Moral Foundations," *Journal of Personality and Social Psychology* 96 (2009): 1029–46.
22 Notice the difference between "ideology" as political ideology — socialism, anarchism, liberalism, fascism, and so forth — and Marxian "ideology" as the collection of values and ideas that serve the interests of the ruling class.

Trotsky once aptly remarked that "the sectarian is satisfied with logical deduction from a victorious revolution supposedly already achieved."[23] Indeed, the ideal-theoretician or utopian sectarian — and all utopianism is sectarian — reasons from the ideal as if it is already achieved to the present, and infers her whole theory from that ideal. But as the ideal is not real, and possibly not even realizable, that theory is a sandcastle; and what's worse, each sect fanatically defends its own sandcastle, based on or inferred from its own ideal. This is, of course, extremely useful to those who profit from the status quo, which is what makes utopianism ideology (in the Marxian sense of "ideology"). A splintered opposition can never be a threat. Even if a majority of people in a society agree that change is necessary but cannot agree on what changes should be made, then nothing will change. In this way, ideal theory supports conservatism and social inertia.

In a famous sectarian attack on competing sects, Lenin called the ideas of those to the "left" of him an "infantile disorder,"[24] but it would be more appropriate to say that the real "infantile disorder" plaguing the radical left is the sectarianism rooted in utopian ideal theory. Marx, Engels, and their followers, including Lenin, aimed to overcome this disease by turning socialism into a science, but much of that "science" (i.e. Marxism) is outdated, confused, or just plain wrong.[25] Nevertheless, Marx and Engels made a serious effort to get acquainted with and even contribute to the most up-to-date science of their day, and there is much to admire in their general idea of overcoming utopianism by turning to science. This, I think, is the path forward, not just for radical Buddhism or for the left, but for humanity as a whole: to try to overcome utopianism and ideal theory. Rather than focusing on the ideal and deriving a theory from that, we should focus on what is possible and what is attainable,[26] and only then ask ourselves which of the really possible alternatives is the best.[27] utopian ideals are counterproductive; what we need are realistic scenarios.[28]

Overcoming utopianism in this way has been made especially urgent by the climate crisis. There are probably no ideal solutions to or outcomes of that crisis, only greater or lesser dystopias. It is, of course, possible to sketch ideal scenarios of environmentally friendly futures in which everyone is happy and healthy, but, as it has

---

23 Leon Trotsky, "Independence of the Ukraine and Sectarian Muddleheads" (1939), in *Writings of Leon Trotsky 1939–40* (New York: Pathfinder, 1977), 44–54.
24 Vladimir Lenin, *"Left-Wing" Communism: An Infantile Disorder* (1920), ed. Ahmed Shawki (Chicago: Haymarket Books, 2014).
25 Which doesn't mean that all Marxist thought is wrong, of course. In the contrary, there is a treasure trove of useful ideas to be found in the writings of Marx, Engels, and their followers. It just means that there are plenty of bad or outdated ideas as well.
26 Without letting our judgments of what is really possible be clouded by ideology presenting itself as "science." See the previous chapter.
27 Wherein the standard of what is "best" is ideally determined by the framework presented in chapters 12 to 14 above.
28 Traditionally, the political right and center accused the left of being driven by ideology, while they considered themselves "realistic"; that is, based on science and common sense. If the real situation ever really was like this, it certainly isn't anymore. On the contrary, with an exception for the most dogmatic Marxists, it is the political left that is realistic in this sense nowadays, while the right and center are entirely driven by ideology. Anti-scientism used to be one of the defining characteristics of fascism, but now characterizes the whole of the right in most countries (and the right has drifted closer to fascism in other respects as well), and the only "science" that right and center tend to accept is mainstream economics, which, as the previous chapter explained, is ideology rather than science.

become exceedingly unlikely that such scenarios sketch attainable futures, they are pointless or even counterproductive.

Mappō

Most of the twelfth and thirteenth century Buddhist reformers in Japan (including Nichiren 日蓮, but not Dōgen 道元) believed that they were living in the beginning of the degenerate era of the end of the Dharma or *mappō* 末法 (Chinese: *mofa*).[29] The idea was based on a common East Asian mythical periodization of the history of Buddhism into three eras: the era of the true Dharma 正法 (*shōbō, zhengfa*) during which people would still be able to genuinely follow the teachings of the Buddha; the era of the semblance Dharma 像法 (*zōhō, xiangfa*) in which only something resembling the true teachings remained; and mappō, the period of decline and, ultimately, disappearance of Buddhism from this world.[30] Fixing the starting date of mappō seems rather debatable, but I think a case can be made that we have at some point in the not-so-distant past entered this era, or something very much like it, indeed. This does not mean that I accept the mythological three-era periodization but that I believe that we have entered an era in history that will probably see the decline and disappearance of Buddhism, along with much else. The cause is very different from anything medieval Buddhists could ever have foreseen, however: human-induced climate breakdown.

To be clear, I'm not claiming that mappō in this sense is inevitable or somehow historically necessary but rather that the hegemonic capitalist hunger for fossil-fuel-driven economic growth is probably too powerful to be stopped and turned around in time. In some circles, it is fashionable to say that for the economic and political elite (i.e., the Transnational Capitalist Class) short-term profits outweigh long-term habitability of the planet,[31] but the problem is much more fundamental than that. There is no real alternative to fossil fuels to feed the capitalist hunger for endless, cheap energy,[32] and therefore, to end our dependence on fossil fuels we must end

---

29 See the section "from Saichō to Nichiren" in chapter 2.
30 Followed eventually by the birth of a new Buddha starting the cycle all over again. As mentioned in the section "From Saichō to Nichiren" in chapter 2, this mythical periodization was probably a Chinese innovation. An interesting question, to which I have not seen an answer, is whether the Buddhist three-era periodization was influenced by or even based on the distinction of three ages in the Confucian classic the *Book of Rites* 禮記, mentioned in the section "China/Taiwan — A Pure Land in the Human World" in chapter 3.
31 Already in 1976 Paul Mattick, "Kapitalismus und Ökologie: Vom Untergang des Kapitals zum Untergang der Welt," *Jahrbuch Arbeiterbewegung* 4 (1976): 220–41, at 237, wrote that "[b]ecause the movement of the world is determined by profit, capitalists concern themselves with ecological problems only insofar as those are related to profit. The capitalists do not care about the destruction of the world; [but] would it turn out that preserving the world can be profitable, then protecting the world will also become a business." (Da die Bewegung der Welt vom Profit bestimmt wird, kümmern sich die Kapitalisten um das ökologische Problem nur insoweit, als es sich auf den Profit bezieht. Den Kapitalisten liegt nichts an der Zerstörung der Welt; sollte es sich herausstellen, daß auch die Erhaltung der Welt profitabel sein kann, dann wird auch der Schutz der Welt zu einem Geschäft.)
32 There are plenty of alternative energy sources, but all of theme come with various other problems, limits, and disadvantages (such as unreliability, low-energy return on energy investment, impossible resource requirements, and so forth), and even together they cannot possibly replace fossil fuels as an energy source *in time*.

capitalism.³³ Unfortunately, for most of us it appears to be "easier to imagine the end of the world than to imagine the end of capitalism"³⁴, or more desirable at least, and so that is what we are heading for: not so much the end of *the* world but the end of *this* world, the end of the world we are used to.

The aforementioned Japanese reformers argued that because the world had entered mappō, Buddhism had to change. According to the Pure Land Buddhists Hōnen 法然 and Shinran 親鸞 one could no longer reach awakening by oneself, but would have to rely on rebirth in the Pure Land of Bliss and Amitābha's saving grace. And according to Nichiren, the only remaining path to salvation was faith in the *Lotus Sūtra*. Neither Amitābha nor the *Lotus Sūtra* are likely to be of much help in the climate crisis, but these reformers were right that if we have entered mappō, then that changes things. If I am right that climate breakdown may lead to some kind of collapse, then a radical Buddhist, especially one who rejects ideal theory, should take that into account. But before considering how collapse might matter, I first need to explain why I believe that this is a likely scenario.

Typically, overly pessimistic scenarios of climate change are based on misunderstandings of climate science or an exaggeration of risks. So, hoping to avoid those pitfalls, I will try to tread carefully. At the time of writing (summer 2020), the global average temperature is more than 1°C above pre-industrial levels.³⁵ According to a 2018 paper by Wangyang Xu and colleagues we can expect to reach 1.5°C around 2030 (with an uncertainty range of 2025–2037) and 2°C around the middle of the 2040s (uncertainty range: 2037–2052).³⁶ Part of this temperature increase is already more or less locked in, but how big that part is exactly is hard to say. The Earth system responds slowly to changes, so some of the warming in the near future is due to emissions in the past and stopping all emissions right now would not immediately stop warming. Estimates of the length of this lag effect differ from much less than a decade to several decades or even longer. It depends on ocean-atmosphere interactions and various other complex interaction effects in the Earth system that are not all equally well understood yet.³⁷ Probably, a more substantial part of the future temperature increase is "locked in" for socioeconomic rather than geophysical reasons, however.

In 2019, Dan Tong and colleagues calculated that existing fossil-fuel-burning infrastructure, electric power plants mainly, commits us to emissions of roughly 658 gigatons of CO_2 (range: 226–1479) and further infrastructure that is planned or al-

---

33 Because, as explained in the section "Misery for the Many" in the previous chapter, capitalism depends on economic growth, and economic growth mainly depends on the substitution of energy for labor in the production process.
34 Fredric Jameson, "Future City," *New Left Review* 21 (2003): 65–79, at 76.
35 Or 1.5°C, depending on what date is chosen to represent the pre-industrial level.
36 Wangyang Xu, Veerabhadran Ramanathan, and David Victor, "Global Warming Will Happen Faster Than We Think," *Nature* 564 (2018): 30–32.
37 Katharine Ricke and Ken Caldeira, "Maximum Warming Occurs about One Decade after a Carbon Dioxide Emission," *Environmental Research Letters* (2014): 9.124002 suggested a peak after roughly a decade, but according to Kirsten Zickfeld and Tyler Herrington, "The Time Lag between a Carbon Dioxide Emission and Maximum Warming Increases with the Size of the Emission," *Environmental Research Letters* (2015): 10.031001, it depends on the size of the emissions, with bigger CO_2 emissions involving a larger time lag between emission and peak warming. More recently, Andrew MacDougall et al., "Is There Warming in the Pipeline? A Multi-model Analysis of the Zero Emissions Commitment from CO2," *Biogeosciences* 17 (2020): 2987–3016, found that the likely length of the time lag depends very much on the model used, with values ranging from almost zero to several decades or even millennia, but they also conclude that most likely the time lag is very short.

ready under construction adds another 188 gigatons (range: 37–427).[38] These emissions lead to atmospheric CO_2 increases of roughly 38 and 11 ppm, respectively.[39] At the time of writing, we are at approximately 416 ppm.[40] Adding these 38+11 ppm results in approximately 475 ppm. In addition to that, emissions due to factors not taken into account in these numbers — such as those related to transport, agriculture, and construction — are also still increasing. If we somehow manage to start bringing those emissions down, and do not build even more fossil-fuel-burning infrastructure in addition to what is planned or under construction already, then we might end up somewhere around 520 to 570 ppm (or even more).[41] However, there are significant uncertainty margins, and because of those, even a best-case scenario could result in much more than that. If we're incredibly lucky, on the other hand, and start decommissioning polluting infrastructure early, it could also be significantly less — perhaps, as low as 450 ppm, although that seems insanely optimistic.

What these numbers mean in terms of warming can be inferred from various reports by the Intergovernmental Panel on Climate Change (IPCC) and the recent refinement of the "climate sensitivity" measure by Steve Sherwood and a long list of associates.[42] Climate sensitivity is the expected average global temperature increase due to a doubling of atmospheric CO_2 from pre-industrial levels of 280 ppm to 560 ppm. In 1979 this was estimated at 1.5–4.5°C, and that range remained unchanged until 2020 when Sherwood and colleagues published the refined measure of 2.6–3.9°C. This means that there is a 66 percent chance that the planet will be warmed up that much if we double atmospheric CO_2 relative to the pre-industrial standard of 280 ppm. The 95 percent likelihood range is 2.3–4.7°C, and the median expected temperature increase is 3.1°C.

Forecasts are littered with roughly bell-curve-shaped graphs depicting the probability of various outcomes. There is uncertainty in policy choices, in their effects with regards to emissions, in the translation from emissions to atmospheric CO_2 increase,[43] in the effects on temperature of the latter, and so forth, and these uncertainties compound. However, the effects of such compounding uncertainties matter most for extreme scenarios. For example, there is a small chance that there are no significant climate policies implemented at all, and a small chance that committed emissions from existing and planned infrastructure end up adding another 80 ppm, close to the upper limit of the ranges mentioned above, which would result

---

38 Dan Tong et al., "Committed Emissions from Existing Energy Infrastructure Jeopardize 1.5 °C Climate Target," *Nature* 572 (2019): 373–77.
39 Uncertainty ranges: 15–76 and 2–22.
40 For the most up-to-date number, see *Earth's CO2 Home Page,* http://www.co2.earth.
41 In a very optimistic scenario that assumes carbon-neutrality by 2050, that ignores residual emissions (i.e., emissions of economically necessary activities or processes for which we have no carbon-neutral alternatives), but that does not assume science fiction "solutions" (such as nuclear fusion or large scale direct air carbon capture and storage), we add another 50 ppm or so to the atmosphere (with the usual large uncertainty margins). In more realistic scenarios that do not ignore residual emissions and that take into account that several countries aim for carbon-neutrality in 2070 or even later, for example, it will probably be closer to 100 ppm (or more if natural carbon sequestration becomes less efficient, which might be the case already).
42 Steve Sherwood et al., "An Assessment of Earth's Climate Sensitivity Using Multiple Lines of Evidence," *Review of Geophysics* 58, no. 4 (2020): e2019RG000678.
43 Largely due to uncertainties about natural carbon sequestering. Only a part of what we emit ends up in the atmosphere, while much is taken up (i.e., sequestered) by land, plants, and oceans. How this will change under the influence of warming is uncertain, but small changes in this respect can have very big effects.

in somewhere around 650 or even 700 ppm in the middle of the century. Likewise, there is a small chance that climate sensitivity is close to the upper limit of the range mentioned as well (i.e., close to 3.9°C for 560 ppm), which would mean that 650 or 700 ppm would lead to warming of well over 4 or even 5°C. However, these small chances need to be multiplied to get the likelihood of the overall scenario. If all of them have a 5 percent likelihood, then the probability of this scenario is 5 percent to the power of 3, which is approximately 0.01 percent. Even if all of them have a 10 percent likelihood, which is *much* higher than what the studies mentioned suggest, the overall scenario has a probability of only 0.1 percent. The same is true for very optimistic scenarios, of course: improbably optimistic to the power of 3 also results in a likelihood approaching zero. Consequently, the effect of all these uncertainties is merely a subtle flattening and widening of the probability curve, and the peak of that curve is likely to be close to the scenario that assumes the most probable outcomes in every step. If we do that, then the expected atmospheric CO_2 level mid-century is between 520 and 570 ppm, resulting in average global warming of around 3°C. As mentioned, this would not be reached immediately, due to time lags in the Earth system's responses to change, but it suggests that Xu and colleagues' forecast of 2°C warming in the mid 2040s might even be slightly optimistic.

I will not attempt to describe the expected effects of 3°C of warming in detail here. Mark Lynas has already done an excellent job at that in his *Our Final Warning*, a thoroughly researched catalog of expected effects of 1 to 6 degrees of average global warming, with a chapter per degree.[44] They are devastating, but what is perhaps most concerning about that prospect is that 3°C is in the range of many tipping points. The classic study on tipping points by Timothy Lenton and colleagues suggests that warming in the range of 3 to 5°C triggers most tipping elements in the Earth system, but according to Sybren Drijfhout and colleagues' inventory of tipping points recognized by the IPCC in 2014 about two thirds of those are triggered at temperature increases *below* 3°C.[45] What this means is that it is almost certain that 3°C of warming will lead to fundamental changes that cause further temperature increases. One of the most worrying of those is permafrost melting because melting permafrost releases methane and rots away, putting more carbon in the atmosphere, leading to more warming. Such tipping points are not runaway effects, however; they do not lead to unlimited warming. Rather, they add additional warming on top of the warming that is directly caused by us. In other words, if we warm up the planet by roughly 3°C, there is a very high likelihood that "natural" processes add further warming — perhaps, only a few tenths of a degree, but it could very well be one degree or possibly even more. (But due to lag effects, this will not happen immediately.) And at 4°C only a relatively small part of the planet will remain inhabitable to humans.

This scenario can still be prevented, but what will be nearly impossible to prevent is much of the warming in the much nearer future. The 1.5°C predicted for 2030 (or a little bit later if we are lucky) is already more or less locked in. And given that it is extremely unlikely that we will decommission a significant portion of fossil-fuel-

---

44 Mark Lynas, *Our Final Warning: Six Degrees of Climate Emergency* (London: 4th Estate, 2020).
45 Timothy Lenton et al., "Tipping Elements in the Earth's Climate System," *PNAS* 105, no. 6 (2008): 1786–93, and Sybren Drijfhout et al., "Catalogue of Abrupt Shifts in Intergovernmental Panel on Climate Change Climate Models," *PNAS* 112, no. 43 (2015): E5777–86. See also Will Steffen et al., "Trajectories of the Earth System in the Anthropocene," *PNAS* 115, no. 33 (2018): 8252–59.

burning infrastructure (such as coal-burning power plants) in the *very* near future (instead, we're just building more) and take other measures to significantly curb emissions, the 2°C increase projected for the 2040s is a near certainty as well, although we *might* be able to postpone it a little bit. The differences may seem to be small — less than half a degree more in 2030, and another half degree at some point in the 2040s — but the effects are not, as several recent special reports by the IPCC make abundantly clear.[46] For example, the risk of water scarcity in already dry lands changes from "moderate" to "high" between 1.2 and 1.5°C; that of land degradation between 1.4 and 2°C; and risks related to food security change from "moderate" to "high" at between 1.3 and 1.7°C of warming.[47] According to another study, 1.5°C of warming will result in aridification (severe drying) affecting approximately 8 percent of the world population, while 2°C will result in aridification that affects between 18 and 24 percent (!) of the global population.[48]

The IPCC report *Global Warming of 1.5°C* explicitly compares the difference half a degree makes: it summarizes the effects of 2°C warming relative to 1.5°C. Two to three times as many species of plants, insects, and vertebrate animals will lose more than half of their geographical area. Many of those will go extinct. Approximately 13 percent of land area will experience ecosystem collapse, compared to half that at 1.5°C. Coral reefs will go virtually extinct and ocean acidification will even more severely threaten mollusks, plankton, algae, and many species of fish. The loss of average annual catch for marine fisheries will be twice as high at 2°C as at 1.5°C. There will be a significantly greater reduction in crop yields for major food crops at 2 than at 1.5°C, especially in economically less developed regions. Several *hundreds of millions* of people *more* will be exposed to climate-related risks such as natural disasters, food- and water-shortage and insecurity, and poverty.

In summary, then, 1.5°C means more droughts, famines, and other "natural" disasters affecting hundreds of millions of people around the planet. And 2°C means *even more* disaster.[49] With increasing temperatures, an ever-growing part of the planet will be hit by more and more, worse and worse disasters (droughts, storms, heatwaves, cold-spells, floods, and so forth). This will produce various secondary disasters, ranging from economic damage or even collapse to widespread famines and violent conflicts, as well as growing refugee flows. The increase of the frequency and intensity of disasters with temperature is not linear, however, as figure 16.1 rather conservatively illustrates.

That figure also shows something else: mitigation capacity — that is, the ability of a country or region to cope with the effects of disaster. This mitigation capacity

---

46 IPCC, *Global Warming of 1.5°C* (Geneva: IPCC, 2018); *Climate Change and Land* (Geneva: IPCC, 2019); and *The Ocean and Cryosphere in a Changing Climate* (Geneva: IPCC, 2019).
47 These numbers come from the report *Climate Change and Land*. They assume a specific scenario (namely, SSP3); in other scenario's the numbers may subtly differ.
48 Chang-Eui Park et al. "Keeping Global Warming within 1.5°C Constrains Emergence of Aridification," *Nature Climate Change* 8 (2018): 70–74.
49 There already has been a significant growth in climate-change-related disasters. In a comparison of the first two decades of the twenty-first century with the last two decades of the twentieth century, the UN Office for Disaster Risk Reduction (UNDRR) reported a 134 percent increase in floods and 40 percent increase in storms, the two most common climate-change-related disasters. Furthermore, there was a 46 percent increase in wildfires, 29 percent increase in droughts, and 232 percent increase in disasters due to extreme temperatures, all of which are also related to climate change (*Human Cost of Disasters: An Overview of the Last 20 Years, 2000–2019* [Geneva: UN Office for Disaster Risk Reduction, 2020]).

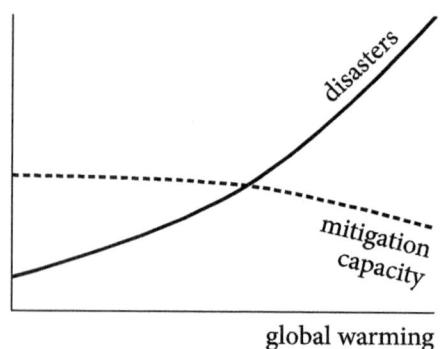

Fig. 16.1. Disaster mitigation.

includes the ability to prevent violent conflict (ranging from riots to civil war), to feed and shelter evacuees and refugees, to repair the damage, and so forth. Mitigation capacity is mainly dependent on economic growth, and as economic growth starts to decline eventually due to disasters or other causes, so will mitigation capacity.[50] At some point, the two lines cross, and that would even be the case if economic growth would not decline. From that time onward, a country or region is no longer able to cope with disaster. It can no longer feed and shelter refugees, it can no longer repair the damage, it can no longer guarantee order. After that point, every next disaster increases the likelihood of a complete collapse of public order, of the economy, and of society. How far in the future that point is differs from country to country. It depends both on a country's economic situation and on its vulnerability to climate-change-related disasters. Unfortunately, many of the poorest countries are also among those that are expected to be most affected by climate breakdown, and it is a near certainty, that a growing number of countries will cross this point in the coming decades.[51] That will set off further refugee flows, leading to human disasters that countries that were already close to collapse cannot deal with, setting off a cascade of societal collapse.[52]

Most likely, rich countries will respond to the growing chaos by trying to turn themselves into fortresses by building walls and other barriers (as they have already been doing). In *Tropic of Chaos*, Christian Parenti suggested that rich nations will develop into "armed lifeboats," trying to stay afloat by keeping out others (i.e., climate refugees and everyone else who does not "belong") by means of barriers and violence. However, no barriers and no amount of violence will be enough to stop refugee flows if those reach many hundreds of millions, and they will almost certainly reach such numbers well before the middle of the current century.

50 It could be argued, of course, that with economic growth, mitigation capacity grows, and thus that mitigation capacity depends on wealth rather than growth, but that is not exactly right because with economic growth mitigation costs also rise, and because disaster damage is more expensive to repair in wealthier countries and regions. Furthermore, as explained in the previous chapter, capitalism needs economic growth to function "properly." With insufficient growth, neither the public nor the private sector can afford disaster mitigation. Hence, even though it is true that wealthier countries have a much greater disaster mitigation capacity, for these reasons, the capacity to fully mitigate a natural disaster depends primarily on the level of economic growth.
51 Some countries may have already crossed it.
52 This paragraph is based on: Lajos Brons, "A Theory of Disaster-Driven Societal Collapse and How to Prevent It," unpublished working paper, 2019, http://dx.doi.org/10.17613/51rk-d378.

There is a real risk that strong states with developed economies will succumb to a politics of xenophobia, racism, police repression, surveillance, and militarism and thus transform themselves into fortress societies while the rest of the world slips into collapse. By that course, developed economies would turn into neofascist islands of relative stability in a sea of chaos. But a world in climatological collapse — marked by hunger, disease, criminality, fanaticism, and violent social breakdown — will overwhelm the armed lifeboat. Eventually, all will sink in the same morass.[53]

It is for this reason that I believe we have entered something like mappō. Not because we'll heat up the planet so much that we'll eventually cause human extinction, although there is a small chance that we'll end up doing that, but because even 2°C of warming will already have such disastrous effects that societal collapse will slowly envelop the planet. Mankind can probably survive that, but Buddhism cannot. There might be temporary "islands of relative stability in a sea of chaos," but as Parenti wrote, they will be neofascist islands in which nothing that even remotely resembles Buddhism can survive, and those islands will eventually "sink in the same morass." After centuries, or possibly even millennia, if mankind eventually reemerges from the chaos and rebuilds something approaching civilization, it will have new myths and new religions.[54]

According to Asaṅga, safeguarding the Dharma belongs to the main duties of a bodhisattva, and failing to do so is among the worst moral transgressions.[55] Consequently, a bodhisattva should do all he can to avoid or turn around a mappō-like decline leading to the disappearance of Buddhism from this world. From a secular or radicalized radical Buddhist perspective, the disappearance of Buddhism may seem a relatively minor concern — surely the immense suffering and hundreds of millions of deaths[56] (or even billions if we really warm up the planet to 4°C or more) that are likely to result from climate change vastly outweigh the badness of the "death" of the Dharma. But that does not mean that a disappearance of Buddhism would not be a bad thing in itself. Admittedly, Buddhism has not always been a force for good,[57] but

---

53 Christian Parenti, *Tropic of Chaos: Climate Change and the New Geography of Violence* (New York: Nation Books, 2011).
54 How long it will take for something like civilization to recover depends on how bad the situation will get. With low levels of warming, collapse may be avoided altogether, but if we warm the planet by more than 4°C, it is possible that the Earth system, after a long unstable period, tips into a new equilibrium that is too hostile for the reemergence of anything resembling civilization at all. And even 3°C would drastically change the face of the planet. Ecosystems cannot move or adapt quickly enough, so new ecosystems will have to develop, which takes a lot of time. Many areas that are now densely populated will (eventually) become effectively uninhabitable, and it takes millennia for fertile soils to develop in areas that might become newly available for human habitation. And given how long CO_2 stays in the atmosphere, it may even take tens of thousands of years to reach a new stable climate. Hence, stability is a thing of the past and of the very distant future. Humanity might not need a completely stable environment to rebuild, of course, but even the relative stability needed to make civilization possible could very well end this century and only be achieved again in several centuries or even millennia from now. The culture of those future people, including their legends, myths, and religious and philosophical ideas, will be nothing like ours. And they will probably live in a world that is more hostile than anything humans ever experienced.
55 Asaṅga, *Bodhisattvabhūmi* (4–5th c.).
56 As well as the suffering of billions of non-human animals.
57 Bernard Faure, *Unmasking Buddhism* (London: Wiley-Blackwell, 2009); Vladimir Tikhonov and Torkel Brekke, *Buddhism and Violence: Militarism and Buddhism in Asia* (New York: Routledge, 2013); and Brian Victoria, *Zen at War*, 2nd edn. (Lanham: Rowamn & Littlefield, 2006).

there can be little doubt that of all available life/world-views,[58] Buddhism is the most consistently committed to the alleviation of suffering. Buddhism's focus on suffering and compassion makes it one of the strongest allies of anyone who believes that our primary moral duty is to try to prevent, limit, or mitigate death and suffering.[59] And if that is right, a disappearance of Buddhism would be morally bad, and thus, Asaṅga was right that a bodhisattva should safeguard the Dharma.[60]

A bodhisattva's work in a world in decline does not end there, however. With the rise of disaster, famine, war, and refugee flows, suffering and death will reach levels never seen before. Universal compassion (or *mettā*) will be needed more than ever. Not just for moral reasons but also out of self-interest. In the previous edition of his catalog of the effects of climate change, Mark Lynas wrote that "in a situation of serious conflict, invaders do not take kindly to residents denying them food: if a stockpile is discovered, the householder and his family — history suggests — may be tortured and killed, both for revenge and as a lesson to others."[61] Something similar will apply on larger spatial scales. Keeping out millions of refugees is not an option. The choice is between helping them or being overrun.

According to the *Lotus Sūtra* we are all in at least some sense bodhisattvas. A bodhisattva's moral duties, then, are our moral duties. Hence, it is the duty of every one of us to practice universal compassion and tear down all walls and barriers. For the sake of those on the outside as well as for ourselves. And not in the least because we might find ourselves on the outside sooner or later.

A Buddha Land in This World

One of the chief arguments against utopianism is that it tends to cause suffering. As mentioned above,[62] poverty and inequality under capitalism are "justified" by the capitalist utopia of freedom and material wealth for all, while suffering in nominally socialist regimes was likewise "justified" by socialist utopias. But radical Buddhism is utopian as well — it strives for a *Buddha land* in this world, and such a Buddha land is a Buddhist utopia — and this opens up the possibility that that utopia might be abused in the same way to justify suffering in the present. Then, rather than a Buddha land in this world, radical Buddhism would deliver its very opposite (assuming that it ever would be able to deliver anything, of course, which does not seem very likely, unfortunately[63]).

There are, however, aspects of radical Buddhism — or at least of the radicalized radical Buddhism advocated in this book — that might prevent that, or make it less likely at least. First, the notion of a Buddha land (or Buddha field, *Buddhakṣetra*; also called "Pure land" 淨土 in East Asia) is closely associated or even identified with

---

58 Strictly speaking, Buddhism is not a single life/world-view but a cluster of related views. On the notion of a "life/world-view" and Buddhism as a life/world-view, see the sections "Defining 'Buddhism' and 'Buddhist'" in chapter 5 and "Between Science and Religion" in chapter 6.
59 If I am right, then chapters 12 to 14 show that almost everyone implicitly believes something very much like that.
60 This raises the question what "the Dharma" is, of course. One answer to that question was given in chapter chapter 5, but for a hypothetical radicalized radical Buddhism it would be more like the ideas presented in this book.
61 Mark Lynas, *Six Degrees: Our Future on a Hotter Planet* (New York: HarperCollins, 2007), 213.
62 In the section "Ideal Theory, Utopia, and Ideology" in chapter 16.
63 See the final section of the next chapter.

ultimate reality.[64] If the metaphysics and epistemology outlined in part II of this book is correct, then ultimate reality is not something we can "reach" or know. And neither can we reach ultimate truth. Our knowledge of reality is always mediated by our conceptual categories. We cut up and classify the world around us and it is only in that cut-up and classified version that we can be consciously aware of the world. That is, the world we are aware of is phenomenal or conventional reality, and ultimate reality is out of reach. The association of Buddha lands with ultimate reality suggests that Buddha lands are similarly out of reach. We can try to approach them, but we can never get or go there. There is a path, but there is no destination, or at least no destination that we can ever arrive at. And for that reason, it is the path that matters, and not the destination.

Second, the pragmatist naturalism that followed from the metaphysical and epistemological investigations in this book implies that all our knowledge claims are merely provisional.[65] As mentioned, truth is out of reach; instead, we should aim for justification.[66] But what we are justified to believe now may turn out to be no longer justified when we learn something new. This forces an anti-dogmatic attitude toward all knowledge claims, which is diametrically opposed to the dogmatic belief in final truths and final goals that comes with utopianism. It implies that not just what appear to be our best options right now might change with changes in what we are justified to believe or changes in circumstances, but that even our images of utopia themselves may change, however subtly, when we learn something new about the world or about ourselves. From the radicalized radical Buddhist perspective, then, not only is a Buddha land not something we can realize, it cannot even be determined what such a Buddha land might be like.

In a sense, a radicalized radical Buddhist demands the impossible, knowing that it is impossible. For the aforementioned reasons, it can only be the path that matters. The "destination" is not real; it is merely a name or symbol on a sign pointing us in the right direction (or a hypothetical benchmark, perhaps). And because a Buddha land is not something determinate and not something that can be reached or realized, it can never justify suffering in the present either.

However, as argued in the final pages of chapter 6, life/world-views have a tendency to become dogmatic,[67] and in the unlikely case that some kind of radicalized radical Buddhism would ever become a significant life/world-view, it is by no means unthinkable that adherents would attempt to "justify" suffering in the present by an appeal to their utopian vision of a future Buddha land in this world.[68] Just because it is a life/world-view radicalized radical Buddhism has an inherent tendency to

---

64 See chapter 2, especially its last section that is not coincidentally titled the same as the present section.
65 See especially the section "Perspectives and Science" in chapter 9 but see also the section "Naturalism" in chapter 1 as well as the introduction to part II.
66 That is, *epistemic* justification; not to be confused with the supposed moral justification mentioned, in scare quotes, in the first paragraph of this section.
67 Some Buddhist thinkers were also well aware of this. The Chinese Yogācāra philosopher Xuanzang 玄奘, for example, warned that attachment to a view is still a form of attachment, and therefore, unhelpful. See the section "Yogācāra Realism" in chapter 8.
68 The pragmatic, scientific attitude of Marx and Engels did not prevent Marxism from becoming dogmatic either.

undermine its own radicality, and therefore, radicalized radical Buddhism is inherently unstable.[69]

---

[69] One might still wonder whether a utopian and thus slightly-less-radicalized radical Buddhism might be preferable to other life/world-views. Given its strong focus on universal compassion and the prevention of suffering, I am inclined to answer "yes" to that question. utopianism is potentially dangerous, but the right kind of utopia(nism) is still better than the wrong kind. See also the last section of chapter 17.

PART IV

CONCLUSION

17

Radical Buddhism for the 21st Century

The term "radical Buddhism" refers to a loose collection of currents in mostly early-twentieth century Buddhism that were radical in two respects. First, radical Buddhists adopted a broadly naturalist stance with respect to Buddhist doctrine and related matters. And second, their political and economic views were radically anti-hegemonic, anti-capitalist, and often even revolutionary. While the naturalist stance is also a core aspect of secularization, the sociopolitical aspect of radical Buddhism is decidedly anti-secular, as secularization denies religion a political role and banishes it to the private sphere. This rejection of secularity-as-privatization is also a defining feature of engaged Buddhism, which is much more moderate (or less radical) than radical Buddhism but which shares many of its social concerns.

Chapters 3 and 4 identified Uchiyama Gudō 内山愚童, early Taixu 太虛, Lin Qiuwu 林秋梧, Seno'o Girō 妹尾義郎, and B.R. Ambedkar as the most prominent radical Buddhists, but chapter 2 showed that key aspects of radical and engaged Buddhism have much older roots. An important precursor of the radical Buddhist political engagement can be found in the thirteenth century Japanese monk Nichiren 日蓮, for example, and social engagement has even older roots within the Buddhist tradition. Furthermore, the naturalist and this-worldly attitude of radical and secular Buddhists is no break with tradition either but is closely related to the rationalist tendency that probably developed in response to Greek and Vedic/Brahmanic thought originally, and that gave birth to the logico-epistemological school of Dignāga and Dharmakīrti.

The aim of this book was not historical but philosophical. It was constructive, rather than re-constructive. Its aim was to develop a position that "radicalizes" radical Buddhism by simultaneously satisfying four related criteria. First, such radicalized radical Buddhism should be radically naturalist in a roughly Quinean or pragmatist sense of "naturalism." Second, it should be politically radical, that is, it should reject neoliberal capitalism, the hegemony of psychopathy, and related aspects of the sociopolitical and economic status quo. Third, it should be recognizably and defensibly Buddhist (because otherwise it would not be a radical *Buddhism*). And fourth, it should be radical in the sense of being uncompromising, rigorous, and consistent.

Lokamātra

Toward this end, part II of this book developed a metaphysical and epistemological foundation for a radicalized radical Buddhism based primarily on Yogācāra thought and the closely related logico-epistemological school, supplemented by ideas found in the broader Tiantai/Tendai 天台 tradition, and further elucidated and supported with the help of "new pragmatist" philosophers such as W.V.O. Quine and Donald Davidson. That foundation, provisionally named "post-Yogācāra Realism" in chapter 10, is a variant of perspectival realism: it is realist in the minimal sense of recognizing the existence of a mind-independent, external reality, but it rejects the idea that there is just one right way of describing that reality. Rather, descriptions of, or views on reality are perspectival: they are views from particular perspectives or constructions due to particular conceptual schemes. And because there is no view from nowhere, they are necessarily perspectival. This does not mean that such perspectives are false views but merely that they are one-sided or incomplete. They do not and cannot radically misrepresent external reality because they are necessarily grounded therein.

Our conscious awareness of the world is mediated by language and conceptually determinate, and because of that, perspectives are to a large extent linguistic. Conceptually determinate, conscious awareness (*pratibhāsa-pratīti*) is constructed (*kalpanā*) out of indeterminate, non-conceptual, and unconscious impressions (*pratibhāsa*) that are caused by external "suchness" (*tathātā*; things and stuffs), but this conceptual construction is not arbitrary because our conceptual categories are themselves formed in a social process of interaction with other speakers in a shared world.

This is, more or less, the standard Yogācāra view, but Yogācāra thinkers inferred from the constructedness of conscious experience that phenomenal reality is a deception, while I argued in chapter 8 that *that* conclusion does not follow. Because kalpanā (conceptual construction) proceeds by applying categories that are necessarily based on real properties of things — because otherwise we could not have those categories — the resulting phenomenal appearances are more like simplifications or caricatures than like illusions or hallucinations. This view is closer to that of the Tiantai/Tendai tradition than to that of Yogācāra, although the difference between the two views is one of attitude more than of substance. According to the founder of Tiantai, Zhiyi 智顗, language misrepresents the world to some extent, but only to some extent; it is not entirely mistaken. And as long as we keep that in mind, we do not have to let language deceive us.

The Tiantai/Tendai tradition also placed greater emphasis on the perspectival implications of conceptual construction than Yogācāra and the logico-epistemological school. Both traditions claimed that different kinds of creatures see the world in different ways, but the former Tendai monk and founder of the Japanese Sōtō 曹洞 Zen sect Dōgen 道元, for example, suggested that we do not have to become a different kind of creature (which is not really possible anyway) to acquire some new perspectives. And this has an important epistemological implication. If a single perspective only gives us a one-sided or partial view, as mentioned above, then combining multiple perspectives gives us a more complete, and therefore probably better understanding of what we're looking at. And if we can acquire new perspectives, as Dōgen suggested, then we can actually do that.

From Dignāga and Dharmakīrti's theories of concept formation through exclusion (*apoha*) and conceptual construction it follows that we cannot form or learn isolated concepts. Concepts are necessarily part of larger clusters that include other, closely related concepts and beliefs. Because of this, all of our concepts and beliefs are directly or indirectly connected, and the content of a concept or belief is to a large extent determined by its location in our webs of belief. This inter-connectivity of our beliefs also plays an important epistemological role. Because we do not have direct access to ultimate reality, there is no way to compare our beliefs with reality, and consequently, all that can justify our beliefs are other beliefs. According to Dharmakīrti, the source of knowledge is coherent or uncontradicted (*avisaṃvādin*) cognition: a cognition or belief is justified in as far as it coheres with other justified beliefs. Nevertheless, all that coherence gives us is epistemic justification — truth is out of reach. The more perspectives we learn to access or create, the more facets of reality we can see and the more evidence or counter-evidence we can collect, but even coherence with all available evidence does not guarantee truth, it merely tells us what we, collectively, are *justified* to believe. Moreover, regardless of how many perspectives we manage to combine, there are always further perspectives including inaccessible ones, and consequently, coherence is contingent: any belief that appears to be perfectly justified now can in principle turn out to be incoherent when we learn something new. And because of that, any belief can only be accepted provisionally.

An important consequence hereof is that we cannot know anything with absolute certainty, but this does not mean that we cannot know anything at all. There is a lot we know, even if all of it is open to revision, and even if there is always more to know. Our most justified beliefs are the beliefs that result from the most rigorous testing for coherence with as many as possible different kinds of perspectives — in one word, science. What does not cohere with scientific findings (provided that those are coherent themselves!) cannot be justified. Because of that, traditional views on karma, rebirth, Pure lands, heavens, and paradises cannot be accepted. There is only this world, and there is only this life, and therefore, if we aim to alleviate suffering, we must do so here and now.

The aim of part III of this book was to built a moral and social philosophy on this metaphysical and epistemological foundation. Key to that project was the aforementioned realization that, because all we ever can achieve is epistemic justification, it really makes no sense to aim for truth. This is especially important in ethics and social philosophy, as there is little agreement on whether there is something like moral truth, and if there is, whether and how we can know it, while moral justification does not face similar difficulties, or at least not to the same extent. As chapter 9 showed, the most justified idea is just the most coherent idea, that is, the idea that most coheres with all available evidence and eligible points of view. Or in other words, epistemic justification depends on combining perspectives, and if all relevant perspectives agree, then that is the strongest possible justification we can have (but even that justification is contingent and may be negated by new findings).

The central question of part III, then, was whether there actually is significant agreement with regards to fundamental aspects of ethics and social philosophy. Chapters 12 to 14 explored three different aspects of this question. Chapter 12 argued that there appears to be widespread agreement that what makes something right or wrong are its expected consequences, even though this is only rarely expressed explicitly in these terms, and that this is a view shared by Mahāyāna ethics as expressed in the writings of Asaṅga and Śāntideva as well. Expected consequences are not a kind of consequence but expectation, that is, they are hypothetical or conditional beliefs about the future, and therefore the resulting view is not a variety of consequentialism but is more appropriately called "expectivism."

The second question focused on the idea that expected consequences determine what is right or wrong is meaningful only if there is a specification of what kind of expected consequences matter. There is a common assumption that everyone aims for their own happiness, but a closer look at this assumption showed that there is no universal agreement that happiness is or should be our ultimate goal. And because of that, expected increases or decreases in happiness cannot be what makes something right or wrong. Neither does there seem to be universal agreement about some other positive standard. What we all do seem to agree about is that death and suffering are bad, suggesting that there is a universal negative standard of right and wrong. What makes something wrong is that it is or should have been expected to lead to death or suffering, and the more death or suffering something causes, the worse it is.

The third question focused on what kind of thing that "something" is. What should we judge for its expected consequences? Acts? Rules? Virtues? Institutions? All of them? Something else? The answer given in chapter 14 is more or less deflationary: in a sense, we can and should judge all of these, but when we do so we are not really judging fundamentally different different things, because all of those things can be reduced to acts. More concretely, rules and institutions and so forth are not really kinds of things, but processes or patterns. They are "maps" of and for behavior (i.e., acts or actions). Strictly speaking there are no such things as rules, virtues, or institutions, but we can still speak of rules in a metaphysically looser sense in reference to these ever-changing maps of and for behavior and the acts that change them.

One of the most important implications hereof is that there is no inconsistency when in one situation we appear to judge a rule or institution and in another situation we appear to judge a particular act. And consequently, the theoretical framework provided by chapters 12 to 14 can be used to assess one of the most distinct characteristics of radical Buddhism: its rejection of capitalism. By the standard provided in these chapters, capitalism is morally wrong to the extent that it is expected to continue to cause more death or suffering than any feasible alternative, and one reason to expect this would be that it already has caused massive suffering. Chapter 15 argues that this is the case indeed but ends with a cautious conclusion that this does not necessarily mean that every aspect of capitalism is equally harmful or should be turned into its opposite. Perhaps, we should aim for some kind of middle path, although that middle path would have to be one that avoids some of the most detrimental aspects of capitalism — such as rent extraction by the financial sector and capitalism's dependency on fossil-fueled economic growth — and would, therefore, not be a capitalist path.

Aside from these general points, what a morally acceptable alternative to neoliberal capitalism could or should be like is a question that is not addressed in this book. The radical Buddhists mentioned above argued for varieties of anarchism, socialism, or social democracy, but the rejection of capitalism does not imply the acceptance of any of these. Instead of advocating a specific alternative to capitalism, the last chapter of part III discussed certain constraints on how to think about such alternatives. The first of these constraints is methodological: it is a rejection of "ideal theory" and utopianism. The second is more contextual and practical, although it could be seen as a special case of the first: the climate crisis changes everything, and social or political thought that does not take climate change and its effects seriously — including the possibility of widespread societal collapse — is unlikely to have much practical relevance in this world.

For ease of reference, and emphasizing its this-worldly focus, I'll call the "radicalized radical Buddhism" developed and defended in this book (and summarized in the foregoing) *lokamātra* in the remainder of this final chapter. *Cittamātra* or *vijñaptimātra*, often translated as "mind only," are sometimes used as alternative names of the Yogācāra school or its most notable doctrine, and similarly, *lokamātra* can be understood as meaning "this world only." The name is not just a tribute to Yogācāra, however, but also to Tanaka Jiroku's 田中治六 term *genseshugi* 現世主義 or "this-world-ism," which referred to a kind of Buddhism that is explicitly focused on this world rather than on death and what comes after.[1] (I am not overly fond of neologisms like this, by the way, but the first draft of this chapter was littered with longer and shorter variants of the phrase "the view developed and defended in this book," which made it nearly unreadable.)

Lokamātra as a whole consists of a metaphysical and epistemological foundation provisionally called "post-Yogācāra realism," a nameless moral and social-philosophical theory built on that foundation that could be described as a kind of "negative expectivism,"[2] a rejection of capitalism based on that moral and social-philosophical theory in turn, and a rejection of ideal theory and utopianism based both on epistemological and ethical considerations. The main question that needs to be answered in this final chapter is whether lokamātra satisfies the four criteria of this book's goal.

Labels, Hesitations, and Rafts

It seems to me that the view defended here is undeniably naturalist and I am reasonably confident that lokamātra is consistent as well, but it is part of the nature of philosophy that the assessment of the consistency of a position is a collective endeavor.[3] This leaves the other two aspects of the book's four-fold goal mentioned above. Is the proposed "radicalized radical Buddhism" (i.e., lokamātra) politically radical indeed? And is it recognizably and defensibly Buddhist?

While lokamātra certainly opposes neoliberal capitalism, the hegemony of psychopathy, and related aspects of the sociopolitical and economic status quo — and thus, satisfies that criterion — it *could* be argued that it is less radical than the views of some of the radical Buddhists mentioned. Uchiyama's primitivist anarchism, for example, seems to imply a more radical rejection of the sociopolitical status quo than the "cautious conclusion" at the end of chapter 15. On the other hand, the demand in that chapter to abolish the financial industry and capitalism itself can hardly be considered a "moderate" demand, and Ambedkar's political views appear to have been significantly less radical than what is argued here. Furthermore, while advocating a complete overhaul of every aspect of society might *seem* very radical, it really is not, because such utopian dreams are unlikely to be realizable in this world, and an attempt to realize what cannot be realized can only lead to a dystopian betrayal of those utopian dreams.[4]

The hardest question in the assessment of this book's project is whether and to what extent lokamātra is really Buddhist, and perhaps, this is also the most important question. It can, of course, be argued that it is much more important whether

---

1   A more literal, part-for-part, translation of *gense-shugi* would be *loka-vāda*, but that compound term exists already. It means something like "public rumor."
2   I referred to it as a "dao of compassion" on a few occasions, but I do not think that that is a useful technical or formal name.
3   There are errors and oversights in any philosophical text including, doubtlessly, in this one. It is much harder to find such errors and oversights in one's own work than in the work of others, however. That's why philosophy is (and *must* be!) a collective effort. That's also why philosophers always argue about everything, and why progress in philosophy is so slow.
4   See chapter 16.

the view developed and defended here is the right view than whether it is a Buddhist view, but that argument would ignore what this book set out to do: to take radical Buddhism seriously and try to figure out whether there is or could be a variety of Buddhism that is radical in all the relevant senses. If lokamātra is not recognizably and defensibly Buddhist, then it would not be a variety of radical Buddhism (and thus not a radicalization thereof) but something else entirely, and that would imply a failure of the project (even if it would not invalidate the substance of the view itself).

As explained in chapter 5, there is no unambiguous and uncontroversial way to decide whether a theory, view, or position is Buddhist. After discussing the various options, it was concluded there that the only feasible criterion is a genetic criterion like the following:

> A theory, doctrine, practice, or idea is Buddhist if most of what it is based on or derived from is Buddhist and if it could not just as well be based on or derived from non-Buddhist sources.[5]

Chapter 10 applied this criterion to the post-Yogācāra realism proposed in chapters 8 and 9. Because this metaphysical and epistemological theory is based mostly on Yogācāra thought, with relatively minor inputs from the larger Tiantai/Tendai tradition and some "new pragmatist" Western philosophers, it satisfies the first part of this criterion. Chapter 10 concluded that it satisfies the second part as well, because post-Yogācāra realism, or anything like it, cannot be based nearly "just as well" on non-Buddhist sources and possibly not at all.

The metaphysical and epistemological foundation, then, is Buddhist, and by the same criterion, what is based on that foundation is Buddhist as well, provided that it satisfies the second sub-criterion, that is, that it cannot be based on non-Buddhist sources just as well. The "negative expectivism" defended in chapters 12 to 14 easily satisfies the first sub-criterion: it is not just based on an extension of important aspects of post-Yogācāra realism into the moral domain, but independently supported by Mahāyāna moral thought as well. However, it might be argued that this moral theory could be based on non-Buddhist sources (although perhaps, not just as well), and if that is the case indeed, then that would imply that this moral theory, by itself, might not be Buddhist by the criterion adopted here, despite its apparent closeness to, for example, Asaṅga's view.[6] This apparent problem evaporates when it is realized that the moral and social philosophy developed in part III is not an isolated theory, but part of a larger whole — namely, lokamātra — that also includes metaphysics and epistemology. And as a whole, lokamātra could not be based on non-Buddhist sources just as well, and most likely not at all.

---

5   See the section "Defining 'Buddhism' and 'Buddhist'."
6   There is an obvious asymmetry between parts II and III of this book with regard to the assessment of the "Buddhist" credentials of the theories developed therein. Part II ended with a chapter that not only included an in-depth assessment of the just-as-well criterion, but that also compared post-Yogācāra realism with similar and related views from other philosophical traditions; but there is no similar chapter in part III. The main reason for that is that the "convergentist" approach of part III makes such a chapter more or less redundant. Because the intersubjectivity criterion at the core of the approach of part III makes comparison an inherent part thereof, no additional comparative chapter is necessary. However, because of the intersubjectivity criterion the theory developed in part III *by itself* — not as a part of a larger whole — also more or less automatically fails the just-as-well criterion. If near universal agreement is the main criterion of epistemic justification, then core ideas must be supported by or in any perspective considered.

Despite that conclusion, I am hesitant to unequivocally call the view developed and defended in this book "Buddhist" for two reasons. The first of those reasons is personal. I cannot sincerely defend a view without making it my own, and consequently this book's view is my view. However, for reasons explained at the end of chapter 5, I do not consider myself a Buddhist, which appears to lead to a contradiction. A socialist, by definition, is someone who adheres to a socialist view. And similarly, if my view is a Buddhist view, then that would seem to imply that I'm a Buddhist as well, but I'm not.[7] This is hardly an argument against the conclusion that lokamātra is Buddhist indeed. My personal hesitations should not matter.

The second reason is related to a problem raised in the final paragraphs of chapters 6 and 16. It was argued there that, because radical Buddhism is a life/world-view, a radicalization thereof is inherently unstable. Due to the psychological roles they play,[8] life/world-views tend to be or become more or less dogmatic. However, even a moderate dogmatism would negate key aspects of the naturalism that is a core element of lokamātra. Consequently, if radicalized radical Buddhism would have adherents, then those adherents would inevitably de-radicalize it in some ways, turning it into something else.[9] The corollary of that problem is that if the naturalist commitment is not compromised, it may be the "Buddhist" identification that has to go instead, and that is my second reason for hesitance.

Given the epistemological framework outlined in chapter 9, a certain kind of naturalism is a cornerstone of lokamātra, if not the very foundation itself.[10] Consequently, *that* element of the view or theory as a whole cannot be changed without changing everything built upon it. But the identification as "Buddhist" plays no similar role. There is nothing in the view presented in this book that demands it to be considered a variety of Buddhism — radicalized radical Buddhism does not care whether it is Buddhist.[11] This, however, is not how the labels of life/world-views work, especially not those that are perceived to be religious labels. Such labels take priority over any other ideological or philosophical commitments the adherent might have. To be a Christian conservative is to be a Christian first and a conservative second; to be a liberal Muslim is to be a Muslim first and liberal second; but to be an adherent of lokamātra (i.e., a *lokamātrin*) is to be some kind of naturalist first, and possibly not a Buddhist at all (if I use myself as an example).

---

7   Strictly speaking, this argument is fallacious because it affirms the consequent, but let's ignore that.
8   Life/world-views give meaning to our lives and play a central role in our mostly unconscious defense against the also mostly unconscious fear of death. See the section "Between Science and Religion" in chapter 6 for further details.
9   An illustration of something like this can be found in the writings of the 14th Dalai Lama, who wrote that "if science proves some belief of Buddhism wrong, then Buddhism will have to change" (Tenzin Gyatso, the 14th Dalai Lama, "Our Faith in Science," *The New York Times,* November 12, 2005, https://www.nytimes.com/2005/11/12/opinion/our-faith-in-science.html). However, when science actually proves some of his supposedly "Buddhist" beliefs wrong, he appeals to the lack of absolute certainty in science, ignoring the fact that this is an inherent feature of science, or makes other evasive moves, thereby compromising or even negating his commitment to science. For further details, see the section "Tibet — Gendun Chopel and the 14th Dalai Lama" in chapter 3.
10 Although it could be argued that the "foundation" is just the claim that there is communication and that even the naturalist method is (indirectly) derived from this claim (see chapters 8 and 9). It must further be noted that the term "foundation" here should not be taken too literally. As a pragmatist (or Quinean naturalist) theory lokamātra has no foundations in a strict sense as nothing is immune to counter-evidence.
11 And I only care myself because it is part of the research question that started this book's project.

Another way of looking at this problem (if it is a problem, indeed) is that the naturalistic commitment of lokamātra may require that view to give up any aspect of Buddhist thought that is incoherent with available evidence. But paradoxically, this willingness to give up aspects of Buddhism is itself a Buddhist doctrine. The Chinese Yogācāra philosopher Xuanzang 玄奘 warned that one should not get overly attached to views because any kind of attachment is unhelpful,[12] but the idea has much older roots. In fact, according to the *Alagaddūpama Sutta*, the Buddha himself argued that the Dharma (i.e., Buddhism) is like a raft that has to be abandoned once it served its purpose (i.e., crossing over a river or "crossing over" toward awakening).[13] There is, of course, a difference between stating that something has to be abandoned once it served its purpose and stating that something would have to be abandoned if and when it is defeated by counter-evidence, but the simile of the raft illustrates that a dogmatic attachment to so-called "Buddhist" doctrines is not a feature of Buddhism. And if that is the case, then the hypothetical possibility that lokamātra might have to reject more "Buddhist" doctrines than it already does,[14] should not in itself be a reason to deny that view the "Buddhist" label either.[15]

Radical Buddhism in This World

A few paragraphs back, I suggested that if something like lokamātra would find adherents, it would almost certainly de-radicalize to at least some extent because the demands following from its life/world-view nature would trump the demands that follow from its "radicality" and particularly, its naturalistic commitments, but probably such de-radicalization would have to take place *before* a view like this could find adherents in the first place. The epistemology that is part of lokamātra entails that any node in a web of belief is revisable, while it is part of the very nature of a life/world-view that core beliefs therein are effectively immune from revision; and the mere existence of such unrevisable nodes in someone's web of belief means that she does not and cannot genuinely accept lokamātra.[16] Furthermore, it is doubtful that lokamātra can offer the kind of "story" that most people unconsciously need to give meaning to their lives and to manage their unconscious fear of death.[17] Humans crave certainty and truth, something firm and fixed to hold on to, and if the world does not provide that, they will invent it themselves. But according to lokamātra epistemology, we cannot even *aim* for truth and absolute certainty is fundamentally impossible. In a sense, lokamātra does not care about human psychological needs — not about these but not about other needs either. The view outlined in this book also completely omits "self-help" aspects of (modernist) Buddhism such as mindfulness meditation and related techniques, for example.[18] In a nutshell, the "problem" is that

---

12 See the section "Yogācāra Realism" in chapter 8.
13 *Alagaddūpama Sutta*, MN 22.13–14.
14 It doesn't reject that much, actually. Lokamātra rejects karma and rebirth, of course, but there are other Buddhists that reject those as well. Overall, lokamātra appears to be mostly consistent with much of Buddhist "core" doctrine or plausible interpretations thereof.
15 In any case, the first thing that should be abandoned after it served its purpose is the term *lokamātra*.
16 An obvious implication is that — despite my statement above that lokamātra is or has become my view — what I really (consciously or unconsciously) believe must in some way or other already deviate from a strict interpretation of lokamātra.
17 See the section "Between Science and Religion" in chapter 6.
18 Of course, "self help" is not the only form Buddhist practice can take (and certainly not the main form it has taken historically), but Buddhist practice has been almost completely ignored in this

lokamātra is neither designed as nor intended to be a life/world-view. It is a philosophical theory developed in response to a hypothetical question.

Nevertheless, one may wonder whether it would be desirable that something like lokamātra, or some other kind or kinds of radical Buddhism, or even some sufficiently similar non-Buddhist radicalism would find adherents and whether there actually is any prospect for a re-emergence of anything like radical Buddhism.

Obviously, we live in a different world now than the worlds the earlier radical Buddhists lived in, although there is at least one disconcerting parallel. Many of the radical Buddhists came in conflict with authoritarian regimes. Seno'o Girō was imprisoned, Uchiyama Gudō executed, and Taixu and Lin Qiuwu also ran into trouble a number of times. Much earlier, Nichiren, a predecessor of radical Buddhist political engagement, was also threatened with execution and banished to Sado Island, which was then a rather remote and inhospitable place. The disconcerting parallel is that authoritarianism is on the rise again, and the toxic mix of ingredients that feed the current authoritarian wave has some worrying similarities to last century's. But there also are fundamental differences, of course, and how similar the current authoritarian wave really is to that which determined the history of the first half of the twentieth century is a question for historians.

The new wave of authoritarianism is fed by a number of interrelated trends that also affect the prospect of the re-emergence of something like radical Buddhism. Seventy years ago, Hannah Arendt observed that early-twentieth-century totalitarianism is rooted in what she called "the mob" and its desire for a "consistent" worldview that explains everything but that ignores reality and rejects science. Because of that, the totalitarian worldview is immune to rational counter-argument and counter-evidence. "Its ingeniousness rests precisely on the elimination of that reality which either unmasks the liar or forces him to live up to his pretense."[19] Additionally, "the mob" also hates science because it is or appears to be the domain of a part of society from which they perceive themselves to be excluded. Unfortunately, it seems that "the mob" has found a home as well as a podium in social media.

Supported by "the mob," authoritarian leaders express a similar disregard for reality and science. "Before mass leaders seize the power to fit reality to their lies, their propaganda is marked by its extreme contempt for facts as such, for in their opinion facts depend entirely on the power of the man who can fabricate it."[20] The substitution of lies and "consistent" fantasy (i.e., conspiracy theories) for reality ties in with a second key trend, but one that is very different, as far as I can see, from a century ago: the death of conservatism and its replacement with something far more dangerous. Of course, there still are people who call themselves "conservatives," but what passes for "conservatism" nowadays has almost nothing in common with the philosophically sophisticated conservatism of Edmund Burke, Alexis de Tocqueville, Leo Strauss, and others. Instead, conservatism has devolved into a brazen defense of the privileges of the privileged (i.e., white people,[21] men, the rich, and so forth) by any means. And those means, indeed, include authoritarianism, ideologically motivated

---

book. (The main exception is the last section of chapter 13.) What lokamātra as practice could look like is an interesting question to which I presently have no good answer. Perhaps, this is something I could try to address in future work.
19 Hannah Arendt, *The Origins of Totalitarianism* (1951; London: Penguin, 2017), 502.
20 Ibid., 458.
21 Or whatever ethnic, racial, or cultural group happens to be the privileged group in some country or territory.

misinformation and lies, and a cynical alliance with "the mob," whose members are generally excluded from the most important privileges that these "conservatives" aim to defend but whose members are not entirely without privilege either. From the mob perspective, the issue is not privilege, of course, but "freedom," *their* "freedom" to be precise. But such "freedom" is nothing but privilege seen from the point of view of the privileged.

This opportunist pseudo-conservatism is further allied to the elite, to the people at the top of the pyramid of privilege, wealth, status, and power, that is, to the Transnational Capitalist Class (TCC).[22] That alliance is itself opportunistic, as much of the TCC is not really "conservative" in this opportunist sense and is instead motivated by a near religious belief in the auspiciousness of markets, free trade, private property, and small government.[23] Such ideological differences tend to be concealed by a shared idolization of "freedom," however, even if different allies may have very different ideas about what exactly "freedom" means (and whose "freedom" they want to protect).

Furthermore, while trickle-down economics is a myth,[24] the worldview of the TCC *does* trickle down. Through their status and power, the ideas of the elite tend, to lesser or greater extent, to become the ideas of the masses. This is what Marx and Engels called "ideology" and what Gramsci called "hegemony."[25] Perhaps, the most pernicious aspect of the dominant ideology, or the *hegemony of psychopathy*, is a kind of pathological selfishness that borders on psychopathy or narcissism and that undermines empathy, care, and genuine engagement with the wellbeing of others.[26]

One of the contextual factors that boosted fascist authoritarianism in the second quarter of the twentieth century was the Great Depression, which lasted from 1929 until approximately 1939. Based on a study of two centuries of economic crises, Richard Vague concluded that most economic crises are caused by unsustainable private debt and that when the sum of debts of households and industry is roughly 150 percent or more of GDP, crisis is almost inevitable.[27] Debt levels are again dangerously high and have been for a while. They caused the Great Recession of 2007–2009, but did not return to safer levels because governments chose to prioritize the interests of the financial industry and the TCC over those of the real economy and the vast majority of people. Because of that, another economic crisis is brewing and is likely to erupt within the next decade or so. Whether governments can afford to bail out the banks again is doubtful, and what will happen when parts of the financial industry collapse is hard to say, but the wider sociopolitical impact is unlikely to be beneficent. Fascism and other forms of authoritarianism are already on the rise again, and another major economic crisis will probably only reinforce that trend.

---

22 Leslie Sklair, *The Transnational Capitalist Class* (New York: Wiley, 2000).
23 See, for example, Peter Phillips, *Giants: The Global Power Elite* (New York: Seven Stories, 2018).
24 John Quiggin, *Zombie Economics: How Dead Ideas Still Walk among Us* (Princeton: Princeton University Press, 2010), and David Hope and Julian Limberg, "The Economic Consequences of Major Tax Cuts for the Rich," LSE International Inequalities Institute Working Paper #55, 2020, https://eprints.lse.ac.uk/107919/.
25 See the sections "Uchiyama Gudō and Early Buddhist Socialism" and "Ideology" in chapters 3 and 4, respectively.
26 Lajos Brons, *The Hegemony of Psychopathy* (Earth: punctum books, 2017), and Jean Twenge and Keith Campbell, *The Narcissism Epidemic: Living in the Age of Entitlement* (New York: Atria, 2009).
27 Richard Vague, *A Brief History of Doom: Two Hundred Years of Financial Crises* (Philadelphia: University of Pennsylvania Press, 2019).

Furthermore, there is another, even bigger crisis brewing, the climate crisis, and that crisis may push the world towards fascism or something very much like it even further. Recent research has shown that natural disasters and other environmental changes that threaten economic security change a society's norms and preferences. They become more hostile towards "deviations" (such as minorities, foreigners, and refugees), less open, more prejudiced, and more authoritarian.[28]

This toxic mix is probably not the fertile soil needed for the reemergence of a radical Buddhism. More likely, it is detrimental. Varieties of Buddhism that appear to be growing, such as secular Buddhism, seem to be thoroughly infected by the hegemony of psychopathy, rather than to go against it and promote a genuine concern for the suffering of others.[29] And engaged Buddhism, radical Buddhism's moderate sister, is not exactly flourishing either. There has been, of course, a steady stream of books and other kinds of publications about engaged Buddhism, but all the movement's leaders are dead or very old, and there is no sight of a new generation. (Similarly, there is no sight of prominent budding radical Buddhists either.) It seems to me, then, that the prospects for a reemergence of anything like radical Buddhism are dim.

But at the same time, and largely for the same reasons, we might need something like radical Buddhism more than ever. Ninety years ago, a proclamation read in the first meeting of Seno'o Girō's Youth League observed that

> [t]his is an era of suffering. Fellow men desire love and trust, but are forced to engage in conflict, while the general public wishes for bread, but is only fed oppression. Either if one [tries to] escape or [engages in] conflict, the present world is fluctuating between chaos and distress.[30]

While the causes of "chaos and distress" may be different this time, all the signs suggest that we are heading for another "era of suffering," or perhaps for a new stage in the same, extended era of suffering. A century ago radical Buddhists were powerless to alleviate the suffering in their time, and it is unlikely that this will be very different now. But still, what might be needed most in circumstances like these are people who refuse to close their eyes for the suffering in this world, and who genuinely want to alleviate that suffering by any effective means available, without falling victim to ideological delusions, and without getting distracted by false promises of otherworldly paradises. Admittedly, not every radical Buddhism fits that mold, but the radicalized radical Buddhism proposed in this book does.

---

28 Joshua Jackson et al., "Ecological and Cultural Factors Underlying the Global Distribution of Prejudice," *PLOS One* 14, no. 9 (2019): 0221953.
29 See the section "Secular Buddhism" in chapter 3.
30 現代は苦悩する。同胞は信愛を欲して闘争を余儀なくされ、大衆はパンを求めて弾圧を食べらわされる。逃避か闘争か、今や世はあげて混沌と窮迫とに彷徨する。— 新興仏教青年同盟 (New Buddhist Youth League),『宣言』[*Proclamation*] (1931), rpt. in Inagaki Masami 稲垣真美,『仏陀を背負いて街頭へ—妹尾義郎と新興仏教青年同盟』(Tokyo: Iwanami 岩波新書, 1974), 3–6, at 3.

References

Pāli Canon Sūtra Collections

Aṅguttara Nikāya [*The Numerical Discourses*]. Abbreviated: AN. Translated by Bhikkhu Boddhi, *The Numerical Discourses of the Buddha: A Translation of the Aṅguttara Nikāya*. Somerville: Wisdom, 2012.

Dīgha Nikāya [*The Long Discourses*]. Abbreviated: DN. Translated by Maurice Walshe, *The Long Discourses of the Buddha: A Translation of the Dīgha Nikāya*. Somerville: Wisdom, 1995.

Majjhima Nikāya [*The Middle-Length Discourses*]. Abbreviated: MN. Translated by Bhikkhu Ñāṇamoli and Bhikkhu Boddhi, *The Middle Length Discourses of the Buddha: A New Translation of the Majjhima Nikāya*. Somerville: Wisdom, 1995.

Saṃyutta Nikāya [*The Connected Discourses*]. Abbreviated: SN. Translated by Bhikkhu Boddhi, *The Connected Discourses of the Buddha: A New Translation of the Samyutta Nikāya*. Somerville: Wisdom, 2000.

Sutta Nipāta. Abbreviated: Sn. Translated by Bhikkhu Boddhi, *The Suttanipāta: An Ancient Collection of the Buddha's Discourses Together with Its Commentaries*. Somerville: Wisdom, 2017.

Sūtras and Other Texts without Attested Authors

Acela Sutta, SN 12.17.
Aggivacchagotta Sutta, MN 72.
Alagaddūpama Sutta, MN 22.
Ariyapariyesanā Sutta, MN 26.
Ārya-saṃdhinirmocana Sūtra.
Attadaṇḍa Sutta, Sn 4.15.
Avataṃsaka Sūtra [*Flower Garland Sūtra*]. Translated by Thomas Cleary, *The Flower Ornament Scripture: A Translation of the Avatamsaka Sutra*. Boston: Shambala, 1984.
Brahmajāla Sutta, DN 1.
Chakkanipāta, AN 63.5.
Cūḷamālunkya Sutta, MN 63.
Dhammacakkappavattana Sutta, SN 56.11.
Dhammapada.
Kaccānagotta, SN 12.15.
Kesamutti Sutta (also known as *Kālāma Sutta*), AN 3.65.
Laṅkāvatāra Sūtra.

Liji《禮記》[*The Book of Rites*].
Mahāsaccaka Sutta, MN 36.
Milinda Pañha [*Questions of King Milinda*].
Saddharma Puṇḍarīka Sūtra [*Lotus Sūtra*]. Translated by Tsugunari Kubo and Akira Yuyama, *The Lotus Sūtra, Translated from the Chinese of Kumārajiva*. Berkeley: Numata Center for Buddhist Translation and Research, 2007; Gene Reeves. *The Lotus Sutra*. Boston: Wisdom, 2008.
Sāmaññaphala Sutta, DN 2.
Vimalakīrti Sūtra. Translated by Robert Thurman, *The Holy Teaching of Vimalakīrti: A Mahāyāna Scripture*. University Park: Pennsylvania State University Press, 1976.

Other References

Adams, Zed. *On the Genealogy of Color: A Case Study in Historicized Conceptual Analysis*. New York: Routledge, 2016.
Ambedkar, B.R. *States and Minorities* (1947). In *Writings and Speeches*, Vol. 1, 381–449. New Delhi: Dr. Ambedkar Foundation, 1979.
———. "Buddha or Karl Marx" (1956). In *Writings and Speeches*, Vol. 3, 441–62. New Delhi: Dr. Ambedkar Foundation, 1987.
———. *The Buddha and His Dhamma* (1957). New Delhi: Oxford University Press, 2011.
———. *The Buddha and His Dhamma* (1957). In *Writings and Speeches*, Vol. 11. New Delhi: Dr. Ambedkar Foundation, 1979.
Anderson, Carol. *Pain and Its Ending: The Four Noble Truths in the Theravāda Buddhist Canon*. London: Routledge, 2013.
Arendt, Hannah. *The Origins of Totalitarianism* (1951). London: Penguin, 2017.
Asaṅga. *Bodhisattvabhūmi* (4–5th c.). Digital Sanskrit Buddhist Canon. http://www.dsbcproject.org/canon-text/book/328. Translated by Artemus Engle, *The Bodhisattva Path to Unsurpassed Enlightenment: A Complete Translation of the Bodhisattvabhūmi*. Boulder: Snow Lion, 2016.
———. *Mahāyānasaṃgraha* (4–5th c.). Digital Sanskrit Buddhist Canon. http://www.dsbcproject.org/canon-text/book/867. Translated by Karl Brunnhölzl, *A Compendium of the Mahāyāna: Asaṅga's Mahāyānasaṃgraha and Its Indian and Tibetan Commentaries*. 3 Vols. Boulder: Snow Lion, 2018.
Asmis, Elizabeth. "Epicurean Epistemology." In *The Cambridge History of Hellenistic Philosophy*, edited by Keimpe Algra, Jonathan Barnes, Jaap Mansfeld, and Malcolm Schofield, 260–94. Cambridge: Cambridge University Press, 1999.
———. "Epicurean Empiricism." In *The Cambridge Companion to Epicureanism*, edited by James Warren, 84–104. Cambridge: Cambridge University Press, 2009.
Axelrod, Robert. "The Dissemination of Culture: A Model with Local Convergence and Global Polarization." *Journal of Conflict Resolution* 41, no. 2 (1997): 203–26. DOI: 10.1177/0022002797041002001.
Bach, Kent. "Do Belief Reports Report Beliefs?" *Pacific Philosophical Quarterly* 78 (1997): 215–41. DOI: 10.1111/1468-0114.00036.
Baghramian, Maria. *Relativism*. New York: Routledge, 2004.
Barsalou, Lawrence. "Situating Concepts." In *The Cambridge Handbook of Situated Cognition*, edited by Philip Robbins and Murat Aydede, 236–63. Cambridge: Cambridge University Press, 2009.

Batchelor, Stephen. *Buddhism without Beliefs: A Contemporary Guide to Awakening.* New York: Riverhead, 1997.

———. *Confessions of a Buddhist Atheist.* New York: Spiegel & Grau, 2011.

———. "A Secular Buddhism." *Journal of Global Buddhism* 13 (2012): 87–107. DOI: 10.5281/zenodo.1306529.

———. *After Buddhism: Rethinking the Dharma for a Secular Age.* New Haven: Yale University Press, 2015.

———. *Secular Buddhism: Imagining the Dharma in an Uncertain World.* New Haven: Yale University Press, 2018.

Batson, C. Daniel. "The Things Called Empathy: Eight Related but Distinct Phenomena." In *The Social Neuroscience of Empathy*, edited by Jean Decety and William Ickes, 3–15. Cambridge: MIT Press, 2011.

———. *Altruism in Humans.* Oxford: Oxford University Press, 2011.

———. *What's Wrong with Morality? A Social-Psychological Perspective.* Oxford: Oxford University Press, 2016.

Bechert, Heinz. *Buddhismus, Staat und Gesellschaft in den Ländern des Theravāda-Buddhismus: Grundlagen. Ceylon.* Berlin: Metzer, 1966.

Becker, Ernest. *The Denial of Death.* New York: Simon & Schuster, 1973.

Beckwith, Christopher. *Greek Buddha: Pyrrho's Encounter with Early Buddhism in Central Asia.* Princeton: Princeton University Press, 2015.

Benatar, David. *Better Never to Have Been: The Harm of Coming into Existence.* Oxford: Oxford University Press, 2006.

Bentham, Jeremy. *An Introduction to the Principles of Morals and Legislation* (1789). Reprint of the 1823 Edition. Oxford: Clarendon, 1952.

Berkson, Mark. "Language: The Guest of Reality – Zhuangzi and Derrida on Language, Reality, and Skillfulness." In *Essays on Skepticism, Relativism, and Ethics in the Zhuangzi*, edited by Paul Kjellberg and Philip Ivanhoe, 97–126. Albany: SUNY Press, 1996.

Bharuch, Filita, and R.V. Kamat. "Syādvāda Theory of Jainism in Terms of a Deviant Logic" (1984) In *Facets of Jain Religion and Culture*, Volume 1: *Anekāntavāda and Syādvāda*, edited by Rai A. Kumar, T.M. Dak, and Anil D. Mishra, 339–44. Ladnun: Jain Vishva Bharati, 1996.

Bhatt, S.R., and Anu Mehrotra. *Buddhist Epistemology.* Westport: Greenwood, 2000.

Bhattacharyya, Narendra. *Jain Philosophy: Historical Outline.* New Delhi: Munshiram Manoharlal, 1999.

Bierstedt, Robert. "Indices of Civilization." *The American Journal of Sociology* 71, no. 5 (1965): 483–90. DOI: 10.1086/224166.

Bingenheimer, Marcus. *Der Mönchsgelehrte Yinshun (*1906) und seine Bedeutung für den Chinesisch-Taiwanischen Buddhismus im 20. Jahrhundert.* Heidelberg: Forum, 2004.

Bloom, Paul. *Against Empathy: The Case for Rational Compassion.* London: Bodley Head, 2016.

Boldt, Hans, Werner Conze, Görg Haverkate, Diethelm Klippel, and Reinhart Koselleck. "Staat und Souveränität." In *Geschichtliche Grundbegriffe: Historisches Lexikon zur politisch-sozialen Sprache in Deutschland*, Vol. 6: *St–Vert*, edited by Otto Brunner, Werner Conze, and Reinhart Koselleck, 1–154. Stuttgart: Klett Cotta, 1990.

Bond, George. *The Buddhist Revival in Sri Lanka: Religious Tradition, Reinterpretation and Response.* Columbia: University of South Carolina Press, 1988.

———. "A.T. Ariyaratne and the Sarvodaya Shramadana Movement in Sri Lanka." In *Engaged Buddhism: Buddhist Liberation Movements in Asia*, edited by Christopher Queen & Sallie King, 121–46. Albany: SUNY Press, 1996.

BonJour, Laurence. *The Structure of Empirical Knowledge*. Cambridge: Harvard University Press, 1985.

Boodberg, Peter. "Philological Notes on Chapter One of The Lao Tzu." *Harvard Journal of Asiatic Studies* 20, nos. 3–4 (1957): 598–618. DOI: 10.2307/2718364.

Bowker, John. *Problems of Suffering in Religions of the World*. Cambridge: Cambridge University Press, 1970.

Braver, Lee. *A Thing of This World: A History of Continental Anti-Realism*. Evanston: Northwestern University Pres, 2007.

Brennan, Jason. *Why Not Capitalism?* New York: Routledge, 2014.

———. *Against Democracy*. Princeton: Princeton University Press, 2016.

Broad, Jacqueline. *Woman Philosophers of the Seventeenth Century*. Cambridge: Cambridge University Press, 2003.

Bronkhorst, Johannes. *Greater Maghada: Studies in the Culture of Early India*. Leiden: Brill, 2007.

———. *Buddhist Teaching in India*. Boston: Wisdom, 2009.

Brons, Lajos. *Rethinking the Culture-Economy Dialectic*. PhD Thesis, University of Groningen, 2005.

———. "Applied Relativism and Davidson's Arguments against Conceptual Schemes." *The Science of Mind* 49 (2011): 221–40. DOI: 10.17613/M6PM42.

———. "Dharmakīrti, Davidson, and Knowing Reality." *Comparative Philosophy* 3, no. 1 (2012): 30–57. DOI: 10.31979/2151-6014(2012).030106.

———. "Meaning and Reality: A Cross-Traditional Encounter." In *Constructive Engagement of Analytic and Continental Approaches in Philosophy*, edited by Bo Mou and R. Tieszen, 199–220. Leiden: Brill, 2013.

———. "Language Death and Diversity: Philosophical and Linguistic Implications." *The Science of Mind* 52 (2014): 243–60. DOI: 10.17613/M6G39X.

———. "The Incoherence of Denying My Death." *Journal of Philosophy of Life* 4, no. 2 (2014): 68–89. DOI: 10.17613/M6KT12.

———. "Facing Death from a Safe Distance: Saṃvega and Moral Psychology." *Journal of Buddhist Ethics* 23 (2016): 83–128. DOI: 10.17613/M6109V.

———. "Putnam and Davidson on Coherence, Truth, and Justification." *The Science of Mind* 54 (2016): 51–70. DOI: 10.17613/M63T1Q.

———. "Recognizing 'Truth' in Chinese Philosophy." *Logos & Episteme* 7, no. 3 (2016): 273–86. DOI: 10.5840/logos-episteme20167328.

———. *The Hegemony of Psychopathy*. Earth: punctum books, 2017.

———. "Postscript: Reply to McLeod." In *Philosophy of Language, Chinese Language, Chinese Philosophy: Constructive Engagement*, edited by Bo Mou, 364–70. Leiden: Brill, 2018.

———. "Patterns, Noise, and Beliefs." *Principia* 23, no. 1 (2019): 19–51. DOI: 10.5007/1808-1711.2019v23n1p19.

———. "A Theory of Disaster-Driven Societal Collapse and How to Prevent It." Unpublished working paper. 2019. DOI: 10.17613/51rk-d378.

Brunnhölzl, Karl. "Preface." In Asaṅga, *A Compendium of the Mahāyāna: Asaṅga's Mahāyānasaṃgraha and Its Indian and Tibetan Commentaries*, Vol. 1, translated by K Brunnhölzl, xv–xxiii. Boulder: Snow Lion, 2018.

Buddhadāsa Bhikkhu. *Another Kind of Birth*. Bangkok: Sivaphorn, 1969.

———. *Dhammic Socialism*. Bangkok: Thai Inter-religious Commission for Development, 1986.

———. *Heartwood of the Bodhi Tree*. Somerville: Wisdom, 2014.

Buddhaghosa. *Visuddhimagga* (5th c.). Translated by Bhikkhu Nyanamoli, Onalaska: BPS Pariyatti, 1999.

Burbelka, Jolanta. "Historical Materialism: General Theory and Forms." In *Poznań Studies in the Philosophy of the Sciences and the Humanities*, Vol. 6: *Social Classes, Action & Historical Materialism*, edited by J. Brzeziński, P. Buczkowki, A. Klawiter, and L. Nowak, 211–35. Amsterdam: Rodopi, 1982.

Burke, Brian, Andy Martens, and Erik Faucher. "Two Decades of Terror Management Theory: A Meta-Analysis of Mortality Salience Research." *Personality and Social Psychology Review* 14, no. 2 (2010): 155–95. DOI: 10.1177/1088868309352321.

Burnouf, Eugène. *Introduction à l'histoire du buddhisme indien*, Vol. 1. Paris: Imprimerie Royale, 1844.

Cabezón, José, and Geshe Lobsang Dargyay. *Freedom from Extremes: Gorampa's "Distinguishing the Views" and the Polemics of Emptiness*. Boston: Wisdom, 2006.

Candrakīrti. *Madhyamakāvatāra* (7th c.). Digital Sanskrit Buddhist Canon. http://www.dsbcproject.org/canon-text/book/243. Translated by the Padmakara Translation Group, *Introduction to the Middle Way: Chandrakirti's Madhyamakavatara with Commentary by Jamgön Mipham*. Boston: Shambhala, 2004.

Caplan, Bryan. *The Myth of the Rational Voter: Why Democracies Choose Bad Policies*. Princeton: Princeton University Press, 2006.

Carnap, Rudolf. *Logische Syntax der Sprache*. Vienna: J. Springer, 1934.

Carnevale, Franco. "A Conceptual and Moral Analysis of Suffering." *Nursing Ethics* 16, no. 2 (2009): 173–83. DOI: 10.1177/0969733008100076.

Carruthers, Peter. *The Opacity of Mind: An Integrative Theory of Self-Knowledge*. Oxford: Oxford University Press, 2011.

Carter, Alan. "Analytical Anarchism: Some Conceptual Foundations." *Political Theory* 28, no. 2 (2000): 230–53. DOI: 10.1177/0090591700028002005.

Carus, Paul. *The Gospel of Buddha*. Chicago: Open Court, 1894.

Casanova, José. *Public Religions in the Modern World*. Chicago: University of Chicago Press, 1994.

Castell, Eric. "The Nature of Suffering and the Goals of Medicine." *The New England Journal of Medicine* 306, no. 11 (1982): 639–45. DOI: 10.1056/NEJM198203183061104.

———. *The Nature of Suffering and the Goals of Medicine*. Oxford: Oxford University Press, 1991.

Chang, Ha-Joon. *Kicking Away the Ladder*. London: Anthem, 2002.

———. *Bad Samaritans: Rich Nations, Poor Policies, and the Threat to the Developing World*. London: Random House Business, 2007.

———. *23 Things They Don't Tell You about Capitalism*. London: Penguin, 2010.

Cho, Francisca. "Buddhism, Science, and the Truth about Karma." *Religion Compass* 8, no. 4 (2014): 117–27. DOI: 10.1111/rec3.12103.

Chomsky, Noam. "Counting the Bodies." *Spectre* 9 (2009). http://www.spectrezine.org/global/chomsky.html.

Clark, J.C.D. "Secularization and Modernization: The Failure of a 'Grand Narrative'." *The Historical Journal* 55, no. 1 (2012): 161–94. DOI: 10.1017/S0018246X11000586.

Clark, Kelly James. "Naturalism and Its Discontents." In *The Blackwell Companion to Naturalism*, edited by Kelly James Clark, 1–15. Chichester: Wiley Blackwell, 2016.

Clifford, Terry. *Tibetan Buddhist Medicine and Psychiatry: The Diamond Healing* (1984). Delhi: Motilal Banarsidass, 1994.

Cohen, G.A. *Why Not Socialism?* Princeton: Princeton University Press, 2009.

Collins, Steven. "On the Very Idea of the Pali Canon" (1990). Reprinted in *Buddhism: Critical Concepts in Religious Studies*, Volume I: *Buddhist Origins and the Early History of Buddhism in South and Southeast Asia*, edited by Paul Williams, 72–95. London: Routledge, 2005.

Confucius 孔子.《論語》 [*The Analects*] (5th c. BCE). Chinese Text Project. https://ctext.org/analects.

Cort, John. "'Intellectual Ahiṃsā' Revisited: Jain Tolerance and Intolerance of Others." *Philosophy East and West* 50, no. 3 (2000): 324–47.

Courtois, Stéphane, ed. *Le livre noir du communisme: Crimes, terreur, répression*. Paris: Robert Laffont, 1997.

Davidson, Donald. "Actions, Reasons, and Causes" (1963). In *Essays on Actions and Events*, 3–19. First Edition. Oxford: Clarendon, 1980; Second Edition. Oxford: Oxford University Press, 2001.

———. "Truth and Meaning" (1967). In *Inquiries into Truth and Interpretation*, 17–36. First Edition. Oxford: Clarendon, 1984; Second Edition. Oxford: Oxford University Press, 2001.

———. "Mental Events" (1970). In *Essays on Actions and Events*, 207–25. First Edition. Oxford: Clarendon, 1980; Second Edition. Oxford: Oxford University Press, 2001.

———. "On the Very Idea of a Conceptual Scheme" (1974). In *Inquiries into Truth and Interpretation*, 183–98. First Edition. Oxford: Clarendon, 1984; Second Edition. Oxford: Oxford University Press, 2001.

———. "Reality without Reference" (1977). In *Inquiries into Truth and Interpretation*, 215–25. First Edition. Oxford: Clarendon, 1984; Second Edition. Oxford: Oxford University Press, 2001.

———. "The Method of Truth in Metaphysics" (1977). In *Inquiries into Truth and Interpretation*, 199–214. First Edition. Oxford: Clarendon, 1984; Second Edition. Oxford: Oxford University Press, 2001.

———. "The Inscrutability of Reference" (1979) In *Inquiries into Truth and Interpretation*, 227–41. First Edition. Oxford: Clarendon, 1984; Second Edition. Oxford: Oxford University Press, 2001.

———. "Empirical Content" (1982). In *Subjective, Intersubjective, Objective*, 159–75. Oxford: Oxford University Press, 2001.

———. "Rational Animals" (1982). In *Subjective, Intersubjective, Objective*, 95–105. Oxford: Oxford University Press, 2001.

———. "A Coherence Theory of Truth and Knowledge" (1983). In *Subjective, Intersubjective, Objective*, 137–53. Oxford: Oxford University Press, 2001.

———. "A Nice Derangement Of Epitaphs" (1986). In *Truth, Language, and History*, 89–107. Oxford: Oxford University Press, 2005.

———. "Deception and Division" (1986). In *Problems of Rationality*, 199–212. Oxford: Oxford University Press, 2004.

———. "Afterthoughts" (1987). In *Subjective, Intersubjective, Objective*, 154–57. Oxford: Oxford University Press, 2001.

———. "Knowing One's Own Mind" (1987). In *Subjective, Intersubjective, Objective*, 15–38. Oxford: Oxford University Press, 2001.

———. "The Myth of the Subjective" (1988). In *Subjective, Intersubjective, Objective*, 39–52. Oxford: Oxford University Press, 2001.

———. "The Conditions of Thought." In *The Mind of Donald Davidson*, edited by J. Brandl and W.L. Gombocz, 193–200. Amsterdam: Rodopi, 1989.

———. "What Is Present to the Mind?" (1989). In *Subjective, Intersubjective, Objective*, 53–56. Oxford: Oxford University Press, 2001.

———. "Epistemology Externalized" (1990). In *Subjective, Intersubjective, Objective*, 193–204. Oxford: Oxford University Press, 2001.

———. "Meaning, Truth and Evidence" (1990). In *Truth, Language, and History*, 47–62. Oxford: Oxford University Press, 2005.

———. "Three Varieties of Knowledge" (1991). In *Subjective, Intersubjective, Objective*, 205–20. Oxford: Oxford University Press, 2001.

———. "The Second Person" (1992). In *Subjective, Intersubjective, Objective*, 107–22. Oxford: Oxford University Press, 2001.

———. "Locating Literary Language" (1993). In *Truth, Language, and History*, 167–81. Oxford: Oxford University Press, 2005.

———. "Thinking Causes" (1993). In *Truth, Language, and History*, 185–200. Oxford: Oxford University Press, 2005.

———. "The Social Aspect of Language" (1994). In *Truth, Language, and History*, 109–25. Oxford: Oxford University Press, 2005.

———. "Laws and Cause" (1995). In *Truth, Language, and History*, 201–19. Oxford: Oxford University Press, 2005.

———. "Pursuit of the Concept of Truth" (1995). In *Truth, Language, and History*, 63–80. Oxford: Oxford University Press, 2005.

———. "The Objectivity of Values" (1995). In *Problems of Rationality*, 39–53. Oxford: Oxford University Press, 2004.

———. "The Problem of Objectivity" (1995). In *Problems of Rationality*, 3–18. Oxford: Oxford University Press, 2004.

———. "The Folly of Trying to Define Truth" (1996). In *Truth, Language, and History*, 19–37. Oxford: Oxford University Press, 2005.

———. "Indeterminism and Antirealism" (1997). In *Subjective, Intersubjective, Objective*, 69–84. Oxford: Oxford University Press, 2001.

———. "Seeing through Language" (1997). In *Truth, Language, and History*, 127–41. Oxford: Oxford University Press, 2005.

———. "The Emergence of Thought" (1997). In *Subjective, Intersubjective, Objective*, 123–34. Oxford: Oxford University Press, 2001.

———. "The Irreducibility of the Concept of the Self" (1998). In *Subjective, Intersubjective, Objective*. Oxford: Oxford University Press, 2001.: 85–91.

———. "Interpretation: Hard in Theory, Easy in Practice." In *Interpretations and Causes*, edited by Mario De Caro, 31–44. Dordrecht: Kluwer, 1999.

———. "Intellectual Autobiography." In *The Philosophy of Donald Davidson*, edited by Lewis E. Hahn, 3–70. Chicago: Open Court, 1999.

———. "Reply to A.C. Genova." In *The Philosophy of Donald Davidson*, edited by Lewis E. Hahn, 192–94. Chicago: Open Court, 1999.

———. "Reply to Pascal Engel." In *The Philosophy of Donald Davidson*, edited by Lewis E. Hahn, 460–61. Chicago: Open Court, 1999.

———. "Reply to Simon J. Evnine." In *The Philosophy of Donald Davidson*, edited by Lewis E. Hahn, 305–10. Chicago: Open Court, 1999.

———. "Comments on Karlovy Vary Papers." In *Interpreting Davidson*, edited by Petr Kotatko, Peter Pagin, and Gabriel Segal, 285–308. Stanford: CSLI, 2001.

———. "Externalisms." In *Interpreting Davidson*, edited by Petr Kotatko, Peter Pagin, and Gabriel Segal, 1–16. Stanford: CSLI, 2001.

———. "What Thought Requires" (2001). In *Problems of Rationality*, 135–49. Oxford: Oxford University Press, 2004.

———. *Truth and Predication*. Cambridge: Belknap, 2005.

Davis, Bret. "The Philosophy of Zen Master Dōgen: Egoless Perspectivism." In *The Oxford Handbook of World Philosophy*, edited by Jay L. Garfield and William Edelglass, 348–60. Oxford: Oxford University Press, 2011.

Davis, Gordon. "Moral Realism and Anti-Realism outside the West: A Meta-Ethical Turn in Buddhist Ethics." *Comparative Philosophy* 4, no. 2 (2013): 24–53. DOI: 10.31979/2151-6014(2013).040205.

Davis, Mike. *Late Victorian Holocausts: El Niño Famines and the Making of the Third World*. London: Verso, 2001.

De Lazari-Radek, Kataryna, and Peter Singer. *The Point of View of the Universe: Sidgwick and Contemporary Ethics*. Oxford: Oxford University Press, 2014.

Deitrick, James. "Engaged Buddhist Ethics: Mistaking the Boat for the Shore." In *Action Dharma: New Studies in Engaged Buddhism*, edited by Christopher Queen, Charles Prebish, and Damien Keown, 252–69. London: RoutledgeCurzon, 2003.

Derrida, Jacques. "Différance" (1968). In *Marges de la philosophie*, 1–29. Paris: Les Éditions de Minuit, 1972.

Dhar, Anup, Anjan Chakrabarti, and Serap Kayatekin. "Crossing Materialism and Religion: An Interview on Marxism and Spirituality with the Fourteenth Dalai Lama." *Rethinking Marxism* 28, nos. 3–4 (2016): 584–98. DOI: 10.1080/08935696.2016.1243426.

Dharmakīrti, *Pramāṇavārttika* (6th/7th c.). *Digital Sanskrit Buddhist Canon*. http://www.dsbcproject.org/canon-text/book/298.

Dharmapāla, Anagarika. "The World's Debt to Buddha" (1893). In *Return to Righteousness: A Collection of Speeches, Essays and Letters of the Anagarika Dharmapala*, edited by Ananda Guruge, 3–22. Colombo: Ministry of Education and Cultural Affairs, 1965.

———. "The Constructive Optimism of Buddhism" (1915). In *Return to Righteousness: A Collection of Speeches, Essays and Letters of the Anagarika Dharmapala*, edited by Ananda Guruge, 391–400. Colombo: Ministry of Education and Cultural Affairs, 1965.

———. "The Repenting God of Horeb" (1922). In *Return to Righteousness: A Collection of Speeches, Essays and Letters of the Anagarika Dharmapala*, edited by Ananda Guruge, 401–25. Colombo: Ministry of Education and Cultural Affairs, 1965.

———. "Message of the Buddha" (1925). In *Return to Righteousness: A Collection of Speeches, Essays and Letters of the Anagarika Dharmapala*, edited by Ananda Guruge, 23–34. Colombo: Ministry of Education and Cultural Affairs, 1965.

Dignāga. *Ālambanaparīkṣā* (4–5th c.). Translated in Duckworth, Douglas, Malcolm David Eckle, Jay L. Garfield, John Powers, Yeshes Thabkhas, and Sonam Thakchöe. *Dignāga's Investigation of the Percept: A Philosophical Legacy in India and Tibet*, 38–39. Oxford: Oxford University Press, 2016.

———. *Ālambanaparīkṣāvṛtti* (4–5th c.). Translated in Duckworth, Douglas, Malcolm David Eckle, Jay L. Garfield, John Powers, Yeshes Thabkhas, and Sonam Thakchöe. *Dignāga's Investigation of the Percept: A Philosophical Legacy in India and Tibet*, 40–46. Oxford: Oxford University Press, 2016.

———. *Pramāṇasamuccaya* (6th c.). Partially translated by Massaaki Hattori, *Dignāga, On Perception, Being the Pratyakṣapariccheda of Dignāga's Pramāṇasamuccaya from the Sanskrit Fragments and the Tibetan Versions*. Cambridge: Harvard University Press, 1968.

———. *Pramāṇasamuccayavṛtti*. Translated by Ole Holten Lind, *Dignāga's Philosophy of Language: Pramāṇasamuccayavṛtti von Anyāpoha*. Vienna: ÖAW, 2015.

Diogenes Laertius. *Lives of Eminent Philosophers* (Βίοι καὶ Γνῶμαι τῶν ἐν Φιλοσοφίᾳ Εὐδοκιμησάντων) (3rd c.). Translated by R.D. Hicks. 2 Vols. Loeb Classical Library. London: William Heineman, 1925.

Dirlik, Alif. *Anarchism in the Chinese Revolution*. Berkeley: University of California Press, 1991.

Dōgen 道元.『正法眼藏』(1231–53). *The SAT Daizōkyō Text Database*, Vol. 82, Text no. 2582. http://21dzk.l.u-tokyo.ac.jp/SAT/index_en.html.

Dolce, Lucia. "Between Duration and Eternity: Hermeneutics of the 'Ancient Buddha' of the Lotus Sutra in Chih-i and Nichiren." In *A Buddhist Kaleidoscope: Essays on the Lotus Sutra*, edited by Gene Reeves, 223–39. Tokyo: Kosei, 2002.

Dooyeweerd, Herman. *A New Critique of Theoretical Thought*, Vol. 1: *The Necessary Presuppositions of Philosophy*. Amsterdam: Paris, 1953.

———. *A New Critique of Theoretical Thought*, Vol. 2: *The General Theory of Modal Spheres*. Amsterdam: Paris, 1955.

Drewes, David. "The Idea of the Historical Buddha." *Journal of the International Association of Buddhist Studies* 40 (2017): 1–25. DOI: 10.2143/JIABS.40.0.3269003.

Dreyfus, Georges. *Recognizing Reality: Dharmakīrti's Philosophy and Its Tibetan Interpretations*. Albany: SUNY Press, 1997.

——— (2011). "Apoha as a Naturalized Account of Concept Formation." In *Apoha: Buddhist Nominalism and Human Cognition*, edited by Mark Siderits, Tom Tillemans, and Arindam Chakrabarti, 207–27. New York: Columbia University Press.

Drijfhout, Sybren, Sebastian Bathiany, Claudie Beaulieu, Victor Brovkin, Martin Claussen, Chris Huntingford, Marten Scheffer, Giovanni Sgubin, and Didier Swingedouw (2015). "Catalogue of Abrupt Shifts in Intergovernmental Panel on Climate Change Climate Models." *PNAS*: E5777–86. DOI: 10.1073/pnas.1511451112.

Driver, Julia. *Uneasy Virtue*. Cambridge: Cambridge University Press, 2001.

———. *Consequentialism*. London: Routledge, 2012.

———. "What the Objective Standard Is Good For." In *Oxford Studies in Normative Ethics*, Volume 2, edited by Mark Timmons, 28–44. Oxford: Oxford University Press, 2012.

Ducheyne, Steffen. "J.S. Mill's Canon of Induction: From True Causes to Provisional Ones." *History and Philosophy of Logic* 29 (2008): 361–76. DOI: 10.1080/01445340802164377.

Duckworth, Douglas, Malcolm David Eckle, Jay L. Garfield, John Powers, Yeshes Thabkhas, and Sonam Thakchöe. *Dignāga's Investigation of the Percept: A Philosophical Legacy in India and Tibet*. Oxford: Oxford University Press, 2016.

Dunne, John. *Foundations of Dharmakīrti's Philosophy*. Boston: Wisdom, 2004.

Dupré, John. *The Disorder of Things: Metaphysical Foundations of the Disunity of Science.* Cambridge: Harvard University Press, 1993.

Edwards, Steven. "Three Concepts of Suffering." *Medicine, Health Care and Philosophy* 6 (2003): 59–66. DOI: 10.1023/A:1022537117643.

Eiteman, W.J, and G.E. Guthrie. "The Shape of the Average Cost Curve." *American Economic Review* 42, no. 5 (1952): 832–38.

Elder-Vass, Dave. *The Reality of Social Construction.* Cambridge: Cambridge University Press, 2012.

Ellis, Brian. "Retrospective and Prospective Utilitarianism." *Noûs* 15, no. 3 (1981): 325–39. DOI: 10.2307/2215436.

Engels, Friedrich. *Der Ursprung der Familie, des Privateigentums und des Staats: im Anschluß an Lewis H. Morgans Forschungen* (1884), MEW 21: 25–173.

Epicurus. *Letter to Herodotus* (3rd c. BCE). In Diogenes Laertius, *Lives of Eminent Philosophers*, translated by R.D Hicks, Vol. 2, Book X, §§35–83. Loeb Classical Library. London: William Heineman, 1925.

Epicurus. *Letter to Pythocles* (3rd c. BCE). In Diogenes Laertius, *Lives of Eminent Philosophers*, translated by R.D Hicks, Vol. 2, Book X, §§84–116. Loeb Classical Library. London: William Heineman, 1925.

Farias, Miguel, and Catherine Wikholm. *The Buddha Pill: Can Meditation Change You?* London: Watkins, 2015.

Faure, Bernard. *Unmasking Buddhism.* London: Wiley-Blackwell, 2009.

Feldman, Simon. *Against Authenticity: Why You Shouldn't Be Yourself.* London: Lexington, 2015.

Field, Hartry. *Science without Numbers: A Defense of Nominalism, Second Edition.* Oxford: Oxford University Press, 2016.

Fine, Arthur. "Fictionalism." *Midwest Studies in Philosophy* 18 (1993): 1–18. DOI: 10.1111/j.1475-4975.1993.tb00254.x.

Flavell, John. "The Development of Children's Understanding of False Belief and the Appearance-Reality Distinction." *International Journal of Psychology* 28, no. 5 (1993): 595–604. DOI: 10.1080/00207599308246944.

Føllesdal, Dagfinn. "Quine on Modality." In *The Cambridge Companion to Quine*, edited by Roger Gibson, 200–213. Cambridge: Cambridge University Press, 2004.

Forte, Victor. "Saichō: Founding Patriarch of Japanese Buddhism." In *The Dao Companion to Japanese Buddhist Philosophy*, edited by Gereon Kopf, 307–35. Dordrecht: Springer, 2019.

Frankfurt, Harry. "Alternate Possibilities and Moral Responsibility" (1969). In *The Importance of What We Care About: Philosophical Essays*, 1–10. Cambridge: Cambridge University Press, 1988.

Frydenlund, Iselin. "'Buddhism Has Made Asia Mild': The Modernist Construction of Buddhims as Pacifism." In *Buddhist Modernities: Re-Inventing Tradition in the Globalizing Modern World*, edited by Hanna Havnevik, Ute Hüsken, Mark Teeuwen, Vladimir Tikhonov, and Koen Wellens, 204–21. New York: Routledge, 2017.

Fung Yu-Lan 馮友蘭. *A Short History of Chinese Philosophy.* Translated and edited by Derk Bodde. New York: MacMillan, 1948.

Furth, Charlotte. "Intellectual Change: From the Reform Movement to the May Fourth Movement, 1895–1920." In *The Cambridge History of China*, Volume 12:

Republican China 1912–1949, Part I, edited by John Fairbank, 322–405. Cambridge: Cambridge University Press, 1983.

Gadamer, Hans-Georg. *Wahrheit und Methode: Grundzüge einer philosophischen Hermeutik*. Second Edition. Tübingen: J.C.B. Mohr, 1965.

Galeo, Sandra, Melissa Tracy, Katherine J. Hogatt, Charles DiMaggio, and Adam Karpati. "Estimated Deaths Attributable to Social Factors in the United States." *American Journal of Public Health* 101, no. 8 (2011): 1456–65. DOI: 10.2105/AJPH.2010.300086.

Galle, Peter. "Gruzalski and Ellis on Utilitarianism." *Australasian Journal of Philosophy* 59, no. 3 (1981): 332–7. DOI: 10.1080/00048408112340291.

Garfield, Jay. "Epochē and Śūnyatā: Skepticism East and West" (1990). In *Empty Words: Buddhist Philosophy and Cross-Cultural Interpretation*, 3–23. Oxford: Oxford University Press, 2002.

———. *Engaging Buddhism: Why It Matters to Philosophy*. New York: Oxford University Press, 2015.

———. "Buddhism and Modernity." In *The Buddhist World*, edited by John Powers, 294–304. London: Routledge, 2016.

Garfield, Jay, Stephen Jenkins, and Graham Priest. "The Śāntideva Passage: Bodhicaryāvatāra VIII.90–103." In Cowherds, *Moonpaths: Ethics and Emptiness*, 55–76. Oxford: Oxford University Press, 2016.

Geertz, Clifford. *Islam Observed: Religious Development in Morocco and Indonesia*. Chicago: University of Chicago Press, 1968.

Gelman, Susan. *The Essential Child: Origins of Essentialism in Everyday Thought*. Oxford: Oxford University Press, 2003.

Gert, Bernard. *Common Morality: Deciding What to Do*. Oxford: Oxford University Press, 2004.

———. *Morality: Its Nature and Justification*. Oxford: Oxford University Press, 2005.

Gettier, Edmund. "Is Justified True Belief Knowledge?" *Analysis* 23 (1963): 121–23. DOI: 10.2307/3326922.

Giere, Ronald. *Scientific Perspectivism*. Chicago: University of Chicago Press, 2006.

Gimello, Robert. "Apophatic and Kataphatic Discourse in Mahāyāna: A Chinese View." *Philosophy East and West* 26, no. 2 (1976): 117–36.

Giridharadas, Anand. *Winners Take All: The Elite Charade of Changing the World*. New York: Knopf, 2018.

Glock, Hans-Johann. *Quine and Davidson on Language, Truth and Reality*. Cambridge: Cambridge University Press, 2003.

Gombrich, Richard. *Buddhist Precept and Practice: Traditional Buddhism in the Rural Highlands of Ceylon*. Oxford: Clarendon, 1971.

———. *Theravāda Buddhism: A Social History from Ancient Benares to Modern Colombo*. Second Edition. London: Routledge, 2006.

Gombrich, Richard, and Gananath Obeyesekere. *Buddhism Transformed: Religious Change in Sri Lanka*. Princeton: Princeton University Press, 1988.

Goodell, Eric. "Taixu's Youth and Years of Romantic Idealism, 1890–1914." *Chung-Hwa Buddhist Journal* 21 (2008): 77–121.

Goodman, Charles. *Consequences of Compassion: An Interpretation & Defense of Buddhist Ethics*. Oxford: Oxford University Press, 2009.

Goonatilake, Susantha. "Review of Collected Works of A.T. Ariyaratne." *Journal of Contemporary Asia* 13, no. 2 (1983): 236–42. DOI: 10.1080/00472338380000161.

———. *Recolonisation: Foreign Funded NGOs in Sri Lanka*. New Delhi: Sage, 2006.

Gorman, W.M. "Community Preference Fields." *Econometrica* 21, no. 1 (1953): 63–80. DOI: 10.2307/1906943.

Graham, Frank. "Some Aspects of Protection Further Considered." *The Quarterly Journal of Economics* 37, no. 2 (1923): 199–227. DOI: 10.2307/1883929.

Graham, Jesse, Jonathan Haidt, and Brian Nosek. "Liberals and Conservatives Rely on Different Sets of Moral Foundations." *Journal of Personality and Social Psychology* 96 (2009): 1029–46. DOI: 10.1037/a0015141.

Gramsci, Antonio. *Selections from the Prison Notebooks*. New York: International Publishers, 1971.

Greenberg, Jeff, and Jamie Arndt. "Terror Management Theory." In *Handbook of Theories of Social Psychology*, Vol. 1, edited by Paul A.M. Van Lange, Arie W. Kruglanski, and E. Tory Higgins, 398–415. London: Sage, 2011.

Greenberg, Jeff, Linda Simon, Tom Pyszczynski, Sheldon Solomon, and Dan Chatel. "Terror Management and Tolerance: Does Mortality Salience Always Intensify Negative Reactions to Others Who Threaten One's Worldview?" *Journal of Personality and Social Psychology* 63, no. 2 (1992): 212–20. DOI: 10.1037/0022-3514.63.2.212.

Gregory, Paul. *Quine's Naturalism: Language, Theory, and the Knowing Subject*. London: Continuum, 2008.

Groner, Paul. *Saichō: The Establishment of the Japanese Tendai School*. Honolulu: University of Hawai'i Press, 2000.

Gruzalski, Bart. "Foreseeable Consequence Utilitarianism." *Australasian Journal of Philosophy* 59, no. 2 (1981): 163–76. DOI: 10.1080/00048408112340131.

Haack, Susan. *Evidence and Inquiry: A Pragmatist Reconstruction of Epistemology*. New York: Prometheus, 2009.

Haidt, Jonathan. *The Righteous Mind: Why Good People Are Divided by Politics and Religion*. New York: Pantheon, 2012.

Hales, Steven, and Rex Welshon. *Nietzsche's Perspectivism*. Urbana: University of Illinois Press, 2000.

Hall, Charles, and Kent Klitgaard. *Energy and the Wealth of Nations: An Introduction to Biophysical Economics*. Second Edition. Berlin: Springer, 2018.

Han Yongun. "The Buddhism I believe In" (1924). In *Selected Writings of Han Yongun: From Social Darwinism to "Socialism with a Buddhist Face,"* translated by Vladimir Tikhonov and Owen Miller, 153–54. Folkestone: Global Oriental, 2008.

———. "Sakyamuni's Spirit: Dialogue with a Journalist" (1931). In *Selected Writings of Han Yongun: From Social Darwinism to "Socialism with a Buddhist Face,"* translated by Vladimir Tikhonov and Owen Miller, 158–64. Folkestone: Global Oriental, 2008.

———. "Meditation and Human Life" (1932). In *Selected Writings of Han Yongun: From Social Darwinism to "Socialism with a Buddhist Face,"* translated by Vladimir Tikhonov and Owen Miller, 165–80. Folkestone: Global Oriental, 2008.

Hansen, Chad. "Classical Chinese Ethics." In *A Companion to Ethics*, edited by Peter Singer, 69–81. Oxford: Blackwell, 1993.

Harbsmeier, Christoph. *Science and Civilization in China*, Vol. 7: *The Social Background*, Part 1: *Language and Logic in Traditional China*. Cambridge: Cambridge University Press, 1998.

Häring, Norbert, and Niall Douglas. *Economists and the Powerful: Convenient Theories, Distorted Facts, Ample Rewards*. London: Anthem, 2012.

Harman, Gilbert. "Moral Philosophy Meets Social Psychology: Virtue Ethics and the Fundamental Attribution Error." *Proceedings of the Aristotelian Society, New Series* 99 (1999): 315–31.

Harman, Graham. "A Festival of Anti-Realism: Braver's History of Continental Thought." *Philosophy Today* 52, no. 2 (2008): 197–210. DOI: 10.5840/philtoday200852234.

Harris, Ian Charles. *The Continuity of Madhyamaka and Yogācāra in Indian Mahāyāna Buddhism.* Leiden: Brill, 1991.

Harris, Stephen. "The Skillful Handling of Poison: Bodhicitta and the Kleśas in Śāntideva's Bodhicaryāvatāra." *Journal of Indian Philosophy* 45 (2017): 331–48. DOI: 10.1007/s10781-016-9311-1.

Harrison, Paul. "Buddhānusmṛti in the Pratyutpanna-Buddha-Saṃmukhāvasthita-Samādhi-Sūtra." *Journal of Indian Philosophy* 6, no. 1 (1978): 35–57.

Harvey, Peter. "Karma." In *The Oxford Handbook of Buddhist Ethics*, edited by Daniel Cozort & James Mark Shields, 7–28. Oxford: Oxford University Press, 2000.

Haslanger, Sally. *Resisting Reality: Social Construction and Social Critique.* Oxford: Oxford University Press, 2012.

Hattori, Massaaki. *Dignāga, On Perception, Being the Pratyakṣapariccheda of Dignāga's Pramāṇasamuccaya from the Sanskrit Fragments and the Tibetan Versions.* Cambridge: Harvard University Press, 1968.

Hegel, G.W.F. *Wissenschaft der Logik,* Vol. 2 (1813). In *Werke,* Vol. 6. Frankfurt a.M.: Suhrkamp, 1969–71.

———. *Vorlesungen über die Geschichte der Philosophie,* Vol. 1 (1837). In *Werke,* Vol. 18. Frankfurt a.M.: Suhrkamp, 1969–71.

Heilbron, Johan, Lars Magnusson, and Björn Wittrock, eds. *The Rise of the Social Sciences and the Formation of Modernity: Conceptual Change in Context, 1750-1850.* Dordrecht: Kluwer, 1998.

Heraclitus. *Fragments* (6–5th c. BCE). In Hermann Diels, *Die Fragmente der Vorsokratiker,* edited by Walther Kranz, Vol. 1, 139–90. Berlin: Wiedmannsche Verlagsbuchhandlung, 1960.

Herman, Edward, and Noam Chomsky. *Manufacturing Consent: The Political Economy of the Mass Media.* London: Vintage, 1988.

Hodgson, Geoffrey. *Conceptualizing Capitalism: Institutions, Evolution, Future.* Chicago: University of Chicago Press, 2015.

———. *Is Socialism Feasible? Towards an Alternative Future.* Cheltenham: Edward Elgar, 2019.

Hope, David, and Julian Limberg. "The Economic Consequences of Major Tax Cuts for the Rich." LSE International Inequalities Institute Working Paper #55. 2020. https://eprints.lse.ac.uk/107919/.

Horkheimer, Max. "Die gegenwärtige Lage der Sozialphilosophie und die Aufgaben eines Instituts für Sozialforschung" (1931). In *Gesammelte Schriften,* Band 3: *Schriften 1931–1936,* 20–35. Frankfurt a.M.: Fischer, 1988.

———. "Materialismus und Moral" (1933). In *Gesammelte Schriften,* Band 3: *Schriften 1931–1936,* 111–49 Frankfurt a.M.: Fischer, 1988.

Hoshino Seiji 星野靖二. "'Rational Religion' and the Shin Bukkyo [New Buddhism] Movement in Late Meiji Japan." In『近代日本における知識人宗教運動の言説空間—「新佛教」の思想史・文化史的研究』, edited by Yoshinaga Shin'ichi, 205–18. Report of Grants-in-Aid for Scientific Research no. 20320016, 2012.

Hudson, Michael. *Killing the Host: How Financial Parasites and Debt Bondage Destroy the Global Economy.* Dresden: Islet, 2015.

———. "Economic Methodology is Ideology, and Implies Policy." In: *J Is for Junk Economics: A Guide to Reality in an Age of Deception,* 291–304. Dresden: Islet, 2017.

Hudson, Wayne. "Historicizing Suffering." In *Perspectives on Human Suffering,* edited by Jeff Malpas and Norelle Lickiss, 171–79. Dordrecht: Springer, 2012.

Hultzsch, E. *Inscriptions of Asoka.* New Edition. Oxford: Clarendon Press, 1925.

Hussey, Edward. "Heraclitus." In *The Cambridge Companion to Early Greek Philosophy,* edited by A.A. Long, 88–112. Cambridge: Cambridge University Press, 1999.

Hylton, Peter. *Quine.* New York: Routledge, 2007.

Ibn Rushd. *Fasl al-Maqal fi ma bayn al-Hikma wa al-Shariah min Ittisal* [*On the Harmony of Religion and Philosophy*] (1179). Translated by George Hourani, *On the Harmony of Religion and Philosophy.* Cambridge: Gibb Memorial Trust, 1961.

———. *Tahāfut al-Tahāfut* [*The Incoherence of the Incoherence*] (1180). Translated by Simon Van den Bergh, *Averroes' Tahafut Al-Tafut.* Cambridge: Gibb Memorial Trust, 1954.

Ichikawa Hakugen 市川白弦.『仏教者の戦争責任』. Tokyo: Shunshūsha 春秋社, 1970.

Inagaki Masami 稲垣真美.『仏陀を背負いて街頭へ―妹尾義郎と新興仏教青年同盟』. Tokyo: Iwanami 岩波新書, 1974.

———, ed.『妹尾義郎宗教論集』. Tokyo: Daizō 大蔵出版, 1975.

Inglehart, Ronald. *The Silent Revolution.* Princeton: Princeton University Press, 1977.

———. *Culture Shift in Advanced Industrial Society.* Princeton: Princeton University Press, 1990.

Inoue Enryō 井上圓了.『哲学要領』(1886). In『井上円了選集』. Vol. 1, 87–215. Tokyo: Tōyō University 東洋大学, 2003.

———.『仏教活論序論』(1887). In『井上円了選集』, Vol. 3: 327–93. Tokyo: Tōyō University 東洋大学, 2003.

———.『仏教活論本論、第二編：顕正活論』(1890). In『井上円了選集』, Vol. 4: 189–37. Tokyo: Tōyō University 東洋大学, 2003.

———.『奮闘哲学』(1917). In『井上円了選集』, Vol. 2: 207–444. Tokyo: Tōyō University 東洋大学, 2003.

Inoue Tetsujirō 井上哲次郎 (1897).「現象即実在論の要領」. In『井上哲次郎集』, Vol. 9, 153–99. Tokyo: Kress クレス出版, 2003.

IPCC. *Global Warming of 1.5°C.* Geneva: IPCC, 2018. https://www.ipcc.ch/sr15/.

———. *Climate Change and Land.* Geneva: IPCC, 2019. https://www.ipcc.ch/srccl/.

———. *The Ocean and Cryosphere in a Changing Climate.* Geneva: IPCC, 2019. https://www.ipcc.ch/srocc/.

Ives, Christopher. *Imperial-way Zen: Ichikawa Hakugen's Critique and Lingering Questions for Buddhist Ethics.* Honolulu: University of Hawai'i Press, 2009.

Iyer, Ravi, Spassena Koleva, Jesse Graham, Peter Ditto, and Jonathan Haidt. "Understanding Libertarian Morality: The Psychological Dispositions of Self-identified Libertarians." *PLOS One* 7, no. 8 (2012): e42366. DOI: 10.1371/journal.pone.0042366.

Jackson, Joshua, Marieke van Egmond, Virginia K. Choi, Carol R. Ember, Jamin Halberstadt, et al. "Ecological and Cultural Factors Underlying the Global Distribution of Prejudice." *PLOS One* (2019): 0221953. DOI: 10.1371/journal.pone.0221953.

James, William. "Pragmatism: A New Name for Some Old Ways of Thinking" (1907). In *Pragmatism and the Meaning of Truth*, 1–166. Cambridge: Harvard University Press, 1978.

Jameson, Fredric. "Future City." *New Left Review* 21 (2003): 65–79.

Jenkins, Stephen. "Do Bodhisattvas Relieve Poverty?" In *Action Dharma: New Studies in Engaged Buddhism*, edited by Christopher Queen, Charles Prebish, and Damien Keown, 38–49. London: RoutledgeCurzon, 2003.

Johnston, Mark. *Saving God: Religion after Idolatry*. Princeton: Princeton University Press, 2009.

———. *Surviving Death*. Princeton: Princeton University Press, 2010.

Jones, Charles. *Buddhism in Taiwan: Religion and the State, 1660–1990*. Honolulu: University of Hawai'i Press, 1999.

———. "Buddhism and Marxism in Taiwan: Lin Qiuwu's Religious Socialism and its Legacy in Modern Times." *Journal of Global Buddhism* 1 (2000): 82–111.

———. "Transitions in the Practice and Defense of Chinese Pure Land Buddhism." In *Buddhism in the Modern World: Adaptations of an Ancient Tradition*, edited by Steven Heine and Charles Prebish, 125–42. Oxford: Oxford University Press, 2003.

Jorgensen, John. "Indra's Network: Zhang Taiyan's Sino-Japanese Personal Networks and the Rise of Yogācāra in Modern China." In *Transforming Consciousness: Yogācāra Thought in Modern China*, edited by John Makeham, 64–99. Oxford: Oxford University Press, 2014.

Josephson, Jason Ānanda. "When Buddhism Became a 'Religion': Religion and Superstition in the Writings of Inoue Enryō." *Japanese Journal of Religious Studies* 33, no. 1 (2006): 143–68. https://www.jstor.org/stable/30233795.

Kallis, Giorgos, Vasilis Kostakis, Steffen Lange, Barbara Muraca, Susan Paulson, and Matthias Schmelzer. "Research on Degrowth." *Annual Review of Environment and Resources* 43 (2018): 291–316. DOI: 10.1146/annurev-environ-102017-025941.

Kant, Immanuel. *Kritik der Reinen Vernunft*. (1781/1787). Hamburg: Felix Meiner, 1998.

———. *Grundlegung zur Metaphysik der Sitten* (1785). Frankfurt a.M.: Suhrkamp, 2019.

Kantor, Hans-Rudolf. "Dynamics of Practice and Understanding – Chinese Tiantai Philosophy of Contemplation and Deconstruction." In *Dao Companion to Chinese Buddhist Philosophy*, edited by Youru Wang and Sandra Wawrytko, 218–92. Dordrecht: Springer, 2018.

Kapstein, Matthew. "Who Wrote the *Trisvabhāvanirdeśa*? Reflections on an Enigmatic Text and Its Place in the History of Buddhist Philosophy." *Journal of Indian Philosophy* 46 (2018): 1–30. DOI: 10.1007/s10781-017-9334-2.

Kashiwahara Yūsen 柏原祐泉.『日本仏教史　現代』. Tokyo: Yoshikawa Kōbunkan 古川弘文館, 1990.

Kashiwagi Ryūhō 柏木隆法.『大逆事件と内山愚童』. Tokyo: JCA, 1979.

Katō Shūichi. "Tominaga Nakamoto, 1715–46: A Tokugawa Iconoclast." *Monumenta Nipponica* 22, nos. 1–2 (1967): 177–93. DOI: 10.2307/2383230.

Katsura, Shōryū. "Dignāga and Dharmakīrti on Apoha." In *Studies in the Buddhist Epistemological Tradition*, edited by Ernst Steinkellner, 129–46. Vienna: ÖAW, 1991.

Keen, Sam. "The Heroics of Everyday Life: A Theorist of Death Confronts His Own End." *Psychology Today*, April 1974, 71–80.

Keen, Steve. *Debunking Economics: The Naked Emperor Dethroned?* Revised and Expanded Edition. London: Zed, 2011.

———. *Can We Avoid Another Financial Crisis?* Cambridge: Polity, 2017.

Kemp, Gary. *Quine versus Davidson: Truth, Reference, & Meaning.* Oxford: Oxford University Press, 2012.

Kern, Hendrik. *Geschiedenis van het Buddhisme in Indië,* Vol. 1. Haarlem: Tjeenk Willink, 1882.

Kim, Hee-Jin. *Eihei Dōgen: Mystical Realist.* Boston: Wisdom, 2004.

———. *Dōgen on Meditation and Thinking: A Reflection on His View of Zen.* Albany: SUNY Press, 2007.

King, Richard. *Orientalism and Religion: Postcolonial Theory, India, and "The Mythic East."* London: Routledge, 1999.

King, Sallie. *Buddha Nature.* New York: SUNY Press, 1991.

———. "Thich Nhat Hanh and the Unified Buddhist Church of Vietnam: Nondualism in Action." In *Engaged Buddhism: Buddhist Liberation Movements in Asia,* edited by Christopher Queen and Sallie King, 321–63. New York: SUNY Press, 1996.

Klein, Naomi. *The Shock Doctrine: The Rise of Disaster Capitalism.* New York: Henry Holt, 2007.

———. *This Changes Everything: Capitalism vs. the Climate.* New York: Simon & Schuster, 2014.

Kohlberg, Lawrence. "From Is to Ought: How to Commit the Naturalistic Fallacy and Get Away With It in the Study of Moral Development." In *Cognitive Development and Epistemology,* edited by Theodore Mischel, 151–235. New York: Academic Press, 1971

———. "The Claim to Moral Adequacy of a Highest Stage of Moral Judgment." *Journal of Philosophy* 70, no. 18 (1973): 630–46. DOI: 10.2307/2025030.

Koller, John. "Syādvāda as the Epistemological Key to the Jaina Middle Way Metaphysics of Anekāntavāda." *Philosophy East and West* 50, no. 3 (2000): 400–407.

Koontz, Amanda. "Constructing Authenticity: A Review of Trends and Influences in the Process of Authentication in Consumption." *Sociology Compass* 4, no. 11 (2009): 977–88. DOI: 10.1111/j.1751-9020.2010.00334.x.

Kosaka Kunitsugu. "Metaphysics in the Meiji Period."『国際哲学研究』(*Journal of International Philosophy*) 3 (2014): 291–307.

Koselleck, Reinhart. "Einleitung." In *Geschichtliche Grundbegriffe: Historisches Lexikon zur politisch-sozialen Sprache in Deutschland,* Vol. 1: A–D, edited by Otto Brunner, Werner Conze, and Reinhart Koselleck, xiii–xxvii. Stuttgart: Klett Cotta, 1972.

Krausz, Michael. "Introduction." In *Relativism: A Contemporary Anthology,* edited by Michael Krausz, 1–10. New York: Columbia University Press, 2010.

Kripke, Saul. *Naming and Necessity.* Cambridge: Harvard University Press, 1972.

———. *Wittgenstein on Rules and Private Language.* Cambridge: Harvard University Press, 1982.

Kritzer, Robert. *Rebirth and Causation in the Yogācāra Abhidharma.* Vienna: Arbeitskreis für Tibetische und Buddhistische Studien, 1999.

Kroeber, Alfred, and Clyde Kluckhohn. *Culture: A Critical Review of Concepts and Definitions.* Cambridge: Peabody Museum of American Archaeology and Ethnology, 1952.

Kropotkin, Peter. *Modern Science and Anarchism.* New York: Mother Earth, 1908.

———. Fields, Factories, and Workshops. London: Swan Sonnenschein, 1909.
Kumārajīva.《中論》(4–5th c.). *The SAT Daizōkyō Text Database*, Vol. 30, Text no. 1564. http://21dzk.l.u-tokyo.ac.jp/SAT/index_en.html.
Ladwig, Patrice, and James Mark Shields. "Introduction." *Politics, Religion & Ideology* 15, no. 2 (2014): 187–204. DOI: 10.1080/21567689.2014.898413.
Lai, Whalen. "Seno'o Girō and the Dilemma of Modern Buddhism – Leftist Prophet of the Lotus Sūtra." *Japanese Journal of Religious Studies* 11, no. 1 (1984): 7–42.
Large, Stephen. "Buddhism, Socialism, and Protest in Prewar Japan: The Career of Seno'o Girō." *Modern Asian Studies* 21, no. 1 (1987): 153–71.
Leaman, Oliver. *Averroes and His Philosophy*. Richmond: Curzon, 1988.
Leiter, Brian. "Perspectivism in Nietzsche's Genealogy of Morals." In *Nietzsche, Genealogy, Morality: Essays on Nietzsche's Genealogy of Morals*, edited by Richard Schacht, 334–57. Berkeley: University of California Press, 1994.
Lenin, Vladimir I. *The State and Revolution*. London: G. Allen & Unwin, 1917.
———. *"Left-Wing" Communism: An Infantile Disorder* (1920). Edited by Ahmed Shawki. Chicago: Haymarket Books, 2014.
Lenman, James. "Consequentialism and Cluelessness." *Philosophy & Public Affairs* 29, no. 4 (2000): 342–70. DOI: 10.1111/j.1088-4963.2000.00342.x.
Lenton, Timothy, Herman Held, Elmar Kriegler, and Hans Joachim Schnellnhuber. "Tipping Elements in the Earth's Climate System." *PNAS* 105, no. 6 (2008): 1786–93. DOI: 10.1073/pnas.0705414105.
Leone, Giuliana. "Epicuro, Della Natura, Libro XIV." *Cronache Ercolanesi* 14 (1984): 17–107.
Levman, Bryan. "Cultural Remnants of the Indigenous Peoples in the Buddhist Scriptures." *Buddhist Studies Review* 30, no. 2 (2013): 145–80. DOI: 10.1558/bsrv.v30i2.145.
———. "The Historical Buddha: Response to Drewes." *Canadian Journal of Buddhist Studies* 14 (2019): 25–56. https://thecjbs.org/archive-document-details/?id=2.
Lewis, C.I. *An Analysis of Knowledge and Valuation*. LaSalle: Open Court, 1946.
Liji《禮記》(The Book of Rites). *Chinese Text Project*. https://ctext.org/liji.
Li Zhenglong 李政隆.〈共建人間淨土的社會福利工作〉,《佛教文化》0 (1990): 2.
———.〈什麼是人間淨土?〉,《佛教文化》1 (1990): 2.
Lin Qiuwu 林秋梧.〈為臺灣佛教熱叫!!〉,《南瀛佛教》6, no. 6 (1928): 50–53.
———.〈階級鬥爭與佛教〉,《南瀛佛教》7, no. 2 (1929): 52–58.
———.〈婦人講座　佛說堅固女經講話(二)〉,《南瀛佛教》11, no. 12 (1933): 18–25.
———.〈婦人講座　佛說堅固女經講話(吾)〉,《南瀛佛教》12, no. 3 (1934): 12–18.
Lin, Pei-ying. "A Survey of the Japanese Influence on Buddhist Education in Taiwan during the Japanese Colonial Period (1895–1945)." *Religions* 11, no. 2 (2020): art. 61. DOI: 10.3390/rel11020061.
Liu, JeeLoo. *An Introduction to Chinese Philosophy: From Ancient Philosophy to Chinese Buddhism*. Malden: Blackwell, 2006.
Lopez, Jr, Donald. *The Madman's Middle Way: Reflections of Reality of the Tibetan Monk Gendun Chopel*. Chicago: University of Chicago Press, 2006.
———. *Buddhism and Science: A Guide for the Perplexed*. Chicago: University of Chicago Press, 2008.

———. *The Scientific Buddha: His Short and Happy Life.* New Haven: Yale University Press, 2012.

———. *The Lotus Sūtra: A Biography.* Princeton: Princeton University Press, 2016.

Lopez, Jr, Donald, and Jacqueline Stone. *Two Buddhas Seated Side by Side: A Guide to the Lotus Sūtra.* Princeton: Princeton University Press, 2019.

Lopez, Jr, Donald, and Thupten Jinpa. "Gendün Chöpel on British Imperialism." In *Sources of Tibetan Tradition*, edited by K. Schaeffer, M. Kapstein, and G. Tuttle, 751–55. New York: Columbia University Press, 2013.

Lusthaus, Dan. *Buddhist Phenomenology: A Philosophical Investigation of Yogācāra Buddhism and the Ch'eng Wei-shih lun.* London: RoutledgeCurzon, 2002.

Lynas, Mark. *Six Degrees: Our Future on a Hotter Planet.* New York: HarperCollins, 2007.

———. *Our Final Warning: Six Degrees of Climate Emergency.* London: 4th Estate, 2020.

MacDougall, Andrew, Thomas L. Frölicher, Chris D. Jones, Joeri Rogelj, H. Damon Matthews, Kirsten Zickfeld, Vivek K. Arora, Noah J. Barrett, Victor Brovkin, Friedrich A. Burger, Micheal Eby, Alexey V. Eliseev, Tomohiro Hajima, Philip B. Holden, Aurich Jeltsch-Thömmes, Charles Koven, Nadine Mengis, Laurie Menviel, Martine Michou, Igor I. Mokhov, Akira Oka, Jörg Schwinger, Roland Séférian, Gary Shaffer, Andrei Sokolov, Kaoru Tachiiri, Jerry Tjiputra, Andrew Wiltshire, and Tilo Ziehn. "Is There Warming in the Pipeline? A Multi-model Analysis of the Zero Emissions Commitment from CO_2." *Biogeosciences* 17 (2020): 2987–3016. DOI: 10.5194/bg-17-2987-2020.

Macfarlane, Alan. *The Origins of English Individualism: The Family, Property and Social Transition.* Oxford: Blackwell, 1978.

Macy, Joanna. "In Indra's Net: Sarvodaya & Our Mutual Efforts for Peace." In *The Path of Compassion: Writings on Socially Engaged Buddhism*, edited by Fred Eppsteiner, 170–81. Berkeley: Parallax, 1985.

Magee, Bryan. *Talking Philosophy: Dialogues with Fifteen Leading Philosophers.* Oxford: Oxford University Press, 1982.

Mahaprajña, Acharya. "The Axioms of Non-Absolutism" (1984). In *Facets of Jain Religion and Culture*, Volume 1: *Anekāntavāda and Syādvāda*, edited by Rai A. Kumar, T.M. Dak, and Anil D. Mishra, 1–32. Ladnun: Jain Vishva Bharati, 1996.

Main, Jessica, and Rongdao Lai. "Introduction: Reformulating 'Socially Engaged Buddhism' as an Analytical Category." *The Eastern Buddhist* 44, no. 2 (2013): 1–34. https://www.jstor.org/stable/44362566.

Malachowski, Alan. *Richard Rorty.* Chesham: Acumen, 2002.

Maraldo, John. "The Japanese Encounter with and Appropriation of Western Philosophy." In *The Oxford Handbook of Japanese Philosophy*, edited by Bret Davis, 333–63. Oxford: Oxford University Press, 2014.

Marx, Karl. *Ökonomisch-philosophische Manuskripte aus dem Jahre 1844.* In Karl Marx and Friedrich Engels, *Werke*, Vol. 40, 465–588. Berlin: Dietz, 1962–68.

———. *Thesen über Feuerbach* (1845). In Karl Marx and Friedrich Engels, *Werke*, Vol. 3, 5–7. Berlin: Dietz, 1962–68.

———. *Das Elend der Philosophie: Antwort auf Proudhons "Philosophie des Elends"* (1847). In Karl Marx and Friedrich Engels, *Werke*, Vol. 4, 63–182. Berlin: Dietz, 1962–68.

———. *Zur Kritik der Politischen Ökonomie* (1859). In Karl Marx and Friedrich Engels, *Werke*, Vol. 13, 1–160. Berlin: Dietz, 1962–68.

——— *Kritik des Gothaer Programms* (1875). In Karl Marx and Friedrich Engels, *Werke*, Vol. 19, 11–32. Berlin: Dietz, 1962–68.

Marx, Karl, and Friedrich Engels. *Die deutsche Ideologie* (1846). In Karl Marx and Friedrich Engels, *Werke*, Vol. 3, 9–530. Berlin: Dietz, 1962–68.

———. *Manifest der Kommunistischen Partei* [*The Communist Manifesto*] (1848). In Karl Marx and Friedrich Engels, *Werke*, Vol. 4, 459–93. Berlin: Dietz, 1962–68.

Mason, Elinor. "Objectivism, Subjectivism, and Prospectivism." In *The Cambridge Companion to Utilitarianism*, edited by Ben Eggleston and Dale Miller, 177–98. Cambridge: Cambridge University Press, 2014.

Matilal, Bimal. *Epistemology, Logic, and Grammar in Indian Philosophical Analysis*. The Hague: Mouton, 1971.

———. *The Central Philosophy of Jainism (Anekānta-Vāda)*. Ahmedabad: LD Institute of Indology, 1981.

Mattick, Paul. "Kapitalismus und Ökologie." *Jahrbuch Arbeiterbewegung* 4 (1976): 220–41.

Mazars, Sylvain. *Le bouddhisme et la médecine traditionnelle de l'Inde*. Paris: Springer, 2008.

McEvilley, Thomas. *The Shape of Ancient Thought: Comparative Studies in Greek and Indian Philosophies*. New York: Allworth, 2002.

McIntyre, Alison. "Doing Away with Double Effect." *Ethics* 111, no. 2 (2001): 219–55. DOI: 10.1086/233472.

McKibben, Bill. *Falter: Has the Human Game Begun to Play Itself Out?* New York: Henry Holt, 2019.

McLeod, Alexus. "A Reappraisal of Wang Chong's Critical Method through the 'Wenkong' Chapter." *Journal of Chinese Philosophy* 34, no. 4 (2007): 581–96. DOI: 10.1111/j.1540-6253.2007.00440.x.

———. *Theories of Truth in Chinese Philosophy*. London: Rowman & Littlefield, 2015.

———. *The Philosophical Thought of Wang Chong*. Cham: Palgrave MacMillan, 2018.

McMahan, David. *The Making of Buddhist Modernism*. Oxford: Oxford University Press, 2008.

Mencius 孟子,《孟子》(4th c. BCE). *Chinese Text Project*. https://ctext.org/mengzi.

Metzinger, Thomas. "Suffering." In *The Return of Consciousness: A New Science on Old Questions*, edited by Kurt Almqvist & Anders Haag, 237–62. Stockholm: Axel and Margaret Ax:son Johnson Foundation, 2017.

Mill, John Stuart. *Utilitarianism* (1861). In *Collected Works*, Vol. X. Toronto: University of Toronto Press, 1969.

Mills, Charles. "'Ideal Theory' as Ideology." *Hypatia* 20, no. 3 (2005): 165–84. https://www.jstor.org/stable/3811121.

Miyazawa Kenji 宮澤賢治.「雨ニモマケズ」(1931). In 『【新】校本・宮澤賢治全集』, Vol. 13. Tokyo: Chikuma Shobō 筑摩書房, 1997.

Mobbs, Dean, and Caroline Watt. "There Is Nothing Paranormal about Near-death Experiences: How Neuroscience Can Explain Seeing Bright Lights, Meeting the Dead, or Being Convinced You Are One of Them." *Trends in Cognitive Sciences* 15, no. 10 (2011): 447–49. DOI: 10.1016/j.tics.2011.07.010.

Mookerjee, Satkari. *The Jaina Philosophy of Non-absolutism*. Delhi: Motilal Banarsidass, 1944.

Morgan, Lewis. *Ancient Society: or, Researches in the Line of Human Progress from Savagery through Barbarism to Civilization*. Chicago: Kerr, 1877.

Mou, Bo. "Searle, Zhuang Zi, and Transcendental Perspectivism." In *Searle's Philosophy and Chinese Philosophy: Constructive Engagement*, edited by Bo Mou, 405–30. Leiden: Brill, 2008.

Mozi 墨子,《墨子》(5th c. BCE). *Chinese Text Project*. https://ctext.org/mozi.

Murthy, Viren. "Equality as Reification: Zhang Taiyan's Yogācāra Reading of Zhuangzi in the Context of Global Modernity." In *Transforming Consciousness: Yogācāra Thought in Modern China*, edited by John Makeham, 123–45. Oxford: Oxford University Press, 2014.

Myrdal, Gunnar. *The Political Element in the Development of Economic Theory*. London: Routledge, 1953.

Nāgārjuna, *Mūlamadhyamakakārikā* (2nd–3rd c.). https://indica-et-buddhica.org/archive/nagarjuna/mulamadhyamakakarikas-sanskrit-digital-text. Translated by Jay Garfield, *The Fundamental Wisdom of the Middle Way: Nāgārjuna's Mūlamadhyamakakārikā*. Oxford: Oxford University Press, 1995; Mark Siderits and Shōryū Katsura. *Nāgārjuna's Middle Way: Mūlamadhyamakārikā*. Boston: Wisdom, 2012.

———. *Ratnāvalī* (2nd–3rd c.). Translated by Jeffrey Hopkins and Lati Rimpoche with Anne Klein in Nāgārjuna & Kaysang Gyatso, *The Precious Garland and The Song of the Four Mindfulnesses*, 13–93. New York: Harper & Row, 1975.

Nagel, Thomas. "What Is it Like to Be a Bat?" *The Philosophical Review* 83, no. 4 (1974): 435–50. DOI: 10.2307/2183914.

Nattier, Jan. *Once Upon a Future Time: Studies in a Buddhist Prophecy of Decline*. Berkeley: Asian Humanities Press, 1991.

Nelson, Robert. *Economics as Religion: From Samuelson to Chicago and Beyond*. Revised Edition. University Park: Penn State University Press, 2014.

Neurath, Otto. "Soziologie im Physikalismus." *Erkenntnis* 2 (1931): 393–431. DOI: 10.1007/BF02028171.

New Buddhist Youth League 新興仏教青年同盟 (1931).『宣言』[Proclamation]. In Inagaki Masami 稲垣真美,『仏陀を背負いて街頭へ―妹尾義郎と新興仏教青年同盟』, 2–6. Tokyo: Iwanami 岩波新書, 1974.

Nhat Hanh, Thich. *Vietnam: The Lotus in the Sea of Fire*. New York: Hill & Wang, 1967.

———. *Being Peace*. Berkeley: Parallax, 1987.

———. "Commentary." In *The Sutra on the Eight Realizations of the Great Beings*, translated by Diem Thanh Truong & Carole Melkonian, 10–25. Loubès-Bernac: Dharma Books, 1987:

———. *The Diamond That Cuts through Illusion*. Revised Edition. Berkeley: Parallax, 2006.

Nichiren 日蓮.『立正安國論』[*Establishing the Peace of the Country*] (1260). *The SAT Daizōkyō Text Database*, Vol. 84, Text no. 2688. http://21dzk.l.u-tokyo.ac.jp/SAT/index_en.html. Translated in Philip Yampolsky, ed. *Selected Writings of Nichiren*. Translated by Burton Watson & Others, 11–47. New York: Columbia University Press, 1990.

———.『開目抄』[*The Opening of the Eyes*] (1272). Translated in Philip Yampolsky, ed. *Selected Writings of Nichiren*. Translated by Burton Watson & Others, 50–147. New York: Columbia University Press, 1990.

———. "Offerings in Principle and Actuality" (also known as "The Gift of Rice," 13th c.). Translated by Jacqueline Stone, *Some Disputed Writings in the Nichiren*

Corpus: Textual, Hermeneutical and Historical Problems. PhD Thesis, University of California at Berkeley, 1990, 483–89.

Nietzsche, Friedrich. *Menschliches Allzumenschliches* (1878). *Digital Critical Edition (eKGWB).* http://www.nietzschesource.org/#eKGWB/MA-I.

———. *Jenseits von Gut und Böse: Vorspiel einer Philosophie der Zukunft* (1886). *Digital Critical Edition (eKGWB).* http://www.nietzschesource.org/#eKGWB/JGB.

Norman, K.R. "The Four Noble Truths: A Problem of Pali Syntax." In *Indological and Buddhist Studies: Volume in Honour of Professor J.W. de Jong on his Sixtieth Birthday,* edited by L.A. Hercus, 377–91. Canberra: Australian National University Press, 1982.

Nottelmann, Nikolaj. "Belief Metaphysics: The Basic Questions." In *New Essays on Belief: Constitution, Content, and Structure,* edited by Nikolaj Nottelmann, 9–29. London: Palgrave MacMillan, 2013.

Nozick, Robert. *Anarchy, State, and Utopia.* Oxford: Blackwell, 1974.

———. "The Holocaust." In *The Examined Life: Philosophical Meditations,* 236–42. New York: Simon and Schuster, 1989.

O'Flaherty, Wendy. "Introduction." In *Karma and Rebirth in Classical Indian Traditions,* edited by Wendy O'Flaherty, ix–xxv. Berkeley: University of California Press, 1980.

Obeyesekere, Gananath. "Religious Symbolism and Political Change in Ceylon." *Modern Ceylon Studies* 1 (1970): 43–63.

Odin, Steve. "The Lotus Sutra in the Writings of Miyazawa Kenji." In *A Buddhist Kaleidoscope: Essays on the Lotus Sutra,* edited by Gene Reeves, 283–96. Tokyo: Kosei, 2002.

Olcott, Henry Steel. *A Buddhist Catechism: According to the Canon of the Southern Church.* Colombo: The Theosophical Society, 1881.

———. *Old Diary Leaves: The Only Authentic History of the Theosophical Society, Fourth Series: 1887–92.* Madras: Theosophical Publishing Society, 1910.

Olsson, Erik. "What Is the Problem of Coherence and Truth?" *The Journal of Philosophy* 99 (2002): 246–72. DOI: 10.2307/3655648.

———. *Against Coherence: Truth, Probability, and Justification.* Oxford: Clarendon, 2005.

Orrell, David. *Economyths: Ten Ways Economics Gets It Wrong.* Ontario: John Wiley, 2010.

Osborne, Catherine. "Heraclitus." In *Routledge History of Philosophy,* Volume I: *From the Beginning to Plato,* edited by C.C.W. Taylor, 88–127. London: Routledge, 1997.

Overgaard, Søren, Paul Gilbert, and Stephen Burwood. *An Introduction to Metaphilosophy.* Cambridge: Cambridge University Press, 2013.

Pacey, Scott. "A Buddhism for the Human World: Interpretations of Renjian Fojiao in Contemporary Taiwan." *Asian Studies Review* 29 (2005): 61–77. DOI: 10.1080/10357820500139505.

———. "Taixu, Yogācāra, and the Buddhist Approach to Modernity." In *Transforming Consciousness: Yogācāra Thought in Modern China,* edited by John Makeham, 150–69. Oxford: Oxford University Press, 2014.

Padmarajiah, Y.J. *A Comparative Study of the Jaina Theories of Reality and Knowledge.* Delhi: Motilal Banarsidass, 1963.

Parenti, Christian. *Tropic of Chaos: Climate Change and the New Geography of Violence.* New York: Nation Books, 2011.

Parenti, Michael. "Friendly Feudalism: The Tibet Myth." *New Political Science* 25, no. 4 (2003): 579–90. DOI: 10.1080/0739314032000145242.

Parfit, Derek. *On What Matters*, Vol. 2. Oxford: Oxford University Press, 2011.

Park, Chang-Eui, Su-Jong Jeong, Manoj Joshi, Timothy J. Osborn, Chang-Hoi Ho, Shilong Piao, Deliang Chen, et al. "Keeping Global Warming within 1.5°C Constrains Emergence of Aridification." *Nature Climate Change* 8 (2018): 70–74. DOI: 10.1038/s41558-017-0034-4.

Peterson, Richard. "Revitalizing the Culture Concept." *Annual Review of Sociology* 5 (1979): 137–66. DOI: 10.1146/annurev.so.05.080179.001033.

Phillips, Peter. *Giants: The Global Power Elite*. New York: Seven Stories, 2018.

Plato. Πολιτεία [*The Republic*] (4th c. BCE). Edited and translated by Christopher Emlyn-Jones and William Preddy. 2 Vols. Loeb Classical Library. Cambridge: Harvard University Press, 1937.

Popper, Karl. *The Open Society and Its Enemies*, Vol. I: *The Spell of Plato* (1943). London: Routledge, 1947.

Puntarigvivat, Tavivat (2013). *Thai Buddhist Social Theory*. Bangkok: World Buddhist University.

Putnam, Hilary. *Reason, Truth and History*. Cambridge: Cambridge University Press, 1981.

———. "Why There Isn't a Ready-Made World" (1981). In *Realism and Reason: Philosophical Papers*, Vol. 3, 205–28. Cambridge: Cambridge University Press, 1983.

———. "Introduction" (1983) In *Realism and Reason: Philosophical Papers*, Volume 3, vii–xviii. Cambridge: Cambridge University Press, 1983.

———. *The Many Faces of Realism*. La Salle: Open Court, 1987.

———. *Representation and Reality*. Cambridge: MIT Press, 1988.

———. *Realism with a Human Face*. Cambridge: Harvard University Press, 1990.

———. *The Threefold Cord: Mind, Body, and World*. New York: Columbia University Press, 1999.

———. *Ethics without Ontology*. Cambridge: Harvard University Press, 2004.

———. "Reply to Tim Maudlin." In *The Philosophy of Hilary Putnam*, edited by Randall Auxier, Douglas Anderson, and Lewis Hahn, 502–9. Chicago: Open Court, 2015.

Quammen, David. *Spillover: Animal Infections and the Next Human Pandemic*. London: Bodley Head, 2012.

Quiggin, John. *Zombie Economics: How Dead Ideas Still Walk among Us*. Princeton: Princeton University Press, 2010.

Quine, W.V.O. "On What There Is" (1948). In *From a Logical Point of View*, 1–19. Cambridge: Harvard University Press, 1964.

———. "Two Dogmas of Empiricism" (1951). In *From a Logical Point of View*, 20–46. Cambridge: Harvard University Press, 1964.

———. "Three Grades of Modal Involvement" (1953). In *The Ways of Paradox and Other Essays*, 158–76. Revised and Enlarged Edition. Cambridge: Harvard University Press, 1976.

———. "Two Dogmas of Empiricism" (1953). In *From a Logical Point of View*, 20–46. Cambridge: Harvard University Press, 1964.

———. "Posits and Reality" (1955). In *The Ways of Paradox and Other Essays*, 246–54. Revised and Enlarged Edition. Cambridge: Harvard University Press, 1976.

———. *Word and Object*. Cambridge: MIT Press, 1960.

———. "Epistemology Naturalized" (1969). In *Ontological Relativity & Other Essays*, 69–90 New York: Columbia University Press, 1969.

———. "Ontological Relativity" (1969). In *Ontological Relativity & Other Essays*, 26–68. New York: Columbia University Press, 1969.

———. "Speaking of Objects" (1969). In *Ontological Relativity & Other Essays*, 1–25. New York: Columbia University Press, 1969.

———. *Philosophy of Logic*. Second Edition. Cambridge: Harvard University Press, 1986.

———. *Pursuit of Truth*. Revised Edition. Cambridge: Harvard University Press, 1992.

———. *From Stimulus to Science*. Cambridge: Harvard University Press, 1995.

———. "I, You, and It: An Epistemological Triangle." In *Knowledge, Language and Logic: Questions for Quine*, edited by Alex Orenstein & Peter Kotatko, 1–6. Dordrecht: Springer, 2000.

Quine, W.V.O., and J.S. Ullian. *The Web of Belief*. Second Edition. New York: Random House, 1978.

Rahula, Walpola. "The Social Teachings of the Buddha." In *The Path of Compassion: Writings on Socially Engaged Buddhism*, edited by Fred Eppsteiner, 103–10. Berkeley: Parallax, 1985.

Railton, Peter. "Alienation, Consequentialism, and the Demands of Morality." *Philosophy & Public Affairs* 13, no. 2 (1984): 134–71.

Rambelli, Fabio. *Zen Anarchism: The Egalitarian Dharma of Uchiyama Gudō*. Berkeley: Institute of Buddhist Studies and BDK America, 2013.

Rapley, John. *Twilight of the Money Gods: Economics as Religion and How It All Went Wrong*. London: Simon & Schuster, 2017.

Rawls, John. *A Theory of Justice*. Cambridge: Belknap, 1971.

Reeves, Gene. "The Lotus Sutra as Radically World-Affirming." In *A Buddhist Kaleidoscope: Essays on the Lotus Sutra*, edited by Gene Reeves, 177–99. Tokyo: Kosei, 2002.

Reinert, Erik. *How Rich Countries Got Rich. and Why Poor Countries Stay Poor*. London: Constable, 2007.

Ricardo, David. *On the Principles of Political Economy and Taxation*. London: Murray, 1817.

Richard, Mark. *Propositional Attitudes: An Essay on Thoughts and How We Ascribe Them*. Cambridge: Cambridge University Press, 1990.

Ricke, Katharine, and Ken Caldeira. "Maximum Warming Occurs about One Decade after a Carbon Dioxide Emission." *Environmental Research Letters* 9.124002 (2014). DOI: 10.1088/1748-9326/9/12/124002.

Riedel, Manfred. "Gesellschaft, bürgerliche." In *Geschichtliche Grundbegriffe: Historisches Lexikon zur politisch-sozialen Sprache in Deutschland*, Vol. 2: E–G, edited by Otto Brunner, Werner Conze, and Reinhart Koselleck, 719–800. Stuttgart: Klett Cotta, 1975.

———. "Gesellschaft, Gemeinschaft." In *Geschichtliche Grundbegriffe: Historisches Lexikon zur politisch-sozialen Sprache in Deutschland*, Vol. 2: E–G, edited by Otto Brunner, Werner Conze, and Reinhart Koselleck, 801–62. Stuttgart: Klett Cotta, 1975.

Riepe, Dale. *The Naturalistic Tradition in Indian Thought*. Delhi: Motilal Banarsidass, 1961.

Ritzinger, Justin. *Anarchy in the Pure Land: Reinventing the Cult of Maitreya in Modern Chinese Buddhism*. Oxford: Oxford University Press, 2017.

Robinson, William. *Global Capitalism and the Crisis of Humanity*. New Edition. Cambridge: Cambridge University Press, 2014.

Roland, Jeffrey. "On Naturalism in the Quinean Tradition." In *Philosophical Methodology: The Armchair or the Laboratory*, edited by Matthew Haug, 43–61. London: Routledge, 2014.

Rorty, Richard. *Philosophy and the Mirror of Nature*. Princeton: Princeton University Press, 1979.

———. *Consequences of Pragmatism*. Minneapolis: University of Minnesota Press, 1982.

———. "Pragmatism, Davidson and Truth" (1986). In *Objectivity, Relativism, and Truth: Philosophical Papers*, Vol. I, 126–50. Cambridge: Cambridge University Press, 1991.

———. *Contingency, Irony, and Solidarity*. Cambridge: Cambridge University Press, 1989.

———. "A World without Substances or Essences" (1994). In *Philosophy and Social Hope*, 47–71. London: Penguin, 1999.

Russell, Bertrand. "William James's Conception of Truth." In *Philosophical Essays*, 127–49. Cambridge: Cambridge University Press, 1910.

Saichō 最澄.『守護國界章』[*Essay on Protecting the Realm*] (818). *The SAT Daizōkyō Text Database*, Vol. 74, Text no. 2362. http://21dzk.l.u-tokyo.ac.jp/SAT/index_en.html..

———.『修禅寺相伝私注』. In『伝教大師全集』, Vol. 3, 661–81. Tokyo: Tendai Sect Publications 天台宗宗典刊行会, 1912.

Said, Edward. *Orientalism*. New York: Pantheon, 1978.

Salomon, Richard. *The Buddhist Literature of Ancient Gandhāra: An Introduction with Selected Translations*. Boston: Wisdom, 2018.

Śāntideva. *The Bodhicaryāvatāra* (8th c.). *Digital Sanskrit Buddhist Canon*. http://www.dsbcproject.org/canon-text/book/258. Translated by Kate Crosby and Andrew Skilton. Oxford: Oxford University Press, 1995.

———. *The Training Anthology of Śāntideva: A Translation of the Śikṣā-samuccaya* (8th c.). Translated by Charles Goodman. Oxford: Oxford University Press, 2016.

Santikaro Bhikkhu. "Buddhadasa Bhikkhu: Life and Society through the Natural Eyes of Voidness." In *Engaged Buddhism: Buddhist Liberation Movements in Asia*, edited by Christopher Queen and Sallie King, 147–93. New York: SUNY Press, 1996.

Sarkisyanz, Emanuel. *Buddhist Backgrounds of the Burmese Revolution*. Dordrecht: Springer, 1965.

Satō Hiroo. "Nichiren's View of Nation and Religion." *Japanese Journal of Religious Studies* 26, nos. 3–4 (1999): 307–23.

Schaaf, Jasper. *Boeddhisme en betrokkenheid: Kan de Boeddha-Darma bijdragen aan een marxistisch georiënteerde inzet van maatschappelijke betrokkenheid?* Groningen: Dialectiek, 2000.

Scheffler, Samuel. *Death and the Afterlife*. Oxford: Oxford University Press, 2013.

Schelling, F.W.J. "Darstellung des Systems meiner Philosophie" (1800). In *Sämtliche Werke*, Vol. 4, 105–212. Stuttgart: Cotta, 1859.

———. *Sämtliche Werke*, Vol. 3. Stuttgart: Cotta, 1858.

Schlick, Moritz. "Über das Fundament der Erkenntnis." *Erkenntnis* 4 (1934): 79–99.

Schmithausen, Lambert. *On the Problem of the External World in the Ch'eng wei shih lun*. Tokyo: International Institute for Buddhist Studies, 2015.

Schopen, Gregory. *Bones, Stones, and Buddhist Monks: Collected Papers on the Archaeology, Epigraphy, and Texts of Monastic Buddhism in India*. Honolulu: University of Hawai'i Press, 1997.

———. *Buddhist Monks and Business Matters: Still More Papers on Monastic Buddhism in India*. Honolulu: University of Hawai'i Press, 2004.

Schulzer, Rainer. "Inoue Enryō's Philosophy of Buddhism." In *The Dao Companion to Japanese Buddhist Philosophy*, edited by Gereon Kopf, 565–73. Dordrecht: Springer, 2019.

———. *Inoue Enryō: A Philosophical Portrait*. New York: SUNY Press, 2019.

Schwitzgebel, Eric. "Zhuangzi's Attitude Toward Language and His Skepticism." In *Essays on Skepticism, Relativism, and Ethics in the Zhuangzi*, edited by Paul Kjellberg and Philip Ivanhoe, 68–96. Albany: State University of New York Press, 1996.

———. "The Unreliability of Naive Introspection." *Philosophical Review* 117, no. 2 (2008): 245–73. DOI: 10.1215/00318108-2007-037.

———. "Introspection, What?" In *Introspection and Consciousness*, edited by Declan Smithies and Daniel Stoljar, 29–47. Oxford: Oxford University Press, 2012.

Searle, John. *The Construction of Social Reality*. London: Allen Lane Penguin, 1995.

———. "The Future of Philosophy." *Philosophical Transactions of the Royal Society of London B* 354 (1999): 2069–80. DOI: 10.1098/rstb.1999.0544.

Sedley, David. *Lucretius and the Transformation of Greek Wisdom*. Cambridge: Cambridge University Press, 1998.

Sellars, Wilfrid. "Empiricism and the Philosophy of Mind" (1956). In *Science, Perception and Reality*, 127–96. London: Routledge and Kegan Paul, 1963.

———. "Abstract Entities" (1963). In *In the Space of Reasons*, 163–205. Cambridge: Harvard University Press, 2007.

Sengzhao 僧肇.《肇論》(5th c.). *The SAT Daizōkyō Text Database*, Vol. 45, Text no. 1858. http://21dzk.l.u-tokyo.ac.jp/SAT/index_en.html.

Seno'o Girō 妹尾義郎 (1931).『新興佛教への転身』. In『妹尾義郎宗教論集』., edited by Inagaki Masami 稲垣真美, 260–301. Tokyo: Daizō 大蔵出版, 1975.

——— (1933) .『社会変革途上の新興佛教』. In『妹尾義郎宗教論集』., edited by Inagaki Masami 稲垣真美, 325–88. Tokyo: Daizō 大蔵出版, 1975.

Sharf, Robert. "The Zen of Japanese Nationalism." *History of Religions* 33, no. 1 (1993): 1–43. https://www.jstor.org/stable/1062782.

———. *Coming to Terms with Chinese Buddhism: A Reading of the Treasure Store Treatise*. Honolulu: Kuroda Institute/University Of Hawai'i Press, 2002.

Sharma, Arvind. "The Doctrine of Syādvāda: Examination of Different Interpretations." In *Facets of Jain Religion and Culture*, Vol. 1: *Anekāntavāda and Syādvāda*, edited by Rai A. Kumar, T.M. Dak, and Anil D. Mishra, 326–38. Ladnun: Jain Vishva Bharati, 1996.

Shen, Haiyan. "Tiantai Integrations of Doctrine and Practice." In *The Wiley Blackwell Companion to East and Inner Asian Buddhism*, edited by Mario Poceski, 127–44. Malden: Wiley Blackwell, 2014.

Sherwood, Steve, M. J. Webb, J. D. Annan, K. C. Armour, P. M. Forster, J. C. Hargreaves, G. Hegerl, et al. "An Assessment of Earth's Climate Sensitivity Using Multiple Lines of Evidence." *Review of Geophysics* 58, no. 4 (2020): e2019RG000678. DOI: 10.1029/2019RG000678.

Shields, James Mark. "Awakening between Science, Art and Ethics: Variations of Japanese Buddhist Modernism, 1890–1945." In *Rethinking Japanese Modernism*, edited by Roy Starrs, 105–24. Leiden: Brill, 2011.

———. "A Blueprint for Buddhist Revolution: The Radical Buddhism of Senoʻo Girō (1889–1961) and the Youth League for Revitalizing Buddhism." *Japanese Journal of Religious Studies* 39, no. 2 (2012): 333–51.

———. "Radical Buddhism, Then and Now: Prospects of a Paradox." *Silva Iaponicarum* 日林 23/24/25/26 (2012): 15–34.

———. "Liberation as Revolutionary Praxis: Rethinking Buddhist Materialism." *Journal of Buddhist Ethics* 20 (2013): 461–99.

———. "Senoʻo Giro: The Life and Thought of a Radical Buddhist." In *Buddhists: Understanding Buddhism through the Lives of Practitioners*, edited by Todd Lewis, 280–88. Chichester: Wiley Blackwell, 2014.

———. "The Scope and Limits of Secular Buddhism: Watanabe Kaikyoku and the Japanese New Buddhist 'Discovery of Society'." In *Buddhist Modernities: Re-Inventing Tradition in the Globalizing Modern World*, edited by Hanna Havnevik, Ute Hüsken, Mark Teeuwen, Vladimir Tikhonov, and Koen Wellens, 15–32. New York: Routledge, 2017.

———. "Immanent Frames: Meiji New Buddhism, Pantheism, and the 'Religious Secular'." *Japan Review* 30 (2017): 7995. https://www.jstor.org/stable/44259462.

———. *Against Harmony: Progressive and Radical Buddhism in Modern Japan*. Oxford: Oxford University Press, 2017.

———. "Buddhist Economics: Problems and Possibilities." In *The Oxford Handbook of Buddhist Ethics*, edited by Daniel Cozort and James Mark Shields, 407–31. Oxford: Oxford University Press, 2018.

Siddhasēna Divākara. *Sanmati-tarka* (5th c.). In *Siddhasēna Divākara's Sanmati Tarka with a Critical Introduction and Original Commentary by Pandita Sukhlālji Saṅghavi and Pandita Bechardāsji Doshi*, edited by Dalsukh Malvania. Bombay: Saubhagyacband Umedcband Doshi, Babalchand Keshavlal Modi, and Shri Jain Shwetambar Education Board, 1939.

Siderits, Mark. *Indian Philosophy of Language*. Dordrecht: Kluwer, 1991.

———. "Buddhism and Techno-Physicalism: Is the Eightfold Path a Program?." *Philosophy East and West* 51, no. 3 (2001): 307–14. https://www.jstor.org/stable/1399844.

———. *Buddhism as Philosophy: An Introduction*. Aldershot: Ashgate, 2007.

———. "Śrughna by Dusk." In *Apoha: Buddhist Nominalism and Human Cognition*, edited by Mark Siderits, Tom Tillemans, and Arindam Chakrabarti, 283–304. New York: Columbia University Press, 2011.

———. "The Case for Discontinuity." In *Madhyamaka and Yogācāra: Allies or Rivals?*, edited by Jay Garfield and Jan Westerhof, 111–26. Oxford: Oxford University Press, 2015.

Sidgwick, Henry. *The Methods of Ethics* (1906). Seventh Edition. Indianapolis: Hacket, 1981.

Simmel, Georg. *Philosophie des Geldes* (1900). In *Gesamtausgabe*, Vol. 6. Frankfurt a.M.: Suhrkamp, 1989.

Singer, Marcus. "Actual Consequence Utilitarianism." *Mind* 86, no. 341 (1977): 67–77. DOI: 10.1093/mind/LXXXVI.341.67.

Singer, Peter. *The Most Good You Can Do: How Effective Altruism Is Changing Ideas about Living Ethically*. New Haven: Yale University Press, 2015.

Sinha, Jadunath. *Indian Realism*. Delhi: Motilal Banarsidass, 1999.
Sivaraksa, Sulak. "Buddhism and Contemporary International Trends." In *Inner Peace, World Peace: Essays on Buddhism and Nonviolence*, edited by Kenneth Kraft, 127–37. New York: SUNY Press, 1992.
———. *Seeds of Peace: A Buddhist Vision for Renewing Society*. Berkeley: Parallax, 1992.
Sklair, Leslie. *The Transnational Capitalist Class*. New York: Wiley, 2000.
Smart, Ninian. "Negative Utilitarianism." *Mind* 67, no. 268 (1958): 542–43. DOI: 10.1093/mind/LXVII.268.542.
Smith, Helmer. *Saddanīti: La grammaire palie d'Aggavaṃsa*, Vol. 1. Lund: Gleerup, 1928.
Solomon, Sheldon, Jeff Greenberg, and Tom Pyszczynski. *The Worm at the Core: On the Role of Death in Life*. New York: Random House, 2015.
Sosa, Ernest. "Knowledge of Self, Others, and World." In *Donald Davidson*, edited by Kirk Ludwig, 163–82. Cambridge: Cambridge University Press, 2003.
Spinoza, Baruch. "Letter 58 (OP): To the Very Learned and Able Mr. G. H. Schuller" (1674). In *The Collected Works of Spinoza*, Vol. 2, edited and translated by Edwin Curley, 427–30. Princeton: Princeton University Press, 1985.
———. "Letter LXII (LVIII): Spinoza to ..., the Hague, October 1674." In *Works of Spinoza*, Vol. 2, reprinted from the 1883 original, 389–92. New York: Dover Publications, 1955.
———. *Ethics* (1677). In *The Collected Works of Spinoza*, edited and translated by Edwin Curley, Vol. 1, 408–617. Princeton: Princeton University Press, 1955.
Stcherbatsky, Theodor. (Фёдор Щербатской). *Buddhist Logic*, Vol. 1. Delhi: Motilal Banarsidass, 1993.
Steffen, Will, Johan Rockström, Katherine Richardson, Timothy M. Lenton, Carl Folke, Diana Liverman, Colin P. Summerhayes, et al. "Trajectories of the Earth System in the Anthropocene." *PNAS* 115, no. 33 (2018): 8252–59. DOI: 10.1073/pnas.1810141115.
Stone, Jacqueline. *Original Enlightenment and the Transformation of Medieval Japanese Buddhism*. Honolulu: University of Hawai'i Press, 1999.
———. "Placing Nichiren in the 'Big Picture': Some Ongoing Issues in Scholarship." *Japanese Journal of Religious Studies* 26, nos. 3–4 (1999): 382–421. https://www.jstor.org/stable/30233632.
Storm, Servaas, and C.W.M. Naastepad. "Europe's Hunger Games: Income Distribution, Cost Competitiveness and Crisis." *Cambridge Journal of Economics* 39, no. 3 (2015): 959–86. DOI: 10.1093/cje/beu037.
Strabo. *The Geography of Strabo*, Vol. 7. Translated by Horace Leonard Jones. Loeb Classical Library. London: Heinemann, 1930.
Strawson, Peter. "Freedom and Resentment" (1962). In *Freedom and Resentment and Other Essays*, 1–28. London: Routledge, 1974.
Streeck, Wolfgang. *How Will Capitalism End? Essays on a Failing System*. London: Verso, 2016.
Swanson, Paul. *Foundations of T'ien-T'ai Philosophy: The Flowering of the Two Truths Theory in Chinese Buddhism*. Berkeley: Asian Humanities Press, 1989.
———. "Zhiyi's Interpretation of Jñeyāvaraṇa: An Application of the Threefold Truth Concept." In *In Search of Clarity: Essays on Translation and Tiantai Buddhism*, 45–62. Nagoya: Chisokudō, 2018.

———. "Dry Dust, Hazy Images, and Missing Pieces: Reflections on Translating Religious Texts." In *In Search of Clarity: Essays on Translation and Tiantai Buddhism*, 213–32. Nagoya: Chisokudō, 2018.

Swearer, Donald. "Bhikkhu Buddhadāsa's Interpretation of the Buddha." *Journal of the American Academy of Religion* 64, no. 2 (1996): 313–36. DOI: 10.1093/jaarel/LXIV.2.313.

———. "Sulak Sivaraksa's Buddhist Vision for Renewing Society." In *Engaged Buddhism: Buddhist Liberation Movements in Asia*, edited by Christopher Queen and Sallie King, 195–235. New York: SUNY Press, 1996.

Taibbi, Matt. "The Great American Bubble Machine." *Rolling Stone*, April 5, 2010. https://www.rollingstone.com/politics/politics-news/the-great-american-bubble-machine-195229/.

Taixu 太虛.〈世界之三大罪惡〉(1913). In《无政府主义思想资料选》, edited by Ge Yichun 葛懋春, Jiang Jun 蒋俊, and Li Xingzhi, 李兴芝, 266–68. Beijing: Peking University Press 北京大学出版社, 1983.

——— (1940).〈我的佛教改進運動略史〉(1940). In《太虛大師全書》, Vol. 19/29, edited by Yinshun 印順. Taipei: Yinshun Culture and Education Foundation 印順文教基金會, 1998.

Takagi Kenmyō 高木顯明. "My Socialism." Translated by Robert Rhodes, *The Eastern Buddhist* 33, no. 2 (2001): 54–61. https://www.jstor.org/stable/44362512.

Tatman, Lucy. "The Other Thing about Suffering." In *Perspectives on Human Suffering*, edited by Jeff Malpas and Norelle Lickiss, 43–48. Dordrecht: Springer, 2012.

Tawney, R.H. *Religion and the Rise of Capitalism: A Historical Study*. London: Murray, 1926.

Tedesco, Frank. "Social Engagement in South Korean Buddhism." In *Action Dharma: New Studies in Engaged Buddhism*, edited by Christopher Queen, Charles Prebish, and Damien Keown, 154–82. London: RoutledgeCurzon, 1991.

Tenzin Gyatso, the 14th Dalai Lama. "Our Faith in Science." *The New York Times*, November 12, 2005. https://www.nytimes.com/2005/11/12/opinion/our-faith-in-science.html.

———. *The Universe in a Single Atom*. New York: Morgan Road, 2005.

———. "Reincarnation." *His Holiness the 14th Dalai Lama of Tibet*, 2011. http://www.dalailama.com/biography/reincarnation.

Tenzin Gyatso, the 14th Dalai Lama, and Marianne Dresser. *Beyond Dogma: Dialogues and Discourses*. Berkeley: North Atlantic, 1996.

Thagard, Paul. *Coherence in Thought and Action*. Cambridge: MIT Press, 2000.

Thapar, Romila. "Ashoka — A Retrospective." *Economic & Political Weekly* 44, no. 45 (November 7, 2009): 31–37. https://www.epw.in/journal/2009/45/perspectives/ashoka-retrospective.html.

Thompson, Evan. *Why I Am Not a Buddhist*. New Haven: Yale University Press, 2020.

Thurman, Robert. "Buddhist Hermeneutics." *Journal of the American Academy of Religion* 46, no. 1 (1978): 19–39. DOI: 10.1093/jaarel/XLVI.1.19.

———. "Nagarjuna's Guidelines for Buddhist Social Activism." In *The Path of Compassion: Writings on Socially Engaged Buddhism*, edited by Fred Eppsteiner, 120–44. Berkeley: Parallax, 1985.

———. "The Edicts of Asoka." In *The Path of Compassion: Writings on Socially Engaged Buddhism*, edited by Fred Eppsteiner, 111–19. Berkeley: Parallax, 1985.

Tikhonov, Vladimir, and Owen Miller. "Introduction." In Han Yongun, *Selected Writings of Han Yongun: From Social Darwinism to "Socialism with a Buddhist Face,"* translated by Vladimir Tikhonov and Owen Miller, 1–36. Folkestone: Global Oriental, 2008.

Tikhonov, Vladimir, and Torkel Brekke. *Buddhism and Violence: Militarism and Buddhism in Asia.* New York: Routledge, 2013.

Tolstoy, Leo. "The End of the Age" (1905). In *Government Is Violence*, 21–52. London: Phoenix, 1990.

Tong, Dan, Qiang Zhang, Yixuan Zheng, Ken Caldeira, Christine Shearer, Chaopeng Hong, Yue Qin, and Steven Davis. "Committed Emissions from Existing Energy Infrastructure Jeopardize 1.5 °C Climate Target." *Nature* 572 (2019): 373–77. DOI: 10.1038/s41586-019-1364-3.

Trentman, Frank. *Empire of Things: How We Became a World of Consumers, from the Fifteenth Century to the Twenty-First.* New York: Harper, 2016.

Trotsky, Leon. "Independence of the Ukraine and Sectarian Muddleheads" (1939). In *Writings of Leon Trotsky 1939–40*, 44–54. New York: Pathfinder, 1977.

Twenge, Jean, and Keith Campbell. *The Narcissism Epidemic: Living in the Age of Entitlement.* New York: Atria, 2009.

Tzohar, Roy. "Imagine Being a 'Preta': Early Indian Yogācāra Approaches to Intersubjectivity." *Sophia* 56 (2017): 337–54. DOI: 10.1007/s11841-016-0544-y.

Uchiyama Gūdo 内山愚童 (1908).『無政府共産革命』[*Anarchist Communist Revolution*]. Translated in Fabio Rambelli, *Zen Anarchism: The Egalitarian Dharma of Uchiyama Gūdo*, 45–51. Berkeley: Institute of Buddhist Studies and BDK America, 2013.

———.『平凡の自覚』[*Common Consciousness*] (1908?). Translated in Fabio Rambelli, *Zen Anarchism: The Egalitarian Dharma of Uchiyama Gūdo*, 53–65. Berkeley: Institute of Buddhist Studies and BDK America, 2013.

Ueda, Noriyuki, and Tenzin Gyatso, the 14th Dalai Lama. *The Dalai Lama on What Matters Most: Conversations on Anger, Compassion, and Action.* Charlottesville: Hampton Roads, 2013.

UNDRR. *Human Cost of Disasters: An Overview of the Last 20 Years, 2000–2019.* Geneva: UN Office for Disaster Risk Reduction.

Vague, Richard. *A Brief History of Doom: Two Hundred Years of Financial Crises.* Philadelphia: University of Pennsylvania Press, 2020.

Vaihinger, Hans. *The Philosophy of 'As if': A System of the Theoretical, Practical and Religious Fictions of Mankind.* Second Edition. London: Kegan Paul, 1935.

Valentini, Laura. "Ideal vs. Non-ideal Theory: A Conceptual Map." *Philosophy Compass* 7, no. 9 (2012): 654–64. DOI: 10.1111/j.1747-9991.2012.00500.x.

Van Bijlert, Vittorio. *Epistemology and Spiritual Authority: The Development of Epistemology and Logic in the Old Nyāya and the Buddhist School of Epistemology with an Annotated Translation of Dharmakīrti's Pramāṇavārttika II (Pramāṇasiddhi) vv. 1–7.* Vienna: ATBS, 1989.

Van Dam, Nicholas, Marieke K. van Vugt, David R. Vago, Laura Schmalzl, Clifford D. Saron, Andrew Olendzki, Ted Meissner et al. "Mind the Hype: A Critical Evaluation and Prescriptive Agenda for Research on Mindfulness and Meditation." *Perspectives on Psychological Science* 13, no. 1 (2018): 36–61. DOI: 10.1177/1745691617709589.

Van Norden, Bryan. *Introduction to Classical Chinese Philosophy.* Indianapolis: Hacket, 2011.

———. *Taking Back Philosophy: A Multicultural Manifesto.* New York: Columbia University Press, 2017.
Varoufakis, Yanis. *Economic Indeterminacy: A Personal Encounter with the Economists' Peculiar Nemesis.* London: Routledge, 2014.
Vasubandhu. *Abhidharmakośabhāṣya* (5th c.). Translated by Gelong Lodrö Sangpo from the French translation by Louis de La Vallee Poussin, 4 Vols. Delhi: Motilal Banarsidass, 2012.
———. *Vādavidhi.* Remaining fragments translated by Stefan Anacker, *Seven Works of Vasubandhu: The Buddhist Psychological Doctor*, 38–47. Revised Edition. Delhi: Motilal Banarsidass, 2005.
———. *Viṃśatikākārikā* (5th c.). *Digital Sanskrit Buddhist Canon.* http://www.dsbcproject.org/canon-text/book/340. Translated by Stefan Anacker, *Seven Works of Vasubandhu: The Buddhist Psychological Doctor*, 159–79. Revised Edition. Delhi: Motilal Banarsidass, 2005.
———. *Viṃśatikāvṛtti* (5th c.). In Stefan Anacker, *Seven Works of Vasubandhu: The Buddhist Psychological Doctor*, 413–21. Revised Edition. Delhi: Motilal Banarsidass, 2005. Translated in ibid., 159–70.
Vasubandhu(?). *Trisvabhāvanirdeśa.* *Digital Sanskrit Buddhist Canon.* http://www.dsbcproject.org/canon-text/book/338. In Stefan Anacker, *Seven Works of Vasubandhu: The Buddhist Psychological Doctor*, 464–66. Revised Edition. Delhi: Motilal Banarsidass, 2005. Translated in ibid., 291–97.
Verburg, Marcel. "Inleiding." In *Herman Dooyeweerd: Grenzen van het theoretisch denken*, edited by Verburg, 11–50. Baarn: Ambo, 1986.
Vergote, Antoine. *Religion, foi, incroyance: Étude psychologique.* Brussels: Pierre Mardaga, 1983.
Verheggen, Claudine. "Language, Thought and Knowledge." In Robert Myers and Claudine Verheggen, *Donald Davidson's Triangulation Argument: A Philosophical Inquiry*, 11–115. New York: Routledge, 2016.
Vetter, Tilman. *The Ideas and Meditative Practices of Early Buddhism.* Leiden: Brill, 1988.
Victoria, Brian. *Zen at War.* Second Edition. Lanham: Rowamn & Littlefield, 2006.
Vinītadeva. *Ālambanaparīkṣāṭīkā* (8th c.). Translated in Douglas Duckworth, Malcolm David Eckel, Jay L. Garfield, John Powers, Yeshes Thabkhas, and Sonam Thakchöe, *Dignāga's Investigation of the Percept: A Philosophical Legacy in India and Tibet*, 78–104. Oxford: Oxford University Press, 2016.
Wang Chong 王充.《論衡》(ca. 80). *Chinese Text Project.* https://ctext.org/lunheng.
Wang Hui. "Zhang Taiyan's Concept of the Individual and Modern Chinese Identity." In *Becoming Chinese: Passages to Modernity and Beyond*, edited by Wen-hsin Yeh, 231–59. Berkeley: University of California Press, 2000.
Weber, Max. *Die Protestantische Etik und der "Geist" des Kapitalismus.* Tübingen: J.C.B. Mohr, 1905.
Weeks, John. *Economics of the 1%: How Mainstream Economics Serves the Rich, Obscures Reality and Distorts Policy.* London: Anthem, 2014.
Welshon, Rex. "Saying Yes to Reality: Skepticism, Antirealism, and Perspectivism in Nietzsche's Epistemology." *Journal of Nietzsche Studies* 37 (2009): 23–43. https://www.jstor.org/stable/20717957.
Westerhoff, Jan. "Buddhism without Reincarnation? Examining the Prospects of a 'Naturalized' Buddhism." In *A Mirror Is for Reflection: Understanding Buddhist Ethics*, edited by Jake David, 146–65. Oxford: Oxford University Press, 2017.

———. *The Golden Age of Indian Buddhist Philosophy*. Oxford: Oxford University Press, 2018.

Wheeler III, Samuel. *Neo-Davidsonian Metaphysics: From the True to the Good*. New York: Routledge, 2014.

Whitehead, Alfred North. *Process and Reality* (1929). Corrected Edition. New York: Free Press, 1978.

Whorf, Benjamin Lee. "Science and Linguistics" (1940). In *Language, Thought, and Reality: Selected Writings of Benjamin Lee Whorf*, edited by John Carroll, 207–19. Cambridge: MIT Press, 1956.

Wierzbicka, Anna. *Semantic Primitives*. Frankfurt: Athenäum, 1972.

———. *Semantics: Primes and Universals*. Oxford: Oxford University Press, 1996.

———. "'Happiness' in Cross-Linguistic & Cross-Cultural Perspective." *Daedalus* 133, no. 2 (2004): 34–43. DOI: 10.1162/001152604323049370.

———. "'Pain' and 'Suffering' in Cross-Linguistic Perspective." *International Journal of Language and Culture* 1, no. 2 (2014): 149–73. DOI: 10.1075/ijolc.1.2.02wie.

Williams, Bernard. "A Critique of Utilitarianism." In J.J.C. Smart & Bernard Williams, *Utilitarianism: For and Against*, 75–150. Cambridge: Cambridge University Press, 1973.

Williams, Paul. "General Introduction: Śāntideva and His World." In Śāntideva. *The Bodhicaryāvatāra* (8th c.), translated by Kate Crosby and Andrew Skilton, vii–xxvi. Oxford: Oxford University Press, 1995.

———. *Mahāyāna Buddhism: The Doctrinal Foundations*. Second Edition. London: Routledge, 2009.

Willis, Janice Dean. *On Knowing Reality: The "Tattvārtha" Chapter of Asaṅga's "Bodhisattvabhūmi."* Delhi: Motilal Banarsidass, 1982.

Wittgenstein, Ludwig. *Logisch-philosophische Abhandlung, Tractatus logico-philosophicus* (1921). Kritische Edition. Frankfurt a.M.: Suhrkamp, 1998.

———. *Philosophische Untersuchungen* (1953). Frankfurt a.M.: Suhrkamp, 1975.

———. *Zettel*. Berkeley: University of California Press, 1967.

Wynne, Alexander. "Did the Buddha Exist?" *Journal of the Oxford Centre for Buddhist Studies* 16 (2019): 98–148.

Xu, Wangyang, Veerabhadran Ramanathan, and David Victor. "Global Warming Will Happen Faster Than We Think." *Nature* 564 (2018): 30–32.

Xuanzang 玄奘.《成唯識論》(7th c.). *The SAT Daizōkyō Text Database*, Vol. 31, Text no. 1585. http://21dzk.l.u-tokyo.ac.jp/SAT/index_en.html.

Yacobi, Hermann. "Ueber Sukha und Duḥkha." *Zeitschrift für vergleichende Sprachforschung auf dem Gebiete der Indogermanischen Sprachen* 25, no. 4 (1881): 438–40.

Yang Huinan 楊惠南.《當代佛教思想展望》. Taipei: Sanmin 三民, 1991.

Yang Jiaqing 楊家青, Teng Jiaqi 滕嘉琦, and Lin Jiamei 林佳美.〈建設人間淨土：座談會〉,《佛教文化》1 (1990): 10–16.

Yarnall, Thomas Freeman. "Engaged Buddhism: New and Improved? Made in the USA of Asian Materials." In *Action Dharma: New Studies in Engaged Buddhism*, edited by Christopher Queen, Charles Prebish, and Damien Keown, 286–344. London: RoutledgeCurzon, 2003.

Ye, Zhengdao. "Why Are There Two 'Joy-like' 'Basic' Emotions in Chinese? Semantic Theory and Empirical Findings." In *Love, Hatred, and Other Passions: Questions and Themes on Emotions in Chinese Civilization*, edited by Paolo Santangelo and Donatella Guida, 59–80. Leiden: Brill, 2006.

Yoshinaga Shin'ichi. "Theosophy and Buddhist Reformers in the Middle of the Meiji Period: An Introduction." *Japanese Religions* 34, no. 2 (2009): 119–31.

Younger, Paul. "The Concept of Duḥkha and the Indian Religious Tradition." *Journal of the American Academy of Religion* 37, no. 2 (1969): 141–52.

Zhanran 湛然.《金剛錍》(8th c.). *The SAT Daizōkyō Text Database,* Vol. 46, Text no. 1932. http://21dzk.l.u-tokyo.ac.jp/SAT/index_en.html.

Zhiyi 智顗.《摩訶止觀》[*The Great Calming and Contemplation*] (594). *The SAT Daizōkyō Text Database,* Vol. 46, Text no. 1911. http://21dzk.l.u-tokyo.ac.jp/SAT/index_en.html.

———.《妙法蓮華經玄義》(6th c.). *The SAT Daizōkyō Text Database,* Vol. 33, Text no. 1716. http://21dzk.l.u-tokyo.ac.jp/SAT/index_en.html.

———.《釋禪波羅蜜次第法門》(6th c.). *The SAT Daizōkyō Text Database,* Vol. 46, Text no. 1916. http://21dzk.l.u-tokyo.ac.jp/SAT/index_en.html.

Zhuangzi 莊子.《莊子》(4th c. BCE). *Chinese Text Project.* https://ctext.org/zhuangzi.

Ziblatt, Daniel. "How Did Europe Democratize?" *World Politics* 58 (2006): 311–38. DOI: 10.1353/wp.2006.0028.

Zickfeld, Kirsten, and Tyler Herrington. "The Time Lag between a Carbon Dioxide Emission and Maximum Warming Increases with the Size of the Emission." *Environmental Research Letters* 10.031001 (2015). DOI: 10.1088/1748-9326/10/3/031001.

Ziporyn, Brook. *Being and Ambiguity: Philosophical Experiments with Tiantai Buddhism.* Chicago: Open Court, 2004.

———. *Emptiness and Omnipresence: An Essential Introduction to Tiantai Buddhism.* Bloomington: Indiana University Press, 2016.

Zysk, Kenneth. *Religious Medicine: The History and Evolution of Indian Medicine.* 1985; London: Routledge, 2017.

———. *Asceticism and Healing in Ancient India: Medicine in the Buddhist Monastery.* Corrected edition. Delhi: Motilal Banarsidass, 1998.

www.ingramcontent.com/pod-product-compliance
Lightning Source LLC
Chambersburg PA
CBHW081943230426
43669CB00019B/2912